CLEOPA

CLEOPATRA'S EGYPT

Age of the Ptolemies

THE BROOKLYN MUSEUM

Exhibition Director: Richard A. Fazzini
Exhibition Curator: Robert S. Bianchi
Research Associates: Donald Spanel, Mary McKercher

This exhibition was organized by The Brooklyn Museum and was made possible, in part, with the generous support of the following agencies and individuals:

National Endowment for the Humanities, a federal agency, Washington, D.C.
National Endowment for the Arts, a federal agency, Washington, D.C.
New York State Council on the Arts

The J.M. Kaplan Fund

Edward H. Merrin
Jack A. Josephson

The Museum Council of The Brooklyn Museum

National Westminster Bank USA, corporate sponsor

In addition, the exhibition is supported by an indemnity from the Federal Council on the Arts and the Humanities.

Exhibition Itinerary
The Brooklyn Museum
October 7, 1988-January 2, 1989
The Detroit Institute of Arts
February 14-April 30, 1989
Kunsthalle der Hypo-Kulturstiftung, in cooperation with the Staatliche Sammlung Ägyptischer Kunst, Munich
June 8-September 10, 1989

293 pages with 37 color- and 212 black-and-white photographs
Frontcover: Cat. 17

Type: Hurler GmbH, Notzingen
Lithography: Witzemann & Schmidt, Wiesbaden
Paper: Papierfabrik Scheufelen, Lenningen
Printed in Germany / Imprimé en Allemagne
Manufactured by Verlag Philipp von Zabern, Mainz on the Rhine
Printed on fade resistant and archival quality (PH 7 neutral)

Library of Congress
Library of Congress Cataloging-in-Publication Data

Cleopatra's Egypt : age of the Ptolemies / Robert S. Bianchi ... [et al.].
p. cm.
Catalog of an exhibition held at the Brooklyn Museum Oct. 7, 1988-Jan. 2, 1989, the Detroit Institute of Arts, Feb. 14-April 30, 1989, and Kunsthalle der Hypo-Kulturstiftung in Munich, Germany June 8-Sept. 10, 1989.
Bibliography: p.
ISBN 0-87273-113-8 : $29.50
1. Egypt–Antiquities–Exhibitions. 2. Ptolemaic dynasty, 305-30 B.C.–Exhibitions. 3. Egypt–Civilization–332 B.C.-337 A.D.–Exhibitions. 4. Cleopatra, Queen of Egypt, d. 30 B.C.–Exhibitions. 5. Ptolemaic dynasty, 305-30 B.C. 6. Egypt–Civilization–332 B.C.-337 A.D. 7. Cleopatra, Queen of Egypt, d. 30 B.C. I. Bianchi, Robert Steven, 1943- . II. Brooklyn Museum. III. Detroit Institute of Arts. IV. Hypo-Kulturstiftung (Munich, Germany). Kunsthalle.
DT58.9.C57 1988
932' .0074014723–dc19 88-2832
CIP

Contents

Lenders to the Exhibition 4

Foreword 6

Egyptian Chronology 8

The Ptolemies: An Abbreviated Genealogy 10

Maps 11

Essays

Ptolemaic Egypt and Rome: An Overview
by Robert S. Bianchi 13

Greeks and Egyptians: Ethnicity, Status, and Culture
by Roger S. Bagnall 21

Ptolemaic Egypt: Priests and the Traditional Religion
by Jean-Claude Goyon 29

Cleopatra VII and the Cults of the Ptolemaic Queens
by Jan Quaegebeur 41

The Pharaonic Art of Ptolemaic Egypt
by Robert S. Bianchi 55

Catalogue 81

Entries 3-9, 12, 13, 19-21, 29, 107, 108, 121, 125-127
by Richard A. Fazzini

Entry 61
by Bernhard H. Overbeck

All Other Entries
by Robert S. Bianchi

Museums and Collections Cited 256

Abbreviations 257

Works Cited 261

Photograph Credits 290

Concordance
(accession numbers : catalogue numbers) 291

Lenders to the Exhibition

Allard Pierson Museum	Amsterdam
Kelsey Museum of Archaeology, University of Michigan	Ann Arbor, Michigan
Staatliche Museen zu Berlin, Hauptstadt der DDR, Ägyptisches Museum/ Papyrussammlung	Berlin/DDR
Staatliche Museen Preußischer Kulturbesitz, Ägyptisches Museum	Berlin/BRD
Verein zur Förderung des Ägyptischen Museums, Staatliche Museen Preußischer Kulturbesitz	Berlin/BRD
Staatliche Museen Preußischer Kulturbesitz, Antikenmuseum	Berlin/BRD
Akademisches Kunstmuseum der Universität Bonn	Bonn
Museum of Fine Arts	Boston
The Brooklyn Museum	Brooklyn
Musées Royaux d'Art et d'Histoire	Brussels
Harvard University Art Museums (Arthur M. Sackler Museum)	Cambridge, Massachusetts
The Cleveland Museum of Art	Cleveland
Ny Carlsberg Glyptotek	Copenhagen
The Detroit Institute of Arts	Detroit
Kestner-Museum	Hannover
Pelizaeus-Museum	Hildesheim
Museum of Fine Arts, Houston	Houston
Staatliche Kunstsammlungen Kassel, Antikensammlung	Kassel
Rijksmuseum van Oudheden	Leiden
The British Museum	London
The J. Paul Getty Museum	Malibu, California
Staatliche Münzsammlung	Munich
Staatliche Sammlung Ägyptischer Kunst	Munich
Wittelsbacher Ausgleichsfonds	Munich
Peabody Museum of Natural History	New Haven
Yale University Art Gallery	New Haven
The Metropolitan Museum of Art	New York
Musée du Louvre	Paris
The University Museum, University of Pennsylvania	Philadelphia
North Carolina Museum of Art	Raleigh
Virginia Museum of Fine Arts	Richmond
Rosicrucian Egyptian Museum	San Jose, California
Württembergisches Landesmuseum, Antikensammlung	Stuttgart
Royal Ontario Museum	Toronto
The Vatican Museums	Vatican City
Kunsthistorisches Museum	Vienna

Private Lenders:
Mr. Christos G. Bastis
The Harer Family Trust
Mr. Jack A. Josephson
Mr. Richard M. Keresey
Mr. Charles Pankow and Mrs. Heide Betz
Anonymous lenders

National Westminster Bank USA is proud to serve as the corporate sponsor of *Cleopatra's Egypt: Age of the Ptolemies*. This exhibition, of both national and international importance, focuses on a period exceptionally rich in masterpieces of art and historical interest. It is a rare occasion when ancient works of such significance are assembled.

The Brooklyn Museum's great collections of ancient Egyptian art have long proved a magnet to visitors. We at NatWest USA are delighted to expand our partnership with the Museum by supporting this unique exhibition as part of our Arts in the Community Program.

William T. Knowles
Chairman and Chief Executive Officer
National Westminster Bank USA

Foreword

Cleopatra VII is one of the most famous rulers of the ancient world and one of the few monarchs of Egypt whose name is a household word. Yet the Ptolemaic Period (305-30 B.C.), when the royal family of Egypt was the Macedonian Greek dynasty of Ptolemy, of which Cleopatra was the last member to rule Egypt, remains poorly known and misunderstood. And the fact that Ptolemaic Egypt was home to an incredible and multifaceted flowering of the arts remains almost a well-kept secret.

Cleopatra's Egypt: Age of the Ptolemies is intended to make Ptolemaic Egypt, its history and cultures and especially its arts, more meaningful and accessible. Those cultures and arts include both the Hellenistic and the pharaonic, and the exhibition includes masterworks illustrative of both artistic styles and the concepts they were used to express. But we have emphasized the native pharaonic because, despite governance by non-Egyptians, it was the culture that remained the dominant force in the country's life as a whole—contrary to much of what has been published. In fact, as the exhibition also demonstrates, native traditions were maintained in Egypt and Egyptian art well after the death of Cleopatra VII and Egypt's conquest by Rome.

For The Brooklyn Museum, *Cleopatra's Egypt* is also maintaining long-lived traditions: an interest in later Egyptian art and the organization of special exhibitions of ancient Egyptian art. Sometimes both traditions have been combined, as in 1941 with *Pagan and Christian Egypt: Egyptian Art from the First to the Tenth Century* A.D. and in 1960 with *Egyptian Sculpture of the Late Period. 700* B.C. *to* A.D. *100*. The former was an important influence on the study of Roman Period and Coptic art; the latter pioneering study remains a standard reference for statuary of Dynasty XXV to the early Roman Period.

Cleopatra's Egypt is a unique introduction to Ptolemaic Egypt in general, providing a synopsis of recent advances in scholarship and presenting some new interpretations of aspects of its history, religion, and art. We trust it will be of value to both the public and the scholarly community.

Preparing the exhibition and its catalogue required considerable effort on the part of many individuals, only some of whom can be mentioned here. In Brooklyn's Department of Egyptian, Classical, and Ancient Middle Eastern Art, *Cleopatra* became almost an additional full-time job for Robert Bianchi, Associate Curator, who wrote most of the catalogue's entries, its historical overview, and its art historical essay; and for Curator Richard Fazzini, who selected the objects with Dr. Bianchi and bore overall administrative responsibility for the exhibition as well as consulting on many aspects of the catalogue and writing several of its entries. Research Associate Donald Spanel was most helpful in preparing and editing the bibliography and in proofreading, as was Research Associate Mary McKercher, who also assisted with many of the administrative details and the preparation of the videotape introduction to the exhibition. Other members of the department, notably Associate Curator James Romano, assisted by handling some tasks that would normally have been done by those working on *Cleopatra's Egypt*.

Others whose contributions to the exhibition or catalogue were invaluable were Diane Guzman, Wilbour Librarian; Rena Zurofsky, Vice Director for Marketing Services; Jeffrey Strean, Chief Exhibition Designer; Ken Moser, Chief Conservator; Ellen Pearlstein, Conservator; Cathryn Anders, Collection Manager; Horace Solomon, Vice Director for Development; Barbara McMahon, Development Manager; Barbara LaSalle,

Registrar; Elizabeth Reynolds, Registrar; Linda Ferber, Chief Curator; Caroline Mortimer, Curatorial Administrator; Deborah Schwartz, Manager, and Missy Sullivan, Assistant Manager, Public Programs and Media; Diana Linden, Education Specialist; Andrea Feeser, intern, Public Programs and Media; and Dara Meyers, Film Coordinator; Sonnet Takahisa, Manager of School, Youth, and Family Programs; and Abigail Ehrlich, Museum Educator.

Special thanks are also owed to Professor Roger Bagnall of Columbia University, Professor Jean-Claude Goyon of the Université Lyon II, and Professor Jan Quaegebeur of the Katholieke Universiteit Leuven for their essays in the catalogue, and to Dr. Bernhard Overbeck of the Staatliche Münzsammlung, Munich who prepared the entry on the coins.

We are also deeply grateful for the cooperation of the other venues for the exhibition, namely The Detroit Institute of Arts and the Kunsthalle der Hypo-Kulturstiftung, Munich, working in cooperation with Munich's Staatliche Sammlung Ägyptischer Kunst. We particularly thank Samuel Sachs, Director of The Detroit Institute of Arts; Joseph Bianco, President of the Founders Society, The Detroit Institute of Arts; and William Peck, Senior Curator and Curator of Ancient Art at The Detroit Institute of Arts; Peter Ade, Director of the Kunsthalle der Hypo-Kulturstiftung; and Professor Dietrich Wildung, Director of the Staatliche Sammlung Ägyptischer Kunst. And of course we thank all those institutions and individuals who agreed to lend their objects to *Cleopatra's Egypt,* without whose cooperation the exhibition would not have been possible.

Finally, we wish to thank those who have provided the funding for the exhibition and its catalogue: the National Endowments for the Humanities and the Arts, the New York State Council on the Arts, Joan Davidson of The J.M. Kaplan Fund, Edward H. Merrin, Jack A. Josephson, the Museum Council of the Brooklyn Museum, The Federal Council on the Arts and the Humanities, and our corporate sponsor, National Westminster Bank USA.

Robert T. Buck
Director
The Brooklyn Museum

Egyptian Chronology

Pre-4000-c. 3000 B.C. PREDYNASTIC PERIOD

c. 3000-2670 B.C. ARCHAIC PERIOD
Dynasties I-II

c. 2670-2160 B.C. OLD KINGDOM
Dynasties III-VIII

c. 2160-2040 B.C. FIRST INTERMEDIATE PERIOD
Dynasties IX-XI (first part)

2040-1781 B.C. MIDDLE KINGDOM
Dynasties XI
(second part)-XII

1781-1550 B.C. SECOND INTERMEDIATE PERIOD
Dynasties XIII-XVII

1550-1075 B.C. NEW KINGDOM

1550-1291 B.C.	Dynasty XVIII
	Ramesside Period
1291-1185 B.C.	Dynasty XIX
1185-1075 B.C.	Dynasty XX

1075-664 B.C. THIRD INTERMEDIATE PERIOD

1075-945 B.C.	Dynasty XXI
945-718 B.C.	Dynasty XXII Libyan Dynasty
820-718 B.C.	Dynasty XXIII
c. 730-712 B.C.	Dynasty XXIV
c. 775-653 B.C.	Dynasty XXV Kushite Dynasty

664 B.C.-337 A.D. LATE PERIOD

664-525 B.C.	Dynasty XXVI Saite Period
525-404/401 B.C.	Dynasty XXVII First Persian Period Dynasty XXVIIA Collateral dynasty of Egyptian kings
c. 404-399 B.C.	Dynasty XXVIII
399-380 B.C.	Dynasty XXIX Mendesian Dynasty
380-342 B.C.	Dynasty XXX Sebennytic Dynasty:
380-362 B.C.	Nectanebo I
362-360 B.C.	Teos
360-342 B.C.	Nectanebo II
342-332 B.C.	Dynasty XXXI Second Persian Period Dynasty XXXIA Putative reign of Chabbash

332-305 B.C. MACEDONIAN PERIOD

332-323 B.C.	Alexander the Great
323-317 B.C.	Philip Arrhidaeus
317-310 B.C.	Alexander II
323-305 B.C.	Ptolemy son of Lagos as satrap

305-30 B.C. PTOLEMAIC PERIOD

(For the relationships among the Ptolemies and their queens, see the Abbreviated Genealogy, following)

305-282 B.C.	Ptolemy I Soter
285/282-246 B.C.	Ptolemy II Philadelphos
246-222 B.C.	Ptolemy III Euergetes I
222-205 B.C.	Ptolemy IV Philopator
205-180 B.C.	Ptolemy V Epiphanes
180-164 B.C. 163-145 B.C.	Ptolemy VI Philometor
145 B.C.	Ptolemy VII Neos Philopator
170-163 B.C. 145-116 B.C.	Ptolemy VIII Euergetes II
116-107 B.C.	Ptolemy IX Soter II
107-88 B.C.	Ptolemy X Alexander I
88-80 B.C.	Ptolemy IX Soter II (reinstated)
80 B.C.	Ptolemy XI Alexander II
80-55 B.C. 55-51 B.C.	Ptolemy XII Neos Dionysos
51-30 B.C.	Cleopatra VII:
51-47 B.C.	with Ptolemy XIII
47-44 B.C.	with Ptolemy XIV
41/36-30 B.C.	with Ptolemy Caesarion
(48-44 B.C.	Cleopatra VII's involvement with Julius Caesar)
(41-30 B.C.	Cleopatra VII's involvement with Marc Antony)

NATIVE EGYPTIAN COUNTER-KINGS AT THEBES

205-199 B.C.	Harwennofre
199-186 B.C.	Ankhwennofre
131/130 B.C.	Horsiese

30 B.C.-337 A.D. ROMAN PERIOD

(Egypt ruled from Rome)

Emperors Mentioned in this Catalogue:

30 B.C.-14 A.D.	Octavian, called Augustus
14-37 A.D.	Tiberius
37-41 A.D.	Caligula
41-54 A.D.	Claudius
54-68 A.D.	Nero
68-69 A.D.	Galba
81-96 A.D.	Domitian
98-117 A.D.	Trajan
117-138 A.D.	Hadrian
138-161 A.D.	Antoninus Pius
180-192 A.D.	Commodus
193-211 A.D.	Septimius Severus
211-217 A.D.	Caracalla
211-212 A.D.	Geta
218-222 A.D.	Elagabalus
222-235 A.D.	Severus Alexander
284-305 A.D.	Diocletian
306-337 A.D.	Constantine the Great

The Ptolemies: An Abbreviated Genealogy

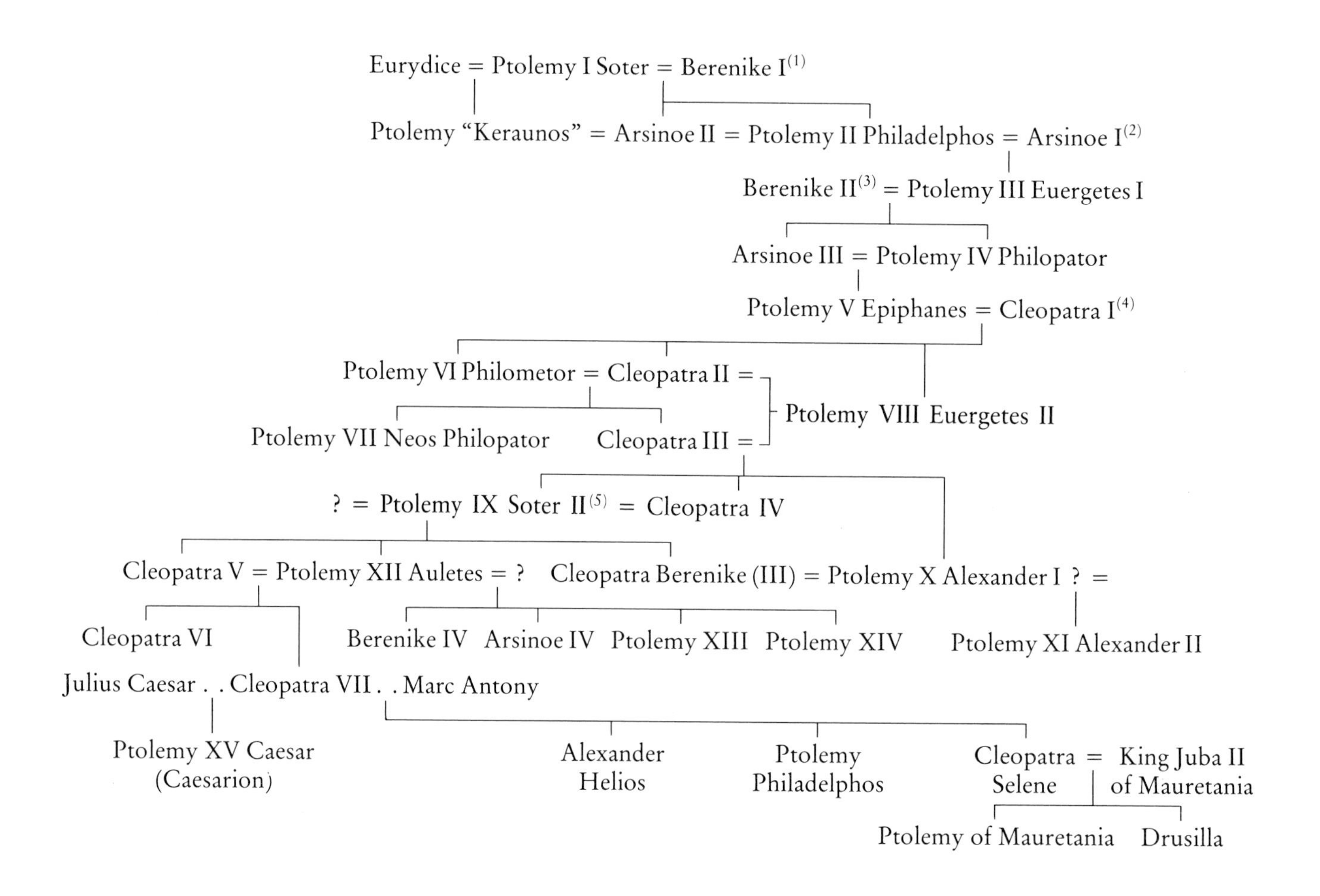

(1) A Macedonian Greek noblewoman
(2) Daughter of King Lysimachos of Thrace (Greece)
(3) Daughter of the Greek King Magas I of Cyrene, the son of Berenike I
(4) Daughter of the Greek King Antiochus III of Syria
(5) It is possible that Ptolemy IX is actually the son of Ptolemy VIII and Cleopatra II (see *RdE* 35. 1984: 47-50)

The Mediterranean World

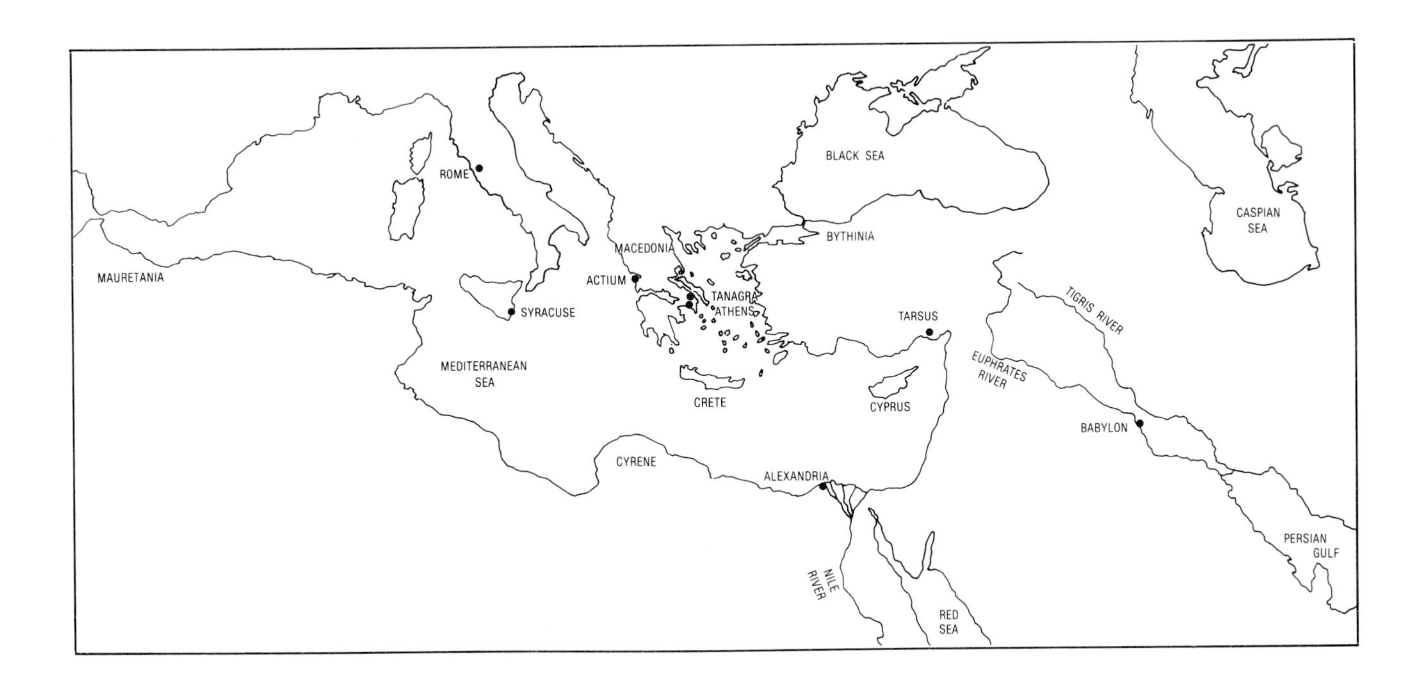

Egypt

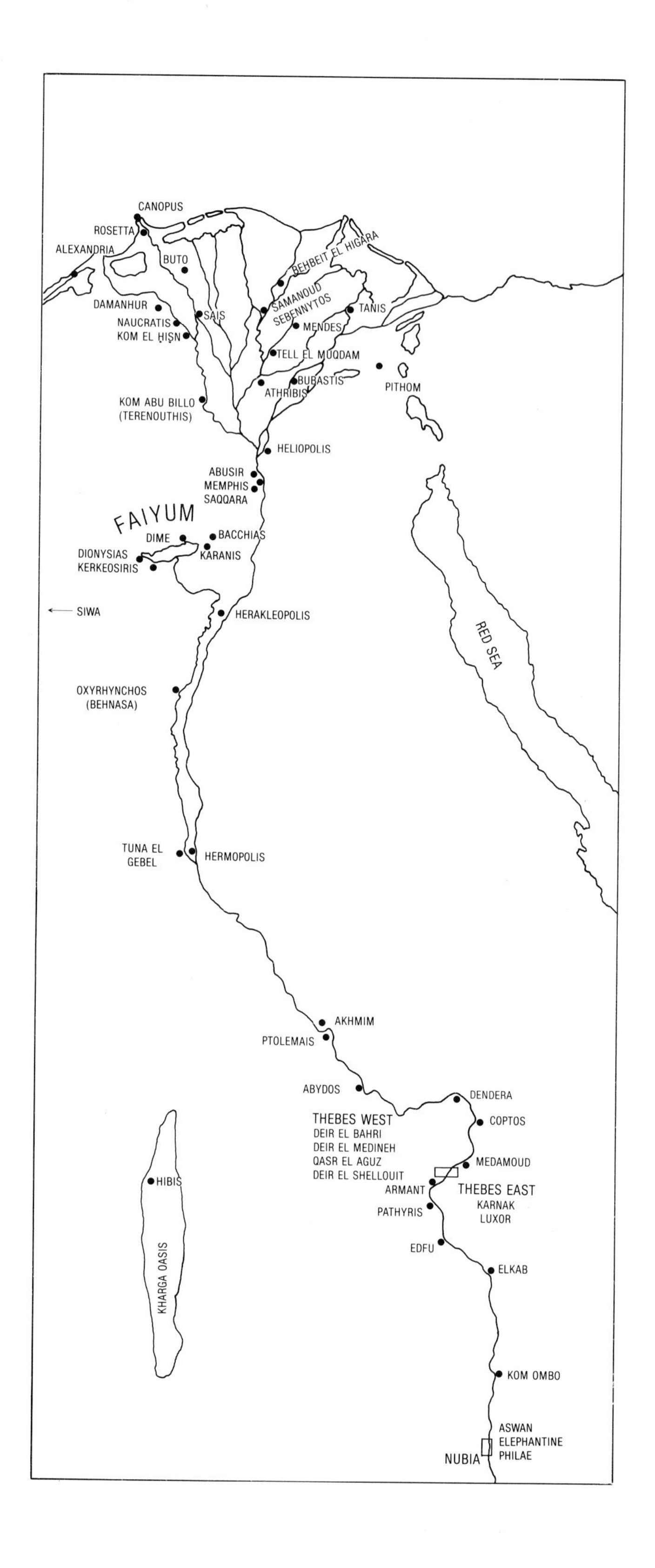
CANOPUS
ROSETTA
ALEXANDRIA
BUTO
BEHBEIT EL HIGARA
SAMANOUD
SEBENNYTOS
TANIS
DAMANHUR
SAIS
NAUCRATIS
KOM EL HISN
MENDES
TELL EL MUQDAM
BUBASTIS
ATHRIBIS
PITHOM
KOM ABU BILLO
(TERENOUTHIS)
HELIOPOLIS
ABUSIR
MEMPHIS
SAQQARA
FAIYUM
DIME
BACCHIAS
KARANIS
DIONYSIAS
KERKEOSIRIS
SIWA
HERAKLEOPOLIS
RED SEA
OXYRHYNCHOS
(BEHNASA)
TUNA EL
GEBEL
HERMOPOLIS
AKHMIM
PTOLEMAIS
ABYDOS
DENDERA
THEBES WEST
DEIR EL BAHRI
DEIR EL MEDINEH
QASR EL AGUZ
DEIR EL SHELLOUIT
COPTOS
MEDAMOUD
HIBIS
ARMANT
THEBES EAST
KARNAK
LUXOR
PATHYRIS
EDFU
ELKAB
KHARGA OASIS
KOM OMBO
ASWAN
ELEPHANTINE
PHILAE
NUBIA

Essays

CAT. 18

II

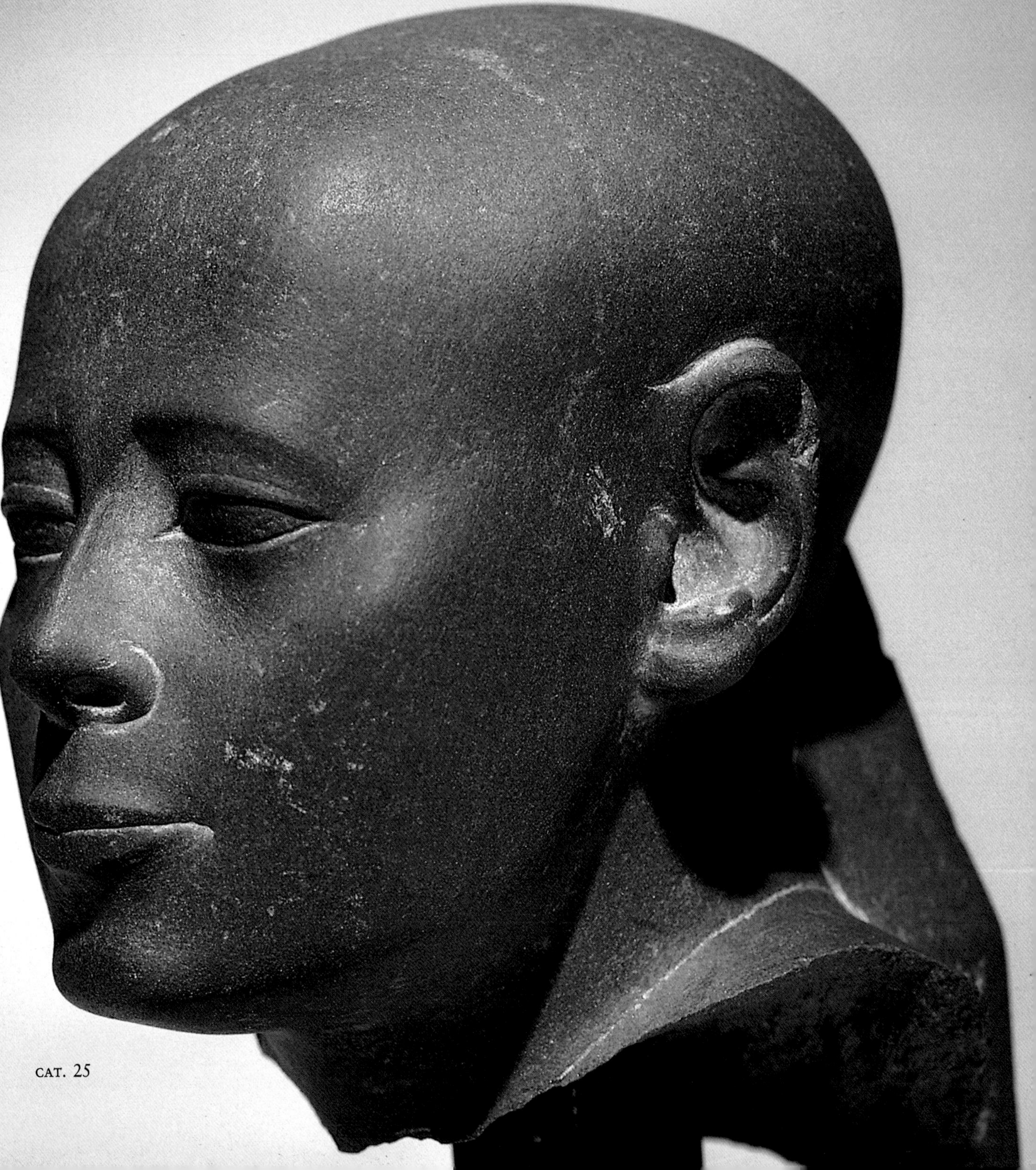

CAT. 25

CAT. 27

IV

CAT. 30

V

CAT. 31

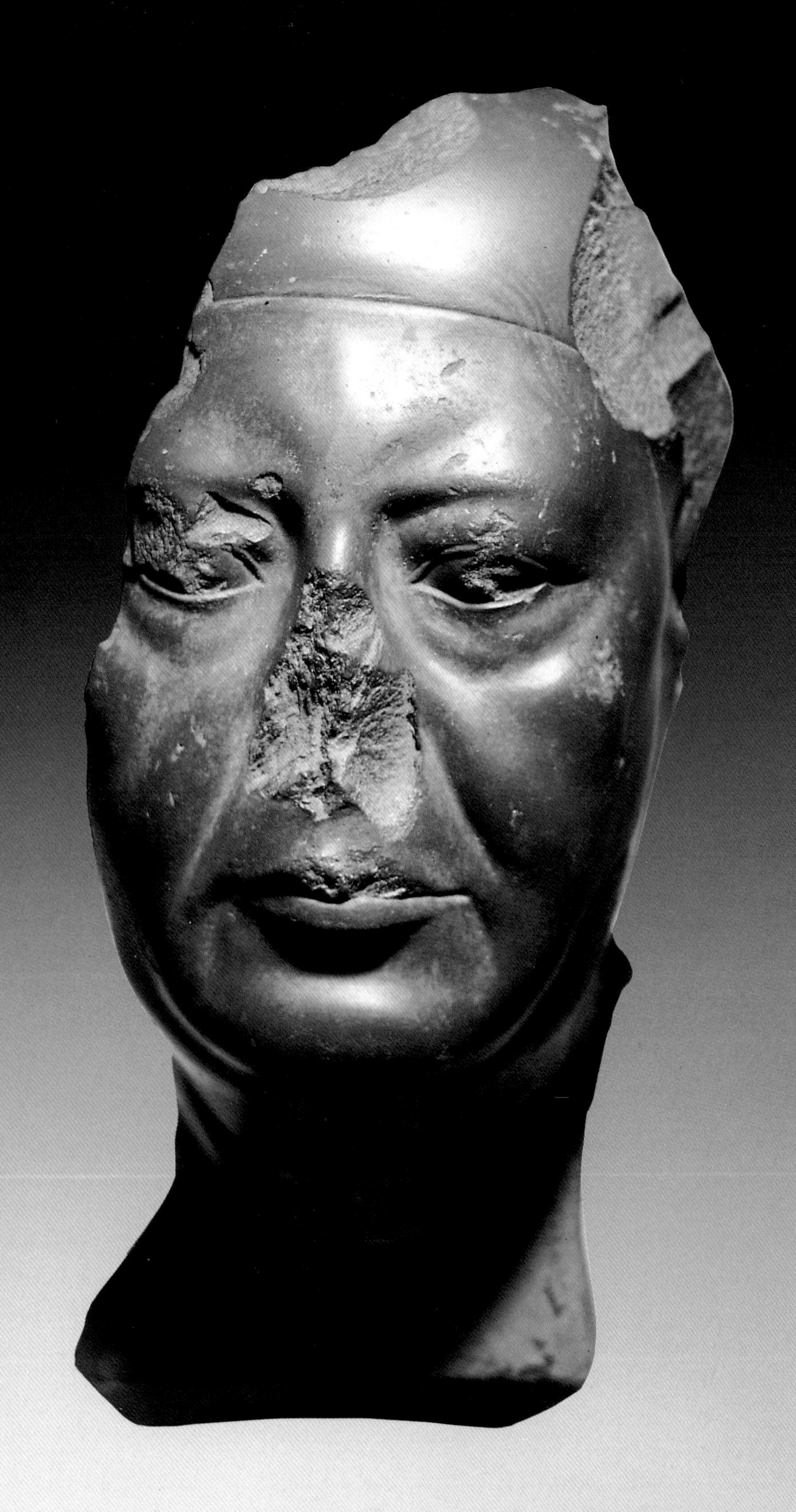

CAT. 35

CAT. 37

CAT. 40

Ptolemaic Egypt and Rome: An Overview

by Robert S. Bianchi

The purpose of the following historical synopsis is to present, in the broadest possible terms, some of the events which transpired between selected royal personalities of Ptolemaic Egypt and the Roman statesmen and generals with whom they interacted. Such an approach provides the international background from which the career of Cleopatra VII emerged. The complexities of the issues may demand fuller treatment, but the contingencies of space dictate both the form and content of the present essay.

The arrival of Alexander the Great (CAT. 49) into Egypt, without a battle, in the winter of 332 B.C. marks a significant continuation, rather than a fundamental turning point, in pharaonic history. Alexander doubtless conspired with Mazaces, the Persian satrap, or governor, and achieved a negotiated settlement whereby Mazaces would cede Egypt to Alexander without a struggle in return for his own continued personal and economic enrichment. Such an arrangement could only have been accomplished with the complicity of certain other highly placed administrators, many of whom were certainly native Egyptians. Alexander soon recognized, as had the Persians before him, that the continued support of this highly entrenched native bureaucracy was the essential component in any plan to seize control of the country and its resources. The loyalty of that privileged class was itself tied to age-old religious expressions and traditions because pharaonic Egypt was a theocracy, its pharaoh serving as both king and chief pontiff. As an extension of this royal model, each pharaonic bureaucrat could be both clerk and cleric and was consequently dependent upon the Crown for his *raison d'être*. Alexander doubtless realized the importance of maintaining this peculiar unity of church and state. One might, therefore, suggest that his alleged coronation according to pharaonic rites at Memphis and his subsequent religious experience with the god Ammon by means of the oracle in the remote Oasis of Siwa in the Western Desert were motivated by his desire to demonstrate, as no Persian king before him had, that he was willing to assume the posture of pharaoh for the benefit of those whose services he so desperately required.

Within months of the death of Alexander in 323 B.C., his longtime supporter and member of his inner council, Ptolemy, the son of Lagus (CATS. 12, 49, 51), assumed *de facto* control of Egypt. Through a series of calculated, astute maneuvers, this Ptolemy ultimately declared himself King of Egypt in 305/304 B.C., thereby founding the Macedonian Greek dynasty whose members were to rule Egypt into the first century B.C. As king, he became known as Ptolemy I Soter and during his reign did nothing to undo the precedent Alexander had established. In fact, members of the family of Nectanebo II (360-342 B.C.), the last native pharaoh in Egypt (CATS. 8, 10), continued to exercise their responsibilities in offices which had become hereditary into the reign of Ptolemy I Soter. Egyptians in other sectors of society, including a quarryman in the Wadi Hammamat, likewise continued in their respective occupations despite changes of dynasty and rulers (CAT. 32). So acceptable and workable had this arrangement become that members of the native Egyptian family attached to the priesthood of Ptah at Memphis (CATS. 121, 122), which appears to have been installed during the reign of Ptolemy I Soter, remained continuously in office until the conquest of Egypt by Octavian, later Augustus, in 30 B.C. In terms therefore of their domestic policy, the Ptolemies seem to have demonstrated a deliberate unwillingness to interfere with existing Egyptian institutions and exhibited a strong desire to avoid change. The consequences of such a position can be

Fig. 1 Pylon of the Temple of the Falcon-God Horus at Edfu
Here, Ptolemy XII Auletes, the father of Cleopatra VII, smites the traditional foes of Egypt in the presence of Horus, the embodiment of divine kingship.

gauged after one surveys their foreign policy, beginning with the reign of Ptolemy I Soter.

Ptolemy I's successful bid to establish Egypt as his realm after the death of Alexander the Great was viewed with envy by the other Diadochoi, as the successors of Alexander are known. Each harbored desires to make himself the single successor to the great conqueror. As a result, a complex, often confusing, and seemingly repetitive series of alliances was made and repudiated; wars were begun, concluded, and renewed; and the same territories seemed to pass into and fall from the same hands time and again. So consumed were the Hellenistic monarchies with their own battles that few recognized the ever increasing military might of Rome to the West.

During the course of the third century B.C., therefore, the Ptolemies continued to rely upon the goodwill of native Egyptian officials interacting with the vast illiterate agrarian population whose continued conformity to established social conditions ensured the stability of the realm. Such apparent domestic tranquility enabled Ptolemy II Philadelphos (CAT. 14) and his son and successor, Ptolemy III Euergetes I, to concentrate their attentions and the resources of the nation on the acquisition of overseas possessions.

During the reign of Ptolemy II, the canal from the Nile River to the Red Sea was again made operational, expeditions brought elephants to Egypt, and diplomatic correspondence was exchanged between the Egyptian court and that of Asoka, the Buddhist emperor whose kingdom occupied the plain of the Ganges River in India. The marriage of Ptolemy II Philadelphos to his sister, Arsinoe II (p. 41 and CATS. 14, 64-66), added to his kingdom the domains which she had earlier acquired independently. She may also have been responsible for bringing Egyptian ideas to Italy since the very first exchange of ambassadors between the Ptolemaic court and Rome took place during the time she ruled with Ptolemy II Philadelphos.

Ptolemy III Euergetes maintained the policy of foreign expansion and gained considerable territories during the course of the Fourth Syrian War. Ties with other courts continued as well, as evidenced by the pleasure yacht, decorated with scenes illustrating the Homeric themes, which Hiero II, Tyrant of Syracuse, sent to Alexandria.

Two sets of documents from the period provide valuable collateral glimpses into the state of affairs in Egypt itself. The first is the Archive of Zenon, a collection of Greek documents consisting of what might be called the discarded memoranda and notes of Zenon, who was the chief administrator in the employ of Apollonius, himself Minister of Finance under Ptolemy II and Ptolemy III. One sees through these documents that Apollonius had extensive personal business interests both in Egypt and the Levant, which could be conducted by means of the merchant fleet he owned. Zenon himself, no doubt due to his association with and knowledge of his employer's affairs, was able to acquire business interests of his own. Both at home and abroad, then, the Ptolemies and the Greeks serving them appear to have enjoyed almost a century of unlimited peace and prosperity.

This picture of advantaged Greeks in the service of the Crown can be compared to that of the native Egyptian priesthood, whose members were also privileged, as revealed in the Decree of Canopus, promulgated in 237 B. C. during the reign of Ptolemy III Euergetes. This decree provided for, among other things, the increase in the number of *phylai*, or clans, to which the native clergy was attached, from four to five and guaranteed the economic support necessary for the maintenance of the cults newly added to their jurisdiction. These apparent concessions to the native clerics were brought into sharper focus by the decision to begin construction of the Temple of Horus at Edfu (Figs. 1, 2). Here the native priests would

Fig. 2 Plan of the Temple of the Falcon-God Horus at Edfu
As with many Egyptian temples the sanctuary containing the naos (Fig. 14) is located at the rear of the temple, behind a series of courts. (Adapted from Cauville 1984. Courtesy of L'Institut Français d'Archéologie Orientale)

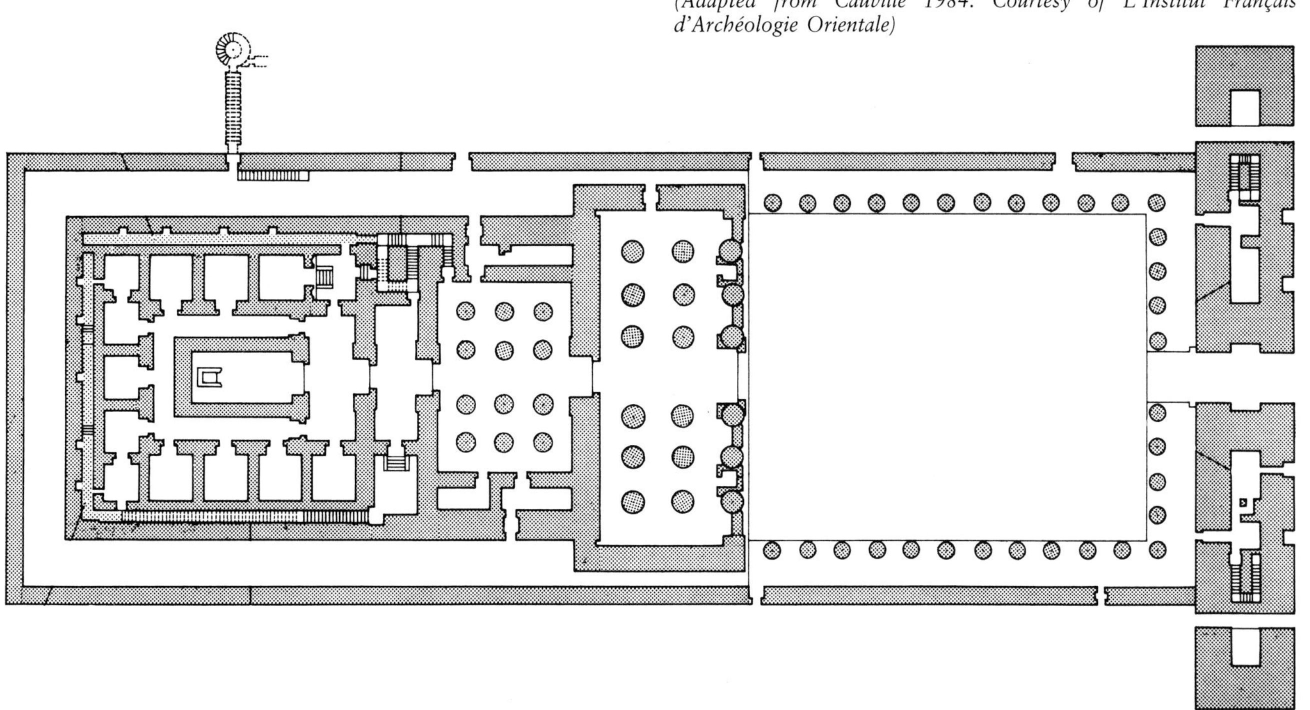

be able to celebrate that aspect of the falcon-god which protected Egypt and ensured the continuation of the native concept of divine royal succession by which Horus was linked to the cults of earlier, native pharaohs, particularly those of Dynasties XIX and XXX (CAT. 9). The priesthood of this, the most important native religious sanctuary of the period, was thus assured of a visible link with its past.

At the end of the third century B. C., Ptolemy IV Philopator (CATS. 15, 54) was apparently unable to secure from among the pool of Hellenistic Greek mercenaries sufficient numbers to staff his needs. As a result, the Ptolemaic garrison at Itanos on Crete was commanded by a Roman. When the foreign possessions of Ptolemy IV Philopator were threatened by Antiochus III, the Hellenistic king of Syria, and he was unable to muster enough troops to meet the challenge, he was forced to employ native Egyptians as soldiers. These native levies, receiving their orders through interpreters, proved the decisive margin of victory at the Battle of Raphia in 216 B. C. But Ptolemy IV's victory was accompanied by political revolt at home. Although an absolute link cannot be forged between the native Egyptian participation in that battle and the subsequent revolt of the Thebaid (the area dependent upon Thebes) in the autumn of 206 B. C., all who have studied these events agree about their causal relationship. That revolt resulted in the virtual secession of Upper Egypt and the establishment of a collateral dynasty of native Egyptians as rulers. Although evidence of such discontent may be lacking from the earlier periods, one might nevertheless adduce its presence from the fact that Ptolemy II Philadelphos banished his first wife, Arsinoe I, to Coptos, just a short distance north of Thebes. He may have selected Coptos as a site of exile because of the perceived hostility of its citizens toward the Crown. In such an environment, any political aspirations of his deposed wife would be curtailed and her life may even have been endangered.

The Theban revolt, and the others which followed, were doubtless possible because those Egyptians who were in positions of responsibility recognized that the administrative mechanisms which they themselves had once directed for the Crown could be easily adjusted to serve nationalistic interests. The revolt suddenly made manifest the latent strengths of the native Egyptians in all sectors of Ptolemaic society. Ptolemy IV Philopator was confronted by a native insurrection that challenged the very principles upon which the administration of the land was based. Almost contemporary with the Theban revolt was an independent intrigue of monstrous proportions at the court in Alexandria, led by the Alexandrian Greek Sosibios, who had risen to the top of the administrative system. Sosibios betrayed his trust by concealing from the country the fact that the king had died, perpetuating the fiction that Ptolemy IV Philopator was only indisposed. He continued to discharge his duties for his own ends. That his charade might fool many, as assuredly it did, is indicative of the extent to which the Crown had abrogated its mandate by distancing itself from its ministers. Both episodes revealed the Crown's inability to govern the land effectively. The plot was discovered by the Alexandrians, who as a group were to become progressively more involved in the feuds between the Ptolemies. That mob proclaimed a mere child king; the fate of Sosibios, however, is moot.

The selection of Ptolemy V Epiphanes (CATS. 55, 56) as king and his installation in 196 B. C. at Memphis according to Egyptian rites, as described on the Rosetta Stone (Fig. 3), appear to have been still another overture to the native Egyptians. Nevertheless, the Egyptians in the Thebaid continued to maintain their independence, and there was a contemporaneous rebellion in the Delta itself. With regard to such revolts, the history of Ptolemaic Egypt is not unlike that of other epochs of ancient Egypt's long history. The collateral dynasties of the Third Intermediate Period, the hint of a native dynast coeval with the First Persian Domination of Dynasty XXVII, and the rival dynasties of the fourth century B. C. reveal that the insurrections of the Ptolemaic Period conformed to a well-established pattern, whereby indigenous political aspirations caused political disjunctions without necessarily prompting corresponding ruptures in other sectors of Egypt's society. Conversely, foreign policy was adversely affected by the revolts of the second century B. C. So preoccupied was the Crown with quelling these insurrections that it lost almost all of Egypt's external possessions.

The history of Ptolemaic Egypt during this century is an involved series of internecine plots punctuated by foreign intervention and the increased involvement of Rome in

Fig. 3 The Rosetta Stone ▷
The installation of Ptolemy V Epiphanes at Memphis in 196 B. C. is recorded on this monument, the very document which enabled J.-F. Champollion to decipher the hieroglyphs in 1822. (London 24)

the destiny of Egypt. That involvement began during the reign of Ptolemy VI Philometor, when Antiochus IV invaded Egypt during the course of the Sixth Syrian War in 168 B.C. The total collapse of Ptolemaic Egypt was averted by the Roman legate Gaius Popilius Laenas, who coerced Antiochus IV into accepting a Roman ultimatum to withdraw from the country. Roman interest in Egypt was thereby firmly established and, although her armies were not to appear on Egyptian soil until the first century B.C., Egypt found it increasingly difficult to act independently of Rome.

But Rome's political and eventual military involvement in Egypt could not countenance the fundamental differences between the two nations. Egypt was, in truth, a land of two cultures, the pharaonic and the Hellenistic, but the Romans were forced to confront the latter since their dealings were with the Ptolemies, as the rulers, and not with the Egyptians, as the ruled. These differences were heightened by an incident that occurred around 140 B.C., when the Roman Scipio Aemilianus, accompanied by the Stoic philosopher Panaetius, visited Alexandria as part of their diplomatic tour of inspection of the East. These men shared the Roman traits of simplicity and conservatism embodied in the principle of *mos maiorum:* adhering to the customs of one's ancestors. Such men and their contemporaries experienced culture shock when they witnessed what they interpreted to be the appalling, by Roman standards, behavior and deportment of Ptolemy VIII Euergetes II (CATS. 19, 53), a grotesquely overweight monarch who insisted on parading about in front of these guests in a gossamer costume. Panaetius and Scipio Aemilianus were, perhaps, incapable of understanding the cultural context of the king's behavior, which was unacceptable from the Roman point of view. Ptolemy VIII Euergetes II was an exponent of the Hellenistic Greek concept of *tryphe*, or luxury, a concept that included, but was not restricted to, a lavish display of luxury, bordering on the ostentatious. It was this facet of Ptolemaic court life that was so attractive to Marc Antony (CAT. 80) and yet simultaneously angered many Romans, so that they held Cleopatra VII (CATS. 76-78) in low esteem.

Ptolemy VIII Euergetes II nevertheless ruled for over fifty years, the longest recorded reign of any Ptolemaic king. He witnessed yet another native insurrection, despite the fact that he was crowned king at Memphis according to pharaonic rites. The internecine rivalries escalated into open hostilities and murder. For instance, Ptolemy VII Neos Philopator, who ruled for less than a year, was eliminated by his uncle, Ptolemy VIII, shortly after the death of Ptolemy VII's father, Ptolemy VI Philometor. The struggle between Ptolemy VIII's wife, Cleopatra II, who was also his sister, and her daughter by an earlier marriage to Ptolemy VI, Cleopatra III, whom he also married, was to continue into the first century B.C. as his sons Ptolemy IX Soter II and Ptolemy X Alexander I vied with each other and with Cleopatra II for control of the country. One might interpret the dearth of coins bearing images of these two Ptolemies as an indication of a partial return to a barter economy by the nation as a whole (see CATS. 60, 61).

During the first half of the first century B.C., the political situation of Egypt relative to Rome was a paradox. Whereas Roman interests in the country waxed so strongly that her generals and statesmen were often responsible for making now one, now another member of the royal family either king or queen, no Roman would venture to take Egypt by force of arms. Ptolemy X Alexander I, perhaps sensing the role Rome might play in support of his cause, even willed Egypt to Rome, but the terms of that testament were never enacted. Upon his death, the Roman dictator Sulla placed Ptolemy X's son, Ptolemy XI Alexander II, along with his stepmother, upon the throne of Egypt. After a little more than fourteen days as king he had his stepmother murdered, a deed that so angered the Alexandrians that they killed him after he had reigned for less than three weeks. Having murdered a candidate supported by Rome, the Alexandrians reacted swiftly and immediately elevated Ptolemy XII Auletes (CATS. 57, 58), a son of Ptolemy IX Soter II, to the throne in an effort to avert reprisals.

Ptolemy XII, too, realized the power of Rome and in 59 B.C., after a heavy bribe to Julius Caesar (CAT. 79) himself in an attempt to secure his throne, received in return the official title of "friend and ally" of Rome. This association did not endear him to the Alexandrians. When the Romans subsequently and unilaterally annexed the island of Cyprus, which had been an Egyptian possession, the incensed Alexandrians immediately deposed Ptolemy XII, and he left for Rome to seek redress. His eldest daughter, Cleopatra VI, and upon her death her sister Berenike IV, each became the monarch of Egypt. Upon payment of yet another bribe, this time to the Roman Gabinius, Ptolemy XII Auletes was reinstated with the help of Roman legions. He died in 51 B.C. after possibly having named his daughter, Cleopatra VII, then sev-

enteen years old, and her brother, Ptolemy XIII, himself only ten years old, to rule the land jointly.
The career of Cleopatra VII can be outlined briefly as follows. The daughter of Ptolemy XII Auletes and, as has been suggested, of Cleopatra V, she had witnessed between the years 60 and 52 B. C. the ever growing influence of Rome on Ptolemaic politics. She understood how Ptolemaic money could buy Roman influence. She witnessed firsthand the rule of a woman, Berenike IV, over Egypt. She could appreciate the value of Roman legions, which had reinstated her father to the throne. A victim of the factions at her own court, she intrigued with Julius Caesar, who entered Egypt and upheld her claim to the throne, to which she was again elevated, but now with her even younger brother, Ptolemy XIV, Ptolemy XIII having been defeated by Caesar and drowned in the Nile. She allegedly bore Caesar a son, Caesarion by name, and subsequently traveled to Rome at the invitation of Julius Caesar. Upon his death, she was rumored to have poisoned her remaining brother, Ptolemy XIV, and returned to Egypt. In 41 B. C. she journeyed to Tarsus, opposite Cyprus on the Turkish coast, to meet Marc Antony. The encounter was lavish; the setting orchestrated by Cleopatra VII conformed to the concept of *tryphe*, which had earlier so outraged Scipio Aemilianus. The mutual drive of Cleopatra and Antony for universal rule set them against the forces of Octavian, who defeated them. They ended their lives by suicide, but Cleopatra's daughter by Antony lived on to marry Juba and become queen of Mauretania.

Fig. 4 The Byzantine Empress Irene
During the twelfth century the legend of Cleopatra VII was again revived, partly due to the personality of Irene, wife of the Byzantine Emperor John II Comnenus, shown here in a mosaic from the South Gallery of the Church of Haghia Sophia in Istanbul.

Today Cleopatra VII emerges from behind these bald facts as an ambitious woman. The historical record reveals that by the time of her involvement with Julius Caesar in 48 B. C. there were virtually two independent states in the Mediterranean world, Egypt and Rome, and there were two headstrong rulers seeking absolute power, Julius Caesar and Cleopatra VII. That scenario and their personalities suggest that both used each other for their own political purposes. The assassination of Julius Caesar placed Cleopatra in an untenable position: she could not approach Octavian because his character was so vehemently antithetical to hers. Like Scipio, he was a product of *mos maiorum*, while she epitomized *tryphe*. The contemporary sources describe her not as a renowned beauty, but rather as a woman possessed of an extraordinary personality and who was an engaging conversationalist. She was, the sources report, monogamous, having admired and loved first Julius Caesar and then Marc Antony, whom she manipulated to her own purposes.
The naval battle between Antony and Octavian at Actium in September of 31 B. C. was of momentous importance for the history of the West because it placed the last two independent states of the Mediterranean world against one another. Cleopatra VII and Antony represented the culture of Ptolemaic Egypt and Octavian that of Rome. That battle, the last naval encounter of Antiquity, changed the destiny of the Western world, which,

had the war been won by Cleopatra VII and Antony, would have been indebted to the traditions of Ptolemaic Egypt. But Cleopatra and Antony lost. Their suicides in 30 B. C. closed one chapter of Egypt's history but opened another.

Octavian, later called Augustus (CAT. 81), fundamentally altered the fabric of ancient Egypt. He closed her borders to all foreigners by decreeing that the country was his personal domain. Travel could only be conducted by special visa. The administration of the land no longer relied upon the complicity of the members of the advantaged classes with the new regime. Rather, it was gradually, but unmistakably, organized along different lines: the Egyptians, native and Greek alike, were confronted with the realities of a government imposed upon all by officials appointed from abroad and supported by legions permanently garrisoned in their land. The Roman administration of Egypt was more ruthless and unrelenting than that of the Ptolemies in its effort to extract the highest possible revenues from a country which became progressively impoverished.

The memory of pharaonic Egypt persisted because the Egyptomania of the Romans, which did so much to keep the spirit of ancient Egypt alive in subsequent ages, was based in large part on the monuments of Ptolemaic Egypt that they encountered on an almost daily basis during their occupation of the land, and which they continued to use as models for their own building projects in Egypt. And so strong was the memory of Cleopatra the Great that later historians confused and conflated her story both with those of Zenobia, Queen of Palmyra, who invaded Egypt in A. D. 269, and the Byzantine Empress Irene, who ruled in her own right in the twelfth century (Fig. 4).

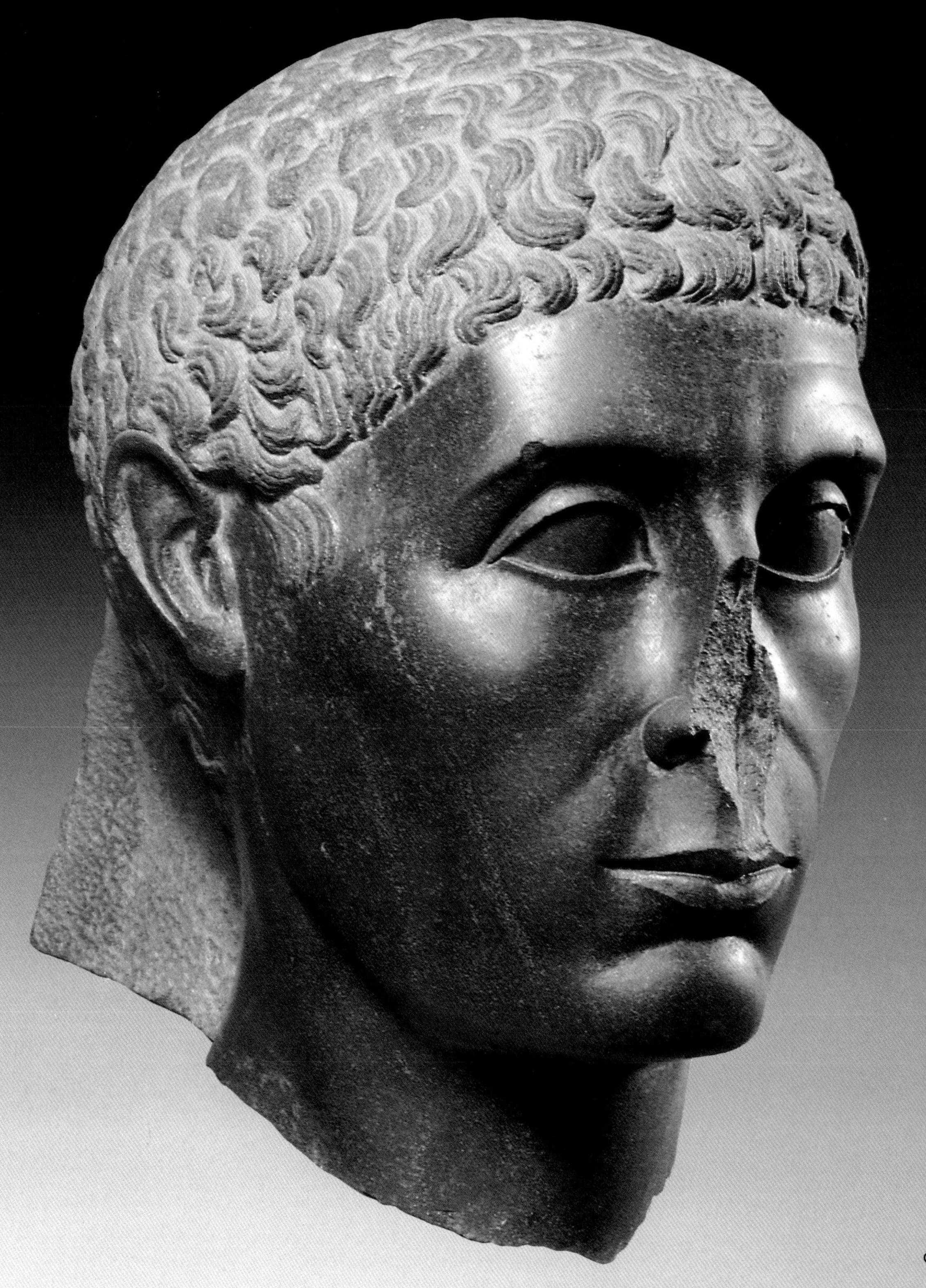

CAT. 43

X

CAT. 45

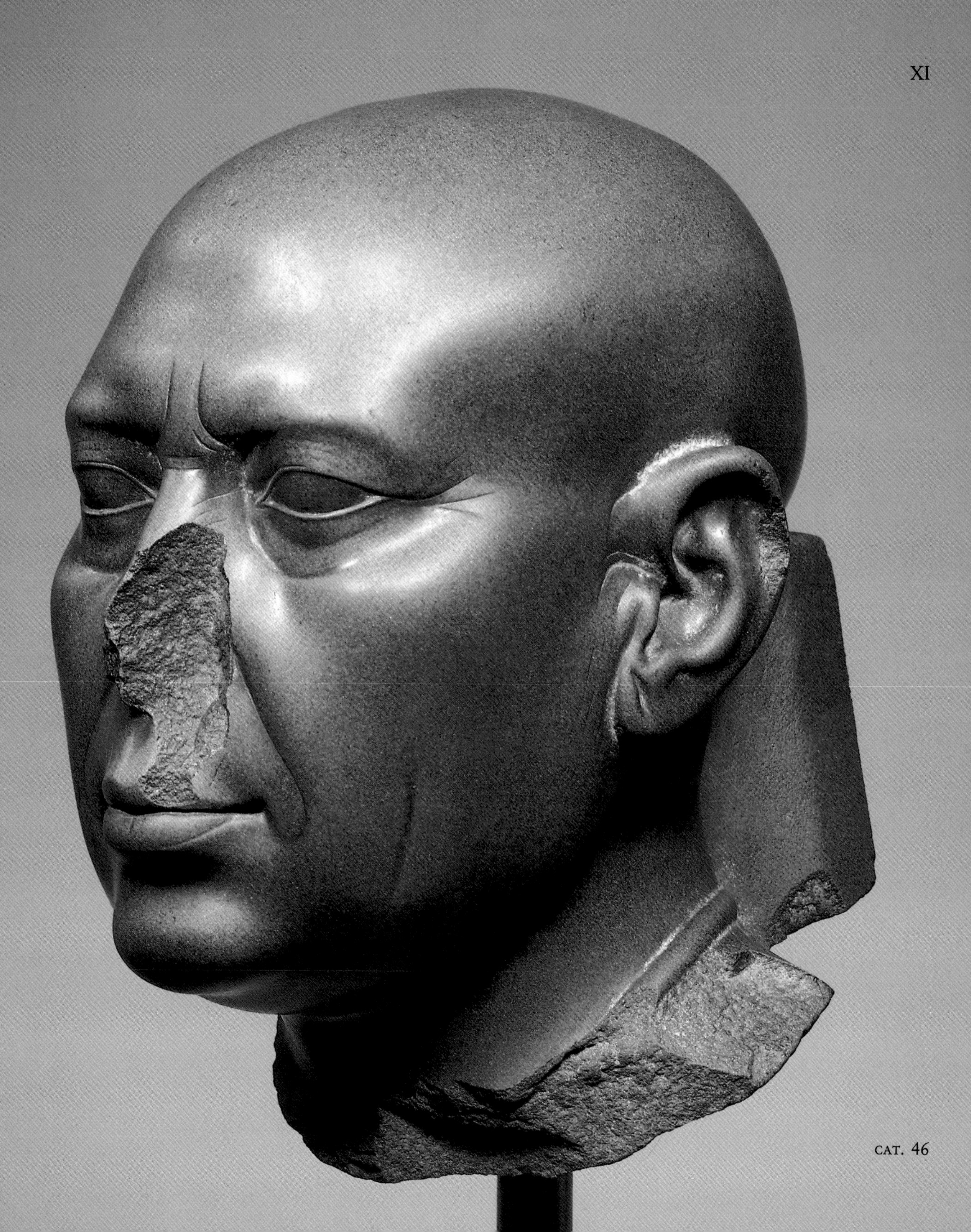

CAT. 46

XII

CAT. 49

XIII

CAT. 62

CAT. 64

XV

CAT. 68

XVI

CAT. 77

Greeks and Egyptians: Ethnicity, Status, and Culture

by Roger S. Bagnall

For more than a half century, the interaction of Greeks and Egyptians, and of Greek and Egyptian cultures, has provided the central interpretive motif for studies of Hellenistic Egypt. From the belief in a mixed society and culture which dominated scholarly thinking for more than a century until the Second World War, scholars have moved to something approaching consensus that by and large Greeks and Egyptians led parallel rather than converging lives, that their cultures coexisted rather than blended.[1] And yet within this consensus there is significant conceptual disarray, visible at the level of detail as well as of generalization. One example will suffice: the Cretan cavalryman Dryton was married in 150 B.C.[2] to a woman named Apollonia, also called Senmonthis, his second wife. She had one Greek name and one Egyptian. Was she a Greek or an Egyptian? The last five years have seen four scholars – two Demoticists and two Hellenists – divide evenly in print on this point, with one Demoticist and one Hellenist on each side.[3] This family has been known for nine decades now, and is the center of a small archive. Several generations and many relatives are known. Why can we not reach consensus on this woman's ethnic identity?

Our difficulties of interpretation stem from three major roots, I think. One of them, perennial and incurable but partially and slowly ameliorable, lies in the sources. We have an abundance of documentation of various sorts for Hellenistic Egypt, but it is very unevenly distributed in time, place, and type of document. Little of it is interpretive except for the occasional literary works, themselves often lacking in sufficient historical context to be fully understandable as cultural documents. The other two difficulties, however, are grounded in our own failures. First, a failure to take into account factors of place and time can cause faulty comparisons and create nonexistent conflicts. We cannot assume that we may interpret a document of the second century on the basis of our understanding of the third, or even that a generalization about Ptolemy I should be seen as being in opposition to a contradictory generalization about Ptolemy II.[4] More important, however, has been the lack of conceptual clarity about our questions. What does the question "Is Apollonia Greek or Egyptian?" mean in the middle of the second century? What do we mean by "Hellenization" or "Egyptianization"? Along with lack of clarity, lack of sophistication; with few exceptions we have not managed to think our way through the conceptual questions to anything but the most obvious results.[5] None of these deficiencies can be remedied in a brief article. My object, rather, is to review selected areas of Greek-Egyptian interaction as they are reflected in recent scholarship and sketch the directions in which these inquiries seem to be leading.

When the Romans took possession of Egypt after three centuries of Ptolemaic rule, they did not find Egyptian vs. Greek a useful distinction. Their lack of such a distinction has been seen as a reflection of their hostility to Egypt,[6] but it may perhaps better be taken as their attempt to make manageable sense in their own juridical framework of a complex situation. They did recognize the claim to separate status on the part of the citizens of the three Greek cities of Egypt (Alexandria, Ptolemais, Naukratis), who are called "Alexandrians" or *astoi*, and who had privileges different from the remainder of the population. The bulk of the people, however, who lived either in the nome capitals or in the countryside, were all "Egyptians."[7] The government did give the residents of the metropoleis (principal towns) of the nomes some special privileges (mostly fiscal), and in the third century A.D. they were to find themselves defined as citizens of municipalities. But for more than two centuries, in legal status they too were Egyptians. It did not matter whether they were descended from Greeks and nothing but Greeks for ten generations or whether their father had learned Greek and given them Greek names. They were Egyptians. Now we may criticize this lumping together as crude, but it surely must reflect the fact that the Romans found no simple way of dividing Greeks and Egyptians. Citizenship did not help much because there were only three Greek cities, and most Greeks did not live in them, as they did in most parts of the Greek world which the Romans acquired. After all, the Roman government had no aversion to dividing society into strata and keeping them separated.[8]

What follows must be prefaced with a crucial point: the problem of ethnicity which we are considering has to do with a narrow segment of society. The large mass of the population, the royal farmers (peasants who held land belonging to the king on a quasi-permanent lease), remained entirely Egyptian, while the urban Greeks and probably most of the military settlers in the countryside remained unequivocally Greek in language and culture (which is not to deny the possibility of intermarriage). Our concern here is with a border region of unknown size and importance, those for whom such an ethnic distinction was no longer clear.[9]

Less than a century before the Roman takeover, Ptolemy VIII had still thought the distinctions usable. In the famous edict of 118 B.C. (*P. Tebt* I 5.207-220=*C. Ord. Ptol.* 53)* about the jurisdiction of Greek and Egyptian courts, the sovereigns speak of Greeks and Egyptians as recognizable groups.[10] The law does not, to be sure, indicate on what basis the status of Greek or of Egyptian is recognized. And the tenor of the law shows that Egyptians and Greeks were making contracts with one another both in Greek and Demotic Egyptian, and that Greeks might even make contracts with Greeks in Demotic. From this it is clear that for the early second century B.C., if not considerably earlier, a definition of ethnicity which rests upon use of language is hopelessly inadequate to the situation.[11] Upon what did ethnic identity rest? In an external, objective sense the answer is easy, at least for men. It was an official status, such as one had been required to give in all legal contexts since at least the time of Ptolemy II.[12] How one came by such status, however, and what it meant subjectively for the individuals, particularly women, at an unofficial level, are much harder questions.

The use of the double name, mentioned above as a symptomatic difficulty of interpretation, is central to our investigation. Recent work has shown that explicit instances of double names are only the tip of the iceberg: we usually cannot detect people who had double names because they generally used only one name at a time – the Greek one in certain contexts, the Egyptian one in others. (One might go so far as to say that they conceived of themselves as having two names, not a "double name" as we term it.) Willy Clarysse has argued that the choice of names depended on the function; that is, the Greek name is used virtually exclusively in the context of documents concerned with official duties or status as a royal functionary, whether administrative or military, while the Egyptian name is used in almost all private acts, particularly in Demotic.[13] For example, Clarysse notes that the "well-known village-scribe of Kerkeosiris [in the Faiyum; perhaps modern Gharaq] in the late 2nd cent., Menches son of Petesouchos, has a proper Egyptian name, just as one would expect from a komogrammateus [village secretary]. Thanks to a single private document in his extensive archives, however, we happen to know that Menches also had a Greek name, Asklepiades, which he never used when acting as village scribe. ... On the other hand, the village epistates** of Kerkeosiris in the same period was a Greek, as was indeed usual during the whole Ptolemaic Period, and as were his predecessors and successors in the village. The funny thing about all this, however, is that the epistates with the Greek name Polemon was probably the father of the village scribe with the Egyptian name Petesouchos (alias Polemon) and the brother of Menches."[14] The *agoranomoi* (notaries) of Pathyris (modern Gebelein) and Krokodilopolis (near Pathyris; perhaps modern Rizagat) all have Greek names, but where we have any evidence for them unrelated to their function as *agoranomoi*, the names of other members of their family are Egyptian. Two of their wives are "endowed wives," *s.ḥm.t sʿnḫ*, a status which can have been established only by a Demotic act under Egyptian law (and which elsewhere is always connected to priestly families).[15]

* All references to papyri follow J. Oates, R. Bagnall, W. Willis, K. Worp, *Checklist of Editions of Greek Papyri and Ostraca* 3rd ed. (*BASP* Suppl. 4, Atlanta, 1985).

** The term epistates is employed for a local magistrate whose authority encompasses, but is not limited to, matters of security comparable to those of a police force.

Another example of the working of double names is found in the archives of Dionysios son of Kephalas.[16] Over the course of his attested career (117/116 to after 104), Dionysios was a soldier, a priest and a cultivator. He was one of three children of a marriage between Demetria and Kephalas, both good Greek names. Kephalas himself was one of four children, the others being Peteharpochrates, Tothoes, and Petenouphis, children of Dionysios and Senobastis. His brothers thus all had Egyptian names. There were no attested aliases on this side of the family, but that may be only a matter of the type of documents preserved. Demetria used the aliases Sarapias and Senabellis and was the daughter of Heliodoros alias Herieus and of Senamounis. Dionysios uses two aliases, Plenis and *Pa-ᶜš3*, and he married Isidora alias Taesis (the Greek name being a translation of the Egyptian), daughter of Hermophilos alias Pachois and of Tetosiris. When Dionysios' brother referred to him in a Greek text, he called him "my brother Plenis." And his Greek name is found only once in his Demotic documents – and that time, tellingly, he calls himself a Greek, with reference to his military status.

More evidence could be cited, but it all points to the validity of Clarysse's conclusions. Double names are found mainly for persons with an official status;[17] they occur as such only occasionally, with the use of one name sufficient in most contexts; the name chosen is the Greek one in official contexts, the Egyptian in private ones. The evidence for this cluster of phenomena comes predominantly from the second half of the second century. It is difficult to avoid the conclusion that at least in the sense of language we are dealing with a context which is Egyptian by choice, Greek only for official purposes. In the case of Dionysios son of Kephalas, Pestman concludes as follows: "Dionysios could write Greek as well as Demotic; he was thus bilingual. This indicates, in our opinion, that he came from an Egyptian cultural sphere, for it was rare that Greeks by origin learned Egyptian and were capable of writing Demotic. On a social level, the reverse situation was more logical, and moreover, learning Demotic writing was so arduous in practice that it was much easier for someone who could already write in Demotic to learn Greek writing as well, than the reverse."[18]

And yet, things are not quite so simple; some people used dual names without holding any official position, and some Greeks probably learned Egyptian. It was, of course, not necessary to master the difficult Demotic script in order to pick up a reasonable spoken command of Egyptian; and scribes could be paid to draft documents.[19] Moreover, cases where our evidence for a particular family is not as extensive as in the examples just cited may leave us unable to determine the "primary" cultural milieu of an individual or a family, let alone original ethnic background. Where an individual functions in both Greek and Egyptian roles, using both languages, can we be confident that some Greek ancestor did not learn Egyptian? In a case like that of Menches' family, one may well be forced to confess that in the later second century neither name nor official ethnic designation tells us much about origins. Each situation must be examined separately, even if we admit that Pestman's presumption is correct.

We return now to Apollonia, wife of the Cretan cavalryman Dryton. Her father's family (we know nothing of her mother) is made up on our family tree[20] almost entirely of double-named men and of women with Egyptian names. The oldest ancestor about whom we know anything is Hermokrates alias Panas, a soldier at Pathyris (attested in 161), the paternal grandfather of Apollonia. Her three sisters, however, all had double names, and her five daughters by Dryton all had double names too. This family, taken by itself, has (as already mentioned) struck some as Hellenic in origin but Egyptianized,[21] others as Egyptian in origin but Hellenized.[22] Clarysse's insight about the use of double names seems to me to show at least that the Greek names are used mainly as a function of military rank in this family, and secondarily as part of the society of such military men. They are usually dropped when no official context is at hand. It is hard to avoid the conclusion that the milieu is predominantly Egyptian in speech, law, and culture: as *persons* these are Egyptians, as *functionaries* they act as Greeks. What their ancestry is, we cannot tell, and the double names as far back as the 180s cannot tell us: they show only that the use of Greek names for official contexts must go back that far.

And yet Apollonia and her sisters insist that they are Greeks; for example, the papyrus *SB* I 4638 tells us that Apollonia and her sisters are Cyrenaeans. Men in military service have Greek or pseudo-Greek ethnic designations.[23] They could have claimed to be Greeks in the terms in which the decree of Ptolemy VIII cited earlier uses the word, and they did operate in both languages. In the case of the women, we cannot detect any motive other than social for the claim of Greek status, which was for them higher and more prestigious. Despite all attempts by the kings to preserve the *laokritai* (native Egyptian judges), they eventually disappeared, while standard Egyptian transactions, increasingly written in Greek, were brought before the *chrematistai* (Greek circuit judges).[24] If the Romans could not tell such people apart from the descendants of Macedonian settlers who knew some Egyptian, it is hardly surprising: Apollonia and her family would not have wanted such a distinction. Nor should we be surprised that the breadth of the possible definitions of Hellenism and indeed the cultural character of Hellenism itself under the later Ptolemies had the ultimate effect of making the term "Hellene" useless. The same thing happened later with Roman citizenship. The point of any mark of distinction, *qua* distinction, is to exclude most people from it; the lowering of barriers does not remove the urge to differentiate oneself from the common herd; it merely creates the need for new barriers. Some other means of distinguishing oneself from others emerges. One does not acquire prestige from being like everyone else.

That, however, is a matter of legal status. When we turn back to social and cultural realities of the Ptolemaic Period, the breakdown of distinctions needs to be examined to see what degree of integration in society we can discern. In Egyptian society, the large mass of peasants was certainly unaffected by Hellenism except as its objects. The propertied class, which we have been discussing,[25] was no doubt a relatively small group, though proportionately very productive of papyrus documents. A significant number among the Egyptian propertied class were priests;[26] we will return to them later. Integration in the reverse direction is almost as difficult to assess: what impact did Egypt have on the Greeks? How "Egyptianized" did the Greeks of Egypt become? In general, the Greek attitude toward Egypt and Egyptians appears to have been an exploitative one, in both the neutral and the negative senses of that word.[27] Even those who have tried to make a strong case for Egyptian influence on the Ptolemies themselves have depicted in essence a use of Egyptian material for royal purposes, not an Egyptianization of the royal family.[28] The Greeks were certainly receptive to the traditions of other countries, and they seem to have absorbed material from Egyptian medicine and wisdom literature, for example.[29]

We must be wary of assuming that such things point to the "Egyptianization" of Greeks. What would such a term mean? At the most superficial level, we have some direct evidence of Greeks learning Egyptian, as has already been pointed out. Dryton, long before he married an Egyptian woman in 150 (an event which is often viewed as an act of "Egyptianizing"), was lending money via Demotic contracts. And the long residence of Ptolemaios the *katochos* in the Sarapieion at Memphis (along with, some of the time, his brother and other Hellenes) certainly led to his deep involvement in the life of an Egyptian temple.[30] That temple milieu, however, was itself increasingly not a purely Egyptian world, but rather one in which Greeks and Greek language and culture were making inroads.

But there is a more important point at stake: Hellenism had always, as far back as we can tell, been local, particularistic, and receptive. The reverse side of the exploitativeness of the Greeks faced with a foreign culture is their ability to adapt and adopt words, products, learning, and gods from foreigners without becoming less Hellenic in the process. Indeed, that openness, combined with deep resistance to absorption, is precisely a mark of Greek culture when compared to Egyptian, which was extremely resistant and yet, by that fact, less able to resist in the long run. The ability of the Greeks to adapt to new circumstances without fundamental cultural alteration, along with their position of power in Egypt, enabled them to take whatever they wished from Egypt without ceasing to become Greeks. It is not obvious that the Egyptians could do the same.

In fact, the almost total lack of visible impact of Greek occupation on Egyptian culture has often been noted, to the point that when two faint echoes (one of Homer, *Iliad* 22, the other of Greek sacrificial customs) were detected in the texts on the walls of the Temple at Edfu, they were greeted with a veritable fanfare.[31] As Claire Préaux pointed out,[32] Egyptian civilization was very closely linked to religion in almost every respect, and Egyptian religion remained essentially closed to foreign influence and persons, even if Greeks might turn up at local temples for festivals. The Egyptian cults remained virtually closed to any novelty not internally generated. In fact, the old cults continued in this hermetic mode right up to their extinction in Late Antiquity, when Christianity (which united an outside influence with a resurgence of the Egyptian language) came to dominate the scene.[33]

There is one curious aspect to this closedness, however. The architects of this policy (if that is not too intentional a word to use) were surely the priests who controlled the cults. And yet we find the priests also represented in the class of the "Hellenizers" – those who turn up with double names and royal functions, and work in Greek. Two instances of this phenomenon have already been cited. Dionysios son of Kephalas is attested as a priest in the period before he enters the army,[34] and the *agoranomoi* use an institution (that of the endowed woman) otherwise found in priestly circles.[35] But the most interesting case is found at a much higher level. A series of Greek metrical epitaphs from the necropolis of Hassaia, near Apollinopolis Magna (Edfu),[36] introduces us to a family holding high military rank in the later second century. Basically these poems come clearly from the Greek poetic tradition, but J. Yoyotte has shown that they incorporate significant Egyptian religious elements.[37] The people involved can, moreover, be convincingly identified with people having Egyptian tombstones on which they bear Egyptian names. One is a *syngenes* (kinsman of the king), and the men are high army officials or, in one case, supervise a granary; but they also are priests of local Egyptian temples (Prophet of Osiris, of Horus, of Harsomtous). The military offices are listed in the hieroglyphic texts as well as in the Greek, but the priestly ones are not listed in the Greek texts. Just like the common soldiers or lower officials, these men turn up with Greek names when acting in an official capacity, but in private life they have Egyptian tombstones, Egyptian names, and Egyptian priesthoods. And they belong to the highest stratum of Egyptian society.

Was Egyptian culture, in its traditional modes of religion and learning, in fact essentially impermeable to foreign influence as is generally thought?[38] Egyptian literature influenced Greek writing, Egyptian gods were worshiped by foreigners (not always in the manner the Egyptians worshiped them, to be sure), Egyptian art eventually acquired popularity with Greek urban populations.[39] Were none of these reciprocally influenced by the Greeks? On one level, they clearly were not. Demotic – a written language largely controlled by priests – was very resistant to borrowing Greek words. Almost all Greek words in Ptolemaic Demotic documents come from a few categories: honorific titles of kings and gods, Greek proper adjectives, official titles (and those only rarely – they were usually translated into Demotic), some technical administrative or military terms, and a few objects of daily life.[40] Demotic literature was essentially free of Greek words altogether; but there is a salient exception in the scientific and medical texts, which borrow very large numbers of Greek words.[41] Broader Greek literary influence is seen in the Demotic literature of the Roman Period;[42] and that influence came from somewhere. Apart from scientific and medical texts, late Ptolemaic Demotic wisdom literature shows clear signs of influence from the contemporary milieu, both Greek and Semitic.[43]

Despite the limits of this cultural borrowing, the people were not untouched by the Greek presence. Even the peasants found their lives affected by the development of a Greek-style market economy and the more generalized use of coinage, among other economic changes, and by the gradual development of the administration from traditional Egyptian models to Greek and then Roman conceptions. The upper classes among the Egyptians underwent the process of at least partial Hellenization described above, which might include some familiarity with Greek poetry on the part of the wealthier, who presumably mixed more with those with a Greek education in the course of their work. (By the Roman Period, the priests needed Greek to function, and even the oracles operated in Greek.) The difference between what happened to the people and what happened to their traditional culture may help to explain the eventual loss of vitality and wide appeal which seems to have afflicted Egyptian culture in the Roman Period; it may even help explain the swiftness with which most of Egypt converted to Christianity. But that is a subject of its own.[44]

All references to papyri follow J. Oates, R. Bagnall, W. Willis, and K. Worp, *Checklist of Editions of Greek Papyri and Ostraca* 3rd ed. (*BASP* Suppl. 4, Atlanta, 1985).

[1] Préaux 1978, vol. II: 543-86.

[2] The date of the marriage is now secure; see Clarysse 1986: 99-103.

[3] See below, pp. 23-24, for discussion of this case.

[4] One example: Clarysse 1985: 64 note 21 contrasts the views of Swinnen (1973) and Koenen (1983; discussed below, note 28). But Swinnen is talking about the religious policies of Ptolemy I, Koenen mainly about the penetration of Egyptian motifs into the propaganda of Ptolemy II and later kings.

[5] An honorable exception has been J. Bingen; see the references given in Bagnall 1982: 16 notes 20, 22. And, as references below will show, the work of Pestman, Clarysse, and Thompson has pointed the way to a more sophisticated understanding of this complex society.

[6] See, e.g., Lewis 1983: 33-35.

[7] On this question, see Modrzejewski 1985, with extensive bibliography.

[8] A fact nowhere clearer than in the *Gnomon of the Idios Logos* (*BGU* V), translated in Lewis/Reinhold 1968: 379-83.

[9] For a summary and bibliography of the literature, one may consult the posthumous article of Peremans (1987).

[10] Pestman (1985) argues that the law's specification that courts are to be used according to the language of agreements shows that ethnicity was no longer determinable. This goes too far and ignores the fact that the edict itself speaks of ethnic groups.

[11] This papyrus is a famous source of controversy. A review with comprehensive bibliography can be found in Modrzejewski 1975, who rejects all of the proposed emendations to the text and argues that the legislator intends all cases involving Egyptians to be tried before the *laokritai* (native Egyptian judges), with language to decide venue in other cases. A different approach, involving major emendation by insertion, is offered by Pestman (above, note 10). Although my view of the social situation is close to Pestman's, I think Modrzejewski is more nearly correct about the essence of the text: Egyptians who make contracts with Greeks in Greek appear before the *chrematistai* (Greek circuit judges); Greeks who make contracts with Greeks in Egyptian appear before the *laokritai*; Egyptians who make contracts with Egyptians in Greek also appear before the *laokritai*. There was no need to talk about Greek vs. Greek in Greek (always *chrematistai*) or Egyptian vs. Egyptian in Egyptian (always *laokritai*); and even Greek vs. Egyptian in Egyptian (*laokritai*). The decree deals with the newer situations, not clearly handled before this time.

[12] Uebel 1968: 11-13; see also Oates 1963: 63, with references. It is impossible to enter here into the complexities of the problems of status designations, particularly the much controverted *Perses tes epigones*. This designation is, however, in my view a question which closer attention to time and place might make it possible to solve in a manner that reconciles the various insights about its use, which have been offered in a spirit of contradiction.

[13] Clarysse 1985.

[14] *Ibid.*, 59.

[15] Pestman in *Das ptol. Äg.*: 203-10.

[16] *Pap-Lugd. Bat.* 22=*P.Dion.*

[17] Archives of persons without such status may have no double names at all, as in the papers of Totoes, for which see Pestman, *Pap.Lugd.Bat.* 23, 145-48, with stemma on 144: not one Greek or double name.

[18] *Pap.Lugd.Bat.* 22, p. 3. "Dionysios pouvait aussi bien écrire le grec que le démotique, il était donc bilingue. Ce qui indique, à notre avis, qu'il était issu de la sphère culturelle égyptienne, car il était rare que les Grecs d'origine apprissent l'égyptien et fussent capables d'écrire le démotique. Sur le plan social, la situation inverse était plus logique, et en outre, l'apprentissage de l'écriture démotique était si ardue en pratique, qu'il était bien plus facile pour quelqu'un, qui pouvait déjà écrire en démotique, d'apprendre aussi l'écriture grecque, que l'inverse."

[19] It would be hard for a Greek who operated a retail trade, even under government monopoly, in an Egyptian village to avoid learning some Egyptian. On the other hand, anyone dealing with the government needed to know Greek. No matter what the ethnic background, then, both spoken languages were necessary for such people. Clarysse will treat this subject in a future volume of the Lille Demotic papyri.

[20] Ritner 1984: 171-84, stemma on pl. 30. Ritner, 185, seems to date the two Mainz papyri concerning the dispute to year 21 of Ptolemy VI, which is incorrect; they belong to Ptolemy V, in 184; see Zauzich 1968: 37, no. 30 and 85, no. 115, with notes.

[21] Ritner 1984: 187: "The papyri of the families of Hermocrates and Dryton provide an unparalleled view of the Egyptianization of Greek colonists under the Ptolemies. The genealogical revisions made possible by the OI papyrus indicate the early date of this assimilation, as the first attested generation of the family already bears a double name (Apollonios/Nakhthor). [This generation is undatable. The next, Hermokrates, is attested in 161, so the phenomenon cannot really be pushed back before the 180s if that far, since a man taking a new or double name might rename his father; cf. *P. Tebt.* I 61a.40.] With the removal of the single instance of the problematic ethnic designation of 'Persian' from the archive's family, there seems no reason to suspect with Oates that the reverse process is documented – the Hellenization of Egyptians. Rather, the stated Cyrenaic and Cretan ethnic designations of Apollonia et al. and Dryton, respectively, should be taken seriously, and the family's use of Demotic legal instruments is all the more striking. The provincial setting of Pathyris, subject to political instabilities and lacking in Greek speakers, must be largely responsible." See also Pomeroy 1984: 103-24, a rather muddled treatment, but essentially in agreement with Ritner on this issue.

[22] Hobson 1987: 72, reviewing Pomeroy 1984: "Are we dealing here with hellenized Egyptians or with egyptianized Greeks? P. inclines toward the latter view and indeed concludes (p. 124) that there is a tendency for women to become more egyptianized and men more hellenized. This is an intriguing hypothesis and well worth further investigation. However, in the present case it would seem more likely that Apollonia was an Egyptian assuming a Greek name because she was married to a Greek (a possibility suggested by Naphtali Lewis when this material was presented by P. at a colloquium on Social History and the Papyri at Columbia University in 1983)." Pestman, *Pap.Lugd.Bat.* XIX, p. 33: "a woman who, while describing herself as 'Cyrenaean,' belongs to a mixed Graeco-Egyptian family all the members of which bear a Greek name and an Egyptian name. The Egyptian element is strongly represented in this family" ("une femme qui, tout en se qualifiant de 'Cyrénéenne,' appartient à une famille mixte gréco-égyptienne dont tous les membres portent un nom grec et un nom égyptien. L'élément égyptien est fortement représenté dans cette famille"). Pestman notes that the witnesses in 126 who sign Dryton's third will sign in Demotic, even though they are military men.

[23] For example, Dionysios son of Kephalas calls himself variously Persian, Macedonian, and *Wjnn* (in Demotic: literally: "Ionian," the Demotic word for Greek), and calls his brother a Libyan.

[24] See Modrzejewski 1975: 708.

[25] See Bingen's discussion (1970) of the archaic lack of political structure in the peasantry, which reduced its options in coping with Greek innovations to acquiescence, refusal, or flight.

[26] On the difficulties of interpreting this fact, see Bagnall 1982: 15.

[27] I have touched on this point briefly: 1981: 21.

[28] Koenen 1983. He describes, 144, his interest as the "mixture of the Egyptian and Greek cultures" ("Vermischung der ägyptischen und der

griechischen Kulturen"). But he admits that the influences he describes run almost entirely one way, from Egyptian to Greek, and his conclusions, 190, describe a purely exploitative attitude on the part of the Ptolemies toward the Egyptian royal ideology, which they used to help justify themselves in the eyes of the Greeks.

[29] Reymond 1976 and 1977.

[30] See D. J. Thompson 1988: chapter 7, "Between Two Worlds: the Sarapieion." This chapter is the most extensive and nuanced discussion known to me of the interactions among Greek and Egyptian people, languages, religion, and culture in a particular setting.

[31] Derchain 1974. Both "reminiscences" of Greek culture are subjectively apprehended rather than clearly demonstrable.

[32] Préaux 1978, vol. II: 550-52.

[33] Koenen 1983: 144.

[34] *P.Dion.*, p. 6.

[35] Moreover, the Egyptian scribal class traditionally was priestly and connected to temples. We do not know the background of the *agoranomoi* very well, but it seems likely enough that they came from the only known body of literate men experienced in writing contracts in Demotic.

[36] Now Bernand 1969: nos. 5-7, 35, and maybe also 8.

[37] Yoyotte 1969.

[38] A somewhat different question is the supposed hostility of the priesthoods to Ptolemaic rule; for a cogent rejection of this hostile attitude, see Johnson 1984. See also Johnson's article on the continued prosperity – indeed, domination of native-held wealth – of the priests in the Ptolemaic Period (Johnson 1986).

[39] Reymond 1976: 62 (not quite agreeing with her own earlier remarks): "The earlier theory was that Greek texts were translated into the Demotic because the question was approached through the study of Greek documents. It is true that our text includes a good number of Greek words; this, however, was an implementation of late date which did not effect [*sic*] the original character of the writing. The essentially Egyptian character of the whole composition is prominent and manifest. New elements incorporated did not break its original and essential features." On the art, see Koenen 1983: 144-45 note 3.

[40] This information comes from Clarysse 1987.

[41] See above, note 29. Coptic, of course, is full of Greek loan-words.

[42] Lichtheim 1980: 8-10, 125, 151-59, 184.

[43] Lichtheim 1983.

[44] Apart from my visible indebtedness to those whose works I have cited, I am grateful to Willy Clarysse and Dorothy J. Thompson for the use of unpublished material and for their comments in conversation and correspondence.

CAT. 80

CAT. 92, 94, 96, 93

CAT. 83

CAT. 84

CAT. 97

CAT. 89

CAT. 90, 91

XXIV

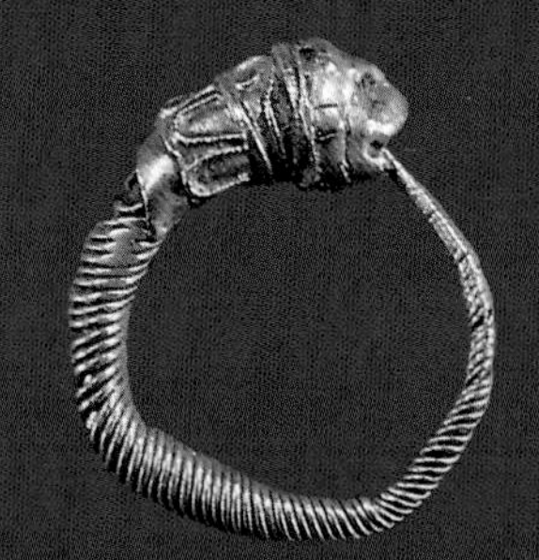

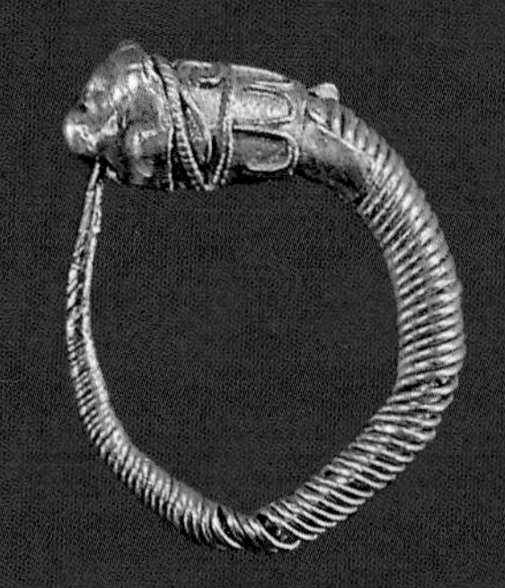

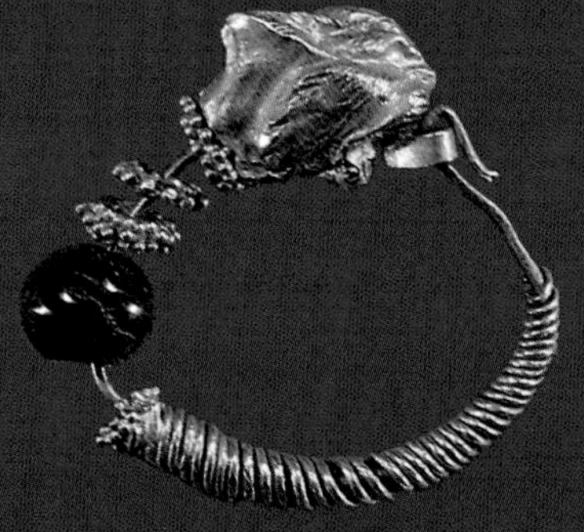

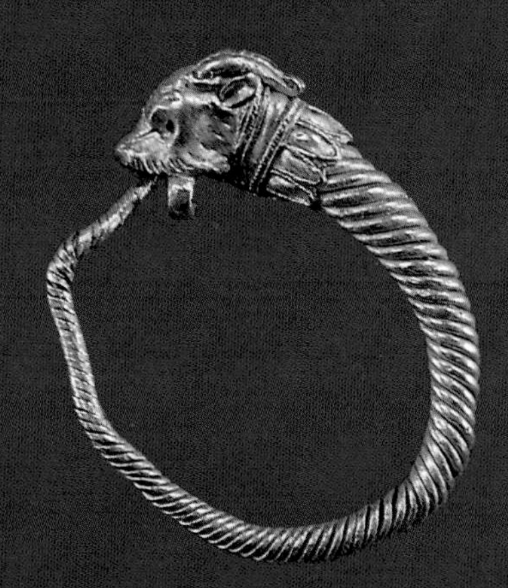

CAT. 85, 88,
86, 87

Ptolemaic Egypt: Priests and the Traditional Religion

by Jean-Claude Goyon

The Creation of the World and the Royal Function

The religion of the ancient Egyptians – the social attitude of a coherent ancient group of people – is based on a special conception of the universe. Brought into focus very early at Heliopolis and widely diffused among Egypt's theological communities, this particular vision of the divine order prevailed until the last days of ancient Egypt's history as a nation. According to this concept, the creation contained within itself a constant menace, that of its own destruction. For an Egyptian in pharaonic times, the religious act and thought that directed him, if he was involved in a cult, constituted a response adapted to this menace, which thus ceased to be ineluctable.

Indeed, the Heliopolitan doctrine had codified the fundamental schema of the created universe thus: drawn from the obscurity of the liquid nothingness (*Nun*) from which all things come by the will and creative thought of a demiurge (Re, Atum), the new world had originally taken the form of an emerging hill (the pyramid; the obelisk of solar temples of Dynasty V at Abusir; or the *Benben* at Thebes) and had welcomed the light and the sun, light's visible form and the source and image of life (Re-Horakhty). Then came living beings to populate the earth. It was in terms of a conflict between the elements – chaos and order, water and earth, shadow and light, death and life – that the daily cycle, governed by the rising and setting of the sun, was established. And in order for that cycle to continue, it was necessary that the demiurge maintain the cosmos in its created state by an act of will. In other words, the creative force had to continue *forever* to will and to think of life and creation in order that it might perpetuate, by unceasingly and untiringly renewing, the act of the First Time, according to the definition of the origins of the world preserved by the hieroglyphic texts.

In the face of imminent destruction should the creative force withdraw and abandon its work, the religious act, supported by words, is the sole salvation. It alone can encourage the deity to perpetuate the universe, and to maintain it in the order established in the beginning, according to the deity's wish and thought. This "original order" the Egyptians conveyed in a figurative manner in their writing and iconography, in the form of a feminine divine principle, the "goddess" Ma'at (a personified abstraction, CAT. 12), who embodied the divine gifts of cosmic equilibrium and of life. By extension, Ma'at also embodied all the factors of political and social order that applied to mankind: Truth, Justice, Authority, and respect for Authority. She was also the means of expressing the existence of the permanent exchange that must be established, and must endure, between the human community (which believes in life) and the force (the godhead) that is its source. Ma'at is thus the essential symbolic expression of the cult in all its aspects, the cult whose celebration must be permanent. One can see how the idea of a gift, of a transmission to humanity of control over its earthly destiny, is intrinsically tied to the origin of Ma'at, the divine principle of equilibrium and life. The godhead thus puts mankind under the obligation to pay respect to its rules, to avoid violating them upon pain of the supreme punishment: man's destruction as well as that of his universe. According to this way of thinking, prime importance is given to the idea of transmission by the divine to the human, and of the responsibility of the group (or of its chief) for the strict observation of the obligations.

In fact, this fundamental schema of transmission is conveyed at a very early date by the Heliopolitan myth of the Children of Re (the Ennead), which is very strongly attested in the Ptolemaic Period in all of the theologies of the South. In this myth, Osiris and Horus, his son, make up the last link in the chain of the transmission of Ma'at from Re, the creator, to his earthly heirs (Fig. 5). Thus, once Horus has punished Seth (the younger brother), thereby depriving him of all rights to the throne, he becomes the victorious successor to the murdered Osiris, and, therefore, the model of the legitimate heir, recognized at once by the gods and by mankind. He is possessed of the power to cause the order of the world (Ma'at) to be respected; he is the guarantor of the divine order in the universe of mankind, and it is this power that he confers on his terrestrial emanation, the pharaoh, "Horus the Living," the king-uniter of the Two Lands.

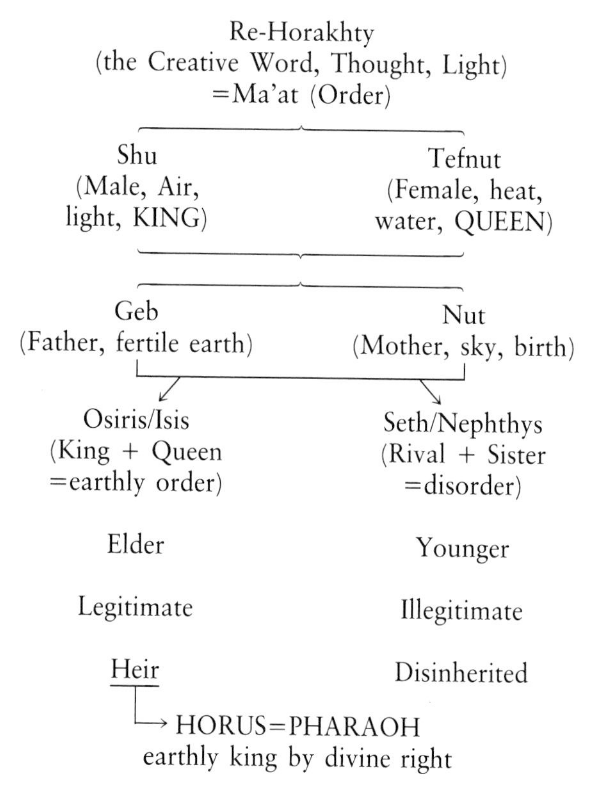

Fig. 5 Divine pedigree of Horus

The titulary of the kings of Egypt, as early as Dynasty I, constantly conveys this unfailing succession: the king is Horus (CATS. 8, 9) and, beyond that, he is also the Son of Re since he is charged with perpetuating, assuring, and transmitting order – Ma'at. Unique and supreme priest, he delegates to the clergy the material charge of ensuring the cult of which he remains the origin and the guarantor.

Consequently, a very special relationship was established between Power and Sacredness. Pharaoh's function, as described, consecrated him to such an extent that he was looked upon as the "perfect god" (*netjer nefer*) on earth, while at the same time being the sole "lord of carrying out the rites" (*neb iret ikhet*). Running like a thread through history, above all during the Ptolemaic Period, this powerful concept embodied by the pharaoh-Horus is based on a *principle* that relegates to second place human questions relating to his person, even to the source of his legitimacy or his ethnic background. For the believing Egyptian – and belief was everything in Egypt for more than three millennia – the existence of the agent of salvation represented by the pharaoh overrode all the political contingencies of this world: there must be a king, no matter by what name you called him, in order to avoid the universal catastrophe that would result if Ma'at were transgressed: the return of creation to chaos.

This faith, founded on an ancestral fear whose importance must be recognized, explains how, in the course of its very long history, Egypt was able to accept and recognize as Horus-sovereign the monarchs of the South (the Mentuhoteps of Dynasty XI) as well as parvenus such as the Ramessides of Dynasty XIX or, even more strangely, "barbarian" kings such as the Libyans of Dynasties XXII-XXIII, the Ethiopians of Dynasty XXV, and finally the Persians such as Darius or Cambyses. The people of the Nile Valley, attached to beliefs that were rooted in the depths of their past, had, in each era, put their confidence in their learned scribes, their theologians, and their clergy. The latter, in fact, never at any time ceased to think and to act in a way that would maintain the national equilibrium according to the ancestral solar tradition that made up their principal doctrinal reference point. The priesthood, therefore, served as an essential agent of political stability in the heart of ancient Egyptian society, for it always enjoyed the confidence of the subjects of the kingdom, for whom it represented the very application of the monarchic principle to the social life of Egypt: by carrying out the cult and the liturgy scrupulously *in the name of the king and for him*, the priests maintained in the universe the presence and the working of the vital creative energy of the First Time.

It was above all at the time of the Lagides (i.e., the Ptolemies), at the time of the construction under the first Ptolemies of the great temples of Edfu (Figs. 1, 2), Dendera (Fig. 6), Philae (Fig. 7), Kom Ombo and Esna, and the renovation of the temples and cults of Thebes

Fig. 6 Facade of the Temple of Hathor at Dendera
The columns with their capitals are in the form of sistra, or rattles, the musical instruments associated with Hathor and other goddesses.

(e.g., the Temple of Amun-Re at Karnak; CAT. 20, Figs. 21, 22) that the clergy began to elaborate and then put in effect *in extenso*, not a new conception of the royal function, but a renewed means of expressing its principles in action. In the golden age of the New Kingdom, it was certainly not rare to see a pharaoh, such as Ramesses II, come to officiate in person at Thebes in the celebration, for instance, of the solemn procession of Amun-Re, king of the gods, in his Beautiful Feast of the Valley. Under the Ptolemies, and then later under the Roman emperors, there is nothing to indicate the effective participation of these human sovereigns in the liturgies of the South. They were, however, recognized there, since it is their cartouches that appear most frequently on contemporary religious edifices.

This lack of participation by the descendants of Alexander's Macedonians in the celebration of the liturgies of Edfu or Philae does not, however, mean that these kings of foreign origin who dominated Egypt after 331 B.C. were completely excluded or cut off from the native cults. The best proof of this is that they took care to reestablish the divine domains in their possessions, to finance new construction, and to assure themselves a place in the pantheon of ancestor-kings or even, as with Alexander the Great or Arsinoe II, in the pantheon of deified heroes. Nevertheless, there seems to have been a split between the South and the North. If the synods of "Graeco-Egyptian" priests were held at Memphis; if the Delta witnessed a blossoming of cults that, while not new, were at least adapted to the beliefs of the Egypto-Greeks (e.g.,

Fig. 7 General view of the Island of Philae in Nubia
The view is from neighboring Bigah Island. To the left of the First (rightmost) Pylon of the Temple of Isis is the mammisi. (From David Roberts 1846)

Isis, Serapis; CATS. 102, 103), the South, from Herakleopolis to Philae, by and large held a privileged position as far as the truly national cults went, and considered itself the true preserver of the pure pharaonic religious tradition.

After 331 B.C. in the temples of the South, the liturgy, above all that of the festivals, tended to take on an essentially sacerdotal character that, at heart, did not differ from what had taken place earlier at the time of the priest-kings of Dynasties XXI-XXIII. At that time, in fact, the Theban High Priests of Amun, above all Herihor (c. 1000 B.C.), were faced with the total decay of Ramesside power and had to institute throughout the "Domain of Amun" an appropriate way of governing and of reuniting the country. These priest-kings based their claim, then, on their supreme function as sacerdotal substitutes for the king in the service of the god. Their legitimacy derived both from their function itself and from an oracle of Amun; that is to say, from the revealed word of the god, which was really only a public reminder of the principle of the transmission of Ma'at. The priest and the king could only become one, according to tradition, after this direct transmission, and the particular deed of the priest only found its true specificity through the force of circumstances and the necessities of the divine cult.

Horus-King and the Triumph of the Falcon King

The adaptation of the sacerdotal functions that had already been germinating, as we have just seen, toward the end of the first millennium at Thebes, was to become the rule in Ptolemaic temples. Thus it is that at Edfu, for example, at the time of the great annual ceremonies, where the titular royal person (a Ptolemy whose throne name we know and whose effigy we may have on coins, but who never ventured so deep into the south) would traditionally have presided and conducted the holy office, a sacerdotal delegate, often the local high priest, took the place of the sovereign and assumed the rank and function of "Priest of the King." This indicates even more clearly the transformation that had taken place in the theological expression of the royal function, although formal appearances were scrupulously kept up in the temple reliefs. There the only names mentioned or images depicted are those of the ruling king, of divine pedigree, who had been crowned King of Egypt in Memphis. We have seen above that the pharaoh-Horus, embodying the principle of the maintenance of Ma'at, was recognized and universally accepted, whatever his name, not because of who he was but for the sake of the fundamental principle of social harmony. By stressing this idea and making use of the imagery of Horus, a vehicle at once of the divine (son of Osiris) and the royal (pharaoh, "Horus of the Living," "Horus of Gold"), the priests of the third century B.C. concentrated in the representation of the Falcon of Horus and its Living Image, the Sacred Falcon, all the properties inherent in the concept of pharaonic royalty; that is, the intrinsic association described above between Power and the Sacred. While the Delta was becoming Hellenized, the South was revitalizing the royal elements of the Heliopolitan doctrine in order to give them a liturgical vigor never before attained.

The walls of the Ptolemaic temples of Edfu and Philae have preserved almost completely the reliefs and texts of the great royal liturgies celebrated in honor of the Living Image, the Living Falcon or the "Animal Sacred to Horakhty." The Living Raptor, whom the vital energy of the great solar king Horus animated, was chosen from among all those of his species housed in the aviary of the temple, and during his lifetime was the incarnate Horus and the earthly royal principle. All the solemn liturgies of the annual royal cycle, celebrated on the day forecast by the calendar of festivals (based on an ancient Heliopolitan model), associated the living Sacred Falcon with the statue of the god-king kept in the temple.

Thus, around the second century B.C., when the construction of the royal temples of the South was practically finished – and in a region completely cut off from the turbulent political world of the distant Ptolemies of Alexandria – the ceremonies of the royal cult, the annual highpoints of the exaltation of the monarchic principle, unrolled in their entirety within the walls of the temple, away from impure contact with the profane world. Only the final phase of the great festivities of the cycle of renewal of royal power at the New Year brought to the people the glorious sight of their god-king.

This cycle harmonized with the astral year; the rites were integrated with the cosmic rhythms and their symbolism was inspired by those rhythms. Weaving their way through the calendar, the rites celebrated the essential acts and events of the endlessly renewed life of the king of the world. The liturgical dramas devoted to the divine birth of Horus-king, to his coronation, his accession, then to the repeated confirmation of his royal power (assuring the perennial nature of the reign) made up the central episodes of the religious year. The clergy based their work on the ancient rituals that came from Heliopolis, where they had been codified well before the time of the pyramids and piously preserved in the sacred archives; the clergy then drew up new copies, completed them and brought them to light to form the *ordo* of the ceremonies. And, under the guidance of the *priest of the king*, the priesthood carried out, with faith and the greatest possible pomp, the celebration of the rituals.

The Royal Rites

The liturgies of Horus-king (some of whose celebrations are described below) most often began, at Edfu at least, at the end of the fourth month of that long Egyptian spring, the season of *Peret* (28 Pharmouthi in the Coptic calendar, or about the end of March). In the "house of birth" (*mammisi*), a special building in the forecourt of the temple, was celebrated the mystery of the divine birth of Horus the heir, legitimate king of the universe, successor to Osiris, the paradigm for all kings. Since Dynasty XVIII a myth of the miraculous birth of the earthly king had been known. In this myth, the creator-god Amun magically took the place of the bodily father, the reigning king, in order to impregnate the queen, a mother sanctified by the divine contact, who would bring the royal child into the world when her time was come. It was this same myth, adapted to fit the legend of Osiris, that was an underlying theme of Ptolemaic times. The mother is Isis: queen, wife of Osiris, rendered pregnant by him after his temporary resurrection; and the longed-for son is Horus, but a Horus perceived as the symbol of the universal king (CATS. 100, 101).

Fig. 8 A scene from the mammisi at Philae
Here the divine child is nursed, modeled by the god Khnum, given years of life by the god Thoth, and, at the right, offered a pectoral by Augustus in his role as pharaoh. (Adapted from Champollion 1835: pl. LXXVI, 1)

It is he whose coming birth is announced by the priestly actors of the liturgy when playing the roles of the divinities involved in the sacred drama; divinities present in the form of their small, portable statues. While the theogamy and the conception of the god-son (denoted modestly by the image of the potter-god Khnum fashioning the body of the child on his wheel) were recalled in secret, the announcement was solemnly made to Isis that she would bring forth into the world the king of Egypt. After being brought to childbed, the mother of the savior-god, under the protection of the genies of birth (Bes, Hytyt) and of the Seven Hathors, the good fairies of universal happiness, gave birth to the divine offspring. The wondrous child, recognized by his father the god, began his life, then, as a royal infant suckled by divine wet nurses (Figs. 8-10).

The entire ritual play was recast with reference to the old myth of the birth of Horus in the papyrus thickets of the Delta, in the secrecy of the swamps of Khemmis near Buto (CAT. 13). Because of this, the focal point of these ceremonies was the presentation, against a backdrop evocative of the Delta marshland, of the effigy of the falcon-god wearing the Crown of Upper and Lower Egypt (Fig. 11). The symbolism of the scene, moreover, was twofold: if it effectively evoked the presentation to the universe of the newly appeared king, it was also intended to recall the mode of the appearance of the king of the universe at Creation. The falcon was also the first living incarnation of Re-Horakhty taking possession of the world that his divine Word had just caused to surge forth from the watery chaos. Once again, Light had been revealed and was guaranteeing life.

Birth and the creation of the world, these were the *idées-forces* behind the celebration of the main mystery of the royal plays of the year. It was then necessary to move on to the acts of the reign. Although we cannot state the precise dates assigned to the festivities, due to the lack of documents, they followed one another in a logical order, from 28 Pharmouthi to the fateful date of the coronation: the first day of the month of Thoth (mid-July).

When Re himself had announced the coming to the world of the heir by saying "Isis has brought into the world her Horus...," the renewed king regained his efficacy, and Ma'at, momentarily menaced, continued to rule the universe. Nevertheless, it was still necessary to confirm the divine decisions about the future of the reign, and to do so at the occasion of the New Year. With the rising of Sothis (Sirius), harbinger of the approach of the Nile flood, the ritualists would prepare for the most important of the ceremonies of the annual *ordo*: the confirmation of Horus' inheritance and the festivals of coronation, coinciding with the New Year (1 Thoth, around July 20). The astrologer-priest having announced the arrival of the new water, the people waited impatiently for

Fig. 9 The birth of the child-god Harpre ("Horus-the-Son") before Amun-Re, the goddess Nekhbet, and Cleopatra VII
The winged scarab above the child is identified as the King of Upper and Lower Egypt, the solar god Khepri, who appears each morning and is identified with Harpre, the son of Amun. The scene is from the destroyed mammisi of Armant. (Adapted from Lepsius 1849–59, pt. IV: pl. 60, a)

the miracle of Egyptian agriculture to renew itself, while from the first hint of dawn on New Year's Day an intense activity animated the temples devoted to Horus throughout the South. The liturgy that was beginning would involve the presence of the two holy symbols of royalty: the divine statue of Horus and his Living Image, the Sacred Raptor (Fig. 12). All the rites, concurrently or consecutively, through the twenty days of the festivities would concern them. Early in the morning of the Egyptian New Year's Day, a procession was organized to bring the actors, adorned and anointed for the festival, to the places of celebration. First it would cross the threshold of the Holy of Holies; then it traversed the vestibule, the hypostyle, and the pronaos to reach the court. In the greatest

Fig. 10 Divine nurses from the destroyed mammisi of Armant (Adapted from Lepsius 1849–59, pt. IV: pl. 59, c)

purity the procession would make its way to the site of the "Pavilion of Bestowing the Inheritance." There, after the sacrament of anointing and the performance of prophylactic acts against "the dangers of the year," Horus-king and his Living Image would watch each other being presented with the emblems of the confirmation of the inheritance, while the lector-priest and choir chanted the verses of the great hymn "The Adoration of Horus Whose Inheritance Is Confirmed."

When the officiating priest had anointed the image of the royal falcon and the head of the Living Falcon, he pronounced the solemn salutation:

Hail to thee, Horus son of Osiris!
May thou be protected! May thou be protected!
Thou art the eldest son of Onnophris,
Adoration to thee, Horus Triumphant! – four times –.[1]

Then the acolytes would proceed to release the first set of messenger birds, who would fly forth to announce to the whole world that the king lived and reigned under the ultimate guarantee of the Creator.

Immediately afterward began the coronation ceremonies. Solemnly, a priest playing the role of Thoth proclaimed Horus king by intoning the powerful words of the "Royal Decree Spoken by Re-Horakhty," conferring on the son of Osiris the government of the earth. Sometimes Isis and Nephthys (personified by female members of the clergy, as at Philae) took up in turn the essential words of the decree, proclaiming them very loudly so that the world of man on the outside could not be in ignorance of their significance. The people, excluded from the secrecy of these rites, were never ignorant of their meaning and were living through the drama of waiting. Inside the sacred precinct, the divine stolists (priests charged with anointments and with dressing the divine statues) would now bring the Crowns, the Red of the North and the White of the South; the scepters and weapons; and would consecrate them for the statue of Horus and for his Living Image who accompanied him. All this time a choir had been chanting the litanies for the protection of the Year, while the sacrament of anointing the statue of Horus was being carried out using a scented chrism called "the greatest rejoicing" (*hekenu*).

Simultaneously, the Living Falcon was also receiving a similar anointment and was being offered the consecrated jewelry, the scepters, and the solar bouquets of Heliopolis, all symbols of the universal life of which he was to become the guarantor.

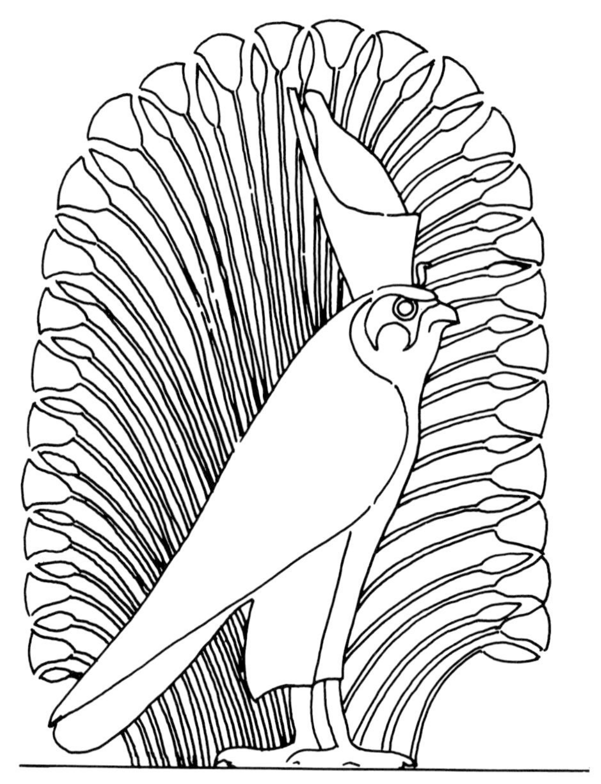

Fig. 11 An image of Horus protected in the marshes
From the mammisi at Philae. (Adapted from Lepsius 1849–59, pt. IV: pl. 36, b)

"Thy Ma'at is with thee, O Living Image, Living Falcon, and thou art its lord..."[2]

When these sacramental words had been pronounced, the principal date of 19 Thoth had arrived, a date which had to coincide with the announcement to the world of men of the consummation of the supreme act for the safeguarding of life. Then, from the aviaries of the temple were brought the messenger birds who would carry the message of salvation to the four cardinal points of the universe. After having received the anointment that sanctified their mission, a falcon (embodying a replica of the Living Falcon of the Year), an ibis, a vulture, and finally another falcon (incarnating Horus son of Osiris), successively took wing. Accompanying their departure the liturgical choir chanted once again the verse of the "Decree of Re," giving to Horus dominion over the Egyptian world and its people. This was made necessary by the fact that the *actual* king, guarantor of Ma'at, was, from this instant on, the Living Image, the Sacred Raptor of

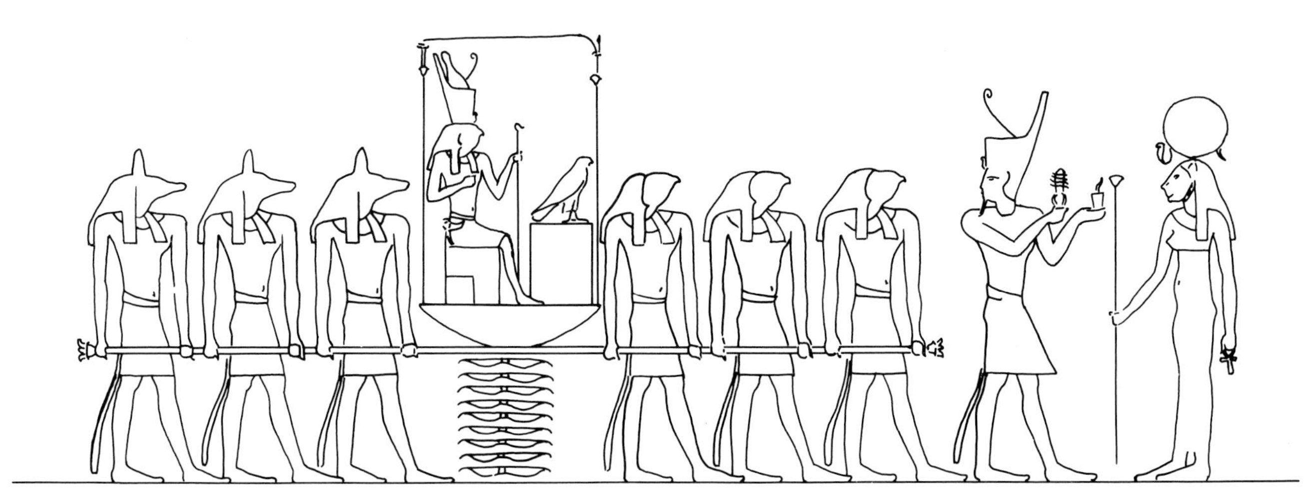

Fig. 12 Procession from the Temple of Horus at Edfu
The train of priests, led by pharaoh, carries divine images of the Living Falcon and the falcon-headed Horakhty ("Horus-of-the-Two-Horizons"). (Adapted from Chassinat 1960b: pl. CLIV)

the Year. It mattered little that, at the appropriate points in the sacramental phrases, the name of the Ptolemy reigning in Alexandria was inserted; it was only pronounced following the evocation of the Sacred Animal of Horakhty. This animal alone played a real role and was, as far as the people of Egypt were concerned, the god-king living on earth. And that is why this sacred hawk, in the company of the processional statue of Horus of Edfu or Philae, would be shown to the people amid a great concourse of joy and of chants invoking grace.

In later days at Edfu and Philae (around the first century B.C.), when the pylons had been built, the procession would form in the Court of Festivals to proceed to the Balcony of Appearances of the Falcon. Formerly constructed for the festival in the front area of the temple, it was now simply a balcony built in the passage over the central door between the two wings of the pylon on the south face of the building (Fig. 1), the side that opened to the world of men. The pylon itself was a symbolic representation of the ancient Egyptian conception of the horizon: a cross-section of the two cliffs bordering the Nile on the east and west. At the center of the pylon, the top of the axial gateway formed a special terrace where the divine effigy and its living counterpart could make their appearance. This appearance was the equivalent of showing the sun inscribing its course over the land of Egypt and of confirming to the assembled throng the renewal of this priceless gift of the light of life. Such a transmission, through such a liturgy, proved beyond a doubt to even the least aware peasants of Upper Egypt gathered for the festival that their world could endure, that it was constantly being protected and recreated because, as had happened since the very beginning of their memories, the king and the god (closely united in the veneration of Egypt), were working together to give Egypt life.

The Union with the Disk

It would be futile to attempt to follow the full course of all the festivals and daily liturgical acts that gave the liturgical year of the temples of Egypt its immutable rhythm down to the days when Christianity finally triumphed over the old religion. However, it remains necessary to describe one major ceremony of the Egyptian religious year in the time of the Lagides, a ceremony whose very existence helped determine the architecture of the ideal Egyptian temple of the later eras. This ceremony was the rite of the Union with the Disk (or Sun). On the first of the year, then at the beginning of the new cycle that marked each change of season and, finally, in the most serious hours of the year, the divine statue in practically every temple, great or small, left the darkness of the Holy of Holies to be carried solemnly to the terrace on the roof of the temple. There it was exposed to the rays of the rising sun. The symbolism of this practice is immediately apparent. The statue in the temple carried within itself – or such was the heartfelt conviction of the ancient Egyptians – a part of the universal cosmic energy that drives the world, an energy embodied by the sun. The cult figure, like a storage battery, stored up this charge of energy; it made it shine forth from the shadow and safety of the sanctuary, and diffused it to the outside world and to humanity. If it was not recharged, the energy would become exhausted, the rays weakened. The idea prevailed, therefore, that according to a set schedule, exposure of the image-battery to the direct rays of the sun would restore to the divine emblem the power of maintaining, spreading and, eventually, recreating the vital energy necessary to the world.

At the time of the Ptolemies, all the temples (Edfu, Dendera, Kom Ombo, Philae, the small Temple of Hathor at Deir el Medineh on the west bank at Thebes or that of Isis at Deir Shellouit) had a specific architectural arrangement for the ceremony of the Union with the Sun. Their plan was drawn to permit inclusion of a stairway that wound to the east. By this means, the statue's climb to the sun (Fig. 13) was accomplished, from the obscurity of the sanctuary by way of the *wabet* (the place of preparation and transition) to the zone of full light on the terraces crowning the building. On these terraces a kiosk draped with curtains was used for the central act of the liturgy: the unveiling of the statue before the rising sun that would bathe it with its dawning rays. From these same terraces, on the west, a straight stairway plunged toward the shadows of the temple itself, toward the hidden Holy of Holies (Fig. 14). Down this stairway the statue would be carried once the liturgy was completed, to the sound of music and chanting. Sealed in its chapel, the

Fig. 13 Procession from the Temple of Hathor at Dendera
The queen and king lead priests carrying a shrine of the goddess Hathor to the roof of her temple in this relief which decorates one of the stairways. (Adapted from Chassinat/Daumas 1978: pl. DCCLXVII)

statue took up once again its function as the nucleus of the universe, giving out its rays and diffusing order and life.

What did it matter, then, if the Ptolemies were tearing themselves to pieces in their terrible internecine quarrels? Or that later the emperors of distant Rome succeeded each other far from the Valley of the Nile? And what difference did it make if the very language of the Greeks and Romans (whose administrators were called strategi or prefects, whose economy was based on stateres or sesterces, and whose soldiers were called hoplites or legionnaires) bore witness to the world that these strangers were Egypt's masters at the moment? The learned priests were fully aware that they carried on their shoulders the faith of the people of whom they were a part. They carried the immense responsibility of having to preserve, by means of their theological knowledge, their archives, their fragile papyri, and the faithful performance of the rites, their national identity, which was linked intrinsically with their prestigious past. Men of tradition, guardians of a language and a writing becoming completely inaccessible to the profane world, they tried, in the last great age of construction in the third century B.C., to make their temples the foundation and unique means of preserving their conception of the Generative Word that creates, captures and carries the vital energy of the universe. Their temples were the world; they contained life on all their walls; the very architectural elements themselves propagated it. With their millions of hieroglyphs, their thousands of divine figures, whether carved in sunk relief or in raised relief, the temples transcribed faithfully and piously all they could of the sacramental knowledge and words of their sacred patrimony. Ptolemaic temples are the books in which the eternal religion of pharaonic Egypt lives and will live until the destruction of the world.

Thus, defying time and the forgetfulness of man, the perennial existence of an Egypt true to the faith that made it strong was assured. The images, words, and phrases graven in stone, the support of that which is eternal, are the most refined human attempt to express the incarnations and activities of the Word that any people of Antiquity ever conceived and brought into being. These witnesses to the monumental act of faith attempted by a people for their salvation ensured through the centuries that, just as they had wished, the equilibrium of the universe was guaranteed and that humanity could still hope to keep that most precious of gifts: the Life given by God.

[1] Brooklyn Papyrus 47.218.50, XVI, 4-5.
[2] Alliot 1954, vol. 2: 661.

Selected Bibliography

Temples and Clergy

H. Stierlin and S. Sauneron, *Les plus beaux temples égyptiens*. Pully, Switzerland, 1980 (reissue of *Derniers temples d'Egypte: Edfou et Philae*. Paris, 1975).

S. Sauneron, *The Priests of Ancient Egypt*, Trans. A. Morrissett. London, 1960.

Theology and Religious Thought

J.-Cl. Goyon, *Les dieux-gardiens et la genèse des temples d'après les textes de l'époque gréco-romaine*. BdE vols. CIII/1-2. 1985.

Dendera

F. Daumas, *Dendera et le temple d'Hathor*. IFAO RAPH 29, 1969.

Edfu

M. Alliot, *Le Culte d'Horus à Edfou au temps des Ptolémées*. BdE vols. XX/1-2. 1948-1954.

S. Cauville, *Edfou*. Guides Archéologiques de l'IFAO, Bibliothèque générale VI. 1984.

S. Cauville, *Essai sur la théologie du temple d'Horus à Edfou*. BdE vols. CII/1-2. 1987.

Esna

S. Sauneron, *Les Fêtes religieuses d'Esna aux derniers siècles du paganisme* (=*Esna* V). Cairo, 1952.

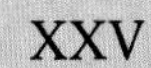

CAT. 82

CAT. 99

CAT. 100

CAT. 101

CAT. 102

XXX

CAT. 111

CAT. 114

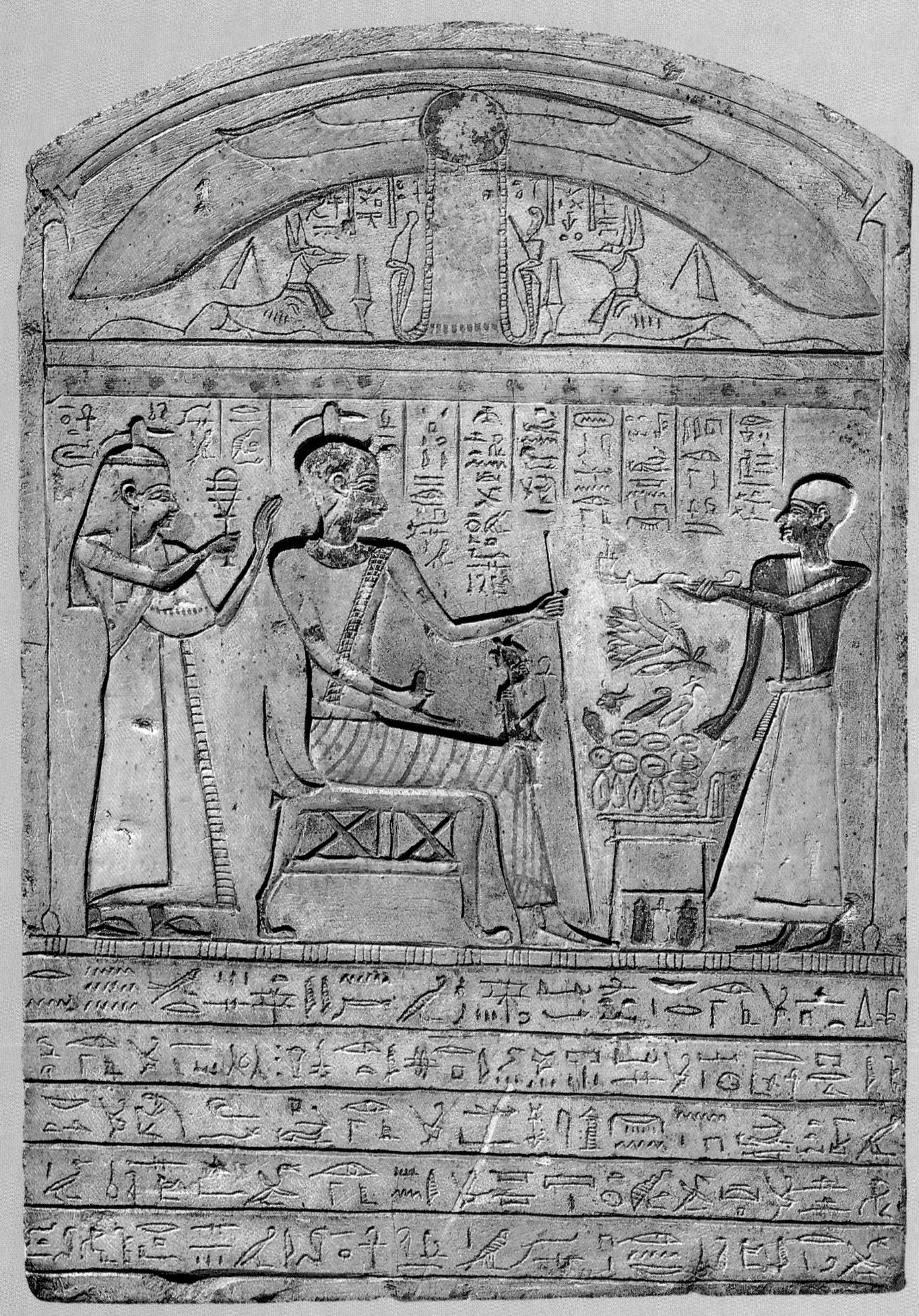

CAT. 123

△ CAT. 126 ▽ CAT. 127

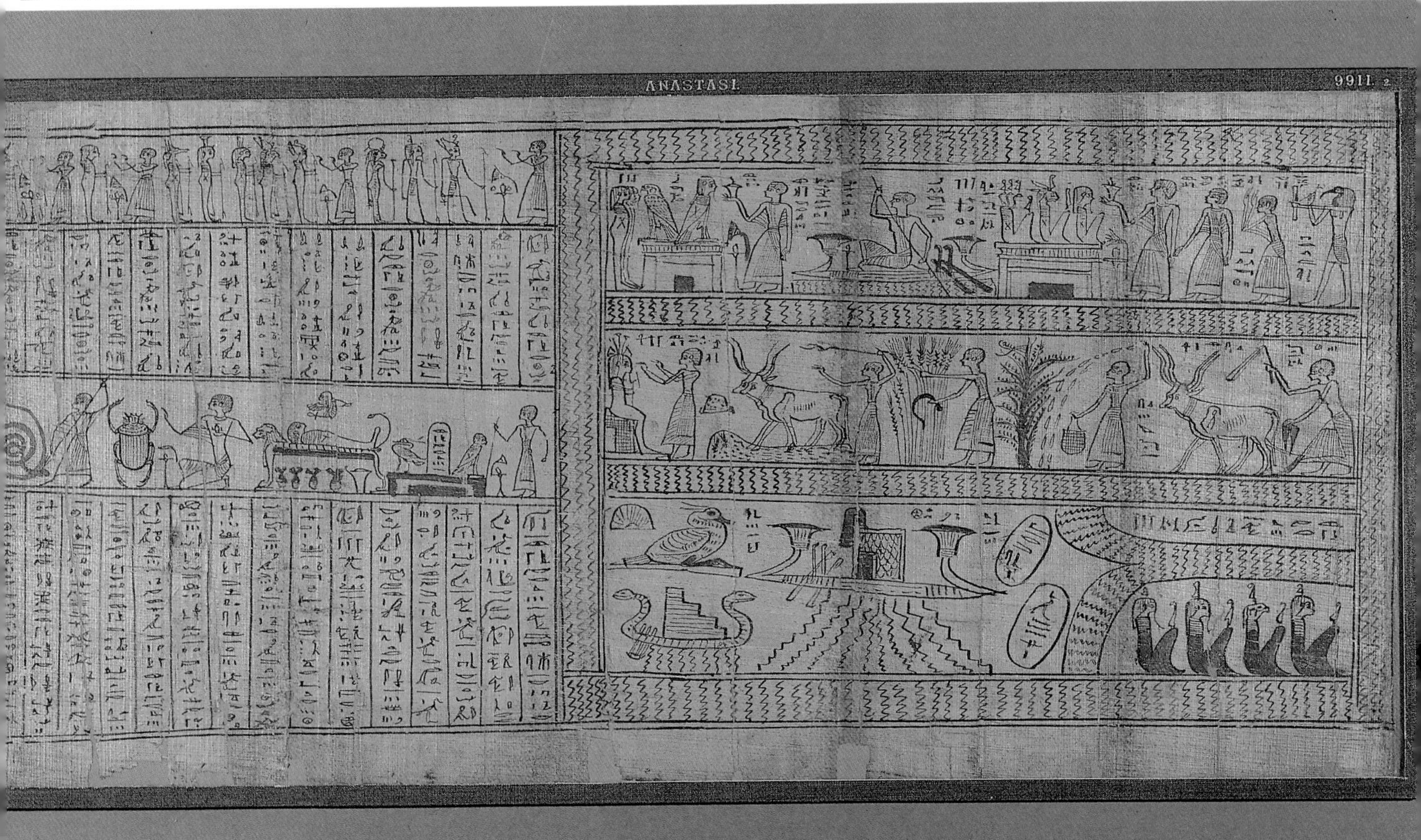

CAT. 130

CAT. 134

CAT. 138

Cleopatra VII and the Cults of the Ptolemaic Queens

by Jan Quaegebeur

The southern island of Philae, with the great Temple of Isis at its center, remained a bulwark of pagan cults during the centuries when Christianity was spreading through Egypt. Only around 536 A. D. would these cults be put to an end by the Byzantine emperor Justinian. Among the numerous, mainly Greek and Demotic, visitors' inscriptions on the Philae temples, mostly built in the Ptolemaic and Roman Periods, one finds a graffito in Demotic script by a certain Petesenufe, scribe of the book of Isis, in which he voices his devotion to Osiris and further declares: "I overlaid the figure of Cleopatra with gold." The text mentions year 90 of Diocles (Diocletian), that is, 373 A. D.[1] F. Ll. Griffith assumes that "Cleopatra" refers to Cleopatra VII, the last Ptolemaic queen, and therefore that almost four hundred years after her death a wooden statue of her – the word appears with the determinative "wood" – was overlaid with precious metal.

Beside this clearly personal attestation from 373 A. D. to a posthumous veneration for the last Ptolemaic ruler, I would like to place another, similarly Demotic, graffito, but one more than six centuries older. A member of an expedition to the quarries of the Wadi Hammamat in the twentieth year of Ptolemy son of Ptolemy (266/265 B. C.) commends his name to Min and the local gods and says of himself: "the handworker of the god, Psenamunis... has come to make a statue of the Pharaoh and an effigy of Arsinoe."[2] Queen Arsinoe II, sister and spouse of Ptolemy II, had died in 270 B. C., which implies a statue of the living monarch and one of the deceased queen.

Both these Demotic graffiti clearly refer to cult statues of Ptolemaic rulers. The honors paid to the queens of Macedonian origin, all of whom bore in Egypt the names Berenike, Arsinoe or Cleopatra, are closely bound up with the worship of the Ptolemaic royal family. This worship is both part of the native religious ritual – which is not very well known and will therefore receive special attention here – and that of the dynastic cult with its Hellenistic Greek background. In either case, there is a variety of textual, archaeological, and iconographic evidence available. As to the veneration of specific queens, a general distinction must be drawn, in both the Egyptian and Greek settings, between the deification of an individual queen – initially upon her decease, later in her lifetime – and her veneration together with her husband as a living royal couple or in their capacity as deceased parents or ancestors. It should also be mentioned that in addition to the official cult a more popular devotion existed, as is apparent, for example, from references to private sanctuaries.

The attribution of specific cult names to king and queen[3] for the purpose of propagating their religious and political program is a purely Greek enterprise, and was, for instance, also a practice of the Seleucid dynasty in Syria. But at the same time it enabled the subjects to distinguish the kings of Egypt, who were all named Ptolemy, as well as their queens. The numbers they now display have been ascribed by historians, although there is no general agreement on that numbering. Thus, Ptolemy (II) son of Ptolemy (I, Soter, the "Savior"), rather belatedly assumed the cognomen Philadelphos, which he took from his sister and wife Arsinoe (II), who upon her deification had received the cult name (*thea*) *philadelphos*, "the brother-loving (goddess)"; together they were revered as *theoi adelphoi*, "brother-sister-gods."

Apart from their respective sources, a few differences can be pointed out between the Hellenistic and native cults of the Ptolemies. In the Greek environment of the new capital on the coast, Alexandria, and of Ptolemais in Upper Egypt, two cities in which the dynastic cult was organized, the priests and priestesses were selected from the ranks of prominent Graeco-Macedonian immigrant families. They were eponymous, which means that their names were used in the dating formulae of official documents, and were changed annually.[4] In Alexandria there was a priest of Alexander (founder of the city) and of the deified Ptolemies, a series that of course grew longer with the passing of history. He was joined by priestesses of the queens, often bearing a specific title, e.g., the *kanephoros* or "bearer of the golden basket" of Arsinoe II Philadelphos, and the *athlophoros* or "bearer of the prize of victory" of Berenike II Euergetis, "the Benefactress." For Alexandria, the eponymous priesthoods are well documented, especially through Greek and Demotic material from all over Egypt, for the period from about 285 to 100 B.C. Toward the end of the second century B.C. some changes can be noted, and the institution tends to disappear. We find that Ptolemy IX Soter II and Ptolemy X Alexander I and also Cleopatra III were themselves priests and priestess, respectively, in the dynastic cult. After 84/83 B.C. there are no more names of eponymous priests. At Ptolemais the dynastic cult is attested only from 215 B.C. (Ptolemy IV Philopator), and it was less elaborately set up than that in Alexandria. As that city's founder, Ptolemy I Soter at Ptolemais took the place of Alexander the Great. Here the last extensive list of priests and priestesses (of Arsinoe II, Cleopatra I, II, III, and IV) dates from 138/137 B.C.

The native clergy, through decisions made at synods, completely incorporated an Egyptian version of the Hellenistic cult of the Ptolemies into the priesthoods and rituals of the local temples.[5] The temple scribes and various priests mention their involvement in the dynastic cult in their titularies on funerary stelae, statues, and papyri.[6] As to individual queens, we have information only on Egyptian priests ministering to the worship of the deified Arsinoe II Philadelphos. Her cult was particularly popular and survived, as will be seen, into the first century B.C. Unlike the Greek counterpart of the cult, Alexander the Great, founder of Alexandria, and Ptolemy I, founder of Ptolemais, were not included in the native cult. For that matter, it is notable that the name Alexandria was rarely rendered in Egyptian; generally, the native name Rakotis was used. Usually the ancestors mentioned ascended to the brother-sister-gods (Ptolemy II and Arsinoe II). The names of the first royal couple, Ptolemy I and Berenike I, do appear in a number of Greek and Egyptian sources, but the rather occasional nature of their inclusion among the deified ancestors is still not wholly explained.

Before placing the numerous Egyptian monuments connected with the cult of the Ptolemaic royal family in a historical perspective, let us first devote some attention to the diversity of Hellenistic sources. There is an abundance of written Greek evidence for the importance of the dynastic cult: papyri, private monuments, place names, and even personal names. The Greek papyri have more to offer than mere dating formulae that include the (Greek) names of eponymous priests and an occasional mention of Egyptian priests connected with the dynastic cult; these are also found in Demotic and even hieroglyphic texts. So, for example, from the so-called Revenue Laws we know that from 263 B.C. onward a considerable portion of the *apomoira* (a tax on orchards and gardens) was destined for the expenses of the cult of Arsinoe II Philadelphos. The great Faiyum oasis, a fertile colonization area where many Greeks settled, was renamed the Arsinoite province, and a number of towns were named after her. She had a temple at Philadelphia, a settlement called after her cult name.

Even outside Egypt proper, in the Ptolemaic empire, private monuments attest to the popularity of her cult, and a good many cities, especially flourishing ports, were named after her.[7] Yet Berenike and Cleopatra, too, will be found in place-names. As to personal names, we encounter both the dynastic name Ptolemy and the Macedonian queens' names in the native environment as well. This quite general occurrence presents an expression of loyalty to the royal house. But in the upper native Egyptian priestly circles of Memphis the names of Berenike and Arsinoe surely had a political tint, expressing an association with the Greek rulers.[8] After the demise of the Ptolemaic dynasty, the name Cleopatra continued to retain a special prestige. In the second century A.D. we encounter it in a prominent native family: the wife of Soter, the Archon of Thebes, is called Cleopatra.[9] Or, even more striking, about 270 A.D., in the period of the Palmyrene occupation, Queen Zenobia presented herself as a new Cleopatra and even assumed that name.[10] Finally, the identification of queens with certain goddesses, especially with Aphrodite and her Egyptian form, Hathor, should not go unmentioned.[11] The wealth of papyrological material is substantially supplemented by the epigraphical texts, among which the dedicatory inscriptions on stone deserve special mention. In addition to these

Greek documentary sources (which are ever increasing in number), we have a much smaller amount of literary material – for example, the famous elegy on the lock of Berenike II by Callimachus, a poet with ties to the Alexandrian library,[12] or the account of the great procession of Ptolemy II Philadelphos by Callixinus.[13]
Among the archaeological sources for queens and their cults, coins (CATS. 60, 61) and sculptures in Hellenistic style occupy a position of importance. The latter category is represented mainly by individual heads of members of the royal house (CATS. 64, 67, 68, 70).[14] The rendering of personal features is in many instances quite remarkable. Accordingly, the identification of these anepigraphic fragmentary statues is in large measure based on a comparative study of the "portraits" on the coins. The portrait value of the coins, on which we find kings or queens as well as royal couples, is manifest. One immediately thinks of the characteristic nose of Cleopatra the Great, of which Pascal wrote; "Le nez de Cléopatre: s'il eût été plus court, toute la face de la terre aurait changé" ("The nose of Cleopatra: had it been shorter, the whole face of the earth would have altered"). The typical aquiline nose of the last Cleopatra is indeed recognizable on coins and so forms a basis for the identification of certain sculptures.[15] Coins can also show a deified queen, e.g., the deceased Arsinoe II (CAT. 61c, d), whose image continued to be struck long after her death.[16] With her diadem and veil, she resembles a Roman matron rather than a deified Egyptian queen. The curled ram's horn behind her ear on these coins emphasizes her divinity and is a reference to Alexander, whose divine nature was defined by the Siwa oracle, which greeted the conqueror as "Son of Ammon." The ram's horn is also a link with the traditional Egyptian chief god, Amun, and with earlier kings like the deified Ramesses II (Dynasty XIX) and pharaohs of Dynasty XVIII, who are shown with this attribute.[17]
This link with the pharaonic past in early Hellenistic iconography is remarkable. Another element is the scepter associated with Arsinoe II on certain coins. It has been recognized as a kind of staff with cobra, a cult object that appears in some Egyptian religious scenes.[18] A number of wine pitchers (oinochoai), or fragments thereof, are called "queens' vases" because they have relief scenes of the queen, sometimes identified by an inscription, holding a cornucopia in her arm like a goddess; adjacent to her sometimes is a horn altar.[19] Some of these elements are also found occasionally on representations in pharaonic style (CAT. 66).

What can we learn from the Egyptian monuments and inscriptions about the veneration of Ptolemaic queens by the native population? The earliest documents that can be dated with certainty appeared after the death of Arsinoe II (270 B.C.), while her brother-husband Ptolemy II was still alive. (Note that we have only posthumous representations of Berenike I in the company of her spouse, Ptolemy I,[20] but that the latter does appear alone as pharaoh on temple reliefs from his reign; see CAT. 12.) Of Arsinoe I, the first wife of Ptolemy II, who was repudiated and banished to Coptos, we have no documentary evidence that refers with certainty to her.[21] First of all, then, our attention must go out to explicit and detailed mentions of the deification of Arsinoe II. The great Mendes Stela now in Cairo (Fig. 15) describes, after her marriage and her death in the king's fifteenth regnal year, the establishment of her cult by Ptolemy II. The relevant hieroglyphic passage may be translated as follows: "His Majesty decreed that her statue be set up in all the temples. This pleased their priests, for they were aware of her noble attitude toward the gods and of her excellent deeds to the benefit of all the people.... Her name was proclaimed as the beloved of the ram, the goddess Philadelphos, Arsinoe."[22] The upper part of the stela depicts the king, who is sacrificing to the ram, a child god, Banebdjed and Hatmehit (the main god and goddess of Mendes), followed by Arsinoe. The king is accompanied by his wife; behind the royal couple appears a third figure with a royal crown, the son and co-regent of Ptolemy II, who was to be assassinated while still young and thus would never succeed to his father's throne.[23] It is significant that the deceased Arsinoe appears among the local gods as well as with her sacrificing husband. This situation – a single person being both subject and object of the cult act – is comparable with Ramesside representations in which Ramesses II stands in adoration before the deified Ramesses II, who can also take the shape of a statue.[24] Besides the Mendes Stela we have a large base, now in the open-air museum at the Serapeum in Alexandria,[25] with the feet of three persons who can be identified by the inscriptions as Amun (in the middle), with Ptolemy II to his right and Arsinoe II Philadelphos to his left. In the fragmentarily preserved inscriptions, Amun addresses Arsinoe with the words: "I will make you a god[dess] at the head of the gods on earth... I give you the breath of life that emanates from my nose to give life to your *ba*, to rejuvenate your body for ever and ever." The funerary terminology makes it clear that Arsinoe is dead.

Fig. 14 The Ptolemaic sanctuary of the Temple of Horus at Edfu
The naos in black granite is an earlier dedication by Nectanebo II of Dynasty XXX. (Photograph by J. P. Sebah [died 1890])

From this period between the death of Arsinoe II in 270 B. C. and the death of Ptolemy II in 246 B. C., we possess a strikingly large number of documents that relate to the worship of this Arsinoe. First of all, there are representations showing Ptolemy II celebrating his sister-wife as goddess. Besides temple reliefs at Philae, only two stelae with Ptolemy II adoring Arsinoe II had been identified until now.[26] Recently, another document of this type, with a horn altar (an element also occurring in the Hellenistic cult) separating the two figures, has come to my attention: a stela in the Royal Ontario Museum (Fig. 16). It derives its importance from the posture of Arsinoe, which has manifestly been influenced by the Hellenistic representations of queens on oinochoai. The long staff that she holds aloft with outstretched arms, in a manner wholly un-Egyptian, may perhaps be linked to the scepter sometimes associated with queens on coins. Apparently, there was some reciprocal influence between the Helle-

Fig. 15 The Mendes Stela
The inscriptions describe how Ptolemy II Philadelphos established the cult of his deified wife, Arsinoe II. (Cairo CG 22181)

nistic and Egyptian forms of the cult of Arsinoe II as an individual goddess. That Arsinoe, as we have learned from the Mendes Stela, was revered in temples alongside the already existing deities as *sunnaos thea* ("resident goddess") can be demonstrated for a good many localities. Cult stelae provide proof for several places in the Delta, but in the limestone quarries of Maᶜṣara, and on walls and gates of several temples of Upper Egypt (e.g., Thebes), Arsinoe was also incorporated into the local pantheon. A number of documents (mostly temple reliefs) have not even been published yet, among them two scenes on the gate of Ptolemy II at Philae (Fig. 17).[27] To Memphis, the second city after Alexandria, only one iconographic document can be ascribed with any probability (CAT. 65). Yet, through a large number of hieroglyphic and Demotic funerary inscriptions of prominent priestly families, we know that Arsinoe II Philadelphos was venerated there alongside the chief god, Ptah, down to about 75 B.C.[28] Members of this family of high priests for a time also ministered to the cult of the prematurely deceased sister of Arsinoe II, the princess Philotera.[29] For that matter, the names of Arsinoe and Philotera are associated on an unpublished seal imprint now in the Metropolitan Museum of Art, New York (10.130.1563).[30] Particularly interesting is a lintel in Stockholm on which the gods of Athribis are worshiped by Ptolemy II, followed by Arsinoe II shaking the sistra.[31] One is inclined to think that Arsinoe is depicted here as a living queen. But since she is not designated by an ordinary royal title, but as "King of Upper and Lower Egypt," it is important to make the comparison with the Mendes Stela, where she is associated with the reigning king after her demise. Similar situations are attested for the New Kingdom too: a deceased and deified king (e.g., Amenhotep I) or queen (Ahmes Nefertari) can be revered not only individually, but also together with local deities; they can also sacrifice to other gods themselves.[32] In another effigy of Arsinoe II in a cultic posture with sistra,[33] her divine situation is made clear by the indication "daughter of Amun," a title with close links to the above-mentioned bond between Arsinoe and Amun. The attribution of the kingly title to Arsinoe on several monuments, presumably posthumous, has been connected with the role she is thought to have played in Ptolemaic naval policy, a policy continued after her death by her brother.[34] Queens with a kingly title or characterized as "daughter of Amun" are also known from pharaonic times, as in the well-known Hatshepsut or the Amun-associated Divine Wives of Dynasty XXVI, who in a sense can be regarded as queens.[35]

Another important piece of evidence for the deification of Arsinoe II is that in each of the above representations she is wearing a particular crown (Fig. 18), one that differs from the traditional queen's crown. It consists of the Crown of Lower Egypt, above which stick out two straight feathers, cow's horns, and a solar disk complemented by ram's horns. A simplified version appears on a remarkable papyrus fragment now in Paris,[36] which shows a queen in a ritual context. This crown would seem to be a variant of the crown of the god Geb, the founding father of the mythical divine dynasty (see Fig. 5), and was presumably designed on the occasion of Arsinoe's deification, as was the crown of the later princess Berenike (see below). In any event, the crown is found on the head of Ptolemaic kings and, exceptionally, on that of certain Cleopatras.[37] As in a few Greek texts, some hieroglyphic inscriptions identify Arsinoe with Isis,[38] instead of with Aphrodite, her more usual identification. This indication would seem to be related to Arsinoe's kingship: Isis, daughter of Geb, is often characterized as queen and, like her brother and spouse Osiris-Onnophris, can also

Fig. 17 The Gate of Ptolemy II Philadelphos at Philae
The relief decoration and inscriptions of this scene belong to a number of documents relating to Arsinoe II which are largely unpublished.

be designated as "King of Upper and Lower Egypt" and can have her name written in a cartouche.[39] On a statue in the Vatican (see below), for that matter, Arsinoe is called "daughter of Geb" and "image of Isis."
We come now to the statues of Arsinoe II Philadelphos.[40] An effigy from the Metropolitan Museum of Art, New York, without crown but with the cornucopia, depicts, according to the inscription on the back pillar, "Arsinoe the goddess Philadelphos, Isis" (CAT. 66). In an anepigraphical sculpture in traditional style in Leiden (CAT. 72), we may very probably recognize Arsinoe with her special headdress. Some bases of statues have also survived; one such is now in Chicago and displays a hieroglyphic inscription dating it to the reign of Ptolemy II and exhibiting in Greek the name "Arsinoes Philadelphou" (genitive). This inclusion of a name written in Greek alongside a hieroglyphic inscription, incidentally, is another element that shows that the native higher clergy was receptive to the Greek language.[41]

◁ *Fig. 16 A stela of Arsinoe II (?) before an altar*
The questions of Hellenistic influences on pharaonic art in Egypt can be explored by studying the treatment of the motifs on such scenes. (Toronto 979.63)

In addition to the Wadi Hammamat graffito quoted at the beginning of the present essay, a passage from the famous Pithom Stela may be cited. It deals with a port called Arsinoe, located at the northern tip of the Red Sea, where "a temple was built for [Arsinoe] Philadelphos; he [Ptolemy II] had [statues of] the brother-sister-gods erected there."[42] One is inclined to think here of a group of three colossi now in the Vatican (Figs. 19, 20), found in Rome but presumably originating from Heliopolis.[43] The king's statue, according to the inscription, represents the living Ptolemy II; the inscription on the Arsinoe statue, containing the epithets "daughter of Geb" and "image of Isis," identifies this statue, from which the crown is missing, as the deified Arsinoe II; the third is almost identical to the second and remains anonymous. Some have suggested that it represents Philotera, but it is equally possible that it was another effigy of Arsinoe, shown once with her brother as the brother-sister-gods and again separately for her own cult. Being her widower, but also perpetually associated with a sister and wife elevated to goddess, it was only a small step for Ptolemy II himself to ascend to divine status within the context of the cult of the *theoi adelphoi*. Only one relief

Fig. 18 The crown of Arsinoe II
Differing from traditional Egyptian headdresses, this insignia consists of the Crown of Lower Egypt, two straight feathers, cow's horns, and a solar disk complemented by ram's horns.

scene of this cult seems to exist for the time of Ptolemy II: a slab from Tanis (CAT. 14) showing the goddess Arsinoe and, in front of her, the deified king depicted as Zeus brandishing the bolt of lightning.

For the reign of Ptolemy III and Berenike II, who adopted the cult name of *theoi euergetai*, "benefactor gods," two important subjects must be mentioned. On the so-called Gate of Euergetes at Karnak we encounter for the first time, divided over two parallel scenes, the dynastic cult relating not only to the living royal couple, but as well to the deceased parents.[44] In one scene (Fig. 21), Ptolemy III burns incense before Ptolemy II, called "father of the king," and before Arsinoe as the goddess Philadelphos,[45] together the brother-sister-gods. In the other (Fig. 22), we see the recognition of the divine kingship of Ptolemy III and Berenike II, who stand at the side of the gods. Both are clothed in a ceremonial attire, which may be viewed as a new version of the jubilee (*heb-sed*) dress,[46] and receive from Khonsu, acting as the god of writing, their titularies and a perpetual reign. A second significant fact from this period of rule is the deification of Berenike, the prematurely deceased daughter of Ptolemy III and Berenike II, an event elaborately related in what is called the trilingual Decree of Canopus, where in 238 B.C. a priestly synod was taking place at the time of the princess' death.[47] Among other matters, it was decided that statues of Berenike were to be erected in all the important temples of Egypt (none of these has yet been identified); this, of course, was by no means an original decision. We also learn that a special crown, which is described in detail, was designed for Berenike,[48] and further that the reigning royal couple were accorded divine honors. The representation at the top of the Stela of Kom el Ḥiṣn (Fig. 23), which contains a version of the Canopus Decree, provides an interesting illustration of the royal cult. On the right are a row of Egyptian gods; facing them on the left are the benefactor-gods, i.e., Ptolemy III and Berenike II, in ceremonial attire and with the crowns of reigning monarchs just as on the Khonsu Gate at Karnak; they are followed by Thoth and Seshat, who note the regnal years of the divine kingship, then by the brother-sister-gods (Ptolemy II and Arsinoe II) and finally by the savior-gods (Ptolemy I and Berenike I).[49]

Fig. 19 Colossal statue of Arsinoe II
This statue, and that in Fig. 20, may have served as actual cult statues. On the back pillar Arsinoe II is called the "daughter of Geb" and the "image of Isis." (Vatican 31)

It is through this analysis of the scenes on the Gate of Euergetes and on the Stela of Kom el Ḥiṣn that the function of Ptolemy IV and Arsinoe III on a London stela (CAT. 15) can be understood. The royal couple are not performing a cultic act before the gods of Imet, near Tanis; their posture and the special dress point to their presence as a divine couple. Similar placings of gods and deified kings are already encountered in the New Kingdom.[50] For the reign of Ptolemy IV we also know of representations that illustrate the various complementary aspects of the dynastic cult. In the great Horus Temple at Edfu we not only find the king together with his wife receiving the divine kingship, but they themselves also perform the rites of the ancestor cult.[51] There is also a great scene in which Ptolemy IV Philopator consecrates the offerings for the local divine Triad of Horus, Hathor, and Harsomtous, the latter followed by Ptolemies III, II and I in the company of their respective wives,[52] all of whom are thus incorporated as *sunnaoi theoi* into the temple's cult.

Such scenes were only introduced in a discussion of the royal cult in the Ptolemaic temples about a decade ago by E. Winter.[53] The Temple of Edfu, dedicated to the theology of divine kingship, provides the most abundant evidence in the scenes from the reigns of Ptolemy IV through IX. In that survey, no representation seems datable to the reign of Ptolemy V Epiphanes, for whom only a limited building activity is known;[54] due to a serious rebellion in the south, work at Edfu came to a standstill.[55] Thus the documentation of the royal cult was influenced by political events, which affected the course of the temple's construction. But we cannot overlook the Stela of Annobeira (near Damanhur) on which Ptolemy V, accompanied by the queen, defeats the enemy before the local gods, followed by three royal couples.[56] Ptolemy V and Cleopatra I are revered at the Edfu Temple as parent couple by both Ptolemy VI and Ptolemy VIII. Elaborate scenes that illustrate the dynastic cult are known at Edfu and elsewhere, especially for Ptolemy VIII. However, the most recent of these scenes at Edfu is the one of Ptolemy IX sacrificing to Ptolemy VIII and Cleopatra III. After Ptolemy IX, there is only a door inscription at Kom Ombo,[57] on which the list of the ancestors of Ptolemy XII Neos Dio-

Fig. 20 Colossal statue of Ptolemy II Philadelphos
This statue, like that in Fig. 19, may have originally come from Heliopolis. The identity of the king is assured from the inscription on the back pillar in which he is named. (Vatican 32)

Fig. 21 The Euergetes Gate at Karnak
This scene depicts Ptolemy III burning incense before both Ptolemy II and Arsinoe II as the goddess Philadelphos. (Adapted from P. Clère 1961: pl. 61)

nysos (nicknamed Auletes, "the flute player") ascends from his parents Ptolemy IX and Cleopatra III all the way back to the brother-sister-gods Ptolemy II and Arsinoe II. At Kom Ombo we also learn that the statues of the ancestors were still carried about in a procession.[58] Although construction of several large temples was continued under Ptolemy XII, we still cannot form a clear idea of his place in the royal cult. Together with his sister and spouse Cleopatra V Tryphaena, he forms the *theoi philopatores philadelphoi*, "the father-loving and brother-sister-loving gods," but the queen disappears from the dating formulae after his twelfth regnal year. Thereafter we have for this reign only a few, rather uncertain, data concerning the queen(s) during the brief period while the king was in Rome.[59]

Before proceeding to the great Cleopatra, the seventh and last queen of that name, let us briefly sum up the position of the queens in the dynastic cult. In the eponymous cult discussed earlier, several queens enjoyed an individual worship, in addition to their place behind their husbands. In the native version we encounter, besides the royal couples, only Arsinoe II Philadelphos. (The princesses Philotera and Berenike, who died before ascending the throne, are not considered here since they never became queens.) The well-developed dynastic cult seems to disappear in the first half of the first century B.C., with the final mentions by name of eponymous priests and of Arsinoe II Philadelphos as *sunnaos thea* at Memphis. There are no more representations of the veneration of ancestors and reigning monarchs. In the latter context,

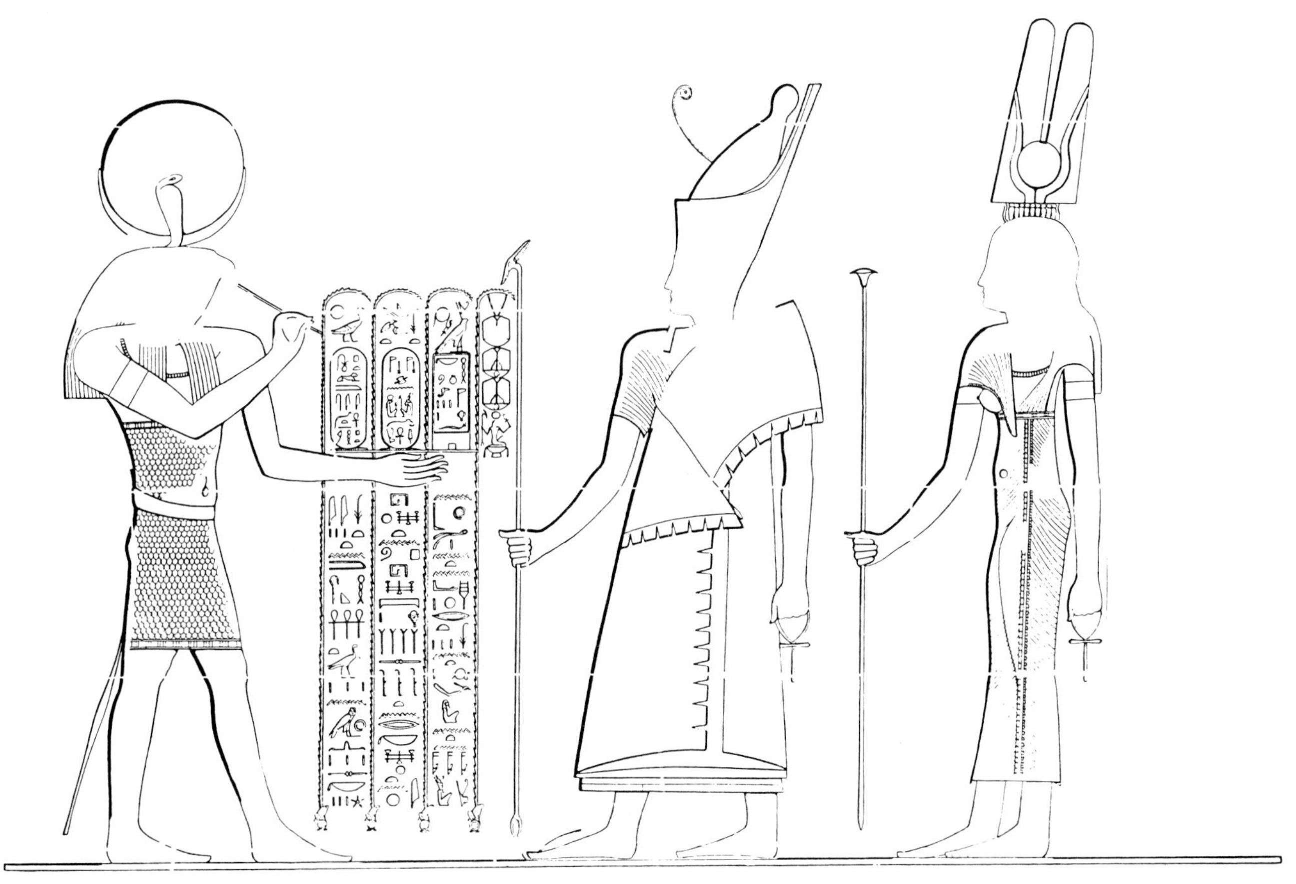

Fig. 22 The Euergetes Gate at Karnak
Ptolemy III and Berenike II receive their titularies and symbols of perpetual reign from the god Khonsu. (Adapted from P. Clère 1961: pl. 43)

the queen always took second place, after her spouse. But there is one exception: Cleopatra III, who as female pharaoh takes precedence in the dating formulae over her sons as co-regents, also precedes Ptolemy IX in a ritual scene at Karnak.[60]

On the veneration of Cleopatra VII during her lifetime and thereafter we are but poorly informed. No representations are known and no statues that could have played a role in the native cult can be attributed to her with certainty.[61] She does appear on temple walls, as in an oracle chapel at Coptos,[62] as officiating queen. The many empty cartouches toward the end of the Ptolemaic Period, as for example, at Dendera and Kom Ombo, often make the identification of the queen difficult. Where her name appears on Egyptian monuments it is usually accompanied by her epithet "the goddess who loves her father" (*thea philopator*), which characterizes her as a goddess, in keeping with the dynastic tradition. On coins with effigies of Antony and Cleopatra she is called *thea neotera* (e.g., CAT. 61w). The meaning of this title (which identifies her with Aphrodite-Hathor or with a new, younger Cleopatra Thea, a Syrian queen of the second century B.C.) remains uncertain. This title also occurs in a Greek papyrus from 36/35 B.C., in which the epithet Philopator is joined by Philopatris, "who loves her fatherland."[63] Unfortunately, we have at present only a provisional description of a royal panegyric in a Demotic literary hand of the first century B.C., for which the following title has been suggested: "Glorification of Cleopatra Philopator": "It exults the good deeds of the Queen and her victories;

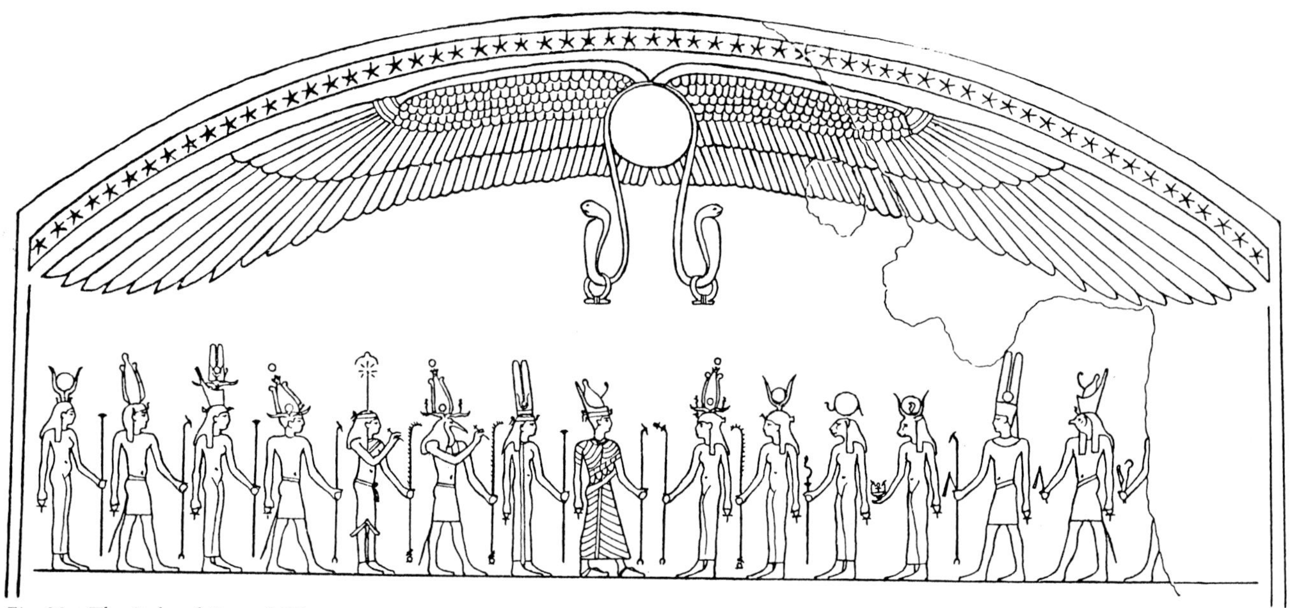

Fig. 23 The Stela of Kom el Ḥiṣn
This scene from the lunette provides an interesting illustration of the royal cult. Ptolemy III and Berenike II face a train of deities (right) and are followed by Thoth, Seshat, and the deified Ptolemy II, Arsinoe II, Ptolemy I, and Berenike I.

it addresses her as the divine protectress of the country."[64] Undoubtedly most familiar is the grand representation on the outside rear wall of the Temple of Hathor at Dendera (Fig. 24), where she quite remarkably appears twice behind her son and co-regent, Ptolemy XV Caesarion.[65] Since she is depicted in a cultic pose, this representation (often claimed to show her as Isis-Hathor) does not particularly emphasize her divinity. As a memorial to the birth of her son, Caesarion, regarded as the son of Re, she had a temple built at Hermonthis, which has not survived into recent times.[66] Fortunately, some old drawings provide interesting clues that suggest some uncertainty as to her position, dependent as it was on the acting coregent. In ritual scenes in general she can appear alone, or in front of the male ruler, or parallel with Ptolemy XV Caesarion. Once she is called "King of Upper and Lower Egypt"; elsewhere she wears, as daughter of Geb, the typical crown that was also borne by the deified Arsinoe II.[67] Inside the Dendera Temple, a queen following a king is depicted wearing this special crown, in alternation with the traditional one.[68] On a stela, too, Cleopatra VII appears with this royal crown,[69] while another stela with a Greek inscription (CAT. 78) portrays her as pharaoh with the Double Crown. A neglected but important piece of information is the mention on the funerary stela of the Memphite High Priest Petobastis-Imuthes (46-30 B.C.) of the title "Prophet of Pharaoh." This office was held by his father, Psenptais, under Ptolemy XII, but because this very young High Priest was appointed by Cleopatra VII in 39 B.C. the priesthood can only refer to that queen.[70]

To what extent this priesthood is a continuation of that of the "Prophet of the Statues of the King" in the late pharaonic period (Dynasties XXVI-XXX) is not clear.[71] It is probably of greater importance to see the connection with the Roman Period, which commenced with the capture of Alexandria and Egypt by Octavian in 30 B.C. In 28/27 B.C., the new *princeps* Augustus appointed the new High Priest, Psenamunis III, as Prophet of the Caesar (i.e., the emperor), which shows that the imperial cult in Egypt in some respects has ties with the Ptolemaic royal cult.[72] On the other hand, the Latin epithet *divi filius*, which Augustus assumed in Rome as (adopted) son of the assassinated and later deified Julius Caesar,[73], also turns up in Egypt in the form "[the god], the son of the [great] god."[74] Of the imperial cult in the native environment we have no representations and only very rare material remains. A fragmentary statue in pharaonic style that probably portrays an emperor as Hercules is, accordingly, worthy of mention.[75] As for the wives of the new rulers, they are no longer objects of veneration. Cleopatra VII, however, the last ruler of an independent Egypt, who upon her defeat at Actium chose death by an asp's poison, continues to captivate the imagination. Many authors hold that the means of her suicide – the bite of a sacred cobra – turned Cleopatra into an immortal goddess in the eyes of those who cherished native religious traditions.[76] As to the value of more concrete testimonials concerning a posthumous cult, there is no agreement. A Greek inscription at Rosetta of 4/5 A. D. that mentions a great temple of Cleopatra has been under discussion, as has a papyrus from the early third century A. D. that refers to Aphrodite-Cleopatra, possibly at Alexandria.[77] Against the backdrop of these disputed data, the Demotic graffito from Philae cited at the outset takes on a special meaning. Indeed, had not Cleopatra also received a golden effigy in the Temple of Venus in Rome itself?[78]

[1] Griffith 1937: 104, no. Ph. 370; 215, no. 465. Note that the continuation of the regnal years of the persecutor Diocletian (284-305 A. D.) was later designated by the Christians as the "Era of the Martyrs."
[2] Thissen 1979: 83-84, no. 35, pl. 22b.
[3] On these epithets, see Koenen 1983: 152ff.
[4] See Clarysse/Van der Veken 1983.
[5] See, e.g., D. Crawford 1980: 27-36.
[6] Pestman 1967: 132ff.; D. Crawford 1980: 29 note 1. This material has not yet been systematically collected.
[7] For the Greek material, see Longega 1968.
[8] Quaegebeur 1986b.
[9] PM I, 2²: 676.
[10] Bowersock 1984: 31.
[11] Cerfaux/Tondriau 1957.
[12] Nachtergael 1980: 240-53.
[13] Rice 1983.
[14] Kyrieleis 1975; Brunelle 1976.
[15] See, e.g., a head in the British Museum, reproduced in Macurdy 1932: 184, fig. 11.
[16] See, e.g., Hildesheim 1979: nos. 85-86.
[17] G. Grimm in *Das ptol. Äg.*: 103-12; L. Bell 1985b: 269-70.
[18] Cheshire 1982: 105-11.
[19] D. B. Thompson 1973.
[20] Quaegebeur in *Das ptol. Äg.*: 247-49.
[21] Quaegebeur 1971b: 215-16.
[22] See De Meulenaere/Mackay 1976: 205-06, no. 111; 174-77, pl. 1 (Cairo CG 22181).
[23] Derchain 1985: 35-36.
[24] Habachi 1969.
[25] Sauneron 1960a: 83-109.
[26] See the stela in Moscow (5375) reproduced in Hodjash/Berlev 1982: 184-86, no. 127; and the stela in a private collection reproduced in *Das ptol. Äg.*: 251-52.
[27] PM VI: 214 (69)-(70). A monograph on Arsinoe Philadelphos in the Egyptian sources is in preparation by the author and P. Dils.
[28] Quaegebeur 1971a: 239-70, esp. 267; see also D. J. Thompson 1988.
[29] Quaegebeur 1983b: 118.
[30] This item was brought to my attention by E. Winter.
[31] George 1982: 11-16.
[32] Quaegebeur in *Das ptol. Äg.*: 259; Osing 1977: pl. 9. For the deified Amenhotep I sacrificing to Min, see Altenmüller 1981: 2.
[33] Hildesheim 1025, reprod. in Hildesheim 1985: no. 176; Quaegebeur 1985: 73-78.
[34] Hauben 1983. For a divergent view, see Burstein 1982.
[35] Quaegebeur 1971b: 204ff.
[36] P. Louvre E. 3308; cf. Devéria 1881: 209, no. XI.15.
[37] Quaegebeur 1983b: 111-13 and notes 67-69.
[38] Quaegebeur 1971b: 202-03; see also the statue in the Metropolitan Museum of Art (CAT. 66).
[39] Bergman 1968: 146-61; Kákosy 1974; Bresciani 1978: 80-81.
[40] For some questionable attributions of statues to Arsinoe see, e.g., Quaegebeur 1983b: 116-17; Iwas 1984.
[41] Fraser 1960: 133-34 no. 2, pl. XXIX (2b) (Chicago, OI 10518). Fraser (1972, vol. I: 70; vol. II: 154 note 234) seems to suppose, wrongly I think, that this statue was dedicated by Greeks of the upper class who were interested in Egyptian cults. Cf. Peremans 1982: 152.
[42] Kamal 1905, vol. I: 171-77; vol. II: pl. LVII (Cairo CG 22183); Quaegebeur 1971a: 242.
[43] Botti/Romanelli 1951: 22-26, nos. 31-33, pl. XXIII; Quaegebeur 1983b: 114-15.
[44] P. Clère 1961: pls. 43, 61.
[45] Ptolemy III was the son of Ptolemy II and Arsinoe I.
[46] Bianchi in *Das ptol. Äg.*: 95-102.
[47] Dunand 1980.
[48] See Desroches-Noblecourt 1952: 35ff.
[49] Kamal 1905, vol. II: pl. LIX (Cairo CG 22186); Quaegebeur in *Das ptol. Äg.*: 247.
[50] See, e.g., Troy 1986: 38, fig. 21; 110, fig. 74.
[51] See note 53 below and Cauville 1987, vol. I: 237-38; vol. II: 57.
[52] Cauville/Devauchelle 1985: pls. 30-33. It is remarkable that Ptolemy III is accompanied by Arsinoe instead of Berenike II, a substitution that also occurs elsewhere. Is it an error or is there a link with the fact that Berenike II was murdered in 221 B. C. by her son Ptolemy IV? She never had a cult in Ptolemais.
[53] Winter in *Das ptol. Äg.*: 147-60. Winter separates the cult of the ancestors too strictly from the deification of the reigning royal couple.
[54] Lanciers 1986: 81-98.
[55] This reason is given in the building inscription; see Cauville/Devauchelle 1984, esp. 35-6. On the revolt, see now Vandorpe 1986: 294-302.
[56] Kamal 1905, vol. II: pl. LXII (Cairo CG 22188).
[57] Winter in *Das ptol. Äg.*: 156.
[58] *Ibid.*
[59] I discussed this question in "Une scène historique méconnue au grand temple d'Edfou," a paper presented at the international colloquium *Egitto e storia antica*, held at Bologna, August-September 1987.
[60] The Epigraphic Survey 1981: pls. 190-91; Quaegebeur in *Das ptol. Äg.*: 255.
[61] Quaegebeur 1983b: 114.
[62] The publication of this chapel is being prepared by Traunecker.
[63] Brashear 1980: no. 2376 (commentary on p. 29).

The Pharaonic Art of Ptolemaic Egypt

by Robert S. Bianchi

For all intents and purposes the history of the art of the Ptolemaic Period begins with Gaston Maspero's critical assessment of the statue of Hor, discovered in Alexandria (Fig. 25). Maspero (1887: 234–37) regarded the coiffure, physiognomy, and particularly the drapery style as effete attempts on the part of native Egyptian craftsmen to capture Hellenistic Greek forms. So convincing were Maspero's pronouncements that they have since become enshrined in the Egyptological literature as the characteristic traits of the so-called Mixed School of Ptolemaic art, defined as an aesthetically weak approximation of Hellenistic forms into a pharaonic framework. Maspero's view was adapted virtually unchanged by Lawrence (1925) and later by Noshy (1937), both of whom never tested the validity of the original premise. In more recent essays, both G. Grimm (1975) and Vandersleyen (1985) have uncritically subscribed to Maspero's view, introducing no new evidence in support of his position.

Within a decade of Maspero's publication, von Bissing (1896) assessed a group of non-ideal heads, many of which had been collected during the course of the nineteenth century without regard for bodies (CAT. 114), inscriptions, or archaeological contexts (Barocas 1974: 113). He termed each such head a representation of a *geron*, an old man (1896: 137), and automatically regarded the group as influenced by the tenets of Classical art (1896: 133-37). Even Edgar (1903: ix), who recognized the Egyptian nature of the bodies belonging to the heads, some of the bodies being inscribed with hieroglyphs, continued to espouse this position when he termed such heads "European," i.e., non-Egyptian. As a result of these initial studies, such non-idealizing images were regarded as "portraits" in the Western sense. Since the basic premise was neither explored nor challenged, the possibility of the Egyptian nature of such images was never raised. Thus Bothmer, discussing one example (Boston 50.3427, ESLP: 128), and more recently Vandersleyen (1985) continued to perceive the heads as indebted to Hellenistic traditions.

So seductive was this position that B. Schweitzer (1948) attempted to intercalcate the image of Horsitutu (CAT. 31) into the development of Roman Republican portraiture of the first century B. C., even though the statue is more obviously datable to the period around 300 B. C. B. Schweitzer's assessment of the physiognomy of Horsitutu as somehow related to a style of Roman Republican portraiture provided the foundation upon which two subsequent premises were based. If one assumed that such images were stylistically related to certain examples of Roman Republican portraiture, then a) those Egyptian images were likewise portraits in their own right (CAT. 44); and b) non-idealizing Egyptian images that could be shown to date to the fourth and third centuries B. C. must, as portraits, have influenced the development of Roman Republican portraiture (Bothmer 1954 and 1987).

The error lies in the assumption that these non-idealizing heads are actually portraits, that is, with features matching those of specific individuals. In fact, in the Egyptian concept of "portraiture" it is not people who are portrayed but rather their ages or stations in life. This principle evolves from what numerous scholars have termed the hieroglyphic basis of Egyptian art – the art as an extension of the hieroglyphic system of writing (Scharff 1939a: 491-97; Moorey 1970: 46; Hornung 1973; Parlebas 1981; Fischer 1986; te Velde 1986). In this view, the rules governing the physical appearance of hieroglyphic signs are also those governing the visual arts. Sign and representation, therefore, exist as interrelated symbols (Hornung 1973; te Velde 1986). This view does not

◁ *Fig. 24 The Temple of Hathor at Dendera*
The scene on the rear wall of this temple shows Cleopatra VII and Caesarion, her putative son by Julius Caesar, offering to the divinities of the temple. The small figure between them represents the Ka *of Caesarion.*

preclude the existence of non-idealizing images, as is demonstrated by an examination of how the ancient Egyptians regarded their world.

From the time of the Old Kingdom, the Egyptians gave visual expression to the passage of time through its effects on the physical appearance of man. Consequently, the door jambs of mastabas of the Old Kingdom generally depict the tomb owner at two distinct stages of life, the one more youthful, perhaps to be termed ideal, and the second more corpulent and aged, perhaps to be termed non-idealizing. The distinction is a modern one; to the ancient Egyptians both images are ideal: each constitutes a hieroglyph symbolizing, in a non-specific way, a generic stage in life rather than a particular moment. And this symbolic contrast between the taut bodies of youth and the corpulence of old age, as found in these Old Kingdom mastabas, was reinterpreted in the Temple of Edfu and there applied to the depictions of the sun at dawn and at dusk (Cauville 1984: 23). In a very similar way, the Egyptian craftsmen of the Late Period developed several typologies for the representations of older men which are nothing more than a later manifestation of this same cultural conceit. The first of these typologies to be identified were the egg-heads, so termed because in profile the contours of their shaven heads resemble hens' eggs (Bianchi 1982a). By employing the stylistic formulae for depicting signs of age (below, pp. 59-60) and relegating them to the frontal planes of such heads, the idealizing variant (Fig. 26) could be readily transformed into the non-idealizing type represented by CATS. 44-47.

Related to the egg-head typology because of similarities in frontal view only are the figure-eight heads. These are so designated because the oval shape of the face has an indentation at the level of the ears which likens its contour to a figure eight. CAT. 42 is a representative example of the type.

A third group, here termed polygonal heads because of the characteristically acute angular changes in the planes of the heads in profile view, is represented by CATS. 33 and 41. Such cranial definition is already encountered during the Old Kingdom, as in the bust of Ankhaef in Boston (Fig. 27; W. Smith 1960: 39), and becomes a fixed feature in the art of the Late Period, as in the head

Fig. 25 Hor, the son of Hor
The initial assessment of the style of this statue has prejudiced subsequent scholarship for over a century. (Cairo CG 697)

of the statue of Psametiksaneith (Cairo CG 726, ESLP: 79) and in the relief from the pronaos of the late fourth century B. C. tomb of Petosiris at Tuna el Gebel (Fig. 28; Bianchi in *Das ptol. Äg.*: 96, ill. A). Working within the

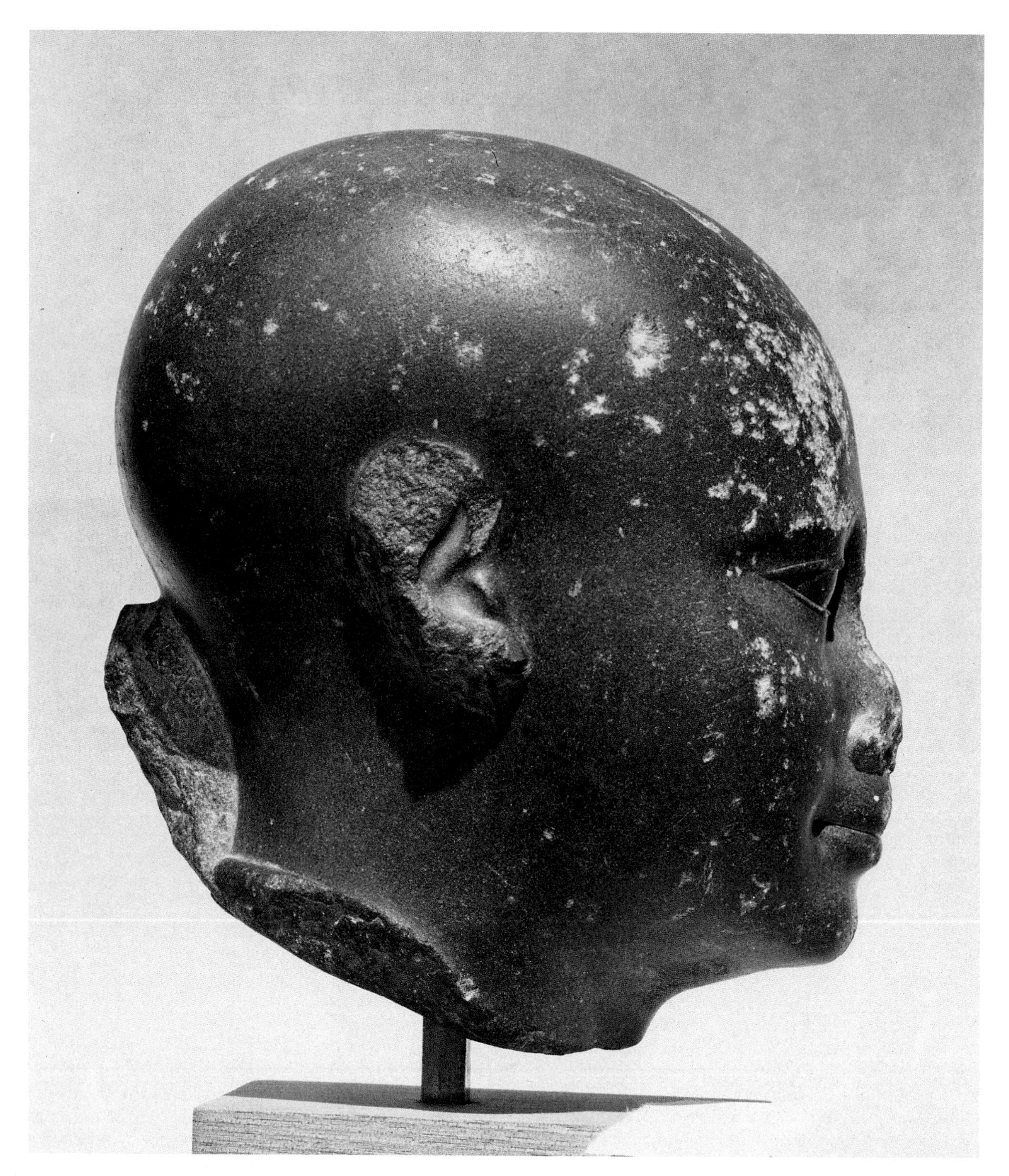

polygonal formula of the head, the Egyptian craftsmen of the Late Period were able to develop a variant, characterized by the addition of an extremely aquiline nose. CAT. 37 is an example of this variation and relates to heads in Venice (284, Leospo 1985: 202) and Brussels (E.5346, ESLP: 142-43).

Idealizing heads other than egg-heads can also be divided into typologies. At present, two such have been identified. The first gained currency during the course of Dynasty XXX and is best exemplified by the Dattari Statue (CAT. 24). The style of the head and its physiognomic details are variations of formulae found on a contemporary head with a valanced wig in Munich (Glyptothek 29, ESLP: 97-98). Such heads conform to the paradigm of the egg-heads, each example representing the range of possibilities inherent in any given form. It is, therefore, an error, as Quaegebeur has shown (1983b: 124 note 88), to regard differences in any one type as indications of wide divergencies in style (ESLP: 98) and to attribute those differences to regional schools (ESLP: 98). The second group of idealizing heads, best exemplified by CAT. 38, demonstrates this point. Its characteristics are an oval face with aquiline nose and closely cropped hair. Similar heads are found both in Stockholm (NME 73, George/Peterson 1982: 100; ESLP: 196) and in Copenhagen (AEIN 293, Roullet 1972: no. 41). The Copenhagen example differs from that in Munich only insofar as its hair is rendered as an undefined mass, lacking articulation of its strands. The absence of such details from one of two otherwise stylistically similar objects is commonplace in the Ptolemaic Period, occurring in relief representations as well (CAT. 65).

The invariable presence of a back pillar, occasionally inscribed with hieroglyphs, removes these heads from the Hellenistic sphere and places them squarely within the cultural milieu of the native Egyptians, who commissioned and crafted the monuments. These Egyptians were always members of the propertied class (p. 23 and note 18, above) who, as the important clerics of the land (Johnson 1986: 72), controlled not only most of the wealth (p. 24 and note 26, above), but also perpetuated the cultural traditions of their ancestors (p. 39, above). It was these very clerics who demanded the non-idealizing images of the Ptolemaic Period, images which find no parallels whatsoever in any representation identified as that of a Ptolemy, either in an Egyptian or a Hellenistic idiom. In this regard, such images are in accord with an observable cultural characteristic for Egyptian art of the Late Period, namely, that the most extreme examples of non-idealizing images are habitually those of private, not royal, individuals. Further, non-idealizing images of women are generally eschewed in Egyptian art of all periods. So it is that not one example of a female figure in pharaonic style from the Ptolemaic Period, not even that of Cleopatra VII herself (Fig. 24) can be adduced as being characterized by signs of age. (An image often reproduced as that of Cleopatra VII [Samson 1985: cover ill.] is in fact a modern pastiche [Quaegebeur 1983b: 121-22].) The non-idealizing corpulence of the faces of CATS. 62 and 69, which are female versions of the *physkon*-type of CAT. 53, is more restrained than that of the cleric in Vienna (CAT. 35). These observations are, then, the strongest stylistic indications of the native, non-Hellenistic nature of such non-idealizing images.

◁ Fig. 26 An idealizing egg-head
The features on such heads could be modified in a number of ways in order to achieve a non-idealizing effect. (Brooklyn 55.178, Charles Edwin Wilbour Fund)

The historiography of these non-idealizing representations must now be presented in order to understand why there has been so much debate about the dating of any given example. In order to justify their contentions that such heads were influenced by the tenets of Classical art, both von Bissing (1896: 133-37) and Edgar (1903: ix) were compelled to identify a cultural climate in which such cross-cultural influences might have been operative. To that end, von Bissing suggested (1923) that details of the Berlin Green Head (CAT. 46) were stylistically similar to those on the relief inscribed for a man named Henat in Berlin (15414) and assumed they were coeval. He then compared those works to the reliefs from the late fourth-century B. C. tomb of Petosiris (Fig. 28), which had recently been discovered and which many felt exhibited Greek influence. Accepting that premise, he concluded that all three Egyptian monuments were indeed contemporary. Von Bissing was in fact comparing only the details of the signs of age without recognizing that the heads did not belong to the same typological groups. His analysis was therefore methodologically unsound because the mimetic principle (p. 64, below) afforded the Egyptian craftsmen the luxury of repeating details at will. His arguments merely affirm that the egg-head and polygonal head types could be coeval and could exist in the fourth century B. C. He failed to realize that the typology takes precedence over the detail in matters of dating and that each head must first be intercalcated into its respective typology in order for its chronological position to be determined. Nevertheless, von Bissing's aesthetic criticism has become entrenched in the literature. Vandersleyen's most recent attempt (1985; so, too, Maehler 1983: 94-95) to impose Classical influence on such portraits is indicative of just how pervasive and long-lived is this unfounded prejudice.

The problems of dating these non-idealizing heads took on an added dimension in the interval between the two World Wars. During the 1930's J. Clère (1934), Gunn (1934), and Kuentz (1934) each contributed studies on the non-idealizing statues of Harwa, and Anthes (1937) wrote on the block statue of Petamenophis in Berlin (Fig. 29), the head of which shows signs of age. Those studies revealed that the statues of Harwa and Petamenophis, each exhibiting non-idealizing features, represented private Egyptian officials whose careers could be securely dated, by their accompanying hieroglyphic inscriptions, to the first half of the seventh century B. C. During this same period, Greek stone sculpture, still in its infancy, was characterized by an abstract idealism. As a result, such Egyptian heads, lacking Greek influence altogether, stood at the beginning of a development which continued into the first century B. C. Anthes (1939a), attempting to define this evolution, next took issue with von Bissing's view and suggested that the stylistic similarities between the Berlin Green Head (CAT. 46) and the heads in the relief of Henat represented artistic choices, not chronological indicators. He then proceeded (1939b) to date both CAT. 46 and the Henat reliefs to the period around 530 B. C., based on his astute assessment that the latter must be regarded as close in time to the reign of Darius I, a dating which has subsequently been reaffirmed (Jelínková 1958: 110-11; De Meulenaere 1966: 15-16). Kaiser's attempt (1966, 1967) to date the Berlin Green Head to the late fifth century B. C., based upon an elaboration of the earlier efforts of Anthes (1939a, 1939b), is flawed because he, like von Bissing earlier, failed to recognize typologies. He, too, assumed that stylistic similarities among heads were sufficient proof of their contemporaneity.

Such studies placed an assessment of Saite art (Dynasty XXVI) into a quandry because it was assumed that nonideal images, like those of Harwa and Petamenophis, cited above, were characteristic of Dynasty XXVI as a whole. As a result, historians such as Pirenne (1963: 209-13) and commentators like Barocas (1974: 149-50) and Wolf (1957: 629) could speak about "Saite realism,"

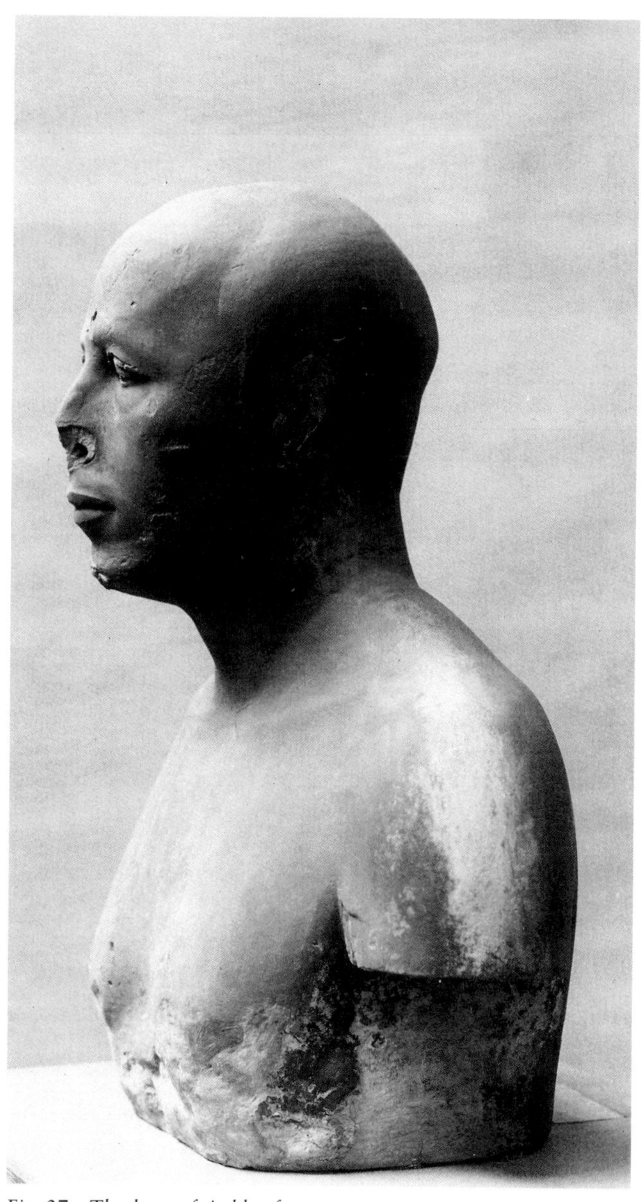

Fig. 27 The bust of Ankhaef
The cranial definition of this non-idealizing head belongs to a tradition which continued into the Ptolemaic Period, when it was used for several non-idealizing images. (Boston 27.442)

despite the fact that the chronological parameters for this artistic phenomenon were not narrowly defined. The term "Saite Period" had become an uncritically applied and imprecise chronological designation for almost any Egyptian phenomenon of the Late Period (Yoyotte 1958: 83-84). The dating of the Berlin Green Head to the Saite

Fig. 28 The Pronaos of the tomb of Petosiris
This scene from the late fourth century B. C. reveals the variety of physiognomies inherent in non-idealizing images of the polygonal head typology.

Period by Spiegelberg (1903: 81) is based, in part, on such arguments and can therefore be dismissed.

A further insight into the nature of pharaonic images from the Ptolemaic Period is provided by a study of the royal representations in the round. These divide readily into the Hellenistic and the pharaonic, and it is to the former that we now turn. Because these images were sculpted in styles more palatable to Western tastes, they have been the subject of greater study than their pharaonic counterparts. The cornerstone in the identification of these images is the establishment of correspondences with coins bearing likenesses and legends of particular rulers (p. 43, above). But simplistic application of such alleged numismatic affinities often leads to unsupportable conclusions. As a result, many still support the identification of a marble in London (1879.7-12.15 [1873]) as Cleopatra VII on the basis of its superficial similarity to her coins (Johansen 1978: 60) despite the fact that this identification was called into question by Wace over eighty years ago (1905: 93; Kyrieleis 1975: 125; Brunelle 1976: 117). Such a simplistic approach fails to take into account the sophisticated differences between a two-dimensional numismatic representation and one sculpted in the round (Brilliant 1971; Kyrieleis 1975: 11, *passim*). Additionally, all the images on coins are temporal; they were created at a given time at a given place and can, therefore, be both precisely identified and dated (R. Smith 1986: 59, *passim*). Nevertheless, images of one and the same monarch may be disconcertingly dissimilar on two different issues. This is certainly the case for Ptolemy V Epiphanes, whose issues from Beirut do not closely resemble those minted in Egypt (compare SV 1296 with var. SV. 1285/6).

Sculpture in the round, on the other hand, is atemporal. Recent investigations have demonstrated that images of the Ptolemies were constantly recut and reused (CATS. 54, 81, 88; R. Smith 1986: 64; Fittschen 1983: 167-68, 170; Krug 1984). All of these considerations must be brought to bear when comparing a sculpture with an image on a coin. But the most important characteristic is one which irrevocably removes the numismatic image from the realm of sculpture. A coin, unlike a statue, has two distinct surfaces on which an image of a ruler and a propagandistic message can be engraved. In numismatic images of Ptolemaic rulers the message is often reserved for the reverse, so that the representation of the ruler can stand prominently, with additional symbolic elaboration, on the obverse. This compartmentalization of function is unique to the nature of coins. In the non-numismatic images of these same rulers, image and message had to be integrated into one and the same visual expression. In such representations, the physical image was subsumed by the desire to express a cultural ideal (R. Smith 1986: 70, and note 32). As a consequence, one habitually discerns explicit references to any number of deities in these images of the Ptolemies. The iconography of some is tied to Pan (Kyrieleis 1975: 66; Laubscher 1985), while that of others is linked to Dionysos (CAT. 58; Kyrieleis 1975: 43). The adherence to iconographic types, however, was never rigid; any Ptolemy might appear in the guise of any deity according to the exigencies of a given circumstance. The variability of iconographic types is no more clearly evident than in the discipline's collective inability to sort them out and identify the sculptural images thought to represent Ptolemy IX, X, and XI on the basis of sealing impressions, themselves extensions of the numismatic evidence (R. Smith 1986). If these images were approximations of the appearances of actual individuals, as the impressions are thought to be, one would have little difficulty in matching the sealings from Edfu with the corresponding sculpture in the round and naming the individual so represented (R. Smith 1986).

Moreover, the Hellenistic engravers of the dies for the numismatic images used certain conventions for creating a profile view. But these conventions do not necessarily facilitate the identification of pharaonic portraits because they are alien to the traditions of the native Egyptian craftsmen of Ptolemaic Egypt. They do, however, enable one to distinguish Hellenistic from pharaonic portraiture. From the fourth century B. C., Greek sculptors had learned how to integrate the various views of a head. As a result, a profile view of a typical Greek work from this period, or later, reveals that the physiognomic features have been pulled back along the side of the face toward the ears. The image thus tends to develop in the round. This approach to the block of stone is significantly different from that of the pharaonic craftsmen. They tend to disregard the volumetric nature of the block and invariably relegate the physiognomic features to the frontal plane. One sees this most emphatically in the baroque orchestrations of planes in non-ideal egg-heads of the third and second centuries B. C., as in the profile views of CATS. 36 and 44. Plasticity of form does not transcend the block of stone as a whole and is noticeably absent in the profile views. The best example of the apparent unwillingness of the Egyptian craftsmen to integrate the views of a head is the trapezoidal configuration of the forehead of CAT. 43. It is this difference in the conception of the volumetric nature of sculpture in the round that separates the productions of the Graeco-Roman world from the coeval productions of pharaonic Egyptian workshops. Therefore, comparing pharaonic images of the Ptolemies to coins as the sole means of adducing an identification may at times be of questionable value (CATS. 33, 53, 69).

Like their counterparts in Hellenistic idiom, these pharaonic images of the Ptolemies subordinate issues of likeness to programmatic statements, as is evident from the prescriptions in the trilingual inscriptions for the erection of royal effigies. In the Rosetta Stone (Fig. 3), for example, one finds the provision for erecting a naos, or shrine, within which is to be placed an image of Ptolemy V Epiphanes (London 24, Sethe 1904, vol. III: no. 36; Kákosy 1983: 59-60). The formula to be followed for the creation of that image focuses on the attributes of the representation and is silent regarding the treatment of the face. The cultic aspect of that effigy, conveyed by symbolic attributes, was the paramount concern. The same conclusions can be drawn from the prescriptions for the statues as recorded both on the Mendes (Fig. 15) and Pithom Stelae (Cairo CG 22181 and CG 22183, respectively, pp. 43, 45, 47, above; Sethe 1904, vol. I: no. 13; 1904, vol. II: 20). Here again one finds elaborate descriptions of the forms of the symbols and attributes necessary to give the statues in question their particular meaning and identity. Such statues were commonplace in Egyptian temples and were often carried about in processions (p. 50, above; Winter in *Das ptol. Äg.*: 148), where their trappings, and not their physiognomies, provided the masses with the means for identification (Daszewski in *Das ptol. Äg.*: 128). These statues became symbols, hieroglyphs if one will, giving visual expression to their underlying religio-political messages. Although the evidence is slender, one may suggest, as Quaegebeur does (p. 47, above), that the statues of Ptolemy II Philadelphos and Arsinoe II (Figs. 19, 20) in the Vatican are representative of the types of images described in those decrees. These are doubtless reflections of the *twt* ("male") and *rpw.t* ("female") statue of Ptolemy II and his deified sister-consort Arsinoe II, for which the prophet (*ḥm-nṯr*) quarried stone in the Wadi Hammamat (Thissen 1979: 83).

Several Greek inscriptions from the Faiyum mention cult statues as well. One such is from Euhemeria, dated to Year XII of Ptolemy XII Auletes (Bernand 1981a: 100-08). It contains a decree of asylum, a peculiar class of document which, as the contents of this one reveal, elucidate the pragmatic *quid pro quo* relationship that existed between officials and the Crown. In exchange for asylum, which the priests of the temple appear to have demanded, the dedicators vow not only to restore images of earlier rulers (see p. 41, above) which had, like the temple, fallen into ruin from disuse, but also to dedicate effigies of Auletes and his family in this sanctuary (Bernand 1981a: 101, 104). Since the images of the king, presumably Ptolemy XII Auletes himself, shown twice in the lunette adoring the crocodile deities of the temple, are in pharaonic style, one can suggest that the images described in the text of this monument would also have been in pharaonic style. Confirmation appears in a Greek inscription on a statue in Egyptian style, also from the Faiyum, which states that it was "made," (Ἐπόη) by one Petese (Alexandria 3199, Bernand 1975: 160-61; compare CAT. 133).

Thus in pharaonic statues of the Ptolemaic Period, where the interaction of the Greeks and the Egyptians in formulating the stylistic idiom can be documented, the pharaonic customarily gets pride of place insofar as the visual representation is concerned. There is never any indication of a so-called Mixed School because the craftsmen were able to keep the two traditions separate, as they were in other social and cultural spheres (p. 25, above). The term Mixed School, coined when the perception of Ptolemaic art was prejudiced by Classical norms, is inappropriate and should be discarded. The term is as irrelevant for figures as it is for faces. The dialectic of pharaonic art that created non-idealizing physiognomic types placed those heads on recognizable body types such as the striding male figure (CATS. 24, 27), the healer (CAT.

Fig. 29 The statue of Petamenophis
The non-idealizing features of this head, datable to Dynasty XXV/XXVI, stand at the beginning of a tradition which was to continue uninterrupted into the Ptolemaic Period. (Berlin/BRD 23728)

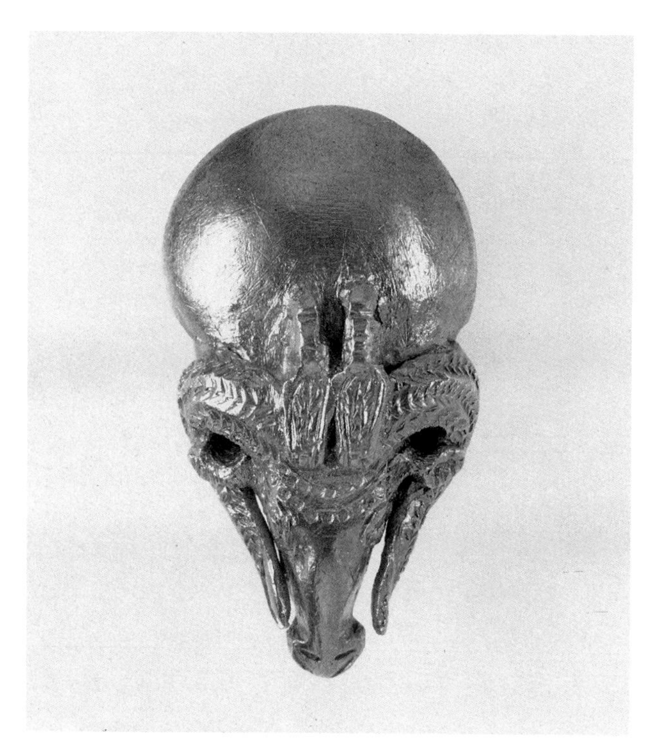

Fig. 30 Ram-headed amulet in gold
Such objects could, via the mimetic principle, be replicated by pharaonic craftsmen in almost any media. (Boston 23.333)

98), the striding draped figure (CATS. 30-32), and the like. The combination of facial and figural type served as symbols and, like the strictly prescribed attributes of the royal sculptures (pp. 62-63, above), the symbolic presentation made a statement about the cultural, religious, and political significance of the monument commissioned. The individual, as Goyon has shown (pp. 33, 36-37, above), was incidental to the process.
Bothmer (1970 and 1987), Russmann (1974: 22-24), Barocas (1974: 126-40), Aldred (in *Crépuscule*: 123-32), and Assmann (1983: 16-7) have all argued that the formal vocabulary necessary for the creation of these non-idealizing images derived from a repertoire of sculptural forms that had a long tradition in Egyptian art. Their arguments establish the mimetic principle in Egyptian art: any stylistic peculiarity can reappear on any Egyptian work at any time subsequent to its introduction. The suggestion of Richter (1954) that there is no artistic continuity between eras in Egyptian art is therefore simply not tenable, as Scharff had long ago shown (1939b: 6-7).

Fig. 31 Bronze statuette of the Kushite Pharaoh Shabaka
The Egyptian craftsmen have here replicated the characteristically Kushite attribute of the ram-headed amulet. (Athens ANE 632)

Similarly, the appearance of non-Egyptian motifs in Egyptian works does not necessarily denote artistic foreign influence. The *dikeras,* or double cornucopia, as an

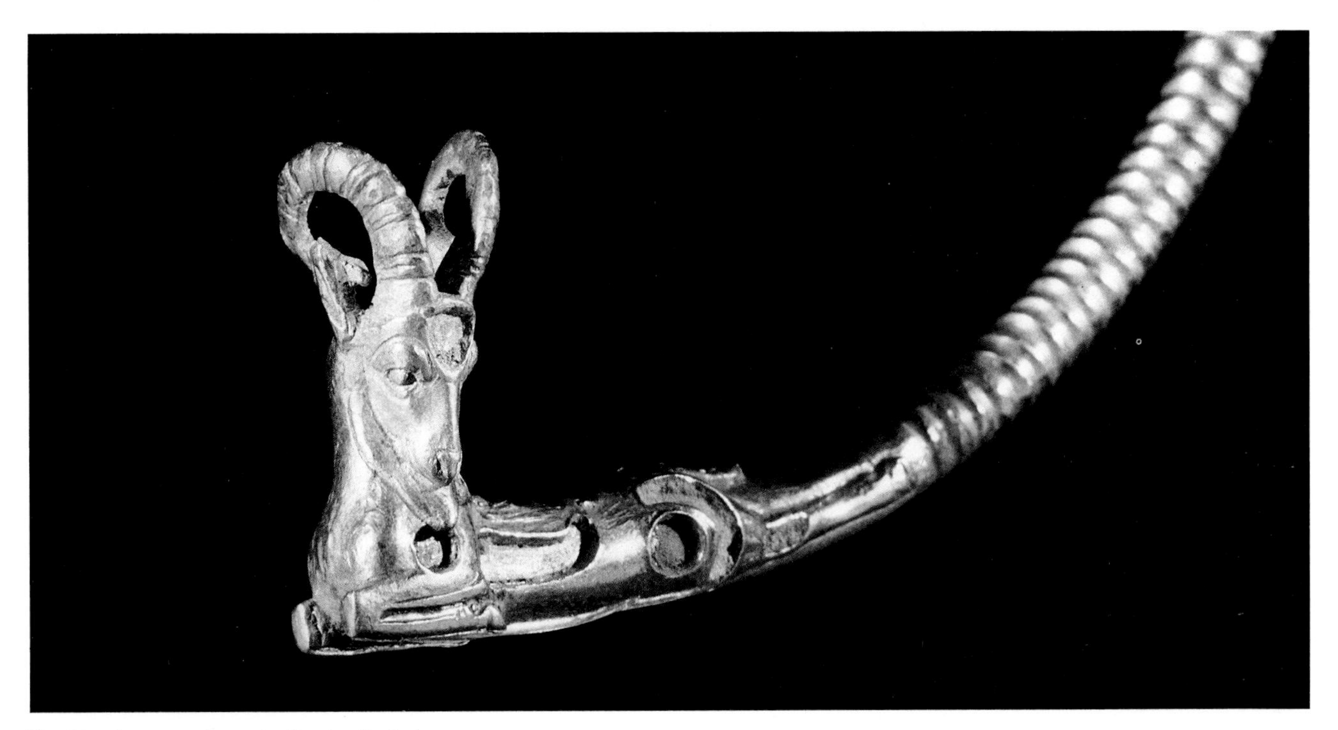

Fig. 32 A torque from the Persian Period
Comparing the treatment of the antlers on this piece of jewelry with that on the Egyptian statue of Ptahhotep (Fig. 33) reveals how foreign motifs were adapted to conform to Egyptian stylistic criteria. (Guennol Collection, on loan to The Brooklyn Museum)

attribute in the pharaonic statue of the deified Arsinoe II (p. 47, above; CAT. 66) or the bolts of lightning in the hand of Ptolemy II on the votive plaque from Tanis (CAT. 14) still follow the mimetic principle. From the time of the Kushites of Dynasty XXV, the ancient Egyptian craftsmen were able to replicate the accessories of foreigners. The amulet in the form of a ram's head (Fig. 30) that often appears on Kushite royal sculpture (Fig. 31) or the Achaemenid torque (Fig. 32) and bracelet on the statue of Ptahhotep (Fig. 33; ESLP: no. 64) amply demonstrate how such non-Egyptian objects could be incorporated into the design and execution of typically pharaonic works of art. The *dikeras* and the bolt of lightning must be regarded in these same terms. The jewelry and ears of wheat shown on the cartonnage of the lady of means (CAT. 82) are but late examples of this characteristically Egyptian artistic phenomenon.

None of these motifs, however, replicates reality, but rather is rendered according to the tenets of ancient Egypt's artistic principles. So, for example, the heads of the ibex serving as terminals on the torque depicted on the statue of Ptahhotep are rotated to conform to the tenets of Egyptian design (compare Figs. 32 and 33) and the shape of the *dikeras* in CAT. 66 has been contracted to conform to the body, in keeping with the Egyptian convention whereby attributes do not project freely into space (D. B. Thompson 1973: pl. I; Kyrieleis 1975: pl. 70, 3). So pervasive was the mimetic principle that Egyptian craftsmen, long after the Persian Empire ceased to exist as a political entity, were still able to create scenes in which typically Achaemenid objects appeared (Fig. 34; Bianchi in *Das ptol. Äg.*: 97; Nakaten 1982).

This same principle is operative for the depiction of those coiffures in which the hair is closely cut and neatly groomed (CAT. 31). The form and execution of such fashions have a long tradition in Egyptian art, going back to the Old Kingdom (Fig. 35). In such depictions, the hair sits on the head as if it were a cap and does not rise organically from the scalp as on Hellenistic Greek examples. Likewise, the depiction of a full beard and mustache on any number of heads in pharaonic style (CAT. 2) must be regarded in this same light, namely, as an Egyptian version of a fashion which appears to gain currency during the second century B. C.

Fig. 33 The jewelry of Ptahhotep
The Egyptian pectoral and the Achaemenid torque are harmoniously integrated into the design of this Egyptian statue. Note how the antlers of the ibexes have been rotated to conform to Egyptian tenets of design. (Brooklyn 37.353, Charles Edwin Wilbour Fund)

Both the fashion of the male garments depicted in CATS. 30-32 and the stylistic means by which they are rendered continue to be ascribed to Greek influence on the basis of Maspero's initial assessment (1887: 234-37). The ensemble usually consists of just three garments, namely, a short-sleeved T-shirt, a wraparound skirt, and a fringed shawl (Bianchi in *Das ptol. Äg.*; and 1980b). But this tripartite costume appears in Egyptian reliefs with private male individuals through Dynasty XXX, at which point it begins to appear in sculpture in the round (Bianchi in *Das ptol. Äg.*: 100). In the following, Ptolemaic, period, this ensemble qualifies as a major category into which sculpture can be divided because over 130 examples with the tripartite costume are known. These range in size from the large scale of Horsitutu (CAT. 31) to a small figurine in glassy faience measuring 12.3 cm in height (Glasgow 13/141, Bianchi in *Das ptol. Äg.*: 95). Although representations in the round of kings wearing this costume are rare during this period, royal relief representations frequently depict a Ptolemaic or Roman ruler in such a costume. (The sole exception to date is a fragment in Berlin/DDR [8810, Berlin 1899: 324] because the nature of the figure so clad beneath a falcon in the court at the Temple of Edfu is equivocal; CAT. 8 and Cantu 1978: ill. facing p. 46.) In some contexts, its significance appears to be linked to the *heb-sed*, or jubilee (p. 48, above), while in others it appears to be funerary (Bruyère 1952: 129 note 15). The female counterpart of this costume, which also consists of three garments, is represented by the statue of Arsinoe II deified (CAT. 66). This ensemble is generally composed of a tunic, a robe, and a shawl draped asymmetrically around the body and knotted at the breast (Bianchi 1980b). Although this female tripartite ensemble first appears in relief representations as early as the fourth century B.C., it appears in sculpture in the round only during the Ptolemaic Period; both costumes are of purely Egyptian origin and development (Bianchi 1980b).

The revelation of the forms of the bodies beneath the folds of these male and female costumes inclined Maspero (1887: 234-37) and most recently Vandersleyen (1985) to suggest that that interplay of flesh and fold was

Fig. 34 Egyptian craftsmen from the tomb of Petosiris
The ability of the Egyptians to replicate foreign motifs is demonstrated in this relief from the late fourth century B.C. in which metal workers craft typically Achaemenid objects at a time when the Persian Empire was no longer a political entity.

Fig. 35 Wooden panel of Hesire
The short coiffure, depicted in this relief from the Old Kingdom, is stylistically related to that found on many Egyptian sculptures of the Ptolemaic Period. (Cairo CG 1428)

the result of Greek influence on these works. Such a suggestion disregards the fundamentally pharaonic way in which the forms emerge from beneath the folds of the garments. One need only compare these statues to the treatment of Egyptian drapery from the earlier pharaonic periods (Figs. 36, 37) to realize that the folds are invariably treated as a series of linear ridges which become more plastically developed as they cross the abdomen. This transition from linear to sculptural folds in the same garment is alien to the stylistic traditions of Greek art from the time of the Parthenon sculptures on and thereby betrays the hand of Egyptian craftsmen.

The attempts to ascribe the corpulence of the male figures in these draped statues to Greek influence (Vandersleyen 1985) is erroneous and fails to recognize a fundamental principle of Egyptian art: the stylized rendering of male corpulence was an artistic convention connoting secular authority and advanced age (Capart 1931: pl. 44a-b; Hildesheim 1962, Schmitz 1982). The immediate Late Period precursor for this convention is found in the torso of Hachoris in Boston (Fig. 38; W. Smith 1960: 177; A. Grimm 1984), which is based in turn on those of Ariketekana (Cairo JE 38018, Wenig 1978: no. 83) and of Harwa (Fig. 39; Michalowski 1968: fig. 598). Egyptian as well is the treatment of the full-figured female body depicted both in the tripartite costume (CAT. 66) and the tightly fitting sheath (CATS. 28, 72). Whereas many commentators persist in regarding such anatomical representations in Egyptian art as the result of Hellenistic Greek influence (ESLP: 119-20; followed by Vandersleyen 1975: 271; 1985), few have placed these figures into the context of Egyptian art and fewer have attempted a direct comparison with contemporary Greek monuments in support of such a position.

During the Late Period, one can document the adherence of the Egyptian craftsman to one of the time-honored attitudes for the depiction of women: the figure wears a tightly fitting sheath and stands with the left leg advanced, the arms generally held close to the body, parallel to the axis of symmetry, with the palms pressed against the thighs, as was encountered in the Old Kingdom (Fig. 40 and Cairo CG 134, Wildung/Schoske 1984: nos. 96 and 5, respectively). This formula is applied in the Late Period, beginning with the Dynasty XXV bronze figure of Takushite (Athens 110, Quaegebeur 1983b: 119-20) and continuing with the wood example dated to Dynasty XXVI (Berlin/BRD 8814, Kaiser 1967: no. 945) and the figures of Isis and Nephthys in the Triad dated to Dynasty XXX (Cairo CG 39220, Wildung/Schoske 1984: no. 192). The anatomical rendition of each of these female figures is uniformly characterized by wide thighs, a swelling pelvic region, a full lower abdomen in which the navel itself is distinctively articulated, a high, pinched waist, and firm, rounded breasts. These are the very same physical characteristics exhibited by the draped statue of Arsinoe II deified (CAT. 66), as well as by the female statues in Brussels (CAT. 28) and Vienna (5809, Vandersleyen 1975: 271; pl. 231).

The suggestion (ESLP: 119-21; Vandersleyen 1985) that the rendering of the female anatomy on figures such as that of CAT. 28 is influenced by Greek art has never been supported by direct comparison with any contemporary Greek work. A comparison with the slightly earlier Praxitelian Knidian Aphrodite, as reflected in several Roman replicas (Fig. 41) (Bieber 1961: figs. 24-31) is instructive because it reveals how different in spirit are the Egyptian and Greek traditions. Each breast in the Egyptian examples is treated singly and lacks the organic unity of those in the Classical statues. The treatment of the lower abdomen and its navel as a stylized bagel is also without parallel in extra-Egyptian contexts, where the emphasis is on a developing contrapposto. The same conclusions might also be drawn by comparing Egyptian female figures to copies of the third century B.C. Kneeling Aphrodite attributed to Doidalsas (Fig. 42) (Lullies 1954), which explores the effects of motion and gravity on the female figure in a way never attempted by variations of the Egyptian formula, as the seated statue of Isis dated to Dynasty XXVI (Cairo CG 38884, Wildung/Schoske 1984: no. 10) and the nude depicted in the Brooklyn symplegma (CAT. 130) clearly demonstrate. The latter belongs to a group of erotica which can only be regarded in terms of Egyptian traditions (Bianchi in Brooklyn 1983: no. 70). Such representations are neither stylistically nor thematically indebted to Classical antecedents. As a result of these comparisons with contemporaneous Greek works, one ought now recognize how erroneous is the ascription of Hellenistic influences to explain the inherent sensuality and perceived eroticism of CAT. 28 (ESLP: 119-20; Quaegebeur 1983b; Vandersleyen 1975: no. 231; 1985).

We conclude this analysis of the ancient Egyptian approach to anatomy with a discussion of tripartition – the rendering of the male torso into the three distinct anatomical divisions of lower abdomen, rib cage, and pectoral region. Such tripartite male torso modeling is not an innovation of the Late Period, as is sometimes claimed (ESLP: 102), but is rather a stylistic feature common to

Fig. 36 The fish bearers of King Amenemhet III
In this rear view, one can begin to appreciate the sensitivity of the Egyptian artists to the rendering of the human body and its emergence from beneath the costume. (Cairo CG 392)

Egyptian sculpture from all epochs (Fischer 1962). It becomes more firmly established in Egyptian statuary from the time of the Third Intermediate Period (Aldred in *Crépuscule*: 123-24) and is occasionally encountered during the course of Dynasties XXV and XXVI (Wildung 1977b: 37-38). Tripartite torsos appear to become the style of choice in royal sculpture of Dynasty XXIX (Fig. 38; W. Smith 1960: 177; A. Grimm 1984) and proliferate during the course of Dynasty XXX for royal and private sculpture (CATS. 24, 26) alike (ESLP: 94; De Meulenaere 1962; H. Müller 1970: 89, 92). Their appearance in the sculpture of the Ptolemaic (CAT. 27) and Roman Periods marks the continuation of a native Egyptian tradition and is not indebted to any foreign influence.
Tripartite torsos are often found in conjunction with the traditional kilted male figure striding forth with the left leg advanced and the arms hanging along the sides of the body (CAT. 24), an attitude ultimately derived from Old Kingdom models (Fig. 40; Saleh/Sourouzian 1987: no. 33). The fisted hands of such statues generally clench an enigmatic object that is often termed an emblematic staff. Despite the recent attempts to redefine the nature of this attribute (Fehlig 1986), there can be no doubt that these cylindrical objects are representations of folded bolts of cloth, as Fischer had already established (1975). Statues of striding, kilted male figures are often paired with female figures wearing tightly fitting sheaths (Fig. 40) which are, themselves, the traditional female fashion of Egypt (CAT. 28).

A continued examination of pharaonic art of the Ptolemaic Period confirms the traditional nature of the craftsmen's conceptions. To begin with sculpture in the round, Ptolemaic works – like Egyptian art of all periods – are often characterized by the phenomenon of asymmetry, a phenomenon which divides into two classifications, compositional and axial. In the former bilateral symmetry is always avoided. For example, two hands are sometimes represented with different gestures,with only one holding an attribute. Such is the compositional asym-

Fig. 37 The Lady Miye
In almost every epoch of Egypt's long history, the sensuality of the female body emerging from beneath the gossamer folds of a garment can be documented. This example from the New Kingdom shows that such artistic concerns were already developed in Egypt almost one thousand years before the sculpting of the Elgin Marbles. (Brooklyn 47.120.3, Charles Edwin Wilbour Fund)

metry discussed by Schäfer (1986: 310-34), which is consistent with the observations of others on the same matter (Fischer 1962; Schoske 1986).

As an artistic phenomenon, axial asymmetry is characterized by noticeable discrepancies in the form and/or mass of corresponding elements on either side of the symmetrical axis (CATS. 39-42) and is documented from the time of the Old Kingdom (Waterman 1958: 28-29, fig. 7). (For a parallel, but unrelated, phenomenon in earlier Greek sculpture, see L. Schneider 1973; Laubscher 1987: 137.) Nevertheless, axial asymmetry begins to become one of the dominant features in Egyptian art of the first century B. C., as revealed not only in CAT. 41, but also in a survey of four heads which belong to the figure-eight typology (p. 57, above; CAT. 42). These four heads include one in Cairo (CG 27493, Montet 1958), which joins to a body in Paris (E. 15683) of Paenmerit, who lived during the time of Ptolemy XII Auletes (Montet 1958); the head on the draped statue of Hor (Fig. 25), found in Alexandria and now in Cairo (CG 697, Terrace/Fischer 1970: 177-80); an uninscribed head in the University Museum, Lipsia (Adriani 1970: 102, and pl. 51, 2); and CAT. 42. A chronological arrangement for these four heads can be suggested, based on the observation that the head of Paenmerit is dated by inscription to the period between 80 and 51 B. C., while the statue of Hor in Cairo is generally datable to the period between 50 and 25 B. C. (ESLP: 171; Terrace/Fischer 1970: 177). In terms of the progressive tendency of this century toward a stylized abstraction and asymmetry, CAT. 42 seems to stand at or near the beginning of the series, in the very late second or early first century B. C. The head in Lipsia, whose left and right halves are volumetrically disparate and whose features are the most stylized of them all, would tend to stand near the end of the series, datable to the turn of the millennium.

Three additional features – plastically rendered eyes, the bichromatic effect of statues in dark stones, and the seeming lack of finish to the surfaces of many statues – characterize the sculpture of the Ptolemaic Period.

Fig. 38 The Pharaoh Hachoris of Dynasty XXIX
Male corpulence was a time-honored Egyptian artistic convention for prosperity and was often employed as an indication of rank in Egyptian art. (Boston 29.732)

Fig. 39 Harwa
The exuberantly baroque delight in the flesh of this statue of Harwa is in keeping with Egyptian traditions that reach back to the Old Kingdom. As such, the rendering of a portly male figure has nothing to do with foreign influence. (Cairo CG 902)

In statues from the Ptolemaic Period (CATS. 31, 42), the plastically rendered eyes, in which the pupil appears as a raised disk, occasionally exhibiting a drilled iris, can be traced back at least to the Middle Kingdom, particularly to Thebes, where it was successively revived from the New Kingdom onward (Fazzini, forthcoming). Such plastically rendered pupils belong to the repertoire of sculptural forms available to Egyptian craftsmen and the mimetic principle enabled them to employ this feature when so motivated. Adriani's observation (1970: 82) that this particular treatment of the eyes is attested in Egypt well before the Hadrianic Period can now be confirmed, and Egyptian works of art exhibiting this feature can no longer be arbitrarily assigned to the Roman Imperial Period (compare CAT. 49).

As for the bichromatic effect, many Egyptian statues of the Late Period are made of hard, dark stones, but the hair appears to be lighter in color than the body – a result of the differing degree of final polish applied to those respective areas. Such bichromy is already current during Dynasty XXX (CAT. 24) and continues unabated into the Ptolemaic Period (CAT. 43). One may cautiously suggest that this bichromy is intentional and may have served as a substitute for paint because, to date, no example of any sculpture in the round in these hard, dark stones appears to have traces of paint preserved. (One has yet to explain satisfactorily why there are no traces of paint on such statues whereas polychromy abounds on some reliefs in hard stone still *in situ* and constantly exposed to the elements – e.g., the Granite Sanctuary of Philip Arrhidaeus at Karnak; Eggebrecht *et al.* 1984: 242-43.)

Related to the bichromatic effect is the tendency on the part of Egyptian craftsmen of all periods, except perhaps for the masters of the finished schist sculptures of Mycerinus of Dynasty IV (Fig. 40), to resist the application of finishing touches to inaccessible areas of their sculptures. This propensity becomes increasingly apparent during the course of the Ptolemaic Period and ultimately characterizes the pharaonic work of the Roman Period. CAT. 133 is perhaps the best example of the last stage of this tendency and, in its lack of final polish, represents the ultimate triumph of the medium in its struggle with the craftsmen. In like manner, the hieroglyphs inscribed on the back pillars of statues exhibit a similar development from the carefully cut signs with interior detail, characteristic of the early Ptolemaic Period (CATS. 25, 26), to the perfunctorily executed signs of the first century B. C., which appear to have been summarily scratched into the surfaces of the stone (CAT. 32).

We now turn our attention to a discussion of relief representations. Here it must be stressed at the outset that both in royal and private reliefs in pharaonic style of the Ptolemaic and Roman Periods the craftsmen habitually avoided non-idealizing representations. These appear to have been used exclusively for male Egyptian clerics in certain representations in the round. There is thus often great conformity between idealizing images of any given monarch in relief and in sculpture, and often those correspondences transcend geographic boundaries and changes in dynasty. So, for example, the sickle-shaped smile that characterizes the canonical form of the face was once thought to be limited to works created for Nectanebo II and Ptolemy II Philadelphos (e.g., CAT. 1). It has now been shown to have developed earlier, in the fourth century B.C., and to have been retained later than the early third century B.C. (CAT. 34). Attempts to discriminate between the images of Ptolemy I Soter and Ptolemy II Philadelphos in relief representations (Myśliwiec 1974) on the basis of stylistic evidence are risky because there is actually little visible variety in such ideal images over time (Daumas in *Crépuscule*: 94) and place (Daumas 1975a: 327; in *Crépuscule*: 96). The same observation applies to certain architectural elements, including column capitals in the form of heads of Hathor (CAT. 6), which so conform to one another that it is often difficult to decide which date to Ptolemaic and which to Roman times (Ziegler 1979). Moreover, one can hardly quantify the differences between the relief style of Ptolemy VIII Euergetes II at Eastern and Western Thebes (Dewachter 1983: 49). As a result, one cannot be dogmatic about the dating and provenance of isolated blocks of royal relief, particularly since the rounded forms of some raised relief are common to all temple sites of Upper Egypt (Daumas 1975a: 330), and certain pre-Ptolemaic conventions for sunk relief continue to dominate the style of such representations from the Ptolemaic Period as well (Daumas in *Crépuscule*: 88-89). It should be emphasized, finally, that royal relief representations of the same monarch, apparently from the same site, which display a congruence of form and composition, very often differ significantly in the treatment of their details (Fig. 43, CAT. 65), a characteristic also noted both for idealizing and non-idealizing heads in their respective typologies (pp. 57-59, above). In contrast to the apparent uniformity between royal relief representations and their occasional correspondences with sculpture in the round, private pharaonic relief depictions, primarily on stelae, offer a different picture. While the majority appear to repeat conventions and are readily grouped into categories sharing similar features, a small number are apparently unique, indicating, perhaps, the creative impulses of the craftsmen and clerics who commissioned them. So, for example, a stela in Leiden (CAT. 108) bears no stylistic resemblance to the Group of Abydos III to which it has been assigned (Munro 1973: 1, 112, 131), whereas that of Pakhaas (CAT. 123) seems to stand outside of all identified groups. Finally, the style of the relief representations on some of these stelae (CAT. 122) is qualitatively finer than that found on any royal relief of the period.

Fig. 40 The Pharaoh Mycerinus and the goddess Hathor
The treatments of both the male and female torsos in this statue from the Old Kingdom stand at the beginning of a tradition that was to continue unbroken into the Ptolemaic Period. (Cairo JE 40679)

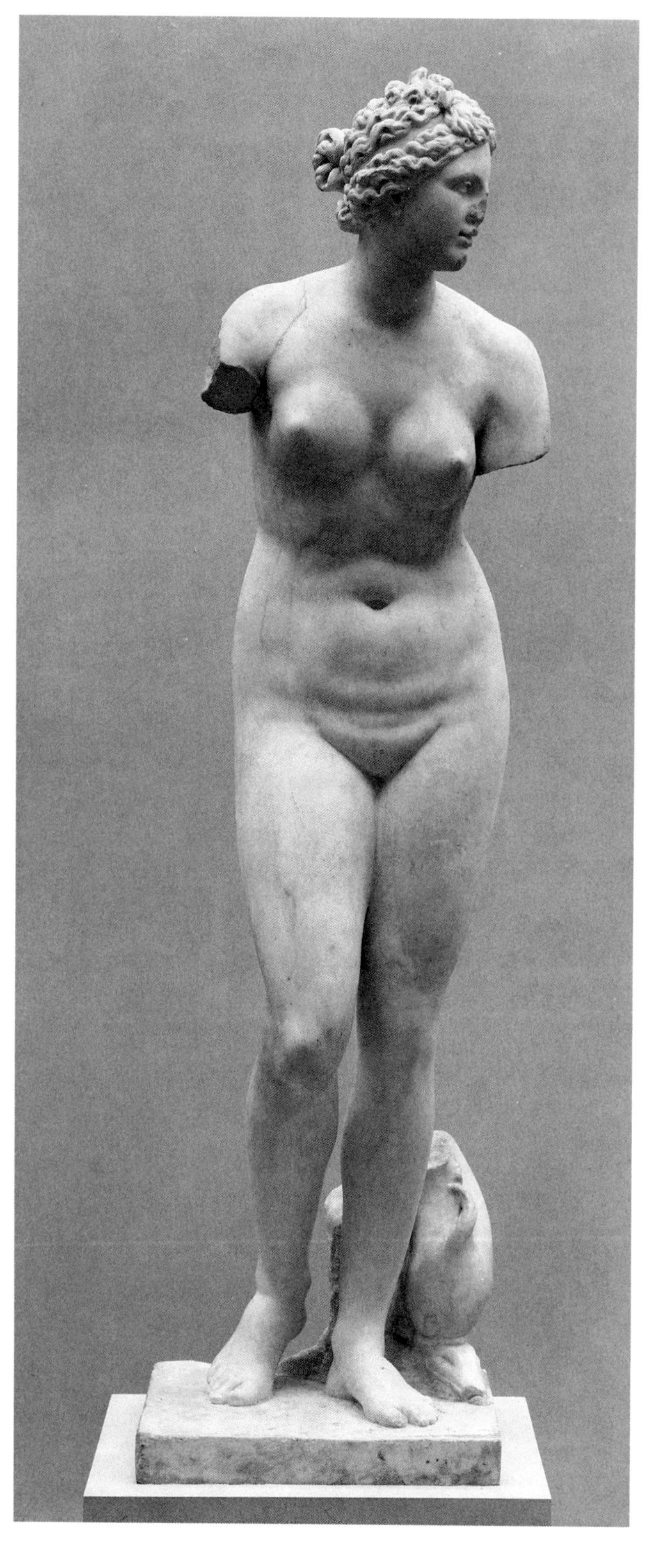

No survey of two-dimensional representations would be complete without commenting on several technical features, the first of which has been characterized by what has been called "perspective," for want of a better term. The presence or absence of perspective in Egyptian art and a workable definition of that term when applied to such Egyptian representations are contested issues (Schäfer 1986: 159-76; Rostem 1948; Baud 1978: 65-76). Nevertheless, the Egyptians were able to render certain details as if they were to be regarded as receding into space. The two most common objects so depicted from the New Kingdom on are sails, as found on the reliefs of Luxor Temple, which correspond to those at Edfu (Fig. 44; Eggebrecht *et al.* 1984: 361), and belt buckles, for example, on the costumes of Amenhorkhepeshef in his tomb in the Valley of the Queens (Fig. 45; Theban Tomb 85, el Mallakh/Bianchi 1980: 81-84). This phenomenon is rooted in the visual vocabulary of the ancient Egyptians and is not indebted to any foreign influence. The treatment of the top of the basin in a scene from Kom Ombo (Daumas in *Crépuscule*: 103), although dated to the second century A. D., may be part of this same tradition, as is the *wadjet*-amulet on the plaque in Boston (CAT. 131) and the horns of the composite crown worn by Arsinoe II on a relief in Cambridge (CAT. 65). The rendering of both of these motifs belongs, therefore, to this established pharaonic vocabulary (Schäfer 1986: 115-17) and ought not be confused with the Western concept of perspective, which, despite the assertions of Baud (1978: 65-75) and Quaegebeur (1985), the ancient Egyptians did not consciously evolve.

In like manner, the attitude of the figure of Ptolemy II Philadelphos on the plaque from Tanis (CAT. 14), which convincingly depicts him in the process of casting bolts of lightning, is indebted to purely Egyptian conventions, as is revealed by comparisons with images of kings smiting the foe on the pylons of temples from the New Kingdom (e.g., Eggebrecht *et al.* 1984: 189). The same is true for the figure identified as Arsinoe II on a stela in Toronto (Fig. 16), which shows an analogous bending at the waist. Comparing this attitude with that of female figures on the Hellenistic queens' vases (CAT. 68), it is clear that

Fig. 41 The goddess Aphrodite standing
Comparisons between this figure and female figures sculpted according to pharaonic norms reveal just how different the approach of an Egyptian artist to the female figure is. (*New York 12.11.5, Fletcher Fund, 1912*)

the figure on the Toronto stela displays none of the contrapposto of those on the vases. This figure is, therefore, devoid of all Greek influence. The mimetic principle enabled the craftsmen of this figure to evoke Hellenistic models (p. 64, above), but the position of the raised far arm is indebted to the pharaonic traditions responsible for the same attitude in the smiting scenes.

Royal and private relief representations of the Ptolemaic and Roman Periods, and to a lesser degree sculpture in the round (p. 72, above), relied for their visual effects upon polychromy and gilding. An idea of the values of those tonalities can be gleaned by examining the traces of paint remaining on the stelae in Brooklyn (CAT. 123) and Leiden (CAT. 125). The perception of these polychromatic values has been negatively prejudiced by the repeated publication of inaccurate modern colored drawings and paintings of the more spectacular of those scenes. Such renditions are so far removed from the actual polychromatic values and hues of the ancient painting that they should be disregarded (Daumas in *Crépuscule*: 104-06), while bearing in mind that color symbolism played a considerable role in conveying the meaning of specific scenes and motifs (Daumas in *Crépuscule*: 105; Manniche 1982). Gilding, too, was imbued with symbolic connotations, for the most part associated with deification (CAT. 123). It was applied to almost every medium from statues (CATS. 66, 100, 132), to reliefs (CAT. 123), to cartonnage (CAT. 82), and even to linen (Brooklyn 75.114, Bruyère 1953: 108-09).

In order to complete the picture of the art of Ptolemaic Egypt, one must examine the developments in Alexandria (Fig. 46), a city which has become synonymous in the literature with the Hellenistic art of Egypt. In the past, Alexandria had been portrayed as the undisputed mistress of a school of art which allegedly produced several distinctively Hellenistic Egyptian categories of art (Fig. 47; Adriani 1965; 1972). It is now recognized that many of these categories were neither introduced nor developed in Ptolemaic Egypt at all. Her craftsmen did not take the lead in the manufacture of glass (CATS. 18, 111) and her central position in the dissemination of Nilotic motifs can no longer be maintained (Daszewski 1985: 165). Tanagra figurines (CATS. 112-114), even the most *outré*, were based on Greek models – if not imported altogether – and at least one classification of Hadra ware is now known to be of Cretan origin (CAT. 119). This revised assessment of Alexandrian art indicates that the Greeks of Hellenistic Egypt were not in the vanguard of artistic developments, but followed the leads of others (CAT. 116).

This revised picture of the so-called Alexandrian School of Hellenistic art and the multivalence of any pharaonic motif (CAT. 111) confounds as well the universally accepted theorem that Alexandria was the undisputed seat

Fig. 42 The Kneeling Aphrodite
Egyptian artists never attempted to explore the effects of motion and gravity on the female figure in the way that Classical sculptors did. (New York 09.221.1, Rogers Fund, 1909)

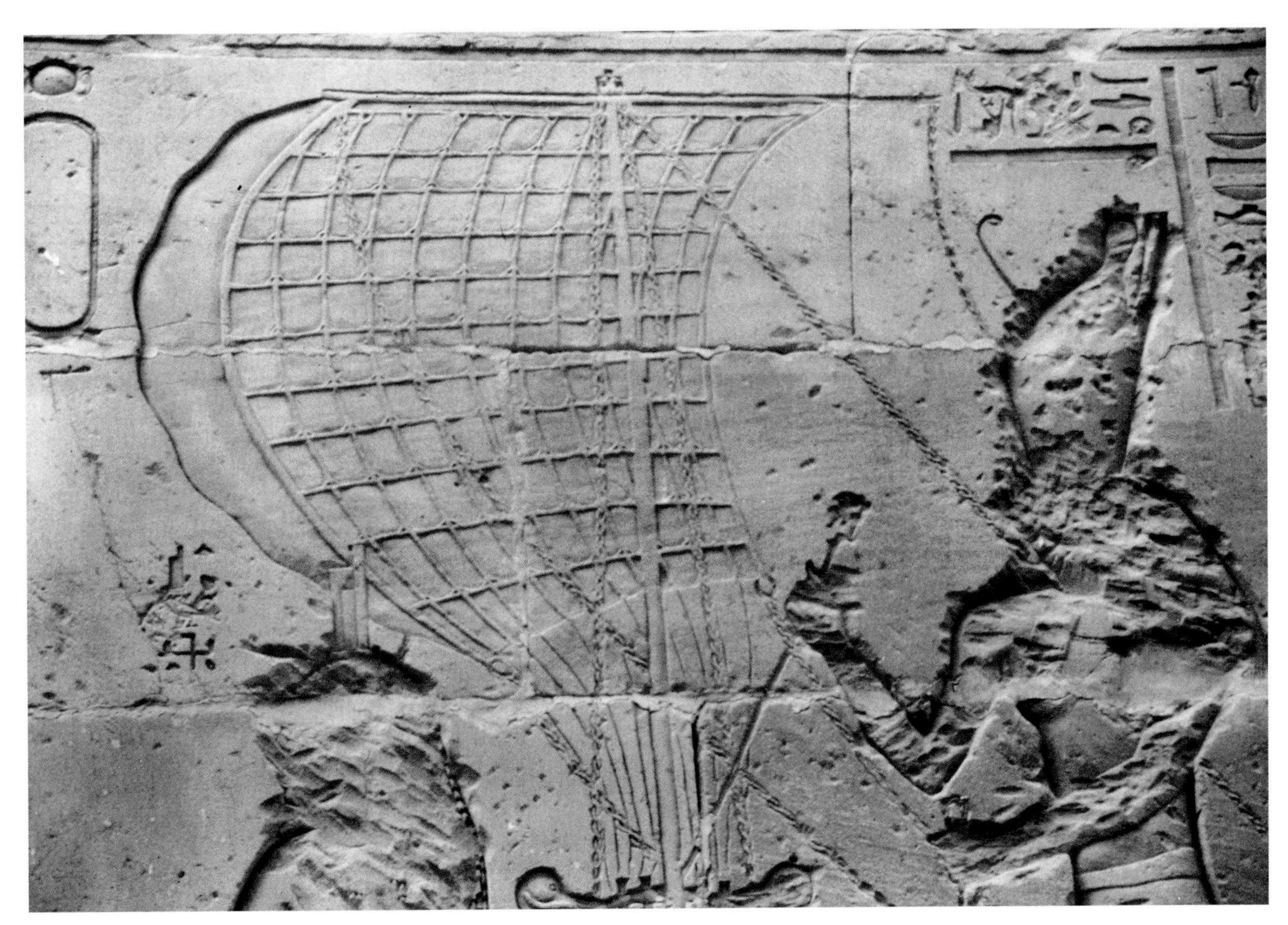

Fig. 44 Sails unfurled
This detail from the reliefs of the Temple of Horus at Edfu represents one of a handful of motifs the ancient Egyptians chose to represent in oblique views.

of a specific school of scholasticism, with uniformly applied tenets that were made manifest in examples of "Alexandrian art," which incorporated into their compositions Egyptianizing elements. As soon as an object is classified as a product of this putative school (CAT. 111), its motifs are subjected to an interpretation whose theoretical basis is erroneous. The creative genius of Hellenistic Alexandria never produced, for want of a better description, an iconology wherein individual motifs had specific, universally understood interpretations. Each such Egyptianizing object or monument must necessarily remain an enigmatic unicum unless its program can be associated with consistently recurring elements derived from the broader spectrum of Egypt's cultural heritage (compare CATS. 136, 140). The same pertains for Alexandrian motifs that appear in non-Egyptian contexts. It is, therefore, academically unsound to seek a uniform pharaonic interpretation of Egyptianizing motifs appearing together in any given composition from Italy dating from the period of Augustus to Domitian (30 B.C.-81 A.D.) because the Romans of that period had a very imperfect understanding of Egypt's pharaonic traditions (p. 219, below).

◁ *Fig. 43 Arsinoe II*
The presence or absence of interior detail in reliefs may not necessarily indicate differences in time or place. This less embellished relief represents the same queen and seems to come from the same monument as CAT. *65. (Hildesheim 1025)*

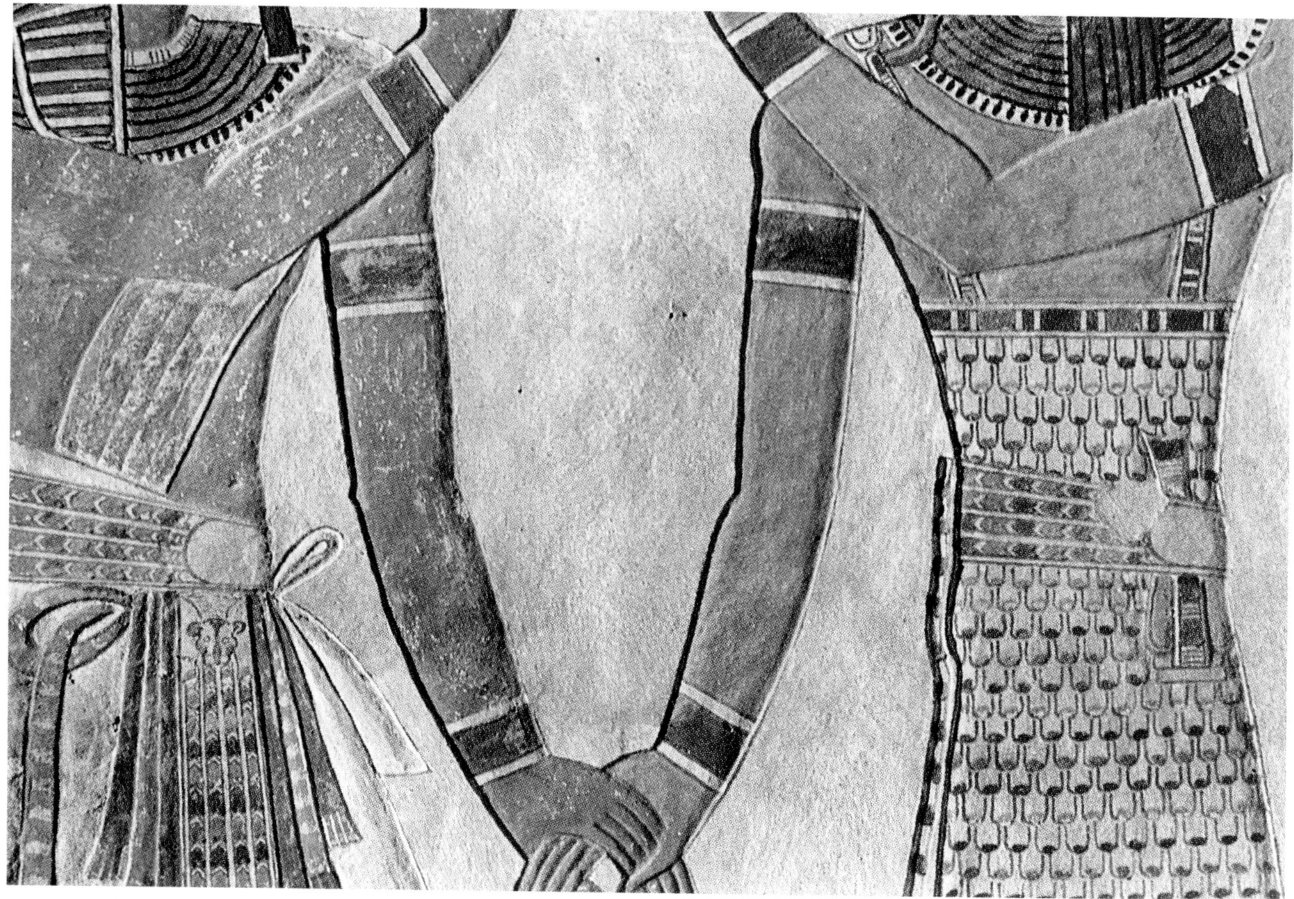

Fig. 45 Belt buckles
The angles from which the belt buckles in this detail from the tomb of Amenhorkhepeshef in the Valley of the Queens are rendered are another example of how the ancient Egyptians depicted selected motifs in oblique views. Such representations are not related to the tenets of Western perspective.

This documented and demonstrable lack of independent artistic initiative on the part of the Hellenistic Greek and the Crown in Alexandria stands in stark contrast to the innovations of the native Egyptian clerics during the same period. These clerics commissioned a plethora of non-idealizing images for their own religious purposes; they also commissioned a series of private funerary stelae, some of which are so unique that they defy placement into categories (CATS. 123, 125), while others display the finest relief sculpture known from the Ptolemaic Period (CAT. 122). This creativity, which has neither parallels in nor interfaces with the artistic milieu of Hellenistic Alexandria, is the most glaring condemnation of any theory regarding foreign influence on the native arts of the period. The pendulum of scholarship has indeed swung fully in the other direction. Just as in Egyptian society of Ptolemaic Egypt, so too in art, the "Greeks and the Egyptians led parallel rather than converging lives" and "their cultures coexisted rather than blended" (p. 21, above).

The suicide of Cleopatra VII in August 30 B.C. and the subsequent incorporation of Egypt as the private property of the Roman Imperial family by Augustus did not at first seriously impair the ability of the native Egyptians to create works of art in traditional styles and techniques. Native ateliers continued to produce such works, as CAT. 133 reveals. The vitality of Egyptian sculpture, however,

Fig. 46 Tomb 1 at Mustapha Pasha, Alexandria
Although the Hellenistic Greeks designed their tombs in Alexandria in accordance with Classical norms, they nevertheless did incorporate Egyptian motifs into the decoration.

traditionally depended upon the interaction of royal patronage with ateliers working for the private and religious sectors of society. The Ptolemies themselves conformed to the earlier models in that regard, but the Roman emperors created a void in that system, because, although pharaoh in name, they did not reside in Egypt. As a result, the history of pharaonic art during the Roman Imperial Period develops along several disparate lines, two of which will now be examined.

The first and most important for the development of pharaonic religion and art during the Roman Imperial Period is that effected by the priesthoods (p. 39-40, 249) of the temples of Upper Egypt, particularly at Esna and Kom Ombo, where one can document an intellectual fervor and creativity that crested during the Severan Period around 200 A. D. Religious expression thrived as the texts from Esna reveal, as did the sculpting of temple relief decoration at both temples. Royal sculpture could also survive, albeit in altered form, according to the proclivities of any given Roman emperor well into the third century A. D. At this point, Caracalla seems to have introduced a new iconographic type which accommodated the established Roman Imperial image to prevailing Egyptian norms (CAT. 140). Far from being an epoch of sterile decline, the Severan Period in Egypt is characterized by an intense interest in the past. So, for example, the Roman Emperor Commodus (180-192 A. D.) usurped at least one statue from the Ptolemaic Period (Vaughan 1960: 146; Kiss 1984; 67) and the theologians at Esna continued to develop religious concepts and exploit the richness

Fig. 47 Pompey's Pillar, Alexandria
Although local legend maintains that the severed head of the Roman general Pompey was once encased in a glass container set on top of this pillar, the existing Greek inscription indicates that the column was erected in honor of the Emperor Diocletian, whose administrative reforms fundamentally altered the fabric of ancient Egyptian society.

of written expression inherent in the hieroglyphs (Sternberg 1983). The Egyptian art of Caracalla represents the highwater mark of that tendency and reveals that at particular intervals throughout the Roman Imperial Period Egypt's cultural traditions could be revived.

The infrastructures enabling a Roman emperor like Caracalla, or more likely his agents, to interact with the native Egyptian priesthoods have not been identified to date. One can suggest, however, that this Severan revival of pharaonic norms was part of a periodic emergence of a highly organized theological administration that presumably enabled some sort of Egyptian synod to communicate directly with members of their confraternity at the Imperial Court in Rome. Such a theory readily explains how a codified theology and a degree of standardization in the image of Isis-in-Hydria (CAT. 136) could be so rapidly developed throughout Egypt (e.g., at Ras el Soda, Alexandria, Adriani 1940: 136-48; and at Luxor, Wagner 1981: 131-32; R. Wild 1981: 12-13, 132) and almost simultaneously transported and adopted in thoroughly Egyptian form in Italy (R. Wild 1981: 128), where Isis-in-Hydria was extremely popular during the second century A. D.

The origins of such close collaboration between the priesthoods of Egypt and the Roman Imperial Court are difficult to trace, but one can suggest that they begin late in the first century A. D., perhaps under Domitian (81-96 A. D.), whose Egyptianizing monuments at Benevento (H. Müller 1969) appear to be closer to actual pharaonic models than the Egyptianizing motifs created in Italy during the reign of Augustus and the Julio-Claudians who followed him. This explains why the hieroglyphic inscriptions on the obelisks erected for Antinous (CAT. 139) are so consummately composed when compared to those adorning the obelisks of Domitian at Benevento (Bresciani 1986) and the pseudo-hieroglyphs on CAT. 111. Such evidence supports the contention that examples of Roman Egyptomania of the first century A. D. are less accurate reflections of actual Egyptian motifs (CATS. 110, 134) than similar representations of the second and third centuries A. D.

The second tendency in pharaonic art of the Roman Imperial Period is the one that rings the death knell: the ultimate triumph of Classical over Egyptian art. The process is gradual but already in place during the first century A. D., as these two disparate artistic tendencies gradually merge (Castiglione 1967: 126) to produce what might be termed the Roman art of Egypt (CAT. 101). The process accelerates with time so that during the course of the third century A. D. it successfully competes against the pharaonic revival (CATS. 129, 140) and ultimately eclipses all traditional Egyptian visual expression. Pharaonic art, which had survived into the Ptolemaic Period and was periodically and vigorously revived during the Roman Empire, virtually ceases altogether during the reign of Diocletian (284-305 A. D.) (Grenier 1983b; Haeny 1985; A. Bowman 1986), whose administrative restructuring of the land deprived the priests of their authority and thereby dismantled the religious and economic bases of Egyptian art (Fig. 47).

Catalogue

In the dimensions of the objects in this catalogue, height precedes width precedes depth, in centimeters, followed by inches. Only height is given for heads and busts; for all other objects dimensions are as complete as was possible at the time the catalogue went to press. Partial dimensions follow the order given above. Unless otherwise indicated, all objects in this exhibition originally came from Egypt, although the exact provenance may not be known.
Full citations for abbreviated bibliographical references may be found in the Works Cited section.
Frequently cited repositories of works of art are indicated by city, followed by museum inventory or accession number. Full citations for these abbreviations appear on p. 256.

CAT. 1
Bust of a Ptolemy

Limestone, 45 (17 11/16)
Late fourth-third century B.C.
Benha (Athribis)
The Brooklyn Museum, 37.37E; Charles Edwin Wilbour Fund

Literature: ESLP: 122; Quaegebeur 1976: 122.

Because objects such as this bust still retain incised grids on their worked surfaces, scholarly opinion has been inclined to regard them as sculptors' models or trial pieces (Quaegebeur 1976: 122). Recent investigation, however, has shown that such a position is, in some instances, indefensible, because the ancient Egyptian definition of a completed work of art was not the same as that formulated by other cultures, even though the incomplete in the Western sense did exist and did function for the ancient Egyptians within the parameters of their cultural traditions (Bianchi 1979b: 19, and notes 41-45; see also CAT. 34). As a result, many objects once summarily dismissed as sculptors' models are now considered to be ex-votos (Myśliwiec 1972b; Bianchi 1979b and 1981). The truncated forms of many of these ex-votos are well within ancient Egyptian definitions for art because Egyptian art is hieroglyphic. The hieroglyphs themselves admit of incomplete forms, and it follows that completed feet, torsos, and busts, even those retaining incised grids, are independent works of art (Fischer 1986: 132-35). It has even been argued that the hieroglyphs *ḥr* ( ) and *tp* ( ) represent aspects of the gods Horus and Seth (Myśliwiec 1972a), and certainly deities, particularly Mestasytmis, were made manifest in bust form rather than as full figures (Wagner/Quaegebeur 1973: 42-44). The inextricable link then between art and hieroglyphs is so strong that the bust in ancient Egyptian art can only be regarded as a conscious, independent creation.

At least as early as the late New Kingdom, the bust was employed by the ancient Egyptians in the cults of their ancestors (Bierbrier 1982: 76, 96; Demarée 1983; Friedman 1985). This practice finds its closest cultural analogy in the use of the ancestor bust in ancient Rome, and both customs ought to be regarded as parallel but independent phenomena (contrary to what is claimed by Fischer 1986: 135; for a similar phenomenon in Greece, see Barr-Sharrar 1985 and 1987). As independent works such busts may have been dedicated in sanctuaries, or may have been used in chapels for private devotion (CAT. 49).

The style of the face and the rendering of its features derive from those in the earlier head of the Dattari Statue (CAT. 24) and are repeated in the Egyptian statues inscribed for Ptolemy II Philadelphos in the Egyptian style (Fig. 20 and ESLP: no. 96); hence the identification of this head as Ptolemy II is possible, but not assured.

CAT. 2
Man with a Lotus Bud Diadem

Granite, 34.5 (13 9/16)
First century B. C.
Said to be from Dime in the Faiyum
Munich, Staatliche Sammlung Ägyptischer Kunst, GL 30

Literature: Hornbostel in Altenmüller/Hornbostel 1982: no. 47; Schoske/Wildung 1985: 120, 122.

Several art historical assessments of this head regard it as one which exhibits a confluence of traditions, combining features belonging to the pharaonic Egyptian and Hellenistic Greek stylistic vocabularies. One must, therefore, examine the individual details of the head in order to test the viability of that hypothesis.

The traces of a back pillar undeniably link this head to the traditions of pharaonic sculpture in general (Hornbostel in Altenmüller/Hornbostel 1982: no. 47), and the disregard for finishing those parts of the head not visible from a strictly frontal view, as seen for example in the back of the ears, the crown and back of the head, and at the juncture of the head, neck, diadem, and back pillar, associate its craftsmen with those working in the late Ptolemaic Period (p. 72, above, and CAT. 32). The treatment of the hair, the individual locks of which do not rise organically from the scalp, is alien to any Hellenistic Greek tradition (p. 65, above, and CATS. 31, 43). The seemingly pensive, introspective expression of the face is achieved by selecting and combining a physiognomic vocabulary from the repertoire of such forms available to the pharaonic craftsmen. Among these are the conception and execution of the linear adjuncts such as the wrinkles on the brow and the deeply etched nasolabial furrows, set into a minimally modeled face; the wide-open eyes, articulated by their lids, characterized by the emphasis given their canthi and set into deep sockets formed by the junction of the brow with the bridge of the nose. It should be stressed that the upper eyelid is creased (CATS. 24, 45) and that the eyebrows themselves are not indicated (CAT. 43). Singly, then, each of these features finds its counterpart in other pharaonic sculptures datable to the first century B. C. The resulting expression may, therefore, appear to Western eyes to be introspective, but one must recall that such an impression is also gained by confronting a group of heads generally assigned to Dynasty XXVII, foremost among which is the head in Boston from Athribis (Boston 37.377; ESLP: no. 60). In context, therefore, the individual stylistic features are combined in a traditionally pharaonic manner to produce a typically Egyptian expression common to other works of art created during the Late Period (CAT. 41). Further demonstration of this position is the failure of the craftsmen to integrate the front and the profile views into an organic whole: all of these physiognomic features are relegated to the frontal plane and do not develop in the round.

The beard and mustache are unusual features which deserve special comment. Stylistically, they are rendered in much the same idiom as the hair on the head–that is, as inorganic elements superimposed on the skin. A three-quarter view from the rear in the direction of the nose reveals that the beard is actually a continuation of the locks of hair falling in front of the ear. The same observation applies to the treatment of the mustache. This execution of the beard and mustache can be regarded as pharaonic. The mustache was fashionable among men in many periods of Egyptian art, both in sculpture in the round and in relief (Desroches-Noblecourt 1947: 187); but a full beard, as opposed to the false beard which is ceremonial and held in place by a strap, although rarely depicted, is generally encountered only in two-dimensional representations (Desroches-Noblecourt 1947; el Tanbouli *et al.* 1978: frontispiece). One might conclude from this summary that the existence of the beard and mustache on this head was prompted by Hellenistic Greek stimuli, were it not for the fact that the full beard appears with greater frequency in Egyptian representations of the Late Period. An interesting *ushabti,* or funerary figure, in faience from Saqqara sports a full beard (Cairo JE 35268; G. Grimm in Hildesheim 1979: no. 74), which can be associated with the Persian presence in Egypt rather than with the Greeks of the Archaic Period, inasmuch as Egyptian craftsmen are known to have replicated via the mimetic principle (pp. 64-65, above) both the costume and accessories of Achaemenid fashion (e.g., Brooklyn 37.353; ESLP: no. 64). The Egyptian replication of the full beard so characteristic of the Persians[1] is in keeping with this phenomenon, as is Osing's suggestion (1980: 1016-19) that the bearded figures shown in some of the tombs of the Eastern Desert (Fakhry 1941: 795, 797; 1973: fig. 75) are depictions of Libyans (see, too, Bresciani 1980: 46-51). It is also a characteristic of the Egyptian Late Period to give plastic expression for the first time to motifs known to have existed earlier exclusively in two-dimensional representations (CATS. 30-32, 66). The appearance of the full beard is to be regarded in this context as well. The beard on the Munich head, therefore, belongs to an established tradition within the tenets of Egyptian art of the Late Period and can be understood in those terms, divorced as they are from Hellenistic influence.

Finally, one should consider the so-called lotus bud diadem shown in the hair of this head. Its rudimentary form, corresponding to the rough treatment of the insignia on the diadem worn by Pakhom (CAT. 32), is sufficiently defined to assure identification. Although parallels are known from other sculptures of the period (ESLP: no. 126), a satisfactory explanation of its significance is yet forthcoming.

[1] A date within the Persian Period for the *ushabti* in Cairo has already been suggested (Bianchi 1982b: 947 note 72). Boardman 1964: 153 associates it with the Greek Archaic Period, and H. Schneider 1977: 347-48 with Cypriote sculpture, but the piece is a more accurate reflection of the Achaemenid fashion, both in the full beard and headdress, than of anything comparable from the Greek orbit.

CAT. 3
Stela with Two Divine Triads

Limestone, 91.5×45.8×7.6 (36×18 1/16×3)
Second century B.C. (?)
Provenance not known
Toronto, Royal Ontario Museum, 910.35.11

Unpublished

Remains of a hieroglyph of heaven are visible along the edge of the rounded top, itself a symbol of heaven and the preeminent stela shape of the Ptolemaic Period, although hardly an innovation of that era. Also an old motif is the winged solar disk with two uraei, a symbol of Horus of Edfu and the tutelary goddesses of Upper and Lower Egypt (CATS. 4, 5). In the Toronto stela, each cobra is looped through a *šn*, symbol of eternity and protection, and holds a feathered fan of the type called *ḫwỉ*, meaning protection (Kees 1912: 126-27), here extended to the figures below (for a somewhat different usage, see L. Bell 1985a: 36-37). According to Munro (1973: 168-69), *ḫwỉ*-fans held by uraei associated with a solar disk are found on some early Ptolemaic royal stelae and begin to appear on private funerary stelae, primarily from Memphis and Northern Egypt, about the middle of the second century B.C. Unfortunately, this does not establish our stela's date nor its general provenance, for there are exceptions to Munro's comments on provenance, and this stela is not clearly funerary.

Equally unfortunate, the identifying texts for the stela's deities and kings–presumably the partially preserved king in the upper register had a counterpart in the scene below–were never carved in the spaces outlined to receive them. Hence it seems simplest to characterize this stela, as has been done for comparable pieces, as "stela of a king" (Pörtner 1908: 13), a votive stela to the gods depicted (Bosticco 1972: figs. 30, 58), or a "stela dedicated to a Ptolemy" (Kamal 1905: 146-47).

That our stela is Ptolemaic is, at least, indicated by its style. That style alone, however, does not permit its precise dating, since there are few detailed studies on Ptolemaic relief styles (pp. 73-75, above), studies which must take into account regional variations and the fact that some "schools" of Ptolemaic relief display very little variation over time (Daumas in *Crépuscule*: 94). Indeed, our figures' "plastic" bodies, the "double chins" on some of them and the forms of the female bodies are the heirs to stylistic tendencies already well developed in early Dynasty XXX (CATS. 10, 11). That this style continues later is evidenced, for instance, by CAT. 15, from the time of Ptolemy IV Philopator (not totally unlike this stela), and by even later works. In general, figures such as ours are often dated to the second century B.C. or later, partly on the basis of the great detail given their attributes and garments.

Despite the lack of texts, the attributes of some of the deities permit their identification as, in the upper register, the Theban Triad of Amun, Mut, and Khonsu and, in the lower, the god Shu, followed by Tefnut, and a form of Horus. Ptolemaic and Roman Period depictions of the latter Triad exist, for example, in temples at Kom Ombo (de Morgan *et al.* 1909: 303), Edfu (Chassinat 1897: 144-45 and pl. XXIIb), Philae (e.g., Junker/Winter 1965: 296-97), and Karnak (De Wit 1958-68, vol. I: 106; vol. II: pl. 3; vol. III: 52-53). That the Theban Triad also appears at Philae (e.g., Junker/Winter 1965: 336-37) as well as Karnak need not mean that either site is the provenance of this stela: the gods of both Triads were worshiped in various parts of Egypt.

CAT. 4

CATS. 4-7
Some Architectural Elements and Decoration

CAT. 4
Upper Part of a Doorway

Limestone, 54.1×93×11.2 (21 5/16×36 5/8×4 7/16)
Ptolemaic Period (?)
Possibly from Tuna el Gebel, near Hermopolis
Hildesheim, Pelizaeus-Museum, 1899

Literature: Derchain 1961: 21-22 and pl. 20, A; Kayser 1973: 115.

CAT. 5
Openwork Window

Limestone, 63.3×69.2×6.6 (24 15/16×27 1/4×2 5/8)
Ptolemaic Period (?)
Said to be from Dendera
London, Courtesy of the Trustees of the British Museum, 1153

Literature: PM VI: 75; E. Bell 1915: 185; Capart 1922: 45 and pl. 191; Jéquier 1924a: 134-35, with fig. 74; Clarke/Engelbach 1930: 176-77.

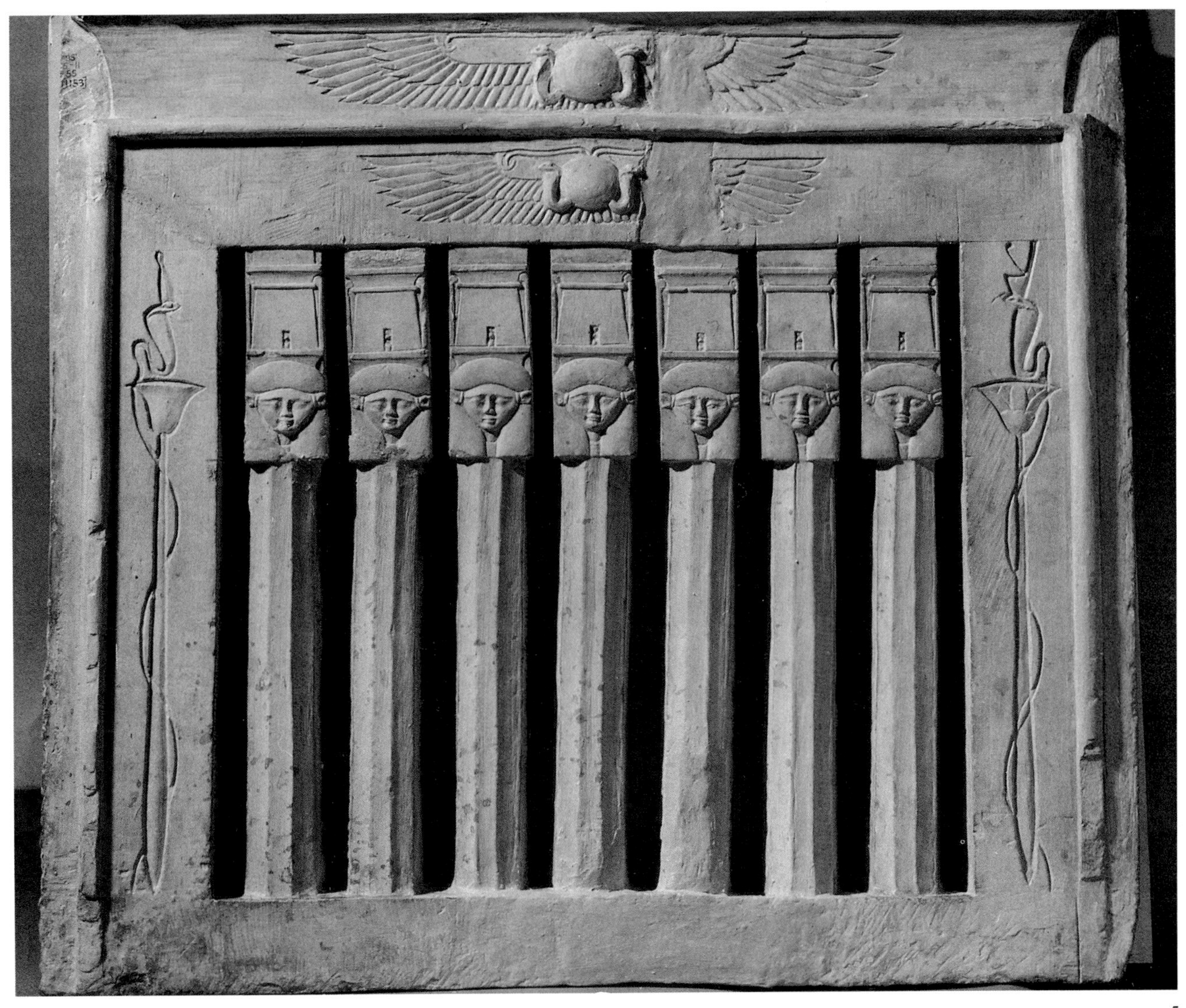

CAT. 5

CAT. 6
Column Capital

Limestone, 35.2×39 (13 7/8×15 3/8)
Ptolemaic-Roman Period
Provenance not known
Hildesheim, Pelizaeus-Museum, 1885

Literature: Roeder/Ippel 1921; 76, fig. 21; 83; Mercklin 1951: 199 and pl. 8a; Kayser 1973: 130 and pl. 90.

CAT. 7
Fragment of a Naos (?)

Gray basalt, 19.7×22×8 (7 3/4×8 11/16×3 1/8)
Probably Ptolemaic Period
Provenance not known
The Brooklyn Museum, 62.46; Charles Edwin Wilbour Fund

Literature: Farkas *et al.* 1964: no. 196 (illus.); Bothmer/Keith 1970: 86-87; 1974: 84-85; Freed 1983: 68, fig. 48.

CAT. 6

As noted in connection with CAT. 3, CATS. 4 and 5 display a common and traditional Egyptian motif, one familiar long before the Ptolemaic Period from the decoration of temples, stelae, and other monuments: the winged sun disk, often with two uraei. As summarized by Wildung (1977a), the winged solar disk with its cobras Nekhbet and Wadjet, the tutelary goddesses of Upper and Lower Egypt, was often shown suspended between heavenly and terrestrial realms (CATS. 3-5, 21, 105, 107, 108, 121, 122, 124), and was a symbol of the kingship that also became a form of manifestation of Horus of Behdet. As Wildung also notes, the Ptolemaic "Legend of the Winged Disk" preserved in the Edfu Temple is in part an attempt to explain the common use of the winged disk on Late Period temples and shrines as an apotropaic image of Horus of Behdet. This lengthy text describes a rebellion against the god Re-Horakhty as King of Egypt by forces of chaos opposed to the divine order, Ma'at (Fairman 1935). The agent of Re-Horakhty's victory is his son, Horus of Behdet, who slays the enemies as "the great winged disk," accompanied by Nekhbet and Wadjet "as two uraei who strike terror in the flesh of the rebels." Victory achieved, Re-Horakhty commands the god Thoth to make an image of the winged disk in every place "in which any gods or goddesses are to this day"; and that disk is defined as "Horus of Behdet" whom "Re-Horakhty has placed in every place of his [in order to] overthrow the rebels" (quotations from Fairman 1935).

But this represents only a partial explanation of the significance of the winged disk as an artistic motif. A few more words must be risked on several complex subjects. To begin, the placement of a solar deity's image on the upper parts of temple walls, doorways, naoi, etc. (cf. CAT. 3) was appropriate to the deity's heavenly nature, especially since a temple, which could embody many concepts in addition to that of a deity's dwelling (Finnestad 1985), was the world in microcosm. This was reflected, for example, in the decoration of ceilings as skies, supported by columns (often with vegetal forms) "growing" from floors associated in various ways with a marshy landscape, as often on the lower parts of walls (Baines 1976: 12). Indeed, temples are directly related to basic ideas concerning The Creation and its daily, seasonal, and annual renewal (pp. 29-39, above), the temples being architectural embodiments of "latent cosmos" and the place of Creation (Finnestad 1985). Hence, according to Finnestad (1985: 94-120, especially 111-12), the series of winged disks marking the theoretical passage of the sun along the main axis of many temples is to be related to ideas about the arrival, with the dawn, of the sun-god. This is equated to his rebirth or transition from "potential being in chaos" to "being," which brings with it all else–that is, his illuminating (i. e., creating) of the world and gods as manifest in the temple's architecture, statuary, and decoration.

The disk with uraei has also been viewed as a solar manifestation of the androgynous nature of the Creator, the disk (normally male) being a "uterine" symbol, and the female uraei "phallic" personifications of the sun's rays (Troy 1986: 20-21).

Since doors (Brunner 1982) in sacred structures are weak points in walls separating the most sacred, the sacred, and the profane, it is understandable that they should receive particular attention in terms of apotropaic imagery. CAT. 4 is the upper part of a "false door," an image of a doorway through which a spiritual entity might come and go. As argued by Derchain (1961: 8, 21-22), the Hildesheim example *may* belong to a subterranean chapel at Tuna el Gebel made for the god Thoth in the time of Ptolemy I (see also Kessler 1983: 108). Nevertheless, its precise provenance, function, and date are unknown. Certainly, however, it shows one door form recessed within another, each having a lintel adorned with a solar disk and two uraei; a typically Egyptian flaring cavetto cornice with winged disk and two uraei; and a frieze of uraei crowned with sun disks above a simulation of rafters.

The uraei on the disks are Nekhbet and Wadjet. The apotropaic frieze of cobras, which could sometimes relate to the concept of uraeus as transporter of the solar disk (K. Martin 1985: 865), is a motif known since the Archaic Period (Kaplony 1977: 188). It became common in the New Kingdom, among other places, on depictions of kiosks consisting of multiple structures, one placed within the other, some with winged disks (e. g., Vandier 1964a: 544-67). These and, for example, a Dynasty XVIII false door at Deir el Bahri (Naville 1895-1908, vol. IV: pl. CIII) are the ancestors of similar two-dimensional depictions in the Third Intermediate and Late Periods (e. g., Munro 1969: 97 and pls. II, IV-IX) and for that era's evolution of multiple false doors in chapels (e. g., Golvin/Goyon 1987: 73 with illus.) and tombs (Assmann 1973: 28-34; Eigner 1984: 120-22, 128-30, 190-91). Some multiple false doors in tombs may be "false temples" and/or depictions of "archetypes of specific shrines" (Assmann 1973: 32-34). They and the multiple false doors in a few chapels must be seen as ancestral to the later doors, false doors (including ours), naoi, and stelae from Egypt of Dynasty XXX (e. g., Traunecker 1982: 341) and later, depicting multiple shrines and/or temples (e. g., Abd el Raziq 1984: 37, 39; Roeder 1914: pl. 39), including monuments of the Ptolemaic and Roman Periods normally associated with Alexandria and its environs (e. g., Le Corsu 1966, 1968), and monuments from the Nile Valley south of Egypt (e. g., Roeder 1911: pls. 82-85; Ricke *et al.* 1967: 25-32; Wenig 1978: 164; Brinks 1983: 27). In fact, CAT. 4 stands within a long pharaonic tradition of quasi-perspectival representations and closely resembles doors made throughout the Ptolemaic and Roman Periods (for some comments on perspectival representations in general, see p. 74, above).

The openwork window of CAT. 5 has a simpler form that evokes a Ptolemaic temple façade (Figs. 1, 7). Here the winged disks with cobras are supplemented by images of Nekhbet (left) and Wadjet (right) on plants symbolizing Upper and Lower Egypt. The mullions are in the form of channeled columns, a reflection of much earlier supports (Jéquier 1924a: 177-84), each with a capital in the shape of a monumental doorway atop a frontal female face with cow's ears: the goddess Hathor (Daumas 1975a). The frontal Hathor face has been viewed as a solar symbol, in keeping with one of her aspects: the female element of the solar theology, with the disk seen as the womb for the solar child, Horus (Troy 1986: 22-23). The two forms together make up an image of the sistrum type called naoform, long associated with Hathor and her cult (cf. CAT. 7), including rituals to appease the goddess and elicit her goodwill (e. g., Daumas 1970: 72-73; George 1978; Germond 1981: 263-64; Ziegler 1984; Tutundjian de Vartavan 1986; the last and LaBranche 1966: 73 would remove this image from the classification of musical instruments). Indeed, this form has been described as symbolic of Hathor as appeased and as the universal goddess (Germond 1981: 263).

Columns with Hathor-head or Hathor-sistrum capitals have a long history inside and outside Egypt (Mercklin 1951; LaBranche 1966; Haeny 1977), including the Ptolemaic Period. This reflects not only Hathor's great importance, but also the association, at least from Dynasty XVIII, of the Hathorean sistrum and capital with other goddesses (J. Clère 1969: 2; Haeny 1977; Ziegler: 1984; 960); and only sometimes in these works is there a clear connection between the goddesses themselves and Hathor. This makes it difficult to identify completely the divine specifications of such symbols of "goddess" unless we know their provenance. Unfortunately, the attribution of our window to Dendera (Budge 1909b: 263; PM VI: 75), a main center of the Hathor cult, is uncertain (E. Bell 1915: 185; Clarke/Engelbach 1930: 176-77), as is Breasted's description of

CAT. 7

it (1936: pl. 324) as coming from an Upper Egyptian temple of about 150 B.C. A clear link with Hathor is, however, perhaps supplied by the seven Hathorean mullions on this window which, as Budge suggested (1914: 22), may refer to the Seven Hathors. They were expressions of Hathor's being who predict fate, their number perhaps connoting totality/perfection (Bleeker 1973: 71-72). They were included in the cults at a number of sites, especially in connection with the temples called *mammisis* (Daumas 1958: 414-18; Gutbub 1973, vol. I: 325).

CAT. 5 has been called a clerestory window (e.g., Budge 1909b: 263; 1914: 22), but this is also doubtful (e.g., Clarke/Engelbach 1930: 173). While our window continues a tradition of openwork windows with fancy forms known from the New

Kingdom and later (e.g., Chevrier 1951: pl. II,2), sometimes as clerestories, if it is from a temple (Clarke/Engelbach 1930: 176-77) it more likely formed a window proper, in a wall, as known in late temples (Jéquier 1924a: 135). Its closest parallel is provided by a very different type of window with Hathor heads in the Ptolemaic Hathor Temple at Deir el Medineh at Thebes (Lepsius 1849-59, pt. I: pl. 88).

For the reasons cited above, it is also impossible to identify the specific divine associations of CAT. 6, the unprovenanced column capital with four Hathor faces surmounted by cavetto cornices. The top of this capital has recesses, quite likely for the attachment of a form on all four sides akin to those in CAT. 5 (Mercklin 1951: 199). In general, this capital may be attributed to the Ptolemaic or early Roman Period, a precise dating made difficult by the considerable similarity among Hathor faces produced at various times (e.g., Ziegler 1979: 40-62, and pp. 72-73, above). As noted by Mercklin (1951: 199), parallels for the rosettes in the coiffures are provided by a capital of related type in the Louvre. Indeed, the rosettes are associated with female jewelry for the head from many periods. When they appear on Hathor's head one might wonder if they symbolize stars, associated with her as a "sky-goddess," or if they are open lotuses, solar and birth symbols (e.g., Barguet 1953: 104-05; Brunner-Traut 1980; Germond 1981: 325), all of which would be appropriate to Hathor, including Hathor of the Four Countenances, or Quadrifrons.

Hathor Quadrifrons has been explained (Derchain 1972) as a representation of universal power comprising the four quarters of the world or of Egypt. It has also been explained as Hathor in association or sometimes even in fusion with other goddesses to personify the sexual excitement that permeates the universe and was necessary to the original demiurge's act of creation, wherein he swallowed his masturbated seed and spit forth a pair of gods who then begot other gods. This excitement must be present for each renewal of creation. Even if the fully evolved idea concerning a female creative power was a late development, some form of it must have been present earlier, and helps explain how even pre-Ptolemaic capitals with four Hathor faces were theological rather than architectural creations (Capart 1944: 226).

CAT. 7 is included in this multiple entry in part because of its subject matter. A king, set within a frame whose top is a hieroglyph for heaven, holds two naoform sistra that he is said "to play" (lit. "make") for his mother so that she will give life. The object of this ritual act, Hathor, appears in human form but is crowned, above a diadem of cobras, with cow's horns supporting a sun disk. She is labeled Hathor, Mistress of the Southern Sycamore, one of her traditional cult epithets since the New Kingdom, and is stated to give the king the "lifetime [of the god] Re," and "years of [the god] Atum," both traditional gifts of goddesses to pharaohs.

The king, alas not named, appears in a traditional gala kilt and wears the Double Crown of Upper and Lower Egypt. The Lower Egyptian part is adorned with circles, which seem to be a feature of this crown mainly for Ptolemaic and Roman times (for disks on the Blue Crown in post-Persian and pre-Ptolemaic times, see ESLP: 88-89; Aldred in *Crépuscule*: 154, fig. 135. Disks can also appear on the Lower Egyptian Crown worn by the goddess Neith in pre-Ptolemaic bronzes). If so, this would help support the attribution of this object to the Ptolemaic Period, perhaps even to the reign of Ptolemy II Philadelphos (Bothmer/Keith 1974: 84). Nevertheless, this fragment is strongly linked stylistically to earlier works. Those links include the bichromatic effect of the lighter carving against the darker polished ground for relief, which is attested ages before the Ptolemaic Period and was very popular during Dynasty XXX for the decoration of sarcophagi (e.g., Maspero 1914: pls. I-VIII) and naoi (e.g., Roeder 1914: pls. 11-33; for bichromy in statuary, see p. 72, above). Moreover, the modeling of the figures' bodies, and even their physiognomies, are not far removed from those on naoi of Dynasty XXX (e.g., Roeder 1914: pls. 19, 23, 32-33). This is one more documentation of the fact, emphasized in this catalogue, that the art of the Ptolemaic Period was closely related to that of Sebennytic times.

Indeed, it is mainly naoi of Dynasty XXX that provide decent parallels in hard stone for our small-scale scene of a king offering (e.g., Roeder 1914: pls. 12, 18, 21, 24, 28) – another reason for including it in this multiple entry. In Brooklyn's accession records, this piece is described as a complete object, perhaps a votive offering, presumably because no fragmentary scene adjoins it as one might expect on a naos. Its rough edges, however, suggest that it might not be an ex-voto, but rather part of a naos broken up before completion (Bothmer/Keith 1970; 1974). In either case, and without precluding the possibility that it is a fragment of a completed naos, it at least calls to mind the Late Period penchant for adorning naoi with images of the divine inhabitants and cult images of their temples or of using them to "illustrate" compendia or "mythological catalogues" on papyri (in temple archives) of the deities, cult objects, etc. for a particular locality (Redford 1981: 94; 1986b: 216). For the naoslike decoration of the sanctuary of the Late Period Hibis Temple, see N. Davies 1953: pls. 2-5; Cruz-Uribe 1987: 219-20.

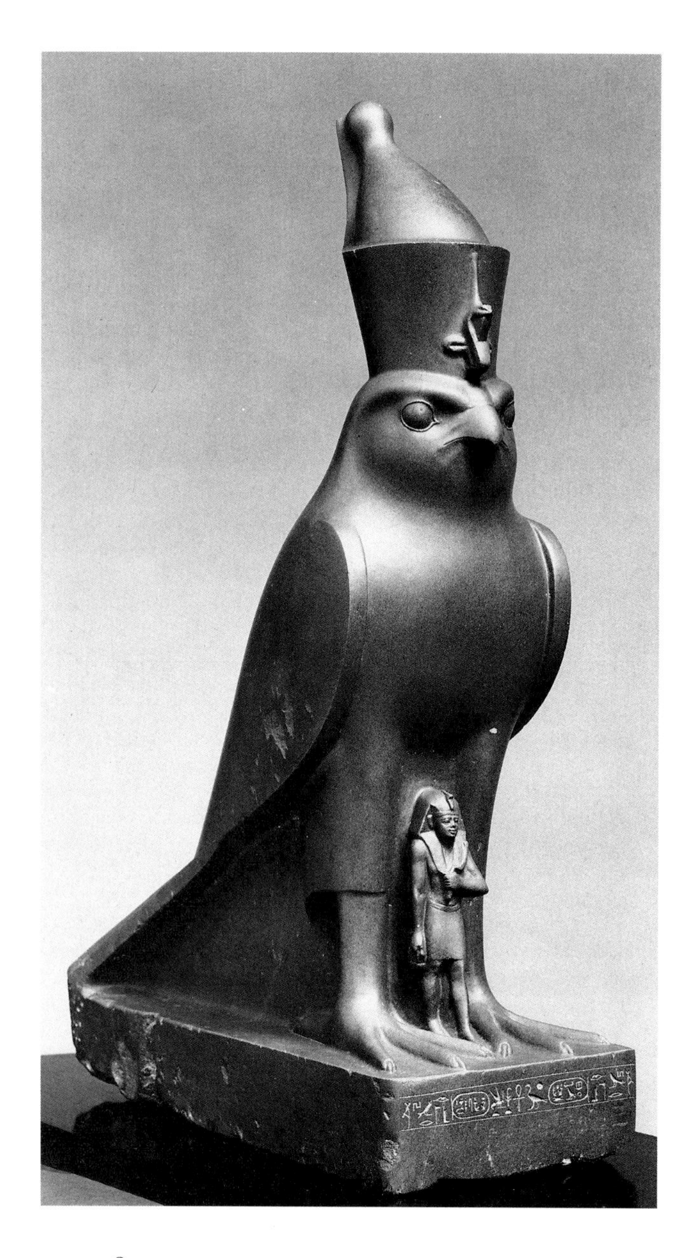

CAT. 8

Nectanebo II before a Falcon

Greenish graywacke, 72×20.5×46.5 (28 3/8×8 1/16×18 5/16)
Reign of Nectanebo II (360-342 B.C.)
Probably from the area of Heliopolis
New York, The Metropolitan Museum of Art, 34.2.1; Rogers Fund, 1934

Literature: Winlock 1934: 186-87; Bosse 1936: 70 and pl. VIIIc; Westendorf 1968: 216; Simpson 1971: 162 and 163, fig. 12; Vandersleyen 1975: 269 and fig. 227a; Holm-Rasmussen 1979: pl. 1.

CAT. 9

A King in Falcon Garb

Blue-glazed faience, 18×6.5×10.5 (7 1/16×2 9/16×4 1/8)
Ptolemaic Period (?)
Provenance not known
Leiden, Rijksmuseum van Oudheden F 1937/6.9

Literature: Wijngaarden 1938; Brunner 1962: 77 and pl. VI; H. Schneider/Raven 1981: 144-45.

CAT. 9

The statue of the last native pharaoh backed by a falcon wearing the Double Crown of Upper and Lower Egypt displays "the predilection so often shown in Late Period statuary for dark, homogeneous materials with smooth, lustrous surfaces modeled in sweeping, freely flowing curves" (Yoyotte 1968: 204; also Winlock 1934: 187). It derives its monumentality from its simple, volumetric forms and suppression of details, including the markings around the eyes found on most depictions of Egypt's preeminent raptor (Simpson 1971: 162). Given the very small scale of the king, all that will be said about his physiognomy is that it displays general affinities with the features given Nectanebo II in *some* of his temple reliefs (CAT. 10).

Iconographically, our sculpture and several related statues of Nectanebo II mentioned below are interesting variations on the always common themes of the relationships between the falcon-god Horus and the pharaoh as his terrestrial emanation (e.g., CATS. 3, 9, 13).

Among the numerous motifs and depictions of kings in these relationships, only a few New Kingdom works provide reasonable prototypes for this image of a king backed by a much larger falcon (Leibovitch 1944: 169; Habachi 1969: 39; Rössler-Köhler 1978; Eaton-Krauss 1981: 15-18; Stadelmann 1987). Given their early dates, the question remains as to whether Nectanebo II's sculpture was influenced by works of the New Kingdom (Scharff 1941: 200-03; 1949: 319-20), was derived from lost post-New Kingdom works, or represents a relatively independent late artistic expression. At the least, the statues of Nectanebo II with falcon are not the only late variation on the theme of pharaoh and/or a private person protected by a larger theriomorphic deity (e.g., Legrain 1894: 56-57, no. 178; Borchardt 1930: nos. 676, 683, 784; Capart 1941: 11-12). One of the most interesting is the later statue of a falcon with human figure (priest or king?) at the Edfu Temple (Chassinat 1934b: pl. DCLV; p. 67, above).

As for the other sculptures of Nectanebo II with a falcon behind him, they differ from each other and from the Metropolitan's statue in terms of material; the precise pose, garb, and attributes of the king; their inscriptions; and their provenances (Tresson 1933: 144-49 and pl. VII; Vigneau 1936: 133; Montet 1952: pl. XI; Barguet 1954: 88-91; Habachi 1963: 47, and pl. VIII). To judge from the plate cited in Montet, one of them also lacked such details as the falcon's facial markings.

In much earlier sculptures of king with falcon, the falcon is small relative to the pharaoh. For this reason some have seen the relative sizes of this statue's figures as reflecting the declining status of the earthly king vis-à-vis the heavenly king (e.g., Westendorf 1968: 216; Lloyd 1983: 291), a process that began well before Dynasty XXX (Spalinger 1978a: 29, 32) and led ultimately to the royal human incumbent becoming secondary to the divine and animal images of the kingship (Alliot 1954: 674-76; p. 32-37, above). Such an interpretation is not impossible. Moreover, as suggested by Johnson (1983: 64), the emphasis Nectanebo II's sculptures place on his identification or association with the Horus-falcon is perhaps to be related to contemporary textual equations of "office of ruler" with "appearance as falcon" and a desire on Nectanebo's part to stress his legitimacy as pharaoh following his ousting of his predecessor.

Nevertheless, the sculptures of Nectanebo II with falcon are open to other interpretations because the text on one calls him "King of Upper and Lower Egypt, the divine falcon born of Isis," whereas the New York sculpture is a rebus of the king's name *Nakht-Hor-heb*, "Horus is Great [lit. strong] of Festivals," with the falcon being Hor(us) and the king holding symbols reading *nakht* (strong) and *heb* (festival).[1] These both suggest identification of the king with the god (Yoyotte 1959: 73-74). As a result, the statues of Nectanebo II with falcon have been linked to a cult of that king attested by inscriptions (some of which call him *p3 bi͗k*: "the falcon") from Dynasty XXX down into Ptolemaic times (e.g., Yoyotte 1959: 73-74; De Meulenaere 1960a: 99-101; Holm-Rasmussen 1979: 22-25). Such a cult of statues would be in keeping with those known for some kings of earlier periods and for Nectanebo I (De Meulenaere 1960a). With Nectanebo II, the cult, during his lifetime and after, would have encompassed the worship of "the falcon," a particular divine form of Nectanebo II as manifest in the statues discussed. Whether this cult was limited to sites where Nectanebo II commissioned significant architectural projects (De Meulenaere 1960a: 100, 107) or reflects his achievements in general (Holm-Rasmussen 1979) has been a subject of discussion. More recently, the cult of Nectanebo II has been linked to the concern he (and Dynasty XXX) displayed for the temples and gods, especially Horus of Edfu; and his sculptures, to which "his soul was believed to return to perpetuate his existence on earth under the auspices of the god Horus" perceived as appropriate forms for commemorating him who proved to be the last native pharaoh (Reymond 1986).[2]

As noted above, pharaoh's association and/or identification with Horus was expressed in Egyptian art in many ways: for example, through the depiction of a falcon by his head or as part of the decoration of his headgear (e.g., Vandier 1958: pls. II, CXXV, CXXXII; Brunner-Traut 1971; Russmann 1981: 151-55; Myśliwiec 1985: pl. VI); and the depiction of king as semi-falcon or in falcon dress (e.g., Brunner 1958, 1962; Giza-Podgórski 1984; Kriéger 1960; Radwan 1975a: 104; 1976: 28-29; 1985: 64-67). Such motifs as falcon images on royal headgear are attested in Ptolemaic times,[3] which have also bequeathed us an image of a priest wearing a falcon costume when playing the role of Horus (Goyon 1985, vol. I: 170).
Another possible Ptolemaic variation on the latter theme is CAT. 9. This faience figure from Leiden shows a king whose headcloth, kilt, and pose are known since the Old Kingdom; whose falcon cloak is best related to New Kingdom images of pharaoh; and the general style of whose faience openwork calls to mind stylistic tendencies common from the Third Intermediate Period on. If the piece is correctly attributed to the Ptolemaic Period, mainly on the basis of its blue glaze color (Wijngaarden 1938; H. Schneider/Raven 1981: 144-45), it would be the one certain three-dimensional image of a king in falcon dress of that era. The one possibly comparable work of the next era is a Roman Egyptianizing bronze that may depict a king as falcon (Leclant/Clerc 1972: 67) but which could be a *ba*-bird (Carducci 1965: 125-26; for *ba*-birds, see CATS. 108, 124).
The kneeling and bound prisoner on each side of the Leiden king's throne is a variation on another basic Egyptian artistic theme: the juxtaposition of the king with symbols, in poses of defeat, of Egypt's actual earthly enemies, who are considered emanations of Isfet ("chaos") in opposition to Ma'at.

[1] And/or "Powerful is Horus of Hebyt," Hebyt being the area of Behbeit el Higara (cf. CAT. 13).
[2] See also Bonhême/Forgeau 1988, which appeared after this entry was written. On pp. 66-67 the falcons of Nectanebo II's statues are described as "transfigured royal effigies," and the composition of the sculptures is seen as expressing a relationship between the physical person of the king and the god. Indeed, these Dynasty XXX sculptures and their texts are viewed as expressing new ideas concerning the total identification of the king and Horus-Son-of-Isis, and as images of the king conceived as the living incarnation of the god (Bonhême/Forgeau 1988: 72).
[3] Brunner-Traut 1971: 21-25 discusses some examples of the motif of a falcon on the rear of royal headgear ranging in date from early Dynasty XVIII to the reign of Trajan. These include a number of small plaques with heads of kings wearing the Blue Crown adorned with a uraeus with double coil, which have normally been labeled Dynasty XXX-Ptolemaic or attributed specifically to the Ptolemaic Period. In a recent study, Bothmer (in New York 1987: 76-79) has argued that these plaques, as well as some with Blue Crown and double-coiled uraeus but without the falcon, are images of Nectanebo II because: (1) at least one Dynasty XXX relief of Nectanebo II depicts him with a Blue Crown with double-coiled uraeus; whereas (2) if the Blue Crown is attested in temple reliefs of Ptolemaic kings, the double-coiled uraeus is not so represented on any crown; and (3) the facial features of many of the images on the plaques are similar to each other and to those in some temple reliefs of Nectanebo II.
Bothmer also views the falcon figures on the crowns as possible references to the cult of Nectanebo II "the Falcon" (CAT. 8), and he suggests that if the plaques are not all the work of Dynasty XXX, then they may be posthumous ex-votos connected with a cult of Nectanebo. Finally, he rejects as "untenable" the dating to the first century B.C. of one of the plaques, where the representation of a king includes the figure of a falcon (Hildesheim 1979: no. 197C), because other stucco reliefs from the same "lot" date to the fourth century B.C.
There are, however, several problems with these interpretations. They include: (1) the fact that the double-coiled uraeus is known from Ptolemaic temple reliefs (Spanel 1988: cat. 45); (2) the facial features on the plaques are also related to those on representations of several post-Dynasty XXX pharaohs; (3) the Blue Crown and the double-coiled uraeus are not clearly associated with monuments definitely connected with cults of Nectanebo II "the Falcon"; (4) the falcon on the rear of a crown has a long history as an expression of various concepts of the relationship between Horus and Pharaoh valid for any king (pp. 30-33, above).
As for the plaster relief in Hildesheim, the "lot" to which it is said to have belonged is that of a Cairo dealer and not a scientifically excavated find (Reinsberg 1980). In fact, the numerous objects in the lot appeared in Cairo over a period of several years, and they include objects that are clearly Ptolemaic (CAT. 51) and later. And it should be noted that CAT. 22, which is clearly Roman in date, was stated to be from near the findspot of the Hildesheim plaque's "lot" (Hildesheim 1979: 197D).

CAT. 10

Nectanebo II before the Bull-Headed Apis

Limestone, 39.6×63.5×8.5 (15 9/16×25×3 3/8)
Reign of Nectanebo II (360-342 B.C.)
Memphis, from the East Temple in the vicinity of the Serapeum
Paris, Musée du Louvre, Département des Antiquités Egyptiennes, N. 423

Literature: PM III², 2: 779 (top); Wibrech 1971: 26; G. Martin 1979: 92, 99.

This rectangular block is decorated in sunk relief and shows the king at left making an offering to the Apis Bull (CAT. 105). The regularly spaced, diagonal traces of the chisel, visible in the lower half of the block, would seem to indicate that the relief was not finished. The inscriptions contain the nomen and prenomen of Nectanebo II and a banal recitation by Apis granting the king all life and all dominion. This block is almost an exact duplicate, down to the appearance of a lone pole wrapped with cloth (Gardiner 1957: Sign List R8) in the field between the two figures, of a second block from this same temple (G. Martin 1973: 92, 99).

The cult of the Apis (Winter 1978) at Memphis gained in importance under the Kushites of Dynasty XXV (Vercoutter 1960) and continued to develop unabated through Dynasties XXVI and XXVII (Posener 1936: 30, *passim*), into the reign of Nectanebo II, who presumably installed the Apis (Lauer 1976: 21-28; Daressy 1908, in which read "Nectanebo II" for "Nectanebo I") that died shortly after the arrival into Egypt of Ptolemy as satrap (Murphy 1985: 110-11, commenting on Diodorus Siculus' *Historical Library*, I, 84-85). During the course of the Ptolemaic Period, the cult of the Apis Bull was an extremely useful vehicle by which the Ptolemies could both associate with and incorporate themselves into the framework of the pharaonic religious traditions at Memphis (D. Crawford 1980; 1983; Fig. 43; CAT. 65). The cult survived until 362 A.D., when it is mentioned for the last time by Ammianus Marcellinus (Hermann 1960).

Despite the apparent lack of finishing touches to the block, the face of Nectanebo II is complete, finely modeled, and perfectly preserved. The buttonhole eye, aquiline nose with flaring nostril and turned-up wing, and pursed mouth with small lips are at variance with the corresponding features of the so-called canonical image of Nectanebo II, so often cited in the literature as the one created during his lifetime and adopted virtually unchanged for the subsequent ideal images of Dynasty XXX and the Ptolemaic Period (CAT. 1). The intense interest in the linear adjuncts of the Paris face, in the form of nasolabial furrows, and the separation of the chin from the lower jaw became fixed stylistic features in the subsequent depictions of faces throughout the Ptolemaic Period. The canonical image, of which the sickle-shaped smile of the lips is the most diagnostic feature (ESLP: no. 96), exists side by side with the more somber depiction of the Paris relief, which is itself indebted to the images of Nectanebo I, as a comparison between the face of Nectanebo II shown here and the preserved faces of Mut and Khonsu on both the Luxor Stela (Abd el Raziq 1968: 156 and pl. XLIVa) and Sphinx 34 of the Dromos of the Luxor Temple reveals (CAT. 120; and Abd el Raziq 1968: pls. XLVb, XLVIa). These same features, but without the developed interest in linear adjuncts, are already established at Thebes during Dynasty XXIX (Traunecker *et al.* 1981: 31, pl. A), a period that is gradually emerging as a heretofore ignored source for some of the stylistic features observed in the art of Dynasty XXX (CATS. 23, 24).

The representation of the theriomorphic Apis in the reliefs from the East Temple at Memphis are consistent in their depiction of the horns which invariably emerge directly from the crown of the head with the near horn almost touching the ear. Dated Ptolemaic images on Memphite stelae depart from this formula (Wildung 1977b: nos. 44, 45). These latter depictions are so stylistically akin to undated representations in other collections that one can suggest, for example, that the stela in Marseilles, questionably assigned to Dynasty XXX (Marseilles 46 [246], Wildung 1977b: no. 19), is to be assigned to the Ptolemaic Period instead.

CAT. 11
Representation of Alexander, Son of Alexander

Granite, 58×78 (22 13/16×30 11/16)
317-311 B.C.
Provenance not known, perhaps from Samanoud
Paris, Musée du Louvre, Département des Antiquités Egyptiennes, E. 10970

Literature: Loyrette 1977.

The identification of this figure as Alexander, the son of Alexander, variously designated either as Alexander II or IV, is assured by his completely preserved titulary in the field above his hands (von Beckerath 1984: 286, no. 3 [T3 and E1]). He offers incense and cool water to "Geb, the son of Re, the count who is at the head of...," as indicated by the text above the *was*-scepter at the far left. Geb bestows "[all life], dominion, health, and joy" to the monarch, who is shown wearing an elaborate headdress of ram's horns, ostrich plumes, sun disk, and uraei. Although the valanced wig, with its echelon curls beneath the headdress, has been described as a conscious evocation of a fashion popular during the Old Kingdom (Munich, Glyptothek 29, a Dynasty XXX head; ESLP: no. 77), the possibility nevertheless exists that such a combination might equally be indebted to the repertoire of standard iconographic attributes (Myśliwiec 1985: 151).

Alexander, eventually assassinated while still a minor, never resided in Egypt, although the country was ruled in his name by Philip Arrhidaeus, a half-brother of Alexander the Great. The scale of this sunk relief indicates that it came from a principal monument commissioned by Philip Arrhidaeus on behalf of the younger Alexander, as was also the case for the granite doorway on Elephantine (PM V, 227). The block might, perhaps, be associated with a temple at Samanoud, where the cartouches of the minor and his regent have been identified in association with the deity Geb (Edgar 1911: 93, block 6).

Stylistically, the relief occupies the transitional phase between one of the artistic styles of Dynasty XXX and that of the subsequent early Ptolemaic Period. The valanced wig with its stepped curls, the delicate plastic brow and paint stripes of the hieroglyphic eye, the angle of the bridge of the nose, its nostril set off by a deep nasolabial furrow, the thin, horizontal lips with drilled corners, and the rounded, offset chin in the form of a golf ball find their exact parallels not only in the head in Munich cited above, but also in the head of CAT. 24, the Dattari statue. This comparison makes it patently clear that the formula operative during the reign of Nectanebo I for the creation of an idealizing, male representation continued to be employed during the Macedonian Period. It is important to stress that this

formula is frequently employed for royal and for non-royal representations both in relief and in the round during the reign of Nectanebo I.

As a result, one can no longer maintain the prevailing opinion that this particular relief style was inaugurated during the reign of Nectanebo II (CATS. 1, 120). As is so often the case with artistic phenomena throughout the history of ancient Egyptian art, the dominant aesthetic trends that become established at the beginning of any particular dynasty are routinely repeated thereafter. Thus the art of Dynasty XXX, particularly that produced under Nectanebo I, must be regarded as the linear ancestor of trends still in place during the early Ptolemaic Period. Egyptian culture of the second half of the fourth century B. C. seems to be characterized by a certain uniformity in its artistic expression and a degree of continuity in its political and religious life (De Meulenaere 1958; 1960a; 1963; Spalinger 1978b) which belies the historical circumstances of a seemingly decentralized administration and relentless confrontations with foreign powers. The resiliency of the native Egyptians and their tenacious grip on their own cultural identity foreshadow the ascendancy of native Egyptian elements in the second and first centuries B. C., when Egypt was again wracked by internal chaos and foreign aggression. These circumstances are yet one more cogent reason to regard native Egyptian culture during the Ptolemaic Period as wholly integrated into the fabric of pharaonic Egypt.

CAT. 12
Ptolemy I Offering Ma'at

Limestone, 36×142 (14 3/16×55 7/8)
Reign of Ptolemy I (305-282 B. C.)
The Temple of Per-kheft in the region of Behnasa/Oxyrhynchos
Leiden, Rijksmuseum van Oudheden, F 1961/12.3

Literature: Braat/Klasens 1968: 42-43 and pl. 77; Sauneron 1968: 24-27 and pl. I; H. Schneider/Raven 1981: 140-41.

Preserved are back-to-back scenes of Ptolemy I offering images of the goddess Ma'at. To the right, Ptolemy wears the Upper Egyptian Crown and his name receives symbols of infinity/eternity and dominion from a hieroglyph for the tutelary goddess of Upper Egypt. To the left such symbolism is all for Lower Egypt. The partially preserved recipient god on the left was Horus, son of Osiris and Isis, and a possible symbol of Lower Egypt. Behind him was presumably a figure of Isis. To the right the recipient god is Dedwen, perhaps originally a Nubian deity (Onasch 1984: 135), but by now long at home in Egypt, often as symbolic of Nubia (Otto 1975b; Goyon *et al.* 1979: 66-67). Here he is labeled "son of Osiris," which suggests that the goddess behind him may be a form of Isis (Braat/Klasens 1968). Nevertheless, she is twice given the name Madjet, which *may* be related to a homonymous Nubian toponym; here she and Dedwen may also represent Nubia, perhaps viewed as part of Upper Egypt, as well as Upper Egypt proper (for Isis south of Egypt, see Leclant 1982).

The relief's texts also associate all these deities with the toponym Per-kheft, which can be located in Middle Egypt (Sauneron 1968: 24-27). In fact, these scenes are not the only reliefs known from the still lost temple of Per-kheft (Dewachter 1983: 45). The star-studded band, presumably part of a large hieroglyph for heaven, suggests that our scenes come from the upper register of scenes on a wall; and it is near the top of a wall, including above doorways, that one often finds such mirror scenes of the offering of Ma'at. It has been suggested that our

scenes came from an east wall of the temple, symbolic north and south corresponding with actual north and south (H. Schneider/Raven 1981: 141).

As a temple scene, the offering of Ma'at is known from Dynasty XVIII onward: Teeter (1986) provides a preliminary history of such scenes, and observes (p. 8) that they are relatively uncommon compared with other cult scenes. Perhaps this is because the Ma'at-offering symbolizes all that the cult signifies, being a declaration that pharaoh has discharged his primary responsibility of helping maintain the fragile divine order (incarnate in Ma'at) as at the time of the Creation, a duty placed in his heart and guaranteed by the Creator (Hornung 1982: 213-16; Graefe 1979).

In a study of royal physiognomies in some reliefs of Ptolemies I and II, Myśliwiec (1974) observed that the former differ from the latter in having more voluminous chins, less arched eyebrows, less distinct and shorter plastic eyebrow and eyepaint lines, more prominent depressions under the eyes, and hence more prominent cheeks, and eyes that are sometimes shorter and more widely opened. To an extent, these distinctions are supported by our relief, which displays one of several variations on a theme known from other reliefs of Ptolemy I (e. g., Bothmer 1952b; Derchain 1961: pls. 5-10). Nevertheless, these are variations on essentially the same theme, variations that permeate many reliefs of Ptolemy II (and later) and grow out of stylistic conventions for faces (e. g., the "puffy" faces with "double chins") and bodies (e. g., tripartite torsos with prominent navels, swelling female bellies, and strongly projecting female breasts), well in place by the beginning of Dynasty XXX (Munro 1973: 177, with reference to Roeder 1954: pls. VII-IX; better photograph in Bianchi 1979b, pl. 3; see also the stela illustrated in Abd el Raziq 1968: pl. XLIV,a). Indeed one can find stylistic prototypes for the rounded faces (Yoyotte 1972: pl. 19B), sometimes with hints of a "double chin" (Bianchi 1979b: pl. 4) and, in statuary, actual tripartite male torso modeling since Dynasty XXVI (ESLP: xxxv); and hints of tripartite modeling with ample forms as early as the Libyan Period (Aldred 1956: 7; Russmann 1981: 152-54).

CAT. 13
Scenes of Offering

Red granite, 86.3×129.5 (33×50)
Fourth-third century B.C.
From Behbeit el Higara (?)
Richmond, Virginia Museum of Fine Arts, 63.45; The Williams Fund

Literature: Steindorff 1945: 54-55, no. 15, fig. 18; Reed/Near 1973: 56-57, no. 65, illus.

Two significant sources of temple reliefs in hard stone, ranging in date from Dynasty XXX to the early Ptolemaic Period, are the central Delta sites of Samanoud (known best by its Greek name, Sebennytos), home of Dynasty XXX, and Behbeit el Higara, nine kilometers away and the site of the Iseion (or Iseum), the main Isis temple of the era. Even in ruins, the Iseion reflects the great veneration for Isis in Sebennytic and Ptolemaic times, a veneration that had been growing for quite a while.[1] Enough is known of the reliefs of the temples at Samanoud and Behbeit el Higara to permit the general attribution to Samanoud/Behbeit el Higara of a group of similar reliefs, such as CAT. 13, whose modern history begins with their appearance in a private collection or on the art market. However, several factors often make it impossible to attribute any of these reliefs specifically to one site or the other. First, neither site has been investigated thoroughly or scientifically, meaning that we lack all sorts of information about the temples and their decorative programs that could facilitate such attributions. Another factor, hardly surprising given the sites' proximity in time and space, is that the temple reliefs of Samanoud and Behbeit el Higara are so similar in style that they cannot be distinguished with certainty on that basis alone (Steindorff 1945: 44-45; Bothmer 1953a: 3). As a result, no more definite provenance than "probably from Behbeit" (Steindorff 1945: 54; Reed/Near 1973: 57) has ever been proposed for the Richmond relief.

CAT. 13 preserves parts of three scenes in sunk relief. In the central scene a king offers incense to a falcon-headed deity who, as noted by Steindorff (1945: 54) could well be the moon-god, Khonsu. The traces of decoration above the king could be the lower part of a device for associating the terrestrial and divine kings: a solar disk from which hang uraei, *ankh*-signs and *was*-signs, framing a writing of "Behdetite, Great God, Lord of Heaven" (Lepsius 1849-59, pt. IV: pl. 26). The scenes to the right and left of the central panel were probably similar in format. Of the scene to the right, all that is preserved is part of the figure of an offering king. Of the scene to the left, it is the divine recipient of an offering who remains. This goddess, wearing a vulture headdress and a circlet of uraei (Troy 1986: 122) crowned with cow's horns and a sun disk, could be Isis, but she might also be Hathor, who can appear in the same guise (CAT. 7), including at Behbeit el Higara (Naville 1930: pl. 9).

Many of the stylistic features of the Richmond relief, as in works cited throughout this catalogue, are common to the art of Dynasty XXX and of the Ptolemaic Period–for example, the slightly smiling faces, the strongly projecting female breast, and the tripartite modeling of the male torso. It is very difficult, therefore, to distinguish between Dynasty XXX and Ptolemaic reliefs at Samanoud and Behbeit el Higara unless royal names are preserved, and very few of the preserved names are from Dynasty XXX (e.g., Steindorff 1945: figs. 2-4). Even for Egyptian art the reliefs display surprisingly little variation.[2] As a result, attributions of the Richmond relief to the time of Nectanebo II (e.g., Steindorff 1945: 54; Reed/Near 1973: 57) remain tentative. In fact, CAT. 13 also resembles some of Behbeit's reliefs inscribed for Ptolemy II and displays some of the physiognomic stylizations Myśliwiec claims as characteristic of reliefs of Ptolemy I at some other sites (CAT. 12).

[1] If, as noted by Lloyd (1983: 294), the first substantial temple to Isis was a Dynasty XXVI construction at Memphis, it should be remembered that this was not her earliest chapel/temple. For example, as argued by De Meulenaere (1982: 25-27), there may have been at least a small structure functioning as a *mammisi* of Isis in Ramesside times at Abydos. In the same period, Buto and nearby Khemmis in the central Delta became important in "cultic topography" because of the myth of Isis hiding her child Horus in the swamps of Khemmis until he was grown and could wrest his inheritance of divine kingship from Seth, murderer of Horus' father, Osiris (Redford 1983: 82-83; pp. 30, 33-36, above). By Dynasty XXII, Karnak had a small Isis temple (Redford 1986a), and from the same general era come the earliest sculptures in the round of Isis with her child Horus (M. Müller 1985: 213-22; for later examples, see CATS. 100, 101). These and the much later construction of great Isis temples such as the Iseion are presumably to be related to the rise in importance, beginning no later than very early Dynasty XXI, of the cults of child-gods, divine Triads, "mammisiac religion," and a "veritable theology of birth." It has been argued (Redford 1983: 83; 1986b: 329-30; M. Müller 1985: 213-22) that these developments were consciously abetted by the less than all-powerful kings of the early Third Intermediate Period. If so, then those kings and their era provided the prototype for what Lloyd (1983: 294) has described as both the "sudden efflorescence" of the cult of Isis in the Late Period and its partial dependence on the cult's significance to the kingship in an era when "the concept of kingship needed all the support it could get." Isis was the mother of Horus, with whom the pharaoh was identified, and as her cult was increasingly popular in general, royal support of it would be well received by the populace.

[2] Even acknowledging the conservative nature of much Egyptian art, it is difficult to accept Steindorff's statement (1945: 44-45) that one need not expect a noticeable change in style over the course of a century. It is perhaps better to describe the stylistic continuity in the reliefs from Samanoud and Behbeit el Higara, as Bothmer did (1953a: 5), in terms of the Egyptian craftsman's ability, when necessary, to imitate exceedingly well the style of an earlier period. The reigns of Ptolemies I and II display a great urge to know and copy the native Egyptian culture, art, and religion, and a desire to conciliate the autochthonous population (cf. Redford 1986b: 204-05), to whom Dynasty XXX was very important.

CAT. 14
Ptolemy II and Arsinoe II as *Theoi Adelphoi*

Limestone, 42.4×34.5 (16 11/16×13 3/16)
200-190 B.C.
From Tanis
London, Courtesy of the Trustees of the British Museum, 1056; Gift of the Egypt Exploration Fund 1885

Literature: Petrie 1885: 31; Quaegebeur 1971a: 239, *passim*; 1971b.

This complete relief, inscribed with the names and titles both of Ptolemy II and Arsinoe II, was found at Tanis with several

CAT. 14

other objects on the ground in front of a brick chapel; a recess in the west wall of the chapel contained a stela inscribed for Ptolemy IV and Arsinoe III (CAT. 15). This stela and several more found scattered in the vicinity of that chapel indicate that a Tanite Triad dedicated to Min, Horsiese, and Wadjet was firmly established at Tanis during the Ptolemaic Period.

Quaegebeur, in his discussions of this relief, has concluded that it is yet one more example of a group of representations that depict Ptolemy II Philadelphos adoring Arsinoe II deified, on the basis of her accompanying inscriptions (Quaegebeur 1971a: 239, *passim*; 1971b). Wearing the tightly fitting sheath, Arsinoe II holds a papyrus, or *wadj*-scepter (Sethe 1929), and the *ankh*-sign (Fischer 1973a), attributes that can be regarded as emblems of deification and which, therefore, support Quaegebeur's philological interpretation. The distinctive crown (Fig. 18), once thought to be the exclusive headdress of Arsinoe II (Quaegebeur 1971b: 198-200), is now known to have been worn by other Ptolemaic queens as well (Quaegebeur 1983b: 110-11).

Although Arsinoe II deified is to be regarded as the principal figure in the relief because she occupies the left-hand side of the composition, which the laws of orientation in Egyptian art deemed the position of primacy, the figure of Ptolemy II Philadelphos is taller, itself an artistic conceit connoting importance. That two artistic conventions are played off against each other would seem to indicate that neither figure is to be regarded as the principal one. This observation is supported by the fact that the inscriptions mention no offerings whatsoever and that other artistic conventions governing offerer and recipient, including the offering table, are totally lacking. As a result, this relief must be removed from the group of depictions of Ptolemy II adoring Arsinoe II deified, to which Quaegebeur has assigned it (Quaegebeur 1971a; 1971b).

Ptolemy II Philadelphos strides forward, holding a *was*-scepter and brandishing a bolt of lightning, represented in typically Hellenistic fashion as a bundle of three rods, which is the traditional attribute of Zeus.[1] By virtue of this attribute, Ptolemy II Philadelphos is assimilated to the god Zeus, thereby affirming his own divinity. The introduction of this Hellenistic motif into the pharaonic repertoire of royal emblems is both unattested and quite unexpected. Since the bolt of lightning does not appear as an attribute either of Ptolemy II or of Arsinoe II, it is doubtful that the artist of this relief was so creative as to introduce it himself. The impetus most likely derives from the reign of Ptolemy V Epiphanes, on the reverse of whose coins, struck between 199 and 197 B. C., is found the bolt of lightning (Kyrieleis 1973: 216-17). The development of the dynastic cult of the Ptolemies, an entirely Greek phenomenon, would certainly allow for the assimilation of Ptolemy II with Zeus. The appearance of the lightning bolt in this typically Egyptian scene has forced the native sculptor to render the figure of Ptolemy II in an attitude of motion commensurate with the act of hurling the bolt. The native artist has successfully rendered the upward thrust of the body and the forward step of an essentially Greek attitude without violating the basic tenets of Egyptian art.

This relief, as R. Fazzini suggested (personal communication), was possibily dedicated to the cult of the *theoi adelphoi*, Ptolemy II and Arsinoe II, the deified "brother-sister-gods," as *sunnaoi theoi* ("resident gods") at Tanis. To judge from the evidence afforded by the bolt of lightning, it may have been made during the early years of the reign of Ptolemy V Epiphanes. Described by Petrie (1885: 31) as a tablet, the relief is complete, but lacks the expected framing elements that generally define the perimeter of stelae or larger relief compositions. As such it may be compared to the ubiquitous limestone plaques decorated in relief which are often, but erroneously, described as "sculptors' models," but are actually ex-votos (CAT. 131).

[1] One should avoid identifying Min with Zeus despite the attempts of Wainwright (1928, 1930, 1931), inasmuch as the Greeks of the Hellenistic and Roman Periods habitually associated Min with Pan. Moreover, Wainwright's attempt to identify the attribute of Min (Gardiner 1957: Sign List R22 and R23) as a bolt of lightning (1931, 1935), although accepted by some (Hummel 1986), is not universally endorsed (Gundlach 1980: 136).

CAT. 15
Ptolemy IV and Arsinoe III Worshiping a Tanite Triad

Limestone, 74×51.3×13.2 ($29\frac{1}{8} \times 20\frac{3}{16} \times 5\frac{3}{16}$)
Reign of Ptolemy IV (222-205 B.C.)
From Tanis
London, Courtesy of the Trustees of the British Museum, 1054

Literature: Petrie 1885: 31-32; James 1962: 171; Quaegebeur 1971a: 201, 216; 1983b: 115; De Meulenaere 1978: 71.

Petrie discovered this stela, with traces of gilding (CAT. 123; Daumas 1956) still preserved, set into a recess of the west wall of a crude brick chapel at Tanis (Petrie 1885: 31). He incorrectly identified the rulers at the right as Ptolemy II and Arsinoe II and assumed that the chapel had been erected and dedicated in their honor. James (1962: 171) correctly identified the king and queen as Ptolemy IV and Arsinoe III.
Arsinoe III stands to the far right. She wears an Egyptian fashion consisting of a three-piece costume, the shawl of which is knotted to the skirt at the breast (pp. 66-67, above; and CAT. 66). Her hair is arranged in a style that may be interpreted as a representation of corkscrew locks (CAT. 74). Her attributes include the *ankh*-sign and a headdress consisting of two ostrich plumes surmounted by bovine horns and a sun disk. She raises her far hand in adoration and is barefoot. Ptolemy IV Philopator, her husband, stands in front of her, wearing sandals and holding a staff, whose finial appears to be an anthropomorphic bust and *ankh*-sign. He wears the Double Crown, around which is tied a diadem fronted with a uraeus. His costume is the Egyptian male fashion that served as the counterpart to that worn by his wife (CATS. 30-32), and which has been suggested, but not demonstrated, to have had *heb-sed*, or jubilee, associations (*Das ptol. Äg.*: 101-02; pp. 48, 67, above).
The royal pair adore the Triad of the ithyphallic Min, at center, the child god Horsiese, and the tutelary goddess of Lower Egypt, Wadjet, wearing the Red Crown symbolic of that region. There is nothing in this stela to support Petrie's contention that the chapel in which it was found was dedicated to Ptolemy IV and Arsinoe III, whom he misidentified (Petrie 1885: 31), nor does the stela associate the chapel with any other royal cult. Moreover, one cannot associate this chapel contextually with the objects found lying on the ground in front of it (CAT. 14), as Petrie implies, because there were no reported architectural or stratigraphic connections between those two loci.
A second stela, found some distance away, also provides evidence of the ways in which the Hellenistic concept of the cult of the ruler was incorporated into the tenets of pharaonic religion. It represents a bilaterally symmetrical scene of a Ptolemaic king, perhaps Ptolemy II; on the right, he is shown offering a spit of land to Min and a Ptolemaic queen (Arsinoe II?) and, on the left, making an offering to Wadjet and Horsiese (Petrie 1885: 31-32). This second stela implies the existence of an important cult of Min, Horsiese, and Wadjet at Tanis during the Ptolemaic Period. So important was this cult of that queen, whatever her identity, that the Crown and priesthood deemed it appropriate to incorporate her cult into that of the Tanite Min as a *sunnaos thea*, one who shares with the existing deities the temple and the concomitant rituals.
The style of CAT. 15, particularly in the rendering of the bodies of Min and Wadjet, is so evocative of the style of Dynasty XXX and the earlier Ptolemaic Period (CATS. 26, 65) that without the accompanying inscriptions one would have difficulty assigning it to a specific period. If the coiffure of Arsinoe III is indeed composed of corkscrew locks, this stela would be the earliest dated example for such a fashion in relief (CAT. 66). This fashion gains currency in the following reign under Ptolemy V Epiphanes, when the coiffure first appears on Ptolemaic coins in depictions of his wife, Cleopatra I.

CAT. 15

CAT. 16

Dyad of a King and a Crocodile-Headed Deity

Limestone, 39×22.6×9.2 (15 3/8×8 7/8×3 5/8)
Third-second century B.C.
Provenance not known
London, Courtesy of the Trustees of the British Museum, 27390

Unpublished.

This composition represents the simplest variety evolved by ancient Egyptian craftsmen for groups of two figures, called dyads. The images are independent creations which are not compositionally united although they share both the pedestal and back slab. In most of these compositions from all periods of Egypt's history (e.g., Cairo CG 133, Saleh/Sourouzian 1987: no. 48; New York 17.2.5, Hayes 1959: fig. 218), the left leg of each figure is advanced,[1] as in this example. The principle of strict symmetry can easily be obviated by altering the types of costumes worn; here asymmetry is achieved by the omission of a central flap on the garment of the crocodile-headed deity.

Through various visual devices, the craftsmen have ensured that the figures emerge as thematic equals. The figure on the left, which in the Egyptian system would be the more important of the two, is shorter than the one on the right, but through a careful adjustment in the height of his Double Crown, the disparity is diminished, making the composition appear to be isocephalic. Yet the crocodile-headed figure *is* taller, itself an artistic device connoting dominance. Thus two independent conventions compete to yield equality (CAT. 14).

The lack of accompanying inscriptions and the fact that any one pharaonic attribute could have a plurality of meanings render the identification of the two figures on this dyad difficult. One can, perhaps, exclude the possibility that the figures represent the gods Horus the Elder and Sobek because the pair, when depicted together in the relief representations at Kom Ombo, invariably appear theriomorphic (e.g., PM VI: 185-86 {51-57}). One might more profitably interpret the dyad as a representation of a king in the company of a crocodile-headed deity, perhaps to be identified in broad terms as Sobek (Kákosy 1963). A more precise identification is virtually impossible because there were at least a dozen local versions of Sobek in the Arsinoite nome alone during the Ptolemaic and Roman Periods (Yoyotte 1957; Gazda *et al.* 1978: 13). Proceeding from the assumption that the craftsmen have purposefully denied each figure primacy, one might tentatively suggest that this dyad is an expression of a king incorporated into the cult of an existing deity as a *sunnaos theos*, one who shares the temple (Quaegebeur 1971a: 242 note 14, citing Nock 1930). Such an interpretation is consistent with that offered for the plaque from Tanis (CAT. 15). The relatively small scale of this modest monument, which may have originally been painted in such a way that the costumes and headdresses would have appeared more interesting, seems to indicate that this dyad was a private, non-royal dedication to just such a cult (as in CAT. 49). The dating of the monument can be suggested on stylistic grounds, particularly in the tripartite modeling of the male torso, which stands closer in its conception to the earlier statue of Amunpayum (CAT. 26) than to the later torso with the enigmatic inscription (CAT. 27). The marked absence of asymmetry in the representation and design of the uraeus on the sun disk of the crocodile-headed figure (compare CAT. 53) would argue for a dating before the end of the second century B.C. One can, therefore, suggest that this private dedication to the cult of a *sunnaos theos* was made between the third and second centuries B.C.

[1]Fischer 1986: 55-56, for an explanation of this characteristic of Egyptian art.

CAT. 17
Plaque of a Queen or Goddess

Gold-plated silver repoussé, 24.5×8 (9 5/8×3 1/8)
Third-first century B.C.
Provenance not known
The Brooklyn Museum, 44.120; Charles Edwin Wilbour Fund
Unpublished.

In 1937 this plaque was in a private collection, along with several other silver objects which were alleged to have come from a common hoard discovered at "a site in the Delta." Over a period of time the objects were dispersed, but the history of their common origin persisted and accompanied each piece as it changed hands. It can now be demonstrated that these silver objects cannot be related archaeologically and that the story of their common origin from a site in the Delta was fabricated in the 1930s when they were found together in that private collection.[1] Unless there are compelling reasons to suggest otherwise, these objects should not be associated with one another in terms either of provenance or of date. Statements about a common findspot for any collection of seemingly related objects that cannot be independently corroborated ought to be questioned, particularly when such statements involve objects made of precious metal (CAT. 117; Bianchi 1985).

This plaque represents a female figure facing left. She wears a vulture headdress over what was apparently a tripartite wig, the individual curls of which are treated as segmented links. Her accessories include a broad collar, the topmost strand of which is composed of pearl-like beads, an armlet, and a bracelet. Her costume is a variant of a haltered sheath without its sleeves (Hall 1981; Hall/Barnett 1985), where the straps of the front and back are knotted over the chest. A feather garment in the form of a vulture, as is evident from the tail feathers appearing at the level of the forearm, is draped over that sheath. The modeling of the body is exceptionally fine, reflecting the full-figured woman so popular in royal relief representations from Ptolemaic Egypt. That corpulence is also evident in the idealizing face with its full cheeks and fleshy throat.

In spirit and style this plaque recalls images of other female figures in relief (CAT. 65), and the fluidity of the modeling and its organic unity conform to a relief style encountered at Kom Ombo during the reign of Ptolemy VIII Euergetes II during the second century B.C. (CAT. 72). In the Roman Imperial Period, these artistic concerns become somewhat mannered and formulaic, as is revealed by a comparison with the figure of a similarly arrayed Isis from the Temple of Mandulis, dated to the time of the Roman Emperor Augustus (Daumas in *Crépuscule*: 38 and fig. 324). These comparisons suggest a dating within the second half of the Ptolemaic Period for this plaque. The dating is corroborated by the results of a spectrographic analysis of the silver, made at the time of its acquisition, which compared favorably to those made of Ptolemaic silver coins minted at Alexandria in the second and first centuries B.C.

Without accompanying inscriptions it is impossible to determine whether a queen or goddess is intended (Riefstahl 1944a).

The function of the plaque is also a matter of speculation because it is unique; no comparable pieces have been identified. In my view, this plaque probably decorated an object associated with a temple, as is suggested by the data provided by the hoard of disparate silver objects found at Dendera.

[1] In addition to the present work, that collection included a small gilded strip inscribed with the cartouche of Ptolemy IX Alexander I (New York 38.6, Lansing 1938: 200; Oliver 1977: 85); a jug with a cover (New York 38.2.18, Lansing 1938: 200; Oliver 1977: 85; and CAT. 117); a silver sistrum inscribed for Ptolemy IX Alexander I (New York 58.5a-b, not published); and a silver bowl (London 66639, Dumbrell 1971; Shore 1965).

CAT. 18
Inlay of a King or Deity

see color plate I

Colored glass, 13×6 (5 1/8×2 3/8)
305-200 B.C.
Provenance not known
The Brooklyn Museum, 49.61.1-.4; Charles Edwin Wilbour Fund

Literature: Bianchi 1983b; 1983c; Bianchi in Brooklyn 1983: no.72.

Since the history of the development of glass inlays has been discussed elsewhere, we will here only recapitulate the salient points. The earliest, dated use of glass inlays appears to be in the form of hieroglyphs decorating the lid of the fourth coffin of Yuaa of Dynasty XVIII (Bianchi 1983b: 29). The technique rapidly expanded during the reign of Tutankhamun, when the use of figural inlays first appeared (Bianchi 1983b: 29). It has been suggested that the colors used for such inlays were imbued with symbolic value (Manniche 1982: 11). The inlays themselves appear to have been individually crafted, rather than mass produced by means of casting (Bianchi 1983b: 29). The use of such inlays continued into the Ramesside Period (Bianchi 1983b: 30) and proliferated during the course of Dynasty XXVI, during which time inlays decorated any number of wooden shrines (Bianchi 1983b: 30-32). For convenience, inlays from this period have been placed into the Saite/Persian Group because their decorative arrangement is characterized by the cellular, or noncontiguous, technique (Bianchi 1983b: 32; 1983c: 10-11). During Dynasty XXX a new facial type was introduced (CAT. 24), which seemed to set the standard for subsequent idealizing physiognomies of the later Ptolemaic and Roman Periods (CAT. 1). Figural inlays of this, the Sebennytic/Ptolemaic Group, are distinguished from the earlier examples in that figures were now composed by contiguously setting or abutting the component elements against one another, as in this glass inlay in Brooklyn (Bianchi 1983c: 13-14). Such figural inlays might have been originally employed to decorate either anthropoid sarcophagi made of cartonnage or wooden shrines (Bianchi 1983c: 14-16). This particular inlay, whose original function is not known, is datable to the early Ptolemaic Period on the basis both of its facial type and contiguous, noncellular composition.

CATS. 19-20

Temple Reliefs of Ptolemy VIII

CAT. 19

Ptolemy VIII and a Cleopatra Offering

Brownish sandstone, 90×80 (35 7/16×31 1/2)
Reign of Ptolemy VIII (170-116 B.C.)
Thebes, West Bank, Qasr el Aguz(?)
Staatliche Museen zu Berlin, Hauptstadt der DDR, Ägyptisches Museum/Papyrussammlung, 2116; erworben durch die Preußische Expedition 1842-1845

Literature: PM II²: 530; Berlin/DDR 1976: 55 and pl. 15; Berlin/DDR 1981: 53 and pl. 17.

CAT. 20

Amun-Re and Ma'at Receive an Offering

Sandstone, 75×62 (29 1/2×24 7/16)
Reign of Ptolemy VIII (170-116 B.C.)
Thebes, East Bank, Precinct of Amun-Re at Central Karnak
Paris, Musée du Louvre, Département des Antiquités Egyptiennes, B. 35 (N. 140)

Literature: PM II²: 212, (40) (a), I.

As in earlier times, the main decorative scheme for Ptolemaic temple walls is a series of registers of square or rectangular scenes, each with little or no indication of setting, depicting the king offering to a deity or deities from whom he is said (and sometimes also shown) to receive blessings (for the basic composition of such Ptolemaic scenes, see Sauneron 1963: XIV-XVIII; Winter 1968). Sometimes, as in CAT. 19, pharaoh is accompanied by a queen (for the queen as priestess, see Troy 1986: 73-102); sometimes the queen even appears alone. Such scenes, especially those with pharaoh and queen, are reasonably well attested from Dynasty XVIII through Dynasty XXII (for the latter, see Fazzini 1988: pls. XI, XIII, XXXII,1). They vanish almost entirely,[1] however, in Dynasties XXV and XXVI, when the royal women depicted in a wide range of cultic acts are the celibate priestesses called God's Wives of Amun (Leclant 1965: 353-86). Judging by the evidence available (which may be misleading), and for reasons still unclear, from Dynasty XXVII through the Macedonian Period images of royal women were absent from temple walls.

CAT. 19 shows Ptolemy VIII, wearing the Crown of Lower Egypt, with both hands raised to offer jars of wine or precious oils. Shown behind him (presumably an artistic convention for beside him), the queen wears a long wig with headband and uraeus (Pécoil/Maher-Taha 1983; Barta 1984; Lillesø 1985) surmounted by a short modius (headdress) supporting two tall plumes with cow's horns and sun disk. This headgear is known for queens well before the Ptolemaic Period but is common for them then as well. It has various religious connotations, most importantly some relating to the goddess Hathor (Malaise 1976; for the plumes, Troy 1986: 126-29). In the queen's hands are two small bouquets of lotus and/or papyrus, both of which may be associated with concepts of birth, renewal, and protection (Dittmar 1986: 132-43; Borghouts 1983). As with the offering of wines or oils, the offering of flowers is a common element of Egyptian temple iconography (Dittmar 1986, *passim*), and can be made by a king or queen alone or, more usually, by a queen while a king makes a different offering.

This half-scene was acquired between 1842 and 1845 by the Royal Prussian expedition directed by Lepsius. According to the Ägyptisches Museum, the expedition's records do not give its provenance, although a catalogue of 1871 says it came from a temple in Western Thebes. Since then it has been attributed to the small Temple of Thoth at Qasr el Aguz built in the name of Ptolemy VIII (PM II²: 530; Dewachter 1983: 49, who accepts the attribution but also indicates the difficulties involved in distinguishing between Thebes East and West in the provenance of some reliefs of Ptolemy VIII). However, the provenance of the Temple of Thoth is not certain, and, according to Dr. Bell of the University of Chicago's Oriental Institute, cannot be confirmed by a comparison of a photograph of Berlin 2116 with Oriental Institute photographs of the Qasr el Aguz temple.[2]

The queen of our relief, named Cleopatra, is normally identified as Cleopatra II, Ptolemy VIII's sister and wife, rather than as his other wife, Cleopatra III, the daughter of Cleopatra II by her earlier marriage to Ptolemy VIII's brother, Ptolemy VI. Ptolemy VIII appears with either Cleopatra at Qasr el Aguz where, to judge from the temple's publication (unfortunately only in drawings and typeset texts: Mallet 1909), Cleopatra is not written, as it is in our relief, with a reed leaf (𓇋) before the lasso (𓍢), although there is one example of a stroke (/) where a reed leaf would occur (Gauthier 1916: 327; he gives non-Theban examples of the writing of the names of Cleopatra II and III with the reed leaf on pp. 304, 309-10, 317-18, 321, 323-24, and 331-33).

In one sense, CAT. 20, a relief from the Louvre, begins where the Berlin relief ends, i.e., with a hand of Ptolemy VIII offering a vessel of oil or unguent to "his father" so that he might give life. The recipient is Amun-Re, holding an *ankh*-sign and *was*-scepter and called "great god since the beginning of time, creator of that which is." With him is Ma'at, holding an *ankh*-sign and with one arm raised protectively. She is labeled "daughter of [the sun] Re, united with Amun, beloved of all the gods."[3] Another *was*-sign forms the right border of the scene. In the texts below their arms, Amun is said to give the king a gift related to Ma'at, whereas Ma'at gives him "the rulership of he who hides his name, Amun" (Amun's name means "the hidden one"). For a related scene in the Temple of Opet at Karnak, see De Wit 1958-68, vol. I: 117; vol. II: pl. 3; vol. III: 61.

As demonstrated by Barguet (1959: 2-3 with figs. 2-3), the Louvre's relief formed part of a doorjamb of another temple at Karnak, a temple at the rear end of the Temple of Amun begun in the New Kingdom and added to later. Unlike most of that main dwelling of the god, it was accessible to ordinary people. Formally a temple for Amun-Re-Horakhty ("Amun-Re, Horus of the Horizons"), it was also dedicated to "Amun-who-hears-

CAT. 19

prayers." In Dynasty XIX, Ramesses II became a "god" who hears prayers there also, and a text in the temple shows that there Ptolemy VIII was either "beloved of Amun-who-hears-prayers" (Barguet 1962: 233) or "hearer of prayers," that is, like Ramesses, a more-than-human intermediary with the god (Nims 1971: 108).

As for the Louvre relief's style, Barguet (1959: 4) has described it as characteristic of its era, with sure outlines and well-denoted body modeling, even if heavy with rounding of forms. The latter features are, however, hardly new to reliefs in the time of Ptolemy VIII; and it is worth noting that even this bold, rounded relief is not very high. In fact, most Ptolemaic reliefs are not much bolder or, in the case of sunk relief, not much deeper than some of their pre-Ptolemaic antecedents, even if their rounding gives that impression (Daumas 1975a: 330). Daumas (in *Crépuscule*: 88-89) also links this rounding mainly to southern Egypt. The Berlin relief displays less rounding and its queen has a less curvilinear body than the Paris relief's Ma'at. Such variations are commonplace, even in works of one reign from the same or related sites. Both treatments of the fe-

CAT. 20

male form remain in the traditions of works of much earlier times. In fact, the figure of Ma'at is related, ultimately, to female figures of Dynasties XXV and XXVI (Munro 1969: 98), which on occasion can have a strongly projecting Dynasty XXX-Roman Period female breast (e.g., Munro 1973: pl. 33, fig. 122).

If Ptolemaic relief styles display regional variations (Daumas 1975a: 327), it is also true that Theban Ptolemaic reliefs differ little from those of nearby cities (Daumas in *Crépuscule*: 96), and one can find good parallels for the style of our Ptolemy VIII reliefs outside Thebes.

[1] A queen of Dynasty XXV may well have appeared in a series of temple reliefs depicting the divine birth of a king (Fazzini 1988: 13).
[2] I am grateful to Dr. Bell for his assistance with this matter.
[3] For Amun or Amun-Re, see Otto 1975a. For Ma'at as the incarnation of the divine order, see CAT. 12 and p. 29, above. For Ma'at as daughter of Re and constant companion of pharaohs and gods, see Troy 1986: 25-28, 61.

CAT. 21

Stela Commemorating Benefactions for Mut by Augustus and Tiberius

Sandstone, 66.3×44×13 (26 1/8×17 5/16×5 1/8)
Reign of Tiberius (14-37 A.D.)
From Thebes, East Bank
Amsterdam, Allard Pierson Museum, 7763

Literature: van Haarlem 1986: 60-62; van Haarlem/Lunsingh Scheurleer 1986: 24, 27.

In the upper field is a winged disk with two cobras (CAT. 4) over a hieroglyph for heaven. The latter, together with the two *was*-scepters supporting it, frames the scene below. Here Tiberius offers to the goddess Mut (te Velde 1980; 1982a; forthcoming) and her son Khonsu. Khonsu holds an *ankh*-sign and *was*. Mut holds the same sign and papyrus staff, associated with various deities and a symbol of renewal and protection (e.g., Werbrouck 1952; Dittmar 1986: 136-37). She wears the vulture headdress (Troy 1986: 116-19) and, as usual for her, the Crown of Upper and Lower Egypt (te Velde 1980: 6). Tiberius wears the helmetlike *khepresh*, symbolic of legitimate succession to the kingship (CAT. 48; and W. Davies 1982: 75) Its relatively squat form with high rear peak relates it to many depictions of this crown (especially in relief) from Dynasty XXVI (e.g., Yoyotte 1972: pl. 19B) down through the age of Augustus and Tiberius (e.g., Junker/Winter 1965: 256, 268, 306, 356), to which it is closest in shape, and later. A similar crown is worn by the sphinx Tiberius holds, which has human hands and clasps a jar.[1] Sometimes a large-scale sphinx clasping a jar appears alone as king (e.g., Barguet/Leclant 1954: pl. LX,A; Barguet 1961). When held by the king, a cult object in the form of a human-handed sphinx clasping a jar is normally identified as an offering of myrrh (for myrrh, see Germer 1985: 106-07), an offering rare in the New Kingdom but frequent in Ptolemaic-Roman times (Žabkar 1980a: 128). In fact, since all three figures on this stela rest on pedestals and not on base lines, they may represent a statue of Tiberius offering to statues of Mut and Khonsu (cf. Schulman 1986: 308-11; for some late images–late in the history of such figures–of comparable type, see Fischer 1956: 34-35; N. Davies 1953: pls. 67-68).

Our stela's main text commemorates Tiberius' completion and/or extension of work begun by Augustus at Mut's main cult center, her precinct at South Karnak (PM II²: 255-75). To take two recent translations, that work consisted either of "a big temenos wall (*s3t/s3w*) protecting her quarters, the temple of the territory of the sun-disk" (van Haarlem 1986: 61), or "a large wall surrounding her venerable sanctuary" (De Meulenaere 1978: 70).

In fact, Amsterdam's stela (Traunecker 1975: 147, stela no. 16) is one of four Tiberius stelae commemorating work variously described as: a great *sbty* surrounding Mut's sanctuaries (*sḫmw*) (De Meulenaere 1978: 69; Budge 1909a: pl. 52; Traunecker 1975: 147, stela no. 15); a great *ỉnb* surrounding Mut's temple (*ḥwt*) (De Meulenaere 1978: 69; Erman 1900: 125; Traunecker 1975: 147, stela no. 17); and a great *ỉnb* around the House of the White Crown (i.e., the Temple of Mut) of the Lady of the South (?) (De Meulenaere 1978: 70-71; Budge 1909a: pl. 51; Traunecker 1975: 147, stela no. 14). In general, most agree that *s3t/s3w*, *sbty* and *ỉnb*, three different words for wall (Spencer 1984: 260-64, 267-78), must all refer to the same construction, which should be defined as a precinct's enclosure, or temenos wall (Traunecker 1975: 145, 153; De Meulenaere 1978: 69). Moreover, although Traunecker's stela no. 17 is not well enough preserved to compare it fully with the other three stelae, it is possible to say that the Amsterdam stela is quite similar to his stelae nos. 14 and 15. As Traunecker has observed and suggested (1975: 145), the texts of the latter two stelae allude to popular rites relating to pious circumambulations of a precinct, and may have formed a pair of stelae that could conceivably have been set into the outer face of the Mut Precinct's temenos wall flanking its main entrance.

On the other hand, and admitting that archaeological investigation has barely begun, there are several good reasons for viewing the Mut Precinct's late enclosure wall in mud brick as, in general, much earlier than Augustus or Tiberius. In fact, the only segment of it that appears to be different from the rest is a small section behind (i. e., south) of all the known temples, where the construction is mud brick over baked brick over stone. This could be a candidate for an early Roman repair of a wall damaged, as the stelae's texts may indicate, by a Nile flood (Erman 1900: 125; Habachi 1976: 249-50; De Meulenaere 1978: 69-70). But it is also true that the thick wall encircling much of the Mut Temple (as opposed to the Mut Precinct) is similar in construction and that there is evidence to suggest its attribution to very late Ptolemaic or early Roman times. Hence, we have speculated that the work commemorated by the Tiberius stelae may refer, at least in part, to the temple wall (Fazzini/Peck 1982: 41, 48; Fazzini 1985: 291-92).

The Amsterdam stela and Traunecker's stelae nos. 14 and 15 are very similar in style and format. Moreover, their small-scale figures with relatively rounded forms, curved eyebrows, smiling mouths, and small chins seem basically relatable to larger scale temple reliefs of their general period (e. g., reliefs of Augustus in the Dendur Temple: Aldred 1978: *passim*).[2]

[1] For sphinxes in general, see Coche-Zivie 1984; and for those with human arms, usually considered an innovation of Dynasty XVIII–but see Bourriau 1986: 180 and pl. XV,1, a possible Old Kingdom example–see Romano 1976: 100, 108; U. Schweitzer 1948: 59-60.

[2] For a very different stela commemorating work on a temenos wall done in the name of Tiberius but also mentioning two Roman officials by name, see Aimé-Giron 1926.

CAT. 22

The Emperor Trajan (?) Offering to Amun and Hathor

Plaster, 19.3×23.4 (7 5/8×9 3/16)
Attributed to the reign of Trajan (98-117 A. D.)
Said to be from Memphis
Hildesheim, Pelizaeus-Museum, 1537

Literature: Castiglione 1967: 127; Derchain 1972: 11; G. Grimm in Hildesheim 1979: 197D; Quaegebeur 1983a: 48.

A frame in the form of three fasciae around the four sides of this plaque indicates that it belongs to an ever-increasing group of independent works of art made of plaster during the Ptolemaic and Roman Periods (CAT. 51; Castiglione 1984; Alexandria 26.6.20.5 [*sic*], a plaster plaque in Classical style, Vermaseren 1986: 12, no. 28; Cairo JE 26620, Reeder 1987: 428, fig. 5). The composition itself is set within an architectural framework consisting of three arches, beneath which are placed the principal figures, supported by two palmiform columns. This setting, fanciful as it is, is neverthelesse evocative of the fountain complex at Dendera (Castel *et al.* 1984). At the right stands the offering ruler, identified as "the King of Upper and Lower Egypt, the Lord of the Two Lands, the Pharaoh, living forever," wearing a *hemhem*-crown (Myśliwiec 1985: 150) and sidelock. An enthroned ram-headed deity identified as "Amun,"[1] wearing an *atef*-crown (Myśliwiec 1985: 149) and accompanied by a ram, occupies the central zone, while a standing figure of Hathor Quadrifrons (Derchain 1972; and CAT. 6) attending a bull completes the scene. Iconographically, the scene can be associated with Memphis (Berlandini 1983), the alleged provenance of the piece (CAT. 51; and Bianchi 1985).

The figures are cast into the plaster with a great deal of attention to interior detail, particularly evident in the coiffure of Hathor and in the throne of Amun. The quality of the modeling is exceptional and links the work to an epoch of great artistic accomplishment. The closest stylistic correspondences are provided by the scenes on the screen walls of the Roman *mammisi* at Dendera (Daumas 1959: pls. L-LIII; Daumas in *Crépuscule*: fig. 49), most of whose decoration is attributed to the early second century A. D. (Daumas 1959: pls. XIX-XXIII). Such a comparison is strengthened by the evocative relationships between the arches of the plaque and those of the fountains at Dendera (Castel *et al.* 1984; Bianchi 1986: 830), which can be linked to the fashionable curved tympana of the second century A. D. (Pensabene 1983: 107, 110). The connections with Dendera are also evident in the treatment of the very elaborate throne of Amun with its bead-and-reel motif (de Vos 1980: pl. 42). The appearance of the genie Nemesis with a paw raised on a wheel within the panel of that throne supports such a dating as well (Quaegebeur 1983a: 45).

[1] On the Egyptian, rather than the Nubian, origin of Amun as a ram, see Hofmann 1984: 122-28, the objections of Kormyschewa-Minkowskaja 1984: 129-34 notwithstanding.

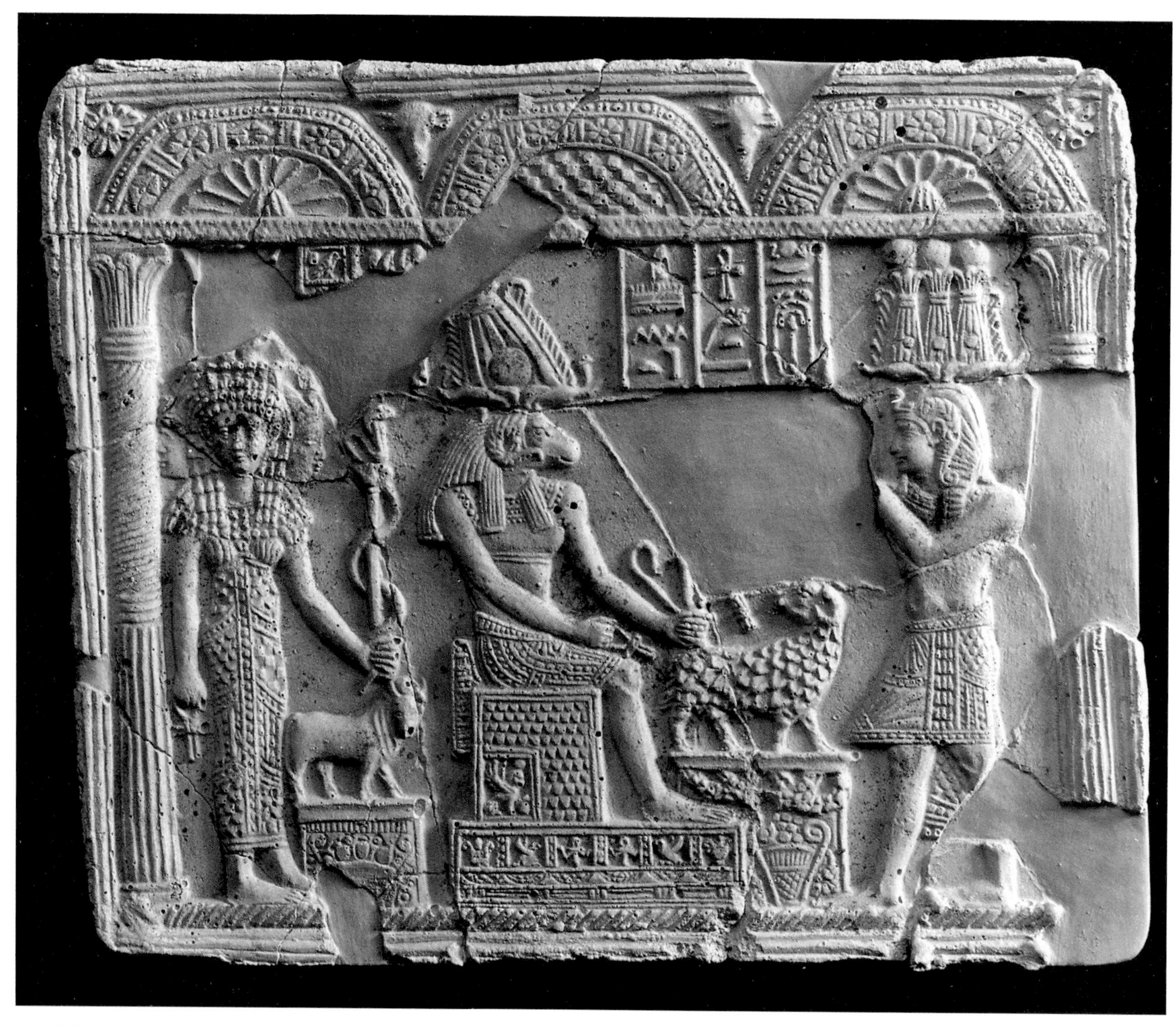

CAT. 22

CAT. 23
Statue of Teos, the Priest

Granite, 33.9×11.8×15.1 (13 3/8×4 7/16×5 15/16)
350-325 B.C.
Karnak, Amun Precinct, the Cachette
Brussels, Musées Royaux d'Art et d'Histoire, E. 7654

Literature: Capart 1941: 58-68.

Teos is here represented as a striding male figure, an attitude which had become a fixed feature in Egyptian art from the time of the Old Kingdom. The verticality of the right side of the statue is formed by the static positions of the rigid right leg and stiff right arm, whose fist holds a stylized bolt of cloth (p. 70, above). The left side conforms to the aesthetic predilections of ancient Egyptian art for violating strict symmetry, and in so doing reveals the left leg advanced and the left arm bent so that its palm steadies an unusual attribute (see below). The bag wig and striated kilt complete the costume. The face of Teos is bland and idealizing, and the rendering of the pectoral muscles is consistent with the convention of ancient Egyptian art for corpulence (p. 68, above).

The inscriptions on the back pillar, although admitting to translation, are difficult to interpret, but do connect Teos with the Cachette at Karnak in which this statue was found, as well as with Elkab, to the south, and Sebennytos in the Delta. The association with Elkab is provided graphically both by the images of Horus, Isis, and Anhur that appear prominently as a group of figures incised into the region of the left collar bone and by the legend *Nḫb.t nb(t) t3wy* ("Nekhbet, Mistress of the Two Lands"), inscribed on the right side of the attribute which, although badly battered, can only be interpreted as a rebus for that same legend. The component elements of that visual pun are the vulture itself (the goddess Nekhbet), which is probably standing on a version of the *neb*-sign ("mistress"), which is in turn supported by the two columns, whose capitals were in all likelihood originally decorated as the lotus and lily, respectively, thereby reflecting the word *t3wy* ("the two lands") in the legend. This rebus relates to that of the statue of Nectanebo II protected by the falcon (CAT. 8), which is itself indebted to Ramesside norms (Bianchi, forthcoming). In fact, like that image, the vulture here protects a male figure snuggling against its breast. The correspondence between this miniature group composition and the colossal version of the same theme excavated at Elkab has led at least one scholar to suggest that this Teos was involved in the erection and dedication of the colossus at Elkab for his Sebennytic sovereign (Capart 1941).

The dating of the Brussels statue is difficult to establish with precision. The problem resides in the proper interpretation of the cartouches appearing in the column of text on the right face of the back pillar. The absence of any framing lines would tend to support the view that this particular text was cut into the statue subsequent to its initial dedication (Capart 1941: 7-9). The scenario, also suggested by Capart, that the first cartouche is a reference to the deceased pharaoh Teos of Dynasty XXX (CAT. 60) is tempting, but inconclusive. Nevertheless, the close correspondences between this statue's rebus and the falcon monuments of Nectanebo II (CAT. 8), and certain stylistic features such as the cutting of the wig over the brow and the configuration of that wig with the back pillar (Chicago, OI 13953, ESLP: no. 89 and New York, private collection) suggest a date within the last half of the fourth century B.C., during Dynasty XXX.

CAT. 24
The Dattari Statue

Diorite, 51.2×16.7×14 (20 3/16×6 9/16×5 1/2)
Reign of Nectanebo I (380-362 B.C.)
Provenance not known, possibly from the Delta (ESLP: 101)
The Brooklyn Museum, 52.89; Charles Edwin Wilbour Fund

Literature: ESLP: no. 80.

Named after its first owner, Giovanni Dattari, this statue is fundamental for an understanding of the subsequent development of Ptolemaic art. The figure is depicted in an attitude that had become canonical for representations of male images in Egyptian art from the time of the Old Kingdom: the left foot advanced, the arms hanging alongside the body, and the fisted hands holding bolts of cloth (p. 70, above). The modeling of the torso in tripartition is a stylistic characteristic common to Egyptian sculpture from all epochs (pp. 69-70, above). The valanced wig with its stylized, echelon curls and a central, undecorated disk on the top of the head is also derived from an older tradition–Old Kingdom models, which had already been modified by the sculptors of Dynasty XXVI (ESLP: 97-98, 101). The style of the head belongs to a type common to the fourth century B.C.

On the basis of its inscription, the Dattari statue has been assigned to the reign of Nectanebo I (De Meulenaere 1962: 42 note 1). The features of the face–the protruding golf-ball chin, the nascent smile, the drilled corners of the lips, the full cheeks, the hieroglyphic, almond-shaped eyes, and the naturalistic brow–are common to representations of kings of Dynasty XXIX (A. Grimm 1984), as well as to those of Nectanebo I, both in sculpture in the round (Vandier 1973: fig. 14; H. Müller 1970: fig. 4) and relief (Abd el Raziq 1968: pl. XLVIII, d). These stylistic features anticipate the style of Nectanebo II, which was continued into the reign of Ptolemy II, as von Bissing first observed (1914: text to pls. 103-04; followed by Steindorff 1945 and Bothmer 1953a). As a result, the *terminus post quem* for such facial features must be pushed back at least to the first quarter of the fourth century B.C., if not earlier (Brooklyn 71.39, Bianchi 1979a: 70-71). Objects once datable to the Ptolemaic Period on the basis of such stylistic features (ESLP: no. 98) might better be assigned to Dynasty XXX (Quaegebeur 1983b: 115-16; also CAT. 62).

The decoration of the top of the back pillar of this Dynasty XXX statue deserves comment because it serves as a chronological indicator. There one sees squatting images of the deities Amun, Mut, and Khonsu, each acting as a visual introduction to a column of text below. Whereas earlier epochs would only show the name of a deity in the top of a back pillar, the sculptors of Dynasty XXX introduced such figures of deities there (De Meulenaere 1986: 142; CAT. 25). On rarer occasions these figures might be replaced by an adoration scene, a feature more common in statues of the Ptolemaic Period (De Meulenaere 1986: 142; CAT. 26).

CAT. 25

see color plate II

Portrait of Wesir-wer, Priest of Montu

Green schist, 15.3 (6)
Dynasty XXX (380-342 B.C.)
Karnak, Amun Precinct, the Cachette
The Brooklyn Museum, 55.175; Charles Edwin Wilbour Fund

Literature: ESLP: no. 83; Bresciani 1960: 109-18; Bothmer 1964: 42-51.

A study of the inscriptions on the back pillar of this head and on a headless statue in Cairo (JE 38064) led H. De Meulenaere to conclude that both belonged to the same monument (Bresciani 1960: 109–18). Bothmer eventually published the statue with both pieces joined (1964: 42-51). The decoration in the truncated triangle at the top of the back pillar (Bothmer in Bothmer/De Meulenaere 1986: 4 note 10, correcting his remarks in ESLP: 79) contains a figure of Osiris (in Egyptian, *Wesir*) seated on a throne decorated with a *wr*-bird (𓅨) ("great"), which is a rebus for Wesir-wer ("Osiris-is-Great"), the name of the statue's owner. Such figural decoration in this place is common for sculpture made during Dynasty XXX (CAT. 24).

Wesir-wer is depicted in a striding stance with the left leg advanced and is clad in a variation of a particular costume (ESLP: no. 63) which, although in vogue during Dynasty XXVI (ESLP: 76), is a reflection of Achaemenid court attire. That ensemble consists of three garments: a round-necked undergarment over which is worn a V-necked tunic with flaring sleeves, around which is wrapped a skirt, which (contary to Laurent 1984: 142-44) has nothing at all in common with the African skirt of the Masai. The opening in the neck of the tunic is indicated by a sharply incised line, which indicates that the raised band at the neck of the Berlin Green Head (CAT. 46) must represent a fashion accessory.

The "broad and squat" shape of Wesir-wer's skull (ESLP: 105) is more brachycephalic than is usual in the non-idealizing egg-head typology (Bianchi 1982a), thereby removing this head from that group of images (CATS. 44-47). In fact, the sculpting of the head of Wesir-wer is unique because it falls into no established typology for such representations. The modeling, executed with restraint as the planes merge subtly into one another, is both abstracted and mannered. The knot at the brow that interrupts the forehead is geometrically rendered as a triangle, and is only vaguely reminiscent of this same feature in late Kushite and early Saite sculpture (Berlin/BRD 23728, Hornbostel in Altenmüller/Hornbostel 1982: 81). The artist has effectively used line to define the wings of the nose, the separation of the lips, the crease in the upper eyelids, and the contours and articulation of the preserved left ear. In these features, the sculptors seem to be imitating the earlier formulae operative in the statue of Ariketekana (Cairo JE 38018, Aldred in *Crépuscule*: fig. 225), which have also been incorporated, but without the emphatic use of linear adjuncts, into the design of the statue of Nectanebo II under the falcon (CAT. 8). The resulting image, which is not a portrait (pp. 55-59, above), reveals the wide variety of coeval styles found in the sculpture of Dynasty XXX (p. 59).

CAT. 26
Torso of Amunpayum

Gray granite, 95.3×35.5×34.3 (37 1/2×13×13 1/2)
280-250 B.C.
Provenance not known, perhaps from Mendes[1]
The Cleveland Museum of Art, 48.141; Gift of the Hanna Fund

Literature: ESLP: no. 197; De Meulenaere/Mackay 1976: 199, no. 61; Chevereau 1985: 190-91.

Amunpayum is here represented in the classic Egyptian pose for male figures (p. 70, above, and CAT. 24). His pleated kilt is held in place by a belt that is inscribed. Such a feature belongs to a long pharaonic tradition for private statuary that goes back to the Old Kingdom (Fischer 1962) and was not, as has been mistakenly suggested (ESLP: 11, 124) first introduced near the end of Dyansty XXV.

The inscriptions on the belt are symmetrically arranged in two rows that converge at the center on the *ḥm*-sign (𓋴), which is aligned almost directly below the navel. The top of the back pillar shows Amunpayum, right, confronting the Mendesian Triad of Harpocrates, Banebdjed, and Hatmehit. The signs of the single horizontal line of inscription beneath these figures are oriented with those on the belt and converge at the spine (ESLP: 124). Although the outlines of all the hieroglyphs are incised into the stone, the interiors of a few selected signs have been articulated. During the course of the Ptolemaic Period one notices, in certain monuments, a gradual abandonment of all interior articulation of the hieroglyphs in favor of an exclusive reliance upon signs which appear to be simply scratched into the surface of the stone (p. 72, above, and CAT. 32).

Amunpayum has been identified as the owner of a second statue, found at Tanis (Cairo 8-2-21-4, Yoyotte 1973: 81; Chevereau 1985: 190), which represents him in the tripartite costume (CATS. 30-32). Amunpayum is, therefore, the earliest datable native Egyptian to have commissioned statues of himself in each of the two traditional fashions, the kilt and the tripartite costume. From the information contained in the inscriptions of those two statues and from that of related monuments (Chevereau 1985: 190-91) one assumes that Amunpayum enjoyed a great deal of mobility in the discharging of his responsibilities, a mobility comparable to that enjoyed by the Greek Apollonios, who served for almost twenty years as Finance Minister of Egypt under Ptolemy II (p. 15, above) and who was in fact a contemporary of Amunpayum. While the interfaces between the native Egyptian and Greek administrators of the land require further investigation, it is now apparent that one of Amunpayum's Egyptian titles, *sn-nsw*, whose translation and meaning are debated, can no longer be equated with the Greek συγγενής ("kinsman"; Mooren 1975: 237; Bresciani 1983b: 19; Fraser 1972, vol. II: 102). Nevertheless, it is clear that the native population could aspire to and hold superior military rank in the period before the Battle of Raphia in 216 B.C. (p. 16, above). Amunpayum was a *mr mšᶜ*, or general, who commanded both infantry and cavalry (Chevereau 1985: 260-63; 340-45). One wonders whether that preeminence is to be ascribed to his own abilities or, as seems more likely, to his family's entrenched position within the administration of the land, positions which the Ptolemies were keen to support (Chevereau 1985: 357-58). Amunpayum's other non-honorific title on this statue is that of *ḥm-nṯr*, "prophet" (Chevereau 1985: 190), whose writing, although resembling a monogram at the belt's center, is curiously not followed by any written form of a deity's name. Since the statue appears to have been dedicated to the Mendesian Triad, as suggested by their presence on its back pillar, perhaps their names were implied as following *ḥm-nṯr*. Since the titulary of Amunpayum is here more fully developed than that on his statue in Cairo, the Cleveland statue was probably commissioned at a later date, perhaps toward the end of the reign of Ptolemy II Philadelphos.

[1] The statue was acquired on the open market. Although De Meulenaere/Mackay (1976: 199, no. 61) assign the statue to the site of Mendes, they admit that it may come from Tanis.

CAT. 27 *see color plate III*

Statue with an Enigmatic Inscription

Limestone, 63×15.5×12 (24 13/16×6 1/8×4 3/4)
Second-first century B. C.
Provenance not known, possibly from Saqqara[1]
Private collection

Literature: ESLP: no. 129.

The mimetic principle (p. 64, above) is no more clearly demonstrated than in this limestone torso of a male figure. It is indebted to norms established during the Old Kingdom for its attitude, as a comparison either with the figures of Mycerinus from the Triad (Cairo JE 40679, Saleh/Sourouzian 1987: no. 33) or of Ranofer (Cairo CG 19 and 18, Saleh/Sourouzian 1987: nos. 45-46) reveals. The modeling of the present figure, however, is closer in spirit to those of Mycerinus than to those of Ranofer in that all display a high, pinched waist and a lower abdomen articulated so that it appears as a raised plane within which is recessed the navel, whose circular form is linearly defined. The pectoral regions are clearly defined in the tradition of representing a well-exercised body, and their outer contours interrupt the upward surge of those of the midriff. A comparison of this torso with those of Amunpayum (CAT. 26) and the Isis Casati (CAT. 30) reveals just how varied the treatment of the male torso can be in Ptolemaic Egypt. Such variety cautions one against using the modeling of a torso *per se* as a dating criterion (ESLP: 168, contradicting an observation made on p. 169).

The plain kilt without striations is encountered with greater frequency at the beginning of the Ptolemaic Period (New York, Spaeth Collection, De Meulenaere/Mackay 1976: pl. 24a; Kansas City 47.12, *ibid.*: pl. 24e; Paris, E.15546, *ibid.*: pl. 25c), when the tendency was to inscribe the belt with the name and titles of the owner (CAT. 26). The back pillar, despite the fact that its top inclines toward the head (ESLP: 168), is again not a criterion for dating because of the variety of back pillar types encountered during this period. The presence of the *pt*-sign ("sky"), however, at the top of the back pillar parallel to its top surface – a surface just below the juncture of the neck and shoulders – is a feature which begins to appear during Dynasty XXXI (Chicago, AI 10.243, ESLP: no. 91). This statue, therefore, shares features with those statues from the late fourth and third centuries B. C. With works from the second and first centuries B. C. it shares a tendency to create striding male statues wearing undecorated kilts with plain belts (e.g., Brooklyn 54.113, ESLP: pl. 127; Berlin 10972, Brooklyn 36.843, De Meulenaere/Bothmer 1974). As such, this torso fits within the development of the type of kilted statue known from the Ptolemaic Period.

A closer dating may ultimately result from a detailed study of the hieroglyphic inscription on the back pillar. The signs, whose arrangement within each line is capricious, vary in their paleography from the careful to the perfunctory. One can easily pick out random snatches of the inscription; it does name, from top to bottom, a series of deities, including Shu, Serapis, Isis, and Thoth. The whole, however, is somewhat unintelligible, the key being an understanding of the recurring phrase 𓏲(?) △ ☥. The inscription ought not, therefore, be termed "cryptographic" (ESLP: 168). Moreover, since the name "Serapis" is intercalcated as the second in a series of four deities, the statue is not likely to be an image of that god, as has been suggested (ESLP: 168). It seems more likely that these four divine names are given prominence of place following the principle of honorific transposition and that their relationship to the owner of this statue is expressed in the garbled composition of signs following the penultimate *n*-sign. Until the information contained in the inscription can be understood, this statue fits more comfortably into the second half of the Ptolemaic Period than into the first half, but a more narrow dating cannot be supported.

[1] ESLP: 168 says that the statue was known to have been found at Saqqara, but offers no documentation.

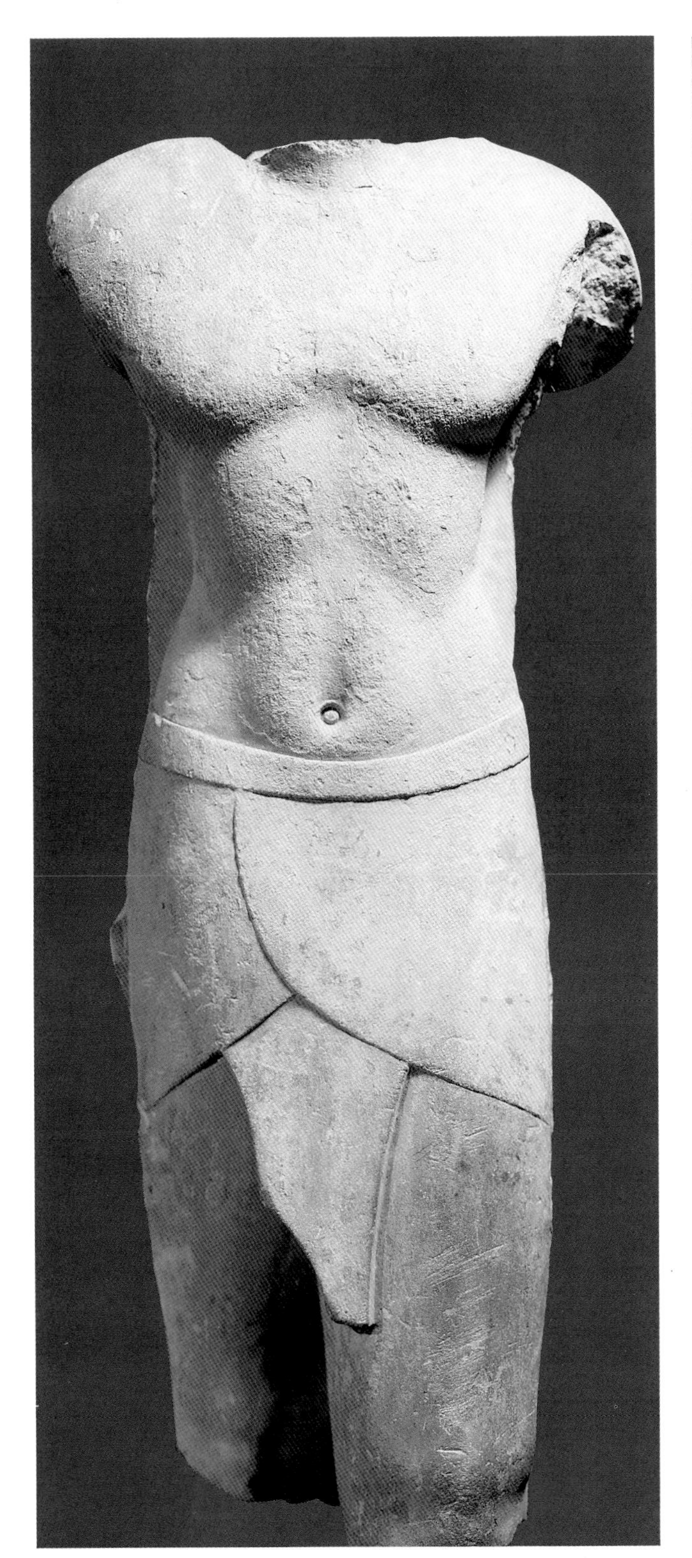

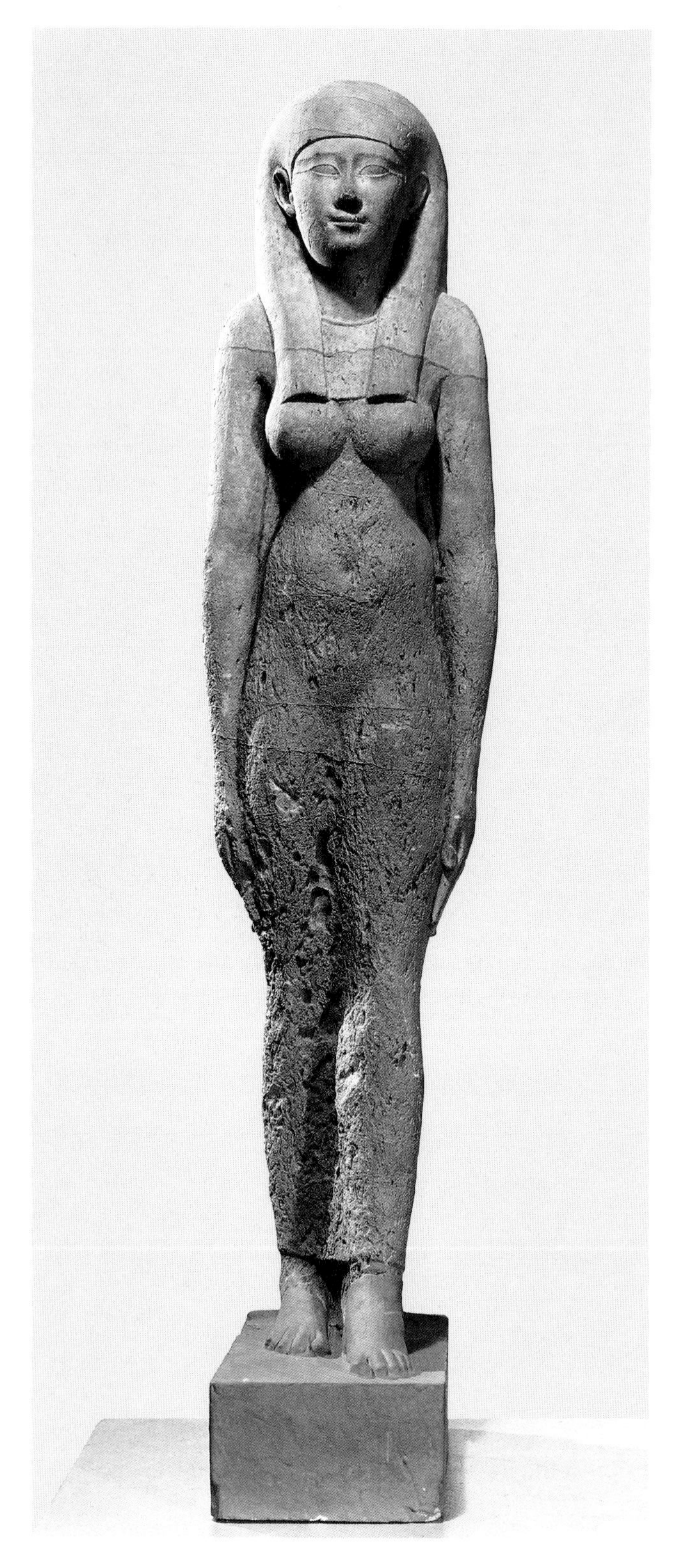

CAT. 28
Statue of a Ptolemaic Woman

Limestone, 78.3×17.8×27.5 (30 13/16×7×10 13/16)
Third century B.C.
Provenance not known
Brussels, Musées Royaux d'Art et d'Histoire, E. 3073

Literature: Quaegebeur 1983b: 122-24; Tefnin 1988: 56-57, no. 19.

The classification of sculptures to which this statue belongs has recently been studied in detail by Quaegebeur; the results of his investigations can be briefly summarized as follows. The woman depicted is probably a private individual rather than a queen or goddess because the statue, as preserved, lacks attributes (Quaegebeur 1983b: 122, with his caveat about its base). The exact congruity of the major stylistic characteristics of this statue with those of a similar statue in Vienna (5809, Vandersleyen 1975: no. 231; Quaegebeur 1983b: 121-22) and an inscribed statue in Paris (N. 2456) suggests a dating in the third century B.C. for all three. So prevalent was this style throughout Egypt at that time for sculpture both in hard and soft stones that one would be hard pressed to assign the Brussels statue to a specific geographical region (Quaegebeur 1983b: 124 note 88).
The importance of such statues for an understanding of the art of Ptolemaic Egypt cannot be underestimated because the ascription of their inherent sensuality and perceived eroticism to Hellenistic influences has been shown to be erroneous (pp. 68-69, above).

CAT. 29

CAT. 29
Block Statue of Wahibre, Priest of Amun at Karnak

Black basalt, 34×13×19.5 (13 3/8×5 1/8×7 11/16)
Third-first century B.C.
Karnak, Amun Precinct, the Cachette
The Harer Family Trust

Literature: PM II^2: 165; Sotheby's, London, December 13, 1977: lot 192 and pl. XXXVII.

The block statue, a distinctly Egyptian blending of abstract and concrete forms, is a sculpture of a man wearing a robe and squatting on the ground, as here, or on a low cushion, with his arms crossed over his drawn-up knees. Known since at least the Middle Kingdom, block statues and other sculptures came to have their bodies or garments covered with texts and figural representations long before the Ptolemaic Period (Young 1967: 277, who sees sculptures with depictions such as the one on the front of this statue as amalgamations of statue and stela; so, too, Fischer 1986: 134). As with most private temple sculptures, even those placed in temples during their owners' lifetimes, our statue's main purpose was funerary and commemorative: to help the deceased partake of the god by sharing in the offerings to the deity and in the deity's daily rebirth, and to remember the dead and thus keep him in the community of ordered being, rather than have him fall away into the unordered reality that exists before and outside Creation (van Dijk 1983: 53-58; te Velde 1982b). Indeed, block statues have been identified not only as depictions of individuals in a typically Egyptian posture indicating modesty and humbleness in the presence of a superior (Radwan 1973: 29), but also as representations of the rebirth of the deceased, revivified by the rays of the sun, assimilated to Osiris at the moment his head emerges from a burial mound or box in the Netherworld (Eggebrecht 1966). The sculptures' back pillars (on their shapes, see Van de Walle 1983) may represent both the deceased and his protective deity as a "pillar-god," who protects the deceased and assists in his rebirth (van Dijk 1983: 56).

Wahibre's block statue and many like it were once ascribed to Dynasties XXII-XXVI, and these mistaken attributions obscured both the stylistic development of the sculptural type and the fact that Upper Egyptians of the Ptolemaic Period enjoyed the affluence and freedom necessary to continue their time-honored tradition of dedicating private temple statuary (ESLP: 152). The same could also be said of Egyptians in other parts of the country. Happily, we have since come to recognize works such as CAT. 29 as creations of the Ptolemaic Period, among other reasons because block statues of earlier periods normally have significantly squatter and deeper forms than those found in Sebennytic-Ptolemaic works (ESLP: nos. 76, 117; for a partial exception, see the statue published by Young 1967). Also indicative of our sculpture's late date is its smiling face, variants of which also abound in Theban sculptures of Dynasty XXX and later (e.g., ESLP: nos. 102, 117, pl. 95, fig. 256, and pl. 108, fig. 292, respectively), although such stylistic features are not necessarily limited to Thebes.

The depiction on the front of the statue of Wahibre adoring Osiris finds parallels on other Karnak block statues of the era (e.g., Steindorff 1946: no. 164), as well as on Theban funerary stelae made before, during, and after the Ptolemaic Period. And it is perhaps worth noting that it is not unusual to find at Karnak priests of Amun, such as Wahibre, worshiping Osiris on statuary made for the Temple of Amun. Osiris was the funerary deity *par excellence*, and by Dynasty XXII the area immediately northeast of the then Amun Temple and Amun Precinct at Central Karnak had become a divine "burial mound" associated with Osiris and Isis (Redford 1986a). Thereafter, Osiris became even more prominent at Karnak, as attested by the construction of numerous chapels dedicated at least in part to him in and around the growing Amun Precinct (Leclant 1965: 216-19), and by the evolving syncretisms between Osiris and Amun (e.g., Traunecker *et al.* 1981: 138).

CAT. 30

CATS. 30-32
Striding, Draped Male Figures

CAT. 30

see color plate IV

Draped Statue of Herybastet, Known as the Isis Casati

Granite, 152.2×40.5×34.5 (59 15/16×15 15/16×13 9/16)
305-150 B.C.
From the Precinct of the Goddess Mut, South Karnak
Private collection

Literature: Gauckler, 1912: 361-62; Stricker 1960: 18, *passim*; Roullet 1972: 136-38; Sotheby's, New York, December 11, 1980: lot 306, illus.

CAT. 31

▷

CAT. 31

see color plate V

Statue of Horsitutu

Granite, 113 (44 1/2)
305-250 B.C.
Provenance not known, said to be from Sais
Staatliche Museen zu Berlin, Hauptstadt der DDR, Ägyptisches Museum/Papyrussammlung, 2271

Literature: von Bissing 1914: text to pl. 108B; B. Schweitzer 1948: 77; Stricker 1959: 1, *passim*; Adriani 1970: 75, *passim*; Bianchi in *Das ptol. Äg.*: 95, *passim*.

CAT. 32

Statue of Pakhom, Governor of Dendera

Black diorite, 69.8×18.5 (27 1/2×7 1/4)
Circa 50 B.C.
From Dendera
The Detroit Institute of Arts, 51.83; Founders Society Purchase, William H. Murphy Fund

Literature: De Meulenaere 1959: 1, 14, 15; ESLP: no. 136; Bianchi in *Das ptol. Äg.*: 98; 1980b: 14-15.

The statue of Horsitutu (CAT. 31), the earliest of the three statues here discussed, wears a well-attested variant of the tripartite costume (pp. 66-67, above) that consists solely of the addition of a V-necked garment worn over the round-necked T-shirt. The statue can be provisionally assigned to Sais, and its dating to the early Ptolemaic Period is suggested both by the orthography of the signs and by the nature of the rebus (CATS. 8, 23, 25) on the back pillar (Bianchi in *Das ptol. Äg.*: 95, *passim*). These observations negate B. Schweitzer's attempt (1948: 77) to place the head stylistically into the framework of Roman Republican portraiture (p. 55, above); they negate as well the subjective reading of the folds as metallic (ESLP: 160), a reading then used as a dating criterion.

This statue is one of the most ambitious private commissions of the Ptolemaic Period. The diadem around the head was made of metal, presumably of gold, and fitted into the depression in the hair so as to accommodate it to the streamers appearing on the sides of the back pillar. A second depression in the V-necked garment was probably for a cord, again perhaps of gold, from which an attribute, now lost, appeared to be suspended, although in fact it was anchored in the slot in the chest. The absence of traces of the left arm along the side of the body suggests that the arm was raised to support this attribute.

Two further details deserve mention. The first is the treatment of the hair which, in accordance with Egyptian stylistic conventions, sits on the scalp like a cap (Kyrieleis 1975: 136; Bianchi in *Das ptol. Äg.*: 99). The second is the rendering of the pupils of the eyes as disks, a stylistic feature with a long tradition in Egyptian art (p. 72, above; CATS. 36, 42, 49; Bianchi in *Das ptol. Äg.*: 99 notes 46-50; Bianchi: forthcoming; Fazzini: forthcoming).

CAT. 30 was most recently published as a representation of a

woman (Sotheby's 1980; see *Literature*) and called the "Isis Casati" because it was formerly in the collection of the Marchesa Casati in Rome. In fact, it depicts the male official Herybastet (De Meulenaere 1982: 28 note 21). He is shown striding in the traditional tripartite costume of the period. The articulation of the pectoral muscles, which affords the appearance of female breasts, is actually an artistic convention of the period to indicate a degree of corpulence commensurate with the status of the official depicted (p. 68, above, and CAT. 24). The attribute held in the clenched left fist may well be flowers, although the damage is too extensive to identify it more specifically, and such floral additions do characterize this group of statues as a whole (Philadelphia 40-19-3, Bianchi in *Das ptol. Äg.*: fig. 61; Cairo 8-2-21-8, Lyons 1896: 51; Bianchi 1976: 3). The shape of the back pillar, the scene at its top, and the orthography of the hieroglyphs suggest a dating in the first half of the Ptolemaic Period.

The information provided by the inscriptions (De Meulenaere 1982: 28 note 21) indicates that this statue was originally dedicated in the Precinct of the Goddess Mut at South Karnak (Fazzini 1985: pl. II). Inscriptions on the back pillars of similar statues show that they were erected near pylons of temples. One can suggest, therefore, that this monument once stood either before the first pylon of the Temple of Mut proper, or before that of Temple A. Sometime after being put in place at South Karnak it was transported to Rome and reerected in the Sanctuary of the Syrian Gods on the Janiculum. It then disappeared from view until published by Gauckler (1912: 361-62) as belonging to the Marchesa Casati. It disappeared again (Roullet 1972: no. 121) until 1980, when it was offered for sale at Sotheby's. Immediately after the sale, its new owner placed it on loan at The Brooklyn Museum.

CAT. 32, the draped statue of Pakhom, Governor of Dendera, is the most recent in date of the three statues in tripartite costume. If one cautiously assumes, as does De Meulenaere (1959: 14-15), that this Pakhom is the father of Pamenkhes (Cairo JE 46320 and CG 50047, Spiegelberg 1932: 19-20), who is known to have lived about 30 B.C., the *floruit* of Pakhom would have been about 50 B.C. Pakhom holds the traditional bolt of cloth (p. 70, above) in his fisted right hand and wears a broad fillet around his head. The latter has been unsuccessfully modified as if the sculptors were groping for a solution to mask what otherwise appears to be a blatant appropriation of the royal Alexandrian wide diadem both in its form (Krug in *Das ptol. Äg.*: 10; Kyrieleis 1975: 69) and its positioning on the head. The apparent lack of final polishing, anticipating the extremely rough surfaces of completed pharaonic sculptures of the first century A.D. (CAT. 133) accords well with the paleography of the hieroglyphs on the back pillar (CATS. 26, 31). The inlaid eyes are a particular feature that gains currency among workshops of the late Ptolemaic and early Roman Periods (CATS. 32, 137). The features of the face are modeled in broad planes and subjected to the principle of asymmetry (pp. 70-71, above), a stylistic pecularity which can be paralleled elsewhere in pharaonic sculpture from the late Ptolemaic and early Roman Periods (CAT. 41).

CAT. 33

Official Holding an Image of Osiris within a Naos

Basalt, 41.9×10.3×13.5 (16 1/2×4 1/16×5 5/16)
Late second-first century B. C.
Provenance not known
Hannover, Kestner-Museum, 1935.200.773

Literature: ESLP: no. 115.

The Egyptians appear to have developed the naophoros as a statue type during the course of Dynasty XVIII in order to express a closer relationship between man and his god (Bonnet 1961; Abitz 1979). The individual represented in such statues physically supports the deity and, thereby, aspires to a metaphysical eternal existence in the retinue of the god represented within the shrine. The owner of such a statue might also hope to gain the eternal benefit of divine protection from that particular deity because of the intimate connection afforded by the naos (Bonnet 1961; Lloyd 1982: 168, *passim*). During the Late Period, certain inscriptions on such naophoroi seem to indicate a particular *quid pro quo*, whereby the owner requests a benefaction from the deity whom he claims to be protecting by carrying the deity in the naos (Cairo JE 30978, Posener 1936: 5-6; van Dijk 1983: 52-58).

The Hannover statue raises several important art historical issues. One involves the costume (Bresciani 1960), whose most important component is a variant of the wraparound skirt (ESLP: no. 63; Bothmer 1964: 45, 51 note 3), generally worn in conjunction with a sleeved coat, characteristic of Achaemenid fashion (Knauer 1978; Roes 1951; Brooklyn 37.353, ESLP: no. 64). This particular skirt always has an accumulation of material on the upper chest, which results from the tuck necessary to hold the skirt in place. Often termed the Persian wraparound skirt, its appearance on statues did not coincide with the arrival of the Persians in Egypt in Dynasty XXVII (ESLP: 76). Examples are known on Egyptian monuments dated to Dynasty XXVI (Paris A. 93, Vandier 1964b; Bresciani 1967; Barocas 1974: 113, *passim*; Vittmann 1976). The type continues into the Roman Imperial Period, as is demonstrated by an infelicitously crafted naophoros with just such a skirt in Paris (N. 849, unpublished). Arranging examples of this costume in chronological order, one observes that the earlier examples are more accurate reflections of the actual appearance of the costume. With the passage of time – and regardless of whether or not the costume remained fashionable in Egyptian wardrobes – the craftsmen evolved formulae with which to evoke it. One stage in the abstract formulation is represented on the statue of Wesir-wer (CAT. 25) of the fourth century B. C., a later stage by the present statue, and a final stage by the statue in Paris (N. 849). This diachronic survey indicates that the progressive stylization of the wraparound skirt owes less to any venerable archaisms (ESLP: 148) and more to the craft of sculpting.

Questions of foreign influence in the rendering of particular details also require comment. Portraying the fingers wrapped around the bottom edge of the naos is an elective, variable feature for naophoroi made after Dynasty XXVII (De Meulenaere 1962: 40). The hair, far from being naturalistic and rendered in a Hellenistic manner (ESLP: no. 115), is a more extreme stylization, without articulation, of a type of coiffure that ultimately derives from models current during the Old Kingdom (e.g., Fig. 35).

The most distinctive feature of this statue is the face, whose features have been characterized as individualistic (ESLP: 149). A closer examination reveals otherwise and relates the shape of this head to the polygonal type already encountered in the Old Kingdom (pp. 57-59, above). Here, the visage, rendered as a series of modeled planes, relies on the addition of incised linear adjuncts – again in the form of nasolabial furrows – for its effect.

The lack of final polish, in conjunction with the seemingly incomplete state of some of the features, most notably the ears (ESLP: 149), and the propensity toward asymmetry, particularly in the face, would suggest a date for this statue in the late second or first centry B. C.

CAT. 34
Plaster Head in Profile

Plaster, 25.4×18.4×6 (10×7 1/4×2 3/8)
Fourth-second century B.C.
Provenance not known
Collection of Richard M. Keresey

Literature: Sotheby's, New York, December 11, 1976 : lot 295, illus.

This enigmatic profile, made of plaster and intentionally crafted as a fragment, is instructive because it belongs to a class of objects which few have studied. From the time of the Old Kingdom, Egyptians had modeled faces in plaster, as attested by the numerous examples believed to have been modeled over the linen wrappings of mummies (Boston 37.644, 39.828, W. Smith 1960: 65). The famous plaster masks from Amarna must be regarded within this tradition (Edwards 1960; Aldred 1973: 35 and note 55), to which belong as well two additional groups of plaster heads that are datable by their style to the Late Period: one group dates to the time of Ptolemy II Philadelphos (Varga 1960), whereas the second was published as representations of Apries of Dynasty XXVI (Aubert 1967), based on the suggested stylistic similarities with other depictions of that king as adduced by H. Müller (1955). The assertion that these plaster heads are to be regarded as death masks (Varga 1960: 12-13; Aubert 1967: 289; Aldred 1973: 35; Rieth 1973: 30-31) cannot be supported (Barocas 1974: 137) because they lack the detailed features of collapsed flesh, as a comparison with known death masks of famous Western personalities would reveal.

This particular stucco head is closest to the group assigned to Ptolemy II by Varga (1960), although one now understands that the stylistic features once ascribed to representations of that particular king were already in place during the fourth century B.C. (CAT. 24). As a result, this plaster profile is datable to the period between the fourth and second centuries B.C. The absence of any distinctive attributes and accompanying inscriptions makes a more exact dating speculative at best.

If one accepts the definition that ancient Egyptian art is hieroglyphic, and if the hieroglyphs themselves allow of the fragmentary and incomplete (Fischer 1977; 1986: 24-30), works which the West might define as unfinished could be complete works of art within the tenets of ancient Egypt's cultural requirements (CATS. 1, 131). There is thus no good reason to consider this work a trial piece or sculptors' model. Until contradictory evidence emerges, it is best to regard this profile either as an ex-voto to the cult of a king (CAT. 1) or as a commemorative monument erected in a private shrine devoted to a ruler (CATS. 49, 55, 56).

CAT. 35

see color plate VI

Head Exhibiting Signs of Age

Schist, 32.5 (12 3/16)
Third century B. C.
Provenance not known
Vienna, Ägyptisch-Orientalische Sammlung des Kunsthistorischen Museums, 42

Literature: Parlasca in *Das ptol. Äg.*: 26; Satzinger 1980: 69, pl. 31.

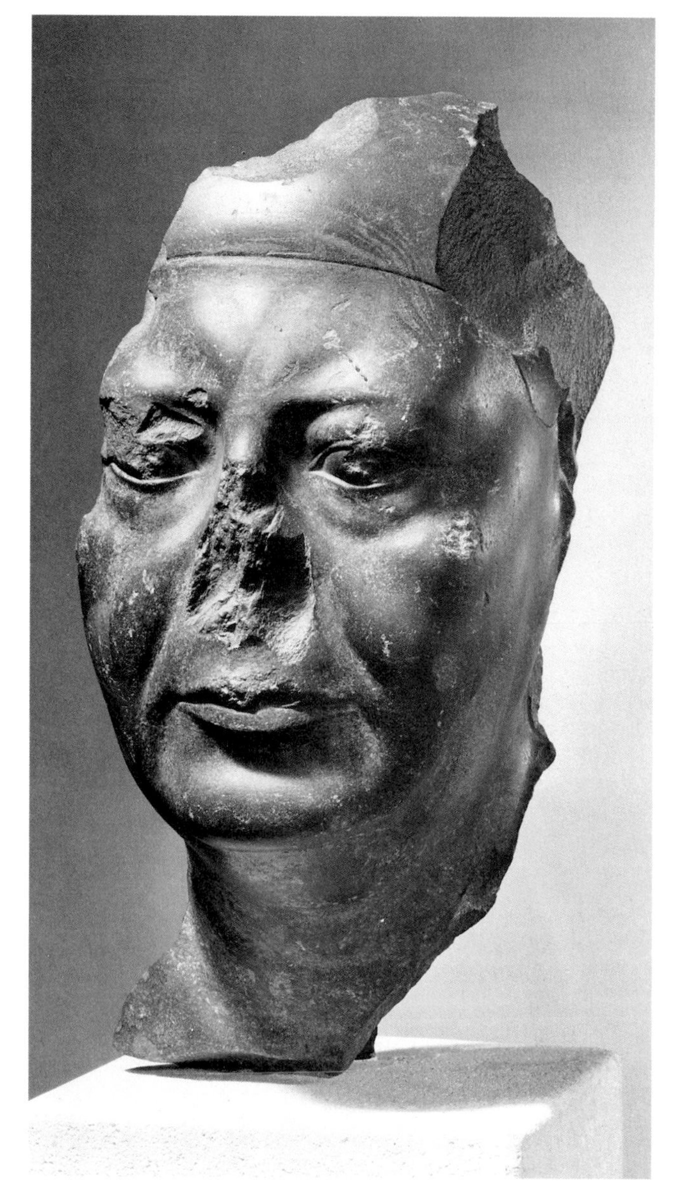

This head is doubtless the finest example known from the Egyptian Late Period of the application of the formulae for rendering signs of age. The individual was wearing a bag wig, whose rounded tab is visible alongside the remains of the left ear. The conception of the head divides into two parts, the front and side views. From the front, the statue exhibits features derived from the traditions to which the Bastis head (CAT. 40) and the Schimmel head (Bothmer 1987) belong. The treatment of the eyes recalls that of the Schimmel head, as does the configuration of the brow with the bridge of the nose, the emphasis on the cheekbones, the nasolabial furrows, and the rendering of the upper lip and chin. The undulating planes of the brow, knotted at each temple and in the center over the nose, are variations of features found in the head of Horsitutu (CAT. 31). The preserved left profile, while still not integrated with the front view, is nevertheless treated with a degree of modeling encountered both in the faces of Horsitutu and the Berlin Green Head (CAT. 46). The two distinctive features that connote a sense of corpulence – the double chin and the two lines on the throat – are both found on female heads of pharaonic style as well. The head of an earlier *physkon*-type (CAT. 48), as well as the quartzite head of a queen or goddess (CAT. 62), display just such a double chin, and the pharaonic female statue (CAT. 69) exhibits the so-called rings of Venus on a fat throat. The resulting image, although recalling the *physkon*, or fat-man type, encountered in Hellenistic depictions of Ptolemaic rulers (Parlasca in *Das ptol. Äg.*: 26; but compare Cairo CG 14, an Old Kingdom statue in which many of these features would still have been visible in the original gessoed and painted state; Saleh/Sourouzian 1987: no. 40), represents a long-established type within the pharaonic art of the Late Period. This head is merely an elaboration of those artistic tenets and fits into the development of Egyptian art of the third century B. C.

Furthermore, the attempt to identify this head as a representation of any Ptolemy, or of Ptolemy X Alexander I (Parlasca in *Das ptol. Äg.*: 26) fails to acknowledge the absence of a uraeus on the brow – the royal insignia always in evidence on such statues – and the presence of a bag wig. To date no example has been adduced of any Ptolemy represented in sculpture in the round who wears the bag wig (cf. CAT. 40). That the headdress is a bag wig and not a *nemes* can be confirmed by the lack of the single band at the brow, which is invariable for the *nemes* (for example, CAT. 1) or the double band, which one associates with the Blue Crown (CAT. 48; Munich ÄS 5339, Parlasca in *Das ptol. Äg.*: fig. 36). The individual represented is thus a private, non-royal person. In this context, it is extremely important to recall that in Egyptian art, from the time of Dynasty XXV on, the most graphic images displaying signs of age are non-royal, private commissions executed in accordance with pharaonic tenets. The phenomenon supports the suggestion that such images were created independently of any foreign influence.

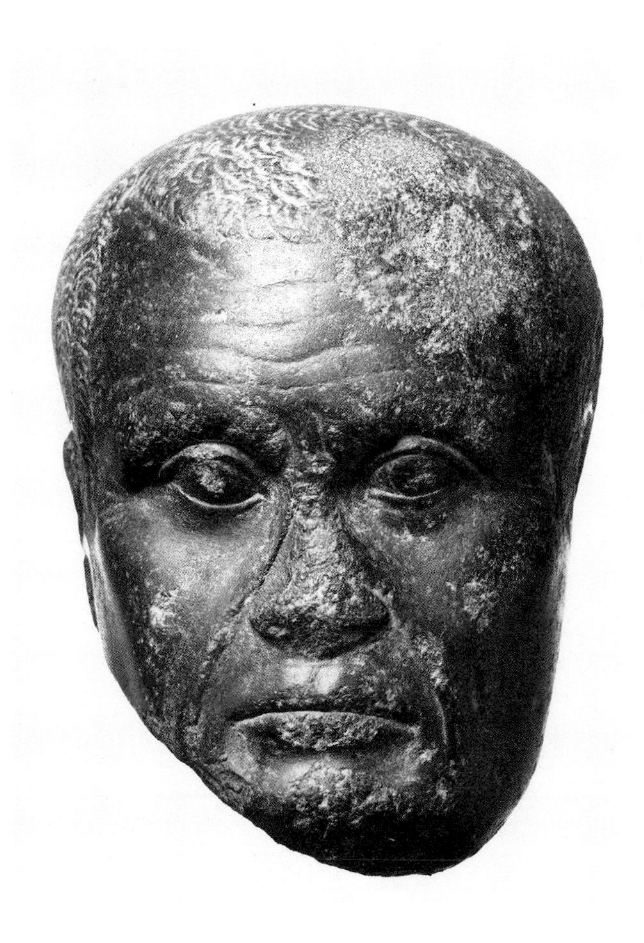

CAT. 36

Head of a Man

Basalt, 18.5 (7 5/16)
Third-second century B.C.
Provenance not known, allegedly from Karnak
Amsterdam, Allard Pierson Museum, 7860

Literature: van Haarlem/Lunsingh Scheurleer 1986: 71.

Many of the stylistic characteristics of the non-ideal egg-head (p. 57, above and CATS. 44-47), belonging as they did to a repertoire of sculptural forms, could be applied to other types of sculpture as well. This head in Amsterdam relies somewhat less heavily than the "Strong Man" (CAT. 44) on the interaction of plastically rendered planes for its effect. At the same time, the linear adjuncts are not as prominent as those encountered in the second century B.C. on examples such as the Boston Green Head (CAT. 45). One is, therefore, tempted to regard the stylistic features of this head as partaking of both traditions, and to suggest a dating for it between the third and second centuries B.C.

An unusual feature of this statue is the appearance of plastically rendered pupils, here in the form of disks. Such a stylistic device has a long tradition in Egyptian art and anticipates a similar phenomenon in Roman Imperial art of the second century A.D. (p. 72, above; CAT. 30).

The depiction of the hair, despite its almost modern appearance, is indebted to Egyptian norms (p. 65, above). It should be noted, however, that the individual locks are only carefully articulated over the face and at either side of the head. The crown of the head, seen from the back, reveals a surface merely roughed out in a way that neglects the definition of individual locks. In some respects, this feature anticipates the treatment of the hair on the Brooklyn Black Head (CAT. 43).

A final note should be added regarding a fundamental difference between Egyptian non-ideal images and representations of individuals in Hellenistic art and, later, in Roman art. The apparent unwillingness of the Egyptian craftsmen to integrate the profile and frontal views into a unified composition, and their insistence on relegating all of the physiognomic features to the frontal plane, fundamentally distinguish their works from those of Hellenistic and Roman workshops (p. 62, above).

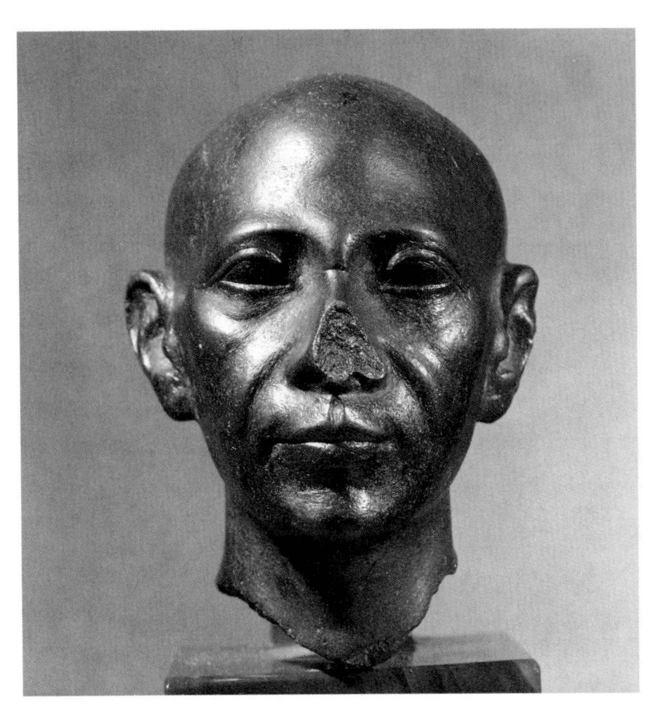

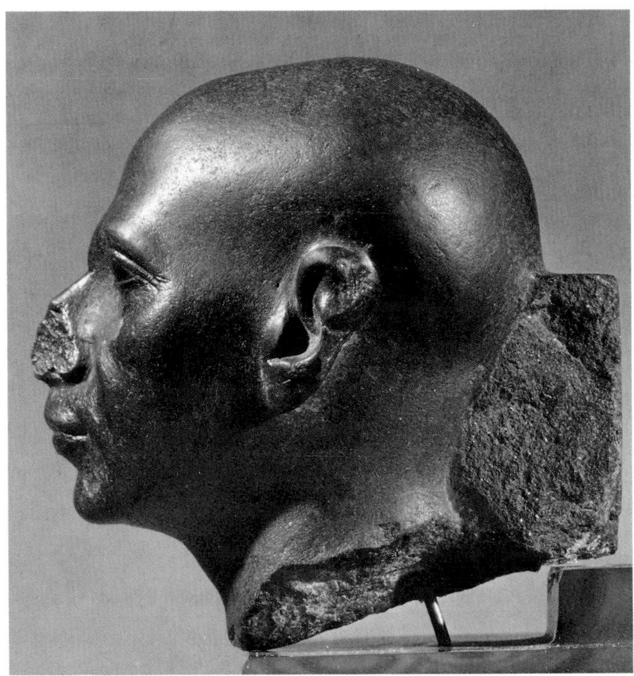

CAT. 37 *see color plate VII*

Head of a Man with an Aquiline Nose

Basalt, 8.7 (3 7/16)
Third-second century B.C.
Provenance not known
The Detroit Institute of Arts, 40.48; City Purchase

Literature: ESLP: no. 111.

This famous head, whose configuration is a variant of the polygonal type (pp. 57-59, above), is one of three similar examples where prominence is given to the aquiline nose. The second is in Brussels (E. 5346, ESLP: no. 110), the third in Venice (284, Leospo 1985: 202). So close are all three in style and execution that they must belong to a type. None are images of distinct individuals, as has been maintained (ESLP: 143-44). The particular slant of the ears of the Detroit head is a feature found in the other two examples as well. The knoblike protrusion at the root of the nose appears earlier on the statue of Petamenophis (Berlin 23728, Hornbostel in Altenmüller/Hornbostel 1982: no. 32). The line across the root of the nose itself and the crow's-feet anticipate the appearance of those features on the Berlin Green Head (CAT. 46). Such features belong to a common repertoire of forms on which Egyptian craftsmen could draw at will. The accentuated philtrum and the prominence given to the Adam's apple, although not as uncommon as the blemish on the Boston Green Head (CAT. 45), reveal how that repertoire could be enlarged from time to time. The Egyptian craftsmen's documented preoccupation with rendering physiognomies in accordance with their own pharaonic traditions during the Ptolemaic Period would quite naturally lead to an enlarged repertoire of such forms.

The lack of linear adjuncts and the inability of the craftsmen to integrate the plastically rendered frontal planes with the profile views are features common to the non-ideal egg-heads of the third and second centuries B.C., to which period this head can likewise be assigned.

CAT. 38
Face of an Official

Basalt, 19.5 (7 11/16)
Second century B. C.
Provenance not known
Munich, Wittelsbacher Ausgleichsfonds, Gl WAF 328

Literature: H. Müller/Wildung 1976: 206-07; Adriani 1978: 121 note 4.

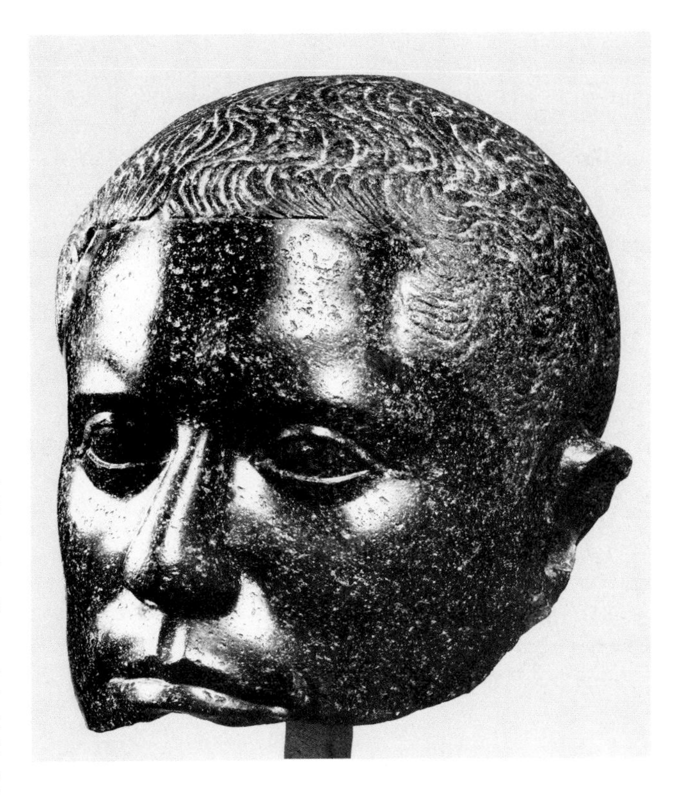

This interesting fragment of a head unquestionably belongs to the pharaonic traditions of the Late Period, as revealed by the faint, but undeniable traces of the back pillar, which may have resembled that found on a statue in Stockholm (NME 73, George/Peterson 1982: 100; ESLP: 156). The contrast between the highly polished surfaces of the skin and the somewhat rougher treatment of the hair, which results in an intentional bichromatic effect (p. 72, above; Bianchi 1979a: no. 80), is a stylistic feature found in sculpture dated to Dynasty XXX (CAT. 24) that continues to characterize certain classifications of sculpture in the round into the first century B. C. (ESLP: 156; and CAT. 43). Relief representations from the Old Kingdom provide exact parallels for the rendering of the hair as short strands (H. Wild 1953: pls. CXX, CXXII) rather than as tight curls, as in the Amsterdam example (CAT. 36), which is itself also indebted to models from the Old Kingdom. In style and execution, then, such coiffures are pharaonic in character and should not necessarily be defined as Egyptian interpretations of prevailing Hellenistic fashions (ESLP: 156). The differences between the pharaonic treatment of such hair, which sits inorganically on the top of the head like a cap (Kyrieleis 1975: 135-36; and Bianchi in *Das ptol. Äg.*: 99), and a Classical treatment of the same feature can best be gauged by comparing this head to that of Julius Caesar (CAT. 79).

Several physiognomic features connect this head to other pharaonic images. The rendering of the aquiline nose and the philtrum derive from the same repertoire of forms employed for the crafting of the head in Detroit (CAT. 37), and the almond shape of the stylized eyes set beneath an arched naturalistic brow finds close parallels on a head in Baltimore (22.226, ESLP: no. 120).

Much more revealing, however, is a comparison with a fragmentary head now in Copenhagen (AEIN 293, Roullet 1972: no. 41). So close in conception and execution are these two heads that they provide further demonstration that the pharaonic sculpture of the Ptolemaic and Roman Periods can be divided into types (pp. 57-59, above). The treatment of the almond-shaped eyes, with the well-defined inner canthi, set into gently receding sockets beneath a slightly arched naturalistic brow, the angle at which the aquiline nose is set off from the forehead, the pronounced philtrum, and the form and treatment of the lips are too close to be coincidental. The similarities are also to be found in the way the hair frames the face as a series of three intersecting circular segments, each one sweeping from ear to temple on either side of the face, with the third spanning the brow. The treatment of the facial features is one of restraint dominated by gently merging planes into which are set discrete nasolabial furrows of subdued linearity. The head in Copenhagen may well be unfinished because the hair is simply rendered as an undefined mass that rises from the surfaces of the skin. So relatively thick is this mass that the craftsmen may have been contemplating completing the head with the addition of tight curls, of the type found on the head of the anonymous official in Stockholm cited above. Indeed, the features on that face might be considered as variants of those found on the Munich/Copenhagen pair. One might suggest, therefore, that all three represent variations on a type of oval face with aquiline nose and short hair. This classification now emerges as yet another type into which heads from the Ptolemaic and Roman Periods can be divided (p. 59, above). The ability to identify objects whose characteristics conform to known typologies is one of the surest indications that the pharaonic images of the Ptolemaic and Roman Periods are not to be regarded as portraits.

The dating of the type to which both the Munich and Copenhagen heads belong is difficult to establish because of the absence of dated *comparanda*. The suggested dating of the somewhat similarly conceived head in Baltimore (cited above) to the second century B.C. has merit inasmuch as the features on the Munich head derive stylistically from those of heads in Detroit (CAT. 37) and Stockholm (cited above), both datable to the third to second centuries B. C. The subdued modulation of the planes and the discrete use of linear adjuncts on the Munich head also suggest a tentative dating to the second century B. C.

CAT. 39
Face Exhibiting Signs of Age

Basalt, 17.3 (6 13/16)
Late second-first century B. C.
Provenance not known
The Brooklyn Museum, 86.226.14; Gift of the Ernest Erickson Foundation

Literature: Bianchi in Brooklyn 1987: no. 87.

Although earlier commentators have contended that such heads ought to be considered as portraits of specific individuals, the artistic environment in which they were created argues against such a position. The treatment of the hair, resting upon the skull as if it were a cap, and of the individual locks of hair, and the lack of finish on those areas of the head not distinctly visible from the frontal view are characteristics which this head shares with a host of others (e.g., CATS. 31, 43) whose pharaonic character is incontestable. The insistence upon line at the expense of plane as the primary expression of physiognomic features characterizes this group of Egyptian faces, which seems to begin during the course of the late second century B. C. The creases on the brow, the knot at the root of the nose, the rudimentary crow's-feet at the outer corners of the eyes, the deeply pronounced nasolabial furrows, straight mouth, and chin set off from the lower jaw by a depression are formulaic features belonging to a set repertoire which the Egyptian craftsmen of the Ptolemaic Period consistently applied. The distinct asymmetry of the face, which causes its left side to be wider than its right, is a violation of axial symmetry that becomes an increasingly prominent feature of pharaonic sculpture in the first century B. C. (CAT. 41 and pp. 70-71, above).

A dating of this head to the period between the late second century and first century B. C. seems probable because the linearity of the forms has not completely negated the plastic qualities of the face, which are particularly evident in the modeling of the cheeks.

CAT. 40 *see color plate VIII*

Head Exhibiting Signs of Age

Basalt, 7.8 (3 1/16)
First century B.C.
Said to be from Kom Abu Billo (Terenouthis) in the Western Delta[1]
Collection of Christos G. Bastis

Literature: Bothmer in New York 1987: no. 36.

This fragment, whose monumental quality belies its small scale, depicts a male figure wearing a bag wig, one tab of which is preserved (cf. CAT. 35). The craftsmen have relied exclusively upon an orchestration of linear adjuncts in order to render the features of the face. The forehead is scored by two lines and a third is cut into the stone immediately above the natural brow. The right eye is set into a deep socket and is articulated by a fold in its upper lid; the crow's-feet at the outer canthus take the form of three incised lines. The bridge of the nose is set off at an acute angle to the brow; its wing is scored, and its nostril clearly visible. A deep nasolabial furrow accentuates a full, everted lower lip, whose center is scored with a single line.

Each of these linear adjuncts is somewhat artificially and decoratively added to the surfaces of the stone in a way not too dissimiliar from the orchestration of such incisions as groups of three in the Berlin Green Head (CAT. 46). In fact, both heads appear to belong to the same tradition, particularly regarding the treatment of the crow's-feet and, as has already been noted (Bothmer in New York 1987: no. 36), in the scored line on the lower lip. One is, therefore, inclined to date this head to the first century B.C.

[1] This is the provenance recorded by Bothmer in New York 1987: no. 36, although he gives no reason for assigning the head to Kom Abu Billo.

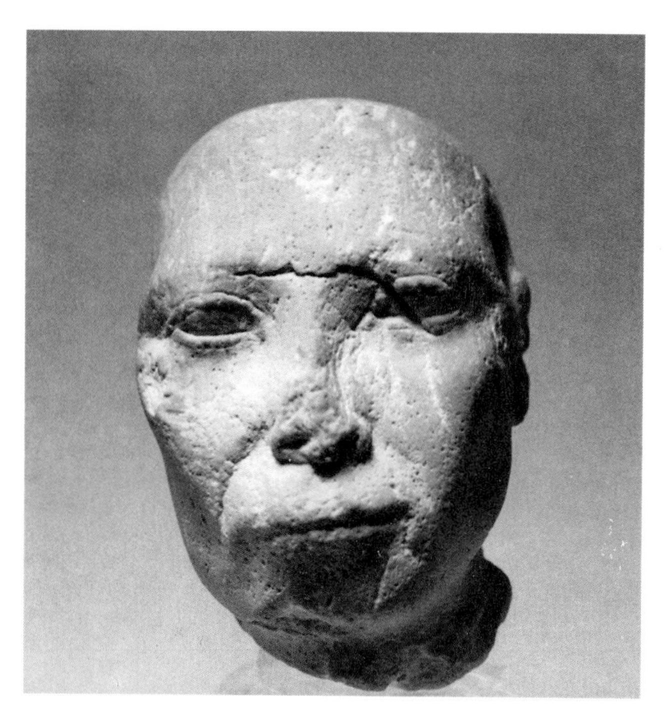

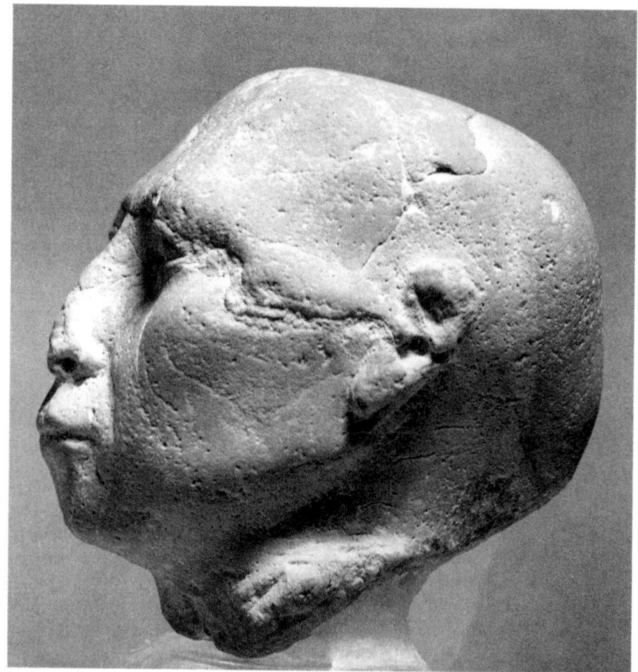

CAT. 41
Asymmetrical Head with Signs of Age

Limestone, c. 9 (3⁹/₁₆)
First century B.C.
Provenance not known
Collection of Jack A. Josephson

Unpublished

This fascinating head is so asymmetrical in its physiognomy that one might at first glance suggest that the artist has consciously created an image of the victim of a bilateral stroke. Such a thought vanishes as soon as the head is intercalcated into the series of polygonal heads (pp. 57-59, above) to which the naophoros in Hannover (CAT. 33) belongs. A comparison between the profiles of both reveals how the skulls are characterized by abrupt changes in the angles of their contours as one moves from the root of the nose to the juncture of the head with the neck. That abstract schema provides the framework into which the formulae for rendering age are set. In both heads, the eyes are outlined with thick lids, the upper running over the lower. This feature is a stylization quite out of place in a naturalistic representation. Further, both heads rely on the transitions between planes to create sunken cheeks. The deeply incised nasolabial furrows, the straight mouth, and the apparently incomplete state of the ears link both heads to one and the same tradition.

There are, of course, differences. The sunken cheeks are here more accentuated, the mouth more protruding, and the head shaved. But these differences are elective, and represent varying approaches to the same repertoire of forms. Far from being a portrait or an artistic response to a neurological disorder, this small limestone head conforms to the principle of axial asymmetry that becomes a hallmark of sculpture made during the Ptolemaic and Roman Periods (pp. 70-71, above).

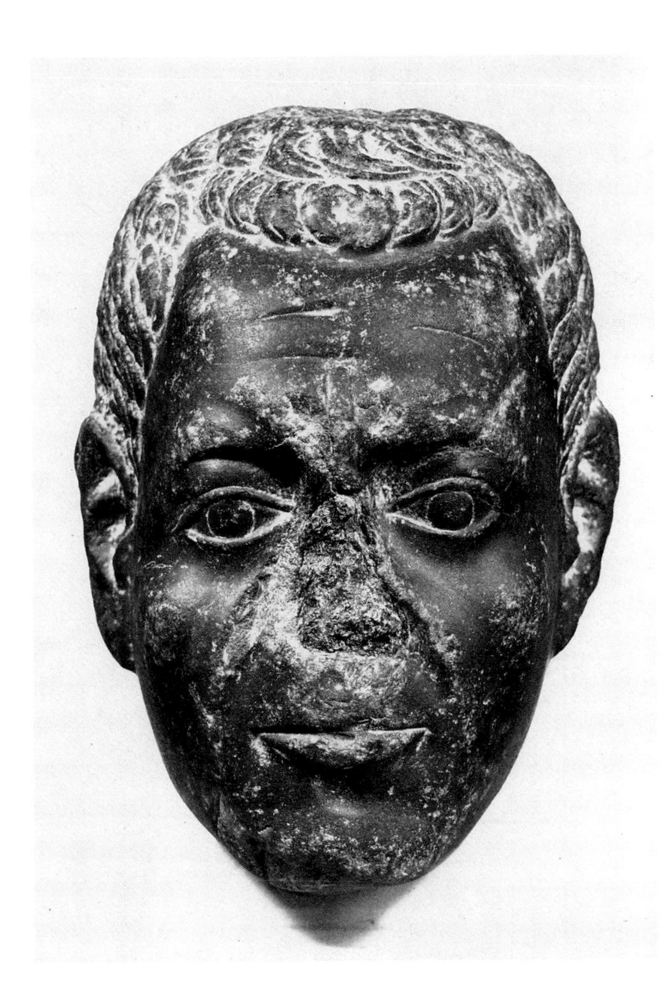

CAT. 42
Head of an Official

Basalt, 25 (9 3/16)
Early first century B.C.
Provenance not known
Paris, Musée du Louvre, Département des Antiquités Grecques et Romaines, MND 2229 (Ma 3565)

Literature: Bothmer 1978: pl. XVI.

Every physiognomic detail of this head is easily integrated into the repertoire of forms available to the pharaonic craftsmen of Ptolemaic Egypt. No stylistic feature is unique. The bichromatic effect achieved by the conscious contrasting of the highly polished surfaces of the face with the rougher treatment of the hair, the plastically rendered disks of the irises, and the caplike hair are all paralleled elsewhere (pp. 72, and 65, respectively). The seemingly careful attention to detail noticeable from a study of the frontal view is deceptive – the sides and back of the head reveal a rather perfunctory approach to completion. Moreover, the outer edge of each ear, simply blocked out, lacks articulation, and the locks of the hair on the crown and at the back of the head are not defined. In fact, one can see how the craftsmen planned to execute the hair in a two-stage operation by observing, particularly in the left profile, how the stone was first laid out as a series of plastically cut lozenges, each corresponding to the size of three locks of hair, which would then be cut as adjacent pairs of intersecting concentric circles. This feature does not necessarily imply that the work is unfinished. Numerous other examples of pharaonic sculpture can be adduced from the Late Ptolemaic and Roman Periods which share this characteristic (CAT. 43). It seems, therefore, that such endemic lack of finish is simply symptomatic of this particular period of Egypt's history.

The plastically rendered planes of the face articulated by a series of linear adjuncts, here including not only the wrinkles on the brow and the nasolabial furrows, but also the articulation of the upper eyelid, belong to the sculptural traditions of the second century B.C. (CATS. 39, 44-46), whereas the marked degree of asymmetry (Bothmer 1978: pl. XVI) in the face is a characteristic more frequently encountered in the first century B.C. (pp. 70-71, above).

The Paris piece belongs to a group of other heads in pharaonic idiom and style from the Ptolemaic and Roman Periods that possess a certain affinity in the configuration of the head. A close examination of the front view of the Paris head reveals that the oval face has an indentation at the level of the ears which likens its contour to a figure eight. The mouth, with its thin lips, is horizontal and the protruding chin is set off from the lower jaw by a faint depression.

These are diagnostic features that can be employed as criteria for defining yet another series of heads (pp. 57-59, above), in which the Paris head seems to stand at or near the beginning. A dating in the very late second century B.C. is, therefore, suggested for this piece.

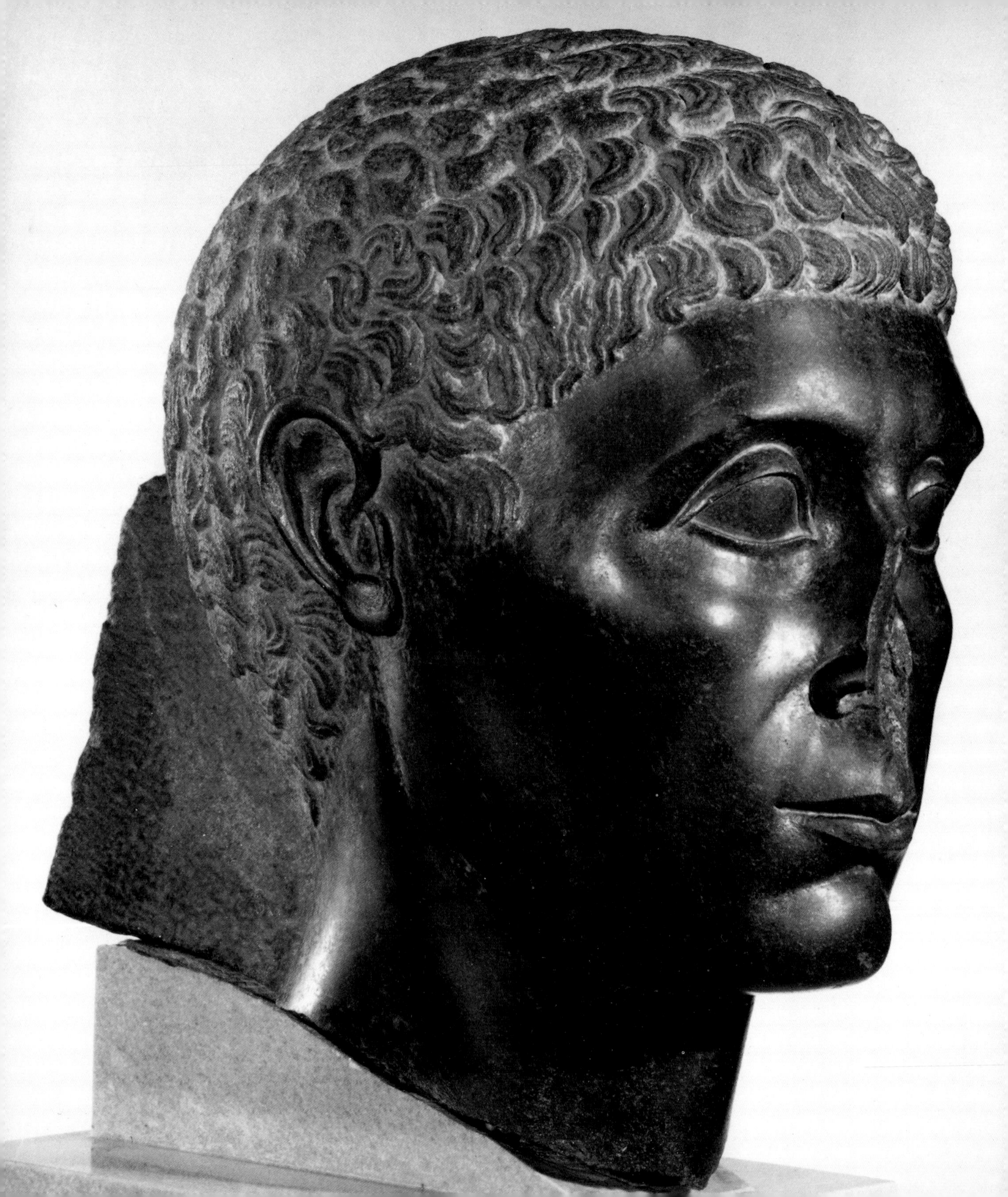

CAT. 43 *see color plate IX*

The Brooklyn Black Head

Diorite, 41.4 (16 5/16)
First century B.C.
Said to be from Mitrahineh
The Brooklyn Museum, 58.30; Charles Edwin Wilbour Fund

Literature: ESLP: no. 132; H. Jucker 1981a: 704-05; Kiss 1984: 25.

The conception and execution of this head are typically Egyptian. So, for example, the coiffure sits on the scalp like a cap (p. 65, above), a feature further emphasized by the sideburns, which are not integrated into the design but appear to be incongruously added tabs. A series of raised half-moon planes forms the basis of the design of the individual strands of hair that are incised into them (compare CAT. 42). Those at the crown of the head are not finished, and the head lacks the final polish at the sides of the neck and back pillar despite its apparent bichromatic effect (p. 72, above) when viewed from the front. Other Egyptian features include the wide-open, staring eyes in which the upper eyelid overlaps the lower.

Traditionally, Egyptian craftsmen respected the rectilinear nature of the block of stone from which the head was carved and therefore failed to develop a consistent formula for integrating the frontal and profile views of the face into a cohesive unit (p. 62, above). In those terms, then, this head displays a very significant feature: the contour of its forehead is trapezoidal, marked at both sides of the face at a point just before the outer corner of the eyes with a distinctive change in plane. This change in plane enabled the craftsmen to experiment with the modeling of the cheeks, the results of which can be appreciated in a profile view – a view, however, which also reveals that the physiognomic features characterizing the face are still relegated to the frontal plane in conformity with Egyptian sculptural tenets. In fact, experimentation with this very same trapezoidal contour of the forehead is encountered, however infrequently, in pharaonic sculpture of the Late Period, as in a head in Munich identified as a representation of Montuemhat and datable to about 650 B.C. (Munich ÄS 1922, H. Müller 1975). Some Egyptian craftsmen, then, did attempt to model the profile views of a small group of heads, but, as the very pronounced, flat, unmodulated horizontal plane of the throat of the Brooklyn Black Head so clearly reveals, they were unsuccessful in their attempts to integrate the planes of the head into a consistent whole.

The Brooklyn Black Head is the central piece in yet another typology of non-idealizing Ptolemaic heads (pp. 57-59, above), characterized by the trapezoidal contour of the forehead. It is identical to a second head in the British Museum (1871), whose surfaces, however, are both less finished and less highly polished. These relate to a head in the Barringer Collection at the Peabody Museum (New Haven YPM 6278, G. Scott 1986: no. 142) and to the much discussed head in Paris (Ma 970), which may or may not represent one of the last Ptolemies (Kyrieleis 1975: 70-71; Krug in *Das ptol. Äg.*: 14 note 44; Parlasca in *Das ptol. Äg.*: 26; R. Smith 1986: 77 note 55). Within that typology, a dating for the Brooklyn Black Head to the middle of the first century B.C. can be suggested. It shares with the Berlin Green Head (CAT. 46) the mannered use of linear adjuncts, especially in the formal line which separates the chin from the jaw, and the parallelism between the crease on the upper eyelids and the corresponding lowermost wrinkles of the brow.

The tantalizing trace of an inscription on the back pillar provides insufficient evidence for identifying the individual represented. Since the piece can be intercalcated into a typology for non-idealizing Egyptian heads, it probably represents a native cleric depicted in a generic stage of life (p. 57, above), rather than one of the more famous historical personages of the era, as was once suggested (Bianchi in Brooklyn 1983: 77). Attempts to associate this cleric with any member of the families of the High Priests of Ptah at Memphis during the first century B.C. (ESLP: 172; Maehler 1983: 95-96) rely too heavily upon the dealer's statement for the head's provenance, made at the time of its acquisition.

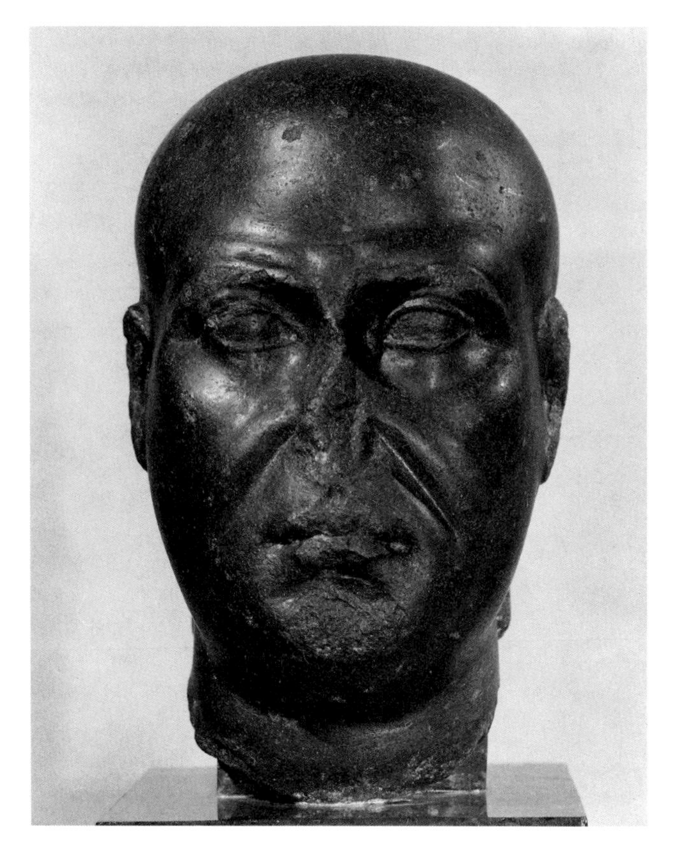

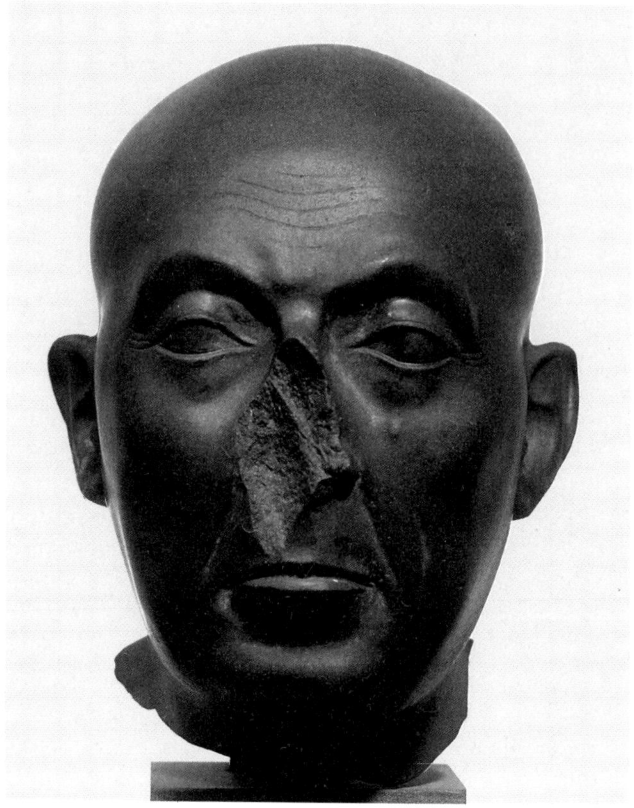

CATS. 44-47
NON-IDEALIZING IMAGES

CAT. 44
The "Detroit Strong Man"

Diorite, 20 (7 7/8)
Third-second century B.C.
Provenance not known
The Detroit Institue of Arts, 40.47; City Purchase

Literature: ESLP: no. 104.

CAT. 45 *see color plate X*
The Boston Green Head

Schist, 10.8 (4 1/4)
Second century B.C.
From Saqqara
Boston, Museum of Fine Arts, 04.1749; Pierce Fund

Literature: ESLP: no. 108.

It is becoming more and more apparent that non-idealizing heads of the Egyptian Late Period conform to developing sculptural types (pp. 57-59, above). The egg-heads, such as CATS. 44-47, have been defined as one type of generic portrait (Bianchi 1982a) whose existence had been earlier hypothesized both by von Bissing (1923) and Anthes (1939a; 1939b). The difficulties with their chronological assessments stemmed from the fact that their *comparanda* could not be narrowly dated. A proposed working hypothesis is that the egg-head, as a type, became a fixed feature of Egyptian art during the fourth century

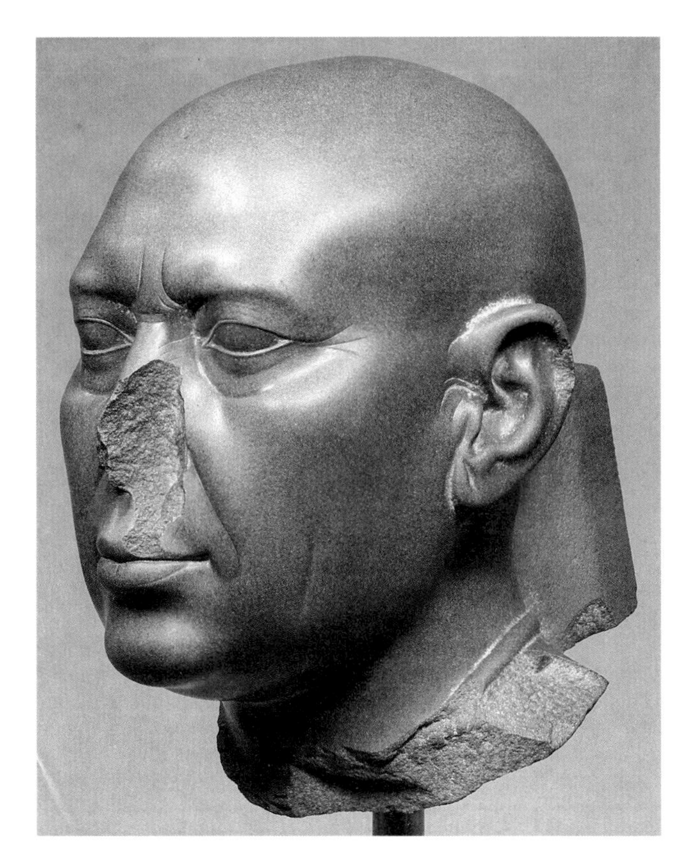

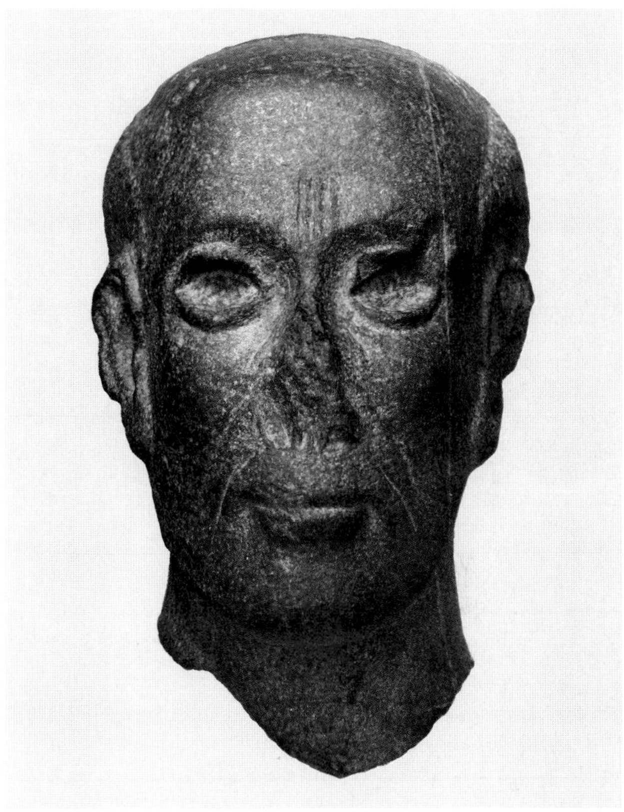

CAT. 46

see color plate XI

The Berlin Green Head

Schist, 21.5 (8 7/16)
First century B.C.
Provenance not known
Berlin/BRD, Staatliche Museen Preußischer Kulturbesitz, Ägyptisches Museum, 12500

Literature: ESLP: no. 127; Küthmann 1962; Kaiser 1966; Bianchi 1982a; Vandersleyen 1985: no. 235.

CAT. 47

Head of an Official

Granite, 26.4 (10 3/8)
Late first century B.C.-first century A.D.
Provenance not known
Brussels, Musées Royaux d'Art et d'Histoire, E. 7946

Unpublished

B.C. (Bianchi 1982a: 149). The Egyptian craftsmen, drawing on a repertoire of forms to indicate signs of age, could transform the surfaces of any given ideal image of an egg-head into a non-ideal image that still retained the shape and contour of an egg-head type (Bianchi 1982a). No example of the type has been adduced for any period prior to the fourth century B.C., when ideal versions of the egg-head become frequent (Bianchi 1982a: 149). A *terminus post quem* for the type may be established by a statue in Cairo (CG 700) inscribed for Teos II, who is known to have discharged his functions during the early third

century B. C. (ESLP: 129). The type may, however, have been developed earlier.
The ideal (Bryn Athyn, without number, ESLP: no. 99), and non-ideal versions of the egg-head type are coeval, but the non-ideal type seems to evolve diachronically from the plastic to the linear. The "Strong Man" in Detroit (CAT. 44) represents the earlier, plastic type. The linear adjuncts, especially the nasolabial furrows, interact with the volumetrically rendered plastic planes to convey a feeling of fleshiness. The Detroit piece has stylistic affinities with a head in Paris (E. 8060, ESLP: 134), which ought not be labeled a caricature. One can see how the formula might be altered to include hair, if one considers the slight change in plane above the temples in the Detroit head as an indication of hair, and compares this feature to the balding indicated on the example in Brussels (CAT. 47).
The Boston Green Head (CAT. 45) may be considered transitional because the baroque plasticity of the "Strong Man" is modified, with the emphasis here placed upon linear adjuncts. The creases on the brow are more stylized, the nasolabial furrows more independent of their surrounding planes, and the lids of the eyes more abstracted in their contours. This development is best paralleled in the features of the face of a statue of an anonymous official in Stockholm (NME 73, George/Peterson 1982: 100; ESLP: 156).
That the craftsmen responsible for the creation of this head were consummate masters of their art is demonstrated by the appearance of a blemish, perhaps to be identified either as a mole or a wart, on the left cheek (ESLP: 140). Such a feature is unique in Egyptian art, but ought to be considered in terms of the crow's-feet at the corners of the eyes, the knot at the root of the nose, and the aquiline nose. Since the Egyptian craftsmen were working within a repertoire of forms and constantly increasing the visual vocabulary for physiognomic details from one generation to the next, one need not look to extra-Egyptian sources for the appearance of the blemish (ESLP: no. 108). Such an effort denies the innovative character of Egyptian art by subjectively invoking the past prejudice for foreign influence. One is dealing not with a portrait, but with a type onto which has been grafted a singular detail. Since that type conforms in all other respects to demonstrable tenets of pharaonic art during the Ptolemaic Period, the ascription of this detail to Greek influence is arbitrary.
No Egyptian work of art from the Late Period has evoked more comment than the Berlin Green Head (CAT. 46), which has been dated to each successive epoch of the last six hundred years of the first millennium B. C. The curious half-round feature appearing on both sides of the base of the neck has never been satisfactorily explained. It appears to be of a diameter too wide to be the seam of a garment (p. 66, above). The alternative suggestion – that it represents a torque – is admissible insofar as this characteristically Persian accessory is known to have survived into the Ptolemaic Period (Naples 490, Donadoni 1981: 270, fig. 2), as did the Persian wraparound skirt (see CATS. 25, 33). An insistence upon the torque, therefore, to establish the dating of the head to the Persian Periods is specious.
As an egg-head, this object cannot, in the present state of knowledge, antedate the fourth century B. C. So dependent upon the linear traditions of the Boston Green Head is the Berlin Head and so cold and calculating is the mannered nature of those linear adjuncts that the head cannot be assigned to any period other than the first century B. C. (Bianchi 1982a). Küthmann's narrower dating to the period 45-35 B. C. and his insistence upon the head's indebtedness to a Graeco-Roman tradition (Küthmann 1962), is based – particularly in its misinterpretation of certain anatomical details – upon a free-association exercise of the presumed interrelationships of stylistic features. It was precisely this prejudice and line of argument that forced B. Schweitzer to interpose the head of Horsitutu (CAT. 31) incorrectly into his development of the Roman Republican portrait of the first century B. C. (1948: 77). The historiography of this group of egg-heads has revealed just how fragile such an art historical appraisal really is.
The head in Brussels belongs to the end of the series. The linear adjuncts that develop from the Boston to the Berlin Green Heads have here become ossified. The lines at the root of the nose and the nasolabial furrows have been routinely incised into the surfaces. The complete abstraction of the planes of the face lacks vitality, while the inlaid eyes are features paralleled on the face of Pakhom (CAT. 32) and anticipate the style of the last pharaonic works of art (see CAT. 133). And yet, the craftsmen are conversant with the possibilities of their tradition to the extent that they were here able to modify the non-ideal egg-head with the representation of a receding hairline.
In conclusion, the series of the non-ideal egg-heads begins at least as late as the third century B. C., at which time the emphasis is on an orchestration of plastic surfaces (CAT. 44). At some point within the second century, the taste for linear adjuncts appears to gain ascendancy (CAT. 45). Eventually, the linear adjuncts become so entrenched in the tradition that examples of the first century B. C. exhibit the artificial repetition of groupings of threes (CAT. 46; and Bianchi 1982a). The series seems to terminate with the integration of the now abstracted linear components into the period's prevailing taste for simplified planes and inlaid eyes (CAT. 47).

CAT. 48
A *Physkon*-Type Wearing a Blue Crown

Basalt, 6.5 (2 9/16)
Reign of Nectanebo I (380-362 B.C.)
Provenance not known
Paris, Musée du Louvre, Département des Antiquités Egyptiennes, E. 8061

Literature: ESLP: no. 73; Curto 1978: 58 note 5; Krug in *Das ptol. Äg.*: 23; Parlasca in *Das ptol. Äg.*: 26.

The suggested identifications of this small head have vacillated considerably over the years. An initial attempt to regard it as Ptolemaic in date, possibly as a depiction of Ptolemy V Epiphanes (Aldred 1962: 209), was countered by the proposal that the head represented Nectanebo I (ESLP: no. 73), until several scholars simultaneously suggested that it might in fact represent a late Ptolemy (Krug in *Das ptol. Äg.*: 23; Parlasca in *Das ptol. Äg.*: 26) as a *physkon*, or fat man (R. Smith 1986). Before proceeding to discuss the stylistic features of the head, it should be noted that the pharaoh is here depicted wearing a Blue Crown (W. Davies 1982; Elie-Lefèbre 1979; Lloyd 1983: 289; Rammant-Peeters 1985; Russmann 1984b: 104-05; Tefnin 1983; Traunecker *et al.* 1981: 73, 89), an attribute which cannot be associated with any securely identifiable sculpture in the round depicting a Ptolemaic king.[1]

The proportions of this face approximate a square, being almost as wide at the cheeks as it is tall, from the juncture of the Blue Crown on the brow to the chin. This configuration of the face seems to characterize non-ideal images of Dynasty XXX as well (CAT. 25), and is at variance with Ptolemaic versions of the *physkon*-type, which tend toward the rectangular, where the height of the face is approximately twice its width, as a comparison with the head in Brussels reveals (CAT. 53). The upper eyelid is set off from its socket by a deeply cut recess which, in light of the small scale of this piece, appears to correspond to the crease found on larger examples of the period (CAT. 25; ESLP: no. 70). The elongated, trapezoidal shape of the back pillar also points to a date within Dynasty XXX (ESLP: 91-92; see also Brooklyn 77.50, Bothmer/De Meulenaere 1986: pl. II, c).

The affinities between the fleshy quality of this head and those found on a plaster sculpture in Munich are undeniable (Munich ÄS 5339, Vandersleyen 1975: no. 224). The rendering of the eyes, the nose, the mouth, the chin, and the double chin are analogous. These shared stylistic traits are also encountered in somewhat modified form, as expected given the disparity in scale, in the sphinxes of the dromos of the Temple of Luxor, which are inscribed for Nectanebo I (ESLP: 92).[2]

Since the features on this small head have more in common with monuments associated with Nectanebo I of Dynasty XXX than they do with those of the Ptolemies, and since the Blue Crown is not securely attested for Ptolemaic sculptures in the round, this piece should be removed from considerations of the Ptolemaic *physkon*-type and reassigned to the fourth century B.C.

[1] Although the Ptolemies (Barocas 1972: figs. 101-02) and the Romans (Daumas in *Crépuscule*: fig. 36) might be represented in relief wearing the Blue Crown, there are no unequivocally identified examples in sculpture in the round of any of those monarchs with that headdress. The heads in Brooklyn (54.68) and Ann Arbor (4971), which have been identified as Ptolemaic rulers wearing the Blue Crown (ESLP: 167-68) are not inscribed and were acquired on the art market without any archaeological provenance. So aberrant are their respective styles that one might be tempted to call both into question. Could not this absence of the Blue Crown on sculpture in the round indicate the paradox in which the native priesthoods found themselves? The performance of the cults within the temples required all of the regalia of the past, whereas the Ptolemies, as usurpers, may have been denied the appearance of the Blue Crown, a known symbol of legitimacy (W. Davies 1982), in their statuary.

[2] I wish to thank Mr. El Sayed Aly Hegazy for allowing me to study these sphinxes in detail and to assist in the collation of the inscriptions on their bases. This firsthand study confirms the identification of these sphinxes proposed in ESLP: 92.

CAT. 49 *see color plate XII*

Portrait of Alexander the Great

Alabaster, 10.5 (4 1/8)
First century B. C.-first century A. D.
Provenance not known
The Brooklyn Museum, 54.162; Charles Edwin Wilbour Fund

Literature: A. Hermann 1980: 118-19; Bianchi in Brooklyn 1983: no. 79.

This statuette, whose small scale indicates that it might have been employed for private rather than public devotion (Krug 1984: 199; see also CAT. 51), is sculpted with a cameolike delicacy evident in the whole as well as in details such as the articulation of the irises and the pupils by incision (A. Hermann 1980: 119). This last feature is common in Egyptian pharaonic art (p. 72, above). Once established within the repertoire of sculptural forms, this treatment of the eyes could be repeated at any subsequent time by the Egyptian sculptors. There is no good reason, therefore, to ascribe this stylistic feature to Egypt's faience industry (Lunsingh Scheurleer in *Das ptol. Äg.*: 6-7, citing the comment of Parlasca regarding Brooklyn 58.1 and 58.79.1). One finds such eyes on a limestone statuette of purely Egyptian style inscribed for a Cleopatra in New York (89.2.660, Kyrieleis 1975: 118, 183 [M1]), as well as on a head of Augustus in Baltimore (Vierneisel/Zanker 1979: 53, no. 5.7). Adriani's observation (1970: 82) that this particular handling of the eyes is attested in Egypt well before the Hadrianic Period is confirmed, and works so sculpted can no longer be arbitrarily assigned to the Roman Imperial Period. Moreover, the eyes themselves are here large, bulging, and wide open, features that likewise characterize Hellenistic ruler portraits from Egypt (Kyrieleis 1976, 85-86.)

This carefully made bust was originally set into a draped body sculpted from a differently colored stone (A. Hermann 1980: 118). The long, flowing locks were tied by a fillet, whose streamers are indicated in relief on the shoulders. The circumference of the head is marked by a series of evenly spaced holes into which spikes, perhaps of gold, were originally set, in imitation of the rays of the solar crown of Helios (A. Hermann 1980: 118). Holes for attaching such a crown also occur on a marble head, in a private Swiss collection, identified as a portrait of Ptolemy III (I. Jucker 1975: 17).

The dating of the piece is problematic, particularly because the style of the sculpting can be paralleled in works from the late first century B. C. to the first century A. D. (A. Hermann 1980: 119).

CAT. 50
Portrait of Ptolemy I Soter

White marble, 26 (10¼)
300-250 B.C.
Reportedly from the Faiyum
Copenhagen, Ny Carlsberg Glyptotek, Cat.-nr. 453 a (IN 2300)

Literature: Poulsen 1951: 322; Kyrieleis 1975: 165 [A3]; Kiss 1984: 23; Maehler 1983: 89, 93.

The remarkably strong resemblance of the features on this marble head to those on coins of Ptolemy I Soter renders the identification certain. The head was anciently completed in plaster (Strocka 1967: 126) and was doubtless attached by means of the same material to a separately made body (Queyrel 1985: 280). The material and technique, therefore, are characteristic of other Hellenistic works made in Egypt during the Ptolemaic Period. By extension, some observers have maintained that the style of this particular head is purely Greek (Maehler 1983: 89, 93); some have gone so far as to attribute the head to the circle of Skopas (Kiss 1984: 23). One need only compare the treatment of the facial features to those on any number of Hellenistic originals, such as the Skopaic works from Tegea (Bieber 1961: fig. 55), the Aegias at Delphi (Sjöqvist 1953), or the "Beautiful Head" in Pergamon (Bieber 1961: fig. 475) to realize that the head of Ptolemy I Soter in Copenhagen relies upon an integration of linear adjuncts with the plastic modeling of the flesh in order to achieve its physiognomic statement. Such a strict reliance upon line is foreign to the Hellenistic formal repertoire. As a result, one can only agree with Kyrieleis (1975: 16) that this linearity is indebted to earlier Egyptian works of Dynasty XXV/XXVI, in which the inherent potential of line, as opposed to plane, for the rendering of flesh was first explored. This linear tradition was further developed during Dynasty XXVII and finally reached its zenith of expression at the end of the Ptolemaic Period (CATS. 40, 46). Moreover, the treatment of the eyes, set into deep sockets, and their clearly articulated lids are within the tradition to which the corresponding features on the royal head of *physkon*-type belong (CAT. 53). The head in Copenhagen is, consequently, an early example of the influence of a native Egyptian sculptural tradition upon a typically Hellenistic Greek idiom and material. On the basis of comparisons with other heads, assigned to the circle of Ptolemy II Philadelphos and Arsinoe II, the Copenhagen head is perhaps best regarded as a posthumous portrait of the dynasty's founder made early in the reign of his successor (Kyrieleis 1975: 16), in order to serve the requirements of the newly founded cult of Ptolemy I as *theos soter* (Kyrieleis 1975: 13).

CAT. 51
Portrait of Ptolemy I Soter

Plaster, 8.3×5.8 (3 1/4×2 5/16)
305-282 B.C.
From Mitrahineh
Hildesheim, Pelizaeus-Museum, 1120

Literature: Kyrieleis 1975: 8-11; Reinsberg 1980: no.36.

There is universal consensus that this bust is a portrait of Ptolemy I (Kyrieleis 1975: 8-11), called Soter at an early period in his reign (Bresciani 1983a: 103-05). The representation, showing the king frontally as a bust, with the locks of his hair characteristically arranged in a Hellenistic fashion, ought to date to the early decades of the third century B.C. on the basis of its position within a series of other portraits so identified (CAT. 50; Kyrieleis 1975: 8-11). The wide fillet with its streamers at the neck imbues the figure with Dionysiac overtones (Kyrieleis 1975: 9), thereby establishing one of the Ptolemaic dynasty's most lasting thematic characteristics (CAT. 58) at a very early date (Heinen 1978: 181).

In a pioneering study, Adriani (1960: 111-25; and, more briefly, 1972: 168, *passim*) demonstrated that in at least one instance a plaster cast was the medium by which a specific motif, encountered on a metal vessel, was transmitted. His findings confirmed a suggestion made earlier (Rubensohn 1911), which has now been expanded to include the use of plaster casts for replicating statues (von Hees-Landwehr 1982). As a result, there is a tendency to regard all such plasters as models of this sort (Dohrn 1985; Queyrel 1984; Lunsingh Scheurleer 1984; Himmelmann 1983: 24; D.B. Thompson 1964). That view has recently been challenged by Burkhalter (1984), who proposed that some of those plaster casts existed as independent works of art. Indeed, Burkhalter's suggestion is confirmed by several other casts (CATS. 22, 34, 128), which indicate that there was a long tradition in Egypt for creating independent works in plaster (CAT. 34). Since the Hildesheim plaque cannot be associated with a workshop with any degree of certainty (Bianchi 1985), it might very well have been such an independent work of art, along the lines suggested by Burkhalter (1984: 341-42) for some of the plasters from Begram.

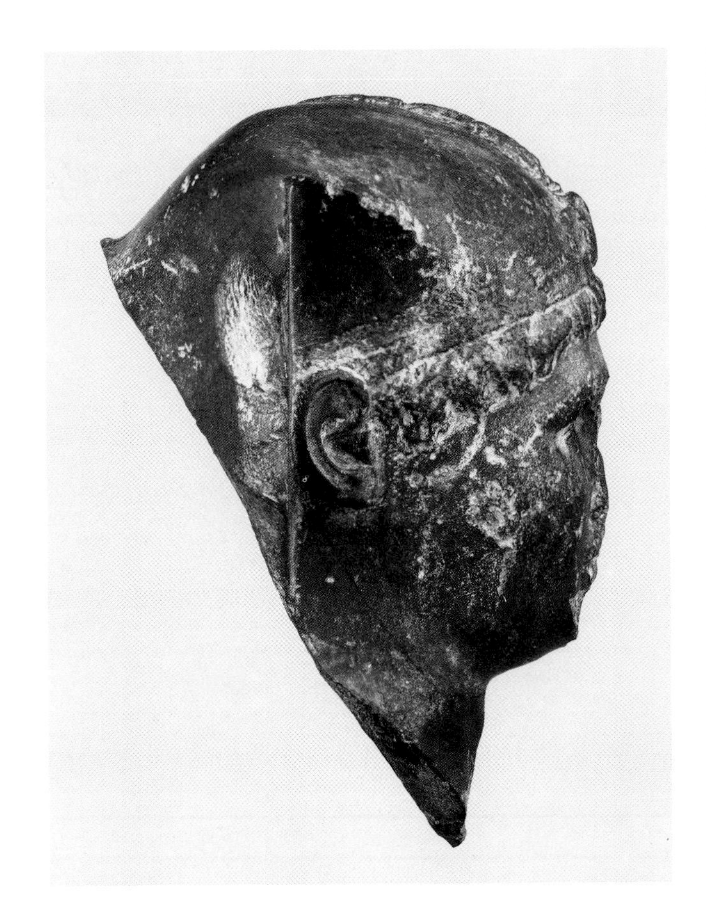

CAT. 52
Head of a Ptolemy

Schist, 37 (14 9/16)
Third century B.C.
Provenance not known
New Haven, Yale University Art Gallery, lent by Peabody Museum of Natural History, 4.1.1953; Barringer Collection

Literature: G. Scott 1986: 170-71.

There are several features about this head which have elicited disparate opinions regarding its dating. Some have noted that the *nemes* is characterized by a swelling of its contours (ESLP: 132), an observation which has then been erroneously interpreted by others, who ascribe the swing of the *nemes* to Hellenistic influence (Maehler 1983: 93). Its unusually narrow band has been purposefully roughened for reasons which are not clear. While it is true that such a feature is an indication of gilding now lost (ESLP: 132), one wonders why gilding, if originally present, was relegated to such a relatively small area. The lack of tabs hanging from the band in front of the ears is not unusual, being almost commonplace in the depiction of the *nemes* on royal sculpture assigned to the Ptolemaic and Roman Periods (Alexandria 362, Kyrieleis 1975: pl. 60, to cite one example without hair on the brow).

The *nemes* is adorned with a uraeus, the bottom of whose hood extends ever so slightly over the lower edge of the band and touches the hair. Its locks, which are an Egyptian rendering of a Hellenistic Greek fashion (CAT. 43), are sculpted according to pharaonic stylistic tenets and were made by native Egyptian craftsmen (ESLP: 132); they have nothing to do with Hellenistic artistic influence as many maintain (Maehler 1983: 93; G. Scott 1986: 170). Since the eyes were originally inlaid, their appearance would have varied markedly from the present one. As a result, it seems presumptuous to characterize the lower lids as heavy and compare them to coin portraits in order to formulate an identification of the pharaoh depicted (Maehler 1983: 93). The damage to the nose and chin, evident in a profile view of the right side of the face, precludes an adequate assessment of the appearance of these features (G. Scott 1986: 170, top). The corners of the mouth are drilled and drawn slightly downward, in a way frequently encountered in Egyptian sculpture of the Late Period (Baltimore 297 and 197, ESLP: nos. 69, 93). It is therefore unwise to interpret this feature, derived from the repertoire of pharaonic formal elements, as an indication of the subject's personal character (G. Scott 1986: 170, citing ESLP: 132). This Egyptian nature of the lips permeates the conception of the head as a whole. The face is designed as a slight oval with almost square proportions (as in CAT. 62). In keeping with pharaonic tenets, there is almost no hint of facial modeling, as revealed in the profile view, where the cheek presents itself as a broad, uninterrupted plane. All of these observations lead one to agree with Kyrieleis (1975: 41) and Aldred (in *Crépuscule*: 160, based on ESLP: 132) that this head is indebted to pharaonic, not Hellenistic, traditions.

The attempt to identify this head as a representation of the Roman Emperor Augustus is based, in part, on its apparent stylistic similarities to other uninscribed heads, thought to represent that monarch, as well as on the mistaken notion that the head exhibits a blending of Egyptian and Hellenistic features (Kiss 1984: 35; Massner 1986: 63-64; but see Strocka 1980: 180). Although it is possible that Augustus might have commissioned an Egyptian statue of himself, the known images of this ruler recovered from Egypt are not so conceived (CAT. 81).

The identification of this head as either Ptolemy IV Philopator, first proposed by Needler (1949: 133-35; Strocka 1980: 180), or Ptolemy V Epiphanes, as Bonacasa suggested (1961: 369), cannot be supported because the head lacks a distinctive physiognomy and attributes. In like manner, an identification as Ptolemy III Euergetes I, which many endorse (I. Jucker 1975: 23; Strocka 1980: 180; Vermeule 1981: 142; Maehler 1983: 93), cannot be proved because the head, whose pharaonic character is established, can no longer be profitably compared to coins which are derived from an entirely different tradition (p. 62, above).

The lack of definite changes of plane within the configuration of the face, the downward turn of the mouth, the absence of linear adjuncts, and the symmetrical character of the face place the work within pharaonic traditions of the third century B. C., as Aldred perceptively maintained (in *Crépuscule*: 160, basing his observations on ESLP: 131-32). A more narrowly defined time span stretches the limits of available data and enters the arena of speculation.

One final observation may affect the eventual identification of the subject. Viewed from the right profile, one sees that the contour of the *nemes* from the crown of the head is interrupted by an upward swing which, seen from the rear, does not appear to be a back pillar, as has been suggested (ESLP: 132). The statue to which this head belonged may thus have been set against a back slab (CAT. 16) or compositionally arranged in an attitude different from that of a striding figure (ESLP: 132); it may even come from a sphinx.

CAT. 53
A *Physkon*-Type as Pharaoh

Diorite, 47 (18 1/2)
Third-second century B. C.
Provenance not known
Brussels, Musées Royaux d'Art et d'Histoire, E. 1839

Literature: ESLP: 177; Kyrieleis 1975: 174 [G2]; Vandersleyen 1975: 270; Heinen 1978: 194, fig. 9; Kiss 1984: 22; R. Smith 1986: 70; Tefnin 1988: 54-55, no. 18.

Although there is almost universal agreement among scholars that this head is a representation of Ptolemy VIII Euergetes II because of its remarkably close physiognomic correspondences to coins struck for that king in 138/137 B.C., commentators seem unable to identify or even to agree on the artistic traditions and styles represented in this extraordinary work. In Vandersleyen's view (1975: 270), many of the head's features are non-Egyptian. Kyrieleis (1975: 64), however, accepts the Egyptian nature of the head, as do Kiss (1984: 22) and R. Smith (1986: 70), although they both reject Kyrieleis' assessment of the head's concomitant psychological intensity and both consider the face to be devoid of any expressive dynamism. Such apparent contradictions must be satisfactorily resolved in order to formulate a more coherent assessment of this work.

The Egyptian artists of the Late Period had earlier developed and repeatedly employed the stylistic vocabulary and technical means for depicting a *physkon*, or obese individual (p. 59, above). It is also true, however, that Hellenistic artists were capable of achieving similar effects, as the correspondences between the Brussels head and the coin portraits of Ptolemy VIII Euergetes II reveal. Such facile stylistic analyses (pp. 43, 61, above) of the rendering of corpulence are consequently a deficient means for establishing the artistic tradition to which this head belongs, because both Hellenistic and pharaonic craftsmen could independently achieve the effect of the *physkon*-type by working exclusively within the confines of their own sculptural traditions.

The question of Egyptian versus Hellenistic components can be resolved by considerations of structure. In general, one fundamental difference between Egyptian and Hellenistic heads is the Egyptian's strict insistence on relegating all of the physiognomic features of the face to the frontal plane (p. 62, above). In the Brussels head, the craftsmen have so tenaciously adhered to this basic Egyptian sculptural principle that there can be no doubt about its Egyptian identity. The extremely arched brows, which lack cosmetic paint stripes, the bulging eyes, the feature of the upper lid crossing the lower, and the failure to give all the surfaces of the stone the same degree of final polish (p. 72, above) are each characteristics of Egyptian, not Hellenistic, art. Kyrieleis and R. Smith are, therefore, correct in their assessment of this head as the product of an Egyptian workshop. It is a native Egyptian version of a *physkon*-type. Readings of psychological intensity, however, remain subjective. Compared with Hellenistic ruler portraits of the Ptolemies, the Brussels head lacks such intensity, as R. Smith observed (1986: 70). But it should not be compared to works belonging to traditions, temperaments, and cultures different from the ones in which it was created.

In terms of non-idealizing images of Ptolemaic rulers created within Egyptian traditions, the Brussels head finds its closest parallels in the statue of a corpulent female (CAT. 69). Both of these works are more ideal versions of the obesity displayed in the head of a private individual (CAT. 35). Since all three belong to a native pharaonic tradition and lack identifying inscriptions, one cannot insist on identifying them with any historical personage. Because the head in Brussels conforms to established pharaonic traditions that were current in the third and second centuries B.C., its resemblance to images of any Ptolemaic ruler in a Hellenistic idiom may be gratuitous.

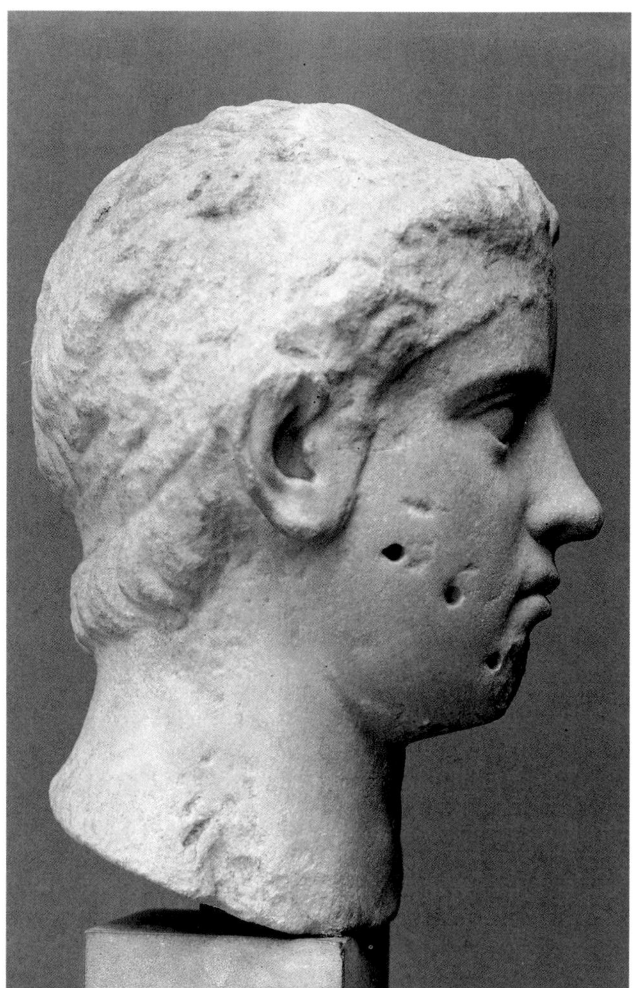

CAT. 54
Portrait of Ptolemy IV Philopator

Marble, 27.5 (10 13/16)
222-205 B.C.
Perhaps from Alexandria, but its association with the district of Hadra (Eleusis) is not certain
Boston, Museum of Fine Arts, 01.8208; H. L. Pierce Fund

Literature: Kyrieleis 1975: 170-71 [D1].

In its present state, the physiognomic details revealed in the profile view of this marble correspond so precisely to those found on numismatic images of Ptolemy IV Philopator that the identification of this head as a portrait of that king is assured. Nevertheless, the Alexandrian image on those coins is here transformed by the appropriation and inclusion of certain formal principles derived from pharaonic art. These include the modeling of the facial features as a series of broad planes, the excessive reliance upon a sharply defined, uniform edge that causes the brow to merge imperceptibly with the nose, and the stylized, expressionless rendering of the eyes set into deep, undefined sockets (CAT. 64; Kyrieleis 1975: 49). One should not, however, ascribe this pharaonic cast of the portrait to the documented ascendancy of Egyptian nationalism during the reign of Ptolemy IV (p. 16, above; Fraser 1972, vol. I: 60-61) because a similar stylistic phenomenon is also operative in earlier portraits of Ptolemy III Euergetes I (Alexandria 3270, Kyrieleis 1975: 169 [C11]), and in those of Arsinoe II (CAT. 64; Kyrieleis 1975: 49).

The forceful impression gained from this blocky, almost four-square mass of the profile is diluted in the frontal view, which is somewhat weaker and more triangular in its configuration. This difference is to be ascribed to the alteration of the head at a later date, when the planes of the chin and cheeks, in particular, were cut back to accommodate the addition of a beard, set into the line of the lower jaw, as the presence of the drilled holes reveals. In order to add the beard, the sideburns, so characteristic of numismatic images of Ptolemy IV on coins, were removed, as indicated by the deeply incised line running from the left earlobe upward along the hairline on the cheek. At the same time, the hair was modified, both in the locks falling over the brow and in those roughly corresponding to the line of the original placement of the headband toward the front. The hair thus removed by the sculptor's chisel was restored in plaster in the subsequently completed portrait. Such usurpation of earlier works and the use of plaster for alterations are phenomena peculiar to the history of Alexandrian ruler portraits from Egypt (CAT. 81).

Three features of this head before alteration deserve comment. The first is the somewhat wide and flat diadem, which was bound tightly around the hair and secured so that it rested high on the head. Similarly shaped and positioned diadems are found on two other portraits of Ptolemy IV (Budapest 4769, Alexandria 22150, Kyrieleis 1975: 47-48; Houghton 1986: 58-59). Secondly, the mouth of the Boston example, with the upper lip in the form of an undulating cupid's bow tightly pressed against the sickle-shaped lower, is given fuller, more sensuous expression in a fourth portrait in Paris, which has long been erroneously identified as a portrait of Ptolemy III (Paris Ma 3168, Kyrieleis 1975: 46-47). Thirdly, the most unusual feature of this portrait of Ptolemy IV is that the teeth are seen from within the open lips. This is a most remarkable detail that recalls the portrait of Ptolemy XII in Paris (CAT. 57), where one can see the impression of the tongue within the slightly parted lips.

The coin portraits of Ptolemy IV deserve special comment as well, because they seem to reflect an ever increasing intrusion of Egyptian motifs into an art form which had theretofore been exclusively indebted to Hellenistic norms. Some jugate portraits depict Ptolemy IV and his wife, Arsinoe III, in the guise of Serapis and Isis crowned with miniature, almost fancy dress, versions of Egyptian crowns (SV: 1124). In these coins, the image of Ptolemy IV habitually overlaps that of his wife. Some (Brunelle 1976: 54-55; Carter 1984: 763) regard this overlapping as evidence for identifying the royal couple on the relief of Archelaos in London (2191) as Ptolemy IV and Arsinoe III, but since the physiognomies of those two faces do not correspond to the ones on the jugate coin portraits of those monarchs the identification has been challenged (Kyrieleis 1975: 44 note 167).

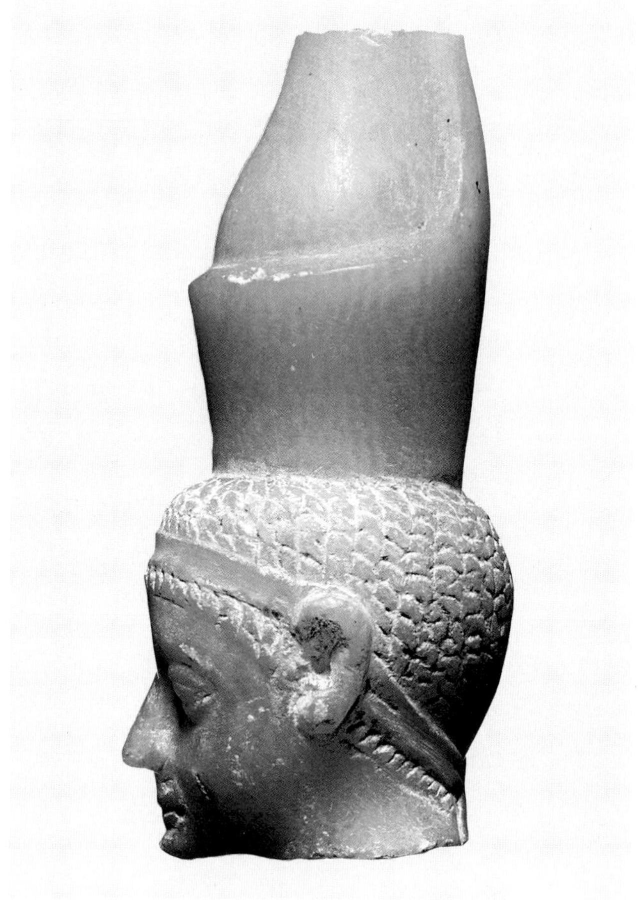

CAT. 55

CAT. 55
Portrait of Ptolemy V Epiphanes as Pharaoh

Alabaster, 10.6 (4 3/8)
Reign of Ptolemy V Epiphanes (205-180 B.C.)
Provenance not known
Berlin/BRD, Staatliche Museen Preußischer Kulturbesitz, Ägyptisches Museum, 14568

Literature: Kyrieleis 1975: 134 [E1]; Parlasca in *Das ptol. Äg.*: 28-29.

CAT. 56
Portrait of Ptolemy V Epiphanes with Uraeus

Alabaster, 7.8 (3 1/16)
Reign of Ptolemy V Epiphanes (205-180 B.C.)
Provenance not known
Berlin/BRD, Staatliche Museen Preußischer Kulturbesitz, Ägyptisches Museum, 13457

Literature: Kyrieleis 1975: 134 [E2]; Parlasca in *Das ptol. Äg.*: 28-29.

These two portraits are presented together because they illustrate some of the problems inherent in understanding and identifying portraits of the Ptolemies. CAT. 55 depicts a youthful face whose physiognomy is so distinctive when compared to other images of children questionably identified as representations of various Ptolemies (Kraus 1983; Vollenweider 1984) that it must represent a specific type. The triangularly shaped face with its pointed, projecting chin, the oblique angle by which the aquiline nose is set off from the forehead, and the

CAT. 56

gaunt, sunken cheeks are also features encountered in CAT. 56 and in a third head (Berlin/BRD 23140, Kyrieleis 1975: 134 [E3]).

Whereas scholars unanimously agree that all three heads represent one and the same individual, there is little agreement about the identity of that individual. The attempt by Parlasca (in *Das ptol. Äg.*: 29) to see these images as representations of Ptolemy Caesarion because of a perceived lack of quality in their execution can be dismissed as subjective. Correspondences between CAT. 55 and the others in this group to coin portraits confirm that the subject can only be Ptolemy V Epiphanes (Kyrieleis 1973; 1975: 52, 54). The fillet is neither wide and flat nor is it worn high on the head, as Houghton (1986: 59) maintains in an attempt to support a dating in the first century B. C. The fillet, as the left profile and rear views show, is actually a thin ribbon wrapped several times around the head before it was secured below the occipital bulge by a knot that allowed the streamers to fall freely about the neck. The rendering of this ribbon finds an exact echo in the numismatic evidence (Kyrieleis 1975: pl. 40, figs. 1-2).

Both Kyrieleis (1975: 54) and Parlasca (in *Das ptol. Äg.*: 28) interpret the sidelock on CATS. 55 and 56 as the insignia of a child, in accordance with Egyptian conventions. Such emphasis is unwarranted because the pharaonic formula for depicting a child demands that the sidelock appear in conjunction with an index finger placed at the lips (Hornung 1973: 43). The appearance of the sidelock alone is the insignia of various classes of priests (Quaegebeur 1971 a: 246; in *Das Ptol. Äg.*: 23; CAT. 130), some of whom are specifically associated with Memphis (Brooklyn 82.23, J. Clère 1983: 29; Brooklyn 82.23 with Brussels E. 7049, Bothmer 1985: 101-02), where Ptolemy V Epiphanes was crowned pharaoh in 196 B. C. in accordance with Egyptian rites (Fig. 3, the Rosetta Stone, Sethe 1904, vol. II: 182-83; Andrews 1981). The sidelock may eventually prove to be an emblem reserved exclusively for images of Ptolemy V Epiphanes that associate him with Memphis (Baltimore 54.1050, Heinen 1978: 195). One might tentatively link the alabaster head in Berlin with the Double Crown (CAT. 55) to the image of Ptolemy V Epiphanes erected in a naos at the time of his coronation (Fig. 3, Sethe 1904, vol. II: 192; Kákosy 1983: 59-60). Stylistically, the rendering of the physiognomy of the three heads identified as representations of Ptolemy V Epiphanes are dependent upon Egyptian sculptural tenets (Kyrieleis 1975: 135). The same conclusion obtains for the treatment of the hair, whose small, tight curls are an Egyptian translation of a Greek fashion (Kyrieleis 1975: 135-36; Bianchi in *Das ptol. Äg.*: 99). This pharaonic character is reinforced by the appearance of a back pillar on CAT. 56.

CAT. 57

Portrait of Ptolemy XII Auletes

Marble, 37.5 ($14\frac{3}{4}$)
55-51 B.C.
Said to be from Alexandria
Paris, Musée du Louvre Département des Antiquités Grecques et Romaines, MND 1960 (Ma 3449)

Literature: Strocka 1967: 126; Kyrieleis 1975: 178 [I1]; Parlasca in *Das ptol Äg.*: 28; R. Smith 1986: 67.

The fundamental assumption in identifying specific images as depictions of individual members of the Ptolemaic royal family is that correspondences exist between the physiognomy of any given representation and that preserved on coins bearing the likeness of the ruler in question. Despite the pitfalls inherent in a simplistic application of this principle (CAT. 53; pp. 61-62, above), its premise is valid and, when applied judiciously, produces results. The identification of this marble as a representation of Ptolemy XII Auletes is assured, because its forehead, virtually undamaged nose, lips, and chin combine into a profile congruent with those found on coin portraits of this monarch.
The portrait nevertheless raises a series of important technical, iconographic, and practical issues. A careful examination of the marble reveals that it was anciently recut from an earlier portrait of this same ruler (R. Smith 1986: 67). Although the reasons for this recutting are moot, an analogy with the theory regarding the recutting of a head in Boston (59.51, R. Smith 1986: 78) suggests that this portrait was modified in the period between Ptolemy XII's return to Egypt and resumption of the crown in 55 B.C. and his death in 51 B.C.
Secondly, the portrait in its final form, if not already in its original version, was completed in plaster, a technical characteristic commonplace among Hellenistic ruler portraits from Ptolemaic Egypt (p. 62, above). Conventional wisdom ascribes such a practice to the paucity of marble, which had to be imported into Egypt since the country had no natural sources of the stone. That suggestion has been challenged on economic and technical grounds (CAT. 81). The completion of a marble portrait with plaster additions represents a convergence of earlier Greek and pharaonic practices in the ateliers of Ptolemaic and Roman Egypt.
Iconographically, the images of Ptolemy XII Auletes bear a striking familial resemblance to those of his daughter and successor, Cleopatra VII (Toynbee 1978: 85). The similarities are most evident on the numismatic portraits in which a gaunt visage highlighted by deeply set eyes, an unnaturally bulbous, projecting chin, and an acutely aquiline nose predominate (Kyrieleis 1975: pls. 68,2 and 107,1-2). The same features characterize some images on issues of Ptolemy VI Philometor (Kyrieleis 1975: pl. 46,1) and ultimately evoke the numismatic likenesses of Ptolemy I Soter himself (Kyrieleis 1975: pls. 1-2). Whether such representations reflect strong genetic traits within the family or are conscious artistic concessions to the image of Ptolemy I Soter, whose posthumous likeness was continually perpetu-

ated by his successors on issues struck in his memory, cannot now be decided. However, it is an inescapable conclusion that the images of Ptolemy XII Auletes and of Cleopatra VII stress their Macedonian Greek origins.

CAT. 58
Ptolemy XII Auletes as Dionysos

Bronze, 4.8 (1 7/8)
80-57 B.C. or 55-51 B.C.
Said to be from Alexandria
Private collection

Literature: Kyrieleis 1975: 178 [I2].

A comparison of this small, well-preserved complete bust with coins (CAT. 61m) and a head in Boston (59.51, Kyrieleis 1975: 175-76 [H6]) confirms the identification of Ptolemy XII, with his characteristic profile, including a distinctive nose, lips, and chin. Ptolemy XII is represented wearing a chlamys, a state mantle serving as a royal insignia (Kyrieleis 1975: 77), which is clasped over the right shoulder by a fibula, or elaborate safety pin. The hair is decorated with an interesting combination of motifs, including ivy arranged around a diadem whose streamers fall onto the shoulders, and the horns of a bull (Kyrieleis 1975: 78). The resulting image is, thereby, imbued with over-

tones of the Greek god Dionysos (Kyrieleis 1975: 77-78), with whom Ptolemy XII himself was identified – one of his epithets was *neos Dionysos*, "the young Dionysos."

This god, whose character is diverse, was at times identified with the Egyptian god Osiris (Kákosy 1983: 57-58), but soon came to represent *tryphe*, or unlimited luxury, the cultural characteristic of the Ptolemaic court at Alexandria (p. 18, above). He came to be regarded as the god with whom the Ptolemies themselves wished to be associated. As a result, one finds that Dionysos and his cult held a special place in the court of Ptolemaic Alexandria: he was given, for example, special prominence in the grand procession of Ptolemy II that wound its way through the streets of Alexandria for several days (Rice 1983: 28-30) and two cities in the Faiyum were renamed Bacchias and Dionysias in his honor (Tondriau 1950). The cult of Dionysos gained momentum during the reign of Ptolemy IV Philopator (Kyrieleis 1975: 43), perhaps at the expense of the Egyptian cult of Osiris (cf. CAT. 104). Some historians would suggest, therefore, that this eclipse of Osiris was unacceptable to the native Egyptians and represented yet another contributing factor to the revolt of the Thebaid (Peremans 1975: 401; p. 16, above). In any event, the associations between Dionysos and the Ptolemies became ever stronger, so that by the time of the ill-fated visit of Scipio to the court of Ptolemy VIII Euergetes II the rift between the irreconcilable Roman and Hellenistic Egyptian cultural values of *mos maiorum* (p. 18, above) and *tryphe* had become unbridgeable (Heinen 1978). For this reason the Romans, unwilling to accept or to understand *tryphe*, continued to hold the Ptolemies in low esteem into the first century B. C., when the cult of Dionysos reached its zenith in Egypt. It was at this time that the Alexandrians gave Ptolemy XII, the father of Cleopatra VII, the epithet Auletes, "the flautist," because of his devotion to the cult of Dionysos (Le Corsu 1978: 25). Somewhat later, Marc Antony, although a Roman, became so acculturated to Alexandrian norms that he himself was associated with Dionysos, to the dismay of the Romans (Becher 1976; Heinen 1978). The defeat of the forces of Cleopatra VII and of Antony at Actium was viewed by the Romans as the triumph of Apollo over Dionysos (Becher 1976) and the concomitant cultural supremacy of the concept of *mos maiorum* over that of *tryphe* (Heinen 1978).

CAT. 59
Statue of One of the Last Ptolemies

Basalt, 82×39 (32 5/16×15 9/16)
First century B. C.
Provenance not known
Paris, Musée du Louvre, Département des Antiquités Egyptiennes A. 28 (N. 28)

Literature: ESLP: 162; Bonicatti 1963: 197.

At first glance, this statue appears to conform in most of its features to artistic norms common to other works of art from the Ptolemaic Period. These characteristics include the plain, undecorated kilt (CAT. 25), the *nemes*, without stripes (CATS. 1, 52), and the tripartition of the torso with the peculiarly Egyptian rendering of the lower abdomen, into which is set the teardrop-shaped depression of the navel (CAT. 27). The sickle-shaped smile of the lips and the different levels on which the eyes are placed even appear to imbue the face of this statue with a certain individuality. Closer examination, however, demonstrates that these facial features are part of the craftsmen's general disregard for axial symmetry (p. 71, above). The median line of the body does not coincide with the body's axis of symmetry: the left side of the statue is wider than the right. This disparity is evident in the disproportionate circumferences of the arcs defining the pectoral regions beneath each lappet of the *nemes*. This asymmetry is carried over into the face and head, where the cheeks and the eyes are placed on different horizontal levels and the band of the *nemes* on the brow and its contour at the top of the head are askew. In the profile views, the proper left side appears to be deeper than the right. Viewed from the back, the kilt's upper band does not form a continuous design as it passes beneath the back pillar. Here one observes that the band is depicted on two different levels, the left side being somewhat higher than the right.

From the present configuration of the back pillar, one gains the distinct impression that the design of the statue was altered while it was being sculpted. The triangular top of the back pillar is superimposed upon a raised rectangular plane. The rough surfaces here, contrasting so emphatically with the polished surfaces of the front and sides of the statue, underline the craftsmen's apparent inability to decide upon the ultimate design of the back pillar. Because the craftsmen were equivocal about their artistic statement, the dating of the statue is somewhat difficult to establish. Nevertheless, the extreme degree of asymmetry would argue in favor of a dating within the first century B. C., as would the relative height of the head in proportion to the body. Such small heads seem characteristic of this period (CAT. 33).

CAT. 60
Coin of One of the Last Native Pharaohs

Gold, 1.8 (11/16) diameter
Fourth century B.C.
Provenance not known
Berlin/BRD, Staatliche Museen Preußischer Kulturbesitz, Verein zur Förderung des Ägyptischen Museums, 1-78

Unpublished.

Whereas a minor academic argument still rages about whether aspects of the economy of the late New Kingdom can justifiably be termed monetary, it is agreed that the use of coinage as a medium of exchange did not become prevalent in Egypt until late in her history. That use was initiated by the Greeks, who had been in Egypt at least as early as Dynasty XXVI, and who were accustomed to the use of coin as the accepted medium of exchange. The account of Herodotus (IV, 152) implies that the Greeks at Naucratis employed the Aegenetian stater (Malibu 1983: 29) for inter-Hellenic commerce during Dynasty XXVI (Lipiński 1982: 24). The arrival of the Persians into Egypt during Dynasty XXVII accelerated the use of coinage in the land. Herodotus (IV, 166) indicates that Aryandes, Satrap of Egypt under Darius the Great, was the first to issue silver coinage that was actually struck in Egypt itself (Milne 1938: 200). Under the Persian domination, coinage in Egypt became more prevalent, and was inextricably linked to the silver Athenian tetradrachm, called the Athenian owl, the earliest textual reference to which is in an Aramaic papyrus in The Brooklyn Museum (47.218.94, Lipiński 1982: 23).[1] By the very end of the fifth century B.C., a second Aramaic papyrus, also in Brooklyn (47.218.95, Lipiński 1982: 24-25), suggests the existence of an active mint at Syene (Aswan) that issued its own versions of the Attic owls, and a second mint at Memphis which, in turn, issued its own versions of those imitations. These coins, again of silver and bearing legends in Aramaic, were struck for use by the Persian administration of the land.

Coins continued to be minted in Egypt throughout the fourth century B.C. Although the evidence is slender, it has been suggested that the Pharaoh Hachoris of Dynasty XXIX was the first native pharaoh to issue his own coinage, but that suggestion is based upon an interpretation of the Demotic legends such coins bear (Daumas 1977). One is on firmer ground with the accession of Teos of Dynasty XXX. Urged by the Greek Chabrias, Teos apparently struck coins in order to pay the Greek mercenaries in his employ (Chassinat 1901; 1910; Meyer 1931: 69-70; Daumas 1977: 432). They represented a radical departure from the norm, a revolutionary break with tradition and with Egyptian religious sensibilities: the coins are of gold, a material long considered to represent the flesh of the gods (Daumas 1977) and consequently one which ought not be polluted by such mundane applications. This attitude was a continuing factor in the reluctance of the native Egyptians to issue and use their own coinage. The gold issues of the fourth century B.C. bear the hieroglyphic legend *nbw nfr*, "the good gold," and the image of a rearing horse[2] as the equivalent for *nbw*, "gold" (Chassinat 1923: 133; Daumas 1977). This may have been a veiled attempt to counter the religiously influenced reluctance to use this metal, because the horse, as a motif, was not associated with the pharaonic pantheon (Meeks 1986: 173).

A series of silver coins bearing Demotic legends long thought to name Teos (Meyer 1931: 69-70; el Khashab 1958) has been shown to be, in fact, issues of the Persian king, Artaxerxes III (Shore 1974).

[1] The only Attic die ever found for these owls was actually one recovered at Athribis (Dattari 1905; Lipiński 1982: 24 note 6).

[2] We are grateful to J. Settgast, Berlin/BRD for making available to us his recent research on this coin, which suggests that its die was carved in Greek, not pharaonic, style.

CAT. 61a-z
Selected Coins of the Ptolemies and Their Contemporaries

This entry should serve to give an impression of the diversity of Ptolemaic portrait coinage, a term descriptive of at least the gold and silver issues of Ptolemaic coins (for Hellenistic royal portrait coins in general, see Newell 1937). Although it cannot be a detailed introduction to the many problems involved in dating and attributing the different coin types to specific rulers, some of those problems must at least be mentioned.

First, all the Egyptian kings were named Ptolemy, and the reverse of all their coins from Ptolemy I to Ptolemy XII and even Caesarion bears only the insufficiently specific label ΠΤΟΛΕΜΑΙΟΥ ΒΑΣΙΛΕΩΣ: "of Ptolemy, the King." In addition, although a few bear Greek numerals that could serve as clues to identify the rulers they portray, it is not always possible to determine whether such numerals are regnal years rather than merely issue marks. Sometimes a special sign appears to indicate a mint – Ptolemaic coinage originated not only in Alexandria but also in Cyprus and Phoenicia – but that also is not an indication of specific date. To add to the confusion, most coins of the period bear the image of the dynasty's founder, Ptolemy I Soter, although the coins of his son Ptolemy II are an exception to this general rule.

The tetradrachm of Ptolemy I (CAT. 61a) shows his typical portrait, a design that would be repeated in the different mints of the Ptolemaic territories until Egypt's conquest by Rome. The portrait often appears in a degenerate (or at least different) style, sometimes probably in an attempt to make it bear some resemblance to the actual ruler under whom it was minted (see, for example, CATS. 61i-n, p).

On the other hand, there are some coins of kings after Ptolemy II on which the portraits differ greatly from that of Ptolemy I. For example, the rather clumsy and massive head on CAT. 61e is clearly an attempt by the die engraver at an individual portrait of Ptolemy III. Moreover, both the portrait coins of Ptolemy V (CAT. 61h) and the coins of this king that bear the likeness of his father, Ptolemy IV, display the high standard of portrait art of the Phoenician mint.

Problems of dating and attribution also confront attempts to identify the coins of the various Berenikes, Arsinoes and Cleopatras. It is hard to distinguish between coins issued during a queen's lifetime and those issued posthumously. And here, too, the image of one queen sometimes influenced the coin portraits of later queens.

In the *Theon-Adelphon* ("brother-sister gods") series of Ptolemy II (CAT. 61b), the king's deified parents, Ptolemy I and Berenike I, are represented on the obverse in the same manner as Ptolemy II and his sister-wife Arsinoe II on the reverse. That there is a strong resemblance between the two couples is surely not due solely to the style of the engraver and is not surprising given the close familial relationship among the rulers.

Family resemblance, however, does not explain how the portrait of Arsinoe II (CATS. 61c-d) became in some way the prototype for royal female portraiture, as in CAT. 61f, a coin of Berenike II. But, as with royal male portraiture, not all queens' coinage followed the Arsinoe model, as may be seen in the image on the obverse of a bronze coin of Cleopatra VII (CAT. 61o), where she is depicted as an independent Hellenistic ruler wearing the diadem.

Also included in this selection of coinage are coins from the reign of Cleopatra VII, including a Roman coin of Julius Caesar (CAT. 61x) and examples reflecting Cleopatra VII's union with Marc Antony (CATS. 61u-w, z). CAT. 61z, an eastern, Roman denarius with the legend *regina regum filiorum regum* ("Queen of Kings [and of the] Sons of Kings"), refers to the events of 34 B.C., when Antony proclaimed Cleopatra "Queen of Kings" and Caesarion (her son by Caesar, shown in typical Ptolemaic style in CAT. 61p) "King of Kings." A late portrait with a rather sharp and marked profile, her image on this coin does not accord with the myth of a woman enchanting a Roman lover by the power of her beauty.

Because Ptolemaic Egypt did not exist in a geographical or political vacuum, we have also included some coins of the Seleucid dynasty in Syria (CATS. 61q-t), descendants of another of Alexander's generals and relatives of the Ptolemies. Antiochus II, for instance (CAT. 61q), married a daughter of Ptolemy III, and Antiochus III of Syria (CAT. 61r) was the father of Cleopatra I. The daughter of Ptolemy VI, Cleopatra Thea, who was deeply involved in the international politics of the second century B.C. appears in CAT. 61s. Her many diplomatic marriages in the Seleucid family, all of which produced offspring (e.g., Antiochus IX Cyzicenus, shown in CAT. 61t), greatly added to the general anarchy that was Syria in the first century B.C.

Note: CATS. 61 o, v, z are from private collections. All remaining coins belong to the Staatliche Münzsammlung, Munich.

CAT. 61a-p

CAT. 61q-z

CAT. 61a
Tetradrachm of Ptolemy I Soter
Silver, 2.6 (1) max. diameter
Circa 300-283 B.C.
Alexandrian mint
Literature: SV: no. 247; Jenkins 1960: 26.

Obverse: Diademed head of Ptolemy I right with aegis; border of dots.
Reverse: Eagle left on thunderbolt; legend ΠΤΟΛΕΜΑΙΟΥ ΒΑΣΙΛΕΩΣ ("of Ptolemy, the King"); in field left P/A; border of dots.

CAT. 61b
Octodrachm of Ptolemy II Philadelphos, *Theon Adelphon* ("of the Brother-Sister Gods")
Gold, 2.6 (1) max. diameter
Circa 270-260 B.C.
Alexandrian mint
Literature: SV: no. 603; Brett 1955: no. 2274; Troxell 1983: 60-62 (for dating).

Obverse: Jugate busts right of Ptolemy I wearing diadem; and of Berenike I veiled and diademed; above, ΘΕΩΝ.
Reverse: Jugate busts right of Ptolemy II diademed and wearing chlamys; and of Arsinoe II diademed and veiled; in field left oval gaulish shield; above ΑΔΕΛΦΩΝ.

CAT. 61c
Octodrachm of Arsinoe II, issued posthumously by Ptolemy II
Gold, 2.6 (1) max. diameter
250/249 B.C.
Sidon mint
Literature: SV: no. 747; Troxell 1983: 52.

Obverse: Veiled and diademed bust of Arsinoe II right wearing small horn; lotus-tipped scepter behind; dotted border.
Reverse: Double cornucopiae bound with fillet; in field Λ⊏ and ΣΙ/ΜΑ; legend ΑΡΣΙΝΟΗΣ ΦΙΛΑΔΕΛΦΟΥ ("of Arsinoe Philadelphos").

CAT. 61d
Decadrachm of Arsinoe II, issued posthumously by Ptolemy II
Silver, 3.3 (1 5/16) max. diameter
Circa 253-246 B.C.
Alexandrian mint
Literature: SV: no. 947; Troxell 1983: 44, group 3.

Obverse: Similar to preceding; in field left issue mark MM.
Reverse: Similar to preceding; no letters or monograms.

CAT. 61e
Coin of Ptolemy III Euergetes
Bronze, 1.8 (11/16) max. diameter
246-221 B.C.
Presumably Alexandrian mint
Literature: SV: no. 1000.

Obverse: Laureate bust of Ptolemy III right with aegis; dotted border.
Reverse: Eagle left on thunderbolt; in field right cornucopiae; legend ΠΤΟΛΕΜΑΙΟΥ ΒΑΣΙΛΕΩΣ ("of Ptolemy, the King"); dotted border.

CAT. 61f
Quarter drachm of Berenike II minted by Ptolemy III
Gold, 1.1 (7/16) max. diameter
246-221 B.C.
Alexandrian mint
Literature: SV: no. 982.

Obverse: Diademed and veiled head of Berenike II; dotted border.
Reverse: Cornucopiae, bound with fillet, between two stars; dotted border; legend ΒΕΡΕΝΙΚΗΣ ΒΑΣΙΛΙΣΣΗΣ ("of Berenike, the Queen").

CAT. 61g
Tetradrachm of Ptolemy IV Philopator, issued posthumously by Ptolemy V
Silver, 2.6 (1) max. diameter
Circa 202-200 B.C.
Phoenician mint
Literature: SV: no. 1276; Kyrieleis 1973: 234, no. 27; Mørkholm 1979: 212, group XIV.

Obverse: Diademed bust of Ptolemy IV right wearing chlamys; dotted border.
Reverse: Eagle left on thunderbolt; B left in field; NI between eagle's legs; legend ΠΤΟΛΕΜΑΙΟΥ ΒΑΣΙΛΕΩΣ ("of Ptolemy, the King").

CAT. 61h
Tetradrachm of Ptolemy V Epiphanes
Silver, 2.6 (1) max. diameter
Circa 202-200 B.C.
Phoenician mint
Literature: SV: no. 1263; Kyrieleis 1973: 216ff; Mørkholm 1979: 209, group IV.

Obverse: Diademed bust of Ptolemy V right, wearing chlamys.
Reverse: As preceding, but left in field is only the mint mark Μ.

CAT. 61i
Tetradrachm of Ptolemy VI Philometor
Silver, 2.5 (1) max. diameter
162 B.C.
Cyprus, Paphos mint
Literature: SV: no. 1431; Mørkholm/Nicolaou/Nicolaou 1976: pl. 14,2.

Obverse: Diademed bust of Ptolemy I, wearing aegis.
Reverse: As preceding but LIΘ-ΠΛ(=ΠΑ) in field.

CAT. 61j
Tetradrachm of Ptolemy VIII Euergetes II
Silver, 2.3 (15/16) max. diameter
126 B.C.
Cyprus, Salamis mint
Literature: SV: no. 1557.

Obverse: As preceding.
Reverse: As preceding, but LMΔ-ΣΑ in field.

CAT. 61k
Tetradrachm of Ptolemy IX Soter II
Silver, 2.4 (15/16) max. diameter
112-111 B.C.
Alexandrian mint
Literature: SV: no. 1667; Kromann/Mørkholm 1977: 351.

Obverse: As preceding.
Reverse: As preceding, but L ⊏-ΠΑ in field.

CAT. 61l
Tetradrachm of Ptolemy X Alexander I
Silver, 2.4 (15/16) max. diameter
96-95 B.C.
Alexandrian mint
Literature: SV: no. 1679; Kromann/Mørkholm 1977: 368.

Obverse: As preceding.
Reverse: As preceding, but LIΘ-ΠΑ in field.

CAT. 61m
Tetradrachm of Ptolemy XII Auletes
Silver, 2.4 (15/16) max. diameter
80-79 B.C.
Alexandrian mint
Literature: SV: no. 1848; Kromann/Mørkholm 1977: 377.

Obverse: As preceding.
Reverse: As preceding, but LB-ΠΑ in field.

CAT. 61n
Tetradrachm of Cleopatra VII Thea
Silver, 2.6 (1) max. diameter
44-43 B.C.
Alexandrian mint
Literature: SV: no. 1823; Kromann/Mørkholm 1977: 403.

Obverse: As preceding.
Reverse: As preceding, but LΘ-ΠΑ in field.

CAT. 61o
Coin of Cleopatra VII Thea
Bronze, 2.7 (1 1/16) max. diameter
51-30 B.C.
Alexandrian mint
Literature: SV: nos. 1871-72; Kromann/Mørkholm 1977: 419-21.

Obverse: Diademed bust of Cleopatra right; dotted border.
Reverse: Eagle left on thunderbolt; in field left cornucopiae; in field right Π; legend ΚΛΕΟΠΑΤΡΑΣ ΒΑΣΙΛΙΣΣΗΣ ("of Cleopatra, the Queen"); dotted border.

CAT. 61p
Tetradrachm of Ptolemy XV Caesarion
Silver, 2.4 (15/16) max. diameter
37/36 B.C.
Alexandrian mint
Literature: SV: no. 1816; Mørkholm 1975: pl. 6,5.

Obverse: As CAT. 61n.
Reverse: As CAT. 61n, but in field left LA with star above; in field right ΠΑ.

CAT. 61q
Tetradrachm of Antiochus II
Silver, 2.8 (1 1/16) max. diameter
Circa 261-246 B.C.
Turkey, Tarsus mint
Literature: Newell 1941: 1310; Houghton 1983: 456.

Obverse: Diademed head of Antiochus II right.
Reverse: Apollo seated left on omphalus holding arrow and bow; legend ΒΑΣΙΛΕΩΣ ΑΝΤΙΟΧΟΥ ("of Antiochus, the King"); in exergue monograms ΝΚ . Α/.

CAT. 61 r
Tetradrachm of Antiochus III
Silver, 2.9 (1 1/8) max. diameter
Circa 223-187 B.C.
Provenance not known; western mint
Literature: Newell 1941: no. 1695.

Obverse: Diademed head of Antiochus III right.
Reverse: As preceding, but no monogram. The style of the reverse is slightly barbaric.

CAT. 61 s
Tetradrachm of Cleopatra Thea and Antiochus VIII
Silver, 2.8 (1 1/16) max. diameter
125 B.C.
Palestine, Ake-Ptolemais mint
Literature: Newell 1939: 13, no. 8.

Obverse: Jugate veiled head of Cleopatra Thea with stephane and diadem and diademed head of Antiochus VIII right; fillet border.
Reverse: Enthroned Zeus Nicephorus left; left in outer field Σ̌; legend on left ΚΑΙ ΒΑΣΙΛΕΩΣ ΑΝΤΙΟΧΟΥ; legend on right ΒΑΣΙΛΙΣΣΗΣ ΚΛΕΟΠΑΤΡΑΣ ΘΕΑΣ ("of Cleopatra Thea, the Queen, and Antiochus, the King").

CAT. 61 t
Tetradrachm of Antiochus IX Cyzicenus
Silver, 2.9 (1 1/8) max. diameter
Probably issued during second reign of Antiochus IX in Tarsus, 110-108 B.C.
Turkey, Tarsus mint
Literature: Houghton 1983: 496.

Obverse: Diademed head of Antiochus IX right, lightly bearded.
Reverse: Garlanded shrine in which appears the god Sandan standing right on back of horned and winged lion; left in outer field Δ/ / ME ; legend ΒΑΣΙΛΕΩΣ ΑΝΤΙΟΧΟΥ ΦΙΛΟΠΑΤΟΡΟΣ ("of Antiochus Philopator, the King").

CAT. 61 u
Tetradrachm of Marc Antony and Cleopatra VII
Silver, 2.8 (1 1/16) max. diameter
34 B.C. or later(?)
Presumably from Turkey, Antioch ad Orontem
Literature: Wroth 1899: 158, no. 53; Buttrey 1954 (attributing this coin type to a Phoenician mint); Mørkholm 1959: 129; Seyrig 1968: 255 f (re-attributing this type to Antioch).

Obverse: Bare head of Marc Antony right; legend ΑΝΤΩΝΙΟC ΑΥΤΟΚΡΑΤΩΡ ΤΡΙΤΟΝ ΤΡΙΩΝ ΑΝΔΡΩΝ ("Antony, Commander-in-Chief for the third time, Triumvir").
Reverse: Diademed bust of Cleopatra right wearing necklace of pearls or fibulae with chain of pearls; legend ΒΑCΙΛΙCCΑ ΚΛΕΟΠΑΤΡΑ ΘΕΑ ΝΕΩΤΕΡΑ ("Queen Cleopatra, *Thea Neotera*" [one of Cleopatra's titles]).

CAT. 61 v
Coin of Marc Antony and Cleopatra VII
Bronze, 2.5 (1) max. diameter
Presumably 34/33 B.C.[1]
Phoenicia, Dora mint
Literature: Baldus 1983.

Obverse: Jugate busts of Cleopatra wearing diadem and jewelry similar to the preceding; and of bareheaded Marc Antony; in left field, border of dots.
Reverse: Turreted Tyche (personification of a city) to left holding caduceus; in field left LΘΙ (= Year 19); in field right Ω above Δ, to be read as ΔΩ[ΡΙΤΩΝ] ("of the Doritons", that is, the inhabitants of Dora).

CAT. 61 w
Coin of Marc Antony and Cleopatra VII
Bronze, 2 (13/16) max. diameter
32/31 B.C.
Phoenicia, Chalkis sub Libano
Literature: G. Hill 1910: 54, no. 15 (wrongly attributed to Berytus), 383; Seyrig 1950: 44-47 (attribution to Chalkis sub Libano); Mørkholm 1961: 383; Martini 1984: 44 (re-attribution to Berytus).

Obverse: Draped bust of Cleopatra right wearing diadem and necklace; legend (partly illegible) ΒΑCΙΛΙCCΗC ΚΛΕΟΠΑΤΡΑC ("of Cleopatra, the Queen"); dotted border.
Reverse: Bare head of Marc Antony right; legend ЄΤΟΥC ΚΑ ΤΟΥ ΚΑΙ ꞆΘΕΑC ΝЄΩΤЄΡΑC ("Year 21, which is also Year 6 of *Thea Neotera*").

CAT. 61 x
Denarius of Julius Caesar
Silver, 1.9 (3/4) max. diameter
44 B.C.
Mint of Rome, moneyer M. Mettius
Literature: M. Crawford 1974: 480 no. 3.

Obverse: Wreathed head of Caesar right; left in field a lituus (augur's crook) and culullus (drinking vessel); right in field CAESAR IMP[ERATOR] ("Caesar, the Commander-in-Chief"); dotted border.
Reverse: Venus Victrix standing left holding small Victory and scepter with left elbow resting on shield set upon globe; right in field M. METTIVS; left in field I; dotted border.

CAT. 62 *see color plate XIII*

Head of a Ptolemaic Queen or Goddess

Quartzite, 18 (7 1/16)
Circa 280-270 B.C.
Provenance not known
Collection of Jack A. Josephson

Unpublished

The stylistic features of this head, sculpted in one of the hardest of stones known to the ancient Egyptians, serve to emphasize the pitfalls inherent in identifying images as specific rulers on the basis of style alone. Although the face is conceived as an oval, the breadth of the forehead exceeds that of the face at the level of the mouth, and the width between the outer surfaces of the cheeks is approximately equal to the height of the face proper from the juncture of the wig with the forehead to the tip of the chin. The face relies for its sculptural effect on the modeling of the planes, which results in both the full cheeks and the protrusion of the globular chin. The naturalistic brow, with a slightly raised ridge over each eye, intersects the bridge of the nose so that the confluence of brow and bridge creates an almost perpendicular depression that forms the socket of each eye, the eyes being originally inlaid. The sickle-shaped smile of the mouth is formed by an upward swing of the lips, the corners of which are drilled. A profile view reveals a thick throat. Abrasions to the surfaces have rendered the treatment of the ears, wig, and headdress somewhat indistinct. That the subject of the sculpture is a woman, either a queen or a goddess, is confirmed by the headdress – a circlet of cobras – atop the wide wig, which is itself fronted by a uraeus.

Stylistically the features of this head relate it to a group of sculptures that have been variously attributed to the fourth century B.C. (New York 30.8.90, ESLP: no. 90) and to the third (Hamburg 1924.170, Hornbostel in Altenmüller/Hornbostel 1982: no. 38; and CAT. 63). The dating of this group as a whole revolves around an assessment of a head in New York that was identified as a representation of Arsinoe II (New York 38.10, ESLP: no. 98) on the basis of its stylistic similarities to the face of a statue, inscribed for Arsinoe II, in the Vatican (Fig. 19; ESLP: 126; Botti/Romanelli 1951: 22-23). Quaegebeur has recently observed (1983b: 116, citing Bisson de la Roque 1924: 65-66) that the New York head was found together with a torso (present whereabouts not known) at Abu Roash (ESLP: 126 records no specific site) in association with worked blocks inscribed for Nectanebo II of Dynasty XXX. He then suggests that the head in New York could be associated with those blocks in order to date that head to Dynasty XXX. Theoretically, his suggestion is well taken because it is a logical extension of the generally accepted premise that the relief style of Dynasty XXX (CATS. 7, 11, 13, and pp. 72-73, above) was adopted virtually unchanged by the early Ptolemies (Quaegebeur 1983b: 116, citing the oft-repeated, but seldom credited, remarks first made by von Bissing 1914: text to pl. 104). Practically, the dating of the New York head to the fourth century B.C. cannot be supported because the archaeological context of the crocodile caverns in which it was found was so disturbed that one frankly cannot insist upon any contextual links between the two. Quaegebeur's hypothesis, however, serves as an important caveat against identifying all such stylistically similar images as Arsinoe II (see also CAT. 63).

Nevertheless, one must admit that there are certain characteristics about CAT. 62 that place it in a class of its own. The choice of stone is exceptional for sculptures of the fourth and third centuries B.C. and would seem to indicate a special commission. The use of inlaid eyes is rare and, although not common until the second century B.C. (CAT. 74), is known in the third (CAT. 71). The circlet of cobras, which is ultimately indebted to models from the New Kingdom, appears to have been consciously adopted from the iconography of the divine consorts of Amun of Dynasty XXV (for example, Omaha 1953.80, ESLP: no. 1) and royal women of the Saite Period (Cairo CG 42205, Legrain 1914; London 775, De Meulenaere 1968: 183-85 and pl. XXIX, 1). It is a distinctive attribute that is subsequently repeated on other representations (Bisson de la Roque *et al.* 1928: 114, inv. no. 2212, fig. 65). Since the underlying formula of the face was current during the fourth and third centuries B.C., one must observe Quaegebeur's caveat and simply suggest that the identification of this head as an image of Arsinoe II is a possibility, but not an exclusive one. The fleshy throat is a particularly telling detail which seems to anticipate the fuller treatment of the fleshy face during the third and second centuries B.C. (CATS. 35, 69).

CAT. 63
Head of a Ptolemaic Queen or Goddess

Limestone, 10.8 (4 1/4)
Late fourth-third century B.C.
Provenance not known
The Brooklyn Museum, 86.226.32; Gift of the Ernest Erickson Foundation

Literature: Bianchi in Brooklyn 1987: no. 86.

The oval configuration of this head, the slight slant to the almond-shaped eyes, and the sickle-shaped smile of the lips relate this head to CAT. 62 and to a head in New York (New York 30.10, ESLP: figs. 244-45). The presence of the clearly defined, plastically rendered brow on the Brooklyn example is a variable detail without chronological implications (compare CAT. 24 to Munich Glyptothek 29, ESLP: figs. 192-94). These features, once established during the course of Dynasty XXX, were repeated through the mimetic principle into the Ptolemaic Period both for images of Arsinoe II (Fig. 19; Botti/Romanelli 1951: 22-24) and subsequent members of the Ptolemaic dynasty, for whom the style of this queen was adopted and occasionally modified (Kyrieleis 1975: 78-94, 97-98; Brunelle 1976: 10-19). Had the attribute, originally set into the mortise in the columnar protrusion resting on top of the wig, been preserved, the identity of the figure might have been more easily determined. Furthermore, the tripartite wig with echelon curls and the single hair band fronted by a uraeus are too general to render a specific identification. One cannot, therefore, rule out the possibility that this head belonged to an image of a goddess. For the time being, it is best to regard it as either a royal or divine image created during the late fourth or early third century B.C. As such it calls into question the generally accepted observation (ESLP: xxxvii, 116, 119-20) that representations of female figures are infrequent in the period between the end of Dynasty XXVI and the beginning of the Ptolemaic Period (Quaegebeur 1983b: 114-16).

CAT. 64 *see color plate XIV*

Portrait of Arsinoe II

Large-crystal, gray-white marble, 24.6 (9 11/16)
Circa 270 B.C.
Provenance not known
Bonn, Akademisches Kunstmuseum der Universität, B 284

Literature: Kyrieleis 1975: 179-80 [J8].

This head is an interesting example of the ways in which a highly skilled Greek sculptor was able to imbue a Hellenistic ruler portrait with pharaonic overtones. His hand is revealed by the treatment of the lips, whose configuration matches the one invariable in the portraiture of Arsinoe II: the upper lip with pronounced undulations; the lower somewhat smaller and distinctively set off from the projecting chin by a marked indentation of the skin beneath it. The resulting profile of this head conforms to the numismatic images of Arsinoe II (CAT. 61 c,d; Kyrieleis 1975: 78-80, 84). The surface of the marble had anciently been subjected to severe polishing (see below), a characteristic found on better Alexandrian royal portraits (R. Smith 1986: 70), and one which Kyrieleis (1975: 40-41, 92) would also ascribe to a conscious attempt on the part of the Hellenistic Greek artists to imitate the polish achieved on pharaonic alabaster sculpture.[1] Such an observation accords well with other Egyptianizing features of this head. Foremost among those additional borrowings are the treatments of the eyes, originally inlaid; of their sockets; and of the brow as it merges into the bridge of the nose (compare CAT. 54). More significantly, the sculptor has attempted to imitate Egyptian sculptural tenets by concentrating the features of the face on the frontal plane and in so doing has modified the underlying Alexandrian schema of the head.

The dating of this head of Arsinoe II is difficult to determine with precision because this queen's stature during her life, and her posthumous reputation, contributed to what statistically must have been the largest number of dedicatory portraits ever erected in honor of any one ruler of Ptolemaic Egypt (Blomfield 1905; Quaegebeur 1971 a: 242 note 12, emending the list of Longega 1968). At least three distinct coin types struck for the living Arsinoe II have been identified (Kyrieleis 1975: 78-80)[2] and subsequent rulers continued to issue commemoratives, loosely based on those original types. That her image persisted, and doubtless changed, through time complicates the task of identifying her surviving portraits. Further, Quaegebeur has observed in a slightly different context (1983 b: 117, 124) that uninscribed images of Arsinoe II do not readily divide into contemporaneous and posthumous groupings. The Egyptianizing features of the Bonn portrait are not themselves a sufficient dating criterion because Arsinoe II, as queen, had recognized the value of employing Egyptian precedents and adapting them to suit her specific requirements. On the other hand, correspondence of the Bonn head with contemporary coin types and its concomitant dissimilarities with posthumous issues do suggest that this portrait was made during the period of her monarchy, which lasted less than a decade.[3]

[1] In this regard, it is interesting to note that in at least one Ptolemaic text Greek marble in general seems to be equated with Egyptian poros, itself then equated in that same text with Parian marble (Thissen 1979).

[2] Cheshire (1982) identifies the scepter on some of those issues with a floral staff, which she identifies as one of the symbols associating Arsinoe's consanguineous marriage to her brother, Ptolemy II Philadelphos. She then associates this marriage with that of the Greek gods Hera and Zeus. Her argument fails, in my estimation, because the serpents, so central to her reasoning, never appear on those coins in association with the scepter, which is itself typologically dissimilar to the staff with which she equates it.

[3] Arsinoe II married her brother, Ptolemy II Philadelphos, and became queen at some point between 279 B.C. and November 2, 274 B.C. (Hauben 1983: 99; Rice 1983: 41; somewhat narrower parameters are suggested by Longega 1968: 79, *passim*).

CAT. 65

Relief of Arsinoe II

Limestone, 42.5×57.7 (16¾×22¾)
After 270 B.C.
Possibly from Memphis
Cambridge, Massachusetts, Harvard University Art Museums (Arthur M. Sackler Museum), 1983.96; Gift of Mr. and Mrs. Samuel H. Lindenbaum

Literature: Quaegebeur 1985: 77 and note 4.

Quaegebeur had astutely recognized this relief, then still on the art market, as a representation of Arsinoe II, and he immediately related it to a second in Hildesheim (Fig. 43; Quaegebeur 1985: 73-78; Martin-Pardey in Hildesheim 1985: 154-55). In both, the queen is shown facing right, wearing the tripartite wig and crowned with the headdress that was originally created for her and subsequently employed in representations of later queens (CAT. 72; Quaegebeur 1985: 74 and note 5). The suggestion that the ram's horns on this particular crown are rendered in perspective (Quaegebeur 1985: 73 and fig. 1) is interesting, but such a rendition of those horns can be traced back at least to the reign of Tuthmosis III of Dynasty XVIII (e.g., Luxor J. 140, Luxor 1979: 52-53; CAT. 131). The facial features of the queen are identical in both scenes and emphasize a fleshy throat, projecting chin, straight mouth, an aquiline nose whose wings are indicated by a firmly incised line, hieroglyphic eyes with paint stripes indicated in relief, and a plastic eyebrow.

This characterization of the face closely approximates the queen's images on coins struck during her lifetime (Kyrieleis 1975: pl. 70), and bears a striking resemblance to the head in Bonn (CAT. 64), which is itself indebted to Egyptian norms. These art historical comparisons suggest that the relief in Cambridge ought to have been sculpted during the reign of the queen (279/274-270 B.C.). While Quaegebeur entertains this possibility, he is at pains to point out that the epithet *s3.t 'Imn*, "the daughter of Amun," seems to imply the posthumous deification of the queen (Quaegebeur 1985: 76). The remains of a second cartouche on the relief in Cambridge, in which one can read traces of the epithet *mr(.t) nṯrw*, "beloved of the gods," would seem to confirm Quaegebeur's suspicion, because both cartouches are employed on the Pithom Stela (Cairo CG 22183) for identifying Arsinoe II, who is there depicted deified (Sethe 1904, vol. II: 82, 14; Sauneron 1960a: 95, *passim*; Quaegebeur 1971a: 242; von Beckerath 1984: 118, 287). As a result, the relief in Cambridge probably dates to the period after 270 B.C., at which time the posthumous cult of the deified Arsinoe II was instituted.

The style of the reliefs in Cambridge and Hildesheim is so similar that one ought to consider the works as coming from one and the same monument. The fact that the treatment of the interior detail in the Cambridge relief is more elaborate than that on the Hildesheim example does not negate this suggestion, particularly since such variations are commonly encountered (Abd el Raziq 1984: pl. 7A-B). Quaegebeur, observing the reference to the Apis Bull (CAT. 105) in the left marginal inscription of the Cambridge relief, has suggested that it might originally have come from Memphis, where the cult of Arsinoe and of the Apis Bull were tightly linked together (Quaegebeur 1985: 77 and note 4). The Cambridge relief is stylistically among the most accomplished produced by the sculptors of Ptolemaic Egypt. The attention to detail, particularly in the rendering of the individual locks of the tripartite wig, is consummate, as is the sensitivity to developing a sense of space by means of overlapping within the narrow confines of the sunk relief. The near hand, holding a lily-scepter, is in front of the lappet of the wig, which is itself placed over the broad collar. Such spatial concerns characterize the finest pharaonic relief style, and in that respect this relief approaches the style of the reliefs of Sety I at Abydos (El Mallakh/Bianchi 1980: 38-44) and anticipates the exquisitely rendered interior detail of the intercolumnar panels of the Roman *mammisi* at Dendera decorated in the name of Trajan (Daumas 1975a: pls. 324-25).

CAT. 66
Statuette of Arsinoe II Deified

Limestone, originally painted and gilded, 38.1 (15)
270-246 B.C.
Provenance not known
New York, The Metropolitan Museum of Art, 20.2.21; Rogers Fund, 1920

Literature: Kyrieleis 1975: 82; Brunelle 1976: 29; Bianchi 1980b.

The statuette represents Queen Arsinoe II deified in a variant of the tripartite costume, which, despite the assessments of Classicists (Bieber 1961: 92 note 23; Stricker 1960; and Brunelle 1976: 29) is of purely Egyptian origin and execution (Bianchi 1980b). The interplay between flesh and fold, once considered a weak attempt at an emulation of Hellenistic plastic values, has elsewhere been argued to be of a purely Egyptian style that adds linear adjuncts to subtly merging sculptural planes (pp. 67-69, above). As a consequence, the drapery style can no longer be regarded as a product of the Mixed School, and the label can be disregarded in this context.

The coiffure consists of elaborately sculpted corkscrew locks (CAT. 74), painted black; those framing the face are drilled at their bottoms, a technique here employed to define the nostrils as well. The origin and development of such locks in Egypt and their subsequent appearance in the art of Greece and Rome are debated issues (von Bissing 1895: 109; Noshy 1937: 125; Kashnitz von Weinberg 1965: 11; Kyrieleis 1975: 118).[1] Depictions of these locks appear in the first indisputably datable context in the reliefs of the fourth century B.C. tomb of Petosiris at Tuna el Gebel (Lefebvre 1924: pl. XIV; Himmelmann 1983: 49 note 139).[2] Drilled locks become common after their elaborate treatment in some of the scenes from the tomb of Pabasa (PM I,1: 357) and recur with great frequency on limestone votive plaques of the Late Period (Lise 1979: no. 87; Bianchi 1979b). As a result, both the locks and their attendant drilling are within the traditions of Egyptian art.

The face and neck were once gilded, a common practice in Ptolemaic Egypt to connote divinity (Daumas 1956; Tefnin 1969: 90). This artistic convention is reinforced by the epithet on the back pillar which defines Arsinoe II as "divine" (Needler 1949: 140). The headdress, in conforming to this characterization, might be reconstructed along the lines suggested by Quaegebeur (1983b: 110; 1985). The *dikeras*, or double cornucopia, retaining traces of red, is the emblem of Arsinoe II and derives from the Hellenistic repertoire of attributes (D.B. Thompson 1973: 32, *passim*; Kyrieleis 1975: 26, 82; Rice 1983: 202-08). The addition of such an attribute to an otherwise Egyptian statuette forces one to consider the Hellenistic cult of the deified Arsinoe II against its Egyptian background (Quaegebeur 1971a; in *Das ptol. Äg.*: 245-62) and to conclude from its presence that the Egyptian statuette was addressed to a Hellenistic audience. On the other hand, Egyptian craftsmen of the Late Period could replicate the cultural regalia of almost any non-Egyptian culture in any medium, as the ram-headed

amulets of the Kushites (Fig. 30; Wenig 1978: 166) and the torques and bracelets of the Persian Period (Fig. 32; ESLP: no. 64) so admirably attest (pp. 64-65, above).

Since the face of this statuette would have been originally gilded, the wide-open eyes, their globular shape, the highly arched brows and the cupid's-bow upper lip are features that would have been emphasized. These are characteristics that belong to the pharaonic (ESLP: nos. 85, 99, 121; Queyrel 1984), not to the Hellenistic (Kyrieleis 1975: 82) tradition. Furthermore, in accordance with Egyptian sculptural tenets, these physiognomic features occupy the frontal plane and are integrated neither into the profile nor the three-quarter view, as they would be had they been indebted to a Hellenistic tradition. The resulting image is so unlike any other image of Arsinoe II (Kyrieleis 1975: 82; Brunelle 1976: 29),[3] that its dating has been debated.

The evidence necessary for the dating of this statuette is contained in the hieroglyphic inscription on the back pillar, whose context parallels the inscriptions on a sculpture in Alexandria, now erected in the Serapeum, wherein Arsinoe II is deified in the company of the god Amun during the lifetime of her brother (Daumas 1956; H. Wild 1954: 176; Sauneron 1960a). On the basis of this correspondence, the New York statuette had to have been dedicated, therefore, between 270 B. C. and 246 B. C., in that period after Arsinoe's own death but before that of her brother. Such a dating is supported by Quaegebeur's observation that commemorative stelae naming both Arsinoe II deified in conjunction with a (living) Ptolemy II date from that time span (Quaegebeur 1971a: 203; in *Das ptol. Äg.*: 245-62; 1983b: 115, whose original position I now support). As a result, one can no longer maintain the earlier suggestion (ESLP: no. 123) to date this statuette to the period after 225 B C. on the basis of a stylistic analysis of its drapery style, which had been termed "metallic" because of its supposed correspondence to the treatment of garments on Hellenistic bronzes.

[1] One can dismiss the equation of the Greek epithet "goodly tressed" with corkscrew locks, as suggested by Hornblower (1929: 44), because that phrase does not describe a specific hairstyle.

[2] This tomb cannot be securely dated, but the inscriptional evidence marshaled by von Bissing (1923) carries more weight than the arguments of Roeder (1939). The suggested chronology for such locks proposed by Tutweiler (1976) cannot be maintained because not one of her examples is dated.

[3] The attempt to relate this head to a second in New York, also identified as that of Arsinoe II (ESLP: no. 98) has recently been challenged (CATS. 62, 63; Quaegebeur 1983b: 116).

CAT. 67
Portrait of Berenike II

White, Greek marble[1] with large crystals, 38 (14 15/16)
246-222 B. C.
Reportedly from Alexandria
Kassel, Staatliche Kunstsammlungen, Antikensammlung, Sk 115

Literature: Berger 1962: no. 5; Kyrieleis 1975: 98, *passim*; Brunelle 1976: 34; Philipp 1979: 773; Krug 1984: 199; Queyrel 1984; Vollenweider 1984: 375; Daszewski 1985: 142-60.

Any discussions of the portraits of Berenike II must, of necessity, begin with her representations on coins. Those issues are modeled on the earlier coinage of Arsinoe II but repeat neither the scepter nor the ram's horn of Amun, which is replaced by an earring (Kyrieleis 1975: pls. 70 and 82). The *stephane*, or circlet, of Arsinoe II is also replaced by a diadem and the veil habitually covers a bulkier and more prominently depicted chignon. Whereas the numismatic images of Arsinoe II concentrate on her face and throat, those of Berenike II include more of her body, so that her image appears, on some issues at least, to resemble a bust (CAT. 61f). Rings of Venus and a necklace of a simple strand of pearl-like beads are variable details on Berenike II's coins as well. Although there is great variety in the renderings of the profiles on those coins (Besques 1984: 275), the overall impression of her physical appearance is that of a large, full-figured woman, corresponding to that of her husband, and one that is less refined and elegant than that projected by the numismatic images of Arsinoe II (CAT. 61c, d).

On the basis of such evidence, this exceptional marble from Alexandria has been identified as undoubtedly the finest representation of Berenike II to have survived from Antiquity (Berger 1962: no. 5; Kyrieleis 1975: 98, *passim*; Hornbostel in Altenmüller/Hornbostel 1982: no. 42). The modeling of the flesh in broad, smooth planes and the treatment of the hair as a series of simple, tightly undulating striations associates this piece with the prevailing currents of early Hellenistic sculpture. In its conception and in its execution, therefore, the Kassel head is exclusively indebted to a purely Hellenistic tradition and, as such, completely lacks any admixture of Egyptian stylistic features. The head is, additionally, more than a formulaic expression of those tenets. It is rather imbued with a matronly corpulence (Kyrieleis 1975: 98), reflecting the individual depicted on the coins. That feeling of chubbiness is conveyed by the full cheeks and by the round, rather than oval, shape of the face itself. In profile, the accentuated folds both at the wing of the nose and the corner of the mouth, the heavy chin, and the thick, fleshy throat correspond remarkably well to the images of Berenike II depicted on contemporary coins. The traces of color, especially the reddish-brown pigment found on the irises, convey better than any other example the expressive quality of Alexandrian royal portraiture at its best.

Although the iconography of Berenike II has caused some scholars difficulty (Tefnin 1969, all of whose attributions save one are rejected by Kyrieleis 1975: 98), most reasoned assess-

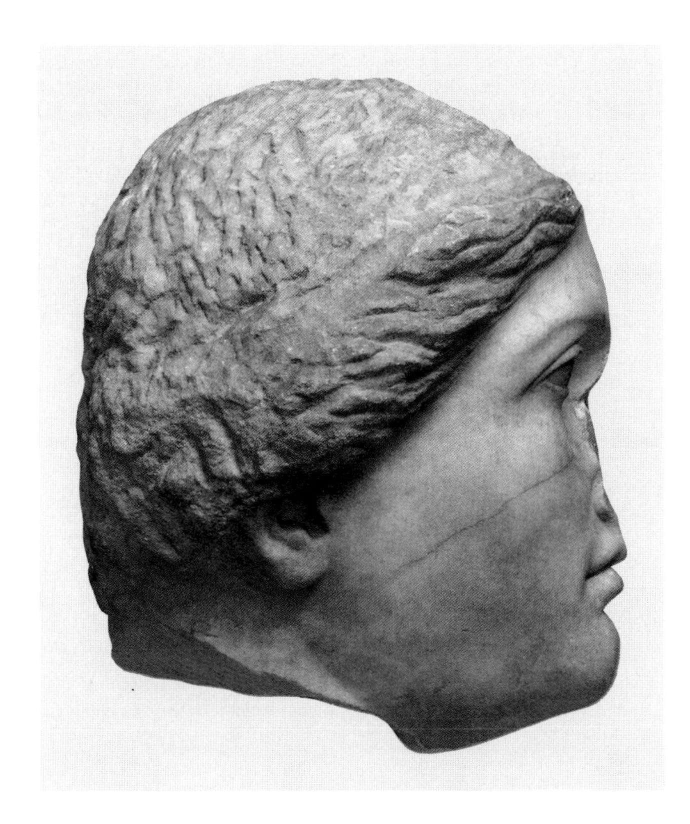

ments of her portraiture consider the Kassel head central to one classification among her portrait types.[2] These images form a closed group. And the presence of the Hellenistic diadem in the profile view of the Kassel head confirms (Kyrieleis 1975: 101) that all were sculpted and dedicated in honor of Berenike II in Alexandria during her lifetime (Berger 1962: no.5; Gercke 1975: 24).

In a reasoned and well-argued exposition, Daszewski has recently identified the images on two mosaics from Thmuis, now in Alexandria, as representations of Berenike II. Although somewhat modified in the transmission to the mosaic medium, they too belong to the Kassel Group (Alexandria 21739 and 21736, Daszewski 1985: 142-60). To this classification may also be added a miniature portrait sculpted from jet, a very rare material, which probably depicts Berenike II as well (Indianapolis 52.26, Brendel 1953, followed by Brunelle 1976: 38-39; and Vermeule 1981: no.109). That miniature shares with the head in Kassel corpulence and a round face, the idiosyncratic features of this queen.

[1] I wish to thank Peter Gercke (letter to the author, October 29, 1986), who reports that the faint traces of red material on the lips of this marble head have been identified as being entirely of red ocher, according to the analysis of E.-L. Richter of Stuttgart.

2 Kyrieleis 1975: 98, *passim*; Brunelle 1976: 34, *passim*; Queyrel 1984; Krug 1984; Vollenwerder 1984. Many of Brunelle's attributions cannot be supported. See R. Smith 1986, who, although discussing a different group of portraits, nevertheless clearly articulates the difficulties inherent in comparing two-dimensional representations with sculpture in the round in an effort to identify the ruler-portraits of the Ptolemies.

CAT. 68 *see color plate XV*

Fragment of an Oinochoe with Berenike II Holding a Cornucopia

Faience, 15.5 (6 1/8)
246-222 B.C.
Probably from Alexandria
New York, The Metropolitan Museum of Art, 26.7.1016; Gift of Edward S. Harkness, 1926

Literature: D.B. Thompson 1973: 132-33; Besques 1984.

Of all the classes of objects uncovered in Alexandria none are more difficult to understand and interpret than these vases because they represent a characteristically Greek vase shape, the oinochoe or wine jug, made in faience,[1] the quintessentially pharaonic medium. Since D.B. Thompson (1973: 1-2) has explored this dialectic, her work provides a convenient beginning for this investigation. Most scholars agree with D. B. Thompson (Simon 1975; Peck 1977) that the female figures decorating the bodies of these vases represent specific Ptolemaic queens, whose identities can be determined with a reasonable degree of accuracy (D.B. Thompson 1973: 19-39); and that the queen here represented is doubtless Berenike II (D. B. Thompson 1973: 132-33; Besques 1984). In general, most would accept D. B. Thompson's relative chronology for the series (Simon 1975; Besques 1984). The difficulties arise when one considers the artistic traditions to which these queens' vases belong and the uses to which they were put (Bosse-Griffiths 1975).

The oinochoai themselves can be understood in terms of the development of Greek ceramics in general (Hochuli-Gysel 1977: 48-49, 51-71), and need not be indebted to any traditions in plate, as D.B. Thompson maintains (1973: 14-15). Moreover, since Alexandria showed a demonstrable artistic dependency on Athens insofar as the Tanagra figurines are concerned (CATS. 112-114), the queens' vases may be an Alexandrian response to the uniquely Attic practice of using actual Tanagra figurines as appliqués on vessels (Higgins 1986: 118-19) – as in the vessels that have been excavated in the Sanctuary of the Nymph on the South Slope of the Acropolis. Another type of relief-decorated vessel, the "Plakettenvasen" uncovered in Alexandria, certainly indicates the predilection of the Alexandrians for this aesthetic (Alexandria P.10877 and 7306, G. Grimm in Hildesheim 1979: nos. 107, 109; Dohrn 1985).

The use of faience deserves special comment. Although the exclusive material in which these queens' vases were made, it does not necessarily imply the presence of native Egyptian artists in the ateliers, as suggested by D.B. Thompson (1973: 18). By 500 B.C., almost every culture of the ancient world was capable of manufacturing faience objects (W. Smith 1965: 38-50; Webb 1978: 9-10; Moorey 1985: 155-58). The Alexandrian faience industry must be regarded in terms of this pan-cultural phenomenon, especially since its craftsman were so technologically sophisticated that they almost certainly adopted this traditionally pharaonic medium as their own. The number and variety of faience vessels in a Hellenistic idiom from the Ptolemaic Period certainly supports such a position (CAT. 116; London 1875.11-10.2 and Berlin/BRD, Antikenmuseum F 2941, Higgins 1986: 59-60).[2]

Since the medium of faience could be effectively manipulated by the Alexandrians themselves, the notion that the style of the figures undergoes a progressive "Egyptianization" (D.B. Thompson 1973: 30-31, 35-39, *passim*) is open to question. One would expect any "Egyptianizing" tendencies to manifest themselves at the beginning of the sequence, when the Alexandrians were theoretically first familiarizing themselves with the medium. Furthermore, the "Egyptianizing" characteristics which D. B. Thompson (1973: 132–33) ascribes to the drapery style of this particular fragment are debatable on several counts. Since she adduces no external parallels in support of her argument, might not this stylistic peculiarity be more accurately ascribed to the mannering of the drapery motif?

Enklaar (1985: 114) has astutely remarked that the rapid development of the Hadra vase and the standardization of its form (CAT. 119) are phenomena which the queens' vases also exhibit. Both classifications of vessels, therefore, are part of an Alexandrian milieu divorced from any native interference. Further, this particular fragment appears to represent Berenike II, a queen whose portrait sculptures tend to be exclusively Hellenistic in idiom without any admixture of Egyptian elements (Kyrieleis 1975: 98-102). In fact, Callaghan (1984) has convincingly argued that the drapery style of the vases of the older Berenike II and certain stylistic elements of the Centaurs Painter are congruent with those of the painting of Tomb 1 at Mustapha Pasha in Alexandria. It appears, therefore, that D. B. Thompson has misunderstood the style of the drapery on this fragment.

One can suggest a reconstruction of the scene to which this fragment belonged. The queen, holding a cornucopia, was doubtless standing before a horned altar offering a libation with a phiale (as in D. B. Thompson 1973: pls. I and IX). The scene may have also contained a depiction of a column (as in D. B. Thompson 1973: fig. 2, and color pl. C). The details of the phiale and horned altar are such that one really cannot distinguish putative Egyptian from Hellenistic forms (D. B. Thompson 1973: 31-36; although Quaegebeur 1971b and Soukiassian 1983 disagree).

D. B. Thompson's theories regarding the rituals related to these queens' vases have not been universally accepted and others have suggested alternative interpretations (Simon 1975; Peck 1977). In this respect, the significance of the queens' vases is as elusive as that of the Tanagra figurines (CATS. 112-114). All theories will remain necessarily speculative until the Greek inscriptions on the queens' vases are fully understood.

[1] See Peck 1977 and Schlick-Nolte 1977, for further discussions of faience.

[2] Maehler (1983: 93-94) is perhaps in error when he suggests that the queens' vase now in the museum in Antalya (inv. 571) was probably made at Xanthos. The fact that this vessel is so well preserved argues that it was from a grave and was probably brought to Turkey by its owner from Alexandria.

CAT. 69

CAT. 69

Statue of a Ptolemaic Queen or Goddess

A hard dark stone, possibly either diorite (Kyrieleis 1975: 184) or basalt, 105 (with modern base)×26.3×39 (41 5/16×10 3/8×15 3/8)
Third century B. C.
Provenance not known
San Jose, California, Rosicrucian Egyptian Museum, 1582

Literature: ESLP: 147; Kyrieleis 1975: 184 [M 7]; Quaegebeur 1983b: 114.

The physical appearance of this statue presently approximates its ancient state since the restorations, particularly of the nose, and the coating of the surfaces with a black material have been removed. One is confronted with the image of a striding female figure, with left leg advanced and arms held along the sides of the body with their fists clenching bolts of cloth (p. 70, above). The figure wears a tripartite wig covered with stylized echelon curls whose ends are not bound; over the wig is a circlet fronted by three uraei. Her costume is the tightly fitting sheath that reveals the form of the body beneath it. In this respect, the statue belongs to the same type as CAT. 72.

Past attempts to identify the woman represented assumed that the face of the statue was in its original state (Kyrieleis 1975: 119). This false impression led to the association of the hawk-like (ESLP: 147) profile with images of Cleopatra VII on her coins (CAT. 61 n, o, u-w, y, z). With the removal of the restored nose, the resulting profile compares favorably neither with those coins (Kyrieleis 1975: pl. 107, figs. 1-4) nor with the known images of Cleopatra VII in Hellenistic style (CATS. 61, 76, 77). As a result, one can dismiss that identification (Kyrieleis 1975: 119; Quaegebeur 1983b: 114).

A distinguishing iconographic feature is the circlet of the triple uraeus, which is attested for the first time during the reign of Amenhotep III on at least one representation of Queen Tiye (ESLP: 147). The view of H. Müller, cited in ESLP: 147, who suggests "that the center uraeus orginated in an assimilation of the queen's vulture head [on a vulture headdress] to the two uraei due to her" is plausible for a statue of a female figure in Turin (1385), whose tripartite wig is covered by a stylized vulture headdress (Scamuzzi 1965: pl. XC). On the other hand, it is difficult to accept this view for those examples on which the triple uraeus appears independent of the vulture headdress. There are at least three such examples of Ptolemaic queens that exhibit this insignia without the vulture cap (CAT. 69; Leningrad 3936; New York, 89.2.660; ESLP: 147). Since the significance of this insignia has yet to be determined (ESLP: 147; Quaegebeur in *Das ptol. Äg.*: 262) and since it is found on stylistically different images, its appearance is perhaps better regarded as connoting an association with a particular goddess rather than as a mark of identification for a specific queen. In addition to the triple uraeus, CAT. 69 was equipped with a second attribute that is no longer extant but whose presence is suggested by the regular contour of the rough, circular depression now visible in the crown of the head. The iconography of CAT. 69, therefore, lacks the specificity necessary for establishing the identity of the figure represented.

The association of CAT. 69 with the female figure in Turin (ESLP: 147; Kyrieleis 1975: 119) cannot be maintained because the faces are conceptually and stylistically dissimilar. The shape of the face of the San Jose figure approximates a square oval (compare CAT. 62), whereas that of the Turin example is almost twice as high as it is wide. Furthermore, the features of the Turin face exhibit signs of age whereas those on the San Jose statue depict a *physkon*-type in ideal terms (CAT. 53, above). The San Jose head also shares with the Vienna head (CAT. 35) a double chin and rings of Venus on the neck. These features are incorporated into the oval face without a reliance on linear adjuncts. The treatment of the body recalls that of the figure in Stockholm (NME 73, ESLP: 156), although the nipples are here more emphasized, as does the configuration of the coiffure falling to the breasts. Both statues also appear to have been worked with the same types of tools to the same degree of completion. As a result, a dating within the third century B. C. is suggested for the San Jose figure.

CAT. 70

Portrait of Arsinoe III

Marble, 35 (13 3/4)
217-203 B.C.
Possibly from Alexandria
Boston, Museum of Fine Arts, 01.8207; H.L. Pierce Fund

Literature: Kyrieleis 1975: 181-82 [L 1]; Brunelle 1976: 43-44; Queyrel 1984.

CAT. 71

Portrait of Arsinoe III

Basalt, 23.5 (9 1/4)
217-203 B.C.
Provenance not known
Copenhagen, Ny Carlsberg Glyptotek, Cat.-nr. 329 (IN 586)

Literature: Kyrieleis 1975: 183 [L 8]

CAT. 70

CAT. 70, like so many other marble images of members of the Ptolemaic royal house, was anciently completed in plaster (Strocka 1967: 128, no. 52). The earlobes are pierced and may have originally been fitted with earrings (as in Stuttgart 1.4, Hornbostel in Altenmüller/Hornbostel 1982: no. 45; and a male in Frankfurt [127], Bol 1981: 90-91). That this head represents Arsinoe III, wearing a *stephane*, or hair band, is universally accepted because of the unmistakable parallels provided by the coin portraits (Kyrieleis 1975: 104).

Nevertheless, there is something diconcerting in the style of the head, which cannot be as easily integrated into the prevailing baroque tendencies of Hellenistic art as one would expect for a sculpture made during this period (Kyrieleis 1975: 110). Its acknowledged stereometric form appears to stand outside of the tenets of Hellenistic sculpture of the late third century B. C. This anomaly can best be explained by comparing the head in Boston to a second, in basalt, now in Copenhagen (CAT. 71), first identified as a representation of this same Arsinoe III Philopator by Brendel (cited in Kyrieleis 1975: 107, 183). Conceived as a series of unmodulated, abstract planes which imperceptibly merge into one another (Kyrieleis 1975: 107), the Copenhagen head finds its closest formal parallels in the head of Wesir-wer (CAT. 25). Here, however, the linear adjuncts have been suppressed in favor of the overriding geometric configuration of the curvilinear forms, which radiate in ever increasing concentric circles from the sharply formed brow, to the first roll of locks, the *stephane*, and finally the crown of the head. This schema has been grafted onto a small face, to which has been added a small, jutting chin, small nose with slender bridge, and a small mouth with pursed lips, whose corners are indented. The resulting image is so close to that in Boston that the same queen must be intended in both representations. In fact, the head in Boston follows the same formal schema as the head in Copenhagen. Its proportions and the plastic expression of its physiognomic features are remarkably like those of the Egyptian head in Copenhagen. The formal details of the mouths, with drilled corners, are indebted to Egyptian norms as well. And yet the head in Boston still retains a Hellenistic rendering of the brow and eyes, while the eyes in the Copenhagen exam-

ple are inlaid, an Egyptian feature that gains in popularity from the second century B.C. on (Tefnin 1969: 96).
These comparisons clearly point up certain formal elements from the pharaonic sculptural tradition that influenced Hellenistic norms (Kyrieleis 1975: 110-12). Recognition of this phenomenon – that influences in Ptolemaic Egypt generally traveled from the pharaonic cultural spheres to the Hellenistic – is of paramount importance for understanding the history of Ptolemaic art. This documented Egyptianizing tendency accelerated incrementally after the Battle of Raphia (216 B.C.), as the analysis of the Boston and Copenhagen heads reveals (Kyrieleis 1975: 112). Such a position has always been maintained by historians and social scientists, who saw the Greeks in Egypt as habitually borrowing cultural values and expressions (Grenier 1983a: 32; Merkelbach 1969: 73). A specific example of that phenomenon is provided by Yoyotte (1969: 131) in his study of a certain class of monuments from Edfu. Here the Greek-speaking population was served by texts in Greek that paraphrased particular pharaonic religious precepts (p. 25, above, and CAT. 78). Those paraphrases were limited to verbal approximations and were not accompanied by pictorial embellishment. It would appear, therefore, that the Greek community was making a concerted effort to reach out and understand their Egyptian contemporaries, at least at Edfu. The remarkable fact is that to date not a single piece of corresponding evidence has been adduced to indicate that the native Egyptians were motivated to follow suit, confirming Pereman's assertion (in *Das ptol. Äg.*: 45) that the Egyptians eschewed almost all forms of Greek culture and became increasingly insular as time passed. As a result, almost every advocate of the so-called Mixed School of Ptolemaic art who has regarded seemingly hybrid creations as the result of Hellenistic Greek influence on pharaonic stylistic tenets (e.g., Vandersleyen 1985) is ill-apprised of the cultural ambience in which those works of art were created, and has hence subscribed to the facile and erroneous interpretation of many artistic forms as "Hellenisms" when they are, in fact, purely Egyptian in their origin and development (Bianchi in *Das ptol. Äg.*: 95-102).

CAT. 71

CAT. 72
Statue of Cleopatra II or III (?)

Limestone, 83×14×20.5 ($32^{11}/_{16}$×$5^{1}/_{2}$×$8^{1}/_{16}$)
Second century B.C.
Provenance not known[1]
Leiden, Rijksmuseum van Oudheden, F 1938/7.20

Literature: Quaegebeur 1983b: 109-27.

Attempts to identify and date uninscribed works of art from the Egyptian Late Period are exceedingly difficult tasks because the development of the formal and visual vocabulary of the craftsmen did not seem to have been interrupted by cultural disjunctions. This figure in Leiden demonstrates that, through the mimetic principle, a stylistic peculiarity or a motif could be repeated at any time after its initial appearance.

The figure wears a tightly fitting sheath, the quintessentially Egyptian female fashion that remained invariable from the time of its introduction in the Old Kingdom (Wildung/Schoske 1984: 194-95). The tripartite wig surmounted by the headdress in the form of a vulture is of a type developed during the New Kingdom (Sourouzian 1981; but see Troy 1986: 117-19). To that headdress has been added the Red Crown, without its stinger; the two plumes; sun disk; cow's horns; and two uraei, each with a sun disk on its head (Quaegebeur 1983b: 111). At first glance, there is little to distinguish this statue from those of Dynasty XXV, as a comparison with the ivory figurine of a Divine Adoratress (?) in Edinburgh reveals (1954.40, ESLP: no. 12; Aldred in *Crépuscule*: fig. 120). Thus, through the mimetic principle, the general formal elements of Dynasty XXV have been transmitted to a later age.

There are, nevertheless, small, but significant differences between the Edinburgh and Leiden works. The sheath of the latter lacks the articulation of a bodice. Although the bodice itself is not a sure index of a date (Wildung/Schoske 1984: nos. 87, 95, 96), the composite crown has the additional attribute of ram's horns (Quaegebeur 1983b: 111). It was on the basis of this feature that Quaegebeur (1971b: 198, *passim*) initially and unequivocally associated this headdress with Arsinoe II, a position he later modified (1983b: 111). Whereas such a crown may originally have been introduced as an attribute for Arsinoe II, it could also be employed as an emblem for later women (Quaegebeur 1983b: 113), and is therefore not a definitive means of identification. The attempt to date this statue to the first quarter of the third century B.C. on the basis of its seeming stylistic similarity to an inscribed and securely dated female sculpture in Paris (Quaegebeur 1983b: 123-24) does not take into account the mimetic principle. That similarity merely provides a *terminus post quem* for the work in Leiden.

The tentative identification of this statue as a depiction of Arsinoe II (Quaegebeur 1983b: 124) must be questioned because it bears little resemblance to the one identified image of the deified Arsinoe II (CAT. 66), and its physiognomic features correspond neither to Hellenistic (Kyrieleis 1975: 78-94) nor to pharaonic representations of that queen (Fig. 19; Botti/Romanelli 1951: 22-24). The straight mouth and heavy jowls are set into an oval-shaped face. These particular features characterize royal representations of the late second and first centuries B. C. (Kyrieleis 1975: 69-75; Van de Walle 1952: 29-31). The Leiden statue may, therefore, be tentatively identified as a representation of a Ptolemaic queen of the second century B. C., perhaps Cleopatra II or III (Quaegebeur 1983b: 117).

[1] See Quaegebeur 1983b: 111 for the difficulty of assigning provenances to Egyptian works of art without known findspots.

CAT. 73
Statue of a Ptolemaic Queen or Goddess

Granite, 65×33.3×26.3 (25 9/16×13 1/4×10 3/8)
Second century B. C.
Provenance not known
Toronto, Royal Ontario Museum, 910.75

Literature: ESLP: no. 105.

The identity of this figure as either a queen or a goddess is moot because the appearance of the uraeus on the hair band is an attribute common to both. A more precise identification would have been possible had the attribute once attached to the mount in the form of two superimposed annulets on the crown of the head been preserved. Such a support is not uncommon in sculpture of the Late Period, as comparisons with two other statues reveal (private collection and Cairo CG 784, ESLP: figs. 127, 128). Such annulets were sculpted as part of the back pillars, whose height was increased above the tops of the heads in order to provide additional support for the attributes, which in many instances were sculpted from the same piece of stone (CAT. 72). The tripartite coiffure with the individual locks articulated is of the type also shown on CAT. 63. A comparison of the two with CAT. 69 suggests what completed examples of this kind of sculpture look like.

Quaegebeur has argued for a dating within the third century B. C. for the type, based on the inscribed example in Paris (N. 2456, Quaegebeur 1983b: 117-18). But types, once established, could be repeated at any time subsequent to their introduction. Recognizing this phenomenon in Egyptian sculpture of the Late Period and acknowledging that studies of the back pillars have so far produced inconclusive dating criteria for female sculpture of the Ptolemaic Period (ESLP: 170), one naturally turns to an examination of the face for chronological criteria. The features are neither portraitlike nor evocative of a pensive mood (compare CAT. 2), which some would derive from an infusion of Hellenistic Greek sculptural concerns (ESLP: 134-35). The face is modeled in broad planes without the addition of linear adjuncts, and the treatment of the eyes, with a creased upper lid which passes over the lower,[1] recalls features common to sculptures assigned to the third and second centuries B. C. The surfaces, having received a lesser degree of polish recall the surfaces of CAT. 74 which likewise preserves similar traces of tool marks. Furthermore, in the Toronto statue and in CAT. 74 the neckline of the garment is treated as a raised concave plane. This feature distinguishes these statues from CAT. 28, where the neckline appears as a raised band. For these reasons, a dating within the second century B. C. is suggested for this example in Toronto.

[1] This is a feature peculiar to Egyptian representations of eyes as both Adriani (1970: 74 and note 4), and Porada (1979: 40) observed in their discussions of Classical and ancient Middle Eastern art, respectively.

CAT. 74

CAT. 74
Statue of a Ptolemaic Queen or Goddess

Basalt, 48.6×23.5×14 (19 1/8×9 1/4×5 1/2)
Second century B. C.
Provenance not known
New Haven, Yale University Art Gallery, 1931.106; Yale University Purchase Fund

Literature: ESLP: no. 130; Kyrieleis 1975: 184 [M8]; G. Scott 1986: 168-69.

CAT. 75
Egyptianizing Statue of a Goddess

Grano-diorite, 66×25.5×15 (25×10 1/16×5 7/8); height 104 (40 15/16) with restoration
Second century A. D.
Provenance not known
Leiden, Rijksmuseum van Oudheden, F 1958/4.3

Literature: H. Schneider/Raven 1981: 141.

Both of these examples depict full-figured women, the rendering of whose anatomy derives from an established pharaonic tradition that developed independently and was not indebted to Greek influence. Each is shown wearing variations of the native Egyptian tripartite female costume that was first given three-dimensional sculptural expression in the Ptolemaic Period (CAT. 66).The very nature of this costume gave the craftsmen an opportunity to explore the interplay of flesh and fold. A careful examination of CAT. 74 underscores the pharaonic aesthetic operative in that orchestration. The forms of the body are modeled as broad planes over which the folds of the garments, almost always in the form of linear adjuncts rather than as plastically rendered planes, are superimposed. The round, spherical forms of the breasts are not interrupted by those linear adjuncts, which simply serve as framing elements beneath, above, and between them. The same observation obtains for the treatment of the folds over the lower abdomen, where the navel emerges uninterrupted by the folds radiating from the medial tie. The characterization of the woman depicted in this statue as "naked" (ESLP: 169) imparts a subjective interpretation to the image, which Quaegebeur (1983b: 121, *passim*) and others have called into question (CAT. 28). This approach to the body and its drapery is pharaonic (pp. 67-69, above). Although the most obvious comparisons derive from Dynasty XVIII (Bianchi in *Das ptol Äg.*: 98-99; 1980b: 19-20), additional examples of this phenomenon can be adduced from earlier periods as well (Cairo CG 392, Saleh/Sourouzian 1987: no. 104). The earlier assessment of Lawrence (1925; 1927: 66-68), who regarded such examples as artistically inferior works of craftsmen inadequately able to emulate Classical models, has certainly prejudiced late appraisals of such statues (ESLP: no. 130; Vandersleyen 1975: 271; 1985). The conception and execution of the interplay of flesh and fold on these examples are purely pharaonic; the sculptures must be considered in terms of Egyptian, rather than Classical, artistic norms.
The coiffures both of CATS. 74 and 75 consist of an elaborately arranged series of corkscrew locks also called "Libyan" (for example, Kyrieleis 1975: 128). The origin of such locks is presently not known (Kaschnitz von Weinberg 1965: 11), although they are depicted in relief in the tomb of Petosiris, datable to the late fourth century B. C. (Daumas in *Crépuscule*: 90 and 290, fig. 306) and appear with increased frequency during the course of the second century B. C. – a result, perhaps, of the use of this particular hairstyle on the coins of Ptolemy V Epiphanes (Noshy 1937: 125). Despite claims to the contrary (for example, Tran Tam Tinh 1984: 1722 and note 53), there is no

evidence for the exclusive association of these particular locks with Isis for monuments made in Egypt. Corkscrew locks, like the tripartite female costume, appear to have gained a degree of popularity as a fashion among native Egyptian women. Thus the tripartite costume, too, cannot be ascribed solely to Isis, since inscribed female statues so arrayed more frequently name goddesses other than Isis (Bianchi 1980b: 18-19; compare CATS. 66 and 82).

The woman represented in CAT. 74 is presumably either a goddess or a queen and not a private individual because of the presence of the uraeus on the hair band (for which see CAT. 28). The facial features are too ideal and the single attribute too general to decide in favor of queen or goddess, although some have regarded this idealization and attribute as reasons for calling her a queen whose precise identitiy cannot be adduced (Kyrieleis 1975: 119). The conception of the tripartite costume appears to be a more abstracted version of that shown on a more plastically rendered example in Cairo (CG 27472, Bianchi 1980b: fig. 12).

The dating of the statue can be established on stylistic grounds. The treatment of the features of the face as a series of gently merging sculptural planes without accentuated linear details would suggest a dating before the first century B. C., as would the complete absence of axial asymmetry. Although traces of tool marks are evident, the craftsmen have attempted to avoid the bichromatic effect by giving every surface of the stone the same degree of final polish. They have failed to achieve that goal only in the locks of hair on the forehead and those framing the neck. All of these features are inconsistent with developments of the first century B. C. and would seem to suggest that this statue be assigned instead to the second century B. C. The Leiden statue (CAT. 75) is in many ways an evocation of that in New Haven, despite the fact that modern restorations have tampered with the back pillar and restored the statue from the knees down (H. Schneider/Raven 1981: 141). Both are indebted to a prototype from which the Cairo statue also derived, but with the addition of the corkscrew locks. This dependency is most evident in the correspondences in the conception of the tripartite costume. In the Leiden and New Haven examples, the vertical fall resulting from the medial tie of the shawl to the skirt serves as the point from which the oblique folds fall. Moreover, the line of the shawl running obliquely over the left forearm and over the right breast almost horizontal to the line of the shoulder is similar in both examples.

There are, however, fundamental differences both in the approach to these motifs and in their execution. In the statue in Leiden, the conception of the hair does not adhere to Egyptian norms, because it closely follows the contour of the crown of the head before evolving into the corkscrew locks at the level of the ears. In this respect, the coiffure is somewhat analogous to that found on a statue from Pompeii (Naples 976, Tran Tam Tinh 1964: 156, no. 81). The representation of the knot is decorative rather than functional, thereby betraying a lack of familiarity with the actual garment. The features of the face, which are truly aberrant from Egyptian norms, are rendered in broad, stylized, highly polished planes which evoke the surfaces of

CAT. 75 ▷

CAT. 137, datable to the Roman Imperial Period. That high degree of polish characterizes the rest of the statue as well. All these features appear to indicate that the Leiden statue is an Egyptianizing work of Roman craftsmen datable to the second century A. D. It finds its closest parallel in a statue from Hadrian's Villa, now in Munich (Gl WAF 26b, Roullet 1972: no. 123). The large hole in the crown of the head doubtless served as a mortise for an attribute that would identify this figure, surely a representation of a goddess rather than a queen, for her Roman audience.

CAT. 76
Portrait of Cleopatra VII

Large-grained marble with a yellowish patina, 35 (13¾)
Circa 50 B. C.
Discovered in 1790 near the Villa Cassia in the neighborhood of the so-called Tomba di Nerone
Vatican City, The Vatican Museums, 38511

Literature: Helbig 1963: 18-19; Kyrieleis 1975: 185 [N 1]; Brunelle 1976: 108, *passim*; Johansen 1978: fig. 7 and note 9; Toynbee 1978: 88; Fittschen 1983: 170.

Cleopatra VII Philopator was born around 69 B. C. to Ptolemy XII Auletes and his wife, Cleopatra V (Thissen 1980: 453-54); she ended her life, perhaps from the venom of a snakebite (Becher 1966: 38, 50, *passim*), on August 12, 30 B. C. (Thissen 1980: 453-54). Although she was anciently identified both with Aphrodite and Isis, it would be an error to ascribe to her any outstandingly beautiful traits (Becher 1966: 71). Her appearance is best described by Plutarch:

> For her actual beauty, it is said, was not in itself so remarkable that none compared with her, or that no one could see her without being struck by it, but the contract of her presence, if you lived with her, was irresistible; the attraction of her person... and the character that attended all she said or did, was something bewitching. (Plutarch, *Lives*, Antony 27,II,3)

Cleopatra's political acumen and intelligence have been appreciated by modern commentators (Le Corsu 1965: 19-20). As for her moral character, she was – accusations to the contrary (Becher 1966) – sexually discreet and monogamous, taking as exclusive lovers only Julius Caesar and, upon his death, Marc Antony.

Her image is preserved on a series of coins (CAT. 61 n, o, u-w, z), once estimated to comprise almost sixty different issues (Wank 1984). Kyrieleis (1975: 125) has soberly cautioned against regarding that variety as the basis for identifying any number of allegorical female representations as images of Cleopatra VII (Adriani 1965: 41; La Rocca 1984; Linfert 1984; Parlasca 1985). In fact, not one of those issues ever depicts the queen in Egyptian regalia (D.B. Thompson 1980: 182). Although these coin portraits differ in detail from issue to issue, their profiles consistently represent a woman with a lightly arched nose and distinctive mouth, with a bowed lower lip (Fittschen 1983: 167; Linfert 1984: 357). These features bear a striking resemblance to those of her father (CATS. 57, 58; Toynbee 1978: 85) and even evoke the likeness of Ptolemy I Soter, the dynasty's founder (CATS. 50, 51). Although most of CAT. 76's nose is missing, what remains of the root and bridge is sufficient to identify it as Cleopatra VII. This identification is confirmed by the close correspondences between this head and some of the finer silver issues of Cleopatra VII, as Curtius (1933) had first suggested.

In the Vatican head, the queen is shown with the melon coiffure, wearing a wide band, suggested by some to represent a golden diadem (Curtius 1933; Trevelyan 1976: 65),[1] but which ought to be regarded rather as the wide diadem so characteristically an insignia of the later Ptoelemies (Kyrieleis 1975: 125). The eyes, wide open and strongly outlined by their lids, are set within a highly arched brow that recalls the configuration of earlier portraits (CATS. 53, 66). The elegant outlines of this highly classicizing portrait (Kyrieleis 1975: 125) evoke an image of the youthful queen, an impression enhanced both by the removal of the modern restorations, which included the nose, and the separation of this head from the draped statue to which it did not belong.

In most marble Ptolemaic ruler portraits parts of the head were originally completed in plaster. The Vatican head of Cleopatra VII, however, is entirely worked in marble, leading Kyrieleis (1975: 125) to suggest that it is a copy of a bronze original, presumably made early in Cleopatra's reign. That suggestion is supported by the blemish on the left cheek, as well as by the amorphous boss at the front of the diadem, both anomalies doubtless representing either attribute(s) or a gesture in the original which the copyist misunderstood in his marble rendering (Curtius 1933).

[1] Trevelyan (1976: 65) suggests that there are close similarities between this depiction of the queen wearing the golden band and a painting, now in Naples (9077), which both he and Johansen (1978: 61) accept as a portrait of Cleopatra VII.

◁ CAT. 76

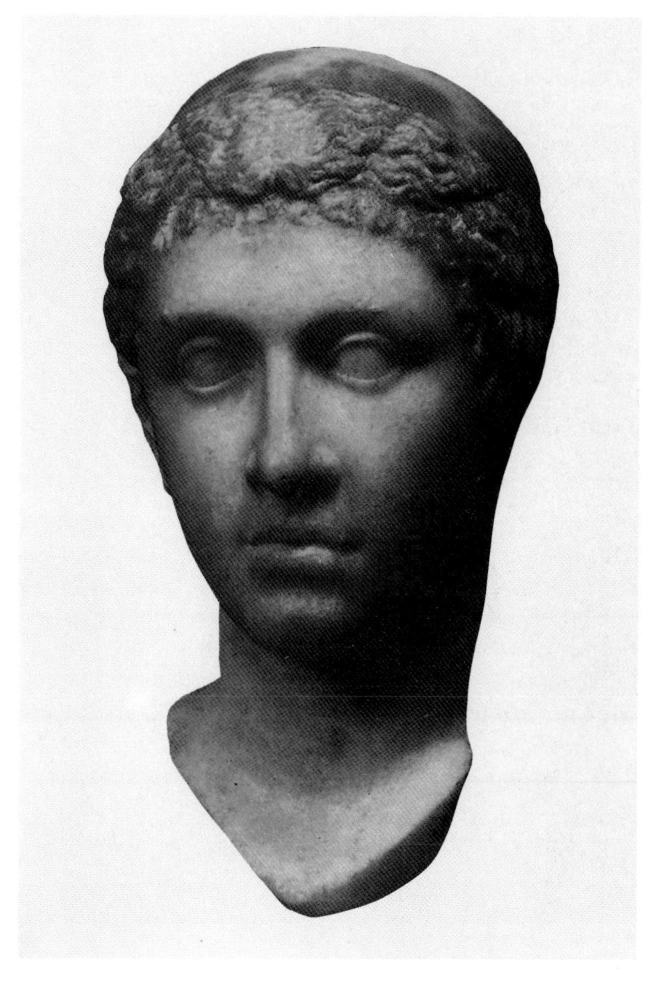

CAT. 77 *see color plate XVI*

Portrait of Cleopatra VII

Marble, 28 (11)
30-11 BC.
Provenance not known
Berlin/BRD, Staatliche Museen Preußischer Kulturbesitz, Antikenmuseum, 1976.10

Literature: Johansen 1978: 61, 62, and fig. 10; G. Grimm in Hildesheim 1979: 131; Heilmeyer 1979; Vierneisel 1980; Hornbostel in Altenmüller/Hornbostel 1982: no. 49; Krug 1984: 199; Fittschen 1983: 168; Maehler 1983: 95-96; Megow 1985: 465, *passim.*

This portrait, extolled as an extraordinarily beautiful, flattering image of Cleopatra VII (Maehler 1983: 95-96) is, nevertheless, somewhat softer and more mannered than the example in the Vatican (CAT. 76). The wide diadem is less naturalistically bound around the hair and does not interact with the bun, here depicted more like a ponytail than a concentric arrangement of braids, at the back of the head. Moreover, unlike the Vatican example, the diadem leaves the ear(s) exposed and does not seem to react to the mass of supple hair tightly bound beneath it. In addition, the diadem interrupts the arrangement of the locks of the melon coiffure, so that those in front of it are not compositionally integrated into the pattern of carefully arranged curvilinear rows of curls behind.

Although the physiognomy is generally that of Cleopatra VII as found both in the coin portraits and the Vatican example, this portrait has closer stylistic affinities with a head in Chercel, Algeria, identified as a representation of the same queen (Chercel 31, Johansen 1978: 60-61, fig. 9 and note 11; Fittschen 1983: 170 note 46; contra Kyrieleis 1975: 125, note 497). As a result, Fittschen has proposed that the Berlin head is a posthumous portrait of Cleopatra VII, erected in Mauretania by her daughter Cleopatra Selene, during the time of the latter's marriage to Juba (Fittschen 1983). That statues of Cleopatra VII were identified as such long after her death is demonstrated by a graffito of a scribe at Philae that mentions his recovery of one of her statues in 373 A. D. (Quaegebeur in *Das ptol. Äg.*: 256; p. 41, above).

CAT. 78
Stela of Cleopatra VII Offering to Isis

Limestone, 52.4×28×4 (20 9/16×11×1 9/16)
July 2, 51 B. C.
Provenance not known, but undoubtedly from the Faiyum
Paris, Musée du Louvre, Département des Antiquités Egyptiennes, E. 27113

Literature: Vandier 1973: 113-15; Wagner 1973; Bernand 1981b: 136-38.

This dedicatory stela depicts the queen, right, whose face and arms are damaged, standing before a sparsely ladened offering table, presenting jars of wine (?) to an image of the enthroned goddess Isis, who is nursing Horus (CATS. 100, 101). The top of the round-topped stela is adorned with a winged sun disk from which are suspended two uraei. The Greek text below translates: "For Queen Cleopatra, the goddess, the father-loving, [has been dedicated] the seat [*topos*] of the association [of Isis; Muszynski 1977] Snonais, the president of which is Onnophris. July 2, 51 B. C." Despite the ambiguities inherent in defining the specific nature of the *topos*, literally "seat", being dedicated and in the exact meaning of the epithet S[o]nonais applied to Isis, this stela is the earliest such dated monument clearly associated with the reign of Cleopatra VII as the sole ruler of the land, because her name stands alone, even though she and her brother Ptolemy XIII may have been co-regents as of July 2, 51 B. C. (Wagner 1973; Bernand 1975: 35-36; CAT. 107). More remarkable still is her epithet, *thea*, "goddess", which here dates to the very beginning of her reign.

The fact that Cleopatra VII is represented as a bare-chested kilted pharaoh wearing the Double Crown deserves comment. The visual precedents for this image derive from an Egyptian repertoire to which the reliefs of the Red Chapel at Karnak, decorated for Hatshepsut and Tuthmosis III, also belong (Eggebrecht *et al.* 1984: 244-45). Moreover, earlier Ptolemaic queens also appeared as pharaohs, as in a stela of asylum inscribed for Berenike IV, whose principal decoration is a bearded bust wearing a *nemes* (Cairo JE 40727, Bernand 1975: 50-58). In addition to the existence of such types, other aspects of the Paris stela suggest that it may not have been originally commissioned for Cleopatra VII. The grid, traces of which are evident between the lines of the Greek inscription within the sunken panel in the lower half of the stela, differs in its arrangement from that incised on the raised border to the left and right of that inscription. Closer examination reveals the apparent inability of the stonemason to fit the Greek text comfortably into the available space – the letters are both diminished and crowded together in lines 7-8. This would indicate that the Greek text was an afterthought. In fact, the scene in the upper half of this stela appears to have been a stock piece; another stela with the same composition, also in Paris, is inscribed for Cleopatra's father, Ptolemy XII Auletes (Paris 14702, Bernand 1975: 37-39 and pl. 9). While there are small differences in composition, typologically these two stelae are the same. Judging from the published photograph of the stela of Ptolemy XII Auletes, it appears that the present inscription was recut over an earlier text, whose characters were not completely chiseled off. Such recutting seems to be characteristic not only of royal stelae of the late Ptolemaic Period (Cairo JE 40720, a stela inscribed for Cleopatra VII and Caesarion, Bernand 1975: 45-47), but also for ruler portraits as well (CATS. 54, 59). The vagaries of the political circumstances of the times demanded the immediate removal of the visible monuments of toppled incumbents and their swift reworking and reerection in the name and/or image of the successful challenger.

This stela is also a valuable document in defining the nature of Ptolemaic culture, specifically in the Faiyum, an agricultural region heavily settled by the Crown with Greek veterans. Despite their Greek heritage and their advantaged status within Ptolemaic Egypt, these Greek cleruchs continually developed the Egyptian cult of Isis in this region to such a degree that the goddess' already diverse Greek epithets became innumerable. This intellectual, and verbal, development outpaced any visual, or iconographic, development. So, for example, one finds on this particular stela the problematic epithet "S[o]nonais" (Bernand 1981b: 137-38) in conjunction with a traditionally pharaonic image of the goddess Isis nursing the Horus child (CAT. 100). A comparable cultural milieu existed at Edfu, where traditional pharaonic religious concepts were paraphrased in Greek for the benefit of the local audience (CATS. 70, 71; pp. 25, 179, above; Yoyotte 1969). Such intellectual exercises on the part of the Greeks have no counterparts in the material cultural expressions of the native Egyptians. One has yet to identify a monument from Egypt with a Greek visual motif accompanied by a pharaonic text. Despite the unresolved question about the language of the original edition of the Ptolemaic royal decrees, the fact remains that their figural decorations are usually conceived in accordance with pharaonic, not Hellenistic, norms.[1] One might conclude from this curious phenomenon, documented in two different geographic and culturally divergent populations in the non-Greek countryside, that the Greek population attempted to cross cultural frontiers to effect a degree of intellectual assimilation by means of the written word, whereas their native Egyptian counterparts were content to remain locked deep within the confines of their own traditions. Such an adamant refusal on the part of the native Egyptians to

integrate with the Hellenes or to accept things Greek characterizes native Egyptian society throughout the Ptolemaic and Roman Periods. Ultimately, it manifests itself both in Egypt's autochthonous creation of monasticism and in its national espousal of the Monophysite doctrine, which led to the unbreachable rift with the Byzantine Church.

[1] The motif of the mounted king on a stela of Ptolemy IV (*Crépuscule*: fig. 68) is indebted to Egyptian norms.

CAT. 79
Portrait of Julius Caesar

Yellow, fine grained marble 26 (10 1/4)
20-1 B.C., after an original of 45-44 B.C.
Provenance not known
Vatican City, The Vatican Museums, 713

Literature: Amelung 1908: 473-74; Helbig 1963: 120, no. 158; Johansen 1987.

This portrait is the product of an extremely talented artist who has successfully subsumed stereometric formulae into a convincing portrayal of an individual (Helbig 1963: 120). The artist proceeded from an ovoid volumetric mass onto which he grafted a succession of specific physiognomic features. The hair, rendered as a series of S-curves radiating from a starfish pattern over the crown of the head, frames a rather wide forehead that is lightly creased with a series of horizontal folds. The root of the nose is marked by two sets of wrinkles, at right angles to one another. Their conjunction emphasizes the penetrating stare of the deeply set eyes, with their rather heavy lids and crow's-feet. The thin bridge of the nose, whose wings are restored, thematically echoes the gaunt, ascetic effect of the sunken cheeks, each of which is scored by vertical, thin creases. The nasolabial furrows, arranged almost on the diagonal axes of the face, frame the expressive mouth with its small lips, and echo the triangular shape of the strong, projecting chin, itself a continuation of the well-defined lower jaw.

Each of these features is not confined to the frontal plane but is integrated into the profile views of the sculpture. It is this very integration of organically interdependent physiognomic features, each relegated to the dominant, stereometric mass, which sets this head and, by extension, other examples of late Roman Republican portraiture, apart from contemporary Egyptian images (e.g., CATS. 43, 46). Further, the artist has been able to combine those characteristic traits into a convincing, hauntingly vibrant image of Julius Caesar, whose features thereby emerge from the marble as those of a specifically recognizable individual. A comparison with coin portraits struck between 45 and 44 B C., during the last year of Caesar's life (e. g., CAT. 61x), assure the identification (Johansen 1987).

And yet, in its very stereometric formulation, this portrait is not naturalistic. It is based, ultimately, on an earlier portrait of Caesar, whose features have here been codified and represented as idealizations of a type. Consequently, it cannot be regarded either as an example of late Republican or of Augustan artistic tendencies. It is, rather, an exception, outside of any artistic trend, that represents a consciously artificial attempt, datable to the first half of the Augustan Principate, to create a recognizable image of Julius Caesar by employing idealized, standardized features which unmistakably evoke only him.

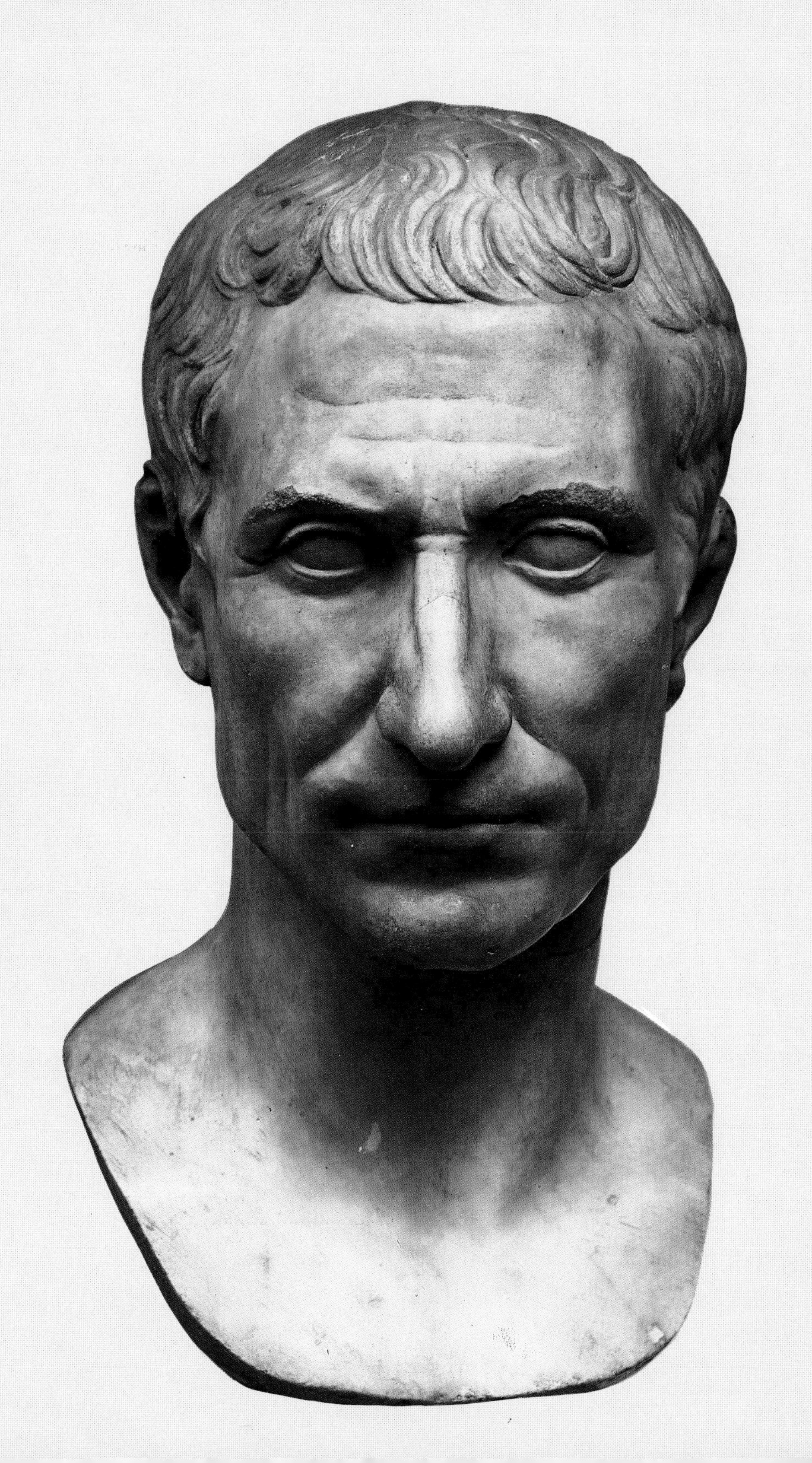

CAT. 80 *see color plate XVII*

Portrait of Marc Antony (?)

Schist, 23.5 (9 1/4)
50 B. C.-50 A. D.
Probably from Alexandria
The Brooklyn Museum, 54.51; Charles Edwin Wilbour Fund

Literature: Cooney 1956: 21-22; Brendel 1962: 365-66; Möbius 1964: 39-40; Johansen 1978; Megow 1985: 490.

After the Battle of Actium, the Romans proscribed statues of Antony and ordered them toppled (Johansen 1978: 70). As a result, his coin portraits (CAT. 61 u-w, y, z) may be the only contemporary images to have survived. These are remarkable because Antony was the second Roman, after Julius Caesar, to mint coins bearing his own image (Johansen 1978: 64). Some of them show Antony with a full beard, whereas his distinctive three-tiered profile – characterized by a receding forehead, an aquiline nose, and a jutting chin – is better represented in those issues on which he appears clean-shaven (Brendel 1962: 361). Later Julio-Claudian emperors of Rome, in the first half of the first century A. D., regarded Antony as one of their ancestors and erected posthumous images in his honor. It may be that the disconcerting lack of correspondence between the coins and some of the later sculptures believed to represent Antony (Brendel 1962: 360) is due to the comparison of non-coeval evidence. The problem is further compounded by the fact that no ancient sculpture inscribed for Antony has survived. Consequently, any sculpture depicting a man with the perceived characteristics of the coin portraits and lacking a diadem – also lacking in the numismatic images – is almost invariably adduced as a depiction of Marc Antony (Kyrieleis 1976).

The Brooklyn bust (compare CAT. 1) is one such image. In profile, it seems to conform to the three-tiered images of the clean-shaven Antony found on the coins. In this regard, it is remarkably similar to a second bust, also in schist, but of somewhat larger scale, now in Kingston Lacy, Dorset (Brendel 1962: 365-66)[1]. The shapes of both of these busts are typologically the same, with a triangular section of the upper chest articulated by the sternum notch and clavicles. Both heads are sharply turned to the right, an attitude accentuated by the prominence given to the muscles of the neck and to the Adam's apple. The example in Brooklyn preserves traces of a cloak draped over the left shoulder. There are also slight differences in the styles of the coiffures and their treatment. The dating of such busts has not been established. Vermeule and von Bothmer (1956), discussing the example in Kingston Lacy, suggest a dating in the Augustan Period (27 B. C.- 14 A. D.), but concede that such a bust could have been created in Egypt in the period before 31 B. C. They further suggest that such busts were either erected on pillars or set into niches.

Although there are many correspondences between these two busts – compare the profile views and the material – opinions nevertheless vary about their respective identities. So it is that Brendel (1962: 365-66) and Johansen (1978: 76) accept both as images of Marc Antony, whereas Toynbee (1978: 45) and Megow (1985: 491) accept only the Kingston Lacy example and Möbius (1964: 42) only the Brooklyn piece. Parlasca (1967: 176 and note 26) admits the impasse: this sculpture might well be a posthumous evocation of Marc Antony.

One final point deserves mention. The bust in Brooklyn appears to have been recut in antiquity because the right side of the face has been worked to a smooth flat surface from the line of the lower jawbone to the level of the top of the brow in the area between the outer corner of the eye and the ear. Such an alteration, while not unexpected (CATS. 54, 81), is nevertheless unusual because it has not radically changed the appearance of the individual represented. One might suggest that the alteration was dictated by the requirements of placing the bust into a niche, in which it would be regarded from either a profile or three-quarter view. The small scale of the piece doubtless indicates that the bust served the needs of a private, rather than a public, monument (compare CAT. 49)

[1] See C. A. Picon in Washington 1985: no. 246. Picon cites an undated letter written in the 1840s that states that the head was found near the site of Canopus in 1780. The head measures 42 cm. in height.

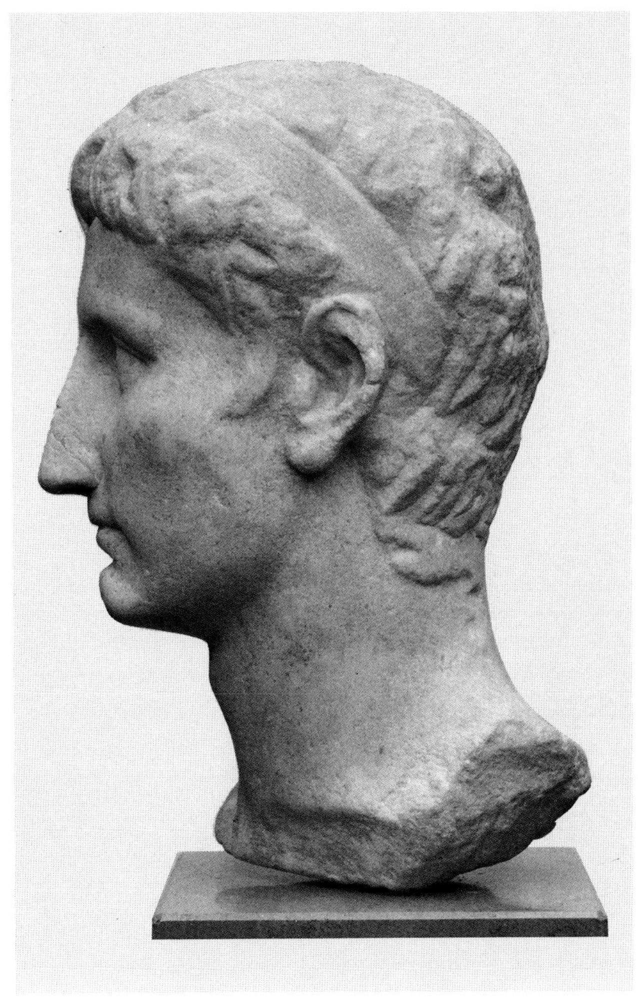

CAT. 81
Portrait of Augustus

White marble with large crystals, 30 (11 13/16)
Late first century B.C.
From Sahha, near Damanhur
Stuttgart, Württembergisches Landesmuseum, Antikensammlung, 1.35

Literature: Bonacasa 1971; Vierneisel/Zanker 1979: 5.15; H. Jucker 1981a: 669-70.

A careful study of this object reveals that it was anciently reworked from an already completed statue (H. Jucker 1981a: 669-70; 1981b: 241-42; Vierneisel/Zanker 1979: 5.15). That reworking is most noticeable in the treatment of the hair and of the nose, both of which were recut and anciently reconstructed with plaster. The preserved diadem, which could not be readily effaced in the reworking process, belonged to the earlier portrait; its width, indicating a date for the original within the first century B.C. (Krug in *Das ptol. Äg.*: 10; H. Jucker 1981b: 241-42; with both H. Jucker 1981a: 669-70 and Kiss 1984: 32-33 opposed), suggests that the portrait initially represented a late Ptolemy – portraits of whom were themselves subjected to alterations (CAT. 54; R. Smith 1986: 78; H. Jucker 1981b: 241-42). It would be futile, therefore, to speculate on the identity of the ruler depicted in the original version.

The head, in its present form, belongs to the Prima Porta Group of Augustan portraits (Vierneisel/Zanker 1979: 5.15; H. Jucker 1981b: 241-42), and is indebted to East Greek traditions for the rendering of its soft, idealizing features, which find their closest parallels in a colossal head of Augustus now in Alexandria (24043, H. Jucker 1981a: 682; Bonacasa 1971). Although the question remains open as to whether this head was set into a body either of a togatus or cuirass type, there is no doubt that such marble heads, and perhaps even busts (H. Jucker 1981b: 241), were inserted into bodies sculpted from different materials. One of the reasons for this practice was the absence of marble, the quintessentially Greek medium for sculpture, in Egypt. That dearth, as has been repeatedly suggested, was a contributing factor both in the practice of recutting marble portraits into second versions, or into totally different images, as here, and for the rampant use of plaster to complete marble statues in general. Such an assumption implies that the economics, and perhaps even the politics, of marble importation dictated the adoption of a technical process which is now regarded as synonymous with Graeco-Roman portraiture in Egypt.

But this assessment needs to be reevaluated. The repertoire of Greek marble sculpture of the sixth and fifth centuries B. C. contains examples of heads which have been similarly finished with painted plaster additions (Blümel 1968: 11-24). A similar phenomenon is observable in Egyptian sculpture from the time of the Old Kingdom. Numerous examples of pharaonic sculpture, carved from the plentiful, local Egyptian varieties of limestone, were likewise completed by the addition of painted plaster (e.g., Boston 27.442, W. Smith 1960: 39). Could the practice of completing Hellenistic and Roman marble portraits in Egypt be ascribed alternatively to an existing artistic tradition common both to Classical Greek and native pharaonic ateliers? This suggestion gains support from a group of almost totally ignored independent sculptures of pharaohs crafted exclusively in plaster (CAT. 34), which come into vogue before and continue to be produced during the Ptolemaic Period. Portrait sculpture produced in Egypt under the Ptolemies and Romans that adds plaster to marble is therefore better regarded as a multi-media creation, motivated by a long-standing artistic tradition. This tradition was shared, perhaps independently, by Greek and Egyptian ateliers, but it remained divorced from politico-economic considerations.

CAT. 82 *see color plate XXV*

Funerary Cartonnage of a Lady of Means

Linen, gilded gesso, glass, and faience,
57.6×37.2×19 (22 11/16×14 3/8×7 1/2)
First century A. D.
Provenance not known, but assigned to Hawara in the Faiyum
The Brooklyn Museum 69.35; Charles Edwin Wilbour Fund

Literature: G. Grimm 1974: 22, 53; Bianchi in Brooklyn 1983: no. 80.

Cartonnage is a combination of layers of papyrus and/or linen (as here) and gesso or plaster, resembling *papier-mâché*. This traditionally Egyptian material enjoyed great popularity for anthropoid mummy coverings made during the Third Intermediate Period, especially at Thebes. It was revived in the late Ptolemaic and Roman Imperial Periods by Egyptian artists who distinguished themselves by embellishing the medium with a great array of secondary materials as inlays.

This example represents a lady of means depicted from the waist upward (G. Grimm 1974: 22 note 80), a form of cartonnage particularly frequent in the Faiyum at the site of Hawara during the first century A. D. (G. Grimm 1974: 55-57). The crown and back of her head are decorated with a painted depiction of a vulture, presumably the goddess Nekhbet, who provides magical protection for the deceased. The corpulently modeled face with fleshy throat derives from an ideal of female beauty current from the fourth century B. C. on (CATS. 36, 48, 69), and its idealism is enhanced by the addition of inlays of faience and glass for the eyes and brows. The coiffure replicates a painstakingly arranged series of tightly spiraled curls framed at the ears by a series of short curls; the costume is the traditionally Egyptian female tripartite ensemble which knots the shawl to the breast (CAT. 66).

The propensity of Egyptian artists to replicate accessories is here given full rein. The earrings reflect a type of S-shaped earrings with pearl-like beads (Segall 1938: no. 134; New York 07.228.170A-B, unpublished); the anguiform ring, bracelets, and armbands find their direct correspondence in the jewelry of CATS. 94-96; and the imitation beryl-bead necklace accurately reflects a fashion common in the first century A. D. (CAT. 97). The second necklace is composed of alternating rosettes and imitation stones in what appear to be gypsy settings (Davidson/Oliver 1984: 154). The three ears of wheat held in the left hand imitate examples in gold (Brooklyn 67.13, Bothmer/Keith 1974: 80-81), and are substitutes for botanical specimens that have actually been found intact between the bandages of at least one mummy from the Roman Imperial Period (New York 25.3.152, N. Scott 1944: fig. 14). The garland, pressed to the left breast with the right hand, is a frequently encountered motif in the funerary arts of Roman Egypt, but its significance has not been established (Wagner 1972: 144; Gaşsowska 1983: 101, who uncritically terms this attribute a *hypothymis*, or neck garland).

There is little doubt that the anguiform motifs on the jewelry and the ears of wheat associate the deceased with Isis and Osiris, respectively, as the deities of resurrection, and that that association is emphasized by the gilding of the entire front of the cartonnage, which imparts a sense of rebirth and eternal permanance (Daumas 1956; CAT. 123). In such a context, the tendency to associate the knotted three-piece costume with the goddess Isis is exceedingly tempting (Bianchi in Brooklyn 1983: no. 80), since statuettes identified as representations of Isis are shown similarly dressed (CAT. 101). On the other hand, figures of private women and of queens are often shown wearing this knotted costume in contexts which are specifically divorced from associations with Isis (CATS. 74, 75; Bianchi 1980b). Moreover, there are numerous non-pharaonic representations of Isis from the Ptolemaic and Roman Periods that represent the goddess in a simpler costume (CAT. 102; Cairo JE 47108, Wildung/Schoske 1984: 40-41). The knotted three-piece costume itself, therefore, should not be associated automatically with the goddess Isis.

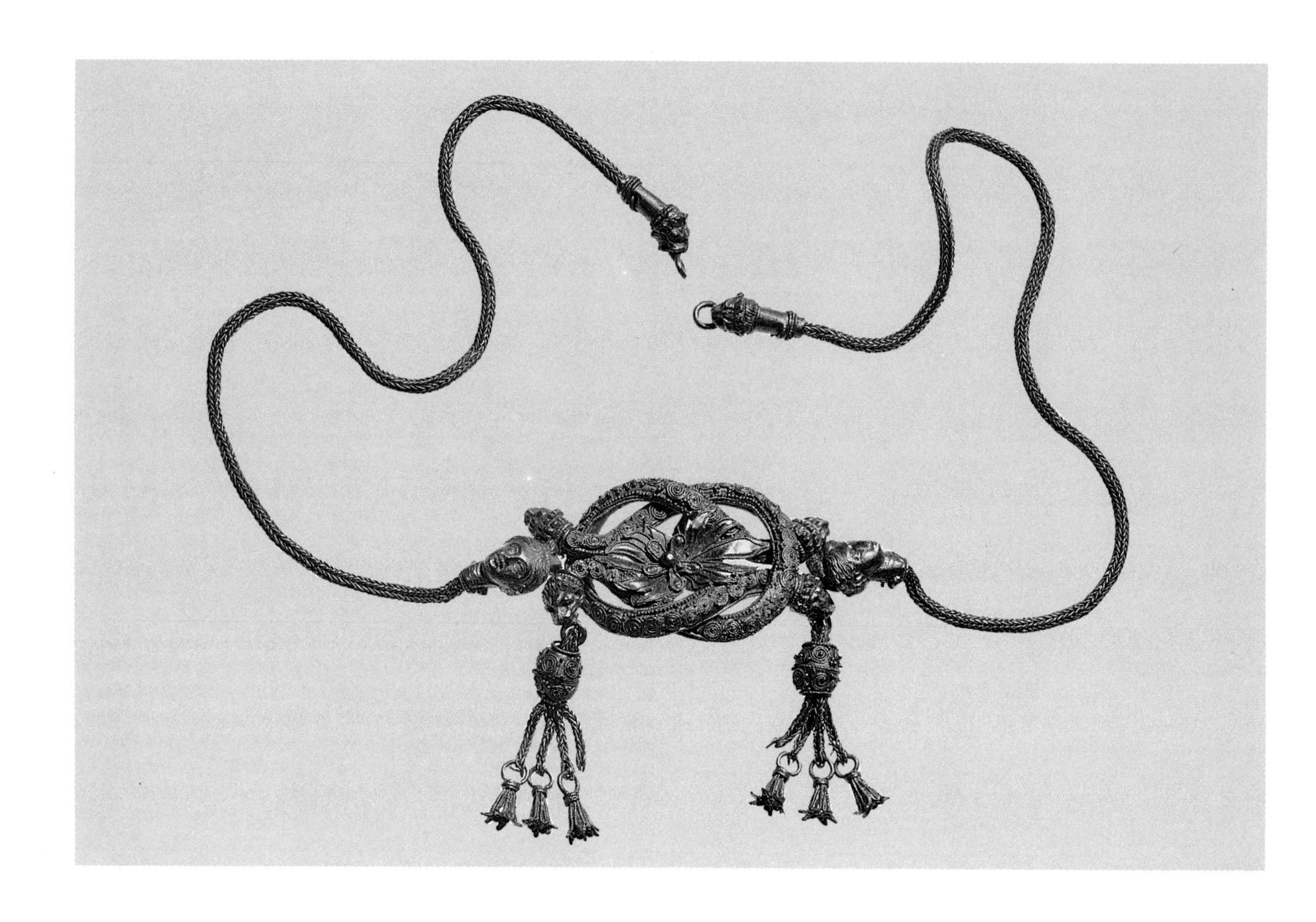

CAT. 83 *see color plate XIX*

Gold Fillet with Herakles Knot

Gold, 40.7 (16) length
Late fourth-third century B.C.
Provenance not known
Collection of Christos G. Bastis

Literature: Davidson/Oliver 1984: 37-39; Oliver in New York 1987: no. 180.

The motif of the square knot, representing an easily tied fastening that holds fast, first appears as a decorative motif in Egyptian art (Davidson/Oliver 1984: 18), where its symbolic value has been variously explained (Schäfer 1943; Day 1967: 57-59). Like the animal heads on the hoop earrings (CAT. 86) that the Macedonian Greeks appropriated as their own, so too this Egyptian motif was adopted by Alexander the Great and his successors as one of their insignia (Buitron 1979: 87), without acknowledgment of its Egyptian origin. The significance of the square knot was then transformed to conform to Greek sensibilities. It became the "Herakles knot", whose ropes symbolized the union of Zeus and Rhea as snakes (Buitron 1979: 87). The Greeks believed the knot to be imbued with amuletic properties particularly efficacious for healing wounds (Buitron 1979: 87). The present work is a particularly splendid example of the Herakles knot. The open space in the center of the knot is closed with a rosette centered in a palmette. The four lion-headed ends of the "rope" are stylistically related to the same motif on the two hoop earrings (CAT. 85). The open mouth of each of the two lions at the bottom holds a ring to which is attached a tassel. The chain of the fillet is joined to the Herakles knot by means of two exquisitely crafted female heads, each in turn attached to the paired lion heads. The clasp, now missing, fitted at the lion-headed terminals at the chain's end. Such an object, which belongs to a class of similar fillets (Davidson/Oliver 1984: 37), indicates the high level of craftsmanship attained by the goldsmiths of the early Hellenistic Period and suggests the degree of luxury which might have existed at the Alexandrian court at this time.

CAT. 84 *see color plate XX*

A Pair of Earrings with Egyptian Crowns

Gold inlaid with semiprecious stones and white and black glass, 7.2 (2 13/16) length
Third or second century B.C.
Provenance not known
Collection of Christos G. Bastis

Literature: Oliver in New York 1987: no. 184.

Each of these earrings consists of two separate parts, the hook and the pendant. The latter is heart-shaped and features a centrally placed stone, bordered by a frame of black and white glass inlays in a setting decorated with gold beading. Although the use of such semiprecious stones in jewelry of the Hellenistic Period is indebted to Achaemenid norms (CATS. 83, 85-88), the colored pieces of opaque glass may derive from pharaonic traditions. In this context, they were employed to imbue the earrings with a technical as well as a visual link with Egypt. That visual link is further elaborated by the principal decoration of the hook: a variation of what Plutarch (*De Iside* 19, Griffiths 1970: 147, 350-51) terms the *basileion*. Its design apparently conforms to what is commonly called the Crown of Isis (Grumach-Shirun 1975: 143, fig. 2), whose canonical form consists of a sun disk surmounted by two plumes and resting on the horns of a cow (compare Fig. 18). Although the horns are not represented in these earrings, the intention of the goldsmith is clear. He was crafting a reflection of the *basileion*, which served as a principal emblem of Isis (Malaise 1976; Berlandini 1983) and could be incorporated into the insignia of queens (Quaegebeur 1983b: 111). One assumes that the individual for whom these earrings were made either participated in an Isis cult in life or aspired to resurrection after death with the assistance of that goddess. The earrings thus reflect the tastes of those Greeks of the Hellenistic Period who embraced Egyptian cults, in somewhat altered form, outside Egypt (Leclant 1984).

CAT. 85 *see color plate XXIV*

Two Lion-Headed Earrings

Gold, 1.6 (5/8) diameter
Late fourth-third century B.C.
From Upper Egypt
The Brooklyn Museum, 37.775E and 37.776E; Charles Edwin Wilbour Fund

Literature: Davidson/Oliver 1984: 40, 43.

CAT. 86 *see color plate XXIV*

Lynx-Headed Earring

Gold, 1.9 (3/4) diameter
Second century B.C.
From Thebes
The Brooklyn Museum 37.783E; Charles Edwin Wilbour Fund

Literature: Davidson/Oliver 1984: 40, 46-47.

CAT. 87 *see color plate XXIV*

Gazelle-Headed Earring

Gold, 2.3 (7/8) diameter
Late fourth-third century B.C.
From Thebes
The Brooklyn Museum, 37.774E; Charles Edwin Wilbour Fund

Literature: Davidson/Oliver 1984: 40-48.

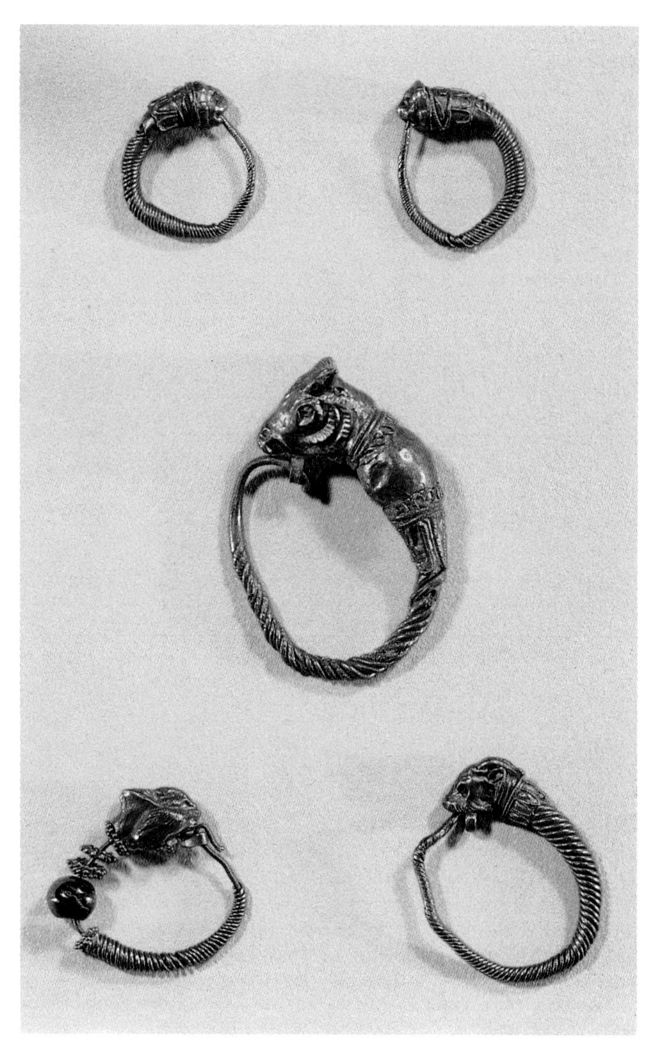

CATS.85 (top); 88 (middle); 86, 87 (bottom)

The great traditions of the pharaonic jewelers appear to have come to an abrupt halt with the close of the Third Intermediate Period. The jewelry that has been recovered from tombs dating from the Saite Period and later, although admittedly not from royal contexts, is somewhat disappointing from a technical point of view, even if it does perpetuate pharaonic motifs and iconographic features (e.g., Barsanti 1900; 1901; 1904). The jewelry recovered from fourth-century tombs is even less interesting (Bresciani 1983c: figs. 35-37). While these examples are by no means all-inclusive and may very well reflect the economic status or individual tastes of the tomb owners, a gradual decline in the craft of native jewelers is nevertheless observable during the course of the early Late Period.

The arrival of the Macedonians with Alexander the Great and the subsequent establishment of the Ptolemaic dynasty seem to have finally and irrevocably destroyed this native tradition of ancient Egypt's material culture and to have replaced it with one that was not particularly pharaonic in nature. Indeed, the vast majority of the jewelry recovered from Ptolemaic Egypt belongs to an idiom common to many countries of the Eastern Mediterranean. Furthermore, many of the motifs encountered in this Hellenistic jewelry are indebted to prototypes borrowed from the repertoire of Persian goldsmiths. The animal heads on the hoop earrings grouped together here are inspired by Persian models encountered by the Macedonian Greeks in the army of Alexander the Great as they fought their way East (Hoffmann/Davidson 1965: 2). It is, however, exceedingly difficult to accept the contention that Achaemenid craftsmen, as refugees from a destroyed Persepolis, migrated immediately to Egypt, or elsewhere, in order to open up new workshops (Parlasca 1979). Each of the animals, particularly the gazelle and lion, had a long association with the royal courts of the ancient Near East. Moreover, it is unlikely that the new Hellenistic audience imparted an Achaemenid meaning to the forms thus borrowed. In fact, the sensibilities of the Hellenistic Greeks demanded that the animal heads on such hoop earrings, which originally faced into the ears of the wearers in conformity with Persian practice, be rotated 180 degrees. That alteration allowed the animal heads to look out into the direction of the viewer rather than at the wearer (Hoffmann/Davidson 1965: 106-10).

CAT. 88 *see color plate XXIV*

Bull-Headed Earring

Gold, 3.3 (1 5/8) length
Late fourth-third century B.C.
Provenance not known
The Brooklyn Museum, 05.459.2; Ella C. Woodward Memorial Fund

Literature: Davidson/Oliver 1984: 40, 54.

CAT. 89

CAT. 90

CAT. 89 *see color plate XXII*
Armlet with Deities

Gold with fused-glass inlays, 4.5×9×4.5 (1 3/4×3 9/16×3/16)
Reign of Queen Amanishakheto (late first century B.C.)
Meroe, North Cemetery, Pyramid 6 at Begrawiya
Munich, Staatliche Sammlung Ägyptischer Kunst, Ant. 2455

Literature: Wenig 1978: no. 170.

CAT. 90 *see color plate XXIII*
Shield-Ring with the God Sebiumeker

Gold with fused-glass inlays, 4.7×3.6 ×1.8 diameter (1 7/8×1 7/16×11/16)
Reign of Queen Amanishakheto (late first century B.C.)
Meroe, North Cemetery, Pyramid 6 at Begrawiya
Munich, Staatliche Sammlung Ägyptischer Kunst, Ant. 2446c

Literature: Wenig 1978: no. 168.

CAT. 91 *see color plate XXIII*
Shield-Ring with Ram's Head and Temple Façade

Gold with fused-glass inlays and carnelian bead, 5.5×5.4×1.8 diameter (2 3/16×2 1/8×11/16)
Reign of Queen Amanishakheto (late first century B.C.)
Munich, Staatliche Sammlung Ägyptischer Kunst, Ant. 2446b

Literature: Wenig 1978: no. 164.

During Dynasty XXV, the Kushites, or Nubians, whose ethnicity Trigger (1978) attempted to define, established themselves as overlords of Egypt, with Thebes and Memphis as their principal strongholds. They were toppled from power by the Assyrians and then replaced as rulers of Egypt by members of a princely family resident in the Delta city of Sais; eventually the Kushites regrouped far to the South (Priese 1978). There they ruled from the city of Napata until about 300 B.C., when the capital was transferred to the city of Meroe (Bianchi 1979c: 65-66) for reasons which are still not absolutely certain (Hintze 1978). By accident, rather than by plan, the common boundary between the Nubian Kingdom of Meroe and that of Ptolemaic Egypt was at Aswan in the region of the First Cataract. The Meroites continued to develop their own native forms of cultural expressions and even invented a system of writing, called Meroitic, which has still to be deciphered (Hintze 1978: 93-94), although many of the inscriptions have been subjected to computer analysis.

As each culture developed along its own lines, their common border provided ample opportunity for interfacing. Politically, the two kingdoms enjoyed a symbiotic relationship (Bianchi 1979c: 65-66) and, although there may have been Meroites involved in the revolt of the Thebaid (p. 16, above), the Meroitic king Asekhraman may have served as a mediator in the ultimate resolution of the conflict in the reign of Ptolemy V Epiphanes (Alliot 1951; Bianchi 1979c: 66). Culturally, some Egyptians may have been xenophobic toward their Meroitic neighbors (Sauneron 1959; 1960c: 123-25); others, living in Thebes, incorporated the name of the Meroitic god Arsennuphis into their own personal names (Quaegebeur 1974b: 51).

CAT. 91

Bronze objects in quantity were continuously exported from Egypt into the Kingdom of Meroe (W. Adams 1981: 6-7). Religiously, the goddess Hathor of Dendera was said to return annually to Egypt from Nubia (Barguet 1977). Conversely, the Ptolemaic god Serapis (CAT. 104) was assimilated to the Meroitic god Apedemak at Meroe (Török 1976) and the Egyptian deities Shu and Tefnut were incorporated into the decorative program of the great temple at Musawarat es Sufra. This picture of peaceful coexistence which the Ptolemies shared with the Meroites for almost three centuries changed abruptly with the arrival into Egypt of the Romans (p. 20, above).

Roman hostility toward the Kingdom of Meroe may, on one level, be regarded as an extension of Roman fear of foreign women aspiring to supreme political power. Having successfully defeated Cleopatra VII and thereby acquiring Egypt, the Romans were simultaneously confronted by the Meroites whose social system of large extended families enabled women to rise to the position of sole monarch (Katznelson 1966; Millet 1981). Coincidently, Augustus' rule over Egypt was contemporary with that of the Meroitic queen Amanishakheto (Vercoutter 1962), and he could have regarded her as a new female threat to his realm. His fears were soon realized when the military forces of Rome, led by one Petronius (Plumley 1975: 16; Weinstein/Turner 1976: 115-16; Hofmann 1977; Burstein 1979; Bagnall 1985), were defeated by those of Queen Amanishakheto, whom the Romans mistakenly called "Candace," assuming that this Meroitic word was a personal name and not a title (Trigger 1974; Hofmann 1981). The Meroitic forces must have stormed across the border at Aswan and perhaps even pillaged the Egyptian sanctuaries there in 25 B.C. That they razed monuments erected in honor of Augustus is certain. A beautiful bronze head of that emperor, once part of a statue and now in London (1911.9-.1.1, Hintze 1978: 101) was found during excavations in the city of Meroe. This bronze had been subjected to an abusive burial, symbolizing the triumph of Meroe over Rome: it had been intentionally interred beneath the floor of a room which contained a painting of a Meroitic throne, beneath which lay depictions of Meroe's hapless foe, a Roman included in their number (Haynes 1983).

CATS. 89, 90 and 91 represent a part of the funeral jewelry of Queen Amanishakheto. The entire ensemble was accidently discovered in 1834 by the Italian physician Giuseppe Ferlini while he was dismantling the queen's pyramid in Begrawiya North, one of two cemeteries in which those ruling from the city of Meroe were buried (Wenig 1978: no. 162). Today, the treasure is divided between Munich and Berlin/DDR (Wenig 1978: 236-54; H. Müller/Wildung 1976: 242-48).

In contrast to the jewelry associated with the Ptolemies of Egypt, which relies on forms and motifs belonging to extra-Egyptian cultural traditions (CATS. 82-88, 92-97), this Meroitic treasure conforms to a time-honored Egyptian aesthetic for jewelry: the gold unites with other materials, here fused glass, to create a dazzling effect which bombards the retinal nerve with an explosion of color. This effect is carried throughout the piece and, unlike Classical and later Western taste, no single stone is isolated in a central setting that becomes the focus of the composition.

CAT. 89 is an armlet crafted from two segments (see Wenig 1978: no. 170 for details) and hinged, with the joint opposite the fastening concealed by a figure of a goddess there identified as Mut. One cannot, however, insist on the strict equation of Egyptian deities with members of the Meroitic pantheon because borrowed motifs often retain the form but not the significance of the original motif (see CAT. 111). Moreover the plurality of meaning for an Egyptian Double Crown precludes a more precise identification. The panels around the band itself are decorated with images of crowned deities, which recall the shape of the shield-rings.

Two such rings are illustrated in CATS. 90 and 91 and both rely for their effect on hinging a broad collar to the shank of the ring. CAT. 90 represents the Meroitic god Sebiumeker, whose iconography, in contrast to that of the winged female of CAT. 89, has been worked out in some detail (Wenig 1978: 241). The god is shown bearded and wearing the Double Crown, and he is flanked by Meroitic versions of the *wadjet*, or eye of protection.

The design of CAT. 91 is the more ambitious of the two shield-rings. It unites the motif of a broad collar with that of a chapel facade (see CAT. 4), an architectural motif that occurs with frequency in Meroitic art (Wenig 1978: 237). The identity of the deity represented by the ram and the significance of its appearance before an architectural setting remain enigmatic. Nevertheless, the Ferlini Treasure affords a fleeting glimpse of the longevity of Egyptian tenets of design and allows one to behold the possessions of a queen who succeeded where Cleopatra VII failed.

Clockwise from upper left: CATS. 92, 94, 96, 93

CATS. 92-96 *see color plate XVIII*

CAT. 92
Finger Ring with Busts of Two Divinities

Gold, 2.2 (7/8) diameter, 3.2 (1 1/4) greatest extension
First century A. D.
Provenance not known
The Brooklyn Museum, 67.2; Charles Edwin Wilbour Fund

Literature: Davidson/Oliver 1984: 154-55.

CAT. 93
Finger Ring with Busts of Two Divinities

Gold, 2.4 (15/16) diameter, 3.1 (1 3/16) greatest extension
First century A. D.
Provenance not known
The Brooklyn Museum, 16.148; Gift of the Estate of Charles Edwin Wilbour

Literature: Davidson/Oliver 1984: 155.

CAT. 94
Anguiform Ring

Gold, 5.1 (2) length
Third century B. C.
Found on the Greek island of Ithaka
The Brooklyn Museum, 37.785E; Charles Edwin Wilbour Fund

Literature: Davidson/Oliver 1984: 74.

CAT. 95
Snake Bracelet

Gold over a metal (bronze?) core with glass enamel inlays, 9.9 (3 7/8) diameter
First century A. D.
Provenance not known
The Museum of Fine Arts, Houston, 37-48; The Annette Finnigan Collection

Literature: Hoffmann 1971: 472-75.

CAT. 95

CAT. 96
Bracelet with Serpent Heads

Gold, 6.6 (2 5/8) diameter
Third century A. D.
Provenance not known
The Brooklyn Museum, 16.146; Gift of the Estate of Charles Edwin Wilbour

Literature: Davidson/Oliver 1984: 150-51.

The available evidence indicates that finger rings decorated with busts of deities were fashionable between the first century B. C. and the first century A. D., although admittedly none have been recovered from controlled excavations (Davidson/Oliver 1984: 154). Such rings exhibit two distinct forms, each illustrated by one of these examples. The first type (CAT. 92) is a penannular hoop ring, whose twisted ends terminate in two or more busts; the second type (CAT. 93) is a ring composed of several spirals, each end of which is formed into a bust (Davidson/Oliver 1984: 154). The decorative use of such divine busts in this context can be regarded as a development from their appearance on coins and medallions (CAT. 102), as well as in other media (CAT. 103).

The identifications of the deities on each ring are rendered somewhat difficult by their small size and by the imprecision with which their attributes have been crafted. The male bust in CAT. 92 may be identified as Osiris because he is wearing an *atef*-crown and is clean-shaven. The corresponding figure is then to be regarded as Isis, whose attribute, although indistinctly formed, is plausibly identified as the throne (Gardiner 1957: Sign List Q1). The full beard and long hair on the male figure of CAT. 93 would indicate that Serapis is there paired with Isis (CAT. 104).

This collection of anguiform, or serpentlike, jewelry reveals the frequency of the serpent motif in Antiquity. Its history can be sketched as follows. The earliest appearance of the motif in jewelry seems to occur in Urartu in the ninth century B. C. (Landenius 1978: 37, citing Maxwell-Hyslop 1971: 205), although allegations abound of earlier appearances in other Near Eastern contexts (Segall 1938: 42; Moorey 1971: 220; contra Maxwell-Hyslop 1971: 205). The motif then appears for the first time in Greece at Eleusis, a suburb of Athens, in the form of an anguiform bracelet from a tomb of the Geometric Period. Despite the association of the serpent with Isis, this bracelet, contrary to what Segall (1938: 116) maintains, cannot be unequivocally related to the goddess, especially since the serpent as a motif was imbued by the Greeks with several different levels of interpretation (Landenius 1978: 38). So, for example, anguiform accessories occasionally appear in the form of armbands on figures on Attic vases of the sixth century B. C. (Landenius 1978: 38 and notes 22 and 23; Würzburg 530, Keuls 1985: 180). Moreover, the veritable explosion of the snake motif on jewelry in the course of the fourth century B. C. cannot historically be connected with the concomitant spread of the cult of Isis, as has been mistakenly maintained in the past (Segall 1978: 38). This phenomenon is rather to be ascribed to the fact that anguiform jewelry is an integral part of the koine of early Hellenistic jewelry, whose character is neither decidedly Ptolemaic nor Egyptian (CATS. 85-88). The natural coiling form of a serpent rendered it an ideal motif for those types of jewelry which provided the allusion of being "wrapped" around a finger or limb.

The finger ring (CAT. 94) is a case in point because its five loops would accommodate it comfortably to a finger. The extremely thin and fragile nature of the gold suggests that it may have been employed solely in a funerary context (Davidson/Oliver 1984: 74). Its dating to the third century B. C. (Davidson/Oliver 1984: 74) cannot be associated with any contemporary cult of Isis on the island of Ithaka (Brown 1975). One should, therefore, regard this anguiform ring in terms of the general chthonic associations serpents had for the Greeks.

The snake bracelet (CAT. 95) derives from types which have been excavated in Egypt, specifically the example found at Sais (Cairo CG 52114, Vilímková *et al.* 1969: no. 87), which were extremely popular in the Hellenistic Period (Higgins 1961: 187). It is not unusual to encounter examples such as this in which each end of the serpent's body terminates in a head. On this example, each head was separately molded and attached to the hoop but the joints have been masked by covering them with a collar of beaded wire. The eyes have been inlaid with glass enamel and imbue the piece with a polychromatic effect that ultimately derives from the Achaemenid repertoire of jewelry (CATS. 85-88). The tongue, separately made from a thin piece of gold, realistically flickers in the open mouth when the hand is moved. Because this unusual detail is also found on one other bracelet now in Athens (Segall 1938: 85, no. 97) and because such bracelets were generally worn in pairs, Andrew Oliver has suggested that CAT. 95 may actually be the mate of the one in Athens (Hoffmann 1971: 473). On the basis of excavated parallels from Pompeii, such examples are datable to the first century A. D. (Higgins 1961: 187 and 193).

Bracelets terminating in two serpents' heads continued to evolve as Roman tastes changed. The solid hoop was soon replaced by a type crafted from twisted wires, as seen in CAT. 96, on which the heads, instead of serving as independent terminals, were now equipped with fasteners. This new type has been found in sites ranging from Lyon in the south of France to Doura Europos on the Euphrates River (Higgins 1961: 188) and was in vogue during the third century A. D.

CAT. 97 *see color plate XXI*

Necklace with Beryl Beads

Gold, with 18 hexagonal beryl beads and a Bes-image, also of beryl, whose eyes are inlaid with silver grains ringed with gold wire, 34.4 (13 9/16) length
First century A. D.
Provenance not known[1]
The Brooklyn Museum, 16.149; Gift of the Estate of Charles Edwin Wilbour

Literature: Davidson/Oliver 1984: 140.

The distinguishing feature of this necklace is the presence of green beryl beads, which were "a standard feature of Roman jewelry" (Davidson/Oliver 1984: 140), although the wire of this piece is modern. Such necklaces were extremely popular throughout the Roman Empire during the first century A. D. and an Egyptian provenance cannot be established for this example. In fact, the Bes-image, which Romano (1980) has demonstrated can no longer be considered a depiction of a bandy-legged dwarf but is rather an image based on a leonine deity, appears to have been added as a pendant in more recent times, when the beryl beads were restrung in their present configuration. It is nevertheless instructive to note that a similar necklace, but without a Bes-image, is represented on the gilded cartonnage of a noblewoman (CAT. 82), which has been independently dated to the first century A. D. as well. The penchant of Egyptian artists to replicate what their eyes beheld continued unabated into the Roman Imperial Period, as this example demonstrates.

[1] This necklace was purchased in 1909 by Miss Theodora Wilbour, the daughter of Charles Edwin Wilbour, at the auction of the collection of Mrs. Garrett Ryckman Pier (Davidson/Oliver 1984: 140).

CAT. 98
Head and Bust from a Magical Statue

Limestone, 18 (7 1/16)
Fourth century B. C.
Provenance not known
Munich, Staatliche Sammlung Ägyptischer Kunst, ÄS 2824

Literature: H. Müller/Wildung 1976: 191.

CAT. 99 *see color plate XXVI*
Cippus of Horus

Steatite, 23.2×13.5×5.6 (9 3/16×5 5/16×2 3/16)
Third century B. C.
Provenance not known
The Brooklyn Museum, 60.73; Charles Edwin Wilbour Fund

Literature: Bianchi in Brooklyn 1983: no. 68.

Both of these sculptures are covered with inscriptions containing variations of a known corpus of apotropaic spells against venomous bites of snakes, scorpions, and other noxious beasts. The principal defender invoked is Horus, who appears in this capacity as early as the Old Kingdom, as the Pyramid Texts reveal (Faulkner 1969; Kákosy 1970: 7). Such spells begin to gain wide currency during the late New Kingdom, as attested by a papyrus from the craftsmen's village at Deir el Medineh (Bierbrier 1982: 83) and a group statue inscribed for Ramesses III (Cairo JE 69771, Drioton 1939). During the course of the Third Intermediate Period, particularly under the Libyan dynasties (Fazzini 1988: 10), the Egyptian theologians began to codify the spells and we have the first stages in the rise in popularity of the type of object called a cippus (Seele 1947; Fazzini 1988: 10; Jacquet-Gordon 1966; Berlandini 1980; Hodjash/Berlev 1982: 244-74). Its canonical form depicts the child Horus in raised relief on a plaque, all of whose surfaces are covered with such magical spells. To the same period apparently belong the first larger private monuments, if the interpretation of a base seemingly used for this purpose can be maintained (Paris, private collection, el Sayed 1983: 219, perhaps the same object discussed by Berlandini 1980: 236, no. 2). Shortly thereafter, during early Dynasty XXVI, a chapel was erected at Karnak in the Precinct of the Goddess Mut, whose walls were inscribed with a magical healing spell elsewhere known only from two works of the fourth century B. C. (Traunecker 1985: 70),[1] including an elaborate cippus known as the Metternich Stela.

During the fourth century B. C., cippi and statues inscribed with magical spells for protection against noxious beasts became more and more frequent. Several methods have been adduced for the ways in which these objects were actually used. On the one hand, a celebrant might pour a liquid, usually water, over the cippus or statue while reciting the spells. As this liquid passed over the hieroglyphs it was magically infused with their efficacious power. Collected in a container, the liquid might be drunk or ritually poured over the celebrant. Alternatively, these objects might also have been touched directly onto a wound or even kissed in order to transmit their powers. Because some cippi have been found in tombs, they may have been thought to protect the dead as well as the living from similar dangers.

The best preserved and most complete collection of these spells known to date is that found on the Metternich Stela now in New York (50.85), which is dated by its inscriptions to the reign of Nectanebo II (N. Scott 1951, for photographs of the monument; Sander-Hansen 1956 and Sternberg-el Hotabi 1987, for the inscriptions). The inscriptions on this monument have been conveniently divided into chapters, which facilitates identification and comparison with other examples. The inscriptions on the Dynasty XXVI chapel at Mut mentioned above is a version of the Metternich Stela's Chapter XIV.

CAT. 99 is a cippus both later in date than the Metternich Stela and with an abridged version of its spells. This cippus can be dated to the Ptolemaic Period, when the sculpting of such monuments reached its height in popularity. The craftsman has rendered the plump, childish body of Horus by indicating rolls of fat in the chest and abdomen.

CAT. 99

CAT. 98 belongs to the fourth-century series of magical healing statues (Lacau 1922; Kákosy 1970; 1985: 91, 130, *passim*). Although the features of the face are extensively damaged, the presence of the nasolabial furrows is sufficient indication that the face originally exhibited signs of age. The head is covered with a bag wig, whose two principal characteristics are the raised plane that separates it from the face and the definition given to its outer corners, visible at the shoulders. The position of the arms, as preserved, suggests that this figure was holding a naos before him (CAT. 33). The closest parallels for this object are the block statue in Cairo inscribed for a man named Djedhor, dated by its inscriptions to the time of Philip Arrhidaeus (Cairo JE 46341, Jelínková-Reymond 1956), and the Tyskiewicz Statue in Paris, whose dating is variously suggested as late fourth or early third century B.C. (Paris, E. 10777, Yoyotte 1953b: 181; 1968: 233; Aldred in *Crépuscule*: fig. 141). The ideal features of the face of the statue of Djedhor have been altered in the Munich work according to the conventions employed for the egg-heads (CATS. 44-47). Its dating to the fourth century is, therefore, consistent with the available evidence.

[1] Evidence linking this monument to early Dynasty XXVI, recently discovered by The Brooklyn Museum's Mut Expedition, will be published by C. Traunecker.

CAT. 100 *see color plate XXVII*

The Goddess Isis Nursing the Child Horus

Faience, 13.5×3.6×6.4 (5 5/16×1 7/16×2 1/2)
Third century B. C.(?)
Provenance not known
Collection of Christos G. Bastis

Literature: Bothmer in New York 1987: no. 27.

CAT. 101 *see color plate XXVIII*

The Goddess Isis Nursing the Child Horus

Serpentine with traces of gilding, set into a base of limestone, 41×17×14.5 (16 1/8×6 11/16×5 3/4)
Late first century B. C.-early first century A. D.
Mataᶜna el Asfun, in the vicinity of Esna
Munich, Staatliche Sammlung Ägyptischer Kunst, ÄS 4201

Literature: H. Müller 1963 a: 9; Schoske/Wildung 1985: 122.

The spectacular rise of Isis (CAT. 13) as the divine nurse was due to two circumstances, the first being the gradual absorption into the cult of Isis of characteristics shared with other goddesses, particularly Hathor (Berlandini 1983). The beginnings of this process are visible at Thebes even in Dynasty XXII (CAT. 9), and accelerated during Dynasty XXV (De Meulenaere 1982; Leclant 1984: 220; Forgeau 1984: 172; M. Müller 1985, with a slightly different emphasis). The Saites continued this process (Haeny 1985: 202) and laid the foundations by which Isis, as the goddess of the Delta, became inextricably linked with each of Egypt's successive dynasties (Lloyd 1983: 294; Moussa 1981). Throughout the Ptolemaic and Roman Periods this linkage continued until the goddess Isis gradually subsumed the powers of other deities. Her popular cult eventually enjoyed an unchallenged universality that lasted into the late third or early fourth century A. D. (Junge 1979; Leclant 1979: 210; Malaise 1980: 117; Morenz 1962; Solmsen 1979).

The faience statuette in the Bastis collection (CAT. 100) represents the goddess Isis in traditionally pharaonic idiom, wearing the tightly fitting sheath (Hall 1981; Hall/Barnett 1985), the tripartite wig, and bearing a throne (Bleeker 1963: 4), her expected attribute, on her head. The paratactic composition, lacking all unifying elements that might formally integrate the two figures, is a direct quotation of a millennia-old formula that ultimately derives from the Old Kingdom statuette of Pharaoh Pepy II on the lap of his mother (Brooklyn 39.119, James 1974: 28).[1] This pharaonic depiction provides a convenient foil against which to examine the alternate treatment of the same theme in CAT. 101.

This representation of Isis nursing Horus conforms to a fundamental characteristic of ancient Egyptian art, the reliance on secondary materials to enhance sculptural compositions. The serpentine has been gilded, doubtless to connote divinity (CATS. 66, 123), the eyes were once inlaid, and the hole in the top of the head was once the socket for a metal attribute, suggested to have been the cow's horns and sun disk (Schoske/Wildung 1985: 122). This polychromatic effect would have been enhanced by placing the statuette into a base, or socle, of a contrasting color.

Pharaonic, too, are Isis' characteristic locks, variously described as "Libyan" or "corkscrew", which can be equated neither with her Greek epithet εὐπλόκαμος, "goodly tressed", (Hornblower 1929: 44) nor with Greek art (Adriani 1978; Horn 1938; D. B. Thompson 1973: 61, *passim*; Tran Tam Tinh 1984: 1722 note 53). Such locks appear for the first time in scenes in the late fourth-century B. C. tomb of Petosiris (Lefebvre 1924: pl. XIV), reappear on works in pharaonic style (CAT. 66), and are habitually associated with works from the Nile Valley (H. Jucker 1983: 144; Kaschnitz von Weinberg 1965: pls. 11-12).

These pharaonic locks are combined with a costume that departs from the traditional Egyptian tripartite female ensemble developed in the course of the Late Period and independent both of Greek influences and the cult of Isis (Bianchi 1980 b). The characteristic vertical, tubular pleats generated by knotting the skirt to the shawl at the level of the breast in the pharaonic ensemble are absent. The resulting costume is to be regarded as a Greek variation of a pharaonic fashion that is more fully exploited in a second statuette in Berlin/BRD, dated to the second century A. D. (Berlin/BRD 1955, H. Müller 1963 a: 25; Quaegebeur 1980: 45; Kaiser 1967: 102). Both are variations on the theme of Isis Lactans, the divine nursing mother, as is a third example, a life-sized marble group of Isis, with a Classical coiffure, nursing the child Horus now in the local museum at Antalya, Turkey (ALEA B-145, 1A, 4A, 5A). The differences among all three, as in the corpus of representations of Isis in general, are so great (Tran Tam Tinh 1984: 1722, who contrasts this situation with those for Serapis, which follow established typologies) that one can hardly support the suggestion that a putative cult statue in Alexandria was behind these variations (H. Müller 1963 b). So pervasive was the image of Isis Lactans that it eventually passed into the repertoire of Christian art as the source for the iconography of Maria Lactans, the Virgin Mary nursing the Christ Child.[2]

The dating of CAT. 101 to the period of Augustus is suggested by the treatment of the inlaid eyes and by the relative lack of final polish to its surfaces (as in CAT. 133). The syntactic composition, wherein the figure of Horus, if restored, would interact with that of Isis, may be indebted to a Hellenistic, rather than a pharaonic, tradition, although one must keep in mind Egyptian symplegmata in which smaller figures are successfully integrated into multifigured, intertwined compositions (CAT. 130). Nevertheless, the contrapposto of Isis' figure and her Greek costume suggest that the statuette is the product of a Roman workshop that has successfully integrated pharaonic and Hellenistic forms into a harmonious composition. Its small size indicates that it may have been placed in a shrine for private devotion (CATS. 49, 51, 80). As such, it serves to demonstrate that the disparate artistic tendencies of the Ptolemaic Period could gradually merge to produce what might be termed the Roman art of Egypt. Despite this current, pharaonic art (CATS. 133, 140) and learning (Sauneron 1982) continued to develop in a vacuum quite unaffected by the changes in other sectors of the culture of Roman Egypt.

CAT. 101

[1] Despite the investigations of Münster (1968), the visual representations of Isis nursing the Horus child appear to derive from the royal iconography of Dynasties IV-VI, a period from which there are virtually no statues of deities. In fact, the inscriptions on the group of Pepy II on the lap of his mother make no reference whatsoever to either Isis or Horus. By the time of the New Kingdom the pharaoh is shown seated on the lap of any number of goddesses, who nurse him (PM III^{2}, 2: 843; Berlandini 1984).

[2] See Graindor 1939: 41; Forgeau 1984: 172; Leclant 1977; H. Müller 1963 a; 1963 b. For the question of ἀγάπη, "Christian love", in this context, see Griffiths 1978 and Solmsen 1979: 112-13. Tran Tam Tinh 1978; 1984b: 1728; Tran Tam Tinh/Labreque 1973 hold that the Christian image is not indebted to that of Isis Lactans.

CAT. 102

CAT. 103
Burlesque of Isis and Serapis

Grayish terracotta with black glaze, 15.2×11.3×8 (5×4 7/16×3 3/16)
Late first century B. C.-first century A. D.
Provenance not known
Munich, Staatliche Sammlung Ägyptischer Kunst, ÄS 3991

Literature: H. Müller/Wildung 1976: 253-54.

CAT. 102 *see color plate XXIX*
Medallion of Isis and Serapis

Gold, 2.8×2.4 (1 1/8×15/16)
Reign of Ptolemy IV or Ptolemy V (222-180 B. C.)
Provenance not known
The Brooklyn Museum, 73.85; Charles Edwin Wilbour Fund

Unpublished

The gold medallion represents two figures in front view. To the left is a female figure wearing the native Egyptian shawl that knots to the skirt (CAT. 66); her hair is arranged in corkscrew locks (CAT. 101); and her attribute consists of two elements, the cow's horns and sun disk. To her right is a male figure in a chiton, with a full beard and mustache, and hair arranged in the Anastole-form, "rising from the brow" (CAT. 104). His headdress consists of a miniature *atef*-crown, usually associated with Osiris, composed of the White Crown of Upper Egypt flanked by an ostrich feather set on top of two ram's horns (Castiglione 1978). The busts seem to be set into a floral motif of indeterminate form. The medallion is framed by a separately applied, horizontally grooved rim (Baltimore 57.539 and 57.1524, Oliver 1979: 110-11). Although not inscribed, the figures are so iconographically precise that they can only represent Isis and Serapis, the latter given prominence because his bust overlaps that of his consort. The medallion is based upon coin types current during the reign of Ptolemy IV Philopator, which represent jugate busts of these two deities, in profile, in an attitude usually reserved for the ruling couple (Stambaugh 1972: 22-23 and pl. I, 2). The presence of corkscrew locks on images of Isis may begin as early as the reign of Ptolemy IV, but is certainly established during the reign of Ptolemy V Epiphanes (CATS. 74, 75). As a result, this medallion is datable to those two reigns. Busts of Isis and Serapis proved to be popular devices for lamps of the Roman Imperial Period (Derksen 1978), as well as for a curious group of shallow bowls (Munich ÄS 5972, H. Müller/Wildung 1976: 199; Alexandria 25519 and Munich ÄS 5972, G. Grimm in Hildesheim 1979: nos. 147-148; and further, Parlasca 1983) which are inexplicably related to stylistically similar examples of Gandhara art (Czuma 1985: 144-54).

CAT. 103

The goddess Isis retained her identity throughout the Graeco-Roman Period as her cult gradually eclipsed those of all other Egyptian goddesses (CATS. 13, 100, 101). She was loosely associated with Serapis (Malaise 1980: 83; and CATS. 93, 104), who at no time, however, was regarded as her true consort since the ties with Osiris, her pharaonic brother and husband, could never be totally severed (Solmsen 1979: 27-29). Nevertheless, the pair came to represent the city of Alexandria and the Ptolemaic, and later Imperial Roman, court.

Although the function of the medallion has not been determined, the deities are treated with respect. In contrast is the depiction on CAT. 103, a jar that appears to present an irreverent burlesque of the images on the gold medallion. The female figure to the right wears a necklace of large, pearl-like beads and coquettishly (H. Müller/Wildung 1976: 254) clutches a corner of her shawl, which is knotted, not as expected at the breast, but over the shoulder. Her companion, who clasps her forearm with one hand while hugging her far shoulder with the other, is represented as a Black with short, curly hair. The cultural bias inherent in such a depiction has been treated at length elsewhere (Brilliant 1979; Snowden 1970). This unflattering burlesque is symptomatic of the Alexandrian love of satire, which may also be in evidence in a drawing added to a clay vessel from Abydos, now in London (52929, Johansen 1978: 58, 60, here identified, after Milne 1914, as Antony and Cleopatra VII [?]; but see Liverpool 49.47.840, Wenig 1978: 278, which suggests that we are dealing with a type rather than with specific individuals). So indiscriminate were the Alexandrians in this regard that they would even mock Roman emperors. Nero was an object of special ridicule, while an outrageous affront to Caracalla caused him to unleash his legions against the Alexandrians. The particular satiric intent of the Munich vase, as a parody of the two most revered deities of Roman Alexandria, is thus more than a simple racial slur. At least two other complete jugs virtually identical to this one have survived from Antiquity (Berlin/DDR, without number, and Leiden AT 29, perhaps from the same mold; Pagenstecher 1913: 39 for the example in Berlin; compare Bresciani 1976: 31 and pl. XXIX [175]). While its thematic content may be elusive, this group appears to be datable to the late first century B. C. or early first century A. D., on the basis of the black glaze (Graindor 1939: 55), which is here artistically employed to represent the skin color of its subjects.

CAT. 104
Head of Serapis

Serpentine, 13.3 (5 1/4)
Antonine or Severan Period, second-third century A. D.
From Karanis, surface find
Ann Arbor, Kelsey Museum of Archaeology, University of Michigan, 8526

Literature: Gazda *et al.* 1978: 37; Vermeule 1981: 217.

The history and development of the cult of Serapis have been rigorously debated issues. Although the nature of the evidence involved is equivocal, a basic picture does tend to emerge. There may very well have been an Egyptian deity, perhaps even Osiris himself, ensconced in the vicinity of Alexandria at the time of its founding, whom Alexander encountered and worshiped as Serapis (Stambaugh 1972: 13, 88). Shortly thereafter, Ptolemy I Soter became a proponent of the cult and was responsible for the introduction of a Hellenized image of Serapis into Egypt (Stambaugh 1972: 6-7, 11-13, 88). The Memphite origin of Serapis (Mussies 1978), first championed by Wilcken (1927: 18-29, 77-89) and repeatedly defended in more recent times (Quaegebeur 1971 a: 244, and note 30; Swinderk 1975), may reflect the syncretistic tendencies at Memphis in the second century B. C. (to which period date the majority of the documents employed for this line of reasoning) rather than the religious circumstances during the reign of Ptolemy I Soter (Stambaugh 1972: 5). The cult of Serapis assimilated to itself aspects of other cults, including that of the Apis Bull at Memphis (CAT. 105; Stambaugh 1972: 26-87), but seemed to respect the distinctions separating it from that of Osiris (CAT. 136; Stambaugh 1972: 44-52). As a result, Serapis came to be associated with the affairs of this world (Malaise 1983: 110; Tran Tam Tinh 1984 b; van den Broek 1978; *contra* Leclant 1979: 210), while his consort of convenience, Isis, and her lawful spouse, Osiris, continued to maintain their funereal associations. Serapis, although extremely popular outside of Egypt, never gained a strong following within the country of his origin. His cult was never popular with the native Egyptians and is not attested within the precincts of purely Egyptian sanctuaries (Winter 1978: 147; Golvin 1986). Derchain, (in *Das ptol. Äg.*: 111) would even ascribe the push to install Dionysos as the dynastic god under Ptolemy III as an effort to curb the growth and influence of the cult of Serapis.

Whereas most would agree that the Hellenized statue of Serapis, the god introduced by Ptolemy I, depicted the deity seated and wearing a chiton with the three-headed Cerberus at his side (Tran Tam Tinh 1984 b: 1715), there is continued debate about the physical appearance of the head on that statue because the preserved examples generally divide into two groups. Castiglione (1958) suggested that the type called the Anastole-form (CAT. 93), which shows the hair "rising from the brow," reflects the original Hellenized cult statue, which was damaged at the time of the Jewish Revolt in 115-117 A. D. and subsequently transformed, after repair, into the image represented by this head, with five distinct locks falling onto the forehead, called the *Fransenfisur*-type. Hornbostel has convincingly refuted this theory by demonstrating that the two types of hairstyles existed side by side during the course of the Roman Imperial Period. In reexamining the evidence, he evinces the *Fransenfisur*-type as the original hairstyle (1973: 79-80, 351), best represented by a statue in Alexandria (3916) which, as Fraser (1976: 214) wittily remarks, Hornbostel "seems almost inclined to regard... as the original itself." As Fraser points out, however, the earliest datable *Fransenfisur*-types are Augustan, whereas the Anastole-form appears in the Ptolemaic Period. Tran Tam Tinh (1984 b: 1734), in light of the present evidence, sees no exit from the impasse and accommodatingly suggests the distinct possibility that there may already have been several iconographically dis-

parate but nevertheless concurrent statues of Serapis in the Hellenistic Period. Castiglione's rejoinder to Hornbostel, which considers an image of Serapis crowned with an *atef*-crown, only muddies the waters (1978). Until new evidence is forthcoming or the existing evidence is reinterpreted, the conundrum regarding the original appearance of the Hellenized Serapis head remains unsolved.

The *Fransenfisur*-type exhibited by this head from Karanis shows one distinct image of Serapis with traces of the characteristic five locks on the brow. The mustache is full and the beard bifurcate, groomed into two distinctive points. The flaring headdress in the form of a conical container, alternately labeled an annona (Gazda *et al.* 1978) or a calathus (Fraser 1984: 348), is here decorated with olive branches (Gazda *et al.* 1978; Munich ÄS 5303, H. Müller/Wildung 1976: 220). A dating for this head to the Antonine or Severan Period, between 150 and 200 A. D., as suggested by Gazda (1978), can be supported by comparisons with contemporary pieces (Hornbostel 1973: 214-83).

CAT. 105
The Apis Bull

Green serpentine, 52.5×58 (20 11/16×22 13/16)
400-100 B. C.
Provenance not known
The Cleveland Museum of Art, 69.118; Purchase, Leonard B. Hanna, Jr., Bequest

Literature: Cooney 1971.

The identification of this sculpture as a depiction of the Apis Bull (CAT. 10) is based upon its very strong stylistic affinities with a second sculpture in limestone, excavated at Saqqara by Mariette (Lauer 1976: 22 note 13; Kater-Sibbes/Vermaseren 1975 a: 4; Ziegler 1981: 29). Faint traces of what the Egyptians considered to be the characteristic markings on the hide of the Apis Bull (Winter 1978: 16-18) are still visible on the Memphite example, as are the remains of a now illegible inscription

in Demotic (Desroches-Noblecourt *et al.* 1981: xi). The two sculptures have in common the wide broad muzzle, the use of a bridge of negative space to support the sun disk, which is itself cradled by the horns, the configuration and placement of the uraeus, and the sweep of the dewlap. Of these features, the treatments of the muzzle, whose front approximates a blocky rectangular form, of the nostrils, the eyes, and the ears are distinctive, and separate these two works from almost all other representations of the Apis Bull in stone. So, for instance, the muzzles of two bovines in private collections are more bulbous (Schildkraut/Merrin 1986; Cambridge, Massachusetts 1954: 18, no. 18; Kater-Sibbes/Vermaseren 1975 b: 45, no. 380), a feature encountered in other examples (Sturtewagen/Bianchi 1982: 180-81), and one which seems to be present as well, but in a more abstracted way, in the head of an Apis Bull datable to the Roman Imperial Period (Kawamura 1976: 12, 22). It is unfortunate that photographs of the two Apis Bulls excavated at the Serapeum in Luxor have never been published (Golvin 1986; Leclant 1951; Wagner 1981), especially since they are dated to the period of Hadrian and would be of utmost value as *comparanda* (Botti 1899). In any event, the shape of the heads of the bulls from Memphis and in Cleveland seems to develop from the bovine type established during Dynasty XXVI, as a comparison with the Hathor Cow protecting Psamtik shows (Cairo CG 784, Aldred in *Crépuscule*: fig. 132).
The statue of the bull from Saqqara is usually assigned to Dynasty XXX (Kater-Sibbes/Vermaseren 1975 a: 5) on the basis of an interpretation of its supposed archaeological context (Wilcken 1917). Although that premise has recently been challenged insofar as the small finds are concerned, there seems to be no firm evidence either for associating or disassociating this object from that period. The inked Demotic inscription on the stone between the forelegs (Desroches-Noblecourt *et al.* 1981: xi) might suggest a slightly later dating for this object, a dating within the Ptolemaic Period, because of the propensity of the Egyptians of that era to add ink inscriptions to works of art in a variety of media (CAT. 119). The bull in Cleveland is to be assigned to the same period because it is so stylistically dependent upon the Memphite example. These two sculptures represent the Apis Bull as an animal, and derive from an iconographic tradition different from that for the representation of standing, anthropomorphic images of the same deity (CAT. 10; Sturtewagen/Bianchi 1982: 180).

CAT. 106
Stela of a Ptolemy Adoring a Lion

Limestone, 51.1×28×9 (20 1/8×11×3 9/16)
200-30 B.C.
Said to be from Tell el Muqdam
Amsterdam, Allard Pierson Museum, 7772

Literature: De Wit 1951: 276-80; Meeks 1979: 685, no. 3; van Haarlem forthcoming: 36-38.

Since van Haarlem has provided a full description of this stela, whose principal composition conforms to a pattern known from other royal stelae dedicated to animals (Cairo JE 54313, G. Grimm 1975: 5), one can now concentrate on certain details in order to assess its style, inscriptions, and dating.
The text, "the King of Upper and Lower Egypt, Ptolemy [living forever]," over the head of the pharaoh, is too damaged to suggest a precise date (van Haarlem forthcoming: 37). On the other hand, the arrangement of the winged sun disk and uraei – with the original form of the royal ring, or *šn*-sign, and a fan suspended from the bottom of their heads – is frequently encountered on stelae dating from the reigns of Ptolemy V Epiphanes into the Roman Imperial Period (CAT. 3; and Cairo CG 22184, Kamal 1905, vol. I: 177-78; London 184, Munro 1973: 338-39). These comparisons suggest a dating for the stela within the second half of the Ptolemaic Period.
This monument and others like it have no documented provenances because they were acquired from the market rather than from controlled excavations (van Haarlem forthcoming: 37-38). While the legend "the living lion" over the figure of that animal cannot be unequivocally associated with Miysis, the leonine deity of Tell el Muqdam (Gomaà 1985; Žabkar 1980b), the Greek graffito "the sacred house of the Tomb of the Lions" in the lower half of this stela corresponds to descriptions of Tell el Muqdam in the Classical sources as the necropolis for lions in Egypt (Blok 1927; De Wit 1951: 276-80; van Haarlem forthcoming: 36-38), although the meaning of the word "house" (οικια) in this context is not encountered in the papyri (G. Husson 1983: 191-206). This Greek graffito, perhaps replacing an original inscription, was certainly added to the stela at a date subsequent to the sculpting of the principal scene, as the chisel marks and reduced depth of the stela in this area reveal (van Haarlem forthcoming: 37-38).

CAT. 107
Buchis Stela

Sandstone, 90×57 (35 5/8×22 7/16)
Presumably 29 B.C.
Found at the Bucheum, Armant
Copenhagen, Ny Carlsberg Glyptotek, AEIN 1681

Literature: Fairman in Mond/Myers *et al.* 1934, vol. II: 11-13 and 32, no. 13; vol. III: pls. XLIII-XLIIIA; Koefoed-Petersen 1948: 43-45 and pl. 58; Quaegebeur 1983c: 264-72.

In the later periods of Egyptian history great prominence was given to religious beliefs relating to sacred animals – each a *Ba* or manifestation of a power or deity – and sacrosanct animals, which were objects of veneration because they were beloved of a deity, who could manifest in the form of a member of their species (Kessler 1985 on animal cults; Meeks 1986). This sometimes elicited astonishment and/or ridicule from foreigners (Smelik/Hemelrijk 1984) and gave rise to the still popular misconception that Egyptians typically and simply worshiped animals. In fact, at least the priests and other educated individuals were aware of the distinction between deities and their "symbols." As with some sacred animals, such as the Apis Bull (CATS. 10, 105), there was only one Buchis[1] at any given time. He remained a living cult image until his death, when the god would be identified as re-manifested in another living bull. The Osiris (or deceased) form of the god would be buried in splendor in the underground galleries called the Bucheum at Armant, not far from Thebes.
Called "living image of Montu" on the Copenhagen stela, Buchis is most simply and commonly identified as the bull of that god, long at home in the region of Thebes. Nevertheless, Buchis' precise origins and nature remain obscure, and he was as-

sociated with other deities.[2] Indeed, his most prominent epithets, such as CAT. 107's "living *Ba* of Re," link Buchis to that sun-god. As also illustrated in this stela's text, at some time he came to encompass deities such as Amun, Horus, Ptah, and others.[3] In fact, elaborate interweavings of deities were common in the Late Period, and the Buchis cult is attested so far only from the time of Nectanebo II until 340 A. D. (Grenier 1983b: 204-05).

The Copenhagen stela commemorates a Buchis that died in Year 1 of Augustus (29 B. C.), who is depicted here in traditional Egyptian royal regalia. He is making a time-honored Egyptian offering of fields to the god, who stands atop a pedestal with an offering table. Stylistically, the decoration is related to other small-scale reliefs of various epochs, including its own. One good parallel is provided by CAT. 78, the stela inscribed for, but perhaps not made for, Cleopatra VII. Iconographically, the Copenhagen stela stands close, in many ways, to the end of one main phase in the development of its genre. Thus, for example, as on earlier Buchis stelae, and on one of Tiberius (Mond/Myers *et al.* 1934, vol. III: pl. XLIV, 15), the image of Buchis (or of a statue of Buchis) is that of a standing bull. Even though labeled "Osiris-Buchis," he is not depicted recumbent and mummiform, as on other Roman Period Buchis stelae, including one from later in the reign of Augustus (Mond/Myers *et al.* 1934, vol. III: pl. XLIII,14). CAT. 107 may have differed from earlier and later Buchis stelae in one important way: it may have been a more complex art form that included a bull or bull's head in wood and plaster, perhaps relating to a line in the stela's text invoking the dead Buchis to rest atop its monument (Mond/Myers *et al.* 1934, vol. I: 130-31, 134-35; vol. II: 12-13).

As the king of Egypt was priest *par excellence* of all the Egyptian gods (p. 30, above) and the theoretical officiant for their cult services, it is not surprising that Augustus is shown conducting ceremonies, from which he was probably absent, in connection with one of the "animal cults" that he reportedly scorned.[4] Because Egyptian monuments often record religious truth as historical fact the Copenhagen stela remains a document of interest for late Ptolemaic studies.

In addition to commemorating the bull's death, the main text records, briefly, the bull's original installation as Buchis at Thebes and his procession three days later to Armant. These events are dated to Year 1 of a queen whose cartouches are blank, but who can only be Cleopatra VII, whose Year 1 was 51 B. C. The description of the events includes mention of a "king," which might or might not also be a reference to Cleopatra (Quaegebeur 1983c: 269-72). As a result, this stela and CAT. 78, another stela with a Year 1 date of Cleopatra VII, are significant for discussions of the nature and dates of possible coregencies between Ptolemy XII, his daughter Cleopatra VII, and her brother Ptolemy XIII (Wagner 1973: 103-05; D. Crawford 1980: 11; Quaegebeur 1983c: 270-72).

Also a subject of discussion is whether, as the Copenhagen stela's text states, Cleopatra VII, with or without co-regent, was actually present for the ceremonies at Thebes and Armant. If she was, it was perhaps as part of a ritual tour of the country's main cult centers, a tour related to the old Egyptian tradition of a new ruler "taking possession" of the country (Quaegebeur 1983c: 272).

[1] The ancient Egyptian name for the bull is *Bḫ*, the "Easterner" (?). The Greek version of this name, Buchis, is far more common in the literature.

[2] On Buchis in general and the development of Buchis stelae, see Myers and Fairman in Mond/Myers *et al.* 1934, vol. I: 1-23; vol. II: 36-50; Otto 1938: 40-57.

[3] Quaegebeur 1983c: 269. It has been suggested that a textual equation of Buchis with Atum, the "setting sun," on one stela explains why the Bucheum was called the "Mansion of Atum"; Hodjash/Berlev 1982: 220.

[4] Smelik/Hemelrijk 1984: 1926-28. Dynasty XXX's concern for animal cults may have been in part an assertion of distinctly Egyptian beliefs in opposition to growing pressures from foreign cultures (e.g., Lloyd 1983: 294-95). Continued support of such cults would have been politically beneficial for later, non-native kings, including Roman emperors. Nevertheless, Ptolemaic royal support of animal cults need not have been simply a means of coopting potential opposition by Egyptian priesthoods, since Greek religious practice included the acceptance of and sacrifice to non-Greek deities (Samuel 1983: 82, 92-93, 106-08).

CAT. 108
Funerary Stela of a Priest of Amun-Re

Limestone, 32×25 (12 5/8×9 13/16)
Late Ptolemaic-Roman Period(?)
Provenance not known
Leiden, Rijksmuseum van Oudheden, CI. 327

Literature: Boeser 1915: 8, no. 23 and pl. XVI, 23; Munro 1973: 112, 301.

Below the winged disk with two uraei are the deceased's mummy, his *Ba* as human-headed bird, and the funerary god Anubis. Variants on the theme of mummy with Anubis and/or *Ba*-bird are not rare adornments on late funerary equipment (CAT. 124; and e.g., Niwiński 1983: 449-50). In the scene below, the deceased raises his hand in worship above a stand with offerings placed before Osiris, Horsiese ("Horus-son-of-Isis") and Isis, deities whose significance was not limited to funerary concerns.

The mummiform Osiris or statue of Osiris (CAT. 21) stands on a trapezoidal base, which may symbolize Ma'at, and holds the usual crook and flail of kingship. He wears an *atef*-crown, also associated with the pharaoh and the sun-god (L. Bell 1985 b: 269), of whom Osiris can be the night form (van Dijk 1980: 20-21). Horsiese wears the Double Crown of Upper and Lower Egypt and holds an *ankh*-sign and a bolt of cloth, possibly a mummy binding likened to the divine garb of the gods for the deceased (Moret 1902: 178-90). Isis, identified by the hieroglyph of a throne atop her head as well as by the text before her, holds an *ankh* and a situla or metal bucket (CAT. 110). Situlae were used for libations meant to purify, nourish, and revive the dead (Cauville 1983; Lichtheim 1947; Evrard-Derricks/Quaegebeur 1979), possibly even coming to symbolize a ritual immersion of the deceased in the holy and revivifying water of the Nile (Evrard-Derricks/Quaegebeur 1979: 53). That Isis holds a situla may also, however, be related to milk libations believed to be made by her for Osiris, especially at Philae, which also influenced the iconography of Meroitic funerary monuments (Junker 1913: 13-14, 51-54; Yellin 1982; Millet *et al.* 1982). Osing (1982: pl. 27) shows an interesting Roman Period scene of Isis libating for the deceased.

The boxed text between the deceased and Osiris remains undeciphered. The lower line of inscription identifies the stela's owner as a "*wab*-priest of the front of Amun-Re, King of the Gods," indicating that he was one of the privileged bearers of the god's processional bark (Kees 1960; Kruchten 1986: 9, 366-67). This may link the priest, but not necessarily his stela, to Amun's main cult center of Thebes.

Munro (1973: 112, 301) has attributed this monument to a mainly Ptolemaic class of stelae he designates as Abydos III – the gods shown in the Leiden stela being of major importance at Abydos. The Leiden work, however, bears no great resemblance to any of the others in this class. If it is from Abydos, chief cult place of Osiris, it would reflect that city's enduring significance as a center of religious pilgrimage (Munro 1973: 110 note 1).

In his discussion of the stela, Munro has noted that it displays characteristics of several major formats for funerary stelae of late times, including the Ptolemaic Period. Problematic, however, are Munro's characterization (1973: 112) of the deceased's features as "Negroid," and of the rendering of his hair as un-Egyptian in its lack of schematization. Even ignoring the questions surrounding the very concepts of race and the problems inherent in making racial distinctions on the basis of ancient artistic representations, the fact remains that our priest's physiognomy and hairstyle, as well as his fringed garment (CATS. 30-32), are most easily and better interpreted as late Egyptian variants of long-known Egyptian themes. Even though Munro's tentative attribution of the stela to "late Ptolemaic-Roman (?)" times is possible, we cannot agree with his identification of a combination of Egyptian and un-Egyptian elements as one of the dating criteria, since the stela is wholly Egyptian in style and iconography.

CAT. 109
Figure in an Egyptianizing Costume

Bronze, 8×3.5 (3 1/8×1 3/8)
First century A. D.
From Gaza
Private collection

Literature: Mitten in Mitten/Doeringer 1967: 124.

There can be little doubt that this bronze depicts a male figure, perhaps a priest or votary of the goddess Isis, as Mitten (in Mitten/Doeringer 1967: 124) suggested, represented in a female costume. The costume consists not only of a Roman variation of the tripartite knotted fashion of Egyptian women (CAT. 66), but also of the headdress fitted with corkscrew locks at the back (CAT. 74). Sandals complete the costume. Comparisons with depictions of priests of Egyptian cults in wall paintings from Herculaneum in Italy (Tran Tam Tinh 1964: 27, 101, and pls. XXIII, XXIV), while confirming the identification, do little to shed light on the interpretation of this enigmatic figure. The suggestion that he represents an actor engaged in a dramatization of an episode in the life of the goddess Isis (Mitten in Mitten/Doeringer 1967: 124) is a seductive one. In fact, this figure finds its closest thematic parallels in equally small bronze figurines of dancing women, wearing the identical costume, which were found at Galjub, some 16 kilometers north of Cairo, and are now in Hildesheim (2251 and 2252, Kayser 1966: 138). The dancing women have thematic correspondences to the Egyptianizing relief from Ariccia, Italy (Rome, Museo Nazionale Romano 77255, Roullet 1972: 27-28). In these examples, as in the bronze under discussion, there is a noticeable absence of masks; masks are also lacking in the pair of terracotta figurines, suggested to represent actors, from Hildesheim (CAT. 114) and in Apuleius' accounts in *The Golden Ass* (Griffiths 1975). Two avenues of identification are now open: either the figures do not represent actors or such actors could be represented in the minor arts without masks. The evidence remains equivocal, as does that for deciding the function of this bronze which, like the Tanagra figurines (CATS. 112-114), might very well have employed one motif to serve different purposes. The lack of an archaeological context certainly precludes speculation in that regard.

The dating of the bronze figurine is open to discussion, as is that of the two dancing women from Galjub. One may, however, tentatively suggest a dating within the first century A. D. for this figure.

CAT. 110
Situla with Egyptianizing Scenes

Gilded silver, 15.2 (5)
62-79 A. D.
Pompeii, from the vicinity of the Triangular Forum near the Temple of Isis, to which the situla is said to have belonged
Munich, Wittelsbacher Ausgleichsfonds, Ant. WAF 512

Literature: H. Müller/Wildung 1976: 219.

During the course of the first millennium B. C., the situla, literally a "bucket" or "pail", became firmly established as a distinctly Egyptian religious vessel (CAT. 108; Lichtheim 1947); it continued in use into the Ptolemaic (Evrard-Derricks/Quaegebeur 1979) and Roman Periods, at which time it became a frequent attribute of the goddess Isis. It is important to observe in this context that the situla is not a shape encountered in contemporary silver services used for secular gatherings (Baratte 1986). As a sacred vessel, then, the situla might hold either water, associating Isis with the Nilitic rites of Osiris (CATS. 108, 136), or milk, emphasizing her maternal qualities as the mother of Horus (CATS. 13, 100, 101). In fact, one of the Egyptian words for situla could also be used as a metonym for breast. Apuleius, the Roman novelist of the second century A. D., was aware of this association when he described a situla as *aureum vasculum in modum papillae rotundatum* ("a small golden vessel in the rounded shape of a breast," *The Golden Ass*, XI, 10; Parlasca 1966: 163 note 73).

In this and other Egyptianizing vessels, architectural elements are employed as vertical compositional devices serving to frame and separate one scene from the other (CAT. 111; Fuhrmann 1941: figs. 108-15). As a result, the figural decoration on this situla naturally divides into two vignettes, the first of which is better preserved. The principal figure is a woman who offers a crocodile on a base to a crested, perhaps crowned, serpent perched on a pedestal. She wears an unusual costume characterized by an oval "apron" on which appears a cross design in a circle. Her coiffure is arranged in corkscrew locks and her headdress, which ought to be the cap in the form of a vulture, is misunderstood and appears to take the form of a duck. The iconography here is so close to that of a second woman on one side of a silver tumbler from Pompeii, now in Naples (without number, Fuhrmann 1941: fig. 110) that both must either represent the same individual, Isis herself, or the same ritual act performed by a priestess of Isis. Behind this figure stands a multi-tiered structure, approached by a stairway, rendered as a ladder, and topped by a flame. One can cautiously suggest that this structure was intended to evoke the famous Pharos, or Lighthouse, at Alexandria.

The second vignette is separated from the first by the fact that the serpent and the ram of the second are back to back, at different levels, and compositionally independent due to the respective heights of their podia. Since this vignette has been damaged, its preserved figural decoration does not conform to the line drawing published at the time of its discovery (Tran Tam Tinh 1964: pl. XII, 4, for an accessible reproduction of the drawing). One can clearly distinguish the ram on a high podium (a composition similar to Fuhrmann 1941: 598 and fig. 112, where the animal is, however, a bull). To the right are the remains of a second architectural structure, but the intervening space is too damaged to permit a detailed description of its composition. (One wonders whether the figural decoration on a stone object identified as a water trough [Fuhrmann 1941: 599-600, and figs. 116-17, present whereabouts not known], may have been a modern forgery based on the original drawing of the situla inasmuch as the apron of the principal figure, her coiffure, headdress, and the crest and bifurcated tongue of the serpent are misunderstood.)

The situla can be dated no later than the third quarter of the first century A. D. by virtue of the fact that it was found in Pompeii. The motifs are free adaptations of Egyptian iconographic themes, rather than faithful copies. Any interpretation of these vignettes must therefore be based on contemporary Roman practices and beliefs. Such an observation would tend to support our suggestion that examples of first-century A. D. Roman Egyptomania (e.g., CAT. 111) are less accurate reflections of actual Egyptian practices than those of the second century A. D. (CAT. 136).

CAT. 111
Perfume Bottle

see color plate XXX

Opaque white over deep blue glass, 7.6×4.2 diameter (3×1 5/8)
25 B. C.-25 A. D.
Said to be from Eskisehir, Turkey (ancient Bithynia)
Malibu, California, The J. Paul Getty Museum, 85.AF.84

Literature: Harden 1987: 83-84.

The base of this vessel is decorated with a five-petaled rosette around which are symmetrically arranged eight triangularly shaped leaves. The figural decoration, respecting a groundline and arranged around the widest part of the vessel, is grouped into three vignettes that are not compositionally integrated. The limbs of the lone tree seem intentionally placed to mark the beginning and end of the decoration, as H. Jucker (1965: 46-53 and fig. 5) rightly observed in his discussion of the theme and in his accompanying line drawing. The naked putto interacts with the ibis and baboon adorning the cylindrical pedestal through eye contact, while the second, draped putto, his back to the first group, seems to engage the Egyptianizing figure who faces him from across the horned altar (CAT. 68), decorated with a uraeus. The attribute in the hands of this putto (H. Jucker 1965: 48; Harden 1987: 83), which may in fact be two separate objects, is indistinct, as are those of the single Egyptianizing figure standing on the other side of the altar. Wearing what has been termed a Double Crown placed upon the *nemes* (H. Jucker 1965: 49; Harden 1987: 83), this kilted, male figure holds a round object, presumed to be a vessel (H. Jucker 1965: 49), and a staff, tapering upward and curved, which might represent either a notched palm frond ( ) (H. Jucker 1965: 49) or the crook ( ), as held by an ibis-headed representation of Thoth in a panel from the tablinium of the Villa dei Misteri (de Vos 1980: 12). The obelisk, whose inscriptions are gibberish, despite attempts at decipherment (H. Jucker 1965: 49), remains isolated, placed as it is behind the back of the Egyptianizing figure and separated from the first scene by the tree. The very nature of these apparently paratactic vignettes – a random intercalcation of Classical and Egyptianizing figures whose enigmatic attributes and inscriptions defy precise identification – seems to preclude any exacting interpretation such as that adduced by H. Jucker (1965: 46-50), who relates the figural scene to a cult of the Egyptian deity Atum-Re localized in the city of Heliopolis.

In formulating his thematic explanation for the scenes on this perfume bottle, Jucker tacitly assumed that Egyptianizing motifs in extra-Egyptian contexts retain a limited pharaonic significance, tempered by Greek traditions (but see Fowden 1986: 45-52). Such an assumption is flawed because it fails to recognize that any given motif from pharaonic Egypt is imbued with a multiplicity of meanings that cannot be distilled into clearly defined Aristotelian categories (CAT. 131). Jucker's thematic interpretation of the scenes on this perfume bottle is therefore an academic exegesis which few, if any, ancients would immediately recognize.

The chronological position of this bottle must be determined from its relative place within the closed classification of cameo glasses to which it belongs (Harden 1987: 55). Contrary to H. Jucker (1965: 50), the cameo glass industry may not have been introduced in Egypt (Harden 1987: 54) and was certainly not operative there during the early Hellenistic Period (Harden 1987: 55). The development of cameo glass, both rapid and short-lived, is suggested to have occurred between 25 B. C. and 100 A. D. (Harden 1987: 55). The Egyptianizing elements on this perfume bottle share the thematic concerns of the Second

Style of Roman wall painting (Harden 1987: 84). To be sure, the tree, as a compositional device, along with the obelisk and its pseudo-hieroglyphs, establishes a sylvan setting for the Egyptianizing motifs in the vignettes. There is no doubt that the pedestal adorned with the ibis and baboon alludes to Thoth (H. Jucker 1965: 48; von Bissing 1922), who is perhaps to be identified as the human-headed (von Bissing 1922: 82) Egyptianizing figure holding a notched palm frond (H. Jucker 1965: 49). The uraeus on the horned altar has overtones of an Isis cult (as in "The Adoration of the Water" from Herculaneum, H. Jucker 1965: 48; R. Wild 1981: pl. XIV). Whatever the identification of the putti, and they may quite simply be playful surrogates for adult worshipers, the vignettes could be nothing more than a simple allusion to Egypt as the source of the perfume that was originally contained in this vessel. As a luxury item, it could very well reflect the pretentious affectations of some wealthy, but boorish, Campanian devotee of an Egyptian cult. Its motifs appear to have been randomly selected for an overall effect in much the same way as the Egyptianizing motifs in the tablinium of the Villa dei Misteri at Pompeii, which are likewise indistinct and do not yield the intelligible program (de Vos 1980: 12) that Le Corsu (1967: 250-51) perceives. Both the perfume bottle and the Pompeian painting are stylistically related and ought to date to the time of Emperor Augustus, despite the bottle's topological affinities with glass vessels of the early Third Style of Roman wall painting (Harden 1987: 84). As a general observation, Egyptianizing motifs in the visual arts of Italy during the reign of Augustus are more fanciful interpretations of pharaonic motifs than those encountered under the emperors of the second half of the first century A. D. (CATS. 110, 136, and pp. 77, 80, above).

CATS. 112-114
A Group of Terracotta Figures

CAT. 112
Statuette of a Woman

Terracotta with a white slip and traces of red paint, 19.5 (7 11/16)
Late fourth-early third century B.C.
Provenance not known
Collection of Christos G. Bastis

Literature: Buitron in New York 1987: no. 71.

CAT. 113
Statuette of a Woman

Terracotta with traces of red and blue paint, 20.3 (7)
Third century B.C.
Provenance not known
Collection of Christos G. Bastis

Literature: Buitron in New York 1987: no. 72.

CAT. 114
see color plate XXXI
Actors (?) Engaged in a Dialogue

Terracotta, 14.5 (5 11/16)
Circa 300-275 B.C.
Provenance not known
Hildesheim, Pelizaeus-Museum, 464

Literature: G. Grimm in Hildesheim 1979: no. 196.

The statuettes of the two women are known as Tanagra figures, after the cemetery in Boeotia in Greece where the type was first identified (Higgins 1986: 117-61; Buitron in New York 1987: no. 71). It has been suggested that such figurines were inspired by theatrical productions in which women such as these played prominent roles to the delight of the public (Buitron in New York 1987: no. 71). The earlier of these two figures (CAT. 112), according to the dating established for them by Buitron (in New York 1987: nos. 71-72), represents a woman enveloped in her himation, an outer garment which is here wrapped around the body like a shawl. The second (CAT. 113) is also enveloped in a himation and holds a fan in her left hand (Buitron in New York 1987: no. 72). Although such female statuettes are statistically the most numerous of the Tanagra figurines to have survived, other types, such as children and erotes, are also known, as are actors (Higgins 1986: 65, 159), as CAT. 114 shows. The composition of the Hildesheim group, which was part of the collection W. Pelizaeus formed in Egypt (Roeder/Ippel 1921: 168, no. 464 and fig. 70), is perhaps the most ambitious

CAT. 112

example of the art of the coroplast, or crafter of terracotta figurines, to have survived from the Hellenistic Period. It represents a pair of male figures engaged in a lively discussion. Since there are no indications that their grotesque physiognomies are due to masks, these dramatic figures must have been only inspired by, not based directly upon, masked characters in contemporary drama (Higgins 1986: 159; CAT. 109). This group is one of the few such compositions of the Tanagra type to have survived virtually intact. Earlier collectors had so coveted such heads that they acquired them by the hundreds, severing them from the bodies, which they discarded (p. 54, above; Adriani 1952: pls. XVII-XX; Graindor 1939: 36-37).

How such Tanagras functioned is a debated issue, especially since any specific type could fulfill different requirements: the same types of Tanagra figurines have been recovered from graves of men, women, and children (Higgins 1986: 65), as well as from sanctuaries and private houses (Higgins 1986: 64), where they could have served as toys or been unspecified personal possessions (Higgins 1986: 65). Conventional wisdom regards such grotesques, which are clearly indebted to the traditions of the theater, as imbued with religious overtones because Greek theater and religion remained closely linked (Higgins 1986: 65). In this view, grotesques with a demonstrable funerary context would have provided the deceased with entertainment and comfort in the hereafter (Higgins 1986: 65). On the other hand, the immense popularity of grotesques in Egypt, which has statistically yielded more examples of this type than any other region, has inclined scholars to seek alternative interpretations. Graindor (1939: 36-37) proposed that the function of grotesques was often one of warding off the evil eye. Higgins, tentatively eschewing any such symbolic interpretation, cautiously suggested that Tanagra figures of women such as CATS. 112 and 113 might have been personal possessions (1986: 65). Here he echoes the sentiments both of Préaux (1983: 5) and D. B. Thompson (1979: 177), who have argued that these "Alexandrian" grotesques, being possessions of this sort, represent native Egyptian fellahin, the impoverished agrarian peasants, and that the deformed physical appearance of the terracottas was a conscious reflection of the peasants' broken spirit. Such a notion is intriguing because it suggests the very real possibility that these grotesque terracotta heads are a Hellenistic Greek response to the native Egyptian non-idealizing heads (CATS. 35-41, 43-47). The issues are necessarily complex and the lack of a documented archaeological context for these loquacious men cloaks their original function and significance in silence.

Despite the fact that quantities of Tanagra figurines have been uncovered at numerous sites on mainland Greece, including both Tanagra and Athens (Higgins 1986: 118-61), as well as in and around Alexandria (Adriani 1952), there can be little doubt about the primacy of Athens, and not Alexandria, as the center responsible for the development of this classification of terracottas in the mid-fourth century B.C. (Buitron in New York 1987: no. 71; Higgins 1986: 105, 107, 118; cf. Fraser

CAT. 113

1972, vol. II: 871). The documented political contacts between Athens and Alexandria during this period not only explain the adoption of this Athenian tradition by the Alexandrians (Fraser 1972, vol. I: 306, 307, 315, *passim*), but also offer an intriguing alternative for the origin of at least some Tanagra figurines with Alexandrian provenances. Himmelmann concluded that the figurines from Chatby and Hadra share great affinities with examples from mainland Greece (1983: 67) and later suggested that the clay for other examples was of an imported, non-local variety (1983: 28). These same observations had been applied earlier to certain classifications of Hadra vases, which are now known to be Cretan, and not Alexandrian, products imported into Egypt (CAT. 119). As the study of these Hadra vases has shown, one would have difficulty supporting a position that espoused the wholesale importation of clay into Ptolemaic Egypt for the local manufacture of such statuettes. It appears extremely possible, therefore, that greater numbers of Tanagra figurines were imported into Egypt than has heretofore been admitted, and that the presence of these figurines in Hellenistic Alexandria reflects a taste for them throughout the Greek-speaking East in the late fourth and early third century B.C. The statistical preponderance of grotesques from Ptolemaic Egypt ought not be taken, *a priori*, as a guarantee of their Egyptian origin. For the present, it can be stated with certainty that the grotesques reflect a particular predilection on the part of the Alexandrians for such figures, but whether it was satisfied by local or foreign workshops cannot be definitely determined.

Aspects of the Ptolemaic royal economy may require closer scrutiny in order to glean data about the regulations for the import and export of works of art. Certainly the suggestion that the Alexandrians exported Egyptian blue pigment to mainland Greece for the Tanagra figures that were painted blue (and that were consequently relatively rare and expensive; Higgins 1986: 70) would imply that the Crown was aware of the value of its natural, uniquely Egyptian resources to foreign artists. Media such as marble and this Egyptian blue, and works of art, including Hadra vases, Tanagra figurines, and mosaics, were evidently part of an extremely brisk commerce between governments and individuals. That commerce, more than any other factor, may have been primarily responsible for the repeated Alexandrian evocations of the artistic tendencies of other Hellenistic Greek centers (CAT. 116).

The technical advances of the coroplasts in the development of segmental molds and the ability of these craftsmen to add separately made pieces to their compositions liberated their work from the laws of frontality, inherent in the use of front-back, two-piece molds (compare CAT. 116). By means of such advances, these craftsmen could create daring archetypes in any medium, from which they then would take their molds (Higgins 1986: 66, 119-20). The compositions were regarded as sculptures and the bases, necessary for the support of the terracottas, were not part of the original designs. They were often added after the creation of the work as separately made plaques (Higgins 1986: 119). The vent holes were more discreetly treated so that their presence would be minimized (Higgins 1986: 119). All of these features characterize the Tanagra productions of the early Hellenistic Period and suggest a dating between 300 and 275 B.C. for the two-figured composition in Hildesheim (Paris MNB 904, Higgins 1986: 159, is a somewhat parallel one-figure piece).

CAT. 115
Fragment of a Clepsydra

Basalt, 16×18.7×5 (6 5/16×7 3/8×1 15/16)
Macedonian Period (332-305 B.C.)
Provenance not known
Private collection

Literature: Bianchi 1983a; Devauchelle 1986: 1156.

Although the clepsydra, or water clock, was apparently invented in Egypt at the very beginning of Dynasty XVIII by an individual named Amenemhet (Devauchelle 1986: 1156 note 1), past attempts to identify the ancient Egyptian name of this instrument have been fruitless (Devauchelle 1986: 1156 notes 3-6). The recent suggestion equating that name with *ḏd.t wnw*,

"that which speaks the hour," on the basis of the ancient Greek word ὡρολόγιον of like meaning (Hodjash/Berlev 1982: 185, no. 129) remains highly speculative.
This fragment preserves traces of three figures, that of a king in the center flanked by the goddesses Sakhmet, left, and Hathor, right, standing beneath a star-spangled sky. The inscriptions in the columns before the deities ("the one beloved of Sakhmet, Lady of Heaven, the Mistress of the Two Lands" and "beloved of Hathor, Mistress of the Two Lands") identify both female figures. A third inscription is found behind Sakhmet ("I have given to thee hundreds of thousands of years..."), while a fourth, dealing with an offering of wine (Götte 1986), identifies the ruler's actions. Among the known examples of clepsydrai (Rome, Museo Barracco 27, Devauchelle 1986: 1156 notes 7-17; Careddu 1985: 31-32), there are at least five with similar scenes (London 938, Quaegebeur 1971 a: 248 note 58; Moscow I.1.a.5955, Hodjash/Berlev 1982: 185; Berlin/BRD 19556; Leningrad 2507 and 2507 b, Roullet 1972: 145-46), the London and Leningrad examples containing inscriptions virtually identical to those on this fragment. On the basis of the close stylistic similarities between this fragment and those inscribed for either Philip Arrhidaeus and/or Alexander, son of Alexander the Great (London 938; London 933, James 1979: 124; Brooklyn 57.21.1, unpublished), this clepsydra is assigned to the Macedonian Period (Bianchi 1983 a). The empty cartouches, a convention adopted by the ancient Egyptians to indicate politically unstable times (Quaegebeur 1983 b: 112; Cauville 1984: 13), are particularly common in the Macedonian Period, especially on clepsydrai (Bianchi 1983 a) and other royal monuments (Cairo CG 22182, the Stela of the Satrap, Spalinger 1980; Bianchi 1983 a).
Since the preserved clepsydrai from the Macedonian Period do not appear to have spouts of any kind and uniformly eschew the image of a baboon found on earlier (Devauchelle 1986) and later examples (Chicago, OI 16875, Quaegebeur 1971 a: 259-62), they probably served as non-functional votive objects. The artistic style of this group of water clocks is one of refinement, whose hallmark is the care lavished on the modeling of the human body (pp. 69-70, above) which, as Quaegebeur has reaffirmed (1983 b: 120), is not indebted to Greek influence but derives directly from the sculptural style of Dynasty XXX (Bothmer 1952 a: 27, elaborating on von Bissing 1914: text to pls. 114-19).

CAT. 116
Vase with Garland and Dolphins

Faience, 33 (12)
Third century B.C.
Provenance not known
Collection of Jack A. Josephson

Literature: Parlasca 1984.

The production of faience vessels in Egypt began to gain momentum during the course of Dynasty XVIII (Boston 1982: 148-51). Almost every period thereafter produced vessels in this material and that production continued unabated into the Roman Imperial Period (CATS. 68, 118). Within this long period of development, the artisans of the Ptolemaic Period exhibited an exuberant creative penchant for extraordinary shapes and decorative elements, as this unique vessel demonstrates. The technical skill with which this vase was formed and fired is remarkable because the vase's relatively large size suggests that the individual parts were made separately, either in molds, as would be the case for the handles in the shape of dolphins, and/or on a wheel for the foot, body, and neck, and by hand for the spout and the garland (compare CATS. 112-114). These individual pieces were then joined together before firing. The shape of CAT. 116, a variant of an amphora of Panathenaic form, appears to be an adaptation of Athenian black-glazed vessels that exhibit the same ribbing of the body and are dated to the last quarter of the fourth century B.C. (Kopcke 1964: 40-41), as comparison with an example now in Hannover reveals (1962.58, Kopcke 1964: 40, no. 122). The garland on the neck of CAT. 116 is an Alexandrian response to the garlands on Athenian examples, often added in gold leaf (Kopcke 1964: 38-39, 58). In CAT. 116, it is so artfully added to the neck that it imitates the position which an actual garland would assume if one had gently laid it over the neck and allowed it to fall naturally onto the shoulder of the vessel. In light of the observations that the Alexandrians adopted their Tanagra figurines from the Greeks (CATS. 112-114) and based their Hadra vases on Cretan types (CAT. 119), it would be understandable that they might

also imitate a popular classification of Attic pottery in faience. This suggestion seems more plausible than the one that regards this vase as an imitation of vessels in precious metal (Parlasca 1984), especially since the relationship of the Attic prototypes to metal is moot (Kopcke 1964: 25-26). It seems preferable, therefore, to consider this faience vessel and the glass amphora from Olbia now in Berlin/BRD (Antikenmuseum 30219, Parlasca 1984: 301) as local responses to Attic models, as Kopcke seems to suggest (1964: 22-23). Although this vessel takes an Attic model as its point of departure, the shape itself – its lip, neck, and foot – appears to be indebted to local taste, as is revealed by a general comparison with the Hadra vases (CAT.

119) and the handles in the form of dolphins, whose preserved spread tails provide the means of attachment to the body.
The dating of this vessel to the third century B. C., perhaps even to the first half of the century, appears certain. The Attic prototypes seem to be limited in time to the last quarter of the fourth century B. C. (Kopcke 1964: 72). That period, then, becomes the *terminus post quem* for the Alexandrian adaptation, which would have developed at a slightly later point in time. Parlasca (1984: 300-01), approaching the problem from a different perspective, suggested a date in the third century B. C. for the glass amphora from Olbia, and placed this vase close to it in time because of their similarities.
In terms of the faience production of vessels in the Ptolemaic Period this vessel is exceptional. A survey in 1987 of over three hundred faience sherds, representing the partial holdings of such material in the Greco-Roman Museum in Alexandria, revealed no comparanda for either the vessel or its handles. The elegantly crafted garland on the shoulder is paralleled perhaps by only one other sherd, a single rim fragment of indeterminate date (Athens MΠ 1346, D. B. Thompson 1973: 39, no. 186).
The function of the vessel remains enigmatic. Parlasca (1984: 301), in his rapid survey of what he considered to be similarly spouted vases, offered no suggestions. Future attempts to adduce the function of this and similar vessels should not place too much emphasis on the dolphins because those mammals are ubiquitous in the Hellenistic art of Alexandria (Barone 1984).

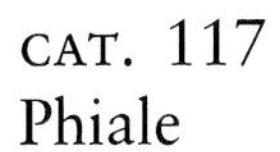

CAT. 117
Phiale

Silver, 3.6×14.6 diameter (1 7/16×5 3/4)
Fourth-third century B. C.
Provenance not known
New York, The Metropolitan Museum of Art, 18.2.16; Rogers Fund, 1918

Literature: Lansing 1938.

This phiale, or shallow bowl, is decorated with twenty-four acorns and two sets of twelve lanceolate leaves radiating from a central rosette, itself composed of fourteen petals. It has been suggested that such phialai developed from silver bowls known from the fourth millennium B. C. (New York 46.11.1, von Bothmer 1984: 16). The type becomes more common about 700 B. C. (New York 1981.11.13, von Bothmer 1984: 21) and continues well into the Hellenistic Period (Byvanck-Quarles von Ufford 1958). The phiale functioned as the vessel from which liquids could be either drunk or ritually spent.
The present phiale was said to have been found at an undisclosed site in the Egyptian Delta, together with four other silver vessels belonging to the same hoard (Lansing 1938). The value of such statements for assessing the individual objects of the hoard is questionable, inasmuch they often prove to be false (CATS. 17, 51). On the other hand, it has been suggested that hoards of just such silver plate discovered in the Delta represent the partial contents of treasuries of temples which, in times of trouble, were buried for safekeeping but never anciently recovered (Shore 1965). These treasuries might very well have included objects that entered at different times, a circumstance which would certainly account for the apparent differences both in style and perhaps even date between two objects from the same hoard, as is revealed by a comparison between this phiale and another found with it (New York 18.2.17, Lansing 1938: fig. 1, bottom row, far right; Shore 1965: 24).
The dating of such hoards and of the individual objects that comprise them is problematic (Shore 1965; Cooney 1956: no. 50, discussing Brooklyn 54.50.32-.42, another hoard of silver objects), but the correspondences between this phiale and other silver vessels from the hoards from Mendes (Cairo CG 3581-3585, De Meulenaere/Mackay 1976: 214, nos. 169-73); and Tuch el Qaramus (Bianchi 1986b), suggest a dating within the fourth or third century.

CAT. 118
Vessel with Appliqués

Faience, 10.7 (4 3/16)
Third century B.C.
Provenance not known
Brussels, Musées Royaux d'Art et d'Histoire, E.4424

Literature: Lunsingh Scheurleer 1979: pl. LI, 4.

The manufacture of faience chalices decorated with relief figural scenes arranged in registers appears to have been extremely popular during the Third Intermediate Period (Tait 1963; Hölbl 1983; H. Müller 1979). Fazzini's suggestion (1972: 66-68) that this production continued to the very end of the period gains support from Russmann's observation (1983: 143 note 43) that the swamp scene, a principal motif on those vessels, seems to disappear toward the end of Dynasty XXV (Cairo JE 58924, a satiric [?] swamp scene from Medamoud associated with Shepenwepet II, Corteggiani 1981: 94-95). Subsequently, new shapes were added to the repertoire of faience vessels, the first being alabastra based on prototypes in precious metal (von Bothmer 1983). Rhytons (Lunsingh Scheurleer 1979; 1986: 148; Munich ÄS 5980, H. Müller 1979: 221, fig. 13), skyphoi (Lunsingh Scheurleer 1979 and 1986), and vessels such as this one in Brussels gradually entered the repertoire. The principal decorative scheme of such vessels relies upon alternating registers of figural and/or floral motifs, applied to the walls in a technique termed sgraffito (D. Hill 1946; Lunsingh Scheurleer 1986: 153; Dayton 1981).

These vessels are universally accepted as products of Egypt exported throughout the Mediterranean basin. Most agree that the center of such faience production was Memphis (Petrie 1911: 34; Fraser 1972, vol. I: 140; G. Grimm 1972; Parlasca 1976), where a group of Helleno-Memphites accommodated the traditional Egyptian medium of faience to foreign shapes and motifs (Lunsingh Scheurleer 1986: 148). But this consensus requires revision in light of the almost one thousand fragments, many unregistered, from sites in and around Alexandria that are presently housed in the magazines of the Greco-Roman Museum in Alexandria. So, for example, the rendering of the feathers of the water fowl on the Brussels vase finds its parallels not only in similar fowl on the vessel in Thessalonike (Andronicos *et al.* 1975: 283), but also on those on sherds in Brooklyn (75.113, unpublished) and two in Alexandria[1] (5824, the second without an inventory number, both unpublished, ALEA B-216, 5). Moreover, the rim decoration, consisting of a tongue pattern separated from the rosettes by a band, is found on two additional sherds in Alexandria (89991 and 16667, the latter incorporating a guilloche), and at least one similarly decorated sherd (Alexandria, without inventory number, ALEA B-219, 12) preserves a head of a Bes-image (Romano 1980), but without plumes. Lunsingh Scheurleer (1986: 148, no. 16) has attempted to connect the Bes-image on such vessels with the work of the pneumatist Ctestibius, but such a comparison may be gratuitous because the figure of *Besas* (a mythical figure that Ctestibius made) is there associated with a rhyton (Fraser 1972, vol. I: 413, 571; Rice 1983: 63). Nevertheless, such Bes-images were popular as appliqués on faience vessels, and one excavated by Breccia has been dated to the third century B.C. on the basis of its archaeological context (Alexandria 19462, Breccia 1922: 271; fig. 181; Lunsingh Scheurleer 1979: 442).

A dating within the third century B.C. consequently accords with the strong similarities between the style of the Bes-images on both the Brussels and Alexandria vases. Such a dating seems to be supported by a comparison with the register of the water fowl on the vase in Thessalonike, dated by its archaeological context to the second century B.C., where the composition is more static. On the basis of the evidence provided, Alexandria may well have been a center for the manufacture of such vases, as correspondences between the decorative motifs of some Hadra vases (CAT. 119) and other types of faience vessels indicate (CAT. 116).

[1] I wish to thank Mme Doreya Said Mahmoud, Director General of the Greco-Roman Museum in Alexandria, for extending every courtesy in allowing me to examine this material.

CAT. 119
Hadra Vase

Red clay with buff slip and brown glaze, 34.1 (13 7/16)
End of the third century B.C., attributed to the Tatillon Painter
Said to be from Alexandria
Raleigh, North Carolina Museum of Art, G. 79.6.15; Gift of Mr. and Mrs. Gordon Hanes

Literature: Bowron 1983: 52.

Despite Cook's observation (1970: 131) that vases of this type were found in quantity on Crete, scholars still support Adriani's opinion (1967: 111) that one or more workshops in Alexandria were responsible for the initial manufacture and subsequent export of these vases (Parlasca 1976: 138-39). But continued excavations on Crete, particularly in the Mesara, led Callaghan (1978: 15) to suggest that many such Hadra vases were in fact manufactured on Crete and were subsequently exported to Alexandria. So revolutionary was this suggestion, that Enklaar (1986) almost immediately recanted his initial rejoinder to Callaghan (1985). Callaghan's view is gradually gaining acceptance (Himmelmann 1983: 29 note 50; Cook 1984: 795); corroborating evidence has been published by La Rosa (1984), who maintains that the Cretan town of Phaistos is perhaps to be regarded as the original center for the production of such Hadra vases.

This new locus for the Hadra vases forces a reconsideration of the function(s) to which such vases were put. The overwhelming majority of the vessels found in Alexandria appear to have been employed as urns for the ashes of the deceased, according to the inscriptions painted on the vases subsequent to their firing (Cook 1970: 119-22; Enklaar 1985: 109). In Alexandria at least such vases do not seem to have been granted as victors' prizes (Forti 1984: 223), but their use in other cultural contexts cannot be excluded.

The inscriptions reveal a close and consistent resemblance to contemporary hands on papyri of the Ptolemaic Period (Fraser 1960) and as such represent a typically Alexandrian phenomenon because pen and ink inscriptions are also known to have been added to some queens' vases (CAT. 68; and D. B. Thompson 1973: 19), and even to some plasters (Hildesheim 1144, D. B. Thompson 1964: 150; Reinsberg 1980: fig. 46). Despite the argument about the chronology for such vases (Enklaar 1985: 111, 116, 145), it is clear that they had been in vogue for a relatively short period. One wonders, therefore, why so many of the deceased who, according to the inked inscriptions, were ambassadors, were dying so closely in time to one another at Alexandria (Braunert 1952; Fraser 1960: 160) and why it had become accepted practice to place their ashes in a particular ware that had to be imported into Alexandria from Crete.

The Raleigh vessel reveals its Cretan origin by its relatively smooth surfaces, which result from the red clay of that island, finer than the coarser clays of Egypt (compare CATS. 112-114). Its slender shape and the style of its painted pattern work associate it with Enklaar's "Workshop L" (1986: 52-56), a Cretan group of painters. More specifically the style of the laurel branch on the neck and the palmette with its lateral spirals on the shoulder is characteristic of the hand that Enklaar identifies as the Tatillon Painter (1985: 136-37). The principal scene found in the panel, placed relatively high up on the belly of the vase, represents a horned ibex confronting a hound. It is only one of two such scenes known on Hadra vases. The second occurs, but without the indications of a landscape, on a vessel attributed to the El Manara Painter (Enklaar 1986: 60-62), now in Alexandria (P. 1885, Adriani 1952: 15, and figs. 15, 19).

The fact that the same motif appears only twice, once each in the work of two different painters, seems to suggest that both sought inspiration in a common prototype rather than that one copied from the other. Since the motifs of the ibex and the dog are common to the iconography of Enklaar's painters of the D Group (1985: 139, 141), it would seem that both the Tatillon and El Manara Painters drew their mutual inspiration from that common source.[1]

[1] I wish to acknowledge my indebtedness to Arnold Enklaar, who kindly read a draft of this entry and provided valuable suggestions and critical advice which have been incorporated into the present version.

CAT. 120
Sphinx of the Officer Wahibre

Limestone, 60.2×32×105.3 (23 11/16×12 5/8×41 7/16)
Reign of Nectanebo II, or shortly thereafter (360-305 B.C.)
Provenance not known
Vienna, Ägyptisch-Orientalische Sammlung des Kunsthistorischen Museums, 76

Literature: Komorzynski; 1955; De Meulenaere 1960a: 93; Satzinger 1980: 67-69.

The sphinx is represented as a harmoniously integrated design of disparate parts in accordance with ancient Egyptian conventions for the design of composite beasts (Fischer 1986: 139-42); the position of its tail on the right side conforms to the rules governing the orientation of elements in Egyptian hieroglyphs (Fischer 1986: 56). The inscriptions are arranged in two lines, each of which diverges to the left and right from their common beginning in the center of the base at the front (CAT. 26). These contain a spell recited by the sphinx,[1] who promises to protect the tomb of Wahibre, son of the mistress of the house Takhut (Komorzynski 1955: 139; Satzinger 1980: 68). Wahibre is known from several other monuments, on which he often bears quite different titles (De Meulenaere 1960a: 93 note 6), although on at least one of these he is tenuously associated with Nectanebo II (Como 28, De Meulenaere 1960a: 93). The bichrome coloring of his *ushabtis,*[2] recording the name of his father, Horwedja (Aubert/Aubert 1974: 250-51), indicates a dating in the second half of the fourth century B.C., when this particular chromatic scheme was in vogue (Aubert/Aubert 1974: 266; New York 26.7.1006, Ricketts 1918; New York 26.7.991, Russmann 1984a: 54). As a result, Wahibre is datable to the fourth century B.C., perhaps contemporary with and slightly later than the reign of Nectanebo II.

This sphinx differs from one of the complete sphinxes inscribed for Nectanebo I that line the dromos of the Temple of Luxor (see CAT. 48). It lacks both a beard and the wide band at the edge of the *nemes* headcloth, whose stripes are clearly indicated and particularly broader in the areas of the ears and jaws. The physiognomic features of the Vienna sphinx correspond to those of the limestone bust identified as that of a Ptolemaic king (CAT. 1), thereby indicating a koine of style for both royal sculpture in the round and in relief during the late fourth and early third centuries B.C. The stylistic characteristics exhibited by this sphinx appear to have been repeated throughout the country, as a comparison with examples from Sanhur and Saqqara reveals (Cairo CG 1166 and CG 1193, Borchardt 1934: 87 and 95 respectively). The apparent uniformity of these sphinxes is a native Egyptian development which has nothing to do with Greek influence, as mistakenly posited by Hassan (1953: 197-98) in his discussions of the last two sphinxes cited.

Sphinxes were employed as guardians of private tombs as early as Dynasty XXVI (Komorzynski 1955: 137) and continued to be used for that purpose throughout the Ptolemaic Period (Alexandria, Anfushi Tomb 2 and Mustapha Pasha Tomb 1, Pensabene 1983: 118), where their form is again Egyptian rather than Greek (Satzinger 1980: 68).

[1] The hieroglyph employed here for "sphinx" is the ideogram depicted in IFAO 1983: 141, nos. 6-9, which also acquired the value *nb*, "lord", during Dynasty XXX (De Meulenaere 1962: 31).

[2] Spanel 1986, for a discussion of this word.

CAT. 121
Funerary Stela of Horemakhet (Harmachis), High Priest of Memphis

Limestone, 58.5×36.7×11 (23 1/16×14 7/16×4 5/16)
Early second century B.C.
Presumably from the Memphite Cemetery of Saqqara
London, Courtesy of the Trustees of the British Museum 391; Salt Collection

Literature: PM III[2], 2: 718-19; Quaegebeur 1971a: 250-51, 268; Munro 1973: 162, 167, 169, 338, 340, 342 and pl. 62, fig. 212; Reymond/Barns 1977: 9-10, 15-17; Quaegebeur 1980: 59, 67, 72; Ray 1980; Reymond 1981: 95-99, no. 9 and pl. VII; Devauchelle 1983a: 138, 143.

This is one of a number of funerary stelae belonging to members of a few closely knit families of the Ptolemaic Period in whose hands were concentrated the most significant Memphite cult offices, including that of High Priest of Memphis (CAT. 122; Reymond 1981). Although the Egyptian priesthoods were not the only areas of economic opportunity for native Egyptians under the Ptolemies (Samuel 1983: 98, 107-08), they represented a main route to prosperity, and priests were the ones who commissioned most private statues and stelae of the era (Johnson 1986: 72; for Egyptian priests in general, see Sauneron 1960c). That the High Priests of Memphis were particularly powerful reflects their city's importance to the Ptolemies as a seat of government, and its tradition as a major religious center since the dawn of Egyptian history (D. Crawford 1980). Indeed, the traditional concern of Memphis for the cults of deified pharaohs may have been one reason for its significance in the establishment of Ptolemaic dynastic cults and the cult of Arsinoe II (pp. 42, 45, 58, above; Quaegebeur 1971a: 245). Political events made Memphis important for the Egyptian priesthood in general, and the Memphite High Priests termed themselves heads of the Egyptian clergy. In fact, Horemakhet, who became High Priest in 223 B.C. and died after 194/193 B.C. (D. Crawford 1980: 20; Quaegebeur 1980: 67-68), would have played a main role in many important political events, including officiating at the crowning of young Ptolemy V Epiphanes (D. Crawford 1980: 31-33). Nevertheless, contrary to some theories (Reymond/Barns 1977), the High Priests of Memphis were not the equivalent of "Prime Ministers" for the Ptolemies (Quaegebeur 1980: 48-49, 77-78), and Horemakhet was not at one time a native rebel king in Upper Egypt (Quaegebeur 1980: 67-68; Ray 1980). He was, however, as evidenced in part by this stela's text, attached to the cults of various Ptolemaic rulers, including Arsinoe II (D. Crawford 1980: 27-29; Quaegebeur 1971a: 251, 263).

The stela has a round top with sky-sign and winged disk, whose significance is discussed in CATS. 3-5. Below is the god Osiris, enthroned. Facing him, Horemakhet censes and pours a libation over offerings on a table, purificatory and revivifying acts hardly an innovation of the Late Pariod, but not commonly depicted on earlier Late Period funerary stelae. Horemakhet wears the sidelock of youth and the panther skin traditionally associated (although not exclusively so) with the High Priests of Ptah (cf. CAT. 130). The main text commemorates his burial and gives some of his titles. Carved during his lifetime, the unfilled blanks left, for example, for his date of death indicate that the stela was never fully finished (Ray 1980).

Horemakhet's stela is part of Munro's Memphis II (Ptolemaic) class of stelae (1973: 161-70, 336-43 and pls. 61-64), made up in part of stelae of the family of High Priests of Ptah and its collateral branches. (For the types of funerary stelae known for the Memphite High Priests, see Reymond 1981: 22-25). Some of those stelae that are proximate in date to Horemakhet's resemble it closely in many ways (Munro 1973: pl. 62, no. 211; Bresciani 1985: pls. 59-60). Munro's Memphis II stelae are related to the pre-Ptolemaic stelae he groups as Memphis I in that they maintain some unity between main texts and figural representa-

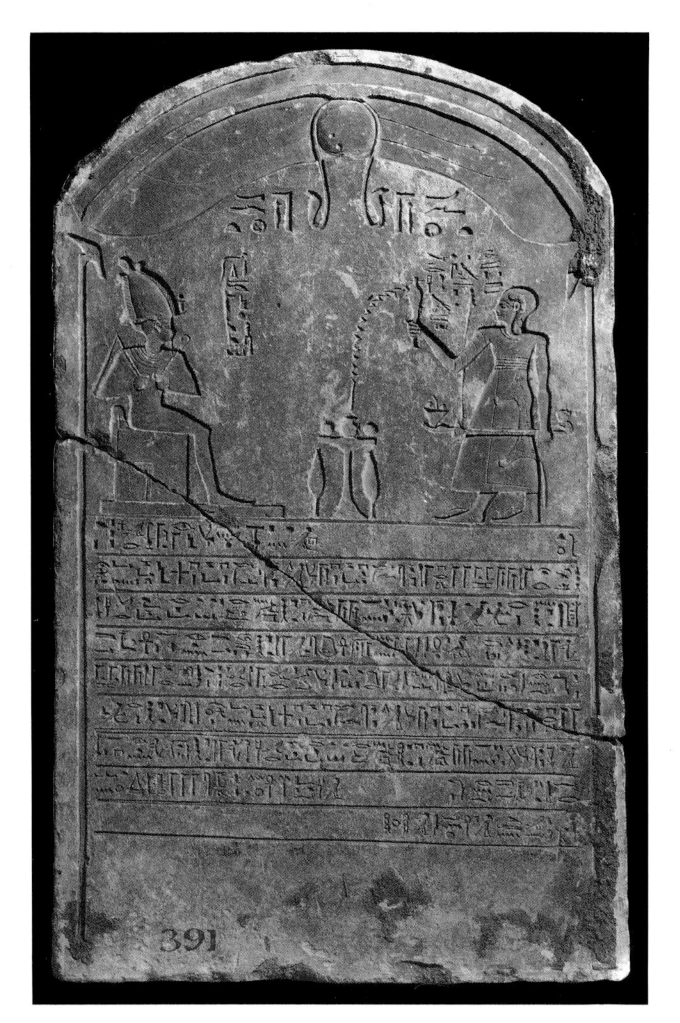

CAT. 121

CAT. 122

tions, heightened in some of the Memphis II stelae by a stronger use of framing elements, such as the *was*-scepters on Horemakhet's stelae (Munro 1973: 165). Like the Memphis I stelae, those in the Memphis II group also show the deceased before Osiris rather than a solar deity such as Re-Horakhty. Unlike almost all late funerary stelae, some Memphis II stelae, of which Horemakhet's is an example, show the deceased before only one god, making for a broad and spacious composition. Munro (1973: 169) also speaks of a tendency, apparent about 200 B.C., toward strong plasticity of forms and deep sunk reliefs, and cites this stela as an early example of a contemporary predilection for making arms too long and heads too large.

CAT. 122
Funerary Stela of Taimhotep

Limestone, 89.2×46×12.5 (35 1/8×18 1/4×4 15/16)
Year 10 of Cleopatra VII (43/42 B.C.)
Presumably from a cemetery at Saqqara
London, Courtesy of the Trustees of the British Museum, 147; Salt Collection 1835

Literature: Munro 1973: 168, 170, 338; Reymond/Barns 1977; Wildung 1977b; 68-70; Lichtheim 1980: 59-65; Quaegebeur 1980: 21, *passim*; Reymond 1981: 165-79; A. Bowman 1986: 187-88, with fig. 116 misidentified as this stela; CAT. 121.

The lively discussions about both the form and content of this important document illustrate the polarity of opinion among scholars about the very nature of Ptolemaic art and culture. The stela is inscribed for the lady Taimhotep, born in Year 9 (73/72 B. C.) of Ptolemy XII Auletes, married to Psenptah III in Year 23 (59/58 B. C.), and died in Year 10 (43/42 B. C.) of Cleopatra VII (Reymond 1981: 165). The last line of the inscription implies that her brother-in-law, one Harimuthis (Quaegebeur 1980: 70 [32]; Lichtheim 1980: 64, 65 note 23, for a different reading of the name), there called *sʿnḫ*, "a sculptor" (Reymond 1981: 252), had a hand in the creation of the monument. The degree of his involvement, however, cannot be judged because of the latitude of meanings inherent in *sš*, "to write", the only verb appearing in that part of the inscription.

The monument is easily intercalcated into a well-defined group, designated Memphis II, by Munro (1973: 161-70; 336-43; CAT. 121). The high artistic merit of the figural decoration of the lunette (Munro 1973: 170; Wildung 1977b: 68) can only be appreciated by an examination of the stela at close range (compare Reymond 1981: 216, fig. 116, to Munro 1973: pl. 64, fig. 217). However, the ascription of the treatment of female anatomy to a Lower Egyptian-Alexandrian School, which implies a degree of Greek influence (Munro 1973: 170), cannot be maintained (Quaegebeur 1983b: 118-20; pp. 68-69, 73, above), especially since one of the monuments cited in support of that theory (Munro 1973: 170 note 1) is no longer regarded as Greek influenced (CAT. 66). The style relates to that of the funerary stela of Taimhotep's husband in London (8856, Munro 1973: 170, 341; Wildung 1977b: 68; Reymond 1981: 139-50). Both are, perhaps, the finest examples of private relief ever made during the Ptolemaic Period.

The group of stelae to which this monument belongs exhibits an interesting phenomenon: the content of the hieroglyphic inscriptions is often repeated in a Demotic version on an independent second stela (London 377, Reymond 1981: 165-94). From the inscriptions of both one learns that Taimhotep and her husband, Psenptah III, had had no male issue, although they had several daughters. The couple subsequently enlisted the assistance of the deity Imhotep, who delivered them of a son (Wildung 1977b: 68-70). The astonishing posthumous advice which Taimhotep addresses to her surviving husband – encouraging him to eat, drink, and be merry (Reymond 1981: 177) – may reflect the wishes of Psenptah and his brother, Harimuthis, rather than the sentiments of their departed relative. In any case, this passage cannot be interpreted, as Reymond (1977: 12-13) and Sauneron (1960c: 39) have done, as an indication that Psenptah and Ptolemy XII caroused together (D. Crawford 1980: 36; Quaegebeur 1980: 76). The evidence suggests, rather, that the king and the prelate enjoyed a mutual and equal respect for one another (D. Crawford 1980: 36, 40) as associates, not as close friends.[1]

The episodes of the birth of the couple's only son and of the *carpe diem* advice to the husband are indebted to Egyptian literary genres. Whether or not one can relate these and other passages in the two stelae of Taimhotep to such Egyptian literary compositions as the "Oracle of the Potter" (Barns in Reymond/Barns 1977: 31-33) and "The Dream of Nectanebo" (Reymond 1981: 166) requires further demonstration. Nevertheless, these themes stand outside the traditions of Hellenistic Greek literary genres. The stela, then, in both its form and content, emerges as an eminently pharaonic document expressing the cultural values of a native Egyptian family.

[1] Quaegebeur (1980) categorically denies the assertions (Reymond/Barns 1977; Reymond 1981) that any members of this family ever married into the Ptolemaic royal family or were buried in the Soma, or royal necropolis, in Alexandria.

CAT. 123 *see color plate XXXII*

Funerary Stela of Pakhaas

Limestone, painted and gilded, 37.5×27×4.2 (14¾×10⅝×1⅝)
Second-first century B.C.
Provenance not known, perhaps Thebes
The Brooklyn Museum, 71.37.2; Charles Edwin Wilbour Fund

Literature: De Meulenaere 1976: 123.

The central figure on this stela, whose theme and style are without parallel (p. 73, above; De Meulenaere 1976: 23), is Pakhaas, the deceased in whose honor the stela was commissioned. Pakhaas, the son of Parui[1] and Nesihor, is shown seated on an elaborate chair and holding a bolt of cloth (p. 70, above), and a staff. His costume consists of a broad collar, belted skirt, adorned with stripes, perhaps representing a patterned textile (Riefstahl 1944b: 46-48), and a sash (Leahy 1980: 170; Kákosy 1983: 59; Cairo JE 37076, Zayed 1962: 150-56; Traunecker 1984). A curious image of what is certainly to be identified as the god Osiris, despite the lack of an identifying inscription, rests on his knees (De Meulenaere 1976: 123). To the right, offering incense and cool water, stands his son Pakhy,[2] while to the far left stands Nesihor II, the wife of Pakhaas and mother of Pakhy. She shakes a sistrum behind her husband.

The image of Osiris on the lap of Pakhaas deserves comment in light of the conflicting views of Morenz (1957, 1969) and Parlasca (1973) regarding the identification of the figures of the deceased with that god in the visual arts of Egypt. In those instances from the Roman Period where one encounters, as here, two distinct images that are clearly those of the deceased and of Osiris, Parlasca (1973: 98-102) would opt for a literal interpretation of the scene, maintaining a distinction between the deceased and Osiris. Morenz (1969: 89), on the other hand, has argued that these same two images are to be understood as an artistic convention ("kontinuierliche Darstellungsweise") by which one is to understand the transformation of the deceased into Osiris. He has perceptively come to terms with one of the most prevalent conceits of Egyptian art for representing different characteristics inherent in one being. So, for example, an emanation of the god Amun may take the form of the deity Bes, whose seven heads collectively represent that deity's *Bau* (Brooklyn 47.218.156, Sauneron 1970: 13, 16, 23).[3] In like manner, the deity Tutu is often depicted with a host of emissary genii, symbolizing the various aspects of his character (Sauneron 1960b). The figure of Osiris on the lap of Pakhaas on the Brooklyn stela is to be understood in light of these parallels. Multiple characteristics and assimilations are often represented in Egyptian art in just such visual terms. It is, therefore, preferable to regard this representation within the development of the visual expressions of ancient Egyptian religion (Fowden 1986: 111), rather than as a phenomenon introduced by the Greeks (Morenz 1957, 1969). By virtue of the fact that an image of Osiris rests on the lap of Pakhaas, Pakhaas becomes Osiris. The image of Nesihor II supports that visual conceit, being couched in the guise of Isis, who is generally shown, sistrum in hand, standing behind her husband Osiris. In this system, Pakhy may be seen as Horus, dutifully ministering to his deceased parent. The traces of gilding on the figure of Pakhaas reinforce the image of his assimilation with the god Osiris (Daumas 1956). The suggested Theban origin of the stela (De Meulenaere 1976: 123) can be supported by the last line of inscription, which in its hortatory expression of life and rejuvenation finds its closest parallel in a Theban statue datable to the Ptolemaic Period (Cairo JE 37076, Zayed 1962: 154). A dating within the second half of the Ptolemaic Period for this stela, as has already been suggested (De Meulenaere 1976: 123), seems consistent with the available evidence.

[1] Compare, perhaps, the name recorded in Ranke 1935: 114, no. 22.

[2] Compare Devauchelle 1983b: 127, 26; and 128, 42(e).

[3] The name of the deity is clearly Bes, as the text shows (Sauneron 1970: 23, 24 note b; Romano 1980).

CAT. 124
Funerary Stela

Limestone, 46×35 (18 1/8×13 3/4)
Second-first century B. C.
Provenance not known
Copenhagen, Ny Carlsberg Glyptotek, AEIN 1071

Literature: Koefoed-Petersen 1948: 60-61; Westendorf 1966: 74-75, 89.

A curved, stippled *pt*-sign conforms to the stela's round top. The lunette contains a winged sun disk from which are suspended two uraei, each holding a fan (CATS. 3-5). The main scene takes place within an embalming booth, whose cavetto cornice is decorated with a second winged sun disk, flanked by uraei, a motif repeated directly beneath in the architrave. The sloping walls of the booth are decorated with uraei, perched upon papyrus umbels. Within the embalming booth is a reed mat employed as a floor covering, upon which stand in adoration Nephthys, left, and Isis, right. The central image is a shrine which, in accordance with Egyptian tenets for two-dimensional representations, is to be understood as containing a lion-shaped bier on which the deceased is placed. Four canopic jars have been placed on the mat alongside, or perhaps under, the bier. Anubis,[1] standing on a support, attends the deceased, whose *ba*-bird flutters about the shrine (Wilkinson 1984). The inscriptions are banal and the name of the deceased is so faintly carved as to be illegible (Koefoed-Petersen 1948: 60-61).

The horizontal lines that describe the top and bottom of the embalming booth are not parallel to one another. Although this feature might reflect the penchant of the Egyptian artists of the Ptolemaic and Roman Periods for asymmetry (pp. 70-71, above), Westendorf (1966) regards it as an intentional device whereby the convergence of the horizontals symbolizes the West and setting sun and the divergence the East and the rising sun.

The scene of Anubis (Meeks 1986: 189) attending the deceased placed on a lion-shaped bier is one of the most traditional and enduring funerary images in Egyptian art from the time of the New Kingdom. It is repeatedly encountered in private tombs of the Ptolemaic and Roman Periods (e.g., Osing *et al.*, 1982: 58-69; 71-94; Adriani 1966: 173-78) and is statistically the most common image on otherwise undecorated "mummy tags" (Quaegebeur 1986 a) and stelae inscribed in Demotic from Dendera (Vittmann 1985; and Petrie 1900). Those commissioning such works must be regarded as staunchly conservative in their religious beliefs and outlooks inasmuch as the character of Anubis underwent an extreme metamorphosis in the hands of the Greeks and Romans in order to render his deeply entrenched theriomorphic nature more palatable to non-Egyptians (Morenz 1954 b; Ristow 1969; Malaise 1972; 1980; 1983: 98-107; Grenier 1977; Tran Tam Tinh 1984: 1731).

The appearance of the uraei with fans in the lunette of the stela may provide a dating criterion. It is a feature that occurs with great frequency during the course of the first century B. C., at

which time a *šn*-sign also appears regularly beneath the hood of the cobra (CAT. 122). The sure outlines of the figures rendered in bold relief and the attention to interior detail tend to support such a dating (compare CAT. 65; Fig. 43), which is also consistent with the dating of the Demotic text at the bottom of the stela. That inscription names an "Osiris Nekhtnebef" and traces his ancestry back at least for two generations. It is unclear whether this Demotic text is to be regarded as a docket, as found on other funerary stelae (compare Reymond 1981: 70, *passim*), in which case Nekhtnebef would have been the original owner of the stela, or whether the Demotic text was added at a subsequent date when the stela was either usurped or appropriated by Nekhtnebef.[2]

[1] The figure of Anubis may represent a priest wearing a jackal-headed mask (Meeks 1986: 180), but the position of Wolinski (1987) regarding the use of masks in ancient Egyptian culture is both inaccurate and misleading because she fails to take into account what the ancient Egyptians themselves had to say on the matter (Meeks 1986).

[2] Dr. Adel Farid, in a letter of July 15, 1987, kindly shared his thoughts on the Demotic text of this stela with me.

CAT. 125
Stela of a Priest before Three Deities

Sandstone, 50×33.5×8 (19 11/16×13 3/16×3 1/8)
Second century B.C. or later
Provenance not known
Amsterdam, Allard Pierson Museum, 7776

Literature: de Bruyn in van Haarlem 1986: 54-57; van Haarlem/Lunsingh Scheurleer 1986: 29, 31-32.

The figure to the right is a priest, the "Osiris" (i.e., deceased) Pa-di-Imhotep, wearing a fringed Egyptian garment (CATS. 30-32), holding an arm-shaped censer, and libating (CATS. 121, 123). On the other side of the stand are figures (or statues; Schulman 1986: 308-11)[1] of three deities: from right to left, Khonsu-[the]-Child, Mut, and Anat. Unlike many of her earlier depictions, Anat, the Near Eastern "war" goddess, does not hold a shield and weapon, but is shown peacefully, as in a few Ptolemaic reliefs (e.g., Chassinat 1947-52: 25 and pl. CCCXL, a scene with Hathor, Horus, Anat, and Khonsu), where she is sometimes assimilated to other goddesses (cf. Junker/Winter 1965: 390-91; C. Husson 1977: 104-05, 239-40).

The text at the top of the stela, informing us that Pa-di-Imhotep was a scribe of the Temple (*ḥwt-nṯr*) of Anat is, contrary to the usual form, oriented not to his figure but to the gods, and is placed above a large hieroglyph for heaven, adorned with zigzag lines (Cairo CG 22137, Kamal: 1905: pl. XL is somewhat similar), which also (and also unusually) fill the register line below the figures. Indeed, this stela displays an "inexorable" use of zigzag lines (von Bissing 1914: text for no. 120 A) on the sides of the throne, where one would expect feather patterns, and on the goddesses' dresses. Rarely are female pleated or feathered garments as abstractly rendered as here. The figures' bodies and faces, however, are far more customary, variants of the latter being found on a number of works ranging in date from the mid-Ptolemaic to the early Roman Periods. The Amsterdam stela is normally dated to the second century B.C., but could be later.

The main text below the figures is an "Appeal to the Living," a type of text with a long history. It invokes benefactions for its subject (here Pa-di-Imhotep) from individuals who find themselves in the presence of his tomb, statue, or stela (C. Müller 1975). The text identifies the monument as "this *snn*": either a statue (de Bruyn in van Haarlem 1986: 55) or other monument (Hornung 1967: 136-37; Ockinga 1984: 57). Here it should refer to the stela, which could have come from his tomb, or from a temple, since the text does not mention a tomb. In fact, it is tempting to associate it with the "Temple" (*ḥwt-nṯr*) of Anat mentioned above, especially as the texts accompanying all three deities link them to a "*pr* (temple or temple estate; de Bruyn in van Haarlem 1986: 55; Spencer 1984: 14-20) of Anat." Unfortunately, Anat's *pr* or *ḥwt-nṯr* cannot be linked to a specific site where all three deities are known to have been venerated.[2] One possible northern provenance is Tanis where, however, Anat was subordinate to Mut, who, with Khonsu-the-Child, retained her Theban epithets (Roemer 1985: 198, 202), which do not include a reference to an Anat Temple. This also makes it difficult to attribute the stela to Thebes, even though von Bissing purchased it in Luxor (de Bruyn in van Haarlem 1986: 55). Another question, too complex to deal with here in detail, is how Anat, Mut, and Khonsu-the-Child became so closely linked as to produce this unique depiction of the three together. The image of two goddesses (other than Isis and Nephthys) with a child-god is also unusual. Among the many possible explanations for the linking of Mut and Anat, two are worth mentioning: Anat, like Mut, is a "daughter of Re" (Roemer 1985: 198), and both can be assimilated to Hathor (C. Bowman 1978: 240, referring to this stela; for Mut and Hathor, see Troy 1986: 60-61). The Mut-Hathor relationships include that of virtuous divine mother and goddess of "good women" (Mut) to goddess of sexual excitement (CAT. 6) and of "bad women" (Hathor) (te Velde 1980: 8; Troy 1984). Anat can be a bridge between the two, or an aspect of both viewed as a unity (van Dijk 1986: 41-42).

[1] I am grateful to Alan Schulman for discussing several aspects of this stela with me, and for several references to the goddess Anat.

[2] Leclant 1975: 255 says that the "Temple of Anat" cited on the stela is also mentioned in an unpublished inscription of Ptolemy VI (Cairo JE 85625). He gives no provenance for the temple. I have not yet been able to investigate this monument and the light it might shed on the provenance of CAT. 125.

CATS. 126-127 *see color plate XXXIII**

Sheets from Two Books of the Dead

CAT. 126

A Last Judgment

Papyrus with ink and paint, 30.3×79.8 (11 15/16×31 7/16)
Third century B. C. (?)
Provenance not known
London, Courtesy of the Trustees of the British Museum, P. 9908,2; Salt Collection

Unpublished

* cf. CATS. 92-96

CAT. 126

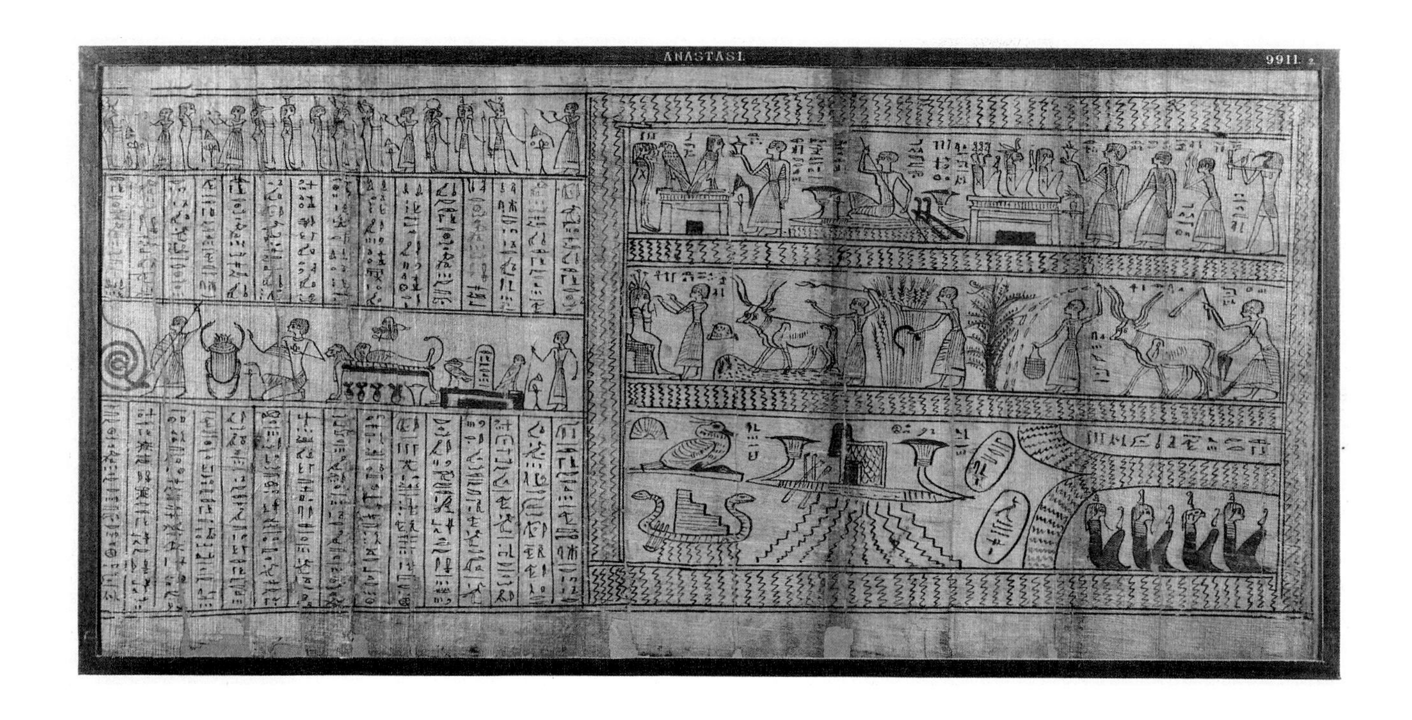

CAT. 127

An Egyptian Paradise and Other Scenes

Papyrus with ink and paint, 40.9×84.2 (16 1/8×33 1/8)
Third-second century B. C.
Provenance not known
London, Courtesy of the Trustees of the British Museum, P. 9911,2; Anastasi Collection 1839

Literature: Faulkner 1985: 9, 105.

Book of the Dead (*BD*) is a name given by Egyptologists to a class of funerary papyri which are first attested in Dynasty XVIII. Each of them is adorned with a selection from a large repertory of spells, often accompanied by vignettes, invoking blessings for their deceased owners. If a well-illustrated Ptolemaic *BD* had a value comparable to that recorded for one such papyrus in Dynasty XIX (Janssen 1975: 245-46), such a book was an expensive item of funerary equipment.

CAT. 126 belongs to a *BD* for a woman named Ta-sherit-min and features a vignette of part of her last judgment, when her heart (believed to be the seat of thought) was weighed against an image of Ma'at (CAT. 12; and p. 29, above), with which it must balance if she was to enjoy a blessed afterlife. In *BD*s this vignette normally accompanies Spell 125 (invoking a positive last judgment) or 30 B (asking the heart not to testify against its owner). Sometimes, however, it accompanies Spell 1 ("Spell for descending to the Council of Osiris on the day of burial...") (Seeber 1976: 12-14), and in Ta-sherit-min's *BD* the text is part of an addition to Spell 1 first attested in Dynasty XXI (T. Allen 1974: 5 note 1; 6, para. 6-7).

Egyptian depictions of the last judgment have been divided into main types with subtypes in a detailed study by C. Seeber (1976). Ta-sherit-min's vignette fits into Type E, known from the Third Intermediate Period to Roman times; coming after a long evolution, it displays a "canonical form" varying only in details (Seeber 1976: 48).

As was long believed but rarely depicted until Type E, the judgment is shown taking place in the Hall of the Two Ma'at Goddesses (Seeber 1976: 49, 63-67, 139-47). Immediately below the hall's roof, Ta-sherit-min is shown adoring a row of divine judges. To the left in the large scene, Ta-sherit-min, one hand to her chest and the other before her face, is flanked by the two Ma'at goddesses who, although incorporating the principle by which she is to be judged, have come to appear as protective goddesses accompanying the deceased. This grouping and Ta-sherit-min's pose make the vignette an example of Seeber's subtype II/2 of Type E (1976: 49, 91-92, 140).

In Type E the actual weighing of the heart can be attended by two gods, here Anubis and Horus. To the left of the balance are: a child-godlike figure on a crook, a symbol of the deceased in the state of rebirth; Meskhenet, personification of a birthing brick and a deity of fate; Thoth recording the positive judgment before Osiris enthroned; the "Devourer" of the damned, who could also signify rejuvenation for the justified; and the four funerary deities known as the Sons of Horus on a lotus symbol of rebirth (Seeber 1976 comments on all these in detail; for the "Devourer" in the context of the "monstrous" in Egyptian art, see Fischer 1987).

The dating of papyri vignettes is made difficult by several factors, such as the relative dearth of their publication and of prosopographical, paleographical, and topographical studies which would enable a more precise charting of their development (Limme 1983: 81, 85, 95-96). However, Ta-sherit-min's vignette has good stylistic and iconographical parallels in several papyri of, or probably of, Ptolemaic date (e.g., Limme 1983, figs. 1, 3 – which Limme notes could be late pre-Ptolemaic – and 5; Seeber 1976: pl. figs. 23-26; Hildesheim 1985: no. 174). The last cited work, Berlin/DDR P.3008, inscribed for a woman named Ta-rudj, is variously attributed to the third century B.C. (Hildesheim 1985) or the second century B.C. (Limme 1983: 90).

CAT. 127, inscribed for a man named Kerquny, has been dated to c. 250-150 B.C. (Faulkner 1985: 9). Needless to say, there are other Ptolemaic *BD*s providing general parallels or counterparts for specific stylistic details. One is published by Limme (1983: 84-85, fig. 1) with discussion of other papyri, mostly of the third century B.C., which display similar figures with striated wigs and garments and, as in the smaller figures to the left in this papyrus, figures with schematically rendered limbs. The papyrus of Ta-rudj (Berlin/DDR P.3008), cited in connection with CAT. 133, also provides good inconographical, stylistic, and compositional parallels for Kerquiny's large vignette with smaller vignettes and text to the left.

The large vignette on this sheet of Kerquny's papyrus is the illustration for *BD* Spell 110. Egypt's agrarian society depended on the Nile's flooding, and on irrigation of the fields by a canal system. Spell 110 concerns a vision of the afterlife in which even the noble dead would have to produce food for their own sustenance and for the gods, as is most clear from the middle register, where Kerquny undertakes his agrarian duties and thanks a god of abundance for a good harvest. In general, the vignette is of Ptolemaic type, dependent in many ways on earlier depictions of the same Egyptian paradise.

The left half of the sheet's decoration relates in part (including the style of the figures and text) to the corresponding adornment of Berlin/DDR P.3008. In the latter, all the texts and vignettes are from *BD* Spell 18, which calls on Thoth to vindicate the papyrus' owner before several divine tribunals against all enemies, just as he had vindicated Osiris against his enemies. The texts in the upper half of this part of Kerquny's *BD* give a quite abbreviated version of Spell 18 and are accompanied by depictions of him adoring some of the deities of the spell.

The texts below are mostly a partial version of *BD* Spell 89 ("Spell for letting a soul regain its corpse in the realm of the dead"). One of the vignettes above these columns is a normal illustration for *BD* 89: a *ba*-bird hovering over its mummy. (For the other vignettes, associated with other *BD* spells, see, e.g., Barguet 1967: 75, 78-79, 88.)

If the precise dating of *BD*s is problematic, the same is true of their precise interpretation and of attempts to answer the question of what a *BD* meant to an ancient Egyptian. For many the answer has been the same as that given for other items of funerary equipment: it was expected to help magically to bring about what it said and depicted, even if this seems incompatible with the emphasis on morality and piety inherent in the concept of a final judgment. Among those holding differing views, H. te Velde (1982b: 142) has argued that a vignette such as Ta-sherit-min's would better be interpreted as "a request, an attempt at persuasion, a profession that the deceased be justified as represented" rather than as a magical means that "would automatically bring about the justification of the deceased." To put it in other words, "it is a prayer not in words but in a drawing" (te Velde 1978: 270).

CAT. 128
Relief of a Heavily Laden Offering Bearer

Limestone, 35.8×28.2 (14 1/8×11 1/8)
Fourth-third century B. C.
Provenance not known
Hildesheim, Pelizaeus-Museum, 2244

Literature: Schäfer 1921; G. Grimm, in Hildesheim 1979: no. 189.

In his initial assessment of this relief, Schäfer concluded that the object was a trial piece, whose style was circumstantially attributed to Greek influence (1921: 19, 22). However, the presence of a relatively wide fascia around three edges of the scene (Schäfer 1921: 19) and the existence of an almost identical piece in Berlin/BRD (Schäfer 1921: 19-20; ESLP: 174), recall the reliefs of the offering bearers in the lowest register of the fourth century B. C. tomb of Petosiris. Such relatively wide fasciae characterize at least three fragments of a stylistically and thematically similar relief discovered at Tod (Vercoutter 1952: pl. IX, 1-3). In Egyptian art, the very nature of offering scenes mandates the repetition of figures and their accoutrements, as even a cursory glance at such scenes from the Late Period in the Asasif reveals (Kuhlmann/Schenkel 1983: pl. 62). In such multiples, it is common to encounter variations in interior detail such as those which distinguish the Berlin from the Hildesheim piece (CAT. 65, Fig. 43). Since there can be no doubt that both pieces are related in style and technique, it would be better to regard these two reliefs as decoration for the walls of the same monument, perhaps a private tomb, rather than as sculptors' studies (G. Grimm in Hildesheim 1979: no. 189).
The circumstantial association of these so-called Neo-Memphite reliefs (ESLP: 110; Bianchi 1980 b: 15-16) with Greek influence can be seriously challenged. Whereas some of these reliefs, published earlier by Maspero (1910) and von Bissing (1914: text to pl. 111) have now been associated with Heliopolis (Yoyotte 1954 a), others have been found at Tod (Vercoutter 1952: pl. VIII) and at Tanis (Montet 1959: pl. XI). Although no one example has been securely dated (Descroches-Noblecourt 1975: 248-50; De Meulenaere 1966: 8, no. 19; el Sayed 1975: 144, 1976: 94-95), the evidence seems to support U. Schweitzer's contention that the series begins in late Saite times (1952: 128), with certain motifs within a papyrus marsh drawn from the repertoire of swamp scenes known from the Third Intermediate Period (CAT. 118). Consequently, the style of those reliefs would have been developed over the course of two and a half centuries. The relief style and themes encountered in the tomb of Petosiris at Tuna el Gebel would then have to be regarded as the culmination of a tradition, rather than as a creation *ab ovo* (Nakaten 1982).
The modeling of the male torsos on the Berlin and Hildesheim reliefs is within the Egyptian tradition for tripartition (pp. 69-70, above); the costume worn by the woman in the Berlin piece has been shown to be a native Egyptian development which has nothing whatsoever to do with the goddess Isis (Bianchi 1980 b; CATS. 66, 100, 101); and the coiffures, both male (Dunham 1957: stela 7; Hassan 1944; pl. XXXIV; Kyrieleis 1975: 76, 135-36; Russmann 1979: 50) and female (CAT. 130) derive from a pharaonic repertoire of formal elements and have good antecedents in the art of the earlier Late Period. The baroque profusion of offerings, evocative of the heavily laden depictions of the god Hapi in the relief in Cleveland (61.205, Cooney 1967), are already in place, lamentably in a very fragmentary state, in the tomb of Ankh-hor (Bietak/Reiser-Haslauer *et al.* 1978: Plan 15, 20). The fashion of a chin beard worn without a mustache is frequently encountered on reliefs from the Old Kingdom, and certainly becomes a fixture of male fashion after the fourth century B. C. (CAT. 2).
The close correspondences between the treatment of the costumes and the presence of earrings on the woman in the relief in Berlin (see also Brussels E. 5335, Brussels 1985: no. 102) incline one to date the Hildesheim relief to the fourth to third centuries B. C.

CAT. 129
Board from a Coffin Decorated in Relief

Wood, 22.3×43.8 (8¾×17¼)
193-212 A. D.
Provenance not known
Hildesheim, Pelizaeus-Museum, 2373

Literature: Kayser 1966: 118.

The scene as preserved depicts four individuals who appear to represent clerics (Kayser 1966: 118), rather than deities (compare CATS. 110, 111), holding the ritual objects for the cult of the deity whom they serve. At the far right stands a male figure wearing what seems to be a late variation of the wraparound skirt that enjoyed great popularity during Dynasty XXVII (CAT. 33). His chest is bare and his head shaved. He holds erect a palm frond, which can be associated with attributes of the priest of Isis depicted in the Meroitic Chamber at Philae (Griffith 1912: pl. XVIII). The second figure is a woman shown with the knotted, tripartite costume and corkscrew locks. Her headdress consists of two feathers and she holds a spouted, squat vessel in each hand. One suspects that the rectangular depression to the left of her head represents insignificant negative space resulting from the carving of the figure. Notice how its left vertical edge coincides with the outer contour of the figure. This rectangle is more articulated than that around the male figure at the right, though it too is doubtless to be understood in the same way. The third figure wears a short skirt wrapped around the body and held in place by one arm, wrapped in the garment's loose end and pressed against the body at the level of the waist; in his other hand he holds a baton. He is bare-chested, has long hair, and wears a headdress consisting of two plumes placed upon the horns of a ram. Only tantalizing traces of the fourth and final figure, at the left of the scene, are preserved; these include an extended arm holding a standard decorated with two oval objects flanking an indistinct central motif.

Thematically, the scene can be profitably compared to similar processions of clerics from Roman Italian contexts; closest are the relief decorations on the four columns from the Iseum Campense (Roullet 1972: 57-58). The column in Florence (Museo Archeologico, without number, Roullet 1972: figs. 37-38) and the three in Rome (Museo Capitolino, Sala dei Monumenti dell'Iseo Campense, Roullet 1972: figs. 39-47) depict such clerics, dissimilarly clad, holding palm fronds and standards (Roullet 1972: figs. 37, 38, 40-42). This temple, destroyed by fire in 80 A. D., was rebuilt by Domitian (Clerc 1978: 256-57). Its rounded pediments, now in Berlin/DDR (16785-16786, Roullet 1972: 59 and figs. 50-51), have been dated to the second century A. D. (Roullet 1972: 59; compare Pensabene 1983: 106, 115). This sanctuary was active into the reigns of the Severans, about 200 A. D., and later under Elagabalus (218-222 A. D.) (Clerc 1978: 256-57).

The style of the wooden board from the coffin is characterized by shallow, sunk relief with incised interior details. The figures tend to be frontal, although one might argue that the cleric to the far right is shown in an approximation of a three-quarter view. These stylistic features are common to the group of so-called stelae from Terenouthis (Abd el Al *et al.* 1985), which have been dated from the first to the third centuries A. D. (Parlasca 1970). The penchant for stricter frontality becomes more common in the late second and third centuries A. D. (Parlasca 1974, and CAT. 135). The one monument which appears to stand closest to this coffin fragment is a relief in Cairo (CG 27569, Kiss 1984: 83-84, and fig. 215), representing an entourage displayed in two registers, the upper one featuring an enthroned figure with a rayed nimbus or halo. Although more accomplished, the Cairo example, datable to the late second or first half of the third century A. D., employs the same approach to the sculpting, which derives from the those employed for the stelae from Terenouthis. One may, therefore, suggest a dating about 200 A. D. for the wooden relief as well.

If this dating is accepted, it would represent one point in a gradual, but incessant departure from pharaonic norms during the course of the third century A. D. One need only compare the coffin and the Cairo relief with the head of Caracalla (CAT. 140) to gauge the impact of this development on pharaonic art of the third century A. D. This trend would eventually become dominant and ultimately eclipse all pharaonic expression, which apparently ceases altogether during the reign of Diocletian (284-305 A. D.; p. 80, above).

CAT. 130 Symplegma

see color plate XXXIV

Limestone, 16.5×17×9.5 (6 1/2×6 11/16×3 3/4)
Ptolemaic Period (305-30 B. C.)
Said to be from the vicinity of Alexandria
The Brooklyn Museum, 58.13; Charles Edwin Wilbour Fund

Literature: Bianchi in Brooklyn 1983: no. 70.

Although group sculptures are known from ancient Egypt, almost every example is characterized by a paratactic composition in which the individual pieces are treated as separate units, related to one another without any integrating compositional devices (Aldred 1949: no. 25, 26, 53) parallel to or perpendicular to the planes of the block of stone employed. These patterns, evolved for group compositions during the course of the Old Kingdom, were invariably repeated throughout Egypt's history (Simpson 1956: 118-19; Freed 1987: 130-31). This paratactic composition was also employed for the statue of Nectanebo II before the falcon (CAT. 8), and paratactic groups continued to be sculpted in the Ptolemaic Period (e.g., Alexandria 11261, now at the Serapeum, Sauneron 1960a: 83-90; p. 43, above).

Given this tradition, the Brooklyn symplegma is atypical for Egyptian statuary types precisely because it relies upon a hypotactic composition in which the secondary figures do interact with the principal ones. The composition develops in the round, and provides from any vantage point an integrated view of the figures. This compositional approach is shared with any number of other symplegmata in limestone or faience that appear to be datable to the Late Period (Bianchi 1978). The female figure in the Brooklyn group can be assigned to the Ptolemaic Period on the basis of her coiffure and the rendering of her face. The bobbed wig is frequently represented in the Late Period (ESLP: nos. 82, 87), but its form as depicted here is typical for examples from the Ptolemaic Period (ESLP: no. 90; Settgast in Altenmüller/Hornbostel, 1982: 90-91). The treatment of the facial features derives from the repertoire of idealizing forms developed as early as the fourth century B. C. and employed for the renderings both of male (CAT. 24) and female images, of which the example in Brussels (CAT. 28) provides the closest stylistic parallels.

The Brooklyn sculpture is the exclusive product of ancient Egypt, its thematic and compositional concerns evolved without any influences from abroad. None of the numerous hypotactically composed symplegmata in limestone and faience that relate to this group have been found in extra-Egyptian contexts. Although an understanding of ancient Egyptian erotica is just beginning to emerge (Störk 1975), this example provides the most complex visual conceits known to date. The focal point of the composition is the large nude woman attended by a retinue of six male figures, each wearing a sidelock (compare CATS. 55, 56, 121). At the front, to the right, are two attendants, who hold a representation of a bound oryx. Thematically this symplegma, through a complex visual vocabulary, must be associated with the cycle of the god Osiris, who posthumously impregnated his consort, Isis, to produce his heir, Horus, and thereby ensure the continuity of his line. The component elements of the allegory are the male figures who, despite their puerile appearances, are in fact *sem*-priests, identifiable by their sidelocks. These priests traditionally performed the final rites of burial at Egyptian funerals (Derchain 1981). The oryx is an animal traditionally associated with evil and destruction (Derchain 1962). To triumph over the oryx was to overcome obstacles, in this context, Death. These individual motifs, grouped around the central female figure who must here be regarded as a Ptolemaic reinterpretation of the Middle Kingdom bride of the dead (Desroches-Noblecourt 1953; Bianchi in Brooklyn 1983: no. 25), represent man's potential for resurrection in the hereafter, through his procreative abilities in life.

CAT. 131
Two-Sided Ex-Voto of a Cat and a Ram

Limestone, 20.5×22.2×1.1 (8 1/16×8 3/4×7/16)
150-100 B.C.
Provenance not known
Boston, Museum of Fine Arts, 51.2474; Helen and Alice Colburn Fund, Martha A. Willcomb Fund, Gift of Mrs. Charles Gaston Smith's Group

Literature: Bothmer 1953b.

Such limestone plaques continue to be called "sculptors' models" or "trial pieces", despite the pioneering suggestion of Bothmer well over a quarter of a century ago (Bothmer 1953b: 83-84, upheld by Bianchi 1979b) that such objects are in fact ex-votos which can be stylistically divided into chronological groupings (Bianchi 1981; and CATS. 1, 131). The exceptionally high relief, which creates an image half in the round, has been erroneously ascribed to Greek influence (Bothmer 1953b: 84). Such bold relief has a long history in Egyptian art and is a particular hallmark at Kom Ombo for works inscribed for Ptolemy VIII Euergetes II. Especially well-preserved examples are to be found on the interior walls of the inner hypostyle (PM VI: 185-89), where the scene of that king accompanied by Cleopatra II and III offering to Harieris (PM VI: 189 [74]; Heinen 1974) provides a particularly good stylistic comparison for dating this ex-voto to the second half of the second century B.C.
Although uninscribed, the deities represented can be adduced

from the necklace worn by the cat, which consists of a series of beads in the form of cowrie shells (*cypraea vitellus*, Seyfried 1983: 111-12), first extensively used in jewelry during the Middle Kingdom (D'Amicone 1985). The cowrie shell acquired erotic overtones (Desroches-Noblescourt 1953: 11 note 1; Seyfried 1983; 111-12; D'Amicone 1985), which in Egyptian culture were related to childbirth (Brooklyn 44.226 and CAT. 130; Bianchi in Brooklyn 1983: nos. 25, 70). The identification of this cat as Bastet is certain since she was habitually depicted in this feline form in her association with women in childbirth during the Ptolemaic and Roman Periods (Cairo, number not known, Bernand 1975: 63-65; and Cairo, Agricultural Museum 601, Wagner 1983).[1] The *wadjet*, or eye of Horus, as a protective amulet is an appropriate pendant on the cowrie shell necklace of the ex-voto (Westendorf 1980) and is frequently depicted on images of cats (Boston 39.593, Simpson 1977: 60-61). As a result, the ram-headed deity (Keimer 1938; Brentjes 1977) on the other side of this plaque must be identified as Khnum, the creator god, rather than as Banebdjed, the ram deity of the Delta city of Mendes (Bothmer 1953 b: 81-82). The ex-voto might, therefore, have been offered in a sanctuary in expectation of or after delivery of a child.

Two unusual features deserve mention. The first is that the trapezodial beard of the ram, which is now missing, was made of a different material (Bothmer 1953 b: 82), which, since there is no evidence of corrosion, may have been faience rather than metal (compare Tübingen 1716, Brunner-Traut/Brunner 1981: 100-01). The second is the apparent perspectival rendering of the *wadjet*-amulet, which is rendered according to time-honored Egyptian conventions for depicting the recession into space of certain motifs (p. 74, above).

[1] Bothmer (1953 b: 81) assumed *a priori* that the cat on this plaque represented Bastet, without offering a demonstration of the assumption. Classicists often blindly follow that lead, refusing to admit alternative identifications for Egyptian cat goddesses (e.g., D. B. Thompson 1984: 311). This note is intended as a caution against such unfounded attributions. The plurality of meanings for any one motif in Egyptian art should be more widely acknowledged; the cat can represent numerous deities (te Velde 1982 a; and Yoyotte 1983: 222).

CAT. 132
Bastet, Goddess of Childbirth

Limestone, gilded and painted, 47 (18)
First century A. D.
Provenance not known
Hildesheim, Pelizaeus-Museum, 748

Literature: Hildesheim 1979: no. 191.

The plurality of meanings inherent in any one Egyptian motif and the fact that the cat can represent more than one divinity (CAT. 131) render the identification of this goddess difficult.

Nevertheless, her attributes seem to revolve around a common theme that confirms her as Bastet, however colored that identification may be by the syncretistic tendencies of the Ptolemaic and Roman Periods.
Her most prominent attribute is a sistrum, of the *sššt*-type (Nagy 1977), which she holds in her left hand. Although such musical instruments are the habitual attributes of Hathor (George 1978; Pécoil 1986) and of Isis, especially in extra-Egyptian contexts (von Bissing 1937; Becher 1966: 49, 53; Balty 1984: 829 note 20), the sistrum is a fundamental attribute of Bastet in her role as the patron of women in childbirth (Cairo CG 69316, Wildung/Schoske 1984: 103). The apotropaic use of the sistrum during the critical period of the actual delivery has long been recognized. Although the figurine of a child, whom the goddess holds against her left forearm and shoulder, has been identified as the god Nefertum (Hildesheim 1979: no. 191), one should perhaps regard it as a visual wish for an offspring in general, in analogy with an inscribed statuette of the Middle Kingdom (Berlin/BRD 14517, Schott 1930; Hornblower 1931: 145). The anomalous pedestal at the front left-hand corner of the plinth once held a small, standing bandy-legged figure without head, whose arms were folded across the chest (ALEA 241, 4-5). This figure appeared in an attitude recalling the companion of Bes on a stela from the chambers at Saqqara in which petitioners would beseech that deity for children (Amsterdam 7762, Lunsingh Scheurleer 1987: 11). The cumulative effect of the sistrum, the child in arms, and the companion of Bes in association with a feline goddess leaves no doubt that the principal figure of this composition is to be identified as Bastet, the goddess of childbirth. This identification seems confirmed by the Greek inscriptions from Egypt, dating from the fourth century B. C. into the Roman Imperial Period, that associated Bastet in cat form with childbirth (Bernand 1975: 63-65; Wagner 1983). The divinity of Bastet is reinforced by the gilding (compare CATS. 66, 123), traces of which appear on the eyes and ears.
Despite earlier assessments (Hildesheim 1979: no. 191), there is no mixing of stylistic traditions in this representation of Bastet. Her attitude is that of a modified S-curve, dependent upon the Greek norms of contrapposto developed during the fourth century B. C. This is evident in the position of her feet relative to that of her head and in the chiasma of opposing shoulders and hips. Such an interest is indebted to Classical, not Egyptian, norms (compare Fig. 41). Moreover, the treatment of the tripartite costume replicates the appearance, but does not conform to the configuration of, the pharaonic fashion (Bianchi 1980 b: 20-21). So close is the conception of the female figure and her drapery to a first century A. D. figure in Brooklyn (74.220, Bianchi 1980 b: 10) that one can suggest a similar dating for this statuette of Bastet.
Despite the syncretistic associations of Isis with Bastet (Bernand 1975: 63-65), the dominant iconography of this group revolves around the cat goddess and is divorced from any direct associations with Isis. The statuette, therefore, provides further evidence for caution in imparting Isidian overtones to every appearance of this native Egyptian costume.

CAT. 133
Seated Official

Basalt, 50×18×29 (19 11/16×7 1/16×11 7/16)
14-50 A. D.
Karanis, on the floor level in a room of a ruined house across the street from the southwest corner of the temenos wall of the Southern Temple; found at the lowest level of occupation
Ann Arbor, Kelsey Museum of Archaeology, University of Michigan, 8218

Literature: ESLP: no. 140; Castiglione 1967: 41; Gazda *et al.* 1978: 41; A. Bowman 1986: 126, fig. 75.

The picture of the survival of private sculpture in Egyptian style into the Roman Imperial Period is far from clear, but may in part be resolved by an examination of the school of sculpture from the Faiyum to which this statue belongs. Its type, that of an enthroned, draped male figure with head preserved, is one of seven known examples. It constitutes a fairly close approximation, one might even say duplicate, of a second in Cairo (CG 1192, Borchardt 1925: 94-95). These two are less abstracted and angular than a third in Alexandria (3203, Castiglione 1967: 123), but equally less naturalistic than a fourth, also in

Alexandria (3193, Castiglione 1967: 123). This last work is itself a duplicate of a fifth statue in Cairo dated to Year 19 of Tiberius by its inscription (CG 1191, Borchardt 1925: 94-95; Castiglione 1967: 123). Acknowledging chronological and geographic differences, one can still profitably compare this Faiyum school of sculpture with the development of the Dendera school (CAT. 32). In both instances, private Egyptian statuary appears to become more abstracted and stylized with time. Consequently, the group to which the Ann Arbor statue belongs should date to the reign of Tiberius, or shortly thereafter. The lack of polish – with the exception of the head – and the obviously unfinished state of the throne are, in themselves, the ultimate triumph of the medium in its struggle with the craftsmen. Egyptian sculpture of all ages, with notable exceptions such as the schist sculptures of Mycerinus of Dynasty IV (Fig. 40; Saleh/Sourouzian 1987: no. 33), exhibits an inherent potential for resisting finishing touches in inaccessible areas (CAT. 43). That potential is here fully realized, and that realization is all the more surprising because this statue of an enthroned private individual was most probably a temple sculpture,[1] as perhaps was Cairo CG 1191, erected in public for all to see. It is interesting, therefore, to observe that the last sculptural expressions of the native Egyptians revert to an enthroned image, a sculptural type which had long since vanished from the repertoire of Egyptian, non-royal statuary. More significant, however, is the observation that tomb sculpture had virtually disappeared from the Faiyum and had, in the end, been supplanted by temple statues. The absence of a resident pharaoh provided the cultural environment in which a private person might appear enthroned in a temple sculpture, a prerogative earlier reserved for depictions of the kings and gods in sculptures in the round.

[1] Although found in a house, the sculpture has so many affinities with other temple statues of the period that it seems reasonable to suggest that it was originally used as a temple statue.

CAT. 134 *see color plate XXXV*

Horus as *Imperator*

Bronze, 46×28.6×6.6 (18 1/8×11 1/4×2 5/8)
First century A. D.
Provenance not known
London, Courtesy of the Trustees of the British Museum, 36062; Purchased 1868

Literature: A. Bowman 1986: 74, fig. 46.

This large and iconographically unusual bronze statuette represents a falcon-headed man in the costume of a Roman *imperator*, or general. The piece of cloth wrapped around his left arm ought to be interpreted as the *palludamentum*, a cloak reserved for generals and officers of superior rank, although its present configuration cannot be paralleled on known examples. The left fist is balled, rather than pierced, so that the attribute, which cannot be a lance, was held diagonally to the outstretched arm and may in fact have been supported by the now missing raised right arm. The *nemes* is so abbreviated that one wonders whether the craftsmen have here conflated its features with those of a striated wig and/or the misunderstood feathering of a falcon's head. The face, dominated by a large beak, is marked on either side with an inverted U-shaped design intended to recall the markings of a falcon (compare Brooklyn 05.394, Fazzini 1975: no. 99). The resultant image appears to be a thoroughly non-Egyptian adaptation of a motif frequently encountered in relief representations of the Ptolemaic Period (e.g., Cairo CG 22182, the Stela of the Satrap, Daumas in *Crépuscule*: fig. 67; and fig. 81, from the Temple of Horus at Edfu) and earlier (Daumas in *Crépuscule*: 89, where Seth is depicted in this scene from the Hypostyle Hall at the Temple of Hibis in Kharga; and Alexandria 20723, Riad *et al.* 1985: 72).

The pharaonic associations of Horus as a warrior (De Meulenaere 1969) were constantly evoked during the Ptolemaic but especially during the Roman Periods, when his initial popularity can be explained by the presence of the Roman legionnaires garrisoned in Egypt. Representations, such as this statuette, that depict the god Horus in the costume of a Roman commander would tend to support such a position. One must, however, never lose sight of the popularity of such deities among the native Egyptians themselves during this very same period. Quaegebeur (1983a: 48) has shown how those natives regarded Horus as an avenger whose intercession in the affairs of men was analogous to that of Nemesis. The subsequent appropriation of the image of Horus as the intercessory warrior by the early Christians in Egypt in their visual representations of saints (Rowe 1946: 43; Parlasca 1983: 157-58) and of Christ (Kákosy 1970: 24) can only be explained as an extension and development of Horus' capacity to intercede in the affairs of men. The genius of these anonymous theologians of the Early Church resided in their remarkable ability to synthesize. They were able to combine the intellectually pharaonic concept of Horus as an intercessor with the tangible trappings of a Roman general, their real life foe during the bloody persecutions of the third century A. D., in order to create a new visual image imbued with traditional, but somewhat altered, meaning. The process was certainly gradual and apparently coeval with the equally gradual transformation of the theriomorphic image of Horus into that of a man (Parlasca 1974; Hildesheim 2242, G. Grimm in Hildesheim 1979: no. 194, although it should be dated considerably later than the first century B. C.; compare Amsterdam 7802 and 7803, Parlasca 1974: pls. 86a-b).

The atypical rendering of the falcon's head and the aberrant form of the *nemes* might suggest a Roman workshop, but the misunderstanding in the form and function of the *palludamentum* and its apparent defiance of the laws of gravity speak for a pharaonic workshop. Since this impasse cannot be broken at this time, one is tentatively inclined to place the piece within the first century A. D. (pp. 77-80, above).

CAT. 135
Cat and Mouse Boxing

Terracotta, 17×13 (6 11/16×5 1/8)
First-second century A. D.
Said to be from Egypt
Copenhagen, Ny Carlsberg Glyptotek, AEIN 449

Literature: Mogensen 1922: 87-88.

As early as the late nineteenth century, Brugsch (1878) and, shortly thereafter, von Lauth (1879) recognized certain similarities between the visual representations of ancient Egyptian animal burlesques and the collective corpus of fables associated with the Greek Aesop (Brunner-Traut 1954; Morenz 1954a; Griffiths 1967, 1969). Whatever the relationships, if any, between these two genres (Curto 1965), the animal fable became a fixed feature in Egyptian culture by the time of the late New Kingdom (Capart 1939; Würfel 1953; Omlin 1973). Such depictions have been considered either within the larger context of the Egyptian literary sense of humor (Van de Walle

1969; Guglielmi 1979) or simply as expression of some native or popular traditions that are devoid of heavy satiric overtones (Brunner-Traut 1968). Whichever argument one supports, it is clear that such fables continued to be produced into Dynasty XXV, as the relief from Medamud indicates (Bisson de la Roque 1931: 73, fig. 54; Curto 1965: fig. 14; Del Francia 1985: 35). Thereafter, in the period between Dynasty XXVI and the Roman conquest of Egypt, such visual representations virtually disappear; they are revived, particularly in mosaics, later in the Roman Imperial Period (Mielsch 1986). The tradition of the animal fable appears, however, to have been continually maintained in the literary tradition (Graindor 1939: 37; Del Francia 1985: 33),[1] as demonstrated by the account by Eudoxos, the Greek author from the city of Cnidos (von Bissing 1949), of the Demotic tale of the vulture and the cat (Franzow 1931), and tales in randomly preserved papyri (Botti 1955; Yarkho 1985). The animals in CAT. 135 are indebted to this long Egyptian tradition, which was also the source for a fresco decorating a monastery at Bawit that humorously depicts the subservience of a delegation of mice before a cat (Cairo, Coptic Museum 8441, Maspero 1913; Badawi 1949: 62, fig. 45; Del Francia 1985).

The casting of this object as a two-piece mold (M. Allen 1985: 9, 51) that adheres to strict frontality (Castiglione 1967: 133-35; M. Allen 1985: 89), the composition of the clay, conforming to that associated with other Faiyumic terracottas (M. Allen 1985: 20), and the motifs of the scene itself certainly point to a dating between the first and second centuries A. D., particularly since there is a perceptible change in the style of Egyptian terracottas after 200 A. D. (Philipp 1972: 13-14).

The cat and mouse square off in an arena indicated both by the empty space between them and the raised viewing area from which the imperfectly preserved eagle, grasping a palm frond – the victor's trophy – regards the event. Although the interpretation of the scene is enigmatic, one can readily dismiss as unfounded the suggestion (Brunner-Traut 1977) that LSD played any role in the work's theme (Vycichl 1983). The attitude of the combatants, recalling that of modern boxers responding to the bell opening a round, has led some scholars to posit a Greek rather than an Egyptian source for the depiction because boxing was not common in ancient Egypt. However, the absence of gloves, which almost certainly would have been worn by Graeco-Roman boxers, and the attitude of the animals do recall the few pharaonic representations of fistfights (Decker 1987: 96) and allow for an Egyptian source for the scene. More important is the observation that the theme illustrated on this terracotta differs from almost every other cat and mouse representation in that neither animal has an advantage. Their attitudes and dimensions are identical. Any interpretation based on an inversion of ethical and/or moral values, on a reversal of the natural order of things, or on perceived juxtapositions of antipodes (Vycichl 1983) must be more fully examined, because the suggested opposing forces are in equilibrium. This equilibrium must be linked to a second observation, namely, that the Egyptian terracottas of the Roman Imperial Period are rarely secular in nature, those serving as children's toys being the only exceptions (Philipp 1972: 12). One might, therefore, consider this theme funereal, and interpret it as a recasting of the psychostasis, or weighing of the heart against the feather of Truth (compare CAT. 126). Throughout the history of Egyptian art, the depiction of the psychostasis in illustrated vignettes in the *Book of the Dead* relied on this equilibrium, as those judging looked on. This terracotta may, therefore, be a Romano-Egyptian version of that time-honored theme, particularly since the eagle may well represent ultimate, divine authority as Serapis (CAT. 104; and Mitten/Doeringer 1967: 278-79, no. 271), and the palm frond salvation, as an attribute of Anubis (Castelli 1979: fig. 9; Malaise 1972: frontis.; 1983: 98).

[1] The association of such scenes with the genre of Egyptian moralistic/didactic literature (Brunner-Traut 1968: 6) is exceedingly tenuous.

CAT. 136
Isis-in-Hydria (Isis-in-a-Jar)

Marble, 22.5×10.8 (8 7/16×4 1/4)
Second century A. D.
Provenance not known
Leiden, Rijksmuseum van Oudheden, F 97/4.1

Literature: Stricker 1943; H. Schneider/Raven 1981: no. 146.

Weber (1911), Panofsky (1961), and more recently R. Wild (1981: 102 and note 6) have admirably demonstrated that the popular designation of such objects as figures of Canopus, a putative deity of like name allegedly associated with the Delta site of Canopus, is unfounded. Such figures are in fact images of Osiris (Weber 1911; R. Wild 1981: 102), and occasionally either of Anubis or, as here, Isis (R. Wild 1981: 113-14 and note 83). The bodies of these composite objects are generally in the form of high-shouldered jars, or hydriai, associated with water (R. Wild 1981: 102, 113; Fouquet 1973: 66; Beinlich 1984: 302). The origin and development of this peculiar divine manifestation is debated, particularly since the earliest dated examples of such images occur on Roman coins of the second half of the first century A. D. (R. Wild 1981: 114). When such vessels were first studied, it was natural to apply the term "canopic jars", as a simple means of identification, that is, pharaonic vessels with human and/or theriomorphic heads in which selected internal organs of the deceased were placed (Fouquet 1973: 66; R. Wild 1981: 116, 156).[1]

Whether or not such traditional canopic jars affected the iconographic and/or symbolic development of the concept of the deity-in-hydria is moot, but the possibility cannot be excluded. The concept of a deity-in-a-vessel is fundamentally pharaonic, although admittedly fairly late, as embodied not only in such vases, but also in a select group of reliefs in Dendera, located in the central room of the East Osiris Chapel (PM VI: 98-100), whose ceiling contained the zodiac now in Paris (D 38). These reliefs represent the various nome deities of Egypt, each bearing a so-called canopic jar (Pantalacci 1986: pls. 39-40, without making this connection, illustrates six such jars), which Beinlich has treated in his monograph (1984; Traunecker 1972). At Dendera such a vessel, which is termed "a relic", itself as infelicitous a term as canopic jar, metaphysically contains that part of the body of Osiris associated with the nome; the nome, personified, bears the jar (Beinlich 1984: 80-81, 209-71). Such vessels are to be understood in terms of the Memphite Theology (Beinlich 1984: 269-71) and relate to the rites of fertility associated with Osiris and the images of the corn-god (Beinlich 1984: 272-89).

The Egyptian antecedents from which this particular visual expression evolved remain to be identified. The representations of Osiris-in-a-jar, which are clearly one part of the tradition fully manifest at Dendera (Beinlich 1984: 302), cannot have begun, as R. Wild argues (1981: 114), at some point during the first century B. C. Beinlich, pointing to the correspondences between the Memphite Theology and the ritual as preserved at Dendera, suggests, but does not insist upon, a Saite origin for this phenomenon (1984: 306). It has, however, been suggested that a cult of Osiris Hydrios is attested in Egypt during Dynasty XXX (Curto 1985: 47) and that the watery deity, Hydreios, existed on the island of Delos during the Hellenistic Period (Malaise 1983: 105 note 67). Until Malaise's announced study is published (Malaise 1983: 105 note 67), one should subscribe to the prevailing opinion that the visual representations of Osiris-in-hydria are an exclusively Roman phenomenon. At the present time, it is evident that this image was widespread in Egypt during the first century A. D., as indicated by the device on coins beginning with the reign of Galba (68-69 A. D.) (R. Wild 1981: 113-14), the reliefs from Dendera (Amer/Morardet 1983; Wilkinson 1984: 344), and a curious monument from Akhmim linking a Greek text with Egyptian images of deities-in-jars (Cairo JE 26093=CG 9267, Milne 1905: 48; Guéraud 1939; R. Wild 1981: 114-15, where the provenance "Alexandria" is in error; Beinlich 1984: 303-04). It is equally clear that a codified theology and a degree of standardization of the image of Isis-in-hydria (Fouquet 1973; R. Wild 1981: 116-17) were developed during the course of the second century A. D. (p. 80, above), to which period this example may be assigned.

The Isis-in-hydria phenomenon would seem to indicate a highly organized theological administration which presumably enabled some sort of Egyptian synod to communicate directly with members of their confraternity at the Imperial Court in Rome. The images of Osiris-in-hydria, which are more common than those of Isis-in-hydria, revolve around a complex thematic conceit, implied in the raised relief decoration characterizing these vessels. That decoration is associated with water, both as a source of life after death and as the means by which the faithful might conquer death (R. Wild 1981: 125-26). The body of Osiris is merged with that water, with the result that both effectively become one (R. Wild 1981: 127). The vessels either of Osiris- or Isis-in-hydria were therefore never intended to be containers. Since the devotees of Isis could make claims similar to those of Osiris regarding water symbolism by virtue of the association of these two deities, the head of Isis could quite comfortably be substituted for that of Osiris without lessening the efficacy of the ritual.

Each jar served (Beinlich 1984: 303) not only as a cult vase for the deity, which could be carried in procession with veiled hands (R. Wild 1981: 127), as indicated at Dendera (Pantalacci 1986: pls. 39-40) and in any number of Roman representations (Vatican, Cortile del Belvedere 55, R. Wild 1981: pls. XIII and *passim*), but could also function as one of the forms in which the deity itself could be worshiped, as the images from Luxor and Ras el Soda show. The smaller images may also have served the needs of individual tombs (R. Wild 1981: 123).

[1] I wish to thank Dr. M. J. Raven for commenting on a draft of this entry.

CAT. 137
A Roman Emperor in the Guise of Pharaoh

Basalt, 31.6×29×25 (12 7/16×11 7/16×9 13/16)
First century A. D.
Provenance not known
Paris, Musée du Louvre, Département des Antiquités Egyptiennes, A. 35 (N. 36)

Literature: Kyrieleis 1975: 177 [H12].

An assessment of this head must first take into consideration the modern restorations to the wings of the nose and both lappets, which adversely affect the appearance of the profile views. What remains, however, is a rather full-faced, ideal image characterized by subtle transitions between planes. The once inlaid eyes are set into sockets that form gentle depressions beneath the arched naturalistic brow, whose lines flow uninterruptedly into the planes of the root of the nose. The lips are thick and inorganic, and the chin is formulaically set off from the lower jaw by means of a horizontally created depression. These features, relegated to the front view, are so divorced from any repertoire of non-ideal physiognomic forms that the resulting image cannot be considered a representation of a specific ruler. Any comparisons with the *physkon*-type (CATS. 48, 53, 69) are gratuitous (Kyrieleis 1975: 75).

This head does, however, exhibit several anomalies. The absence of a tab on the *nemes* along the ear is not without precedent for the Ptolemaic Period (CAT. 52). The locks of hair on the brow were cut into a raised plane, whose lower ridge is still visible running from ear to ear (Mantua 20, Donatelli in Donatelli/Curto 1983: 47-48). Such a feature is invariably absent from the depictions of similar locks in other statues from the Ptolemaic Period (Brooklyn 54.117, ESLP: no. 135; CATS. 43, 52). The configuration and placement of the uraeus on the unadorned *nemes* is atypical for the pharaonic periods. The loops

are of different diameters, the left one being smaller, and the hood, in order to render it more prominent, is supported by an unexpected bridge of negative stone characteristic of Egyptianizing statues of the Roman Imperial Period (Dresden 33, Wenig 1977: fig. 90). The serpent's tail is arbitrarily truncated before it reaches the crown of the head. Elements of this approach to the uraeus are found on Egyptianizing statues of the Roman Imperial Period, as in CAT. 139 and a statue in the Vatican (101, Botti/Romanelli 1951: no. 161). More diagnostic is the treatment of the eyes, particularly of the lids as undefined planes within which the inlays were originally set. With regard to such lids and inlays, the Paris head comes closest to an Egyptianizing statue in Benevento associated with the Roman Emperor Domitian (260, H. Müller 1969: pl. VIII, 1). A first century A. D. dating for this head seems to be confirmed by the imprint of the tool marks at the juncture of the neck with the *nemes* and within the loops formed by the body of the uraeus; these marks recall those left on other Egyptianizing sculptures of the same century (Brooklyn 74.220, Bianchi 1980b: 10 and note 4). A dating within the first century A. D. for this head is thus consistent with the evidence, especially when one considers that the modeling of the face in such broad planes, the treatment of the lips, the upper in the shape of a cupid's bow, and the separation of the chin from the lower jaw by a depression seem to anticipate the more fully developed form of these features in CAT. 139.

CAT. 138

see color plate XXXVI

Egyptianizing Statue of a Roman Emperor as Pharaoh

Serpentine, 117×36.8×27.3 (46×14½×10¾)
Second century A. D., perhaps from the reign of Emperor Hadrian
Provenance not known
Collection of Charles Pankow and Heide Betz

Literature: Kamer 1975: 8-9.

This statue takes as its point of departure a type of Ptolemaic royal sculpture best exemplified by an example in the Barringer Collection (New Haven, 1.1.1953, G. Scott 1986: 165-67). Comparisons between the pose, the configuration of the pigtail of the *nemes*, and the shape of the back pillar reveal the dependency of this statue on pharaonic models. Moreover, the use of serpentine, a stone employed by the Egyptians but never on such a large scale for sculpture, is an indication of the extra-Egyptian origin of this statue, as are the narrow lappets of the *nemes*; the wide irregular shape of the kilt's belt, whose top and bottom edges are not parallel; and the form and configuration of the uraeus. Although the left fist is damaged, the shape of the break is such that one can reasonably conclude that both hands originally held a bolt of cloth (p. 70, above). The kilt, belt, and *nemes* are unadorned. The artist(s) responsible for the design of this statue fully understood the pharaonic artistic tenets for the creation of an ideal image. One need only compare its face to that of a bust in Brooklyn (CAT. 1) to understand how the naturalistic brow, slightly slanted, almond-shaped hieroglyphic eyes, characteristic nose, horizontal mouth with lips drawn into a slight smile, and the protruding chin, are within the best traditions of Sebennytic/Ptolemaic royal representations. The somewhat hard treatment of the eyelids and the lack of attention to the definition of their canthi betray a foreign hand. Although the form of the uraeus is based on known types (CATS. 53, 56), its hood is too decorative and conforms, in this respect, to the hoods of other Egyptianizing statues of the Roman Imperial Period (CATS. 137, 139). The most telling feature of a Roman hand is the treatment of the modeling of the torso, which is derived from the tripartition of Dynasty XXX (CAT. 24). A comparison with a limestone torso, assigned to the second to first centuries B. C. (CAT. 27), reveals the differences in these two approaches to such tripartition. Although both schools attempt to depict the swell of the lower abdomen at the level of the hips, the Roman Egyptianizing examples do not accentuate the region of the navel. As a result, such works rarely show the teardrop-shaped depression into the bottom of which is set the navel itself.

The dating of such Roman Egyptianizing statues is difficult to establish with certainty because of the absence of a precedent class of dated monuments. In general, examples from the first century A. D. tend to be less well-crafted adaptations (CAT. 111; Benevento 260 and 264, H. Müller 1969: pls. VIII,1, XIX; and XXI,1, respectively)[1] rather than more accurate reflections of pharaonic originals. The number of stylistically similar statues from the vicinity of Tivoli, now in the Vatican (71, 82, 93, 103, Botti/Romanelli 1951: nos. 158, 159, 160, 162, respectively) seem to confirm this dating.

The Roman artist(s) did not necessarily have to travel to Egypt in order to consult the models. Sanctuaries such as that of the Syrian Gods on the Janiculum in Rome contained Ptolemaic originals transported from Egypt to Italy. This particular site has yielded not only a draped male statue of Ptolemaic date (CAT. 30), but also a striding representation of Ptolemy in an ideal style wearing both *nemes* and kilt. Despite its inlaid eyes, the statue belongs to the type from which such Roman Egyptianizing images are ultimately derived (Rome, Museo Nazionale Romano 60921, Roullet 1972: fig. 182 = Leclant/Clerc 1974: pl. V).

[1] Despite the tentative suggestion of H. Müller (1969: 61-62) Benevento 264 bears no resemblance to any others identified as Caracalla (CAT. 140).

CAT. 139
Egyptianizing Statue of Antinous

Red marble (*rosso antico*), 135×46×42 (53 1/8×18 1/8×16 1/2)
Circa 135 A. D.
Tivoli, from Hadrian's Villa[1]
Munich, Wittelsbacher Ausgleichsfonds, Gl WAF 24

Literature: Roullet 1972: 86; Schoske/Wildung 1985: 128-30.

The association of this colossal figure with the villa of the Emperor Hadrian at Tivoli (Schoske/Wildung 1985: 130; Roullet 1972: 86) suggests that the statue represents Hadrian's favorite, Antinous (Sturtewagen/Bianchi 1982: 181-82). Many of the restorations, visible in earlier illustrations of this sculpture (Roullet 1972: fig. 116) have now been removed, with the exception of parts of the ears, nose, and mouth (Parlasca 1973: 96; Schoske/Wildung 1985: fig. 92; compare Roullet 1972: 86 and fig. 117). The choice of *rosso antico* has been regarded as a conscious attempt on the part of non-Egyptian sculptors working in Italy to imitate the darker, polychromatic stones used in pharaonic sculpture (Roullet 1972: 86). Those sculptors seem to have taken as their model a second colossal figure of Antinous, also from Hadrian's Villa and now in the Vatican collections (Sturtewagen/Bianchi 1982: 181-82; Roullet 1972: 87 and fig. 118).[2] The attitude of both images is that of a modified Polycleitan contrapposto, with the chest thrust forward and the arms held away from the sides of the body. Similar as well in both are the form and treatment of the kilt and its undecorated belt. The hand of the copyist in the Munich example is revealed in the mechanical rendering of the flesh bulging out over the belt, as well as in the forms of the navel and nipples. The *nemes* is misunderstood and maladroitly rendered.

The physiognomy of this statue, despite the repairs, is bland and idealizing, and as such has nothing in common with the individualized features of those Classical heads which have been identified as depictions of Antinous himself (Clairmont 1966; Sturtewagen/Bianchi 1982: 182). As a result, Kiss would tend to dismiss such indistinct Egyptianizing works as products of Roman exoticism bordering on bad taste (1984: 69-71), although he rightly regards the presence of a uraeus and *nemes* as suitable emblems for such depictions of Antinous (1975: 300). Given Hadrian's Villa as the provenance of both the Munich and Vatican examples, there can be little doubt that both represent Antinous. One should, however, as Parlasca cautions (1973: 96-97), refrain from identifying all such uninscribed representations of male figures with kilt and *nemes* from the Roman Period as depictions of Hadrian's favorite without additional supporting evidence.

Parlasca (1973: 96-97), followed by Kákosy (1983: 58), regards the kilt and *nemes* as attributes that impart Osirian overtones to images so adorned. While one may question how pervasive the acceptance of that symbolism was in extra-Egyptian contexts of the Roman Imperial Period in general (CAT. 138), the suggestion seems valid as it applies to these Egyptianizing images of Antinous. Hadrian's Egyptomania was not limited to the mere borrowing of the external trappings of ancient Egypt, as the hieroglyphic inscriptions on the obelisk erected in Italy for Antinous reveal (Derchain 1975). Certain cultural aspects in Italy during the reign of Hadrian, as in that of Augustus before him, were characterized by a genuine attempt to come to terms with the legacy of ancient Egypt.

[1] The statue was acquired in Paris from the collections of the Villa Albani (ESLP: 98) by Crown Prince Ludwig, who later became King Ludwig I of Bavaria.

[2] The principal figure in "La Fontaine de l'Egyptien" on the rue de Sèvres, Paris (Arsenault-Plessis 1969: 28 and fig. 13) is apparently based on one or both of these statues, in the same way that the waterspout in the form of a lion's head in that same fountain is modeled on the statues of the lions of Nectanebo I, now in the Vatican collections (Sturtewagen/Bianchi 1982: 178-79).

CAT. 140
Portrait of the Emperor Caracalla

Red granite, 51×37.5×52.2 (20 1/16×14 3/4×20 9/16)
211-217 A. D.
Found at the steps of the Temple of Isis at Coptos
Philadelphia, The University Museum, University of Pennsylvania, E. 976

Literature: Petrie 1896: 23; Stevenson 1895: 347-51; H. Jucker 1981 a: 721-22; Kiss 1984: 82.

Caracalla visited Egypt twice, once in 200 A. D. in the entourage of his father, Septimius Severus, and again as emperor between 211 and 217 A. D., at which time he unleashed his armies in a massacre lasting several days against the citizens of Alexandria who had mocked him by ridiculing his personal habits (Alcock 1982). Despite this unpleasant affair, Caracalla was a true Egyptophile (Malaise 1972: 439-42) and closely associated himself with the god Serapis (CAT. 104; Hornbostel 1973: 501-18). He restored the colossus of Memnon in Western Thebes (Bianchi 1980 a; E. Bowman *et al.* 1984; Sauneron 1952 a: 114), and ordered the removal of the name of Geta, his brother whom he had murdered, from the Temple of Khnum at Esna (Alliot 1946; Sauneron 1952 a: 111-12). That proscription may have also been accompanied by the wholesale destruction or appropriation of other Severan monuments, as suggested by Reinach regarding a seated statue from Coptos, originally intended for Commodus (Reinach 1913: 9-10). Whether as a result of such usurpations of the monuments of others, or of happenstance, Caracalla seems to have littered the Egyptian landscape with his image (H. Jucker 1981 a: 722).[1]

This colossal head, which seems to verge on caricature, deeply etches the demonic grimace of Caracalla into the granite (H. Jucker 1981 a: 721). Jucker relates the thick, globular forms of these heads to a similar development in Severan portraiture in Rome, but Kiss (1984) regards this head, and its congeners in Alexandria (G. Grimm in Hildesheim 1979: no. 172) and Cairo (Kiss 1984: 81), as products of a new style, perhaps better termed a new iconographic type (pp. 79-80, above), which Caracalla himself may have introduced to accommodate the established imperial image to prevailing Egyptian norms (Castiglione 1967: 110). Indeed, the adherence to line is certainly within pharaonic norms for sculpture, as is the treatment of the hair, only the foremost locks of which are finished (compare CAT. 43). The eyes themselves are sculpted at an angle to the frontal plane of the face so that they appear to be cast down toward a spectator. This peculiarity, which is intended to reduce the discrepancies of scale and space between the image and those who behold it, is characteristic of pharaonic Egyptian monumental sculpture and can best be compared to the analogous treatment of the eyes on the colossal statue of Ramesses II from Mitrahineh, once on view in Memphis, Tennessee (Freed 1987: 5, 7). The uraeus is decoratively treated, especially in the asymmetrical arrangement of one large loop, which would be exceptional for pharaonic monuments.

[1] See A. Bowman 1986: 170 for an account, from a temple at Arsinoe in the Faiyum, of the sale of iron removed from a machine used to erect such colossal statues.

Museums and Collections Cited

Listed below are the museums and collections cited in the text by city only.

City	*Museum*
Alexandria	Greco-Roman Museum
Amsterdam	Allard Pierson Museum
Ann Arbor	The Kelsey Museum of Archaeology, University of Michigan
Athens	National Archaeological Museum
Baltimore	Walters Art Gallery
Benevento	Museo del Sannio
Berlin/BRD	Staatliche Museen Preußischer Kulturbesitz, Ägyptisches Museum
Berlin/DDR	Staatliche Museen zu Berlin, Hauptstadt der DDR, Ägyptisches Museum und Papyrussammlung
Bologna	Museo Civico Archeologico di Bologna
Boston	Museum of Fine Arts
Brooklyn	The Brooklyn Museum
Brussels	Musées Royaux d'Art et d'Histoire
Bryn Athyn	Academy of the New Church Museum
Budapest	Szépmüvészeti Múzeum
Cairo	Egyptian Museum
Cambridge, England	Fitzwilliam Museum
Chercel	Musée Archéologique
Chicago, AI	Art Institute of Chicago
Chicago, OI	Oriental Institute Museum of the University of Chicago
Cleveland	The Cleveland Museum of Art
Como	Museo Civico Storico G. Garibaldi
Copenhagen	Ny Carlsberg Glyptotek
Dresden	Staatliche Kunstsammlungen Dresden
Edinburgh	The Royal Museum of Scotland
Frankfurt	Liebieghaus (Museum alter Plastik)
Glasgow	The Glasgow Art Gallery, Burrell Collection
Hamburg	Museum für Kunst- und Gewerbe
Hannover	Kestner-Museum
Hildesheim	Roemer- und Pelizaeus-Museum
Indianapolis	Indianapolis Museum of Art
Kansas City	William Rockhill Nelson Gallery of Art and Mary Atkins Museum of Fine Arts
Leningrad	The State Hermitage
Leiden	Rijksmuseum van Oudheden
Liverpool	Merseyside County Museums
London	The British Museum
Luxor	The Luxor Museum of Ancient Egyptian Art
Mantua	Museo Civico di Palazzo Te
Marseilles	Musée Borély
Moscow	Pushkin Museum of Fine Arts
Munich, ÄS	Staatliche Sammlung Ägyptischer Kunst München
Munich Gl WAF or WAF	Wittelsbacher Ausgleichsfonds
Naples	Museo Archeologico Nazionale di Napoli
New Haven	Yale University Art Galleries
New York	The Metropolitan Museum of Art
Omaha	Joslyn Memorial Art Museum
Paris	Musée du Louvre
Philadelphia	The University Museum, University of Pennsylvania
Stockholm	Medelhavsmuseet
Stuttgart	Württembergisches Landesmuseum, Antikensammlung
Thessalonike	Thessalonike Archaeological Museum
Toronto	Royal Ontario Museum
Tübingen	Sammlung des Ägyptologischen Instituts der Universität Tübingen
Turin	Museo Egizio di Torino
The Vatican	Museo Gregoriano Egizio
Venice	Museo Archeologico
Vienna	Kunsthistorisches Museum, Ägyptisch-Orientalische Sammlung
Würzburg	Martin-von-Wagner-Museum der Universität Würzburg

Abbreviations

AA	*Archäologischer Anzeiger*. Beiblatt zum *JDAI*.
AAASH	*Acta Antiqua Academiae Scientiarum Hungaricae*.
ABAW	Abhandlungen der Bayerischen Akademie der Wissenschaften. Munich.
AbhBerl	Abhandlungen der Deutschen Akademie der Wissenschaften zu Berlin. Klasse für Sprachen, Literatur und Kunst. Berlin/BRD.
ADAIK	Abhandlungen des Deutschen Archäologischen Instituts, Abteilung Kairo. Glückstadt.
ÄA	Ägyptologische Abhandlungen. Wiesbaden.
ÄAT	Ägypten und Altes Testament: Studien zu Geschichte, Kultur und Religion Ägyptens und des Alten Testaments. Wiesbaden.
ÄF	Ägyptologische Forschungen. Glückstadt.
Ägypten und Kusch	*Ägypten und Kusch*. Akademie der Wissenschaften der DDR. Zentralinstitut für alte Geschichte und Archäologie. Schriften zur Geschichte und Kultur des Alten Orients, 13. Eds. E. Endesfelder *et al.* Berlin/DDR.
AfO	*Archiv für Orientforschung*.
AH	Aegyptiaca Helvetica. Basel and Geneva.
AJA	*American Journal of Archaeology*.
ALEA	Archive of Late Egyptian Art. Bibliographic and photographic inventory maintained by R.S. Bianchi, New York.
Das alte Ägypten	*Das alte Ägypten*. Ed. C. Vandersleyen. Propyläen Kunstgeschichte, 15. Berlin/BRD, 1975.
AM	*Mitteilungen des Deutschen Archäologischen Instituts, Abteilung Athen*.
AMGR	*Annuaire du Musée Gréco-Romain*. Alexandria.
ANSMN	*American Numismatic Society Museum Notes*
AntK	*Antike Kunst*.
AntW	*Antike Welt*.
Artibus Aegypti	*Artibus Aegypti: Studia in honorem Bernardi V. Bothmer a collegis amicis discipulis conscripta*. Eds. H. De Meulenaere and L. Limme. Brussels, 1983.
ASAE	*Annales du Service des Antiquités de l'Egypte*.
ASAtene	*Annuario della Scuola Archeologica di Atene e delle Missioni Italiane in Oriente*.
ASE	Archaeological Survey of Egypt. London.
AT	Aegyptiaca Treverensia. Trierer Studien zum Griechisch-Römischen Ägypten. Mainz.
Aufstieg und Niedergang	*Aufstieg und Niedergang der Römischen Welt. Geschichte und Kultur Roms im Spiegel der neueren Forschung*. Eds. H. Temporini and W. Haase. Teil II: *Principat*. Bd. 12: *Künste*. 2 fascicles. Berlin/BRD, 1984. Bd. 17: *Heidentum: Römische Götterkulte, Orientalische Kulte in der Römischen Welt [Forts.]*. 4 fascicles. Berlin/BRD, 1984.
AV	Deutsches Archäologisches Institut, Abteilung Kairo. Archäologische Veröffentlichungen. Mainz.
BABesch	*Bulletin Antieke Beschaving*.
BAR	British Archaeological Reports. Oxford.
BASP	*Bulletin of the American Society of Papyrologists*.
BCH	*Bulletin de Correspondance Hellénique*.
BdE	Institut Français d'Archéologie Orientale. Bibliothèque d'Etude. Cairo.
BES	*Bulletin of the Egyptological Seminar*.
BIFAO	*Bulletin de l'Institut Français d'Archéologie Orientale*.
BiOr	*Bibliotheca Orientalis*.
BMA	*Brooklyn Museum Annual*.
BMFA	*Bulletin of the Museum of Fine Arts*.
BMMA	*Metropolitan Museum of Art Bulletin*.
BMQ	*British Museum Quarterly*.
BSAA	*British School in Athens Annual*.
BSAE	British School of Archaeology in Egypt.
BSEG	*Bulletin de la Société d'Egyptologie, Genève*.
BSFE	*Bulletin de la Société Française d'Egyptologie*.
BSRAA	*Bulletin de la Société Royale d'Archéologie d'Alexandrie*.
CAA	Corpus Antiquitatum Aegyptiacarum. Mainz.
CdE	*Chronique d'Egypte*.

CFETK — Centre Franco-Egyptien d'Etude des Temples de Karnak.

CGC — SAE. Catalogue Général des Antiquités Egyptiennes du Musée du Caire.

CMA Bulletin — *Bulletin of the Cleveland Museum of Art.*

CP — *Classical Philology.*

CRAIBL — *Comptes Rendus de l'Académie des Inscriptions et Belles-Lettres.*

Crépuscule — *L'Egypte du crépuscule.* L'univers des formes. Le monde égyptien: les pharaons. Ed. Jean Leclant. Paris, 1980.

CRIPEL — *Cahiers de Recherches de l'Institut de Papyrologie et d'Egyptologie de Lille.*

CW — *Classical World.*

DAIK — Deutsches Archäologisches Institut, Abteilung Kairo.

Dunham Studies — *Studies in Ancient Egypt, the Aegean, and the Sudan. Essays in Honor of Dows Dunham on the Occasion of his 90th Birthday, June 1, 1980.* Eds. W.K. Simpson and W.M. Davis. Boston, 1981.

EEF — Egypt Exploration Fund.

EES — Egypt Exploration Society.

Egypt and the Hellenistic World — *Egypt and the Hellenistic World. Proceedings of the International Colloquium, Leuven – 24-26 May 1982.* Eds. E. van 'T Dack *et al.* SH 27.

Egypte Eternelle — *Egypte Eternelle: Chefs d'œuvre du Brooklyn Museum.* Exh. cat. by H. De Meulenaere *et al.* Organized by the Service de la Diffusion des Arts, du Ministère de la Culture, Belgium. Brussels.

Eikones — *Eikones. Studien zum griechischen und römischen Bildnis. Hans Jucker zum sechzigsten Geburtstag gewidmet.* = Zwölftes Beiheft zur Halbjahresschrift *AntK.*

E.P.H.E. Ve Section. *Annuaire* — Ecole Pratique des Hautes Etudes. Ve Section – Sciences Religieuses. *Annuaire: Résumés des conférences et travaux.*

EPRO — Etudes préliminaires aux religions orientales dans l'empire romain. Leiden.

ESLP — B. V. Bothmer *et al., Egyptian Sculpture of the Late Period, 700 B.C. to A.D. 100.* Exh. cat. The Brooklyn Museum. Brooklyn, 1960.

EVO — *Egitto e Vicino Oriente.* Pisa.

Festschrift Ägyptisches Museum Berlin — *Festschrift zum 150jährigen Bestehen des Berliner Ägyptischen Museums, Berlin.* Mitteilungen aus der Ägyptischen Sammlung, 8. Berlin/DDR, 1974.

FIFAO — Fouilles de l'Institut Français d'Archéologie Orientale. Cairo.

FuB — *Forschungen und Berichte.*

5000 Jahre Ägypten — *5000 Jahre Ägypten – Genese und Permanenz pharaonischer Kunst.* Eds. J. Assmann and G. Burkard. Nussloch, 1983.

FuF — *Forschungen und Fortschritte.*

GGA — Göttinger Gelehrte Anzeiger. Göttingen.

GM — *Göttinger Miszellen.*

GOF — Göttinger Orientforschungen. Wiesbaden.

Gram. Dem. — *Grammata Demotika: Festschrift für Erich Lüddeckens zum 15. Juni 1983.* Eds. H.-J. Thissen and K.-Th. Zauzich. Würzburg, 1984.

HÄB — Hildesheimer Ägyptologische Beiträge. Hildesheim.

Hommages Vermaseren — *Hommages à Maarten J. Vermaseren. Recueil d'études offert par les auteurs de la série études préliminaires aux religions orientales dans l'empire romain à Maarten J. Vermaseren à l'occasion de son soixantième anniversaire, le 7 avril 1978,* 3 vols. Eds. M.B. de Boer and T.A. Eldridge. EPRO 68.

HSCP — *Harvard Studies in Classical Philology.*

IEJ — *Israel Exploration Journal.*

IFAO — Institut Français d'Archeólogie Orientale.

ILN — *Illustrated London News.*

JAOS — *Journal of the American Oriental Society.*

JARCE — *Journal of the American Research Center in Egypt.*

JBerlMus — *Jahrbuch der Berliner Museen.*

JDAI — *Jahrbuch des Deutschen Archäologischen Instituts.*

JEA — *Journal of Egyptian Archaeology.*

JEOL — *Jaarbericht van het Vooraziatisch-Egyptisch Genootschap "Ex Oriente Lux".* Leiden.

JHS — *Journal of Hellenic Studies.*

JKSW — *Jahrbuch der Kunsthistorischen Sammlungen in Wien.*

JNES — *Journal of Near Eastern Studies.*

JPK — *Jahrbuch Preußischer Kulturbesitz.*

JRS — *Journal of Roman Studies.*

JSSEA — *Journal of the Society for the Study of Egyptian Antiquities.*

Karnak — *Karnak V = Karnak V (1970-1972).* CFETK. Cairo, 1975.
Karnak VI = Cahiers de Karnak VI (1973-1977). CFETK. Cairo, 1980.
Karnak VII = Cahiers de Karnak VII. CFETK. Paris, 1982.

KölnJb — *Köln Jahrbuch für Vor- und Frühgeschichte.*

Kush — *Kush: Journal of the Sudan Antiquities Service.*

LÄ	*Lexikon der Ägyptologie.* 6 vols. Eds. H. W. Helck and W. Westendorf. Wiesbaden, 1975-1986.
MÄS	Münchner Ägyptologische Studien. Munich and Berlin/BRD.
MAFC	Mémoires publiés par les Membres de la Mission Archéologique Française au Caire. Paris and Cairo.
MDAIK	*Mitteilungen des Deutschen Archäologischen Instituts, Abteilung Kairo.*
Mélanges Mokhtar	*Mélanges Gamal Eddin Mokhtar.* 2 vols. BdE 97/1-2.
Meroitica 2	*Meroitic North and South. A Study in Cultural Contrasts.* Ed. W.Y. Adams. Berlin/DDR, 1976.
Meroitica 5	*Africa in Antiquity. The Arts of Ancient Nubia and the Sudan. Proceedings of the Symposium Held in Conjunction with the Exhibition, Brooklyn, September 29-October 1, 1978.* Ed. F. Hintze. Berlin/DDR, 1979.
Meroitica 6	*Meroitic Studies. Proceedings of the Third International Meroitic Conference. Toronto 1977.* Eds. N.B. Millet and A.L. Kelley. Berlin/DDR, 1982.
Meroitica 7	*Meroitische Forschungen 1980. Akten der 4. Internationalen Tagung für meroitische Forschungen vom 24. bis 29. November 1980 in Berlin.* Berlin/DDR, 1984.
MIFAO	Mémoires publiés par les membres de l'Institut Français d'Archéologie Orientale du Caire. Cairo.
MMJ	*The Metropolitan Museum Journal.*
Le monde grec	*Le monde grec. Pensée. Littérature. Histoire. Documents. Hommages à Claire Préaux.* Université Libre de Bruxelles. Faculté de Philosophie et Lettres. Eds. J. Bingen *et al.* Brussels, 1975.
MonPiot	*Monuments et mémoires publiés par l'Académie des Inscriptions et Belles-Lettres Fondation Eugène Piot.*
MPER	Mitteilungen aus der Papyrussammlung der Österreichischen Nationalbibliothek (Papyrus Erzherzog Rainer), Neue Serie. Vienna.
MüJb	*Münchner Jahrbuch der bildenden Kunst.*
MW	*Miscellanea Wilbouriana*, vol. I. Brooklyn, 1972.
NARCE	*Newsletter of the American Research Center in Egypt.*
Newsletter SSEA	*Newsletter of the Society for the Study of Egyptian Antiquities.*
NNM	Numismatic Notes and Monographs. New York.
OBO	Orbis Biblicus et Orientalis. Freiburg and Göttingen.
ÖJh	*Jahreshefte des Österreichischen Archäologischen Instituts in Wien.*
OIP	Oriental Institute Publications. Chicago.
OLA	Orientalia Lovaniensia Analecta. Louvain.
OLP	*Orientalia Lovaniensia Periodica.*
OLZ	*Orientalische Literaturzeitung.*
OMRO	*Oudheidkundige Mededelingen uit het Rijksmuseum van Oudheden te Leiden.*
OpAth	*Opuscula Atheniensia.*
Or	*Orientalia.*
OrAnt	*Oriens Antiquus.*
Parker Studies	*Egyptological Studies in Honor of Richard A. Parker. Presented on the Occasion of his 78th Birthday, December 10, 1983.* Ed. L. Lesko. Hanover, New Hampshire, and London, 1986.
PLB	Papyrologica Lugduno-Batava. Leiden.
PM	B. Porter and R.L.B. Moss. *Topographical Bibliography of Ancient Egyptian Hieroglyphic Texts, Reliefs, and Paintings.*
PM I,1	———. I: *The Theban Necropolis, Part 1: Private Tombs.* Oxford, 1960.
PM I,2^{2}	———. I: *The Theban Necropolis, Part 2: Royal Tombs and Smaller Cemeteries.* 2nd rev. ed. Oxford, 1964.
PM II^{2}	———. II: *Theban Temples*, 2nd rev. ed. Ed. J. Málek. Oxford, 1972.
PM III^{2},1	———. III: *Memphis, Part. 1. Abû Rawâsh to Abûsir.* 2nd rev. ed. Ed. J. Málek. Oxford, 1974.
PM III^{2},2	———. III: *Memphis, Part 2. Ṣaqqarâ to Dahshûr.* 2nd rev. ed. 3 fascicles. Ed. J. Málek. Oxford, 1978-81.
PM IV	———. IV: *Lower and Middle Egypt.* Oxford, 1934.
PM V	———. V: *Upper Egypt.* Oxford, 1937.
PM VI	———. VI: *Upper Egypt: Chief Temples, Excluding Thebes.* Oxford, 1939.
PM VII	———. VII: *Nubia, The Deserts, and Outside Egypt.* Oxford, 1951.
Das ptol. Äg.	*Das ptolemäische Ägypten. Akten des internationalen Symposions 27.-29. September 1976.* Eds. H. Maehler and V.M. Strocka. Mainz, 1978.
RA	*Revue Archéologique.*
RAPH	IFAO. Recherches d'Archéologie, de Philologie et d'Histoire. Cairo.
RdE	*Revue d'Egyptologie.*
Religions	*Religions en Egypte hellénistique et romaine. Colloque de Strasbourg 16-18 mai 1967.* Ed. Ph. Derchain. Paris, 1969.

La Revue du Louvre	*La Revue du Louvre et des Musées de France.*
RHR	*Revue de l'Histoire des Religions.*
RM	*Mitteilungen des Deutschen Archäologischen Instituts, Abteilung Rom.*
Das röm.-byz. Ägypt.	*Das römisch-byzantinische Ägypten. Akten des internationalen Symposions 26.-30. September 1978 in Trier.* Eds. G. Grimm *et al.* AT 2.
RSO	*Rivista degli Studi Orientali.*
RT	*Recueil de Travaux Relatifs à la Philologie et à l'Archéologie Egyptiennes et Assyriennes.*
SAE	Service des Antiquités de l'Egypte.
SAK	*Studien zur altägyptischen Kultur.*
SAOC	Studies in Ancient Oriental Civilization. Chicago.
Schrijvend Verleden	*Schrijvend Verleden. Documenten uit het Oude Nabije Oosten vertaald en toeglicht.* Ed. K. Veenhof. Mededelingen en Verhandelingen van het Vooraziatisch-Egyptisch Genootschap "Ex Oriente Lux", 24. Leiden.
SH	Studia Hellenistica. Louvain.
SNG Copenhagen	*Sylloge Nummorum Graecorum. The Royal Collection of Coins and Medals, Danish Royal Museum.* Copenhagen.
Studi Adriani	*Alessandria e il mondo ellenistico-romano: Studi in onore di Achille Adriani.* 3 vols. Rome, 1983-84. 1 = *Studi e Materiali* 4 (1983). 2 = *Studi e Materiali* 5 (1984). 3 = *Studi e Materiali* 6 (1984).
Studia Naster	*Studia Paulo Naster Oblata.* I: *Numismatica Antiqua.* Ed. S. Scheers. II: *Orientalia Antiqua.* Ed. J. Quaegebeur. OLA 13.
Studies in Classical Art and Archaeology	*Studies in Classical Art and Archaeology: A Tribute to Peter Heinrich von Blanckenhagen.* Eds. G. Kopcke and M. B. Moore. Locust Valley, New York.
SV	J. Svoronos, *Ta nomismata tou kratous ton Ptolemaion.* 3 vols. Athens, 1904 (German translation of vol. 1, with commentaries, published as vol. 4. Athens, 1908).
Syncrétismes	*Les syncrétismes dans les religions grecques et romaines.* Paris, 1973.
UGAÄ	Untersuchungen zur Geschichte und Altertumskunde Ägyptens. Leipzig.
VA	*Varia Aegyptiaca.*
VDI	*Vestnik Drevnei Istorii.*
Wepwawet	*Wepwawet. Papers in Egyptology.*
YCS	*Yale Classical Studies.*
ZÄS	*Zeitschrift für Ägyptische Sprache und Altertumskunde.*
ZDMG	*Zeitschrift der Deutschen Morgenländischen Gesellschaft.*
ZPE	*Zeitschrift für Papyrologie und Epigraphik.*

Works Cited

Abd el Al *et al.* 1985 — Abd el Hafeez Abd el Al *et al. Stèles funéraires de Kom Abu Bellou.* Editions Recherche sur les Civilisations, Mémoire 55. Paris.

Abd el Raziq 1968 — Mahmud Abd el Raziq. "Study on Nectanebo Ist in Luxor Temple and Karnak." *MDAIK* 23, 156-59.

1984 — ———. *Die Darstellungen und Texte des Sanktuars Alexanders des Großen im Tempel von Luxor.* AV 16.

Abitz 1979 — F. Abitz. *Statuetten in Schreinen als Grabbeigaben in den ägyptischen Königsgräbern der 18. und 19. Dynastie.* ÄA, 35.

N. Adams 1987 — N. Adams. "The Furnishings and Ritual Objects of a Newly Discovered Temple from Qasr Ibrim, Nubia." In *Program and Abstracts of the Annual Meeting of the American Research Center in Egypt, Memphis, Tennessee, April 1987,* 20-21.

W. Adams 1981 — W.Y. Adams. "Ecology and Economy in the Empire of Kush." *ZÄS* 108, 1-11.

Adriani 1940 — A. Adriani. "Sanctuaire de l'époque romaine à Ras el-Soda." *AMGR* 2 (1935-39), 136-48.

1952 — ———. "Nouvelles découvertes dans la nécropole de Hadra." *AMGR* 3 (1940-50), 1-27.

1960 — ———. "Il vaso argenteo di Ingolstadt e un suo modello alessandrino." *RM* 67, 111-25.

1961 — ———. *Repertorio d'arte dell'Egitto greco-romano,* Ser. A., vol. II. Palermo.

1965 — ———. "Appunti su alcuni aspetti del grottesco alessandrino." In *Gli archeologi italiani in onore di Amedeo Maiuri a cura del Centro Studi Ciociaria.* Cava di Tirreni, 37-62.

1966 — ———. *Repertorio d'arte dell'Egitto greco-romano,* Ser. C, 2 vols. Palermo.

1967 — ———. "Un vetro dorato alessandrino dal Caucaso." *BSRAA* 42, 105-27.

1970 — ———. Ritratti dell'Egitto greco-romano." *RM* 77, 72-109.

1972 — ———. *Lezioni sull'arte alessandrina.* Naples.

1978 — ———. "Il negretto di Chalon-sur-Saône e la statuina Dimitriu." *AM* 93, 119-31.

Aimé-Giron 1926 — N. Aimé-Giron. "Réfection du mur d'enceinte du grand temple de Dendérah sous Tibère." *ASAE* 26, 109-12.

Alcock 1982 — A. Alcock. "Persecution under Septimius Severus." *Enchoria* 11, 1-5.

Aldred 1949 — C. Aldred. *Old Kingdom Art in Ancient Egypt.* London.

1952 — ———. *The Development of Ancient Egyptian Art from 3200 to 1315 B.C.* London.

1956 — ———. "The Carnarvon Statuette of Amun." *JEA* 42, 3-7.

1962 — ———. Rev. of ESLP in *AJA* 66, 207-09.

1973 — ———. *Akhenaten and Nefertiti.* Exh. cat. The Brooklyn Museum.

1978 — ———. "The Temple of Dendur." *BMMA* 36/1, 1-80.

M. Allen 1985 — M.L. Allen. "The Terracotta Figurines from Karanis: A Study of Technique, Style, and Chronology in Fayoumic Coroplastics." PhD diss. University of Michigan, Ann Arbor.

T. Allen 1974 — T. Allen. *The Book of the Dead or Going Forth by Day. Ideas of the Ancient Egyptians Concerning the Hereafter as Expressed in Their Own Terms.* SAOC 37.

Alliot 1946 — M. Alliot. "Les rites de la chasse au filet, aux temples de Karnak, d'Edfou, et d'Esneh." *RdE* 5, 57-118.

1951 — ———. "La Thébaïde en lutte contre les rois d'Alexandrie sous Philopator et Epiphane (216-184)." *Revue Belge de Philologie et d'Histoire* 29, 421-43.

1954 — ———. *Le culte d'Horus à Edfou au temps des Ptolémées,* 2 vols. BdE 20.

Altenmüller 1981 — H. Altenmüller. "Amenophis I. als Mittler." *MDAIK* 37, 1-7.

Altenmüller/Hornbostel 1982 — H. Altenmüller and W. Hornbostel. *Das Menschenbild im alten Ägypten. Porträts aus vier Jahrtausenden.* Exh. cat. organized by INTERVERSA Gesellschaft für Beteiligungen mbH, Hamburg.

Amelung 1908 — W. Amelung. *Die Skulpturen der Vatikanischen Museen,* vol. II. Rome.

Amer/Morardet 1983 — Hassan Ibrahim Amer and B. Morardet. "Les dates de la construction du temple majeur d'Hathor à Dendara à l'époque gréco-romaine." *ASAE* 69, 255-58.

D'Amicone 1985 — E. D'Amicone. "Cowrie-Shells and Pearl-Oysters: Two Iconographic Repertoires of Middle Kingdom Gold-Work." *BSEG* 9-10, 63-70.

Andrews 1981 — C. Andrews. *The Rosetta Stone.* London.

Andronicos *et al.* 1975 — M. Andronicos *et al. The Greek Museums.* Athens.

Anthes 1937 — R. Anthes. "Der Berliner Hocker des Petamenophis." *ZÄS* 73, 25-35.

1939a — ———. "Das Berliner Henat-Relief." *ZÄS* 75, 21-31.

1939b — ———. "Sitzung am 2. Mai 1939." *AA* 54, 376-402.

Apuleius — Apuleius. *The Golden Ass.* See Schnur 1962.

———. *Isiaca.* See Griffiths 1975.

Arsenault-Plessis 1969 — Arsenault-Plessis. "Le Paris Impérial." *Plaisirs de France* 64, 24-29.

Assmann 1973 — J. Assmann. *Grabung im Asasif 1963-1970,* vol. II: *Das Grab des Basa (Nr. 389) in der thebanischen Nekropole.* AV 6.

1983 — ———. "Einführung: Die Gestalt der Zeit in der ägyptischen Kunst." In *5000 Jahre Ägypten,* 11-32.

Aubert 1967 — J.-F. Aubert. "Deux masques de plâtre présumés d'Apriès." *CdE* 42, 281-96.

Aubert/Aubert 1974 — J.-F. Aubert and L. Aubert. *Statuettes égyptiennes: chaouabtis, ouchebtis.* Paris.

Badawi 1949 — A. Badawi. *L'Art Copte. Les influences égyptiennes.* Cairo.

Bagnall 1981 — R.S. Bagnall. "Egypt, the Ptolemies and the Greek World." *BES* 3, 5-21.

1982 — ———. "Papyrology and Ptolemaic History, 1956-1980." *CW* 76, 13-21.

1985 — ———. "Publius Petronius, Augustan Prefect of Egypt." *YCS* 28, 85-93.

Baines 1976 — J. Baines. "Temple Symbolism." *Royal Anthropological Institute News* 15, 10-15.

Baldus 1983 — H. R. Baldus. "Eine Münzprägung auf das Ehepaar Mark Anton-Kleopatra VII." *Schweizer Münzblätter* 33, no. 129, 5-10.

Balty 1984 — J. Balty. "Thèmes nilotiques dans la mosaïque tardive du Proche-Orient." In *Studi Adriani* 3, 827-34.

Baratte 1986 — F. Baratte. *Le trésor d'orfèvrerie romaine de Boscoreale.* Paris.

Barguet 1953 — P. Barguet. "L'origine et la signification du contrepoids de collier de collier-menat." *BIFAO* 52, 103-11.

1954 — ———. "Quelques fragments nouveaux au nom de Nekhthorheb." *Kêmi* 13, 87-91.

1959 — ———. "Bas-reliefs inédits de Karnak au Musée du Louvre et au Musée Borély à Marseille." *La Revue des Arts. Musées de France* 9, 2-8.

1961 — ———. "Bas-reliefs provenant de Karnak au Musée du Louvre." *La Revue du Louvre* 11, 1-4.

1962 — ———. *Le temple d'Amon-Rê à Karnak: Essai d'exégèse.* RAPH 21.

1967 — ———. *Le livre des morts des anciens Egyptiens.* Paris.

1977 — ———. "Le cycle lunaire d'après deux textes d'Edfou." *RdE* 29, 14-20.

Barguet/Leclant 1954 — P. Barguet and J. Leclant. *Karnak-Nord IV (1949-1951).* FIFAO 25.

Barocas 1972 — C. Barocas. *Monuments of Civilization: Egypt.* New York.

1974 — ———. "Les statues 'réalistes' et l'arrivée des Perses dans l'Egypte saïte." In *Gururājamañjarikā. Studi in onore di Giuseppe Tucci.* Naples, 113-61.

Barone 1984 — G. Barone. "Due modelli di gesso del Museo Greco-Romano di Alessandria." In *Studi Adriani* 2, 329-33.

Barr-Sharrar 1985 — B. Barr-Sharrar. "The Anticythera Fulcrum Bust: A Portrait of Arsinoë III." *AJA* 89, 689-92.

1987 — ———. *The Hellenistic and Early Imperial Decorative Bust.* Mainz.

Barsanti 1900 — A. Barsanti. "Tombeau de Zannehibou." *ASAE* 1, 262-71.

1901 — ———. "Tombeau de Péténéit." *ASAE* 2, 97-104.

1904 — ———. "Le tombeau de Hikaoumsaf." *ASAE* 5, 69-78.

Barta 1974 — W. Barta. "Der Terminus *twt* auf den Grenzstelen Sesostris III. in Nubien." In *Festschrift Ägyptisches Museum Berlin,* 51-54.

1984 — ———. "Zur Bedeutung des Stirnband-Diadems *sšd.*" *GM* 72, 7-8.

Baud 1978 — M. Baud. *Le caractère du dessin en Egypte ancienne.* Paris.

Beaud forthcoming — R. Beaud. "Offrande des colliers et des plaques pectorales dans les temples d'époque gréco-romaine: iconographie et textes."

Becher 1966 — I. Becher. *Das Bild der Kleopatra in der griechischen und lateinischen Literatur.* Berlin/DDR.

1976 — ———. "Augustus und Dionysos — Ein Feindverhältnis?" *ZÄS* 103, 88-101.

von Beckerath 1984 — J. von Beckerath. *Handbuch der ägyptischen Königsnamen.* MÄS 20.

Beinlich 1984 — H. Beinlich. *Die "Osirisreliquien": zum Motiv der Körperzergliederung in der altägyptischen Religion.* ÄA 42.

E. Bell 1915 — E. Bell. *The Architecture of Ancient Egypt: A Historical Outline.* London.

L. Bell 1985a — L. Bell. "Aspects of the Cult of the Deified Tutankhamun." In *Mélanges Mokthar*, vol. I, 31-59.

1985b — ———. "Luxor Temple and the Cult of the Royal *Ka*." *JNES* 44, 251-94.

Berger 1962 — E. Berger. *Antike Kunstwerke; Neuerwerbungen 1961*. Staatliche Kunstsammlungen Kassel.

Bergman 1968 — J. Bergman. *Ich bin Isis: Studien zum memphitischen Hintergrund der griechischen Isisaretologien*. Acta Universitatis Upsaliensis, Historia-Religionum, 3. Uppsala.

Berlandini 1979 — J. Berlandini. "Petits monuments royaux de la XXIe à la XXVe dynastie." In *Hommages à la mémoire de Serge Sauneron, 1927-1976*, vol. I: *Egypte pharaonique*. BdE 81, 89-114.

1980 — ———. "Une stèle d'Horus sur les crocodiles du supérieur des prêtres de Sekhmet, Padiimennebnesouttaouy." In *Karnak VI*, 235-45.

1983 — ———. "La déesse bucéphale: une iconographie particulière de l'Hathor memphite." *BIFAO* 83, 33-50.

1984 — ———. "La chapelle de Séthi I. Nouvelles découvertes: les déesses *Ismt* et *Mn-nfr*." *BSFE* 99, 28-52.

Berlin 1899 — Königliche Museen zu Berlin. *Ausführliches Verzeichnis der ägyptischen Altertümer und Gipsabgüsse*.

Berlin/DDR 1976 — Staatliche Museen zu Berlin/DDR. *Kleiner Führer durch die Ausstellung des Ägyptischen Museums*.

1981 — ———. *Kleiner Führer durch die Ausstellung des Ägyptischen Museums*. Rev. ed.

Bernand 1969 — E. Bernand. *Inscriptions métriques de l'Egypte gréco-romaine: recherches sur la poésie épigrammatique des Grecs en Egypte*. Paris.

1975 — ———. *Recueil des inscriptions grecques du Fayoum*, vol. 1: *La "Méris" de Hérakleidès*. Leiden.

1981a — ———. *Recueil des inscriptions grecques du Fayoum*, vol. 2: *La "Méris" de Thémistos*. BdE 79.

1981b — ———. *Recueil des inscriptions grecques du Fayoum*, vol. 3. *La "Méris" de Polémôn*. BdE 80.

Besques 1984 — S. Besques. "Un nouveau fragment d'œnochoé ptolémaïque en faïence." In *Studi Adriani* 2, 273-76.

Bianchi 1976 — R. S. Bianchi. "Flower and Fetish: Two Identifications." In "1975 Annual Meeting Abstracts of Papers." *NARCE* 95, 3.

1978 — ———. "Erotic Representations in Ancient Egyptian Art." In *The Archaeological Institute of America, Abstracts 3, Thirtieth General Meeting. Vancouver, British Columbia, December 28-30, 1978*, 22.

1979a — ———. *Ancient Egyptian Sculpture from the Brooklyn Museum*. Exh. cat. Fundación Arqueológica, Antropológica e Histórica de Puerto Rico, San Juan.

1979b — ———. "Ex-Votos of Dynasty XXVI." *MDAIK* 35, 15-22.

1979c — ———. "Ptolemaic Influences on the Arts of the Late Napatan and Early Meroitic Periods." *Meroitica* 5, 65-70.

1980a — ———. "Memnonskolosse." *LÄ* 4, 23-24.

1980b — ———. "Not the Isis Knot." *BES* 2, 9-31.

1981 — ———. "Two Ex-Votos from the Sebennytic Group." *JSSEA* 11, 31-36.

1982a — ———. "The Egg-Heads: One Type of Generic Portrait from the Egyptian Late Period." In *Römisches Porträt: Wege zur Erforschung eines gesellschaftlichen Phänomens. Wissenschaftliche Konferenz 12.-15. Mai 1981 = Wissenschaftliche Zeitschrift der Humboldt-Universität zu Berlin* 2/3, 149-51.

1982b — ———. "Perser in Ägypten." *LÄ* 4, 943-951.

1983a — ———. "Satrapenstele." *LÄ* 5, 492-93.

1983b — ———. "Those Ubiquitous Glass Inlays from Pharaonic Egypt: Suggestions about Their Functions and Dates." *Journal of Glass Studies* 25, 29-35.

1983c — ———. "Those Ubiquitous Glass Inlays, Part II." *BES* 5, 9-29.

1985 — ———. Rev. of Reinsberg 1980. *JEA* reviews supplement 71, 59-60.

1986a — ———. Rev. of Castel *et al.* 1984. *JAOS* 106, 829-830.

1986b — ———. "Tuch el-Qaramus." *LÄ* 6, 777-78.

forthcoming — ———. "Ptolemaic Uses and Abuses of Ramesside Monuments." In *Proceedings of the International Symposium on Ramesses the Great, April 20-23, 1987, Memphis State University*.

Bieber 1961 — M. Bieber. *The Sculpture of the Hellenistic Age*, 2nd ed. New York.

Bierbrier 1982 — M. Bierbrier. *The Tomb-Builders of the Pharaohs*. London.

Bietak/Reiser-Haslauer *et al.* 1978 — M. Bietak and E. Reiser-Haslauer *et al. Das Grab des 'Anch-Hor, Obersthofmeister der Gottesgemahlin Nitokris*, vol. I. Untersuchungen der Zweigstelle Kairo des Österreichischen Archäologischen Instituts, IV. = Österreichische Akademie der Wissenschaften. Denkschriften der Gesamtakademie, VI. Vienna.

Bingen 1970 — J. Bingen. "Grecs et Egyptiens d'après PSI 502." In *Proceedings of the XII. International Congress of Papyrologists*. Toronto, 35-40.

von Bissing 1895 — F. von Bissing. "Sur une statue de la collection Barracco." *RT* 17, 105-13.

1896 — ———. "Ein Kopf des Museo Civico in Venedig." *RT* 18, 132-44.

1914 ———. *Denkmäler ägyptischer Sculptur.* Munich.

1922 ———. "Ein Kultbild des Hermer-Thot." *ZÄS* 57, 79-86.

1923 ———. "Die Datierung des griechisch-ägyptischen Grabes von Mellaui." *OLZ* 26, 1-4.

1937 ———. "Sul tipo dei sistri trovati nel Tevere." *BSRAA* 9/31, 211-24.

1949 ———. "Eudoxos von Knidos' Aufenthalt in Ägypten und seine Übertragung ägyptischer Tierfabeln." *FuF* 25, 225-30.

Bisson de la Roque 1924 F. Bisson de la Roque. *Rapport sur les fouilles d'Abou Roasch (1922-1923).* FIFAO 1.

1931 ———. *Rapport sur les fouilles de Médamoud (1930), Première Partie: Les Fouilles.* FIFAO 8.

Bisson de la Roque *et al.* 1928 F. Bisson de la Roque *et al. Rapport sur les fouilles de Médamoud (1927).* FIFAO 5/1.

Bleeker 1963 C. J. Bleeker. "Isis as a Saviour-Goddess." In *The Saviour God: Comparative Studies in the Concept of Salvation Presented to Edwin Oliver James.* Ed. S.G.F. Brandon. Manchester, England, 1-16.

1973 ———. *Hathor and Thoth. Two Key Figures of the Ancient Egyptian Religion.* Studies in the History of Religions (Supplements to *Numen*), 26. Leiden.

Blok 1927 H. P. Blok. "Het huis der Leeuwen in Leontopolis." *BABesch* 2/2, 10-13.

Blomfield 1905 R.M. Blomfield. "Alexandria Topography: The Arsinoeum and Its Obelisk." *BSRAA* 8, 27-45.

Blümel 1968 C. Blümel. "Stuckfrisuren an Köpfen griechischer Skulpturen des sechsten und fünften Jahrhunderts vor Chr." *RA*, 11-24.

Boardman 1964 J. Boardman. *The Greeks Overseas.* Baltimore.

Boeser 1915 P. A. A. Boeser. *Beschreibung der ägyptischen Sammlung des niederländischen Reichsmuseums der Altertümer in Leiden,* vol. 7: *Die Denkmäler der saïtischen, griechisch-römischen und koptischen Zeit.* The Hague.

Bol 1981 P. Bol. *Liebieghaus – Museum alter Plastik. Guide to the Collection. Ancient Art.* Frankfurt.

Bonacasa 1961 N. Bonacasa. "Per l'iconografia di Tolomeo IV." *ASAtene* 37/38 (1959-60), 367-80.

1971 ———. *Due note sul ritratto romano imperiale dell'Egitto.* Palermo.

Bonhême/Forgeau 1988 M.-A. Bonhême and A. Forgeau. *Pharaon: Les secrets du Pouvoir.* Paris.

Bonicatti 1963 M. Bonicatti. *Chefs-d'œuvre de l'art, I: de la naissance de l'art à l'Egypte ancienne.* Paris.

Bonneau 1964 D. Bonneau. *La crue du Nil: divinité égyptienne, à travers mille ans d'histoire (332 av.-641 ap. J.-C.).* Paris.

Bonnet 1961 H. Bonnet. "Herkunft und Bedeutung der naophoren Statue." *MDAIK* 17, 91-98.

Borchardt 1925 L. Borchardt. *Statuen und Statuetten von Königen und Privatleuten im Museum von Kairo (CGC 1-1294),* vol. 2. Berlin.

1930 ———. vol. 3. Berlin.

1934 ———. vol. 4. Berlin.

1937 ———. *Denkmäler des Alten Reiches (außer den Statuen) im Museum von Kairo (CGC 1295-1808),* vol. 1. Berlin.

Borghouts 1983 J. Borghouts. "Het aanbieden van de Lotus: een laategyptische Tempelrite." In *Schrijvend Verleden,* 253-62.

Bosse 1936 K. Bosse. *Die menschliche Figur in der Rundplastik der ägyptischen Spätzeit von der XXII. bis zur XXX. Dynastie.* ÄF 1.

Bosse-Griffiths 1975 K. Bosse-Griffiths. Rev. of D.B. Thompson 1973. *JEA* 61, 291-92.

Bosticco 1972 S. Bosticco. *Museo Archeologico di Firenze. Le stele egiziane di epoca tarda.* Cataloghi dei Musei e Gallerie d'Italia. Rome.

Boston 1982 Museum of Fine Arts, Boston. *Egypt's Golden Age: The Art of Living in the New Kingdom, 1558-1085 B.C.* Exh. cat. by E. Brovarski, S. Doll, R. Freed, *et al.*

Bothmer 1952a B. V. Bothmer. "Ptolemaic Reliefs I: A Granite Block of Philip Arrhidaeus." *BMFA* 50, 19-27.

1952b ———. "Ptolemaic Reliefs II: Temple Decorations of Ptolemy I Soter." *BMFA* 50, 49-56.

1953a ———. "Ptolemaic Reliefs III: Deities from the Time of Ptolemy II Philadelphus." *BMFA* 51, 2-7.

1953b ———. "Ptolemaic Reliefs IV: A Votive Tablet." *BMFA* 51, 80-84.

1954 ———. "Scope and Progress of the Corpus of Late Egyptian Sculpture." In *Proceedings of the Twenty-Third International Congress of Orientalists. Cambridge. 21st-28th August 1954.* Ed. D. Sinor. London, 69-70.

1964 ———. "A Brooklyn Head on a Cairo Statue: The Egyptian Priest Wesir-Wer." *BMA* 4 (1962-63), 42-51.

1970 ———. "Apotheosis in Late Egyptian Sculpture." *Kêmi* 20, 37-48.

1978 ———. "On Photographing Egyptian Art." *SAK* 6, 51-53.

1985 ———. "The Brussels-Brooklyn Statue of Bakenrenef (Membra Dispersa VI)." In *Mélanges Mokhtar,* vol. 1, 99-103.

1987 ———. "Egyptian Antecedents of Roman Republican Verism." In *Ritratto Ufficiale e Ritratto Privato. Atti II Conferenza Internazionale sul Ritratto Romano = Quaderni de 'La Ricerca scientifica'* n.116. Rome, 47-65.

Bothmer/Keith 1974 — B. V. Bothmer and J. Keith. *Brief Guide to the Department of Egyptian and Classical Art.* The Brooklyn Museum.

Bothmer/De Meulenaere 1986 — B. V. Bothmer and H. De Meulenaere. "The Brooklyn Statuette of Hor, Son of Pawen (with an Excursus on Eggheads)." In *Parker Studies,* 1-15.

von Bothmer 1983 — D. von Bothmer. "Echoes from Egypt." In *Artibus Aegypti,* 15-23.

1984 — ———. "A Greek and Roman Treasury." *BMMA* 42, 1-72.

Botti 1899 — G. Botti (Sr.). "L'Apis de l'empereur Adrien trouvé dans le Sérapéum d'Alexandrie." *BSRAA* 2, 27-36.

Botti 1955 — G. Botti (Jr.). "Quello che anche l'Egittologia deve a Carlo Anti." In *Anthemon: Scritti di Archeologia e di Antichità Classiche in onore di Carlo Anti.* Florence, 1-6.

Botti/Romanelli 1951 — G. Botti (Jr.) and P. Romanelli. *Le sculture del Museo Gregoriano Egizio.* Monumenti Vaticani di archeologia e d'arte... a cura della Direzione Generale dei Musei e Gallerie Pontificie e della Pontificia Accademia Romana di Archeologia, 9. Vatican City.

du Bourguet 1971 — P. du Bourguet. *Coptic Art.* London.

Bourriau 1986 — J. Bourriau. "Museum Acquisitions, 1984. Egyptian Antiquities Acquired in 1984 by Museums in the United Kingdom." *JEA* 72, 179-84.

Bowersock 1984 — G. W. Bowersock. "The Miracle of Memnon." *BASP* 21, 31.

A. Bowman 1986 — A. K. Bowman. *Egypt after the Pharaohs, 332 B.C.-A.D. 642, from Alexander to the Arab Conquest.* Berkeley and London.

C. Bowman 1978 — C. Bowman, III. "The Goddess 'Anatu in the Ancient Near East." PhD diss. Graduate Theological Union. Berkeley.

E. Bowman *et al.* 1984 — E. Bowman *et al.* "The Northern Colossus of Memnon: new slants." *Archaeometry* 26, 218-99.

Bowron 1983 — E. P. Bowron, ed. *Introduction to the Collections.* Ackland Art Museum, University of North Carolina at Chapel Hill. Chapel Hill.

Braat/Klasens 1968. — W. Braat and A. Klasens. *Artefact. 150 jaar Rijksmuseum van Oudheden, 1818-1968. Een keuze uit de verzamelingen.* Leiden.

Brady 1978 — T. A. Brady. In *Serapis and Isis: Collected Essays.* Ed. C. F. Mullet. Chicago.

Brashear 1980 — W. M. Brashear. *Ptolemäische Urkunden aus Mumienkartonnage.* Ägyptische Urkunden aus den Staatlichen Museen Berlin. Griechische Urkunden, 14. Berlin/BRD.

Braunert 1952 — H. Braunert. "Auswärtige Gäste am Ptolemäerhofe: zu den sogenannten Hadra-Vasen." *JDAI* 65/66 (1950-51), 231-63.

Breasted 1936 — J. H. Breasted. *Geschichte Ägyptens.* Vienna.

Breccia 1915 — E. Breccia. "Ghirlandomania alessandrina." In *Le Musée égyptien: recueil de monuments et de notices sur les fouilles d'Egypte,* vol. 3. Ed. G. Maspero. Cairo, 13-25.

1922 — ———. *Alexandria municipality. Alexandrea ad Aegyptum: a guide to the ancient and modern town and to its Graeco-Roman museum.* Bergamo.

Brendel 1953 — O. J. Brendel. "Two Acquisitions of Egyptian Art." *Bulletin of the Art Association of Indianapolis/John Herron Art Institute* 40, 5-8.

1962 — ———. "The Iconography of Marc Antony." In *Hommages à Albert Grenier = Collection Latomus* 58, 359-67.

Brentjes 1977 — B. Brentjes. "Eine Glaspaste-Statuette aus der ehemaligen Golenischeff-Sammlung." In *Ägypten und Kusch,* 97.

Bresciani 1960 — E. Bresciani. "Una statua in 'abito persiano' al Museo del Cairo." *Studi Classici e Orientali* 9, 109-18.

1967 — ———. "Una statua della XXVI dinastia con il cosidetto 'abito persiano'." *Studi Classici e Orientali* 16, 273-80.

1976 — ———. "Rapporto preliminare delle campagne di scavo 1968 e 1969." In E. Bresciani and D. Foraboschi. *Missione di scavo a Medinet Madi (Fayum-Egitto).* Milan.

1978 — ———. In E. Bresciani *et al. Il tempio tolemaico di Isi ad Assuan.* Biblioteca di studi antichi, 16. Pisa, 11-152.

1980 — ———. *Kom Madi 1977 e 1978: Le pitture murali del cenotafio di Alessandro Magno.* Supplemento a *EVO* 2 (1979), Serie Archeologica I, 3-68.

1983a — ———. "Un Nouveau Texte Démotique daté du 28 Nov. 304 a. J.-C. à Deir el Bahari." *MDAIK* 39, 103-05.

1983b — ———. "Registrazione catastale e ideologia politica nell'Egitto tolemaico. A completamento di 'La spedizione di Tolomeo II in Siria in un ostrakon demotico inedito da Karnak'." *EVO* 6, 15-31.

1983c — ———. In E. Bresciani *et al. Saqqara,* vol. I: *Tomba di Boccori. La galleria di Padineit, visir di Nectanebo I.* Supplemento a EVO 3 (1980).

1985 — ———. *Le stele egiziane del Museo civico archeologico di Bologna.* Cataloghi delle collezione del Museo civico archeologico di Bologna.

1986 — ———. "Tra Egitto e Roma: Aspetti della cultura egiziana in rapporto col mondo romano." In *Gli interscambi culturali e socio-economici fra l'Africa settentrionale e l'Europa mediterranea: Atti del Congresso Internazionale di Amalfi, 5-8 dicembre 1983.* Naples, 83-96.

Brett 1955 A. B. Brett. *Catalogue of Greek Coins. Museum of Fine Arts.* Boston.

Brilliant 1971 R. Brilliant. "On Portraits." *Zeitschrift für Ästhetik und Allgemeine Kunstwissenschaft* 16, 11-20.

1979 ———. "Africa and the Arts of Greece and Rome." *Meroitica* 5, 55-64.

Brinks 1983 J. Brinks. *Die Löwentempel von Naqá in der Butana (Sudan)*, vol. II: *Baubeschreibung*. Eds. H. Gaube and W. Röllig. Beihefte zum Tübinger Atlas des Vorderen Orients, Reihe B (Geisteswissenschaften), 48/2. Wiesbaden.

van den Broek 1978 R. van den Broek. "The Sarapis Oracle in Macrobius, *Sat.*, I, 20, 16-17." In *Hommages Vermaseren* I, 123-41.

Broekhuis 1971 J. Broekhuis. *De godin Renenwetet.* Assen, The Netherlands.

Brooklyn 1983 The Brooklyn Museum. *Neferut net Kemit: Egyptian Art from the Brooklyn Museum.* Exh. cat. organized for Japanese venues.

1987 ———. *The Collector's Eye: The Ernest Erickson Collections at the Brooklyn Museum.* Exh. cat. by L. S. Ferber *et al.*

Brown 1975 R. B. Brown. "A Provisional Catalogue of and Commentary on Egyptian and Egyptianizing Artifacts Found on Greek Sites." PhD diss., University of Minnesota, Minneapolis.

Brugsch 1878 H. Brugsch. "Aesopische Fabeln in einem ägyptischen Papyrus." *ZÄS* 16, 47-50.

Brunelle 1976 E. Brunelle. *Die Bildnisse der Ptolemäerinnen.* Frankfurt.

Brunner 1958 H. Brunner. "Der König im Falkenkleid." *ZÄS* 83, 74-75.

1962 ———. "Nochmals der König im Falkenkleid." *ZÄS* 87, 76-77.

1970 ———. "Die Sonnenbahn in ägyptischen Tempeln." In *Archäologie und Altes Testament. Festschrift für Kurt Galling zum 8. Januar 1970.* Eds. A. Kuschke and E. Kutsch. Tübingen, 27-34.

1982 ———. "Die Rolle von Tür und Tor im alten Ägypten." *Symbolon* 6, 37-59.

Brunner-Traut 1954 E. Brunner-Traut. "Der Katzenmäusekrieg im Alten und Neuen Orient." *ZDMG* 104, 347-51.

1968 ———. *Altägyptische Tiergeschichte und Fabel: Gestalt und Strahlkraft.* Darmstadt.

1971 ———. "Ein Königskopf der Spätzeit mit dem 'Blauen Helm' in Tübingen." *ZÄS* 97, 18-30.

1977 ———. "Der Katzmäusekrieg – Folge von Rauschgift." *GM* 25, 47-51.

1980 ———. "Lotus." *LÄ* 3, 1091-96.

Brunner-Traut/Brunner 1981 E. Brunner-Traut and H. Brunner. *Die Ägyptische Sammlung der Universität Tübingen.* Mainz.

Brunner-Traut *et al.* 1984 E. Brunner-Traut *et al. Osiris.Kreuz.Halbmond.* Exh. cat. organized by the Landeshauptstadt Stuttgart. Mainz.

Brussels 1985 Brussels, Musées Royaux d'Art et d'Histoire. *La femme au temps des pharaons: six œuvres d'art de la collection égyptienne des Musées Royaux d'Art et d'Histoire.* Exh. cat. by L. De Roy and A. Rammant-Peeters.

Bruyère 1952 B. Bruyère. *Rapport sur les fouilles de Deir el Médineh (1935-1940).* FIFAO 20/3.

1953 ———. *Rapport sur les fouilles de Deir el Médineh (Années 1948 à 1951).* FIFAO 26.

Budge 1909a E.A.W. Budge. *A Guide to the Egyptian Collections in the British Museum.* London.

1909b ———. *British Museum. A Guide to the Egyptian Galleries (Sculpture).* London.

1914 ———. *Egyptian Sculptures in the British Museum.* London.

Buhl 1955 M.-L. Buhl. "Remarks on a Group of Late Egyptian Faience Vases." *Acta Archaeologica* 26, 188-97.

Buitron 1979 D.A. Buitron. In Walters Art Gallery, Baltimore. *Jewelry. Ancient to Modern.* New York, 72-93.

Burkhalter 1984 F. Burkhalter. "Moulages en plâtre antiques et toreutique Alexandrine." In *Studi Adriani* 2, 334-47.

Burstein 1979 S. M. Burstein. "The Nubian Campaigns of C. Petronius and George Reisner's Second Meroitic Kingdom of Napata." *ZÄS* 106, 95-105.

1982 ———. "Arsinoe II Philadelphos: A Revisionist View." In *Philip II, Alexander the Great and the Macedonian Heritage.* Eds. W. L. Adams and E. N. Borza. Washington, D.C., 197-212.

Buschor 1949 E. Buschor. *Das hellenistische Bildnis.* Munich.

1960 ———. *Das Porträt. Bildniswege und Bildnisstufen in fünf Jahrtausenden.* Munich.

Buttrey 1954 T. V. Buttrey, Jr. "*Thea Neotera* on Coins of Antony and Cleopatra," *ANSMN* 6, 95-109.

Byvanck-Quarles van Ufford 1958 L. Byvanck-Quarles van Ufford. "Le trésor de Tarente." *BABesch* 33, 43-52.

Callaghan 1978 P. Callaghan. "Excavations at a Shrine of Glaukos." *BSAA* 73, 1-30.

1984 ———. "Knossian Artists and Ptolemaic Alexandria." In *Studi Adriani* 3, 789-94.

Cambridge, Massachusetts 1954 Cambridge, Massachusetts, Fogg Art Museum. *Ancient Art in American Private Collections: A Loan Exhibition at the Fogg Art Museum of Harvard University*... Exh. cat.

Canby 1979 J. V. Canby. In Walters Art Gallery, Baltimore. *Jewelry. Ancient to Modern.* New York, 10-51.

Cantu 1978 G. Cantu. *Les mystères de l'archéologie: la civilisation des pharaons. Réalité et magie dans l'Egypte de l'antiquité.* Paris.

Capart 1922 J. Capart. *L'art égyptien,* vol. I: *L'architecture.* Brussels and Paris.

1931 ———. *Documents pour servir à l'étude de l'art égyptien,* vol. 2. Paris.

1939 ———. "Enquêtes: les fables d'animaux." *CdE* 14, 340-41.

1941 ———. "Téos, prêtre et roi?" *Académie Royale de Belgique. Bulletin de la Classe des Lettres et des Sciences Morales et Politiques,* 5e sér., 27, 3-13.

1944 ———. "Sur un texte d'Hérodote." *CdE* 19, 219-27.

Carcopino 1958 J. Carcopino. *Passion et politique chez les Césars.* Paris.

Carducci 1965 C. Carducci. "Un bronzetto egiziano trovato ad Aosta." In *Gli archeologi italiani in onore di Amedeo Maiuri.* Rome, 119-26.

Careddu 1985 G. Careddu. *La Collezione Egizia. Museo Barracco di scultura antica.* Rome.

Carter 1984 J. Carter. "The Date of the Altar at Priene and Its Reliefs." In *Studi Adriani* 3, 748-64.

Castel *et al.* 1984 G. Castel *et al. Dendara – Monuments de l'enceinte sacrée: les fontaines de la porte nord.* Cairo.

Castelli 1979 P. Castelli. *I geroglifici e il mito dell'Egitto nel rinascimento.* Florence.

Castiglione 1958 L. Castiglione. "La statue de culte hellénistique du Sarapieion d'Alexandrie." *Bulletin du Musée national hongrois des Beaux-Arts* 12, 17-39.

1967 ———. "Kunst und Gesellschaft im römischen Ägypten." *AAASH* 25, 107-34.

1974 ———. "Zwei verschollene Reliefs aus der Römerzeit." In *Festschrift Ägyptisches Museum Berlin,* 465-72.

1978 ———. "Nouvelles données archéologiques concernant la genèse du culte de Sarapis." In *Hommages Vermaseren* I, 208-32.

1984 ———. "Sarapis-Gesichter. Ein Versuch die Ikonographie des Gottes zu vermehren." In *Studi Adriani* 1, 139-45.

Cauville 1983 S. Cauville. "*irt:* un nom de la situle?" *RdE* 34, 137.

1984 ———. *Edfou.* Les guides archéologiques de l'Institut Français du Caire. Cairo.

1987 ———. *Essai sur la théologie du temple d'Horus à Edfou.* BdE 102, 2 vols.

Cauville/Devauchelle 1984 S. Cauville and D. Devauchelle. "Le temple d'Edfou: étapes de la construction. Nouvelles données historiques." *RdE* 35, 31-55.

1985 ———. *Le temple d'Edfou,* vol. XV. MAFC 32.

Cerfaux/Tondriau 1957 L. Cerfaux and J. Tondriau. *Le culte des souverains dans la civilisation gréco-romaine.* Bibliothèque de Théologie, III/5. Tournai.

Cesaretti 1985 M. P. Cesaretti. "Nerone a el-Maharraqa." In *Studi in onore di Edda Bresciani.* Eds. S. F. Bondi *et al.* Pisa, 119-25.

Champollion 1835 J.-F. Champollion. *Monuments de l'Egypte et de la Nubie,* vol. I. Paris.

Chassinat 1897 E. Chassinat. *Le temple d'Edfou,* vol. I. MAFC 10.

1901 ———. "Une monnaie d'or à légendes hiéroglyphiques trouvée en Egypte." *BIFAO* 1, 78-86.

1910 ———. "Une nouvelle monnaie à légende hiéroglyphique." *BIFAO* 7, 165-67.

1923 ———. "Les trouvailles de monnaies égyptiennes à légendes hiéroglyphiques." *RT* 40, 131-57.

1934a ———. *Le temple de Dendara,* vols. I-II. Cairo.

1934b ———. *Le temple d'Edfou,* vol. XIV. MAFC 31.

1947-52 ———. *Le temple de Dendara,* vol. V/1-2. Cairo.

1960 ———. *Le temple d'Edfou,* vol. X/2. MAFC 27.

1968 ———. *Le mystère d'Osiris au mois de Khoiak,* vol. II. Cairo.

Chassinat/Daumas 1978 E. Chassinat and F. Daumas. *Le temple de Dendara,* vol. VIII. Cairo.

Cheshire 1982 W. Cheshire. "Zur Deutung eines Szepters der Arsinoe II. Philadelphos." *ZPE* 48, 105-11.

Chevereau 1985 P.-M. Chevereau. *Prosopographie des cadres militaires égyptiens de la Basse Epoque: carrières militaires et carrières sacerdotales en Egypte du XIe au IIe siècle avant J.-C.* Dijon.

Chevrier 1929 H. Chevrier. "Rapport sur les travaux de Karnak." *ASAE* 29, 133-49.

1951 ———. "Rapport sur les travaux de Karnak, 1950-1951." *ASAE* 51, 549-64.

Clairmont 1966 C. W. Clairmont. *Die Bildnisse des Antinous: Ein Beitrag zur Porträtplastik unter Kaiser Hadrian.* Bibliotheca Helvetica Romana 6. Bern.

Clarke/Engelbach 1930 S. Clarke and R. Engelbach. *Ancient Egyptian Masonry: The Building Craft.* London.

Clarysse 1985 W. Clarysse. "Greeks and Egyptians in the Ptolemaic Army and Administration." *Aegyptus* 65, 57-66.

1986 ———. "Le mariage et le testament de Dryton en 150 avant J.-C." *CdE* 61, 99-103.

1987 ———. "Greek Loan-Words in Demotic." In *Aspects of Demotic Lexicography: Acts of the Second International Conference for Demotic Studies, Leiden, 19-21 September 1984.* Ed. S. P. Vleeming. Louvain, 9-33.

Clarysse/Van der Veken 1983 W. Clarysse and G. Van der Veken. *The Eponymous Priests of Ptolemaic Egypt (P. L. Bat. 24): Chronological Lists of the Priests of Alexandria and Ptolemais with a Study of the Demotic Transcriptions of their Names.* PLB 24. Leiden.

Clerc 1978 G. Clerc. "Isis-Sothis dans le monde romain." In *Hommages Vermaseren* I, 247-81.

J. Clère 1934 J.-J. Clère. "A propos des monuments de Haroua." *BIFAO* 34, 129-33.

1969 ———. "Propos sur un corpus des statues sistrophores égyptiennes." *ZÄS* 96, 1-4.

1983 ———. "Une statuette du vizir Bakenrénef." In *Artibus Aegypti,* 25-33.

P. Clère 1961 P. Clère. *La porte d'Evergète à Karnak,* vol. 2: Planches. MIFAO 84/2.

Coche-Zivie 1984 C. M. Coche-Zivie. "Sphinx." *LÄ* 5, 1139-47.

Cook 1970 B. F. Cook. "A Dated Hadra Vase in the Brooklyn Museum." *BMA* 10 (1968-69), 114-38.

1984 ———. "Some Groups of Hadra Vases." In *Studi Adriani* 3, 795-803.

Cooney 1956 J. D. Cooney. *Five Years of Collecting Egyptian Art, 1951-1956.* Exh. cat. The Brooklyn Museum.

1967 ———. "Gods Bearing Gifts for the King." *CMA Bulletin* 54, 279-89.

1971 ———. "Medley of Bulls." *CMA Bulletin* 58, 10-19.

Corteggiani 1981 J.-P. Corteggiani. *Centenaire de l'Institut Français d'Archéologie Orientale. Musée du Caire, 8 Janvier-8 Février 1981.* Exh. cat. Cairo, Egyptian Museum.

D. Crawford 1980 D. J. Crawford. "Ptolemy, Ptah and Apis in Hellenistic Memphis." In D. J. Crawford, J. Quaegebeur, W. Clarysse. *Studies on Ptolemaic Memphis.* SH. 24, 1-42.

1983 ———. "Hellenistic Memphis: City and Necropolis." In *Studi Adriani* 1, 16-24.

M. Crawford 1974 M. H. Crawford. *Roman Republican Coinage,* 2 vols. London.

O. Crawford/Addison 1951 O. G. S. Crawford and F. Addison. *Abu Geili and Saqadi & Dar el Mek.* Wellcome Excavations in the Sudan, 3. Oxford.

Cruz-Uribe 1987 E. Cruz-Uribe. "Hibis Temple Project: Preliminary Report, 1985-1986 and Summer 1986 Field Seasons." *VA* 3, 215-30.

Curtius 1933 L. Curtius. "Ikonographische Beiträge zum Porträt der römischen Republik und der julisch-claudischen Familie, IV. Kleopatra VII. Philopator." *RM* 48, 182-92.

Curto 1965 S. Curto. *La satira nell'antico Egitto.* Museo Egizio di Torino, Quaderno 1.

1978 ———. "Statua egittizzante nel Museo delle Terme." *SAK* 6, 55-61.

1985 ———. *Le sculture egizie ed egittizzanti nelle Ville Torlonia in Roma.* EPRO 105.

Czuma 1985 S. J. Czuma. *Kushan Sculpture: Images from Early India.* Exh. cat. The Cleveland Museum of Art.

Daressy 1908 G. Daressy. "Construction d'un temple d'Apis par Nectanébo Ier." *ASAE* 9, 154-57.

Daszewski 1985 W.A. Daszewski. *Corpus of Mosaics from Egypt,* vol. I: *Hellenistic and Early Roman Period.* AT 3.

Dattari 1905 G. Dattari. "Comments on a Hoard of Athenian Tetradrachms Found in Egypt." *Journal International d'Archéologie numismatique* 8, 103-14.

Daumas 1956 F. Daumas. "La valeur de l'or dans la pensée égyptienne." *RHR* 149, 1-17.

1958 ———. *Les mammisis des temples égyptiens.* Annales de l'Université de Lyon, 3ème Sér., Lettres, fasc. 32. Paris.

1959 ———. *Les mammisis de Dendara.* Cairo.

1970 ———. "Les objets sacrés de la déesse Hathor à Dendara." *RdE* 22, 62-78.

1975a ———. "Flachbildkunst der Spätzeit." In *Das alte Ägypten,* 325-38.

1975b ———. "Hathor." *LÄ* 2, 1024-33.

1977 ———. "Le problème de la monnaie dans l'Egypte antique avant Alexandre." *Mélanges de l'Ecole Française de Rome. Antiquité* 89, 426-42.

Davidson/Oliver 1984 P. F. Davidson and A. Oliver. *Ancient Greek and Roman Gold Jewelry in the Brooklyn Museum.* = Wilbour Monographs VIII. Brooklyn.

N. Davies 1953 N. de Garis Davies. *The Metropolitan Museum of Art Egyptian Expedition. The Temple of Hibis in El Khargeh Oasis,* vol. III: *The Decoration.* New York.

W. Davies 1982 W.V. Davies. "The Origin of the Blue Crown." *JEA* 68, 69-76.

Dawson/Uphill 1972 W. R. Dawson and E. P. Uphill. *Who Was Who in Egyptology,* 2nd rev. ed. London.

Day 1967 C. L. Day. *Quipus and Witches' Knots: The Role of the Knot in Primitive and Ancient Cultures.* Lawrence, Kansas.

Dayton 1981 J. E. Dayton. "Appendix D: Faience." In G. Martin *et al.* 1981, 135-37.

Decker 1987 W. Decker. *Sport und Spiel im Alten Ägypten.* Beck's Archäologische Bibliothek. Munich.

Demarée 1983 R. J. Demarée. *The 3ḫ iḳr n R*^{c} *Stelae: On Ancestor Worship in Ancient Egypt.* Egyptologische uitgaven 3. Leiden.

Demel 1936 H. Demel. "Einige ägyptische Porträtköpfe der Spätzeit." *JKSW* 10, 1-8.

Dennison 1905 W. Dennison. "A New Head of the So-called Scipio Type: An Attempt at its Identification." *AJA* 9, 11-43.

Derchain 1955 Ph. Derchain. "La couronne de la justification: essai d'analyse d'un rite ptolémaïque." *CdE* 30, 225-87.

1961 ———. *Zwei Kapellen des Ptolemäus I Soter in Hildesheim.* Zeitschrift des Museums zu Hildesheim 13.

1962 ———. *Rites égyptiens I: Le sacrifice de l'oryx.* Brussels.

1972 ———. *Hathor quadrifrons: recherches sur la syntaxe d'un mythe égyptien.* Publications de l'Institut Historique et Archéologique de Stamboul, 28. Istanbul.

1974 ———. "Miettes, 4: Homère à Edfou." *RdE* 26, 15-19.

1975 ———. "A propos de l'obélisque d'Antinous." In *Le monde grec,* 808-13.

1981 ———. "Appendix K: Observations sur les erotica." In G. Martin *et al.* 1981, 166-70.

1985 ———. "Une mention méconnue de Ptolémée 'le fils'." *ZPE* 61, 35-36.

Derksen 1978 J. J. V. M. Derksen. "Isis and Serapis on Lamps from North Africa." In *Hommages Vermaseren* I, 296-304.

Deschênes 1978 G. Deschênes. "Isis Thermouthis: à propos d'une statuette dans la collection du Professeur M. J. Vermaseren." In *Hommages Vermaseren* I, 305-15.

Desroches-Noblecourt 1947 C. Desroches-Noblecourt. "Une coutume égyptienne méconnue." *BIFAO* 45, 185-232.

1952 ———. "Hommage d'un poète à la princesse lointaine." *Kêmi* 12, 34-45.

1953 ———. "'Concubines du mort' et mères de famille au Moyen Empire: à propos d'une supplique pour une naissance." *BIFAO* 53, 7-47.

1975 ———. "Musée du Louvre. Département des Antiquités Égyptiennes. Les récentes acquisitions." *La Revue du Louvre* 25, 248-54.

Desroches-Noblecourt *et al.* 1981 C. Desroches-Noblecourt *et al. Un siècle de fouilles françaises en Egypte, 1880-1980.* Exh. cat. Paris, Musée du Louvre.

Devauchelle 1983a D. Devauchelle. Rev. of Reymond 1981. *CdE* 58, 135-45.

1983b ———. "Les graffites démotiques du toit du temple d'Edfou." *BIFAO* 83, 123-31.

1986 ———. "Wasseruhr." *LÄ* 6, 1156-57.

Devéria 1881 Th. Devéria. *Catalogue des manuscrits égyptiens écrits sur papyrus, toile, tablettes et ostraca en caractères hiéroglyphiques, hiératiques, démotiques, grecs, coptes, arabes et latins qui sont conservés au Musée égyptien du Louvre.* Paris; repr. Hildesheim 1980.

Dewachter 1983 M. Dewachter. "Remarques à propos d'un bas-relief ptolémaïque détruit: le bloc Boulogne Inv. 117.2." In *Artibus Aegypti,* 45-50.

1985 ———. "A propos du temple de Thoth à Karnak Nord." *RdE* 36, 175-77.

van Dijk 1980 J. van Dijk. "The birth of Horus according to the Ebers Papyrus." *JEOL* 26, 10-25.

1983 ———. "A Ramesside Naophorous Statue from the Teti Pyramid Cemetery." *OMRO* 64, 49-60.

1986 ———. "ᶜAnat, Seth and the Seed of Preᶜ." In *Scripta Signa Vocis: Studies about Scripts, Scriptures, Scribes and Languages in the Near East, presented to J. H. Hospers by his pupils, colleagues and friends.* Eds. H. Vanstiphont *et al.* Groningen, 31-51.

Dittmar 1986 J. Dittmar. *Blumen und Blumensträuße als Opfergabe im alten Ägypten.* MÄS 43.

Dohrn 1985 T. Dohrn. "Schwarzgefirnißte Plakettenvasen." *RM* 92, 77-106.

Donadoni 1981 S. Donadoni, *L'Egitto.* Storia Universale dell'Arte. Sezione Prima. Le civiltà antiche e primitive. Turin.

Donadoni-Roveri 1978 A. M. Donadoni-Roveri. "Due vasi imperiali di faience al Museo Egizio di Torino." In *Hommages Vermaseren* I, 316-21.

Donatelli/Curto 1983 L. Donatelli and S. Curto. *La raccolta egizia di Giuseppe Acerbi.* Mantua.

Drerup 1950 H. Drerup. "Aegyptische Bildnisköpfe griechischer und römischer Zeit." *Orbis Antiquus* 3, 1-28.

Drioton 1939 E. Drioton. "Une statue prophylactique de Ramsès III." *ASAE* 39, 57-89.

Dumbrell 1971 W. J. Dumbrell. "The Tell el-Maskhuṭa Bowls and the 'Kingdom' of Qedar in the Persian Period." *BASOR* 203, 33-44.

Dunand 1980 F. Dunand. "Fête, tradition, propagande: Les cérémonies en l'honneur de Bérénice, fille de Ptolémée III, en 238 a. C." In *Livre du Centenaire, 1880-1980.* MIFAO 104, 287-301.

1983 ———. "Culte royal et culte impérial en Egypte. Continuités et ruptures." In *Das röm-byz. Ägypt.,* 47-56.

Dunham 1929 D. Dunham. "Three Inscribed Statues in Boston." *JEA* 15, 164-66.

1950 ———. *The Royal Cemeteries of Kush,* vol. I: *El Kurru.* Boston.

1957 ———. *The Royal Cemeteries of Kush,* vol. IV: *Royal Tombs at Meroë and Barkal.* Boston.

Duthuit 1931 G. Duthuit. *La sculpture copte: statues, bas-reliefs, masques.* Paris.

Eaton-Krauss 1981 M. Eaton-Krauss. "The Dating of the 'Hierakonpolis Falcon'." *GM* 42, 15-18.

Edgar 1903 C. C. Edgar. *Greek Sculpture (CGC 27425-27630).*

1906 ———. *Sculptors' Studies and Unfinished Works (CGC 33301-33506).*

1911 ———. "Notes from the Delta, II: The Temple of Samanoud." *ASAE* 11, 90-96.

Edwards 1960 I. E. S. Edwards. "An Egyptian Plaster Cast." *BMQ* 22, 27-29.

Eggebrecht 1966 A. Eggebrecht. "Zur Bedeutung des Würfelhockers." In *Festgabe für Dr. Walter Will, Ehrensenator der Universität München, zum 70. Geburtstag am 12. November 1966*. Cologne, 143-63.

Eggebrecht *et al.* 1984 A. Eggebrecht *et al., Das alte Ägypten: 3000 Jahre Geschichte und Kultur des Pharaonenreiches*. Munich.

Eigner 1984 D. Eigner. *Die monumentalen Grabbauten der Spätzeit in der thebanischen Nekropole*. Untersuchungen der Zweigstelle Kairo des Österreichischen Archäologischen Institutes VI = Österreichische Akademie der Wissenschaften. Denkschriften der Gesamtakademie, VIII. Vienna.

Elie-Lefèbre 1979 M.-N. Elie-Lefèbre. "La couronne bleue ou khépresh: évolution de la forme." *Revue des archéologues et historiens d'art de Louvain* 12, 246-47.

Emery 1970 W. B. Emery. "Preliminary Report on the Excavations at North Saqqara, 1968-9." *JEA* 56, 5-11.

Enklaar 1985 A. Enklaar. "Chronologie et peintres des hydries de Hadra." *BABesch* 60, 106-51.

1986 ———. "Les hydries de Hadra II: Formes et ateliers." *BABesch* 61, 41-63.

The Epigraphic Survey 1981 The Epigraphic Survey, Oriental Institute of the University of Chicago. *The Temple of Khonsu*, vol. 2. *Plates 111-207: Scenes and Inscriptions in the Court and the First Hypostyle Hall. With Translations of Texts and Glossary for Vols. 1 and 2.* OIP 103.

Erman 1900 A. Erman. "Augustus und Tiberius in Karnak." *ZÄS* 38, 123-26.

Evrard-Derriks/Quaegebeur 1979 C. Evrard-Derriks and J. Quaegebeur. "La situle décorée de Nesnakhetiou au Musée Royal de Mariemont." *CdE* 54, 26-56.

Fairman 1935 H. Fairman. "The Myth of Horus at Edfu–I." *JEA* 21, 26-36.

Fakhry 1941 A. Fakhry. "The Necropolis of 'Gabal el-Môta' at Siwa." *ASAE* 40, 779-99.

1973 ———. *The Oases of Egypt*, vol. I: *Siwa Oasis*. Cairo.

Farkas *et al.* 1964 A. Farkas *et al. Thou Shalt Have No Other Gods Before Me*. Exh. cat. New York, The Jewish Museum.

Faulkner 1969 R. O. Faulkner. *The Ancient Egyptian Pyramid Texts*. Oxford.

1985 ———. *The Ancient Egyptian Book of the Dead*. Rev. ed. London.

Fazzini 1972 R. A. Fazzini. "Some Egyptian Reliefs in Brooklyn." *MW*, 33-70.

1975 ———. *Images for Eternity: Egyptian Art from Berkeley and Brooklyn*. Exh. cat. The Fine Arts Museums of San Francisco and The Brooklyn Museum. Brooklyn.

1985 ———. "The Brooklyn Museum. Report on the 1983 Season of Excavation at the Precinct of the Goddess Mut." *ASAE* 70, 287-307.

1988 ———. *Egypt. Dynasty XXII-XXV*. Iconography of Religions, XVI: *Egypt*, fascicle 10. Leiden.

forthcoming ———. "Osiris-Ruler-of-Eternity and the Art of the Third Intermediate Period." In D. B. Redford, G. E. Kadish, *et al. The XXIIIrd Dynasty Chapel of Osiris Heka-Djet*. SSEA Publications. Mississauga, Ontario.

Fazzini/Peck 1982 R. A. Fazzini and W. H. Peck. "The 1982 Season at Mut." *NARCE* 120, 37-58.

Fehlig 1986 A. Fehlig. "Das sogenannte Taschentuch in den ägyptischen Darstellungen des Alten Reiches." *SAK* 13, 55-94.

Feucht 1986 E. Feucht. *Vom Nil zum Neckar: Kunstschätze Ägyptens aus pharaonischer und koptischer Zeit an der Universität Heidelberg*. Berlin/BRD.

Finnestad 1985 R. G. Finnestad. *Image of the World and Symbol of the Creator: On the Cosmological and Iconological Values of the Temple of Edfu*. Studies in Oriental Religions, 10. Wiesbaden.

Fischer 1956 H. G. Fischer. "Prostrate Figures of Egyptian Kings." *The University Museum Bulletin* 20, 26-42.

1962 ———. Rev. of ESLP. *Archaeology* 15, 136.

1973a ———. "An Eleventh Dynasty Couple Holding the Sign of Life." *ZÄS* 100, 16-28.

1973b ———. "Further Evidence for the Logic of Ancient Egyptian: Diminishing Progression." *JARCE* 10, 5-9.

1975 ———. "An Elusive Shape within the Fisted Hands of Egyptian Statues." *MMJ* 10, 9-21.

1977 ———. "The Evolution of Composite Hieroglyphs in Ancient Egypt." *MMJ* 12, 5-19.

1986 ———. *L'écriture et l'art de l'Egypte ancienne: quatre leçons sur la paléographie et l'épigraphie pharaonique*. Paris.

1987 ———. "The Ancient Egyptian Attitude Towards the Monstrous." In *Monsters and Demons in the Ancient and Medieval Worlds. Papers Presented in Honor of Edith Porada*. Eds. A. Farkas *et al.* Mainz, 13-26.

Fittschen 1983 K. Fittschen. "Zwei Ptolemäerbildnisse in Cherchel." In *Studi Adriani* 1, 165-71.

Forgeau 1984 A. Forgeau. "Prêtres Isiaques: Essai d'anthropologie religieuse." *BIFAO* 84, 155-87.

Forti 1984 L. Forti. "Appunti sul ceramica di Hadra." In *Studi Adriani* 2, 222-41.

Fouquet 1973 A. Fouquet. "Quelques représentations d'Osiris-canope au Musée du Louvre." *BIFAO* 73, 61-70.

Fowden 1986 G. Fowden. *The Egyptian Hermes: A Historical Approach to the Late Pagan Mind.* Cambridge, 1986.

del Francia 1985 L. del Francia. "Scènes d'animaux personnifiés dans l'Egypte pharaonique et copte: à propos d'une peinture de Baouit." In *Acts of the Second International Congress of Coptic Study, Rome, 22-26 September 1980.* Eds. T. Orlandi and F. Wisse, 31-57.

Franzow 1931 G. Franzow. "Zu der demotischen Fabel vom Geier und der Katze." *ZÄS* 66, 46-49.

Fraser 1960 P. M. Fraser. "Inscriptions from Ptolemaic Egypt." *Berytus* 13, 123-61.

1972 ———. *Ptolemaic Alexandria,* vols. 1-2. Oxford.

1976 ———. Rev. of Hornbostel 1973. *JHS* 96, 213-15.

1984 ———. "A Plaster Anguiform Serapis." In *Studi Adriani* 2, 348-50.

Freed 1983 R. E. Freed. *A Divine Tour of Ancient Egypt.* Exh. cat. Memphis, The University Gallery, Memphis State University.

1987 ———. *Ramesses the Great.* Exh. cat. Memphis, Brooks Museum of Art and the Institute of Egyptian Art and Archaeology, Memphis State University.

Friedman 1985 F. Friedman. "On the Meaning of Some Anthropoid Busts from Deir el-Medîna." *JEA* 71, 82-97.

Fuhrmann 1941 H. Fuhrmann. "Archäologische Grabungen und Funde in Italien, Albanien und Libyen. Oktober 1939-Oktober 1941." *AA* 56, 329-732.

Gardiner 1944 A. H. Gardiner. "Horus the Beḥdetite." *JEA* 30, 23-60.

1951 ———. "Addendum to 'The Baptism of Pharaoh', *JEA* 36, 3-12." *JEA* 37, 111.

1957 ———. *Egyptian Grammar, Being an Introduction to the Study of Hieroglyphs.* 3rd rev. ed. Oxford.

Gaşsowska 1983 B. Gaşsowska. "Remarques sur le tricliniarque d'Aboukir et autres monuments analogues de l'Egypte romaine." *Etudes et Travaux* 13, 100-09.

Gauckler 1912 P. Gauckler. *Le sanctuaire syrien du janicule.* Paris.

Gauthier 1916 H. Gauthier. *Le livre des rois d'Egypte. Recueil de titres et protocoles royaux, noms propres de rois, reines, princes et princesses, noms de pyramides et de temples solaires,* vol. 4: *De la XXVe dynastie à la fin des Ptolémées.* MIFAO 20.

Gazda *et al.* 1978 E. K. Gazda *et al. Guardians of the Nile: Sculptures from Karanis in the Fayoum (c. 250 B.C.-A.D. 450).* Exh. cat. Ann Arbor, Kelsey Museum of Archaeology, The University of Michigan.

George 1978 B. George. "Hathor, Herrin der Sistren." *Medelhavsmuseet Bulletin* 13, 25-31.

1982 ———. "Ptolemaios II und Arsionoe II vor den Göttern von Athribis." *Medelhavsmuseet Bulletin* 17, 11-16.

George/Peterson 1982 B. George and B. Peterson. "Egypten." In *Medelhavsmuseet: Introduction.* Stockholm, 9-116.

Gercke 1975 P. Gercke. *Antiken in Kassel aus dem Alltag der Griechen und Römer.* Staatliche Kunstsammlungen Kassel.

Germer 1985 R. Germer. *Flora des pharaonischen Ägypten.* DAIK, Sonderschrift 14.

Germond 1981 P. Germond. *Sekhmet et la protection du monde.* AH 9.

Gesche 1968 H. Gesche. *Die Vergötterung Caesars.* Frankfurter Althistorische Studien, 1. Frankfurt.

Giza-Podgórski 1984 T. Giza-Podgórski. "Royal Plume Dress of XVIII Dynasty." *MDAIK* 40, 103-21.

Goedicke 1973 H. Goedicke. "Hippopotamus – An Egyptian Word." *The Journal of Indo-European Studies* 1, 316-17.

Götte 1986 K. Götte. "Eine Individualcharakteristik ptolemäischer Herrscher anhand der Epitheta-Sequenzen beim Weinopfer." *RdE* 37, 63-80.

Golvin 1986 J.-Cl. Golvin. "Le petit sérapéum de l'époque d'Hadrien." *Egypte: Louqsor – temple du ka royal = Dossiers. histoire et archéologie* 101, 66-68.

Golvin/Goyon 1987 J.-Cl. Golvin and J.-Cl. Goyon. *Les bâtisseurs de Karnak.* CNRS, France.

Gomaà 1985 F. Gomaà. "Tell el-Moqdam." *LÄ 6, 351-52.*

Goyon 1972 J.-Cl. Goyon. *Confirmation du pouvoir royal au nouvel an [Brooklyn Museum Papyrus 47.218.50].* BdE 52.

1985 ———. *Les dieux-gardiens et la genèse des temples (d'après les textes égyptiens de l'époque gréco-romaine). Les soixante d'Edfou et les soixante-dix-sept dieux de Pharbaethos,* 2 vols. BdE 93.

Goyon *et al.* 1979 J.-Cl. Goyon *et al. The Edifice of Taharqa by the Sacred Lake of Karnak.* Brown Egyptological Studies 8. London and Providence.

Graefe 1979 E. Graefe. "König und Gott als Garanten der Zukunft (notwendiger Ritualvollzug neben göttlicher Selbstbildung) nach Inschriften der griechisch-römischen Tempel, mit einem Anhang: Eine Hypothese zur Erklärung der sogenannten Pektoralopferszenen und dem Verhältnis zwischen Ritualgeschehen und bildlicher Darstellung in den späten Tempeln." In

Aspekte der spätägyptischen Religion. Ed. W. Westendorf. GOF, IV. Reihe: Ägypten, 9, 47-78.

Graindor 1939 P. Graindor. *Terres cuites de l'Egypte gréco-romaine.* Rijksuniversiteit te Gent. Werken uitgegeven door de Faculteit van de Wijsbegeerte en Letteren, 86. Antwerp and the Hague.

Grenier 1977 J.-C. Grenier. *Anubis alexandrin et romain.* EPRO 57.

1983a ———. "Ptolémée Evergète II et Cléopâtre d'après les textes du temple de Tôd." In *Studi Adriani* 1, 32-37.

1983b ———. "La stèle funéraire du dernier taureau Bouchis (Cairo JE 31901=Stèle *Bucheum* 20)." *BIFAO* 83, 197-208.

1986 ———. "Le prophète et l'autokratôr." *RdE* 37, 81-89.

Griffith 1912 F. Ll. Griffith. *Meroitic Inscriptions,* vol. II: *Napata to Philae and Miscellaneous.* ASE, Twentieth Memoir.

1937 ———. *Catalogue of the Demotic Graffiti of the Dodecaschoenus,* vol. II. SAE. Les temples immergés de la Nubie. Oxford.

Griffiths 1967 J. G. Griffiths. "Allegory in Greece and Egypt." *JEA* 53, 79-102.

1969 ———. "The Tradition of Allegory in Egypt." In *Religions,* 45-57.

1970 ———, ed. *Plutarch's De Iside et Osiride.* Swansea, Wales.

1973 ———. "Triune Conceptions of Deity in Ancient Egypt." *ZÄS* 100, 28-32.

1975 ———. *Apuleius of Madauros: The Isis-Book (Metamorphoses, Book XI).* Leiden.

1978 ———. "Xenophon of Ephesus on Isis and Alexandria." In *Hommages Vermaseren* I, 409-37.

A. Grimm 1984 A. Grimm. "Ein Statuentorso des Hakoris aus Ahnas el-Medineh im Ägyptischen Museum zu Kairo." *GM* 77, 13-18.

G. Grimm 1972 G. Grimm. "Two Early Imperial Faience Vessels from Egypt." *MW* I, 71-100.

1974 ———. *Die römischen Mumienmasken aus Ägypten.* Wiesbaden.

1975 ———. *Kunst der Ptolemäer- und Römerzeit im Ägyptischen Museum Kairo.* Mainz.

Grumach-Shirun 1975 I. Grumach-Shirun. "Federn und Federkrone." *LÄ* 2, 142-45.

Guéraud 1939 O. Guéraud. "Le monument d'Agrios au Musée du Caire." *ASAE* 39, 279-311.

Guglielmi 1979 W. Guglielmi. "Humor in Wort und Bild auf altägyptischen Grabdarstellungen." In *Wort und Bild. Symposion des Fachbereichs Altertums- und Kulturwissenschaften zum 500jährigen Jubiläum der Eberhard-Karls-Universität Tübingen, 1977.* Eds. H. Brunner *et al.* Munich, 181-200.

Grundlach 1980 R. Grundlach. "Min." *LÄ* 4, 136-40.

Gunn 1934 B. G. Gunn. "The Berlin Statue of Harwa and Some Notes on Other Harwa Statues." *BIFAO* 34, 135-42.

Gutbub 1973 G. Gutbub. *Textes fondamentaux de la théologie de Kom Ombo,* 2 vols. BdE 47.

van Haarlem 1986 W. M. van Haarlem. *Allard Pierson Museum, Amsterdam: Selection from the Collection,* vol. I. CAA. Mainz.

forthcoming ———. *Allard Pierson Museum, Amsterdam: Selection from the Collection,* vol. II.

van Haarlem/Lunsingh Scheurleer 1986 W.M. van Haarlem and R.A. Lunsingh Scheurleer. *Gids voor de Afdeling Egypte: Allard Pierson Museum, Amsterdam.* Vooraziatisch-egyptisch Genootschaap. Phoenix 32/1. Amsterdam.

Habachi 1955 L. Habachi. "A Strange Monument of the Ptolemaic Period from Crocodilopolis." *JEA* 41, 106-11.

1963 ———. "Edjo, Mistress of Nebt (Bilifiya, near to Ihnâsya El-Medîneh)." *ZÄS* 90, 41-49.

1969 ———. *Features of the Deification of Ramesses II.* ADAIK 5.

1976 ———. "Two More Stelae of King Tiberius Unearthed in the Eastern Side of the Luxor Temple." In *Miscellanea in honorem Josephi Vergote.* Eds. P. Naster *et al.*=*OLP* 6/7, 247-52.

Habachi/Biers 1969 L. Habachi and J. Biers. "An Agate Bowl from Egypt." *Muse, Annual of the Museum of Art and Archaeology, University of Missouri–Columbia* 3, 29-33.

Haeny 1977 G. Haeny. "Hathor-Kapitell." *LÄ* 2, 1039-41.

1985 ———. "A Short Architectural History of Philae." *BIFAO* 85, 197-233.

van Haften/Manchip White 1980 J. van Haften and J. E. Manchip White. *Egypt and the Holy Land in Historic Photographs: 77 Views by Francis Frith.* New York.

Hall 1981 R. M. Hall. "Two Linen Dresses from the Fifth Dynasty Site of Deshasheh now in the Petrie Museum of Egyptian Archaeology, University College London." *JEA* 67, 168-71.

Hall/Barnett 1985 R. M. Hall and J. Barnett. "A Fifth Dynasty Funerary Dress in the Petrie Museum of Egyptian Archaeology: Its Discovery and Conservation." *Textile History* 16, 5-22.

Harden 1987 D. B. Harden. *Glass of the Caesars.* Milan.

Hassan 1944 Selim Hassan. *Excavations at Giza,* vol. V: *(1933-1934).* Cairo.

1953 ———. *The Great Sphinx and Its Secrets: Historical Studies in the Light of Recent Excavations,* vol. VIII: *(1936-1937).* Cairo.

Hauben 1983 H. Hauben. "Arsinoé II et la politique extérieure de l'Egypte." In *Egypt and the Hellenistic World,* 99-127.

Hauser 1908 F. Hauser. "The Heads of the 'Scipio' Type." *AJA* 12, 56-57.

Hayes 1959 W. C. Hayes. *The Scepter of Egypt. A Background for the Study of the Egyptian Antiquities in The Metropolitan Museum of Art. Part II: The Hyksos Period and the New Kingdom (1675-1080 B.C.),* Cambridge, Massachusetts.

Haynes 1983 D.E.L. Haynes. "The Date of the Bronze Head of Augustus from Meroë." In *Studi Adriani* 2, 177-81.

von Hees-Landwehr 1982 C. von Hees-Landwehr. *Griechische Meisterwerke in römischen Abgüssen: Der Fund von Baia.* Frankfurt.

Heilmeyer 1979 W.-D. Heilmeyer. "Augustus und Kleopatra." *Berliner Museen* 16, 6-7.

Heinen 1974 H. Heinen. "Les mariages de Ptolémée VIII Evergète et leur chronologie: étude comparative de papyrus et d'inscriptions grecs, démotiques et hiéroglyphiques." In *Akten des XIII. Internationalen Papyrologenkongresses Marburg/Lahn, 2.-6. August 1971.* Eds. E. Kiessling and H.-A. Rupprecht. Munich, 147-55.

1978 ———. "Aspects et problèmes de la monarchie ptolémaïque." *KTEMA* 3, 177-99.

Helbig 1963 W. Helbig, ed. *Führer durch die öffentlichen Sammlungen klassischer Altertümer in Rom,* vol. I: *Die Päpstlichen Sammlungen im Vatikan und Lateran.* 4th rev. ed. Ed. H. Speier. Tübingen.

Hermann 1960 A. Hermann. "Der letzte Apisstier." *Jahrbuch für Antike und Christentum* 3, 34-50.

A. Hermann 1980 A. Hermann. Entries in *The Search for Alexander.* Supplement II to the Catalogue. Exh. cat. by C. C. Vermeule *et al.* Organized by the Museum of Fine Arts, Boston.

Higgins 1961 R. A. Higgins. *Greek and Roman Jewellery.* London.

1986 ———. *Tanagra and the Figurines.* Princeton.

Hildesheim 1979 Hildesheim, Roemer- und Pelizaeus-Museum, *Götter und Pharaonen.* Exh. cat. by D. Wildung, G. Grimm, *et al.* Mainz.

1985 ———. *Nofret. Die Schöne: Die Frau im alten Ägypten,* vol. 2: *"Wahrheit" und Wirklichkeit.* Exh. cat. Mainz.

1986 ———. *Das alte Reich. Ägypten im Zeitalter der Pyramiden.*

D. Hill 1946 D. K. Hill. "Some Late Egyptian Ceramics in the Walters Art Gallery." *Gazette des Beaux-Arts* 30, 193-98.

G. Hill 1910 G. F. Hill. British Museum, Department of Coins and Medals. *Catalogue of the Greek Coins of Phoenicia.* London.

Himmelmann 1983 N. Himmelmann. *Alexandria und der Realismus in der griechischen Kunst.* Tübingen.

Hintze 1978 F. Hintze. "The Kingdom of Kush: The Meroitic Period." In *Africa in Antiquity. The Arts of Ancient Nubia and the Sudan,* vol. II: *The Essays.* Exh. cat. The Brooklyn Museum, 89-105.

Hirayama 1984 I. Hirayama. *Kings in Pharaoh's Land.* Tokyo.

Hobson 1987 D. W. Hobson. Rev. of Pomeroy 1984. *CP* 82, 69-74.

Hochuli-Gysel 1977 A. Hochuli-Gysel. *Kleinasiatische glasierte Reliefkeramik (50 v. Chr. bis 50 n. Chr.) und ihre oberitalischen Nachahmungen.* Bern.

Hodjash/Berlev 1982 S. Hodjash and O. Berlev. *The Egyptian Reliefs and Stelae in the Pushkin Museum of Fine Arts, Moscow.* Leningrad.

Hölbl 1983 G. Hölbl. "Aegyptischer Einfluß in der griechischen Kleinkunst." *ÖJh* 54, 1-17.

Hoffmann 1971 H. Hoffmann. *Ten Centuries that Shaped the West: Greek and Roman Art in Texas Collections.* Exh. cat. Dallas, Institute for the Arts, Rice University. Mainz.

Hoffmann/Davidson 1965 H. Hoffmann and P. A. Davidson. *Greek Gold: Jewelry from the Age of Alexander.* Exh. cat. The Brooklyn Museum. Mainz.

Hofmann 1977 I. Hofmann. "Der Feldzug des C. Petronius nach Nubien und seine Bedeutung für die meroitische Chronologie." In *Ägypten und Kusch,* 189-205.

1981 ———. "Kleopatra–Kandake." *GM* 52, 33-35.

1984 ———. "Einige Probleme der meroitischen Religion." *Meroitica* 7, 122-28.

Holm-Rasmussen 1979 T. Holm-Rasmussen. "On the Statue Cult of Nektanebos II." *Acta Orientalia* 40, 21-25.

Hondoussa 1981 T. Hondoussa. "Le collier ousekh." *SAK* 9, 143-50.

Horn 1938 R. Horn. "Hellenistische Köpfe, III." *RM* 53, 87-89.

Hornblower 1929 G. D. Hornblower. "Predynastic Figures of Women and Their Successors." *JEA* 15, 29-47.

1931 ———. "Notes and News." *JEA* 17, 145.

Hornbostel 1973 W. Hornbostel. *Sarapis: Studien zur Überlieferungsgeschichte, den Erscheinungsformen und Wandlungen der Gestalt eines Gottes.* EPRO 32.

1978 ———. "Sarapiaca I." In *Hommages Vermaseren* II, 501-18.

Hornung 1967 E. Hornung. "Der Mensch als 'Bild Gottes' in Ägypten." In *Die Gottebenbildlichkeit des Menschen.* Ed. O. Loretz = Schriften des Deutschen Instituts für Wissenschaftliche Pädagogik. Munich, 123-56.

1973 ———. "Bedeutung und Wirklichkeit des Bildes im alten Ägypten." In *Kunst und Realität*. E. Schmid *et al.* Akademische Vorträge der Universität Basel, 8, 35-46.

1982 ———. *Conceptions of God in Ancient Egypt: The One and the Many*. Trans. J. R. Baines. Ithaca.

Houghton 1983 A. Houghton. *Coins of the Seleucid Empire from the Collection of Arthur Houghton*. Ancient Coins in North American Collections No. 4. New York.

1986 ———. "A Colossal Head in Antakya and the Portraits of Seleucus I." *AntK* 29, 52-62.

Hummel 1986 S. Hummel. "Notizen zu Min." *Acta Orientalia* 47, 7-12.

C. Husson 1977 C. Husson. *L'offrande du miroir dans les temples égyptiens de l'époque gréco-romaine*. Lyon.

G. Husson 1983 G. Husson. *Oikia: le vocabulaire de la maison privée en Egypte d'après les papyrus grecs*. Paris.

IFAO 1983 *Catalogue de la fonte hiéroglyphique de l'imprimerie de l'I.F.A.O.* Cairo.

Ishiguro 1975 K. Ishiguro. *The Ishiguro Collection of Ancient Art*, vol. I. Tokyo.

Iwas 1984 W. Iwas. "Aphrodite Arsinoe Philadelphos: Eine Orakelstatue hadrianischer Zeit im Ägyptischen Museum Berlin." *AAASH* 29, 385-91.

Jacquet-Gordon 1966 H. Jacquet-Gordon. "Two Stelae of Horus-on-the-Crocodiles." *BMA* 7, 53-64.

James 1962 T. G. H. James. Rev. of ESLP. *JEA* 48, 169-71.

1974 ———. *Corpus of Hieroglyphic Inscriptions in The Brooklyn Museum*, vol. I: *From Dynasty I to the End of Dynasty XVIII*. Wilbour Monographs VI.

1979 ———. *An Introduction to Ancient Egypt*. London.

Janssen 1975 J. J. Janssen. *Commodity Prices from the Ramessid Period; an Economic Study of the Village of Necropolis Workmen at Thebes*. Leiden.

Jelínková 1958 E. Jelínková. "Un titre saïte emprunté à l'Ancien Empire." *ASAE* 55, 79-125.

Jelínková-Reymond 1956 E. Jelínková-Reymond. *Les inscriptions de la statue guérisseuse de Djed-Hor-le-Sauveur*. BdE 23.

Jenkins 1960 G. K. Jenkins. "An Early Ptolemaic Hoard from Phacous." *ANSMN* 9, 17-37.

Jéquier 1924a G. Jéquier. *Manuel d'archéologie égyptienne*, vol. III: *Les éléments de l'architecture*. Paris.

1924b ———. *L'architecture et la décoration dans l'ancienne Egypte*, vol. III: *Les temples ptolémaïques et romains*. Paris.

Johansen 1967 F. S. Johansen. "Antichi ritratti di Caio Giulio Cesare nella scultura." *Analecta Romana* 4, 7-68.

1978 ———. "Antike portrætter af Kleopatra VII og Marcus Antonius." *Meddelelser fra Ny Carlsberg Glyptotek* 35, 55-81.

1987 ———. "The Portraits in Marble of Gaius Julius Caesar: A Review." In *Ancient Portraits in the J. Paul Getty Museum*, vol. I. Occasional Papers on Antiquity 4, 17-40.

Johnson 1983 J. Johnson. "The Demotic Chronicle as a Statement of a Theory of Kingship." *JSSEA* 13, 61-72.

1984 ———. "Is the Demotic Chronicle an Anti-Greek Tract?" In *Gram. Dem.*, 107-24.

1986 ———. "The Role of the Egyptian Priesthood in Ptolemaic Egypt." In *Parker Studies*, 70-84.

H. Jucker 1965 H. Jucker. "'Promenade archéologique' durch die Ausstellung der Sammlung Kofler im Kunsthaus Zürich." *AntK* 8, 40-55.

1981a ———. "Römische Herrscherbildnisse aus Ägypten." In *Aufstieg und Niedergang. Principat*, Bd. 12/2, 667-724.

1981b ———. "Julisch-Claudische Kaiser- und Prinzenporträts als 'Palimpseste'." *JDAI* 96, 236-316.

1983 ———. "Marmorporträts aus dem römischen Ägypten: Beobachtungen, Vorschläge und Fragen." In *Das röm.-byz. Ägypt.*, 139-49.

I. Jucker 1975 I. Jucker. "Zum Bildnis Ptolemaios' III. Euergetes I." *AntK* 18, 17-25.

Junge 1979 F. Junge. "Isis und die ägyptischen Mysterien." In *Aspekte der spätägyptischen Religion*. Ed. W. Westendorf. GOF, IV. Reihe: Ägypten, 9, 93-115.

Junker 1913 H. Junker. *Das Götterdekret über das Abaton*. Denkschriften der Kaiserlichen Akademie der Wissenschaften in Wien. Phil.-hist. Kl., 56, Abh. 4. Vienna.

Junker/Winter 1965 H. Junker and E. Winter. *Das Geburtshaus des Tempels der Isis in Philä*. Österreichische Akademie der Wissenschaften. Phil.-hist. Kl., Denkschriften. Sonderband = Philä – Publikation II. Vienna.

Kadri 1978 Ahmed Kadri. "Discovery of Limestone Blocks of the Late Period between Shebin el-Qantir and Bilbeis." *SAK* 6, 93-96.

Kaiser 1966 W. Kaiser. "Ein Statuenkopf der Ägyptischen Spätzeit." *JBerlMus* 8, 5-33.

1967 ———. *Ägyptisches Museum Berlin*. Berlin/BRD.

Kákosy 1963 L. Kákosy. "Krokodil mit Menschenkopf." *ZÄS* 90, 66-74.

1970 ———. "Les stèles d' 'Horus sur les crocodiles' du Musée des Beaux-Arts." *Bulletin du Musée Hongrois des Beaux-Arts* 34-35, 7-24.

1974 ———. "Isis Regina." *Studia Aegyptiaca* 1, 221-30.

1982 ———. "The Nile, Euthenia, and the Nymphs." *JEA* 68, 290-98.

1983 ———. "Die Kronen im spätägyptischen Totenglauben." In *Das röm.-byz. Ägypt.*, 57-60.

1985 ———. *La magia in Egitto ai tempi dei faraoni.* Milan.

Kamal 1905 Ahmed Bey Kamal. *Stèles ptolémaïques et romaines (CGC 22001-22203)*, 2 vols.

Kamer 1975 H. Kamer. *Kamer et Cie, Qualité.* Paris.

Kaplony 1977 P. Kaplony. *Die Rollsiegel des Alten Reichs*, vol. I: *Allgemeiner Teil mit Studien zum Königtum des Alten Reichs.* Monumenta Aegyptiaca, 2. Brussels.

Kaschnitz von Weinberg 1965 G. Kaschnitz von Weinberg. *Ausgewählte Schriften*, vol. II. *Römische Bildnisse.* Berlin/BRD.

Kater-Sibbes 1973 G. J. F. Kater-Sibbes. *Preliminary Catalogue of Sarapis Monuments.* EPRO 36.

Kater-Sibbes/Vermaseren 1975a G. J. F. Kater-Sibbes and M. J. Vermaseren. *Apis*, vol. I: *The Monuments of the Hellenistic-Roman Period from Egypt.* EPRO 48/1.

1975b ———. *Apis*, vol. II: *Monuments from Outside Egypt.* EPRO 48/2.

Katznelson 1966 I. S. Katznelson. "Kandaka i perezhitki materniteta v Kushe." [Candace and the Survivals of the Maternality in Kush]. *Palestinskiy Sbornik* 15, 35-40.

Kawamura 1976 K. Kawamura. "A Preliminary Report of Excavations by the Waseda University Expedition Party at Malkata, Luxor, Egypt." *Orient* 12, 15-26.

Kayser 1966 H. Kayser. *Die ägyptischen Altertümer im Roemer-Pelizaeus-Museum in Hildesheim.*

1973 ———. *Die ägyptischen Altertümer im Roemer-Pelizaeus-Museum in Hildesheim*, 2nd ed.

Kees 1912 H. Kees. *Der Opfertanz des ägyptischen Königs.* Munich.

1960 ———. "Wêbpriester der 18. Dynastie im Trägerdienst bei Prozessionen." *ZÄS* 85, 45-56.

Keimer 1938 L. Keimer "Remarques sur quelques représentations de divinités-béliers et sur un groupe d'objets de culte conservés au Musée du Caire." *ASAE* 38, 297-331.

Kessler 1983 D. Kessler. "Die Galerie C von Tuna el-Gebel." *MDAIK* 39, 107-23.

1985 ———. "Tierkult." *LÄ* 6, 571-87.

el Khashab 1958 Abd el Mohsen el Khashab. "Money and Coins in Egypt." *Egypt Travel Magazine* 49, 21-28.

Kiss 1975 Z. Kiss. "Notes sur le portrait impérial romain en Egypte." *MDAIK* 31, 293-302.

1984 ———. *Etudes sur le portrait impérial romain en Egypte.* Warsaw.

Knauer 1978 E. R. Knauer. "Toward a History of the Sleeved Coat." *Expedition* 21, 18-36.

Koefoed-Petersen 1948 O. Koefoed-Petersen. *Publications de la Glyptothèque Ny Carlsberg*, vol. 1: *les stèles égyptiennes.* Copenhagen.

Koenen 1983 L. Koenen. "Die Adaptation ägyptischer Königsideologie am Ptolemäerhof." In *Egypt and the Hellenistic World*, 143-90.

Komorzynski 1955 E. Komorzynski. "Ein Sphinx als Wächter eines Privatgrabes." *AfO* 17, 137-40.

Kopcke 1964 G. Kopcke. "Golddekorierte attische Schwarzfirniskeramik des vierten Jahrhunderts v. Chr." *AM* 79, 22-84.

Kormyschewa-Minkowskaja 1984 E. Y. Kormyschewa-Minkowskaja. "Bemerkungen zu einigen Problemen der Religion von Kusch." *Meroitica* 7, 129-34.

Kraeling 1955 C. H. Kraeling. "Hellenistic Gold Jewelry in Chicago." *Archaeology* 8, 252-59.

Kraus 1983 T. Kraus. "Bildnis eines jungen Ptolemäers." In *Studi Adriani* 1, 190-91.

Kriéger 1960 P. Kriéger. "Une statuette du roi-faucon au Musée du Louvre." *RdE* 12, 37-58.

Kromann/Mørkholm 1977 A. Kromann and O. Mørkholm, eds. *SNG Copenhagen. Egypt. The Ptolemies.*

Kruchten 1986 J.-M. Kruchten. *Le grand texte oraculaire de Djéhoutymose, intendant du domaine d'Amon sous le pontificat de Pinedjem II.* Monographies Reine Elisabeth 5. Brussels.

Krug 1984 A. Krug. "Ein Bildnis der Arsinoe II. Philadelphos." In *Studi Adriani* 1, 192-200.

Kuentz 1934 C. Kuentz. "Remarques sur les statues de Harwa." *BIFAO* 34, 143-63.

Küthmann 1962 C. Küthmann. "Der grüne Kopf des Berliner Ägyptischen Museums." *ZÄS* 88, 37-42.

Kuhlmann/Schenkel 1983 K. P. Kuhlmann and W. Schenkel. *Das Grab des Ibi, Obergutsverwalters der Gottesgemahlin des Amun (thebanisches Grab Nr. 36)*, vol. I: *Beschreibung der unterirdischen Kult- und Bestattungsanlage.* AV 15.

Kurth 1975 D. Kurth. *Rites Egyptiens II: Den Himmel stützen. Die "Tw3.pt"-Szenen in den ägyptischen Tempeln der griechisch-römischen Epoche.* Brussels.

Kyrieleis 1973 H. Kyrieleis. "Die Porträtmünzen Ptolemaios' V. und seiner Eltern – zur Datierung und historischen Interpretation." *JDAI* 88, 213-46.

1975 ———. *Bildnisse der Ptolemäer.* Berlin.

1976 ———. "Ein Bildnis des Marcus Antonius." *AA*, 85-90.

LaBranche 1966 C. LaBranche. "The Greek Figural Capital." *Berytus* 16, 71-96.

Lacau 1922 — P. Lacau. "Les statues 'guérisseuses' dans l'ancienne Egypte." *MonPiot* 25/1, 189-209.

Lanciers 1986 — E. Lanciers. "Die Ägyptischen Tempelbauten zur Zeit des Ptolemaios V. Epiphanes (204-180 v.Chr.)." *MDAIK* 42, 81-98.

Landenius 1978 — H. Landenius. "Two Spiral Snake Armbands." *Medelhavsmuseet Bulletin* 13, 37-40.

Lansing 1938 — A. Lansing. "A Silver Bottle of the Ptolemaic Period." *BMMA* 33, 199-200.

La Rocca 1984 — E. La Rocca. *L'età d'oro di Cleopatra – Indagine sulla Tazza Farnese*. Documenti e Ricerche d'Arte Alessandrina, V. Rome.

La Rosa 1984 — V. La Rosa. "Ceramiche del tipo Hadra da Fèstos." In *Studi Adriani* 3, 804-18.

Laubscher 1985 — H. P. Laubscher. "Hellenistische Herrscher und Pan." *AM* 100, 333-53.

1987 — ———. "Ein ptolemäisches Gallierdenkmal." *AntK* 30, 131-54.

Lauer 1976 — J.-P. Lauer. *Saqqarah: The Royal Necropolis of Memphis*. London.

Laurent 1984 — V. Laurent. "Une statue provenant de Tell el-Maskoutah." *RdE* 35, 139-58.

von Lauth 1879 — F. J. von Lauth. "An die Redaktion." *ZÄS* 17, 92-93.

Lawrence 1925 — A. W. Lawrence. "Greek Sculpture in Ptolemaic Egypt." *JEA* 11, 179-90.

1927 — ———. *Later Greek Sculpture and Its Influence on East and West*. New York.

Leahy 1980 — A. Leahy. "Two Late Period Stelae in the Fitzwilliam Museum." *SAK* 8, 169-80.

Leclant 1951 — J. Leclant. "Fouilles et travaux en Egypte, 1950-1951." *Or 20*, 454-57.

1954 — ———. *Enquêtes sur les sacerdotes et les sanctuaires égyptiens à l'époque dite "éthiopienne" (XXVe Dynastie)*. BdE 17.

1965 — ———. *Recherches sur les monuments thébains de la XXVe dynastie dite éthiopienne*. BdE 36.

1975 — ———. "Anat." *LÄ* 1, 253-58.

1977 — ———. In *Annales de l'Université de Lyon* 3 (1976), 89-101.

1979 — ———. "A propos des antiquités égyptiennes découvertes dans les sanctuaires isiaques d'Asie Mineure." In *Florilegium Anatolicum: Mélanges offerts à Emmanuel Laroche*. Paris, 207-17.

1982 — ———. "Isis au pays de Koush." E.P.H.E. Ve Section. *Annuaire* 90, 39-59.

1984 — ———. "Aegyptiaca et milieux isiaques. Recherches sur la diffusion du matériel et des idées égyptiennes." In *Aufstieg und Niedergang. Principat*, Bd. 17/3, 1692-1709.

Leclant/Clerc 1972 — J. Leclant and G. Clerc. *Inventaire bibliographique des Isiaca (IBIS). Répertoire analytique des travaux relatifs à la diffusion des cultes isiaques. 1940-1969*, vol. 1: *A-D*. EPRO 18/1.

1974 — ———. *Inventaire bibliographique des Isiaca (IBIS). Répertoire analytique des travaux relatifs à la diffusion des cultes isiaques. 1940-1969*, vol. 2: *E-K*. EPRO 18/2.

Le Corsu 1965 — F. Le Corsu. "Cléopâtre était-elle laide?" *BSFE* 42, 19-27.

1966 — ———. "Quelques motifs égyptiens survivant dans l'architecture religieuse alexandrine." *RdE* 18, 37-44.

1967 — ———. "Un oratoire pompéien consacré à Dionysos-Osiris." *RA*, 239-54.

1968 — ———. "Stèles-portes égyptiennes à éléments emboîtés d'époque gréco-romaine." *RdE* 20, 109-25.

1978 — ———. "Cléopatre-Isis." *BSFE* 82, 22-33.

Lefebvre 1924 — G. Lefebvre. *Le tombeau de Petosiris*, vol. III: *vocabulaire et planches*. Cairo.

Legrain 1894 — G. Legrain. *Collection H. Hoffmann: Catalogue des antiquités égyptiennes*. Paris.

1914 — ———. *Statues et statuettes de rois et de particuliers (CGC 42001-42250)*, vol. III.

Leibovitch 1944 — J. Leibovitch. "Amon-Ra^c, Rechef et Houroun sur une stèle." *ASAE* 44, 163-72.

1968 — ———. "Quelques griffons demeurés inédits." *IEJ* 18, 126-29.

Leospo 1985 — E. Leospo. "Antichità egizie in Venezia." In *Viaggiatori veneti alla scoperta dell'Egitto*. Ed. A. Siliotti. Venice, 197-210.

Lepsius 1849-59 — C. R. Lepsius. *Denkmaeler aus Aegypten und Aethiopien nach den Zeichnungen der von seiner Majestät dem Koenige von Preußen Friedrich Wilhelm IV nach diesen Ländern gesendeten und in den Jahren 1842-1845 ausgefuehrten wissenschaftlichen Expedition*, pts. I-V. Berlin.

Lewis 1983 — N. Lewis. *Life in Egypt under Roman Rule*. Oxford.

Lewis/Reinhold 1968 — N. Lewis and M. Reinhold. *Roman Civilization*, vol. II. 2nd ed. New York.

Lichtheim 1947 — M. Lichtheim. "Oriental Institute Museum Notes: Situla No. 11395 and Some Remarks on Egyptian Situlae." *JNES* 6, 169-79.

1980 — ———. *Ancient Egyptian Literature. A Book of Readings*, vol. III: *The Late Period*. Berkeley and London.

1983 — ———. *Late Egyptian Wisdom Literature in the International Context: A Study of Demotic Instructions*. OBO 52.

Lillesø 1985 — E. K. Lillesø. "Stirnband und Diademe." *LÄ* 6, 45-49.

Limme 1983 — L. Limme. "Trois 'Livres des Morts' illustrés des Musées royaux d'Art et d'Histoire à Bruxelles." In *Artibus Aegypti*, 81-99.

Linfert 1984 — A. Linfert. "Die Tochter, nicht die Mutter. Nochmals zur "Afrika"-schale von Boscoreale." In *Studi Adriani* 2, 351-58.

Lipiński 1982 E. Lipiński. "Egyptian Aramaic Coins from the Fifth and Fourth Centuries B.C." In *Studia Naster* I, 23-33.

Lise 1979 G. Lise. *Museo archeologico raccolta Egizia.* Milan.

Lloyd 1982 A. B. Lloyd. "The Inscription of Udjaḥorresnet: A Collaborator's Testament." *JEA* 68, 166-80.

1983 ———. "The Late Period, 664-323 B.C." In *Ancient Egypt: A Social History.* Ed. B.G. Trigger *et al.* Cambridge, 279-364.

Longega 1968 G. Longega. *Arsinoe, II.* Università degli Studi di Padova. Pubblicazioni dell'Istituto di Storia Antica, 6. Rome.

Loyrette 1977 A.-M. Loyrette. "L'Egypte des pharaons." *Archeologia* 113, 58-66.

Lullies 1954 R. Lullies. *Die kauernde Aphrodite.* Munich.

Lunsingh Scheurleer 1979 R. A. Lunsingh Scheurleer. "La Faience de Mît Rahîneh." In *Acts. First International Congress of Egyptology. Cairo, October 2-10, 1976.* Ed. W. F. Reineke. Schriften zur Geschichte und Kultur des Alten Orients, 14. Berlin/DDR, 441-42.

1984. ———. "A Note on Two Casts in the Allard Pierson Museum." In *Studi Adriani* 2, 359-62.

1986 ———. "Thirteen Drinking Cups." In *Enthousiasmos: Essays on Greek and Related Pottery Presented to J. M. Hemelrijk.* Ed. H. A. G. Brijder *et al.* Allard Pierson Series. Studies in Ancient Civilization 6. Amsterdam, 147-56.

1987 ———. *Vereniging van Vrienden Allard Pierson Museum Amsterdam Mededelingenblad* 39, 2-13.

Lunsingh Scheurleer *et al.* 1984 R.A. Lunsingh Scheurleer *et al. Egypte: Eender en anders. Tentoonstelling ter viering van het vijftigjarig bestaan van het Allard Pierson Museum gesticht 12 October 1934.* Amsterdam.

Luxor 1979 Luxor Museum of Ancient Egyptian Art. *Catalogue of the Luxor Museum of Ancient Egyptian Art.* Cairo.

Lyons 1896 H. G. Lyons. *A Report on the Islands and Temples of Philae.* London.

Macurdy 1932 G. H. Macurdy. *Hellenistic Queens: A Study of Woman-power in Macedonia, Seleucid Syria, and Ptolemaic Egypt.* The Johns Hopkins University Studies in Archaeology, 14. Baltimore.

Maehler 1983 H.G.T. Maehler. "Alexandria." In *Ancient Centres of Egyptian Civilization.* Eds. H.S. Smith and R.M. Hall. London, 87-96.

Malaise 1972 M. Malaise. *Les conditions de pénétration et de diffusion des cultes égyptiens en Italie.* EPRO 22, 439-42.

1976 ———. "Histoire et signification de la coiffure hathorique à plumes." *SAK* 4, 215-36.

1980 ———. "La piété personnelle dans la religion isiaque." In *L'expérience de la prière dans les grandes religions. Actes du Colloque de Louvain-la-Neuve et Liège (22-23 Novembre 1978).* Eds. H. Limet and J. Ries. Louvain-la-Neuve, 1980=*Homo Religiosus* 5, 83-117.

1983 ———. "La survie isiaque." In *Vie et survie dans les civilisations orientales.* Eds. A. Théodorides *et al.*=*Acta Orientalia Belgica* 3, 97-112.

Malibu 1983 Malibu, California, The J. Paul Getty Museum. *Archaic Coins: An Exhibition at the J. Paul Getty Museum and the Brooklyn Museum from the Collection of Jonathan Rosen.* Exh. cat.

el Mallakh/Bianchi 1980 Kamal el Mallakh and R. S. Bianchi. *Treasures of the Nile.* New York.

Mallet 1909 D. Mallet. *Le Kasr el-Agoûz.* MIFAO 11.

Manniche 1978 L. Manniche, "Symbolic Blindness." *CdE* 53, 13-21.

1982 ———. "The Body Colours of Gods and Men in Inlaid Jewellery and Related Objects from the Tomb of Tutankhamun." *Acta Orientalia* 43, 5-12.

G. Martin 1979 G. T. Martin. *The Tomb of Hetepka and Other Reliefs and Inscriptions from the Sacred Animal Necropolis, North Saqqâra, 1964-1973.* EES. Excavations at North Saqqâra, Documentary Series, 2. London.

G. Martin *et al.* 1981 G. T. Martin *et al. The Sacred Animal Necropolis at North Saqqâra: The Southern Dependencies of the Main Temple Complex.* EES. Excavations at North Saqqâra, Excavation Memoir 50. London.

K. Martin 1985 K. Martin. "Uräus." *LÄ* 6, 864-68.

Martini 1983 R. Martini. "Monetazione bronzea orientale di Marcus Antonius-I," *Rivista Italiana di Numismatica e Scienze Affini* 85, 49-72.

1984 ———. "Monetazione bronzea orientale di Marcus Antonius-II," *Rivista Italiana di Numismatica e Scienze Affini* 86, 17-60.

Maspero 1887 G.C.C. Maspero. *Egyptian Archaeology.* Trans. A. B. Edwards. London.

1910 ———. *Le musée égyptien. Recueil de monuments et de notices sur les fouilles d'Egypte.* Cairo.

1913 ———. "Rapport sur les fouilles entreprises à Baouit." *CRAIBL* 1913, 287-301.

1914 ———. *Sarcophages des époques persane et ptolémaïque (CGC 29301-29306),* vol. I.

Massner 1986 A.-K. Massner. "Ägyptisierende Bildnisse des Kaisers Claudius." *AntK* 29, 63-67.

Maxwell-Hyslop 1971 K. R. Maxwell-Hyslop. *Western Asiatic Jewellery*. London.

Meeks 1979 D. Meeks. "Les donations aux temples dans l'Egypte du Ier millénaire avant J.-C." In *State and Temple Economy in the Ancient Near East. Proceedings of the International State and Temple Economy Conference Organized by the Katholieke Universiteit, Leuven, from the 10th to the 14th April 1978*. 2 vols. Ed. E. Lipiński=OLA 5-6, 605-87.

1986 ———. "Zoomorphie et image des dieux dans l'Egypte ancienne." *Les temps de la réflection, 7: corps des dieux*, 171-91.

Megow 1985 W.-R. Megow. "Zu einigen Kameen späthellenistischer und frühaugusteischer Zeit." *JDAI* 100, 445-96.

Mercklin 1951 E. Mercklin. "Das ägyptische Figuralkapitell." In *Studies Presented to David Moore Robinson*, vol. I. Eds. G. Mylonas and D. Raymond. St. Louis, 198-214.

Merkelbach 1969 R. Merkelbach. "Ein griechisch-ägyptischer Priestereid und das Totenbuch." In *Religions*, 69-73.

De Meulenaere 1958 H. De Meulenaere. "Le Vizir Harsiêsis de la 30e Dynastie." *MDAIK* 16, 230-36.

1959 ———. "Les stratèges indigènes du nome tentyrite à la fin de l'époque ptolémaïque et au début de l'occupation romaine." *RSO* 34, 1-25.

1960a ———. "Les monuments du culte des rois Nectanébo." *CdE* 35, 92-107.

1960b ———. "Notes d'onomastique tardive." *RdE* 12, 67-74.

1962 ———. "Une statue de prêtre héliopolitain." *BIFAO* 61, 29-42.

1963 ———. "La famille royale des Nectanébo." *ZÄS* 90, 90-93.

1966 ———. *Le surnom égyptien à la Basse Epoque*. Uitgaven van het Nederlands Historisch-Archaeologisch Instituut in het Nabije Oosten, 19. Istanbul.

1968 ———. "La famille du roi Amasis." *JEA* 54, 183-87.

1969 ———. "Horus de Hebenou et son prophète." In *Religions*, 21-29.

1976 ———. Entries in *Egypte éternelle*.

1978 ———. "L'œuvre architecturale de Tibère à Thèbes." *OLP* 9, 69-73.

1982 ———. "Isis et Mout du Mammisi." In *Studia Naster* II, 25-29.

1986 ———. "Une famille sacerdotale thébaine." *BIFAO* 86, 135-42.

De Meulenaere/Bothmer 1974 H. De Meulenaere and B. V. Bothmer. "Une statue thébaine de la fin de l'époque ptolémaïque." *ZÄS* 101, 109-13.

De Meulenaere/Mackay 1976 H. De Meulenaere and P. Mackay. *Mendes II*. The Brooklyn Museum and the Institute of Fine Arts, New York University. Warminster, England.

Meyer 1931 E. Meyer. "Zur Geschichte der 30. Dynastie." *ZÄS* 67, 68-70.

Michalowski 1968 K. Michalowski. *L'art de l'ancienne Egypte*. Paris.

Mielsch 1986 H. Mielsch. "Hellenistische Tieranekdoten in der römischen Kunst." *Archäologische Gesellschaft zu Berlin 1984/85=AA* 1986, 747-63.

Millet 1981 N. B. Millet. "Social and Political Organisation in Meroe." *ZÄS* 108, 124-41.

Millet *et al.* 1982 N. B. Millet *et al.* "Discussion: Meroitic funerary customs." *Meroitica* 6, 156-59.

Milne 1905 J. G. Milne. *Greek Inscriptions (CGC 9201-9400, 26001-26123, 33001-33037)*. Oxford.

1914 ———. "Antony and Cleopatra?" *JEA* 1, 99.

1938 ———. "The Currency of Egypt under the Ptolemies." *JEA* 24, 200-07.

1945 ———. "Alexandrian Coins Acquired by the Ashmolean Museum, Oxford." *JEA* 31, 85-91.

Mitten/Doeringer 1967 D. G. Mitten and S. F. Doeringer. *Master Bronzes from the Classical World*. Exh. cat. Fogg Art Museum, Harvard University, Cambridge, Massachusetts. Mainz.

Modrzejewski 1975 J. Modrzejewski. "Chrématistes et laocrites." In *Le monde grec*, 699-708.

1985 ———. "Entre la cité et le fisc: le statut grec dans l'Egypte romaine." In *Symposion 1982 (Santander, 1-4 Septiembre. 1982)*. Akten der Gesellschaft für griechische und hellenistische Rechtsgeschichte, 5. Valencia, 241-80.

Möbius 1964 H. Möbius. *Alexandria und Rom*. ABAW, phil.-hist. Kl. 59. Munich.

Mogensen 1922 M. Mogensen. "Ein altägyptischer Boxkampf." *ZÄS* 57, 87-88.

Mond/Myers *et al.* 1934 R. Mond and O. Myers *et al. The Bucheum*, 3 vols. EES, 41st Memoir. London.

Montet 1952 P. Montet. *Les énigmes de Tanis*. Paris.

1958 ———. "Un chef-d'œuvre de l'art gréco-égyptien. La statue de Panemerit." *MonPiot* 50, 1-10.

1959 ———. "Inscriptions de basse époque trouvées à Tanis, troisième série." *Kêmi* 15, 42-64.

Mooren 1975 L. Mooren. "Die angebliche Verwandtschaft zwischen den ptolemäischen und pharaonischen Hofrangtiteln." In *Proceedings of the XIVth International Congress of Papyrologists*. London, 233-37.

Moorey 1970 P. R. S. Moorey. *Ancient Egypt*. Oxford.

1971 ———. *Catalogue of the Ancient Persian Bronzes in the Ashmolean Museum*. Oxford.

1985 ———. *Materials and Manufacture in Ancient Mesopotamia: The Evidence of Archae-*

ology and Art, Metals and Metalwork, Glazed Materials and Glass. BAR International Series, 237. London.

Morenz 1954a S. Morenz. "Ägyptische Tierkriege und die Batrachomyomachie." In *Neue Beiträge zur klassischen Altertumswissenschaft. Festschrift zum 60. Geburtstag von Bernhard Schweizer.* Ed. R. Lullies. Stuttgart, 87-94.

1954b ———. "Anubis mit dem Schlüssel." *Wissenschaftliche Zeitschrift der Karl-Marx-Universität, Leipzig, 3. Gesellschafts- und Sprachwissenschaftliche Reihe,* I, 127-31.

1957 ———. "Das Werden zu Osiris. Die Darstellungen auf einem Leinentuch der römischen Kaiserzeit (Berlin 11651) und verwandten Stücken." *FuB* 1, 52-70.

1962 ———. "Ägyptische Nationalreligion und sogenannte Isismission." *ZDMG* 111 (1961), 432-36.

1969 ———. "Das Problem des Werdens zu Osiris in der griechisch-römischen Zeit Ägyptens." In *Religions,* 75-91.

Moret 1902 A. Moret. *Le rituel du culte divin journalier en Egypte d'après les papyrus de Berlin et les textes du temple de Séti Ier à Abydos.* Annales du Musée Guimet. Bibliothèque d'Etudes, 14. Paris.

de Morgan *et al.* 1909 J. de Morgan *et al. Catalogue des monuments et inscriptions de l'Egypte antique, première série,* vol. III: *Kom Ombos,* 2. Vienna.

Mørkholm 1959 O. Mørkholm. *SNG Copenhagen. Syria. Cities.*

1961 ———. *SNG Copenhagen. Phoenicia.*

1975 ———. "Ptolemaic Coins and Chronology. The Dated Silver Coinage of Alexandria." *ANSMN* 20, 7-24.

1979 ———. "The Portrait Coinage of Ptolemy V. The Main Series." In *Greek Numismatics and Archaeology. Essays in Honor of Margaret Thompson.* Eds. O. Mørkholm and N. M. Waggoner. Wetteren, Begium.

Mørkholm/ Nicolaou/ Nicolaou 1976 O. Mørkholm, I. Nicolaou, and K. Nicolaou. *Paphos,* vol. I: *A Ptolemaic Coin Hoard.* Nicosia.

Moussa 1981 Ahmed Mahmoud Moussa. "Excavations in the Valley Temple of Unas at Saqqara." *ASAE* 64, 75-77.

C. Müller 1975 C. Müller. "Anruf an Lebende." *LÄ* 1, 293-99.

H. Müller 1955 H. W. Müller. "Ein Königbildnis der 26. Dynastie mit der 'Blauen Krone' im Museo Civico zu Bologna (Inv. Nr. 1801)." *ZÄS* 80, 46-68.

1963a ———. "Isis mit dem Horuskinde. Ein Beitrag zur Ikonographie der stillenden Gottesmutter im hellenistischen und römischen Ägypten." *MüJb* 14, 7-38.

1963b ———. *Die stillende Gottesmutter in Ägypten.* Materia Medica Nordmark, 2. Sonderheft 1963. Hamburg.

1969 ———. *Der Isiskult im antiken Benevent und Katalog der Skulpturen aus den ägyptischen Heiligtümern im Museo del Sannio zu Benevent.* MÄS 16.

1970 ———. "Bildnisse König Nektanebos' I. (380-362 v. Chr.)." *Pantheon* 28, 89-99.

1975 ———. "Der 'Stadtfürst von Theben' Montemhêt." *MüJb* 26, 7-36.

1979 ———. "Goldschmuck und ein Fayencekelch aus dem Grab des Herihor (?)." *Pantheon* 38, 237-46.

H. Müller/ Wildung 1976 H. W. Müller and D. Wildung. *Staatliche Sammlung Ägyptischer Kunst.* Munich.

M. Müller 1985 M. Müller "Zwei Bildwerke aus der dritten Zwischenzeit." *BSEG* 9-10, 199-222.

Münster 1968 M. Münster. *Untersuchungen zur Göttin Isis vom Alten Reich bis zum Ende des Neuen Reiches.* MÄS 11.

Munro 1969 P. Munro. "Eine Gruppe spätägyptischer Bronzespiegel." *ZÄS* 95, 92-109.

1973 ———. *Die spätägyptischen Totenstelen.* ÄF 25.

Murnane 1986 W. J. Murnane. "Pour visiter le temple." In *Egypte: Louqsor, temple du ka royal=Dossiers: histoire et archéologie* 101, 12-16.

Murphy 1985 E. Murphy. *Diodorus Siculus: Diodorus "On Egypt".* Jefferson, Missouri.

Muscettola 1983 A. Muscettola. "Due sculture alessandrine al Museo Archeologico Nazionale di Napoli." In *Studi Adriani* 1, 120-24.

Mussies 1978 G. Mussies. "Some Notes on the Name of Sarapis." In *Hommages Vermaseren* II, 821-32.

Muszynski 1977 M. Muszynski. "Les 'Associations religieuses' en Egypte d'après les sources hiéroglyphiques, démotiques et grecques." *OLP* 8, 145-74.

Myśliwiec 1972a K. Myśliwiec. "A propos des signes hiéroglyphiques *'ḥr'* et *'tp'.*" *ZÄS* 98, 85-99.

1972b ———. "Towards a Definition of the 'Sculptor's Model' in Egyptian Art." *Etudes et Travaux* 6, 71-75.

1974 ———. "Un portrait ptolémaïque de Coptos au Musée des Beaux-Arts de Lyon." *Musées et Monuments Lyonnais* 5, 29-34.

1985 ———. "Quelques remarques sur les couronnes à plumes de Thoutmosis III." In *Mélanges Mokhtar* 2, 149-60.

Nachtergael 1980 G. Nachtergael. "Bérénice II, Arsinoé III et l'offrande de la boucle." *CdE* 55, 240-53.

Nagy 1977 E. Nagy. "Fragments de sistres au Musée des Beaux-Arts." *Bulletin du Musée Hongrois des Beaux-Arts* 48-49, 49-70.

Nakaten 1982 S. Nakaten. "Petosiris." *LÄ* 4, 995-98.

Naville 1895-1908 E. Naville. *The Temple of Deir el-Bahari,* 6 vols. EEF. Memoirs 13, 14, 16, 19, 27, 29. London.

1930 ———. *Détails relevés dans les ruines de quelques temples égyptiens: Abydos, Behbeit-El-Hagher. Appendix: Samanoud.* Paris.

Needler 1949 W. Needler. "Some Ptolemaic Sculptures in the Yale University Art Gallery." *Berytus* 9, 129-41.

Newell 1937 E. T. Newell. *Royal Greek Portrait Coins.* New York.

1939 ———. *Late Seleucid Mints in Ake-Ptolemais and Damascus.* NNM 84.

1941 ———. *The Coinage of the Western Seleucid Mints. Seleucus I to Antiochus III.* Numismatic Studies 4. New York.

New York 1975 New York, The Metropolitan Museum of Art. *Notable Acquisitions 1965-1975.*

1987 ———. *Antiquities from the Collection of Christos G. Bastis.* Exh. cat. Ed. D. von Bothmer *et al.* Mainz.

Nims 1971 C. Nims. "The Eastern Temple at Karnak." In *Aufsätze zum 70. Geburtstag von Herbert Ricke.* Beiträge zur ägyptischen Bauforschung und Altertumskunde, 12. Wiesbaden, 107-11.

Niwiński 1983 A. Niwiński. "Sarg. N[eues) R[eich]-Sp[ät]-z[ei]t." *LÄ* 5, 434-68.

Nock 1930 A. D. Nock. "Σύνναος Θεός." *HSCP* 41, 1-62.

1953 ———. "Neotera, Queen or Goddess?" *Aegyptus* 33, 283-96.

Noshy 1937 Ibrahim Noshy. *The Arts in Ptolemaic Egypt: A Study of Greek and Egyptian Influences in Ptolemaic Architecture and Sculpture.* Oxford.

Oates 1963 J.F. Oates, "The Status Designation ΠΕΡΣΗΣ, ΤΗΣ ΕΠΙΓΟΝΗΣ." *YCS* 18, 1-129.

Ockinga 1984 B. Ockinga. *Die Gottebenbildlichkeit im alten Ägypten und im Alten Testament,* ÄAT 7.

Oliver 1977 A. Oliver. *Silver for the Gods: 800 Years of Greek and Roman Silver.* Exh. cat. The Toledo Museum of Art.

1979 ———. In Walters Art Gallery, Baltimore. *Jewelry. Ancient to Modern.* New York, 104-27.

Omlin 1973 J. A. Omlin. *Der Papyrus 55001 und seine satirisch-erotischen Zeichnungen und Inschriften.* Catalogo del Museo Egizio di Torino. Monumenti e testi, 3. Turin.

Onasch 1984 C. Onasch. "Zur Struktur der meroitischen Religion." *Meroitica* 7, 135-42.

Oriental Institute 1986 Oriental Institute. *The University of Chicago. The Oriental Institute, 1985-1986. Annual Report.* Chicago.

Osing 1977 J. Osing. *Der Tempel Sethos' I. in Gurna: Die Reliefs und Inschriften,* vol. I. AV 20.

1980 ———. "Libyen, Libyer." *LÄ* 3, 1015-33.

Osing *et al.* 1982 J. Osing *et al. Denkmäler der Oase Dachla. Aus dem Nachlaß von Ahmed Fakhry.* AV 28.

Otto 1938 E. Otto. *Beiträge zur Geschichte der Stierkulte in Ägypten.* UGAÄ 13.

1975a ———. "Amun." *LÄ* 1, 237-48.

1975b ———. "Dedun." *LÄ* 1, 1003-04.

Pagenstecher 1913 R. Pagenstecher. In *Die griechisch-ägyptische Sammlung Ernst von Sieglin,* vol. II, part 3: *Die Gefäße in Stein und Ton. Knochenschnitzereien.* Leipzig.

Panofsky 1961 E. Panofsky. "'Canopus Deus'. The Iconography of a Non-Existent God." *Gazette des Beaux-Arts* 57, 193-216.

Pantalacci 1986 L. Pantalacci. "Remarques sur les méthodes de travail des décorateurs tentyrites." *BIFAO* 86, 267-75.

Parlasca 1966 K. Parlasca. *Mumienporträts und verwandte Denkmäler.* Wiesbaden.

1967 ———. "Ein verkanntes hellenistisches Herrscherbildnis. Ein Kolossalkopf Ptolemaios' IX. in Boston." *JDAI* 82, 167-94.

1970 ———. "Zur Stellung der Terenuthis-Stelen. Eine Gruppe römischer Grabreliefs aus Ägypten in Berlin." *MDAIK* 26, 173-98.

1973 ———. "Osiris und Osirisglaube in der Kaiserzeit." In *Syncrétismes,* 95-102.

1974 ———. "Falkenstelen aus Edfu. Bemerkungen zu einer Gruppe zerstörter Reliefs des Berliner Museums." In *Festschrift Ägyptisches Museum Berlin,* 483-88.

1975 ———. "Zur archaisch-griechischen Kleinplastik aus Ägypten." In *Wandlungen: Studien zur Antiken und neuren Kunst,* 57-61.

1976 ———. "Zur Verbreitung ptolemäischer Fayencekeramik außerhalb Ägyptens." *JDAI* 91, 135-56.

1979 ———. "Persische Elemente in der frühptolemäischen Kunst." In *Akten des 7. Internationalen Kongresses für iranische Kunst und Archäologie, München 7.-10. 9. 1976.* Munich, 317-23.

1982 ———. "Zur hellenistischen Reliefkeramik Kleinasiens." *BABesch* 57, 176-80.

1983 ———. "Griechisch-römische Steinschälchen aus Ägypten, mit einem Exkurs von Michael Pfrommer." In *Das röm.-byz. Ägypt.,* 151-60.

1984 ———. "Neues zur ptolemäischen Fayencekeramik." In *Studi Adriani* 2, 300-02.

1985 ———. "Neue Beobachtungen zu den hellenistischen Achatgefäßen aus Ägypten." *The J. Paul Getty Museum Journal* 13, 19-22.

Parlebas 1981 J. Parlebas. "Ecriture idéographique, écriture cursive et iconographie dans l'Egypte pharaonique." In *Méthodologie iconographique. Actes du Colloque de Strasbourg. 27-28 Avril 1979*. Ed. G. Siebert. Groupe de recherche d'histoire romaine de l'Université des Sciences Humaines de Strasbourg, Etudes et Travaux IV, 107-13.

Peck 1977 W.H. Peck. Rev. of D.B. Thompson 1973. *JNES* 36, 73-74.

Pécoil 1986 J. F. Pécoil. "Le soleil et la cour d'Edfou." *BIFAO* 86, 277-301.

Pécoil/Maher-Taha 1983 J. F. Pécoil and M. Maher-Taha. "Quelques aspects du bandeau-*seched*." *BSEG* 8, 67-69.

Pensabene 1983 P. Pensabene. "Lastre di chiusura di loculi con *naiskoi* egizi e stele funerarie con ritratto del Museo di Alessandria." In *Studi Adriani* 1, 91-119.

Peremans 1975 W. Peremans. "Ptolémée IV et les Egyptiens." In *Le monde grec*, 393-402.

1982 ———. "Sur le bilinguisme dans l'Egypte des Lagides." In *Studia Naster* II, 143-54.

1987 ———. "Vreemdelingen en Egyptenaren in ptolemaeïsch Egypte." In *Mededelingen van de Koninklijke Academie voor Wetenschappen, Letteren en Schone Kunsten van België.* Klasse der Letteren, Jg. 49/1, 3–27.

Pernigotti 1980 S. Pernigotti. *La statuaria egiziana nel Museo Civico Archeologico di Bologna*. Bologna.

Pestman 1967 P. W. Pestman. *Chronologie égyptienne d'après les textes démotiques (332 av. J.-C.-453 ap. J.-C.)*. PLB 15.

1985 ———. "The Competence of Greek and Egyptian Tribunals According to the Decree of 118 B.C.." *BASP* 22, 265-69.

Petrie 1885 W. M. F. Petrie. *Tanis, Part. I. 1883-1884*. EEF, 2nd Memoir. London.

1896 ———. *Koptos*. London.

1900 ———. *Dendereh 1898. Extra Plates*. London.

1911 ———. "Roman Glazing Kilns." In *Historical Studies*. E. B. Knobel *et al.* BSAE Studies 2. London, 34-37.

Philipp 1972 H. Philipp. *Terrakotten aus Ägypten im Ägyptischen Museum Berlin*. Berlin/BRD.

1979 ———. Rev. of Kyrieleis 1975. *Bonner Jahrbücher* 179, 770-76.

Pietryzkowski 1978 M. Pietryzkowski. "Sarapis-Agathos Daimon." In *Hommages Vermaseren* III, 959-66.

Pirenne 1963 J. Pirenne. *Histoire de la civilisation de l'Egypte ancienne. Troisième cycle: de la XXIe Dynastie aux Ptolémées (1085-30 av. J.-C.)*. Paris.

Plumley 1975 J. M. Plumley. "Qaṣr Ibrîm, 1974." *JEA* 61, 5-27.

Pörtner 1908 B. Pörtner. *Ägyptische Grabsteine und Denksteine aus Athen und Konstantinopel*. Strassburg.

Pomeroy 1984 S. Pomeroy. *Women in Hellenistic Egypt from Alexander to Cleopatra*. New York.

Porada 1979 E. Porada. "Some Thoughts on the Audience Reliefs of Persepolis." In *Studies in Classical Art and Archaeology*, 37-44.

Posener 1936 G. Posener. *La première domination perse en Egypte: Recueil d'inscriptions hiéroglyphiques*. BdE 11.

Poulsen 1951 F. Poulsen. *Catalogue of the Ancient Sculpture in the Ny Carlsberg Glyptotek*. Copenhagen.

Préaux 1978 Cl. Préaux. *Le monde hellénistique* vol. II. Paris.

1983 ———. "L'attache à la terre: continuités de l'Egypte ptolémaïque à l'Egypte romaine." In *Das röm.-byz. Ägypt.*, 1-6.

Priese 1978 K.-H. Priese. "The Kingdom of Kush: The Napatan Period." In *Africa in Antiquity. The Arts of Ancient Nubia and the Sudan*, vol. II: *The Essays*. Exh. cat. The Brooklyn Museum, 74-88.

Quaegebeur 1971a J. Quaegebeur. "Documents concerning a Cult of Arsinoe Philadelphos at Memphis." *JNES* 30, 239-70.

1971b ———. "Ptolémée II en adoration devant Arsinoé II divinisée." *BIFAO* 69, 191-217.

1972 ———. "Contribution à la prosopographie des prêtres memphites à l'époque ptolémaïque." *Ancient Society* 3, 77-109.

1974a ———. "Inventaire des stèles funéraires memphites d'époque ptolémaïque." *CdE* 49, 59-79.

1974b ———. "Prêtres et cultes thébains à la lumière de documents égyptiens et grecs." *BSFE* 70-71, 37-55.

1975 ———. *Le dieu égyptien Shaï dans la religion et l'onomastique*. OLA 2.

1976 ———. Entries in *Egypte éternelle*.

1977 ———. "Tithoes, dieu oraculaire?" *Enchoria* 7, 103-08.

1980 ———. "The Genealogy of the Memphite High Priest Family in the Hellenistic Period." In D. J. Crawford, J. Quaegebeur, W. Clarysse. *Studies on Ptolemaic Memphis*. SH 24, 43-81.

1983a ———. "De l'origine égyptienne du griffon némésis." In *Visages du destin dans les mythologies: Mélanges Jacqueline Duchemin*. Travaux et Mémoires: Actes du Colloque de Chantilly, 1-2 Mai, 1980. Paris, 41-54.

1983b ———. "Trois statues de femmes d'époque ptolémaïque." In *Artibus Aegypti*, 109-27.

1983c ———. "Twee laat-egyptische teksten rond dierenverering. Stèle Ny Carlsberg Glyptotheek 1681 en Papyrus BMM 10845." In *Schrijvend Verleden,* 263-76.

1985 ———. "Arsinoé Philadelphe, reine, 'roi' et déesse, à Hildesheim." *GM* 87, 73-78.

1986a ———. "La question des étiquettes de momies." In *Sociétés Urbaines en Egypte et au Soudan = CRIPEL* 8, 99-102.

1986b ———. "Osservazioni sul titolare di un Libro dei Morti conservato ad Assissi." *OrAnt* 25, 69-80.

Queyrel 1984 F. Queyrel. "Portraits de souverains lagides à Pompeï et à Délos." *BCH* 108, 267-300.

1985 ———. "Un portrait de Ptolémée III: problèmes d'iconographie." *La Revue du Louvre* 4, 278-82.

Radwan 1973 Ali Radwan. "Gedanken zum 'Würfelhocker'." *GM* 8, 27-31.

1975a ———. "Zur bildlichen Gleichsetzung des ägyptischen Königs mit der Gottheit." *MDAIK* 31, 99-108.

1975b ———. "Der Königsname. Epigraphisches zum göttlichen Königtum im alten Ägypten." *SAK* 2, 213-34.

1976 ———. "Concerning the Identification of the King with the God." *Magazine of the Faculty of Archaeology, Cairo University* 1, 24-36.

1985 ———. "Einige Aspekte der Vergöttlichung des ägyptischen Königs." In *Ägypten. Dauer und Wandel. Symposium anläßlich des 75jährigen Bestehens des Deutschen Archäologischen Instituts Kairo am 10. und 11. Oktober 1982.* DAIK, Sonderschrift 18. Mainz, 53-69.

Rammant-Peeters 1985 A. Rammant-Peeters. "Les couronnes de Nefertiti à El-Amarna." *OLP* 16, 21-48.

Ranke 1935 H. Ranke. *Die ägyptischen Personennamen,* vol. I. Glückstadt.

1945 ———. "A Late Statue of Hathor from her Temple at Dendereh." *JAOS* 65, 238-48.

Ray 1980 J. D. Ray. "Harmachis, the High Priest of Memphis: Wilkinson's Copy of BM 391." *JEA* 66, 170-71.

1986 ———. "Psammuthis and Hakoris." *JEA* 72, 149-58.

Redford 1981 D. B. Redford. "A Royal Speech from the Blocks of the 10th Pylon." *BES* 3, 87-102.

1983 ———. "Notes on the History of Ancient Buto." *BES* 5, 67-101.

1986a ———. "New Light on Temple J at Karnak." *Or* 55, 1-15.

1986b ———. *Pharaonic King-Lists, Annals and Day-Books: A Contribution to the Study of the Egyptian Sense of History.* SSEA Publications, 4. Mississauga, Ontario.

Reed/Near 1973 H. S. T. Reed and P. Near. *Ancient Art in the Virginia Museum.* Richmond.

Reeder 1987 E. D. Reeder. "The Mother of the Gods and a Hellenistic Bronze Matrix." *AJA* 91, 423-40.

Reinach 1913 A. Reinach. *Catalogue des antiquités égyptiennes recueillies dans les fouilles de Koptos en 1910 et 1911 exposées au Musée Guimet de Lyon.* Chalon-sur-Sâone.

Reinsberg 1980 C. Reinsberg. *Studien zur hellenistischen Toreutik. Die antiken Gipsabgüsse aus Memphis.* HÄB 9.

Reymond 1976 E. A. E. Reymond. *From the Contents of the Libraries of the Suchos Temples of the Fayyum,* Part I: *A Medical Book from Crocodilopolis. P. Vindob. D. 6257.* MPER 10.

1977 ———. *From the Contents of the Libraries of the Suchos Temples of the Fayyum,* Part II: *From Ancient Hermetic Writings.* MPER 11.

1981 ———. *From the Records of a Priestly Family from Memphis,* vol. I. ÄA 38.

1983 ———. "Demotic Literary Works of Graeco-Roman Date in the Rainer Collection of Papyri in Vienna." In *Papyrus Erzherzog Rainer (P. Rainer Cent.). Festschrift zum 100jährigen Bestehen der Papyrussammlung der österreichischen Nationalbiliothek.* Vienna, 42-60.

1986 ———. "The King's Effigy." In *Hommages à François Daumas.* Montpellier, 551-57.

Reymond/Barns 1977 E. A. E. Reymond and J. W. B. Barns. "Alexandria and Memphis. Some Historical Observations." *Or* 46, 1-33.

Riad *et al.* 1985 H. Riad *et al. Alexandria: An Archaeological Guide to the City and the Graeco-Roman Museum.* Rev. ed. Ed. Daoud Abdo Daoud. Cairo.

Rice 1983 E. E. Rice. *The Grand Procession of Ptolemy Philadelphus.* Oxford.

Richter 1954 G. M. A. Richter. "The Origin of Verism in Roman Portraits." *JRS* 44, 39-46.

Ricke *et al.* 1967 H. Ricke *et al. Ausgrabungen von Khor-Dehmit bis Bet el-Wali.* The University of Chicago, Oriental Institute Nubian Expedition, vol. II. Chicago.

Ricketts 1918 C. Ricketts. "Bas-relief Figure of a King of the Ptolemaic Period in Blue Faience." *JEA* 5, 77-78.

Riefstahl 1944a E. Riefstahl. "Doll, Queen, or Goddess?" *The Brooklyn Museum Journal* 2, 5-23.

1944b ———. *Patterned Textiles in Pharaonic Egypt.* Brooklyn.

Rieth 1973 A. Rieth, "Antike Goldmasken." *AntW* 4, 28-34.

Ristow 1969 G. Ristow. "Denkmäler hellenistischer Mysterienkulte in Kölner Museumsbesitz – Ägyptische Kultgruppe." *KölnJb* 10, 68-75.

Ritner 1984 R. K. Ritner. "A Property Transfer from the Erbstreit Archives." In *Gram. Dem.,* 171-88.

Roberts 1846 D. Roberts. *Egypt and Nubia.* London.

de Rochemonteix/Chassinat 1987 — M. de Rochemonteix and E. Chassinat. *Le temple d'Edfou*, vol. I, fasc. 3, 2nd ed. Rev. by S. Cauville and D. Devauchelle. MAFC 10/I^3.

Roeder 1911 — G. Roeder. *Debod bis Bab Kalabsche*, vol. II. SAE. Les temples immergés de la Nubie. Cairo.

1914 — ———. *Naos (CGC 70001-70050)*. Leipzig.

1939 — ———. "Die Ausgrabungen in Hermopolis im Frühjahr 1939." *ASAE* 39, 727-65.

1954 — ———. "Zwei hieroglyphische Inschriften aus Hermopolis (Ober-Ägypten)." *ASAE* 52, 315-442.

Roeder/Ippel 1921 — G. Roeder and A. Ippel. *Die Denkmäler des Pelizaeus-Museums zu Hildesheim.*

Roemer 1985 — M. Roemer. "Tanis." *LÄ* 6/2, 194-209.

Roes 1951 — A. Roes. "The Achaemenid Robe." *BiOr* 8, 137-41.

Rössler-Köhler 1978 — U. Rössler-Köhler. "Zur Datierung des Falkenbildes von Hierakonpolis (CGC 14717)." *MDAIK* 34, 117-25.

Romano 1976 — J. F. Romano. "Observations on Early Eighteenth Dynasty Royal Sculpture." *JARCE* 13, 97-111.

1980 — ———. "The Origin of the Bes-Image." *BES* 2, 39-56.

Rostem 1948 — O. R. Rostem. "Remarkable Drawings with Examples in True Perspective." *ASAE* 48, 167-77.

Roullet 1972 — A. Roullet. *The Egyptian and Egyptianizing Monuments of Imperial Rome.* EPRO 20.

Rowe 1946 — A. Rowe. *Discovery of the Famous Temple and Enclosure of Serapis at Alexandria.* Supplément aux *ASAE,* Cahier 2. Cairo.

Rubensohn 1911 — O. Rubensohn. *Hellenistisches Silbergerät in antiken Gipsabgüssen aus dem Pelizaeus-Museum zu Hildesheim.* Berlin.

Russmann 1974 — E. R. Russmann. *The Representation of the King in the XXVth Dynasty.* Monographies Reine Elisabeth 3. Brooklyn and Brussels.

1979 — ———. "Some Reflections on the Regalia of the Kushite Kings of Egypt." *Meroitica* 5, 49-54.

1981 — ———. "An Egyptian Royal Statuette of the Eighth Century B.C." In *Dunham Studies,* 149-55.

1983 — ———. "Harwa as Precursor of Mentuemhat." In *Artibus Aegypti,* 137-46.

1984a — ———. In *Egyptian Art. BMMA* 41/3.

1984b — ———. Rev. of The Epigraphic Survey, 1981. *Serapis* 7, 103-06.

Saleh/Sourouzian 1987 — Mohammed Saleh and H. Sourouzian. *The Egyptian Museum Cairo. Official Catalogue.* Mainz.

Samson 1985 — J. Samson. *Nefertiti and Cleopatra: Queen-Monarchs of Ancient Egypt.* London.

Samuel 1983 — A. Samuel. *From Athens to Alexandria: Hellenism and Social Goals in Ptolemaic Egypt.* SH 26.

Sander-Hansen 1956 — C. E. Sander-Hansen. *Die Texte der Metternichstele.* Analecta Aegyptiaca 7. Copenhagen.

Satzinger 1980 — H. Satzinger. *Ägyptische Kunst in Wien.* Kunsthistorisches Museum, Vienna.

Sauneron 1952a — S. Sauneron. "Les querelles impériales vues à travers les scènes du temple d'Esné." *BIFAO* 51, 111-21.

1952b — ———. "Un thème littéraire de l'antiquité classique: le Nil et la pluie." *BIFAO* 51, 41-48.

1959 — ———. "L'avis des Egyptiens sur la cuisine Soudanaise." *Kush* 7, 63-69.

1960a — ———. "Un document égyptien relatif à la divinisation de la reine Arsinoé II." *BIFAO* 60, 83-109.

1960b — ———. Le nouveau sphinx composite du Brooklyn Museum et le rôle du dieu Toutou-Tithoès." *JNES* 19, 269-87.

1960c — ———. *The Priests of Ancient Egypt.* Trans. A. Morrissett. New York and London.

1963 — ———. *Esna,* vol. II: *Le temple d'Esna.* Cairo.

1968 — ———. Villes et légendes d'Egypte (§ xv-xxiv)." *BIFAO* 66, 11-35.

1970 — ———. *Le papyrus magique illustré de Brooklyn (Brooklyn Museum 47.218.156).* Brooklyn.

1982 — ———. *Esna,* vol. VIII: *L'écriture figurative dans les textes d'Esna.* Cairo.

Sauneron/Stierlin 1975 — S. Sauneron and H. Stierlin. *Edfu et Philae: Derniers temples d'Egypte.* Paris.

Sauneron *et al.*1983 — ———. *La porte ptolémaïque de l'enceinte de Mout à Karnak.* MIFAO 107.

el Sayed 1975 — Ramadan el Sayed. *Documents relatifs à Saïs et ses divinités.* BdE 69.

1976 — ———. "Deux aspects nouveaux du culte à Saïs–Un prophète du nain de Neith–Des châteaux d'Ageb." *BIFAO* 76, 91-100.

1983 — ———. "Nekhtefmout, supérieur des porte-encensoirs." *ASAE* 69, 219-40.

Scamuzzi 1965 — E. Scamuzzi. *Egyptian Art in the Egyptian Museum of Turin.* Trans. B. Arnett Melchiori. New York.

Schäfer 1921 — J. H. Schäfer. "Ein griechisch-ägyptisches Relief." *Berliner Museen. Berichte aus den Preußischen Kunstsammlungen.* Beiblatt zum Jahrbuch der Preußischen Kunstsammlungen. 42, 15-22.

1939 — ———. "Wieder neue ungewöhnliche Darstellungen von Sonnenschiffen und das Viergespann des Brandenburger Tores." *MDAIK* 8, 147-55.

1943 — ———. "Die 'Vereinigung der beiden Länder'. Ursprung, Gehalt und Form eines ägyptischen

Sinnbildes im Wandel der Geschichte." *MDAIK* 12, 73-95.

1986 ———. *Principles of Egyptian Art.* 2nd ed. Ed. E. Brunner-Traut. Trans. J. Baines. Oxford.

Scharff 1939a A. Scharff. "Ägypten." In *Handbuch der Archäologie,* vol. 1. Ed. W. Otto. Munich, 433-639.

1939b ———. "Typus und Persönlichkeit in der ägyptischen Kunst." *Archiv für Kultur-Geschichte* 29/1-2, 1-24.

1941 ———. "Bemerkungen zur Kunst der 30. Dynastie." In *Miscellanea Gregoriana. Raccolta di scritti pubblicati nel I centenario dalla fondazione del Pont. Museo Egizio (1838-1939).* Vatican City, 195-203.

1949 ———. "Gott und König in ägyptischen Gruppenplastiken." In *Studi in memoria di Ippolito Rosellini nel primo centenario della morte (4 Giugno 1843),* vol. I. Pisa, 303-21.

Schienerl 1977 P. W. Schienerl. "Erinnerungen an die Isisverehrung im traditionellen Schmuck Ägyptens." *Baessler-Archiv,* N.F., 25, 205-28.

Schildkraut/Merrin 1986 L. Schildkraut and E. Merrin. *The Majesty of Ancient Egypt and the Classical World.* New York.

Schlick-Nolte 1977 B. Schlick-Nolte. "Fayence." *LÄ* 2, 138-42.

Schmitz 1982 B. Schmitz. "Ein dicker Mann aus Ägypten." *Journal für Geschichte* 5, 48-49.

H. Schneider 1977 H. Schneider. *Shabtis: An Introduction to the History of Ancient Egyptian Funerary Statuettes with a Catalogue of the Collection of Shabtis in the National Museum of Antiquities at Leiden,* vol. 1. Leiden.

H. Schneider/Raven 1981 H. Schneider and M. Raven. *De Egyptische Oudheid. Een inleiding aan de hand van de Egyptische verzameling in het Rijksmuseum van Oudheden te Leiden.* The Hague.

L. Schneider 1973 L. A. Schneider. *Asymmetrie griechischer Köpfe vom 5. Jh. bis zum Hellenismus.* Wiesbaden.

Schnur 1962 Apuleius' *The Golden Ass.* Trans. and ed. H. C. Schnur. New York.

Schoske 1986 S. Schoske. "Symmetrophobia – Symmetrie und Asymmetrie in der altägyptischen Kunst." In *Symmetrie in Kunst, Natur und Wissenschaft,* vol. 1: *Texte.* Darmstadt, 151-56.

Schoske/Wildung 1985 S. Schoske and D. Wildung. *Ägyptische Kunst München. Katalog-Handbuch zur Staatlichen Sammlung Ägyptischer Kunst München.* Munich.

Schott 1930 S. Schott. "Die Bitte um ein Kind auf einer Grabfigur des frühen Mittleren Reiches." *JEA* 16, 23.

Schulman 1977 A. R. Schulman. "Reshep on Horseback?" *Newsletter SSEA* 7, 13-17.

1986 ———. "Some Observations on the *3ḫ ikr n R*ᶜ-stela." *BiOr* 43, 302-48.

Schwaller de Lubicz 1982 R. A. Schwaller de Lubicz. *Les temples de Karnak. Contribution à l'étude de la pensée pharaonique,* 2 vols. Paris.

B. Schweitzer 1948 B. Schweitzer. *Die Bildniskunst der römischen Republik.* Leipzig.

U. Schweitzer 1948 U. Schweitzer. *Löwe und Sphinx im alten Ägypten.* ÄF 15.

1952 ———. "Ein spätzeitlicher Königskopf in Basel." *BIFAO* 50, 119-32.

G. Scott 1986 G. D. Scott, III. *Ancient Egyptian Art at Yale.* Yale University Art Gallery. New Haven.

N. Scott 1944 N. E. Scott. *The Home Life of the Ancient Egyptians.* New York.

1951 ———. "The Metternich Stela." *BMMA* 9, 201-17.

Seeber 1976 C. Seeber. *Untersuchung zur Darstellung des Totengerichts im Alten Ägypten.* MÄS 35.

Seele 1947 K. C. Seele. "Horus on the Crocodiles." *JNES* 6, 43-52.

Segall 1938 B. Segall. *Museum Benaki Athen. Katalog der Goldschmiede-Arbeiten.* Athens.

Sethe 1904 K. Sethe. *Hieroglyphische Urkunden der griechisch-römischen Zeit,* vols. I-III. Leipzig.

1929 ———. "Das Papyruszepter der ägyptischen Göttinnen und seine Entstehung." *ZÄS* 64, 6-9.

Seyfried 1983 K. J. Seyfried. "Thebanisches Kaleidoskop. Ausgewählte Funde aus der Grabung des Heidelberger Ramessidenprojekts." In *5000 Jahre Ägypten,* 103-16.

Seyrig 1950 H. Seyrig. "Antiquités syriennes, 42. Sur les ères de quelques villes de Syrie: Antioche, Apamée, Aréthuse, Balanée, Epiphanie, Laodicée, Rhosos, Damas, Béryte, Tripolis, l'ère de Cléopâtre, Chalcis du Liban, Doliché." *Syria* 27, 5-56.

1968 ———. "Un petit portrait royal." In *Etudes de sculpture antique offertes à Jean Charbonneaux,* vol. 1 = *RA 1968,* 251-56.

Shore 1965 A. F. Shore. "A Silver Libation Bowl from Egypt." *BMQ* 29, 21-24.

1974 ———. "The Demotic Inscription on a Coin of Artaxerxes." *Numismatic Chronicle,* seventh series, vol. 14, 5-8.

Simon 1975 E. Simon. Rev. of D. B. Thompson 1973. *GGA* 227, 206-16.

Simpson 1956 W. K. Simpson. "On the statue group: Amūn affixing the crown of the king." *JEA* 42, 118-19.

1971 ———. "A Horus-of-Nekhen Statue of Amunhotpe III from Soleb." *BMFA* 69, 152-64.

1976 ———. *The Offering Chapel of Sekhem-ankh-Ptah in the Museum of Fine Arts, Boston.* Boston.

1977 ———. *The Face of Egypt: Permanence and Change in Egyptian Art.* Exh. cat. Katonah, New York, The Katonah Gallery.

Sjöqvist 1953 E. Sjöqvist. "The Early Style of Lysippos." *OpAth* 1, 87-97.

Smelik 1979 K. Smelik. "The Cult of the Ibis in the Graeco-Roman Period, with Special Attention to the Data from the Papyri." In *Studies in Hellenistic Religions.* Ed. M. J. Vermaseren. EPRO 78, 225-43.

Smelik/Hemelrijk 1984 K. Smelik and E. Hemelrijk. "'Who knows not what monsters demented Egypt worships?' Opinions on Egyptian Animal Worship in Antiquity as Part of the Ancient Conception of Egypt." In *Aufstieg und Niedergang, Principat.* Bd. 17/4, 1852-2000.

H. Smith 1979 H. S. Smith. "Varia Ptolemaica." In *Glimpses of Ancient Egypt: Studies in Honor of H. W. Fairman.* Ed. H. Ruffle *et al.* Warminster, England, 164-66.

R. Smith 1986 R. R. R. Smith. "Three Hellenistic Rulers at the Getty." *The J. Paul Getty Museum Journal* 14, 59-78.

W. Smith 1960 W. S. Smith. *Ancient Egypt as Represented in the Museum of Fine Arts, Boston.* 4th ed. Boston.

1965 ———. *Interconnections in the Ancient Near East: A Study of the Relationships between the Arts of Egypt, the Aegean, and Western Asia.* New Haven and London.

Snijder 1956 G. A. S. Snijder, ed. *Algemene Gids Allard Pierson Museum, Amsterdam,* 2nd ed.

Snowden 1970 F. Snowden. *Blacks in Antiquity: Ethiopians in the Graeco-Roman Experience.* Cambridge, Massachusetts.

Solmsen 1979 F. Solmsen. *Isis among the Greeks and Romans.* Cambridge, Massachusetts.

Soukiassian 1983 G. Soukiassian. "Les autels 'à cornes' ou 'à acrotères' en Egypte." *BIFAO* 83, 317-33.

Sourouzian 1981 H. Sourouzian, "Une tête de la reine Touy à Gourna." *MDAIK* 37, 445-55.

forthcoming ———. "The Statues of Merenptah." In *Proceedings of the International Symposium on Ramesses the Great, April 20-23, 1987, Memphis State University.*

Spalinger 1978a A. Spalinger. "The Concept of the Monarchy during the Saite Epoch – An Essay of Synthesis." *Or* 47, 12-36.

1978b ———. "The Reign of King Chabbash: An Interpretation." *ZÄS* 105, 142-54.

1980 ———. "Addenda to 'The Reign of King Chabbash: An Interpretation'." *ZÄS* 107, 87.

Spanel 1986 D. B. Spanel. "Notes on the Terminology for Funerary Figurines." *SAK* 13, 249-53.

1988 ———. *Through Ancient Eyes: Egyptian Portraiture.* Exh. cat. Birmingham Museum of Art, Birmingham, Alabama.

Spencer 1984 P. Spencer. *The Egyptian Temple: A Lexicographical Study.* London.

Spiegelberg 1903 W. Spiegelberg. *Geschichte der Ägyptischen Kunst bis zum Hellenismus.* Leipzig.

1932 ———. *Die demotischen Denkmäler,* vol. III: *Demotische Inschriften und Papyri. (Fortsetzung) (CGC 50023-50165).* Berlin.

Stadelmann 1987 R. Stadelmann. "Ramses II., Harmachis and Hauron." In *Form und Maß: Beiträge zur Literatur, Sprache und Kunst des alten Ägypten. Festschrift für Gerhard Fecht zum 65. Geburtstag am 6. Februar 1987.* ÄAT 12.

Stambaugh 1972 J. E. Stambaugh. *Sarapis under the Early Ptolemies.* EPRO 25.

Steindorff 1945 G. Steindorff. "Reliefs from the Temples of Sebennytos and Iseion in American Collections." *Journal of the Walters Art Gallery* 7-8, 39-59.

1946 ———. *Catalogue of the Egyptian Sculpture in the Walters Art Gallery.* Baltimore.

Sternberg 1983 H. Sternberg, "Die Geburt des göttlichen Kindes als mythisches Motiv in den Texten von Esna." *GM* 61, 31-48.

Sternberg-el Hotabi 1987 H. Sternberg-el Hotabi. "Die Götterdarstellungen der Metternichstele: Ein Neuansatz zu ihrer Interpretation als Elemente eines Kontinuitätsmodells." *GM* 97, 25-70.

Stevenson 1895 S. Y. Stevenson. "Some Sculpture from Koptos in Philadelphia." *AJA* 10, 347-51.

Störk 1975 L. Störk. "Erotik." *LÄ* 2, 4-11.

1981 ———. "Zur Etymologie von *Ḫ3B* 'Flußpferd'." *GM* 43, 61.

Stricker 1943 B. H. Stricker. "Een egyptisch cultusbeeld uit Grieksch-Romeinschen tijd." *OMRO* 24, 1-10.

1959 ———. "Graeco-Egyptische private sculptuur." *OMRO* 40, 1-16.

1960 ———. "Graeco-Egyptische private sculptuur." *OMRO* 41, 18-30.

Strocka 1967 V. M. Strocka. "Aphroditekopf in Brescia." *JDAI* 82, 110-56.

1980 ———. "Augustus als Pharao." In *Eikones,* 177-80.

Sturtewagen/Bianchi 1982 C. Sturtewagen and R. S. Bianchi. "Museo Gregoriano Egizio." In *The Vatican Collections: The Papacy and Art.* Exh. cat. New York, The Metropolitan Museum of Art, 175-82.

Swinderk 1975 A. Swinderk. "Sarapis et les Hellénomemphites." In *Le monde grec,* 670-75.

Swinnen 1973 W. Swinnen. "Sur la politique religieuse de Ptolémée Ier." In *Syncrétismes,* 115-33.

Tait 1963 — G. A. D. Tait. "The Egyptian Relief Chalice." *JEA* 49, 93-139.

el Tanbouli et al. 1978 — M. A. L. el Tanbouli *et al. Gerf Hussein,* vol. IV: *la grande salle (E), murs sud, nord et ouest – les niches.* Cairo.

Teeter 1986 — E. Teeter. "The Search for Truth: A Preliminary Report on the Presentation of Maat." *NARCE* 134, 3-12.

Tefnin 1969 — R. Tefnin. "Un portrait de la reine Bérénice trouvé en Egypte." *L'Antiquité Classique* 38, 89-100.

1983 — ———. "Essai d'analyse formelle du visage royal égyptien: un relief de Touthmosis III aux Musées royaux d'Art et d'Histoire de Bruxelles." In *Artibus Aegypti,* 153-77.

1988 — ———. *Statues et statuettes de l'Ancienne Egypte.* Musées royaux d'Art et d'Histoire. Guides du département égyptien, 6. Brussels.

Terrace/Fischer 1970 — E. L. B. Terrace and H. G. Fischer. *Treasures of Egyptian Art from the Cairo Museum.* Boston.

Testa 1986 — P. Testa. "Un 'collare' in faïence nel Museo Archeologico di Napoli." *JEA* 72, 91-100.

Thissen 1979 — H.-J. Thissen. "Demotische Graffiti des Paneions im Wadi Hammamat." *Enchoria* 9, 63-92.

1980 — ———. "Kleopatra." *LÄ* 3, 452-54.

D. B. Thompson 1952 — D. B. Thompson. "Are Tanagras Athenians?" *AJA* 56, 177.

1964 — ———. "ΠΑΝΝΥΧΙΣ." *JEA* 50, 147-63.

1973 — ———. *Ptolemaic Oinochoai and Portraits in Faience: Aspects of the Ruler Cult.* Oxford.

1979 — ———. "A Faience Fellah." In *Studies in Classical Art and Archaeology,* 175-78.

1980 — ———. "More Ptolemaic Queens." In *Eikones,* 181-84.

1984 — ———. "Quae saga; quis magus?" In *Studi Adriani* 2, 309-17.

D. J. Thompson 1988 — D. J. Thompson. *Memphis under the Ptolemies.* Princeton.

Tondriau 1950 — J. T. Tondriau. "Esquisse de l'histoire des cultes royaux ptolémaïques," *RHR* 137, 207-35.

Török 1976 — L. Török. In *Meroitica* 2, 95-102.

Toynbee 1978 — J. M. C. Toynbee. *Roman Historical Portraits.* Ithaca, New York.

Tran Tam Tinh 1964 — V. Tran Tam Tinh. *Essai sur le culte d'Isis à Pompéi. Images et cultes.* Paris.

1978 — ———. "De nouveau Isis lactans (supplément I)." In *Hommages Vermaseren* III, 1231-68.

1984a — ———. "Le baiser d'Helios." In *Studi Adriani* 2, 318-28.

1984b — ———. "Etat des études iconographiques relatives à Isis, Sérapis et Sunnaoi Theoi." In *Aufstieg und Niedergang. Principat* Bd. 17/4, 1710-38.

Tran Tam Tinh/Labrecque 1973 — V. Tran Tam Tinh and Y. Labrecque. *Isis lactans. Corpus des monuments gréco-romains d'Isis allaitant Harpocrates.* EPRO 37.

Traunecker 1972 — C. Traunecker. "Les rites de l'eau à Karnak d'après les textes de la rampe de Taharqa." *BIFAO* 72, 195-236.

1975 — ———. "Une stèle commémorant la construction de l'enceinte d'un temple de Montou." In *Karnak V,* 141-58.

1982 — ———. "Un exemple de rite de substitution: une stèle de Nectanébo Ier." In *Karnak VII,* 339-54.

1984 — ———. "L'étoile diaconale copte et ses antécédents." In *Deuxième journée d'études coptes, Strasbourg. 25 Mai 1984 = Cahiers de la Bibliothèque Copte* 3, 93-110.

1985 — ———. "Une chapelle de magie guérisseuse sur le parvis du temple de Mout à Karnak." *JARCE* 20, 65-92.

Traunecker et al. 1981 — C. Traunecker *et al. La chapelle d'Achôris à Karnak,* vol. II: *Texte.* CFETK. Recherche sur les grandes civilisations. Synthèse 5. Paris.

Tresson 1933 — P. Tresson. "Sur deux monuments égyptiens inédits de l'époque d'Amasis et de Nectanébo Ier." *Kêmi* 4 (1931), 126-50.

Trevelyan 1976 — R. Trevelyan. "The Story of Pompeii." *ILN* 6940, 61-69.

Trigger 1974 — B. G. Trigger. "La Candace, personnage mystérieux." *Archeologia* 77, 10-17.

Troxell 1983 — H. A. Troxell. "Arsinoe's Non-Era," *ANSMN* 28, 35-70.

Troy 1984 — L. Troy. "Good and Bad Women. Maxim 18/284-288 of the Instructions of Ptahhotep." *GM* 80, 77-82.

1986 — ———. *Patterns of Queenship in Ancient Egyptian Myth and History.* Uppsala Studies in Ancient Mediterranean and Near Eastern Civilizations, Boreas 14. Uppsala.

Tutundjian de Vartavan 1986 — C. Tutundjian de Vartavan. "The origin, evolution and function of the *SḪM*, known as the *naos*-sistrum: preliminary researches." *Wepwawet* 2, 26-29.

Tutweiler 1976 — S. Tutweiler. "A Ptolemaic Portrait Head." *Expedition* 18/2, 22-23.

Uebel 1968 — F. Uebel. *Die Kleruchen Ägyptens unter den ersten sechs Ptolemäern.* AbhBerlin 3.

Vanderlip 1972 — V. F. Vanderlip. *The Four Greek Hymns of Isidorus and the Cult of Isis.* American Studies in Papyrology, 12. Toronto.

Vandersleyen 1975 — C. Vandersleyen. "Rundplastik der Spätzeit." In *Das alte Ägypten,* 255-73.

1985 — ———. "De l'influence grecque sur l'art égyptien. Plis de vêtements et plis de peau." *CdE* 60, 358-70.

Vandier 1958 J. Vandier. *Manuel d'archéologie égyptienne,* vol. III: *Les grandes époques. La statuaire.* Paris.

1964a ———. *Manuel d'archéologie égyptienne,* vol. IV: *Bas reliefs et peintures. Scènes de la vie quotidienne.* Paris.

1964b ———. "La statue de Hékatefnakht." *La Revue du Louvre* 14, 57-66.

1973 ———. "Nouvelles acquisitions. Musée du Louvre. Département des Antiquités Egyptiennes." *La Revue du Louvre* 23, 107-16.

Vandorpe 1986 K. Vandorpe. "The Chronology of the Reigns of Hurgonaphor and Chaonnophris." *CdE* 61, 294-302.

Varga 1960 E. Varga. "Contributions à l'histoire des modèles de sculpture en stuc de l'ancienne Egypte." *Bulletin du Musée national Hongrois des Beaux-Arts* 16, 3-20.

Varille 1943 A. Varille. *Karnak I.* FIFAO 19.

Vaughan 1960 M. Vaughan. "The Connoisseur in America." *The Connoisseur* 146/588, 146-50.

te Velde 1971 H. te Velde. "Some Remarks on the Structure of Egyptian Divine Triads." *JEA* 57, 80-86.

1978 ———. Rev. of Seeber 1976. *CdE* 53, 267-70.

1980 ———. "Towards a Minimal Definition of the Goddess Mut." *JEOL* 26, 3-9.

1982a ———. "The Cat as Sacred Animal of the Goddess Mut." In *Studies in Egyptian Religion Dedicated to Professor Jan Zandee.* Eds. M. Heerma van Voss *et al.* Studies in the History of Religions (Supplements to *Numen*) 43, 127-37.

1982b ———. "Commemoration in Ancient Egypt." In *Commemorative Figures. Papers presented to Dr. Th. P. van Baaren on the occasion of his seventieth birthday, May 13, 1982. Visible Religion* I, 135-53.

1986 ———. "Egyptian hieroglyphs as signs, symbols and gods." In *Approaches to Iconology. Visible Religions* IV-V, 63-72.

forthcoming ———. "Mut, the Eye of Re."

Vercoutter 1952 J. Vercoutter. "Tôd (1946-1949). Rapport succinct des fouilles." BIFAO 50, 69-87.

1960 ———. "The Napatan Kings and Apis Worship (Serapeum Burials of the Napatan Period)." *Kush* 8, 62-76.

1962 ———. "Un palais des 'Candaces', contemporain d'Auguste (Fouilles à Wad-ban-Naga 1958-1960)." *Syria* 39, 263-99.

Vermaseren 1986 M. J. Vermaseren. *Corpus Cultus Cybelae Attidisque (CCCA),* vol. V: *Aegyptus, Africa, Hispania, Gallia et Britannia.* EPRO 50.

Vermeule 1981 C. C. Vermeule. *Greek and Roman Sculpture in America. Masterpieces in Public Collections in the United States and Canada.* Berkeley.

Vermeule/von Bothmer 1956 C. C. Vermeule and D. von Bothmer. "Notes on a new edition of Michaelis: Ancient marbles in Great Britain." *AJA* 60, 321-50.

Vernier 1927 E. Vernier. *Bijoux et orfèvreries (CGC 52001-53855).*

Vernus 1976 P. Vernus. "Inscriptions de la Troisième Période Intermédiaire (II)." *BIFAO* 76, 1-15.

Vierneisel 1980 K. Vierneisel. "Der berliner Kleopatra." *JBerlMus* 22, 5-25.

Vierneisel/Zanker 1979 K. Vierneisel and P. Zanker. *Die Bildnisse des Augustus: Herrscherbild und Politik im kaiserlichen Rom.* Munich.

Vigneau 1936 A. Vigneau. *Encyclopédie photographique de l'art,* vol. I. Paris.

Vilímková *et al.* 1969 M. Vilímková *et al. Egyptian Jewellery.* London.

Vittmann 1976 G. Vittmann. "Ein Denkmal mit dem Namen der Königsmutter Esenchēbe (Berlin 10192)." *ZÄS* 103, 143-47.

1977 ———. "Zu den 'Schönen Namen' in der Spätzeit." *GM* 23, 71-73.

1985 ———. "Die Mumienschilder in Petries Dendereh." *ZÄS* 112, 153-68.

Vogliano 1938 A. Vogliano. "Rapporto preliminare della IVa campagna di scavo a Madînet Mâdi (R. Università di Milano)." *ASAE* 38, 533-49.

Volkmann 1958 H. Volkmann. *Cleopatra: A Study in Politics and Propaganda.* Trans. T.J. Cadoux. London.

Vollenweider 1984 M.-L. Vollenweider. "Portraits d'enfants en miniature de la dynastie des Ptolémées." In *Studi Adriani* 2, 363-77.

de Vos 1980 M. de Vos. *L'egittomania in pitture e mosaici romano-campani della prima età imperiale.* EPRO 84.

Vycichl 1983 W. Vycichl. "Histoires de chats et de souris, un problème de la littérature égyptienne." *BSFE* 8, 101-07.

Wace 1905 A. J. B. Wace. "Hellenistic Royal Portraits." *JHS* 25, 86-98.

Wagner 1972 G. Wagner. "Inscriptions grecques d'Egypte." *BIFAO* 72, 139-67.

1973 ———. "Une dédicace à la Grande Cléopâtre de la part du synode snonaïtiaque. 2 Juillet 51 av. J.-C. – Fayoum. Soknopéonèse." *BIFAO* 73, 103-08.

1981 ———. "L'inscription grecque et le martelage du nom du préfet Titus Flavius Titianus." *BIFAO* 81, 129-34.

1983 ———. "Une nouvelle dédicace à Boubastis." *ASAE* 69, 247-52.

Wagner/Quaegebeur 1973 G. Wagner and J. Quaegebeur. "Une dédicace grecque au dieu égyptien Mestasytmis de la part de son synode (Fayoum–époque romaine)." *BIFAO* 73, 41-60.

Wainwright 1928 — G. Wainwright. "The Aniconic Form of Amon in the New Kingdom." *ASAE* 28, 175-89.

1930 — ———. "The Relationship of Amūn to Zeus and His Connection with Meteorites." *JEA* 16, 35-38.

1931 — ———. "The Emblem of Min." *JEA* 17, 185-95.

1935 — ———. "Some Celestial Associations of Min." *JEA* 152-70.

1947 — ———. "Some Ancient Records of Kordofan." *Sudan Notes and Records* 28, 11-24.

Van de Walle 1952 — B. Van de Walle. "Antiquités égyptiennes." In *Les antiquités égyptiennes, grecques, étrusques, romaines et gallo-romaines du Musée de Mariemont.* Brussels.

1969 — ———. *L'humour dans la littérature et dans l'art de l'ancienne Egypte = Scholae Adriani de Buck Memoriae Dicatae.* Eds. A. A. Kampman and A. Klasens IV. Leiden.

1983 — ———. "Rückenpfeiler." *LÄ* 5, 315-18.

Wank 1984 — M. Wank. "The Coinage of Cleopatra." *Collector's Journal of Ancient Art* 5, 26-35.

Washington 1985 — National Gallery of Art, Washington, D.C. *The Treasure Houses of Britain: Five Hundred Years of Private Patronage and Art Collecting.* Exh. cat. Ed. G. Jackson-Stops.

Watermann 1958 — R. Watermann. *Bilder aus dem Lande des Ptah und Imhotep. Naturbeobachtung, Realismus und Humanität der Alten Ägypter, besprochen an zahlreichen Darstellungen alter, kranker und körperbehinderter Menschen und am mißgebildeten Göttern.* Cologne.

Webb 1978 — V. Webb. *Archaic Greek Faience. Miniature Scent Bottles and Related Objects from East Greece, 650-500 B.C.* Warminster, England.

Weber 1911 — W. Weber. "Zwei Formen des Osiris." In *Drei Untersuchungen zur ägyptisch-griechischen Religion.* Heidelberg, 29-48.

Weinstein/Turner 1976 — M. E. Weinstein and E. G. Turner. "Greek and Latin Papyri from Qaṣr Ibrîm." *JEA* 62, 115-30.

Wenig 1977 — S. Wenig. *Ägyptische Altertümer aus der Skulpturensammlung Dresden.*

1978 — ———. *Africa in Antiquity. The Arts of Ancient Nubia and the Sudan,* vol. I: *The Catalogue.* Exh. cat. The Brooklyn Museum.

Werbrouck 1952 — M. Werbrouck. "La déesse Nechbet et la reine d'Egypte." *Archiv Orientální* 20, 197-203.

Wessetzky 1977 — V. Wessetzky. "Reliefs aus dem Tempel Ptolemaios' I. in Kom el Ahmar-Sharuna in der Budapester und Wiener Ägyptischen Sammlung." *MDAIK* 33, 133-41.

Westendorf 1966 — W. Westendorf. *Altägyptische Darstellungen des Sonnenlaufes auf der abschüssigen Himmelsbahn.* MÄS 10.

1968 — ———. *Painting, Sculpture, and Architecture of Ancient Egypt.* Trans. L. Mins. New York.

1978 — ———. "Uräus und Sonnenscheibe." *SAK* 6, 201-25.

1980 — ———. "Horusauge." *LÄ* 3, 48-51.

Wibrech 1971 — M. Wibrech. *Auguste Mariette.* Boulogne-sur-mer.

Wijngaarden 1938 — W. Wijngaarden. "Een Egyptisch koningsbeeldje van blauwe fayence." *OMRO* 19, 1-4.

Wilcken 1917 — U. Wilcken. "Die griechischen Denkmäler vom Dromos des Serapeums von Memphis." *JDAI* 32, 156-60.

1927 — ———. *Urkunden der Ptolemäerzeit (Ältere Funde),* vol. 1: *Papyri aus Unterägypten.* Berlin and Leipzig.

H. Wild 1953 — H. Wild. *Le tombeau de Ti,* fasc. II: *La chapelle.* MIFAO 65.

1954 — ———. "Statue de Hor-néfer au Musée des Beaux-Arts de Lausanne." *BIFAO* 54, 173-222.

R. Wild 1981 — R. A. Wild. *Water in the Cultic Worship of Isis and Sarapis.* Leiden.

Wildung 1972 — D. Wildung. "Two Representations of Gods from the Early Old Kingdom." *MW,* 145-60.

1977a — ———. "Flügelsonne." *LÄ* 2, 277-79.

1977b — ———. *Imhotep and Amenhotep: Gottwerdung im alten Ägypten.* MÄS 36.

Wildung/Schoske 1984 — D. Wildung and S. Schoske. *Nofret. Die Schöne. Die Frau im alten Ägypten.* Exh. cat. Munich, Haus der Kunst and Staatliche Sammlung Ägyptischer Kunst.

Wilkinson 1984 — A. Wilkinson. "Jewellery for a Procession in the Bed-Chamber in the Tomb of Tutankhamon." *BIFAO* 84, 335-45.

Williams 1924 — C. L. Ransom Williams. *New-York Historical Society. Catalogue of Egyptian Antiquities, Nos. 1-160: Gold and Silver Jewelry and Related Objects.* New York.

Winlock 1934 — H. E. Winlock. "Recent Purchases of Egyptian Sculpture." *BMMA* 29, 184-87.

Winter 1968 — E. Winter. *Untersuchungen zu den ägyptischen Tempelreliefs der Griechisch-Römischen Zeit.* Österreichische Akademie der Wissenschaften in Wien. Phil.-hist. Kl., Denkschriften, 98. Vienna.

1978 — ———. *Der Apiskult im alten Ägypten.* Mainz.

1979 — ———. "Das Kalabsha-Tor in Berlin." *JPK* 14, 59-71.

De Wit 1951 — C. De Wit. *Le rôle et le sens du lion dans l'Egypte ancienne.* Leiden.

1958-68 — ———. *Les inscriptions du temple d'Opet à Karnak.* 3 vols. Bibliotheca Aegyptiaca 11-13. Brussels.

Wolf 1957 — W. Wolf. *Die Kunst Aegyptens: Gestalt und Geschichte.* Stuttgart.

Wolinski 1987 A. Wolinski. "Egyptian Masks: The Priest and His Role." *Archaeology* 40/1, 22-29.

Wroth 1899 W. Wroth. *Catalogue of the Greek Coins of Galatia, Cappadocia, and Syria.* British Museum, Department of Coins and Medals. London.

Würfel 1953 R. Würfel. "Die ägyptische Fabel in Bildkunst und Literatur." *Wissenschaftliche Zeitschrift der Universität Leipzig, Jahrgang 1952/1953,* Heft 3, 63-77.

Yarkho 1985 V.N. Yarkho. "A New Papyrus Fragment of Ancient Greek Mock-Heroic Epos." *VDI* 2, 65-66.

Yellin 1982 J. Yellin. "Abaton-Style Milk Libation at Meroe." *Meroitica* 6, 151-55.

Young 1967 E. Young. "An Offering to Thoth: A Votive Statue from the Gallatin Collection." *BMMA* 25, 273-82.

Yoyotte 1953a J. Yoyotte. "Pour une localisation du pays *IAM.*" *BIFAO* 52, 173-78.

1953b ———. "La ville de 'Taremou' (Tell el-Muqdâm)." *BIFAO* 52, 179-92.

1954a ———. "La provenance des reliefs de Tjanefer." *CdE* 29, 278-80.

1954b ———. "Prêtres et sanctuaires du nome héliopolite à la basse époque." *BIFAO* 54, 83-115.

1957 ———. "Le Soukhos de la Maréotide et d'autres cultes régionaux du dieu-crocodile d'après les cylindres au Moyen Empire." *BIFAO* 56, 81-95.

1958 ———. "Le dénommé Mosou." *BIFAO* 57, 81-89.

1959 ———. "Nectanébo II comme faucon divin?" *Kêmi* 15, 70-74.

1968 ———. *Treasures of the Pharaohs: The Early Period, the New Kingdom, the Late Period.* Trans. R. Allen. Geneva.

1969 ———. "Bakhtis–religion égyptienne et culture grecque à Edfou." In *Religions,* 127-41.

1972 ———. "Pétoubastis III." *RdE* 24, 216-23.

1973 ———. "Fouilles à Tanis–rapport sur la XXIVe campagne." *ASAE* 61, 79-86.

1983 ———. "Religion de l'Egypte ancienne." E.P.H.E. Ve Section. *Annuaire* 91, 217-23.

Žabkar 1980a L. V. Žabkar. "Adaptation of Ancient Egyptian Texts to the Temple Ritual at Philae." *JEA* 66, 127-36.

1980b ———. "Miysis." *LÄ* 4, 163-65.

Zauzich 1968 K.-Th. Zauzich. *Die ägyptische Schreibertradition in Aufbau, Sprache und Schrift der demotischen Kaufverträge aus ptolemäischer Zeit,* vol. 1. AA 19.

Zayed 1962 Abd el Hamid Zayed. "Réflexions sur deux statuettes inédites de l'époque ptolémaïque." *ASAE* 57, 143-59.

Ziegler 1979 C. Ziegler. *Musée du Louvre. Département des Antiquités Egyptiennes. Catalogue des instruments de musique égyptiens.* Paris.

1981 ———. "Une découverte inédite de Mariette, les bronzes du Sérapéum." *BSFE* 90, 29-45.

1984 ———. "Sistrum." *LÄ 5, 959-63.*

Photograph Credits

Unless otherwise noted, photographs are courtesy of owner or photographer.
Allard Pierson Museum: CATS. 21, 36, 106, 125; Kelsey Museum of Archaeology, University of Michigan: CATS. 104, 133; Staatliche Museen zu Berlin/DDR, Ägyptisches Museum, photograph Staatliche Museen: CATS. 19, 31; © Ägyptisches Museum, Staatliche Museen Preußischer Kulturbesitz, Berlin/BRD: Fig. 29; CATS. 46, 55, 56; photograph Margarete Busing: CAT. 60; Antikenmuseum, Staatliche Museen Preußischer Kulturbesitz, Berlin/BRD: CAT. 77; Archäologisches Institut und Akademisches Kunstmuseum der Universität Bonn, photograph Wolfgang Klein: CAT. 64; Museum of Fine Arts, Boston: Figs. 27, 30, 38; CATS. 45, 54, 70, 131; The Brooklyn Museum: Figs. 7, 14, 26, 31-33, 37; CATS. 1, 7, 17, 18, 24, 25, 30, 39, 40, 43, 49, 63, 80, 82-88, 92-94, 96, 97, 99, 102, 115, 123, 130; Musées Royaux d'Art et d'Histoire and A. C. L. – Brussels: CATS. 23, 28, 47, 53, 118; The Harvard University Art Museums (Arthur M. Sackler Museum): CAT. 65; The Cleveland Museum of Art: CATS. 26, 105; © Ole Woldbye, Copenhagen, courtesy of Ny Carlsberg Glyptotek: CATS. 50, 71, 107, 124, 135; © The Detroit Institute of Arts: CATS. 32, 37, 44; Kestner-Museum, Hannover: CAT. 33; Pelizaeus-Museum, Hildesheim: Fig. 43; CATS. 4, 6, 22, 51, 114, 128, 129, 132; The Museum of Fine Arts, Houston: CAT. 95; Staatliche Kunstsammlungen Kassel, Antikensammlung: CAT. 67; © Rijksmuseum van Oudheden: CATS. 9, 12, 72, 75, 108, 136; © Trustees of the British Museum: Fig. 3; CATS. 5, 14-16, 121, 122, 126, 127, 134; The J. Paul Getty Museum: CAT. 111; Staatliche Münzsammlung, München: CAT. 61; Staatliche Sammlung Ägyptischer Kunst München: CATS. 2, 89-91, 98, 101, 103; Wittelsbacher Ausgleichsfonds, photographs courtesy of the Staatliche Sammlung Ägyptischer Kunst München: CATS. 38, 110, 139; Yale University Art Gallery: CATS. 52, 74; The Metropolitan Museum of Art: Figs: 41, 42; CATS. 8, 66, 68, 117; © Chuzeville, Paris, courtesy of Musée du Louvre: CATS. 10, 11, 20, 42, 48, 57, 59, 78, 137; The University Museum, University of Pennsylvania: CAT. 140; North Carolina Museum of Art: CAT. 119; Virginia Museum of Fine Arts: CAT. 13; Safani Gallery, New York: CAT. 27; Schopplein Studio, courtesy of Charles Pankow and Heide Betz: CAT. 138; Sotheby's, New York: CAT. 34; Rosicrucian Egyptian Museum: CAT. 79; Württembergisches Landesmuseum Stuttgart, Antikensammlung: CAT. 81; Royal Ontario Museum: Fig 16; CATS. 3, 73; The Vatican Museums: Figs. 19, 20; CATS. 76, 79; Kunsthistorisches Museum Vienna: CATS. 35, 120; Robert S. Bianchi: Figs. 1, 4, 6, 24, 25, 28, 34-36, 39, 40, 44-47; CATS. 27, 58, 109; J. DiClemente: Figs. 21, 22; Richard A. Fazzini: Figs. 2, 8-13; W. Benson Harer: CAT. 29; Jack A. Josephson: CATS. 41, 62; Jan Quaegebeur: Figs. 17, 18, 23; Elliott M. Sanger, Jr.: CAT. 116; © Sarah Wells, courtesy of Christos G. Bastis: CATS. 83, 100, 112, 113.

Concordance

(accession numbers : catalogue numbers)

CITY Lender Accession no.	CAT. NO.
AMSTERDAM	
Allard Pierson Museum	
7763	21
7772	106
7776	125
7860	36
ANN ARBOR	
Kelsey Museum of Archaeology, University of Michigan	
8218	133
8526	104
BERLIN/BRD	
Staatliche Museen Preußischer Kulturbesitz: Ägyptisches Museum	
12500	46
13457	56
14568	55
Antikenmuseum	
1976.10	77
Verein zur Förderung des Ägyptischen Museums	
1-78	60
BERLIN/DDR	
Staatliche Museen zu Berlin, Hauptstadt der DDR, Ägyptisches Museum/Papyrussammlung	
2116	19
2271	31
BONN	
Akademisches Kunstmuseum der Universität Bonn	
B 284	64

CITY Lender Accession no.	CAT. NO.
BOSTON	
Museum of Fine Arts	
01.8207	70
01.8208	54
04.1749	45
51.2474	131
BROOKLYN	
The Brooklyn Museum	
05.459.2	88
16.146	96
16.148	93
16.149	97
37.37E	1
37.774E	87
37.775E-.776E	85
37.783E	86
37.785E	94
44.120	17
49.61.1-.4	18
52.89	24
54.51	80
54.162	49
55.175	25
58.13	130
58.30	43
60.73	99
62.46	7
67.2	92
69.35	82
71.37.2	123
73.85	102
86.226.14	39
86.226.32	63

CITY Lender Accession no.	CAT. NO.
BRUSSELS	
Musées Royaux d'Art et d'Histoire	
E.1839	53
E.3073	28
E.4424	118
E.7654	23
E.7946	47
CAMBRIDGE, MASSACHUSETTS	
Harvard University Art Museums (Arthur M. Sackler Museum)	
1983.96	65
CLEVELAND	
The Cleveland Museum of Art	
48.141	26
69.118	105
COPENHAGEN	
Ny Carlsberg Glyptotek	
Cat. nr. 329 (IN 586)	71
Cat. nr. 453a (IN 2300)	50
AEIN 449	135
AEIN 1071	124
AEIN 1681	107
DETROIT	
The Detroit Institute of Arts	
40.47	44
40.48	37
51.83	32
HANNOVER	
Kestner-Museum	
1935.200.773	33
HILDESHEIM	
Pelizaeus-Museum	
464	114
748	132
1120	51
1537	22
1885	6
1899	4
2244	128
2373	129

CITY Lender Accession no.	CAT. NO.
HOUSTON	
Museum of Fine Arts, Houston	
37-48	95
KASSEL	
Staatliche Kunstsammlungen Kassel, Antikensammlung	
SK 115	67
LEIDEN	
Rijksmuseum van Oudheden	
CI. 327	108
F 97/4.1	136
F 1937/6.9	9
F 1938/7.20	72
F 1958/4.3	75
F 1961/12.3	12
LONDON	
The British Museum	
147	122
391	121
1054	15
1056	14
1153	5
27390	16
36062	134
BM9908,2	126
BM9911,2	127
MALIBU, CALIFORNIA	
The J. Paul Getty Museum	
85.AF.84	111
MUNICH	
Staatliche Münzsammlung	
Coins	61
Staatliche Sammlung Ägyptischer Kunst	
Ant. 2446b	91
Ant. 2446c	90
Ant. 2455	89
ÄS 2824	98
ÄS 3991	103
ÄS 4201	101
Gl 30	2
Wittelsbacher Ausgleichsfonds	
Ant. WAF 512	110
Gl WAF 24	139
Gl WAF 328	38

CITY Lender Accession no.	CAT. NO.
NEW HAVEN	
Peabody Museum of Natural History	
4.1.1953	52
Yale University Art Gallery	
1931.106	74
NEW YORK	
The Metropolitan Museum of Art	
18.2.16	117
20.2.21	66
26.7.1016	68
34.2.1	8
PARIS	
Musée du Louvre:	
Département des Antiquités Egyptiennes	
A.28 (N.28)	59
A.35 (N.36)	137
B.35 (N.140)	20
E.8061	48
E.10970	11
E.27113	78
N.423	10
Département des Antiquités Grecques et Romaines	
MND 1960 (Ma 3449)	57
MND 2229 (Ma 3565)	42
PHILADELPHIA	
The University Museum, University of Pennsylvania	
E 976	140
RALEIGH	
North Carolina Museum of Art	
G.79.6.15	119
RICHMOND	
Virginia Museum of Fine Arts	
63.45	13
SAN JOSE, CALIFORNIA	
Rosicrucian Egyptian Museum	
1582	79
STUTTGART	
Württembergisches Landesmuseum, Antikensammlung	
1.35	81

CITY Lender Accession no.	CAT. NO.
TORONTO	
Royal Ontario Museum	
910.35.11	3
910.75	73
VATICAN CITY	
The Vatican Museums:	
Museo Chiarmonti	
713	79
Museo Pio Clementino	
38511	76
VIENNA	
Kunsthistorisches Museum, Ägyptisch-Orientalische Sammlung	
42	35
76	120
PRIVATE COLLECTIONS	
Christos G. Bastis	
Head of a man	40
Fillet	83
Earrings	84
Tanagra figures	112, 113
Isis with Horus	100
Harer Family Trust	
Block statue	29
Jack A. Josephson	
Head of a man	41
Head of queen or goddess	62
Vase	116
Richard M. Keresey	
Plaster head in profile	34
Charles Pankow and Heide Betz	
Statue of Roman Emperor	138
Anonymous	
Torso of a man	27
The Isis Casati	30
Bust of Ptolemy XII	58
Egyptianizing figure	109
Clepsydra fragment	115